CHILTON BOOK COMPANY
REPAIR & TUNE-UP GUIDE
DATSUN/NISSAN Z and ZX 1970-86

All U.S. and Canadian models of 240Z • 260Z • 280Z • 280ZX
280ZX Turbo • 300ZX • 300ZX Turbo

President LAWRENCE A. FORNASIERI
Vice President and General Manager JOHN P. KUSHNERICK
Executive Editor KERRY A. FREEMAN, S.A.E.
Senior Editor RICHARD J. RIVELE, S.A.E.
Editor RICHARD T. SMITH

CHILTON BOOK COMPANY
Radnor, Pennsylvania
19089

SAFETY NOTICE

Proper service and repair procedures are vital to the safe, reliable operation of all motor vehicles, as well as the personal safety of those performing repairs. This book outlines procedures for servicing and repairing vehicles using safe, effective methods. The procedures contain many NOTES, CAUTIONS and WARNINGS which should be followed along with standard safety procedures to eliminate the possibility of personal injury or improper service which could damage the vehicle or compromise its safety.

It is important to note that repair procedures and techniques, tools and parts for servicing motor vehicles, as well as the skill and experience of the individual performing the work vary widely. It is not possible to anticipate all of the conceivable ways or conditions under which vehicles may be serviced, or to provide cautions as to all of the possible hazards that may result. Standard and accepted safety precautions and equipment should be used when handling toxic or flammable fluids, and safety goggles or other protection should be used during cutting, grinding, chiseling, prying, or any other process that can cause material removal or projectiles.

Some procedures require the use of tools specially designed for a specific purpose. Before substituting another tool or procedure, you must be completely satisfied that neither your personal safety, nor the performance of the vehicle will be endangered.

Although information in this guide is based on industry sources and is as complete as possible at the time of publication, the possibility exists that the manufacturer made later changes which could not be included here. While striving for total accuracy, Chilton Book Company cannot assume responsibility for any errors, changes, or omissions that may occur in the compilation of this data.

PART NUMBERS

Part numbers listed in this reference are not recommendations by Chilton for any product by brand name. They are references that can be used with interchange manuals and aftermarket supplier catalogs to locate each brand supplier's discrete part number.

SPECIAL TOOLS

Special tools are recommended by the vehicle manufacturer to perform their specific job. Use has been kept to a minimum, but where absolutely necessary, they are referred to in the text by the part number of the tool manufacturer. These tools can be purchased, under the appropriate part number, from Kent-Moor Corporation, 29784 Little Mack, Roseville, Michigan 48066. In Canada: Kent-Moore of Canada, Ltd., 2395 Cawthra, Mississauga, Ontario, Canada L5A 3P2 or an equivalent tool can be purchased locally from a tool supplier or parts outlet. Before substituting any tool for the one recommended, read the SAFETY NOTICE at the top of this page.

ACKNOWLEDGMENTS

The Chilton Book Company expresses its appreciation to the Nissan Motor Corporation for their generous assistance in the preparation of this book.

Copyright © 1986 by Chilton Book Company
All Rights Reserved
Published in Radnor, Pennsylvania 19089 by Chilton Book Company

Manufactured in the United States of America
1234567890   5432109876

Chilton's Repair & Tune-up Guide: Datsun/Nissan Z & ZX 1970–86
ISBN 0-8019-7664-2 pbk.
Library of Congress Catalog Card No. 85-47965

CONTENTS

1 General Information and Maintenance
- **1** How to Use this Book
- **2** Tools and Equipment
- **8** Routine Maintenance and Lubrication

2 Tune-Up and Performance Maintenance
- **37** Tune-Up Procedures
- **38** Tune-Up Specifications

3 Engine and Engine Overhaul
- **62** Engine Electrical System
- **76** Engine Service and Specifications

4 Emission Controls and Fuel System
- **132** Emission Control System and Service
- **150** Carbureted Fuel System
- **158** Fuel Injection System

5 Chassis Electrical
- **170** Accessory Service
- **179** Instruments Panel Service
- **182** Lights, Fuses and Flashers

6 Drive Train

- **186** Manual Transmission
- **187** Clutch
- **193** Automatic Transmission
- **198** Driveshaft and U-Joints
- **199** Rear Axle

7 Suspension and Steering

- **209** Front Suspension
- **219** Rear Suspension
- **225** Steering

8 Brakes

- **238** Front Disc Brakes
- **243** Rear Drum Brakes
- **247** Rear Disc Brakes
- **250** Parking Brakes
- **252** Brake Specifications

9 Body and Trim

- **253** Exterior
- **265** Interior

10 Troubleshooting

- **272** Problem Diagnosis

- **306** Mechanic's Data
- **308** Index

- **156** Chilton's Fuel Economy and Tune-Up Tips

- **284** Chilton's Body Repair Tips

Quick Reference Specifications For Your Vehicle

Fill in this chart with the most commonly used specifications for your vehicle. Specifications can be found in Chapters 1 through 3 or on the tune-up decal under the hood of the vehicle.

Tune-Up

Firing Order___

Spark Plugs:

    Type___

    Gap (in.)___

Torque (ft. lbs.)___

Idle Speed (rpm)___

Ignition Timing (°)___

    Vacuum or Electronic Advance (Connected/Disconnected)___

Valve Clearance (in.)

    Intake___   Exhaust___

Capacities

Engine Oil Type (API Rating)___

    With Filter Change (qts)___

    Without Filter Change (qts)___

Cooling System (qts)___

Manual Transmission (pts)___

    Type___

Automatic Transmission (pts)___

    Type___

Front Differential (pts)___

    Type___

Rear Differential (pts)___

    Type___

Transfer Case (pts)___

    Type___

FREQUENTLY REPLACED PARTS

Use these spaces to record the part numbers of frequently replaced parts.

PCV VALVE	OIL FILTER	AIR FILTER	FUEL FILTER
Type___	Type___	Type___	Type___
Part No.___	Part No.___	Part No.___	Part No.___

General Information and Maintenance

HOW TO USE THIS BOOK

This book is organized so that the most often used portions appear at the front, the least used portions at the rear. The first chapter covers all the information that may be required at a moment's notice—information like the locations of the various serial numbers and proper towing instructions. Chapter 1 will probably be the most often used part of the book because of the need to carefully follow the maintenance schedule which it includes to ensure good performance and long component life. Chapter 2 covers tuneup and will be used regularly to keep the engine running at peak performance and to restore operation in case of failure of any of the more delicate components. Chapters 3–9 cover repairs (rather than maintenance) for various portions of the vehicle, with each chapter covering either one system or two related systems. Chapter 10 is designed to diagnose automotive problems. The mechanic's data then lists general information which may be used in rebuilding the engine or performing some other operation on any vehicle.

In using the Table of Contents, refer to the bold listings for the beginning of the chapter. See the smaller listings or the index for information on a particular component or specifications.

In general, there are three things a proficient mechanic has which must be allowed for when a nonprofessional does work on his vehicle. These are:

1. A sound knowledge of the construction of the parts he is working with, their order of assembly, etc.
2. A knowledge of potentially hazardous situations.
3. Manual dexterity, which includes the ability to put the right amount of torque on a part to ensure that it will not be damaged or warped.

This book provides step-by-step instructions and illustrations wherever possible. Use them carefully and wisely. Do not just jump headlong into disassembly. Where you are not sure about being able to readily reassemble something, make a careful drawing of it before beginning to take it apart. Assembly always looks simple when everything is still assembled.

Cautions and notes will be provided where appropriate to help keep you from injuring yourself or damaging the vehicle. Therefore, you should read through the entire procedure before beginning work and make sure that you are aware of the warnings. Since no number of warnings could cover every possible situation, you should work slowly and try to envision what is going to happen in each operation ahead of time.

When it comes to tightening things, there is generally a slim area between too loose to properly seal or resist vibration and so tight as to risk damage or warping. When dealing with major engine parts or with any aluminum component, it pays to procure a torque wrench and go by the recommended figures.

When reference is made in this book to the right-side or left-side of the vehicle, it should be understood that these positions are to be viewed from the front seat. Thus, the left-side of the vehicle is always the driver's side, even when one is facing the vehicle, as when working on the engine.

We have attempted to eliminate the use of special tools wherever possible, substituting more readily available hand tools. However, in some cases, the special tools are necessary. These can be purchased from your Datsun/Nissan dealer or from an automotive parts store.

Always be conscious of the need for safety in your work. Never crawl under the vehicle unless it is firmly supported by jackstands or ramps. Never smoke near or allow a flame to get near

2 GENERAL INFORMATION AND MAINTENANCE

the battery or fuel system. Keep your clothing, hands and hair clear of the fan and pulleys when working near the engine, when in operation. Most importantly, try to be patient, even in the midst of an argument with a particularly stubborn bolt; reaching for the largest hammer in the garage is usually a cause for later regret and more extensive repair. As you gain confidence and experience, working on your vehicle will become a source of pride and satisfaction.

TOOLS AND EQUIPMENT

The service procedures in this book presuppose a familiarity with hand tools and their proper use. However, it is possible that you may have a limited amount of experience with the sort of equipment needed to work on an automobile. This section is designed to help you assemble a basic set of tools that will handle most of the jobs you may undertake.

In addition to the normal assortment of screwdrivers and pliers, automotive service work requires an investment in wrenches, sockets and the handles needed to drive them, plus various measuring tools such as torque wrenches and feeler gauges.

You will find that virtually every nut and bolt on your vehicle is metric. Therefore, despite a few close size similarities, standard inch-size tools will not fit and must not be used. You will need a set of metric wrenches as your most basic tool kit, ranging from about 6–17mm in size. High quality forged wrenches are available in three styles: open end, box end and combination open/box end. The combination tools are generally the most desirable as a starter set; the wrenches shown in the accompanying illustration are of the combination type.

The other set of tools inevitably required is a ratchet handle and socket set. This set should have the same size range as your wrench set. The ratchet, extensions and flex drives for the sockets are available in many sizes; it is advisable to choose a $3/8$ inch drive set initially. One break in the inch/metric sizing war is that metric sized sockets sold in the U.S. have inch-sized drive ($1/4$, $3/8$, $1/2$ and etc.). Thus, if you already have an inch-sized socket set, you need only buy new metric sockets in the sizes needed. Sockets are available in six and twelve point versions; six point types are stronger and are a good choice for a first set. The choice of a drive handle for the sockets should be made with some care. If this is your first set, take the plunge and invest in a flex-head ratchet; it will get into many places otherwise accessible only through a long chain of universal joints, extensions and adapters. An alternative is a flex handle, which lacks the ratcheting feature but has a head which pivots 180°; such a tool is shown below the ratchet handle in the illustration. In addition to the range of sockets mentioned, a rubber lined spark plug socket should be purchased. The correct size for the plugs in your vehicle's engine is $13/16$ inch.

The most important thing to consider when purchasing hand tools is quality. Don't be misled by the low cost of bargain tools. Forged wrenches, tempered screwdriver blades and fine tooth ratchets are much better investments than their less expensive counterparts. The skinned knuckles and frustration inflicted by poor quality tools make any job an unhappy chore. Another consideration is that quality tools come with an unbeatable replacement guarantee–if the tool breaks, you get a new one, no questions asked.

Most jobs can be accomplished using the tools on the accompanying lists. There will be an occasional need for a special tool, such as snap ring pliers; that need will be mentioned in the text. It would not be wise to buy a large assortment of tools on the premise that someday they will be needed. Instead, the tools should be acquired one at a time, each for a specific job, both to avoid unnecessary expense and to be certain that you have the right tool.

The tools needed for basic maintenance jobs, in addition to the wrenches and sockets mentioned, include:
1. Jackstands, for support.
2. Oil filter wrench.
3. Oil filter spout or funnel.
4. Grease gun.
5. Battery post and clamp cleaner.
6. Container for draining oil.
7. Many rags for the inevitable spills.

In addition to these items there are several others which are not absolutely necessary but handy to have around. These include a transmission funnel and filler tube, a drop (trouble) light on a long cord, an adjustable (crescent) wrench and slip joint pliers.

A more advanced list of tools, suitable for tune-up work, can be drawn up easily. While the tools are slightly more sophisticated, they need not be outrageously expensive. The key to these purchases is to make them with an eye towards adaptability and wide range. A basic list of tune-up tools could include:
1. Tachometer/dwell meter.
2. Spark plug gauge and gapping tool.
3. Feeler gauges for valve adjustment.
4. Timing light.

Note that if your vehicle has electronic ignition, you will have no need for a dwell meter and of course a tachometer is provided on the

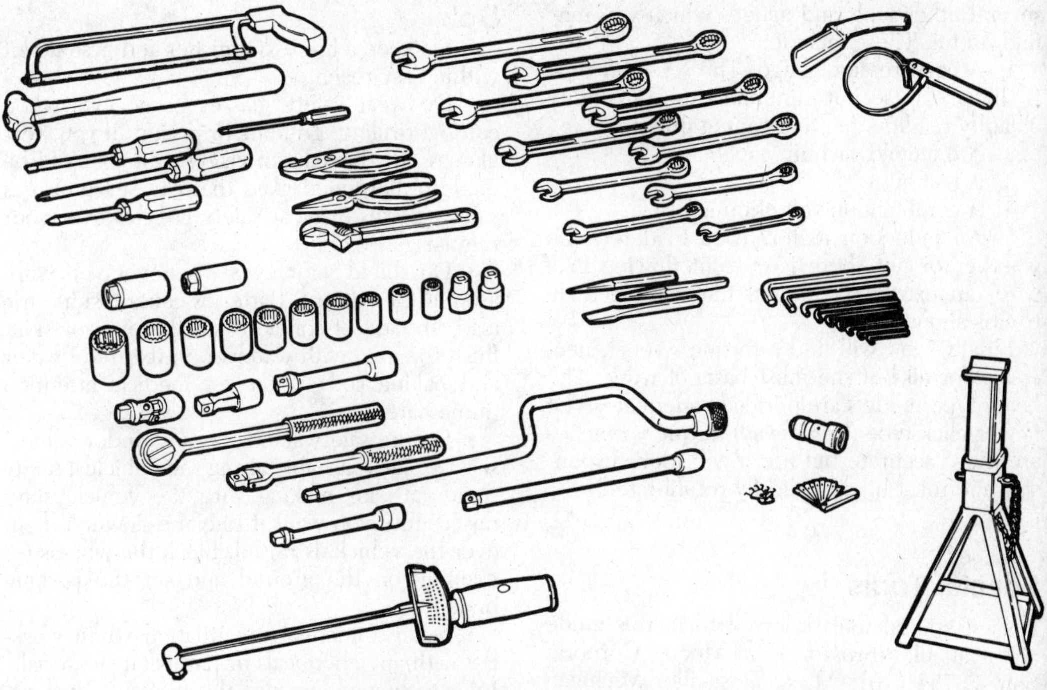

GENERAL INFORMATION AND MAINTENANCE

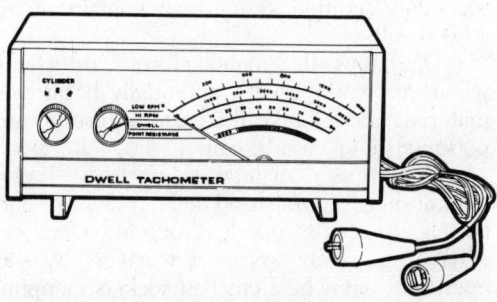

A basic collection of hand tools is necessary for automotive service

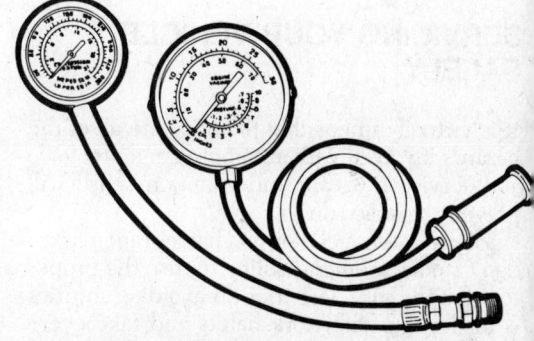

A dwell/tachometer is useful for tune-up work; you won't need a dwell meter if your car has electronic ignition

A compression gauge and a combination vacuum/fuel pressure gauge are handy for troubleshooting and tune-up work

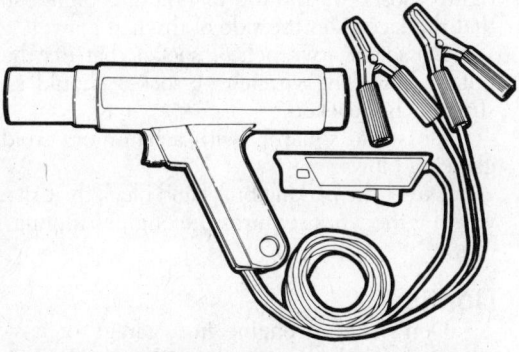

An inductive pickup simplifies timing light connection to the spark plug wire

instrument panel of the vehicle. You will need both the wire type (spark plugs) and the flat type (valves) feeler gauges. The choice of a timing light should be made carefully. A light which works on the DC current supplied by the vehicle battery is the best choice; it should have a xenon tube for brightness. Since most of the vehicles have electronic ignition or will have it in the future, the light should have an inductive pickup which clamps around the No. 1 spark plug cable (the timing light illustrated has one of these pickups).

In addition to these basic tools, there are

4 GENERAL INFORMATION AND MAINTENANCE

several other tools and gauges which you may find useful. These include:

1. A compression gauge. The screw-in type is slower to use but eliminates the possibility of faulty reading due to escaping pressure.
2. A manifold vacuum gauge.
3. A test light.
4. A combination volt/ohmmeter.
5. An induction meter, used to determine whether or not there is current flowing in a wire, an extremely helpful tool for electrical troubleshooting.

Finally, you will find a torque wrench necessary for all but the most basic of work. The beam type models are perfectly adequate. The newer click type (breakaway) torque wrenches are more accurate but are much more expensive and must be periodically recalibrated.

Special Tools

Datsun special tools referred to in this guide are available through Kent-Moore Corporation, 29784 Little Mack, Roseville, Michigan 48066. For Canada, contact Kent-Moore of Canada, Ltd., 2395 Cawthra Mississauga, Ontario, Canada L5A 3Ps.

SERVICING YOUR VEHICLE SAFELY

It is virtually impossible to anticipate all of the hazards involved with automotive maintenance and service but care and common sense will prevent most accidents.

The rules of safety for mechanics range from, don't smoke around gasoline to, use the proper tool for the job. The trick to avoiding injuries is to develop safe work habits and take every possible precaution.

Always support the car on jackstands when working under it

Do's

• Do keep a fire extinguisher and first aid kit within easy reach.

• Do wear safety glasses or goggles when cutting, drilling, grinding or prying. If you wear glasses (for the sake of vision), they should be made of hardened glass that can serve also as safety glasses or wear safety goggles over your regular glasses.

• Do shield your eyes whenever you work around the battery. Batteries contain sulphuric acid. In case of contact with the eyes or skin, flush the area with water or a mixture of water and baking soda, then get medical attention immediately.

• Do use safety stands for any under vehicle service. Jacks are for raising the vehicles; safety stands are for making sure the vehicle stays raised until you want it to come down. Whenever the vehicle is raised, block the wheels remaining on the ground and set the parking brake.

• Do use adequate ventilation when working with any chemicals or hazardous materials. Like carbon monoxide, the asbestos dust resulting from brake lining wear can be poisonous in sufficient quantities.

• Do disconnect the negative battery cable when working on the electrical system. The secondary ignition system can contain up to 40,000 volts.

• Do follow the manufacturer's directions whenever working with potentially hazardous materials. Both brake fluid and antifreeze are poisonous if taken internally.

• Do properly maintain your tools. Loose hammerheads, mushroomed punches and chisels, frayed or poorly grounded electrical cords, excessively worn screwdrivers, spread open end wrenches, cracked sockets, slipping ratchets or faulty droplight sockets can cause accidents.

• Do use the proper size and type of tool for the job being done.

• Do be sure that adjustable wrenches are tightly closed on the nut or bolt and pulled so that the face is on the side of the fixed jaw.

• Do select a wrench or socket that fits the nut or bolt. The wrench or socket should sit straight, not cocked.

• Do strike squarely with a hammer; avoid glancing blows.

• Do set the parking brake and block the drive wheel if the work requires the engine running.

Don'ts

• Don't run an engine in a garage or anywhere else without proper ventilation—EVER! Carbon monoxide is poisonous; it takes a long

GENERAL INFORMATION AND MAINTENANCE

time to leave the body and can build up a deadly supply in your system by simply breathing in a little every day. You may not realize that you are slowly poisoning yourself. Always use power vents, windows, fans or open the garage doors.
- Don't work around moving parts while wearing a necktie or other loose clothing. Short sleeves are much safer than long, loose sleeves; hard toed shoes with neoprene soles protect your toes and give a better grip on slippery surfaces. Jewelry, such as, watches, fancy belt buckles, beads or body adornment of any kind are not safe when working around a vehicle. Long hair should be hidden under a hat or cap.
- Don't use pockets for toolboxes. A fall or bump can drive a screwdriver deep into your body. Even a wiping cloth hanging from the back pocket can wrap around a spinning shaft or fan.
- Don't smoke when working around gasoline, cleaning solvent or other flammable material.
- Don't smoke when working around the battery. When the battery is being charged, it gives off explosive hydrogen gas.
- Don't use gasoline to wash your hands; there are excellent soaps available. Gasoline may contain lead which can enter the body through a cut and can accumulate in the body until you are very ill. Gasoline also removes all the natural oils from the skin so that bone dry hands will suck up oil and grease.
- Don't service the air conditioning system unless you are equipped with the necessary tools and training. The refrigerant, R-12, is extremely cold when released into the air and will instantly freeze any surface it contacts, including your eyes. Although the refrigerant is normally non-toxic, R-12 becomes a deadly poisonous gas in the presence of an open flame. One good whiff of the vapors from burning refrigerant can be fatal.

HISTORY

It was not long after the introduction of the Datsun 240-Z in 1969 that the term, Z-car, became a part of the language. For many, the Z-car represented a perfect compromise between the large size of American "personal" vehicles and the primitiveness of the traditional sports car. The 240-Z was within the financial reach of many who could not afford a traditional grand touring car; it sported the overhead cam, fully independent suspension, exciting appearance and performance which had been dreamed of.

Datsun called the 260-Z an encore to the 240-Z. While it was not a radical departure from the 240-Z, it represented a surprising change in direction. While most vehicles simply continued to sport more and more modest performance, the 260-Z's slight increase in displacement and fully redesigned emission control system meant full performance with a minimal penalty in fuel economy, hitting the Z-car owner or potential owner right where he wanted to be hit.

The 260-Z (2 + 2) allowed the Z-car to become an exciting alternative to the conventional family sedan, while formerly, it sometimes had to be dismissed because the entire family could not be accommodated. The 280-Z was introduced in 1975 and was equipped with a larger 2,800cc, fuel injected engine. A 5-speed transmission was made optional in 1977. The 280-Z (2 + 2) model continued to be the choice in passenger accommodations.

When the 240-Z was introduced, it had virtually no direct competition but instead created an entirely new class of vehicle. Over the years, however, more and more vehicles were introduced by other manufacturers in successful attempts to cash in on the Z-car's market position. Additionally, inevitable price increases slowly but irreversibly moved the Z-car away from it's original market segment, toward a new class of more affluent buyers. Nissan determined that this new breed of buyer valued attributes, traditionally considered part of a luxury car's appeal, not a sports car's.

Accordingly, in 1979, an entirely new Z-car was introduced, the 280-ZX. Conceding the sports car market to the Mazda RX-7, Volkswagen Scirocco, Triumph TR-7 and similar vehicles, the ZX offered luxury in place of sports car performance. Although similar in appearance to the Z, the ZX shared few components other than the engine and transmission. The crisp lines of the Z-car (originally designed by either Albrecht Goertz, according to Goertz or by a Nissan committee, according to Nissan) gave way to a bulkier, more rounded committee form, which shared basic styling elements with the Z but nothing else. The suspension was completely revised for a more luxurious ride, at some expense of handling; the rear suspension was directly lifted from the Datsun 810 and the front suspension was hybridized from various existing designs. Inside the vehicle, elements of both luxury and gimmickry competed for attention. Functional and pleasing touches, such as automatic checkout of fluid levels and light operation or low distortion stereo, nestled next to dual meter gasoline gauges.

Overall, the 280-ZX hit the mark for which Nissan aimed. Although it's price had risen to a level unimaginable ten years before, it offered the new type of ZX buyer the exact blend

6 GENERAL INFORMATION AND MAINTENANCE

of comfort, luxury and performance unavailable in other vehicles.

In 1984, the Nissan 300 ZX was introduced which marks the third generation of Z cars. The first complete redesign occurred with the 1979, 280 ZX. With a new V6 engine, more aerodynamic body, revised suspension and brake systems among other changes, the 300 ZX was designed to surpass both the sportiness of the original Z-car and the luxury of the current ZX.

SERIAL NUMBER IDENTIFICATION

Vehicle

1970–78

The identification number is located on the top of the instrument panel so that it can be seen from outside the vehicle. This number also appears on the vehicle identification plate, which is located on the right front strut housing on (1970–72) and on the right hood ledge panel (1973–78).

The model identification code of the serial number may be interpreted as follows:

1. The first letter will be either an H (for L24 or L28 engine) or an R (for L26 engine). The 2 + 2 models will start with a G.
2. Following this, an L will appear if the vehicle is left hand drive.

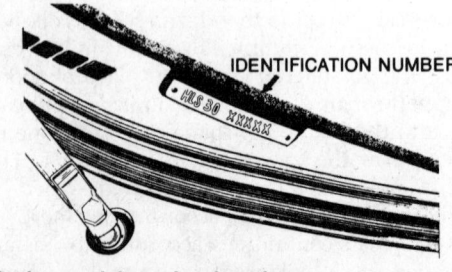

Vehicle serial number location

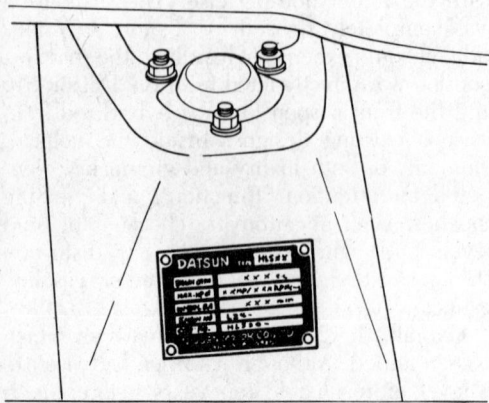

1970–72 car identification plate location

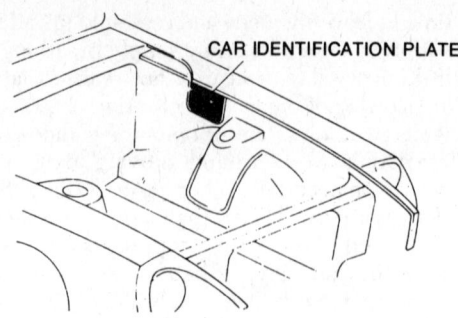

1973–78 car identification plate location

3. Then the designation S30 will appear for all models.
4. If the vehicle has an automatic transmission, an A will then appear. The F designates a 5-speed.
5. The letter U will then appear for all vehicles designed for U.S. and Canadian markets.
6. An N will then appear for Canadian vehicles. California vehicles are designated by a V.
7. If the vehicle is air conditioned, a C will appear at the end of the suffix.
8. On 1970–73 vehicles, a dash will follow the S30 designation. The L24 engine is the 2400cc engine used in the 240-Z, the L26 engine refers to the 2600cc engine in the 260-Z and the L28 for the 2800cc engine.

NOTE: *A Canadian 260-Z, equipped with an automatic transmission and air conditioning would have the code: RLS30AUNC*

1979–83

The Vehicle Identification Number (VIN) is stamped on a plate located on the left front of the instrument panel and is visible through the windshield. The serial number also appears on the firewall, just behind the engine's valve cover. The vehicle identification, engine, vehicle serial numbers and other information, is located on the cowl in the engine compartment, just behind the battery.

The vehicle type identification can be interpreted as follows:

1. The first letter will be a K or a blank; K indicates a T-bar roof.
2. The second letter is an H, for the L28 engine.
3. The third letter is an L, for left-hand drive.
4. The fourth letter is a G or a blank; G indicates a 2 + 2 models.
5. The fifth letter is an S; the prefix for all 280-ZX models.
6. The designation for all 280-ZX models is 130.

GENERAL INFORMATION AND MAINTENANCE

7. The sixth letter is a J, for Grand Luxury model.
8. The seventh letter is either an A (automatic transmission), an F (5-speed transmission) or a blank (4-speed transmission).
9. The eighth letter is a V (California model), a U (U.S.A.–non-California model), a UD (U.S.A.–non-California model with a catalytic converter: 1979 ONLY) or an N (Canadian model).
NOTE: *On models equipped with a turbocharger (1981 and later) the eighth letter (third suffix) is a T.*
10. The ninth letter is a B, for power steering.
11. The tenth letter is a C (air conditioning) or a C1 (air conditioning with automatic temperature control).

1984 and Later

On the 300 ZX the various identification plates are located as illustrated. The Vehicle Identification Number (VIN) Plate is located on the left-front of the instrument panel and can be interpreted as follows:
1. The first letter will be a K or a blank; K indicates a T-bar roof.
2. The second letter is an H, for the VG30E engine.
3. The third letter is an L, for left-hand drive.
4. The fourth is a G or a blank; G indicates a 2 + 2 model.
5. The fifth letter is a Z, a prefix for all 300 ZX models.
6. The number 31 is the designation for all 300 ZX models.
7. The sixth letter is a J, X or a blank; J indicates the GL model, the X indicates the GL-L model or the blank indicates the SF model.
8. The seventh letter is an A (automatic transmission) or a blank (manual transmission).
9. The eighth letter is a T or blank; the T is for turbocharger.
10. The ninth letter is a V (California model), a U (U.S.A., except California) or an N (Canadian model).

Engine

1970–83

The engine serial number is located on the right-rear of the block at the cylinder head contact surface. The prefix will be L24, L26 or L28, depending on the engine displacement and the three digit (1970–73), four digit (1974) or six digit (1975 and later) serial number will appear next to it.

1984 and Later

The engine serial number is located on the right-rear of the block below the cylinder head. The

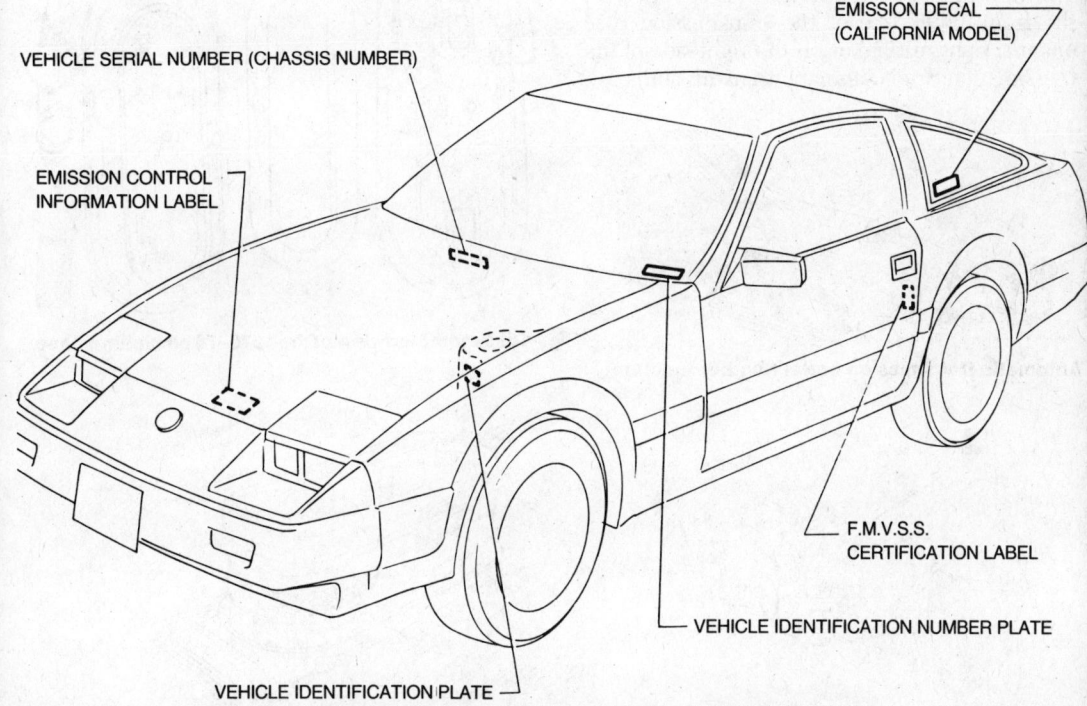

Various identification plate locations—1984 and later

8 GENERAL INFORMATION AND MAINTENANCE

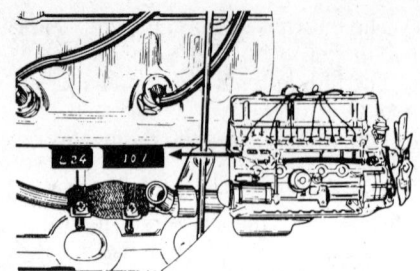
Engine serial number location—1980–83

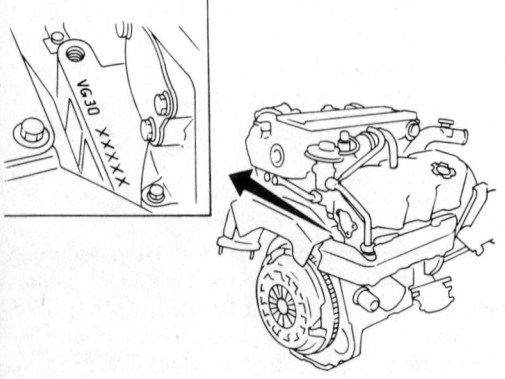
Engine serial number location—1984 and later

prefix will be VG30 which designates the V6 engine followed by a five digit serial number.

Transmission

The transmission serial number is stamped on the front-upper face of the transmission case (manual transmission) or on the right-side of the transmission case (automatic transmission).

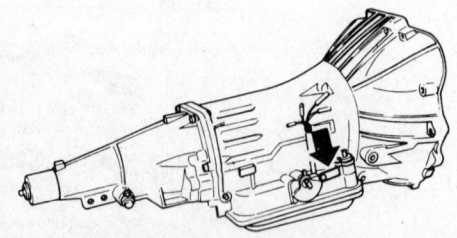
Automatic transmission serial number location

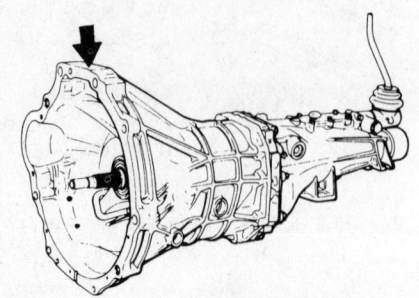
Manual transmission serial number location

ROUTINE MAINTENANCE

Air Cleaner

An air cleaner is used to keep airborne dirt and dust out of the air flowing through the engine. Proper maintenance is vital, as a clogged element will undesirably enrich the fuel mixture, restrict airflow and power, plus allowing excessive contamination of the oil with abrasives. To remove the air cleaner on 1970–83 models, remove the 2–3 thumbscrews, pull off the air cleaner cover and pull out the element. On the 1984 and later models, the cover is retained by four phillips head screws.

The element must be replaced every 24,000 miles (30,000 miles: 1979 and later) or more often if the vehicle is driven in dusty areas. The condition of the element should be checked at every tune-up. Replace the element if it is so heavily coated with dust that you cannot see light through it. The element has been specially treated to eliminate the need for cleaning between replacement intervals; no attempt should be made to clean it with compressed air.

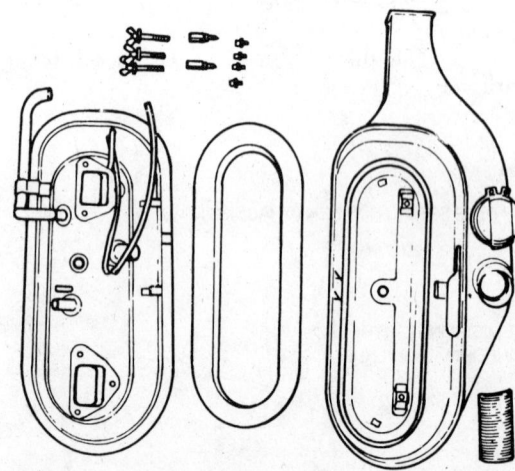
Disassembled view of the 1970–74 air cleaner case

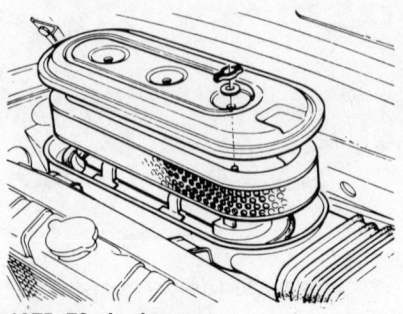
1975–78 air cleaner

GENERAL INFORMATION AND MAINTENANCE

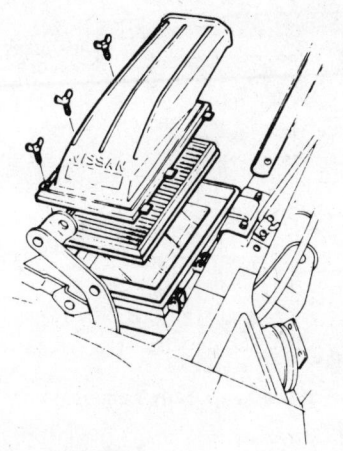

Air Cleaner—1979–83

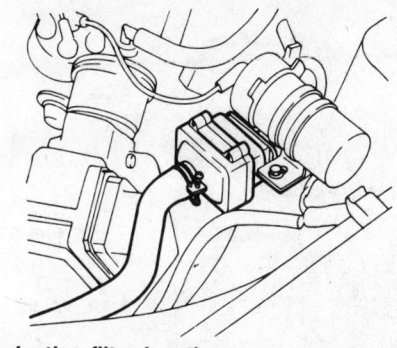

Air induction filter location

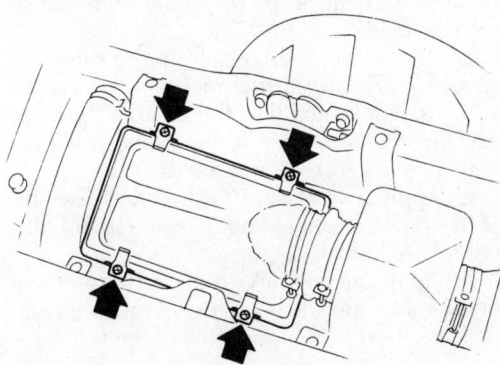

1984 and later air cleaner

Air Induction Filter

1980 Only

Most 1980 ZX models sold in the U.S. have an air induction system for the purpose of emission controls. Vehicles sold in California and Canada do not have the air induction system. The system relies on exhaust pulses to siphon fresh air into the exhaust manifold to continue combustion of any unburned mixtures. More details on this system, which resembles an ordinary air injection system except for the air pump, can be found in Chapter 4.

Every 24 months or 30,000 miles, the air induction valve filter must be replaced.

1. Disconnect the negative cable from the battery.
2. Remove the ignition coil to facilitate access to the air induction filter.
3. Unscrew the clamps and disconnect the hoses from the valve assembly. Remove the valve assembly, noting it's position before removal.
4. Remove the four retaining screws and disassemble the air induction valve. Remove the old filter and discard.

Exploded view of the air induction filter

5. To install, use a new filter and reverse the removal procedures.

NOTE: *Be certain the valve is facing in the correct direction, so that the exhaust gases do not flow backward.*

PCV System

Every 12,000 miles or 1 year, whichever comes first, perform the following checks on the function of the PCV system:

1. Check the ventilation hoses for leaks or clogging and clean or replace as necessary.
2. Remove the ventilator hose from the PCV valve with the engine idling and place a finger over the valve inlet. If a strong vacuum is felt and a hissing noise is evident, the valve is functional; otherwise, replace it.

• On the 1970–74 models, the PCV valve must be replaced every 12 months or 12,000 miles, whichever comes first. To replace the valve, unscrew it from it's fitting on the intake manifold with the proper size wrench and screw the replacement valve into the manifold. Replace any brittle or cracked hoses at the same time.

• On the 1975–79 models, the valve must be replaced every 24 months or 24,000 miles. To replace the valve, simply disconnect it from it's hose fittings and install a new valve into the hoses. Replace any brittle or cracked hoses at the same time.

10 GENERAL INFORMATION AND MAINTENANCE

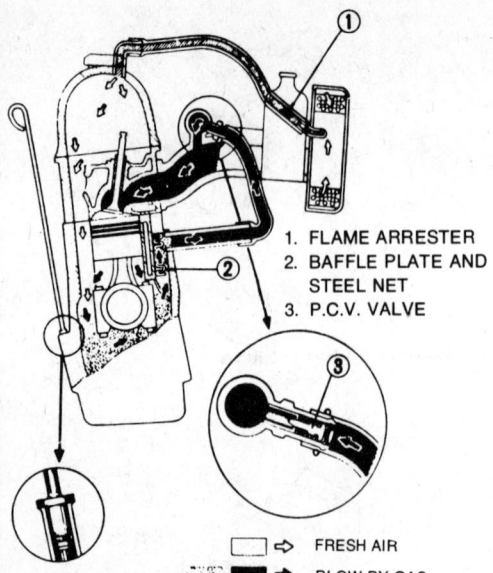

1. FLAME ARRESTER
2. BAFFLE PLATE AND STEEL NET
3. P.C.V. VALVE

□ ⇨ FRESH AIR
■ ➡ BLOW-BY GAS

1970–74 PCV system

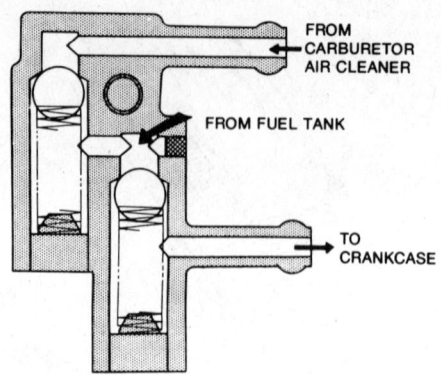

Diagram of the evaporative emission check valve

- On the 1980 and later models, no regularly scheduled replacement of the valve is called for. The valve must be replaced whenever it is clogged, as determined by the test given in Step 2. The valve is of the same type used on the 1975–79 models.

Evaporative Emissions System

Check the evaporation control system every 12,000 miles. Check the fuel and vapor lines/hoses for proper connections, routing and condition; replace the damaged or deteriorated parts as necessary.

1970–74

Remove and check the operation of the check valve as follows:

1. Disconnect the hoses from the valve and apply air pressure to the fuel tank side of the valve; the air should flow through the valve and exit the crankcase side of the valve. If the operation is not correct, replace the valve.
2. Apply air pressure to the crankcase side of the valve; air should not pass to either of the other two outlets.
3. Apply air pressure to the carburetor side of the valve; the air should exit through the fuel tank and/or the crankcase side of the valve.

1975 and Later

The flow guide is replaced with a carbon filled canister which stores fuel vapors until the engine is started; vapors are then drawn into the combustion chambers and burned.

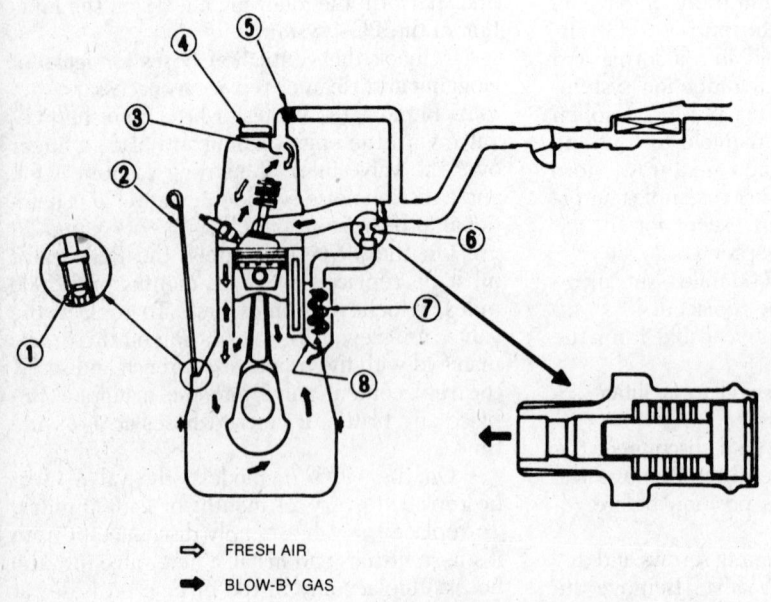

1. O-ring
2. Oil level gauge
3. Baffle plate
4. Oil cap
5. Flame arrester
6. Throttle chamber
7. P.C.V. valve
8. Steel net
9. Baffle plate

⇨ FRESH AIR
➡ BLOW-BY GAS

PCV system—1975–83

GENERAL INFORMATION AND MAINTENANCE

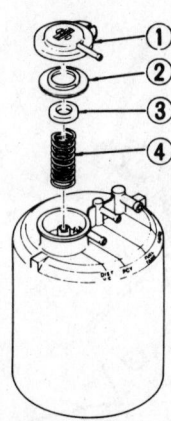

1. Cover
2. Diaphragm
3. Retainer
4. Diaphragm spring

Components of the carbon canister purge control valve

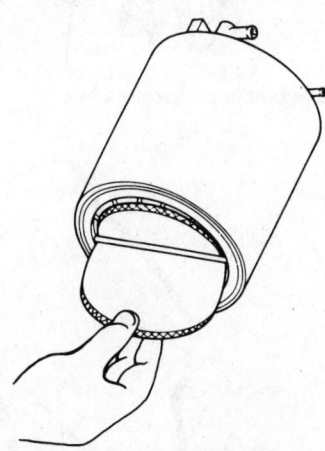

Replacing the carbon canister filter

To check the operation of the carbon canister purge control valve, proceed as follows:
1. Disconnect the rubber hose between the canister control valve and the T-fitting at the T-fitting.
2. Apply vacuum to the hose leading to the control valve. The vacuum should be maintained indefinitely.
NOTE: *If the control valve leaks, remove the top cover of the valve and check for a dislocated or cracked diaphragm. If the diaphragm is damaged, a repair kit containing a new diaphragm, retainer and spring is available and should be installed.*

The carbon canister has an air filter in the bottom of the canister. The filter element should be checked and replaced as indicated on the Maintenance Intervals chart. Replace the filter by removing the canister, pulling the filter out of the bottom of the canister and installing a new filter.
NOTE: *Sealant has been applied to the base of the canister and the canister tray on 1979 and later ZXs. To remove, pull the tray from*

the canister, while twisting the canister at the same time. Apply sealer to the canister tray before replacement. Note that the filter replacement is not a regularly scheduled emissions service on 1980 and later models. On these vehicles, the filter must be replaced only when it is clogged.

For further information on the Evaporative Emissions System, refer to Chapter 4.

Battery

FLUID LEVEL (EXCEPT MAINTENANCE FREE BATTERIES)

Check the battery electrolyte level at least once a month, more often in hot weather or during periods of extended vehicle operation. The level can be checked through the case on translucent polypropylene batteries; the cell caps must be removed on other models. The electrolyte level in each cell should be kept filled to the split ring inside or the line marked on the outside of the case.

If the level is low, add only distilled water or colorless, odorless drinking water, through the opening until the level is correct. Each cell is completely separate from the others, so each must be checked and filled individually.

If water is added in freezing weather, the vehicle should be driven several miles to allow the water to mix with the electrolyte. Otherwise, the battery could freeze.

SPECIFIC GRAVITY (EXCEPT MAINTENANCE FREE BATTERIES)

At least once a year, check the specific gravity of the battery; it should be 1.20–1.26 at room temperature.

The specific gravity can be checked with the use of an hydrometer, an inexpensive instrument available from many sources, including auto parts stores. The hydrometer has a squeeze bulb at one end and a nozzle at the other. Battery electrolyte is sucked into the hydrometer

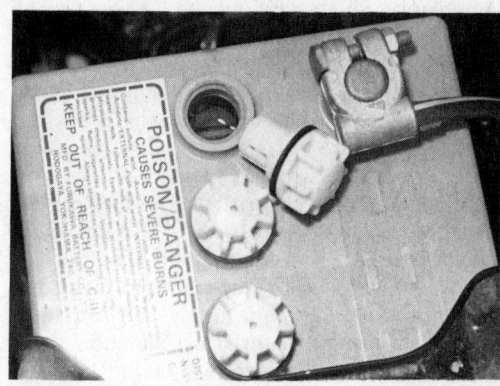

Fill the battery to the bottom of the split ring

12 GENERAL INFORMATION AND MAINTENANCE

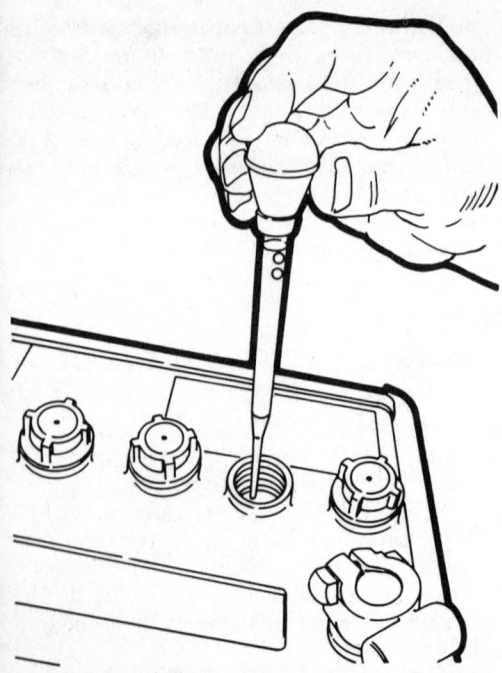

Specific gravity can be checked with an hydrometer

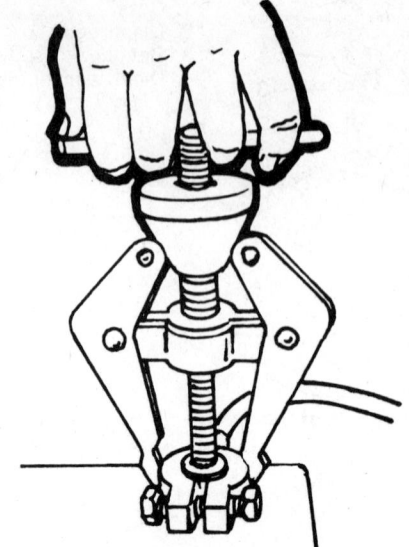

Pullers make clamp removal easier

until the float is lifted from it's seat. The specific gravity is then read by noting the position of the float. Generally, if (after charging) the specific gravity between any two cells varies more than 50 points (0.050), the battery is bad and should be replaced.

It is not possible to check the specific gravity in this manner on sealed (maintenance free) batteries. Instead, the indicator built into the top of the case must be relied on to display any signs of battery deterioration. If the indicator is dark, the battery can be assumed to be OK. If the indicator is light, the specific gravity is low and the battery should be charged or replaced.

CABLES AND CLAMPS

Once a year, the battery terminals and the cable clamps should be cleaned. Loosen the clamps and remove the cables, the negative cable first. On batteries with posts on top, the use of a puller specially made for the purpose is recommended. These are inexpensive and available in auto parts stores. Side terminal battery cables are secured with a bolt.

Clean the cable clamps and the battery terminal with a wire brush, until all corrosion, grease and etc. is removed and the metal is shiny. It is especially important to clean the inside of the clamp thoroughly, since a small deposit of foreign material or oxidation there will prevent a sound electrical connection and inhibit either starting or charging. Special tools

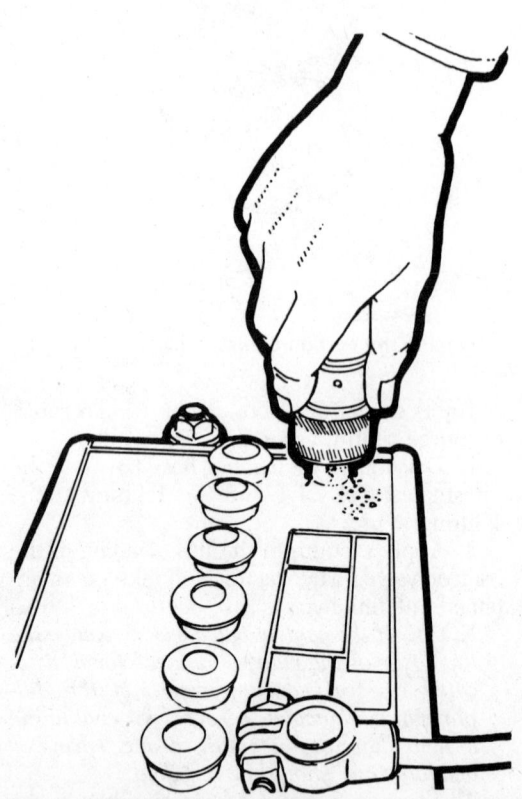

Clean the posts with a wire brush, or a terminal cleaner made for the purpose (shown)

are available for cleaning these parts, one type for conventional batteries and another type for side terminal batteries.

Before installing the cables, loosen the battery hold down clamp or strap, remove the battery and check the battery tray. Clear it of any

GENERAL INFORMATION AND MAINTENANCE

Clean the inside of the clamps with a wire brush, or the special tool

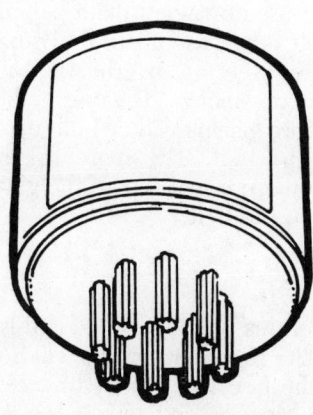

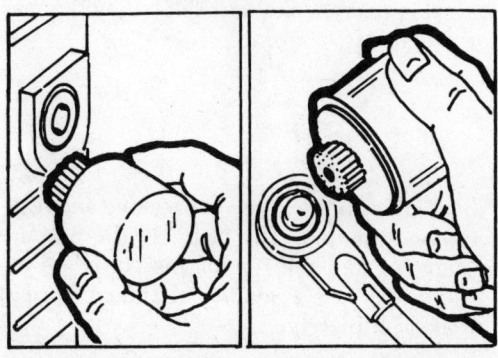

Special tools are also available for cleaning the posts and clamps on side terminal batteries

debris and check it for soundness. Rust should be wire brushed away and the metal be given a coat of antirust paint. Replace the battery and tighten the hold down clamp or strap securely but be careful not to overtighten, which will crack the battery case.

After the clamps and terminals are clean, reinstall the cables (negative cable last); DO NOT hammer on the clamps to install. Tighten the clamps securely but do not distort them. Give the clamps and terminals a thin external coat of grease after installation, to retard corrosion.

Check the cables at the same time that the terminals are cleaned. If the cable insulation is cracked, broken or the ends are frayed, the cable should be replaced with a new cable of the same length and gauge.

NOTE: *Keep flames or sparks away from the battery; it gives off explosive hydrogen gas. Battery electrolyte contains sulphuric acid. If you should splash any on your skin or in your eyes, flush the affected area with plenty of clear water; if it lands in your eyes, get medical help immediately.*

REPLACEMENT

When it becomes necessary to replace the battery, select a battery with a rating equal to or greater than the battery originally installed. Deterioration, embrittlement and just plain aging of the battery cables, starter motor and associated wires, makes the battery's job harder in successive years. The slow increase in electrical resistance over time makes it prudent to install a new battery with a greater capacity than the old. Details on battery removal and installation are covered in Chapter 3.

Belts

TENSION CHECKING, ADJUSTING AND REPLACEMENT

Check the belts driving the fan, air pump, air conditioning compressor and the alternator for cracks, fraying, wear and tension every 6,000 miles. It is recommended that the belts be replaced every 24 months or 24,000 miles. Belt deflection at the midpoint of the longest span between pulleys should not be more than $7/16$ inch with 22 lbs. of pressure applied to the belt.

To adjust the tension on all components except the air conditioning compressor, power steering pump and some late model air pumps, loosen the pivot and mounting bolts of the component which the belt is driving, then, using a wooden lever, pry the component toward or away from the engine until the proper tension is achieved.

14 GENERAL INFORMATION AND MAINTENANCE

HOW TO SPOT WORN V-BELTS

V-Belts are vital to efficient engine operation—they drive the fan, water pump and other accessories. They require little maintenance (occasional tightening) but they will not last forever. Slipping or failure of the V-belt will lead to overheating. If your V-belt looks like any of these, it should be replaced.

Cracking or weathering

This belt has deep cracks, which cause it to flex. Too much flexing leads to heat build-up and premature failure. These cracks can be caused by using the belt on a pulley that is too small. Notched belts are available for small diameter pulleys.

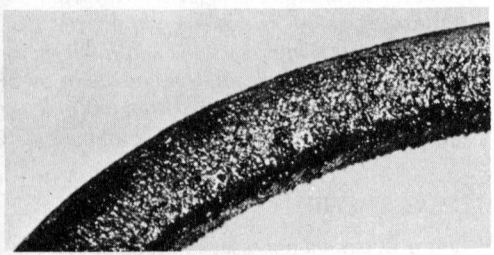

Softening (grease and oil)

Oil and grease on a belt can cause the belt's rubber compounds to soften and separate from the reinforcing cords that hold the belt together. The belt will first slip, then finally fail altogether.

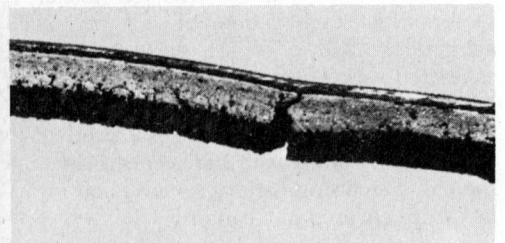

Glazing

Glazing is caused by a belt that is slipping. A slipping belt can cause a run-down battery, erratic power steering, overheating or poor accessory performance. The more the belt slips, the more glazing will be built up on the surface of the belt. The more the belt is glazed, the more it will slip. If the glazing is light, tighten the belt.

Worn cover

The cover of this belt is worn off and is peeling away. The reinforcing cords will begin to wear and the belt will shortly break. When the belt cover wears in spots or has a rough jagged appearance, check the pulley grooves for roughness.

Separation

This belt is on the verge of breaking and leaving you stranded. The layers of the belt are separating and the reinforcing cords are exposed. It's just a matter of time before it breaks completely.

GENERAL INFORMATION AND MAINTENANCE

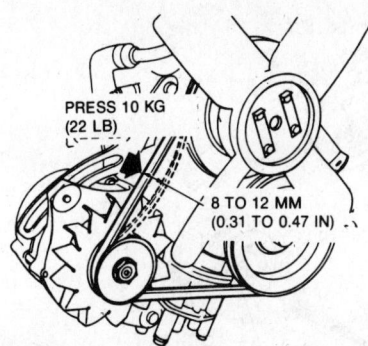

Belt tension

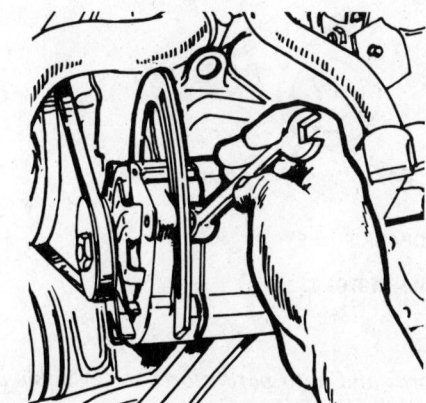

Loosen the pivot bolt—1970–83

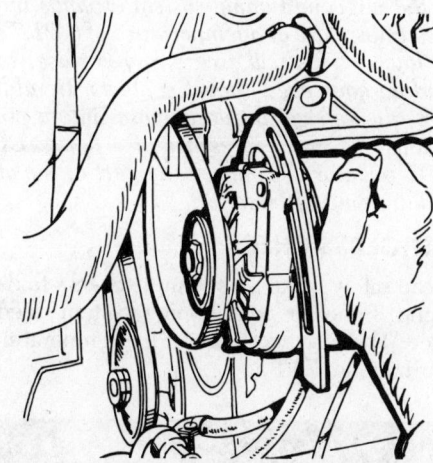

Push the component inwards—1970–83

CAUTION: *An overtight belt will wear out the pulley bearings on the assorted components.*

Tighten the component mounting bolts securely. If a new belt is installed, recheck the tension after driving about 1,000 miles.

NOTE: *The replacement of the inner belt on multi-belted engines may require the removal of the outer belts.*

Belt tension adjustments for the factory installed air conditioning compressor and power steering pump are made at the idler pulley.

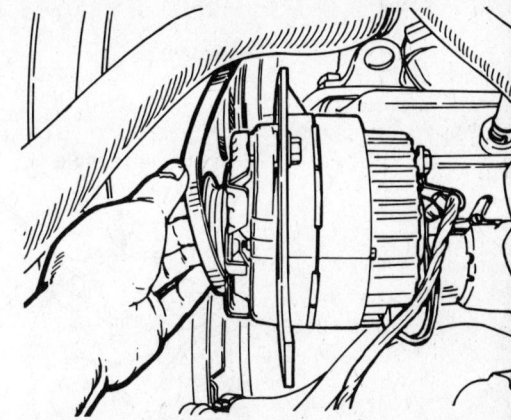

Slip the old belt off and the new one on—1970–83

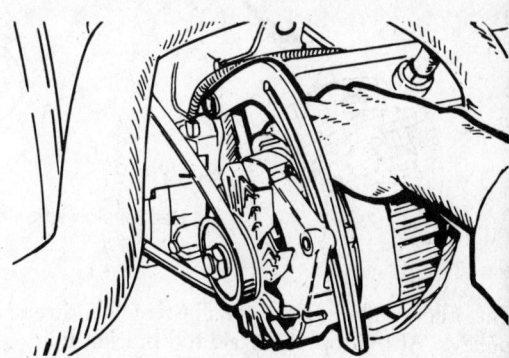

Pull outwards to tension the belt—1970–83

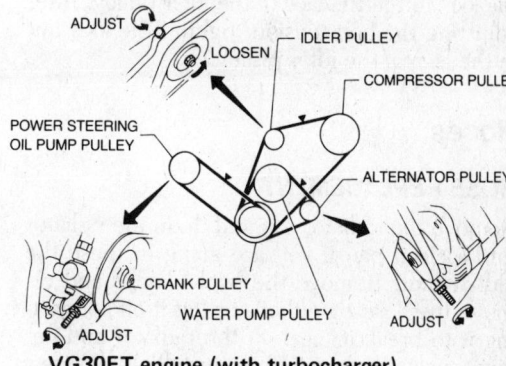

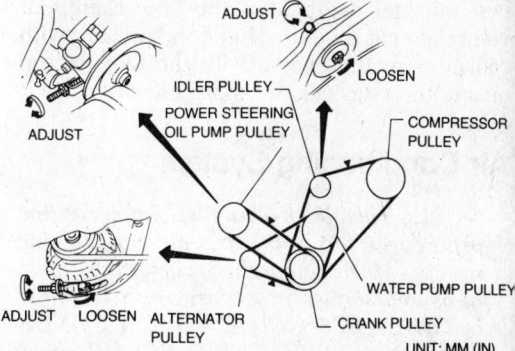

Adjustment points for belt tension—1984 and later

16 GENERAL INFORMATION AND MAINTENANCE

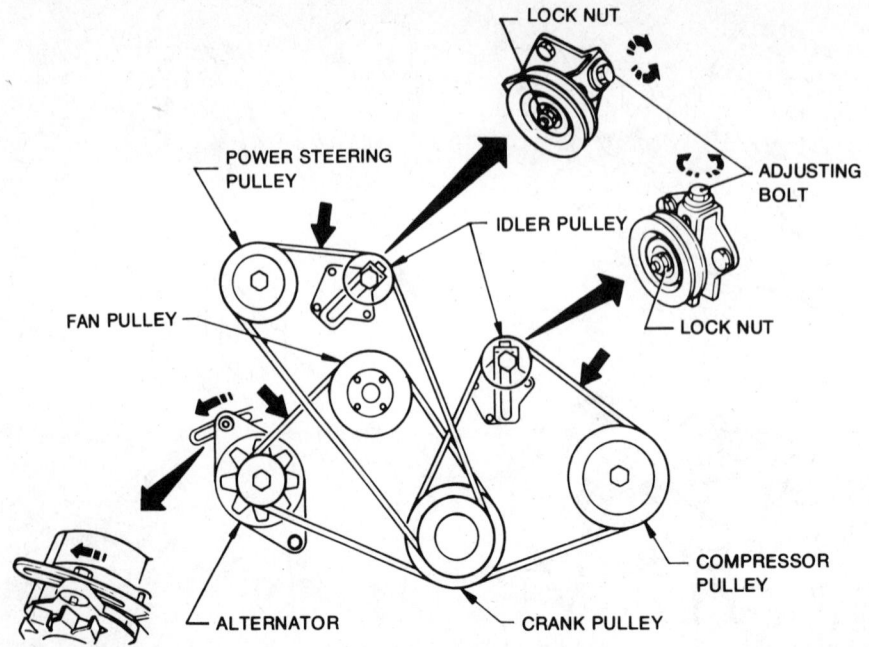

Belt tension adjustment points—1970-83

The idler pulley is the smallest of the three pulleys. At the top of the slotted bracket holding the idler pulley there is a bolt which is used to either raise or lower the pulley. To free the bolt for adjustment, it is necessary to loosen the lock nut in the face of the idler pulley. After adjusting the belt tension, tighten the lock nut in the face of the idler pulley.

Hoses

HOSE REPLACEMENT

Remove the radiator cap and drain the radiator into a clean pan if you are going to reuse the old coolant. Remove the hose clamps and remove the hose by either cutting it off or twisting it to break its seal on the radiator and engine coolant inlets. When installing the new hose, do not overtighten the hose clamps or you might cut the hose. Refill the radiator with coolant, run the engine with the radiator cap on and then recheck the coolant level.

Air Conditioning System

NOTE: *This book contains simple testing procedures for your car's air conditioning system. More comprehensive testing, diagnosis and service procedures may be found in CHILTON'S GUIDE TO AIR CONDITIONING SERVICE AND REPAIR, book part number 7535, available at most book stores and auto parts stores or available directly from Chilton Co.*

CAUTION: *The compressed refrigerant used in the air conditioning system expands into the atmosphere at a temperature of (-)21.7°F or lower. This will freeze any surface, including your eyes, that it contacts. In addition, the refrigerant decomposes into a poisonous gas in the presence of a flame. DO NOT open or disconnect any part of the air conditioning system.*

SIGHT GLASS CHECK

You can safely make a few simple checks to determine if the air conditioning system needs service. The tests work best if the temperature is warm (about 70°F).

Air conditioner receiver-dehydrator sight glass

GENERAL INFORMATION AND MAINTENANCE

HOW TO SPOT BAD HOSES

Both the upper and lower radiator hoses are called upon to perform difficult jobs in an inhospitable environment. They are subject to nearly 18 psi at under hood temperatures often over 280°F., and must circulate nearly 7500 gallons of coolant an hour—3 good reasons to have good hoses.

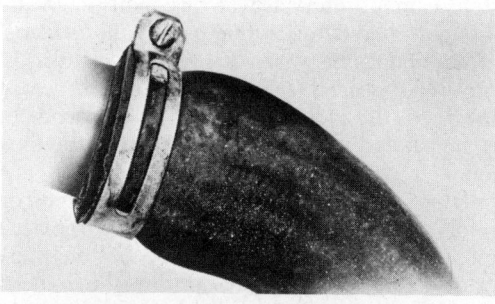

Swollen hose

A good test for any hose is to feel it for soft or spongy spots. Frequently these will appear as swollen areas of the hose. The most likely cause is oil soaking. This hose could burst at any time, when hot or under pressure.

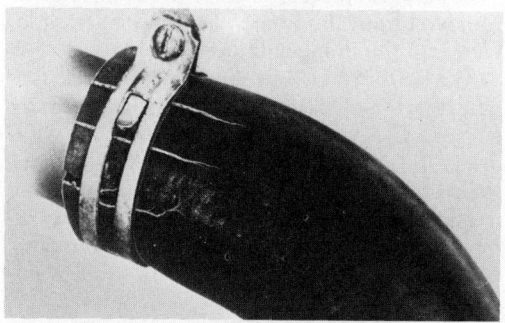

Cracked hose

Cracked hoses can usually be seen but feel the hoses to be sure they have not hardened; a prime cause of cracking. This hose has cracked down to the reinforcing cords and could split at any of the cracks.

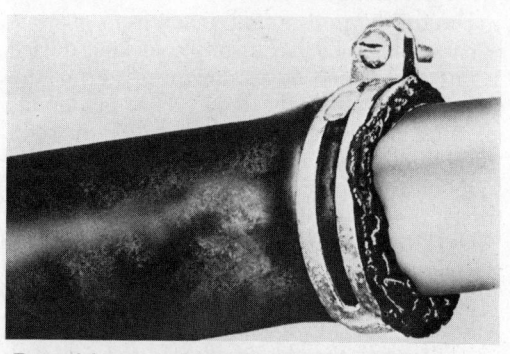

Frayed hose end (due to weak clamp)

Weakened clamps frequently are the cause of hose and cooling system failure. The connection between the pipe and hose has deteriorated enough to allow coolant to escape when the engine is hot.

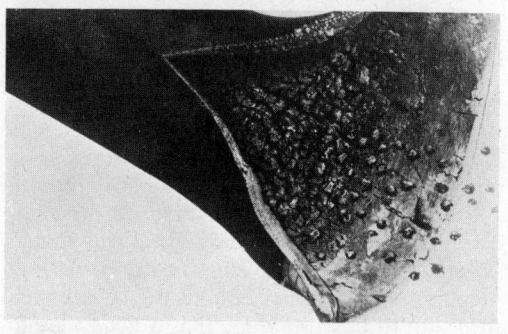

Debris in cooling system

Debris, rust and scale in the cooling system can cause the inside of a hose to weaken. This can usually be felt on the outside of the hose as soft or thinner areas.

GENERAL INFORMATION AND MAINTENANCE

NOTE: *If your vehicle is equipped with an after market air conditioner, the following system check may not apply. You should contact the manufacturer of the unit for instructions on systems checks.*

1. Place the automatic transmission in Park or the manual transmission in Neutral. Set the parking brake.
2. Run the engine at a fast idle (about 1,500 rpm) either with the help of a friend or by temporarily readjusting the idle speed screw.
3. Set the controls for maximum cold with the blower on High.
4. Locate the sight glass in one of the system lines. Usually it is on the left-side, along the top of the radiator.
5. If you see bubbles, the system must be recharged. Very likely there is a leak at some point.
6. If there are no bubbles, there is either no refrigerant at all or the system is fully charged. Feel the two hoses going to the belt driven compressor. If they are both at the same temperature, the system is empty and must be recharged.
7. If one hose (high pressure) is warm and the other (low pressure) is cold, the system may be all right. However, you are probably making these tests because you think there is something wrong, so proceed to the next step.
8. Have an assistant in the vehicle turn the fan control ON and OFF to operate the compressor clutch. Watch the sight glass.
9. If bubbles appear when the clutch is disengaged and disappear when it is engaged, the system is properly charged.
10. If the refrigerant takes more than 45 seconds to bubble when the clutch is disengaged, the system is overcharged. This usually causes poor cooling at low speeds.

CAUTION: *If it is determined that the system has a leak, it should be corrected as soon as possible. Leaks may allow moisture to enter and cause a very expensive rust problem.*

NOTE: *Exercise the air conditioner for a few minutes, every two weeks or so, during the cold months. This avoids the possibility of the compressor seals drying out from lack of lubrication.*

Windshield Wipers

For maximum effectiveness and longest element life, the windshield and wiper blades should be kept clean. Dirt, tree sap, road tar and etc. will cause streaking, smearing and blade deterioration if left on the glass. It is advisable to wash the windshield carefully with a commercial glass cleaner at least once a month. Wipe off the rubber blades with the wet rag afterwards.

CAUTION: *DO NOT attempt to move the wipers by hand; damage to the motor and drive mechanism will result.*

If the blades are found to be cracked, broken or torn, they should be replaced immediately. Replacement intervals will vary with usage, although ozone deterioration usually limits blade life to about one year. If the wiper pattern is smeared, streaked or if the blade chatters across the glass, the elements should be replaced. It is easiest and most sensible to replace the elements in pairs.

There are basically three different types of refills, which differ in their method of replacement. One type has two release buttons, approximately ⅓ of the way up from the ends of the blade frame. Pushing the buttons down releases a lock and allows the rubber filler to be removed from the frame. The new filler slides back into the frame and locks in place.

The second type of refill has two metal tabs which are unlocked by squeezing them together. The rubber filler can then be withdrawn from the frame jaws. A new refill is installed by inserting the refill into the front frame jaws and sliding it rearward to engage the remaining frame jaws. There are usually four jaws; be certain when installing that the refill is engaged in all of them. At the end of its travel, the tabs will lock into place on the front jaws of the wiper blade frame.

The third type is a refill made from polycarbonate. The refill has a simple locking device at one end which flexes downward out of the groove into which the jaws of the holder fit, allowing easy release. By sliding the new refill through all the jaws and pushing through the slight resistance when it reaches the end of its travel, the refill will lock into position.

NOTE: *Regardless of the type of refill used, make sure that all of the frame jaws are engaged as the refill is pushed into place and locked. The metal blade holder and frame will scratch the glass if allowed to touch it.*

Tires

Tires should be checked weekly for proper air pressure. A chart, located either in the glove compartment or on the driver's or passenger's door, gives the recommended inflation pressures. Maximum fuel economy and tire life will result if the pressure is maintained at the highest figure given on the chart. Pressures should be checked before driving since pressure can increase as much as six pounds per square inch (psi) due to heat buildup. It is a good idea to have your own accurate pressure gauge, be-

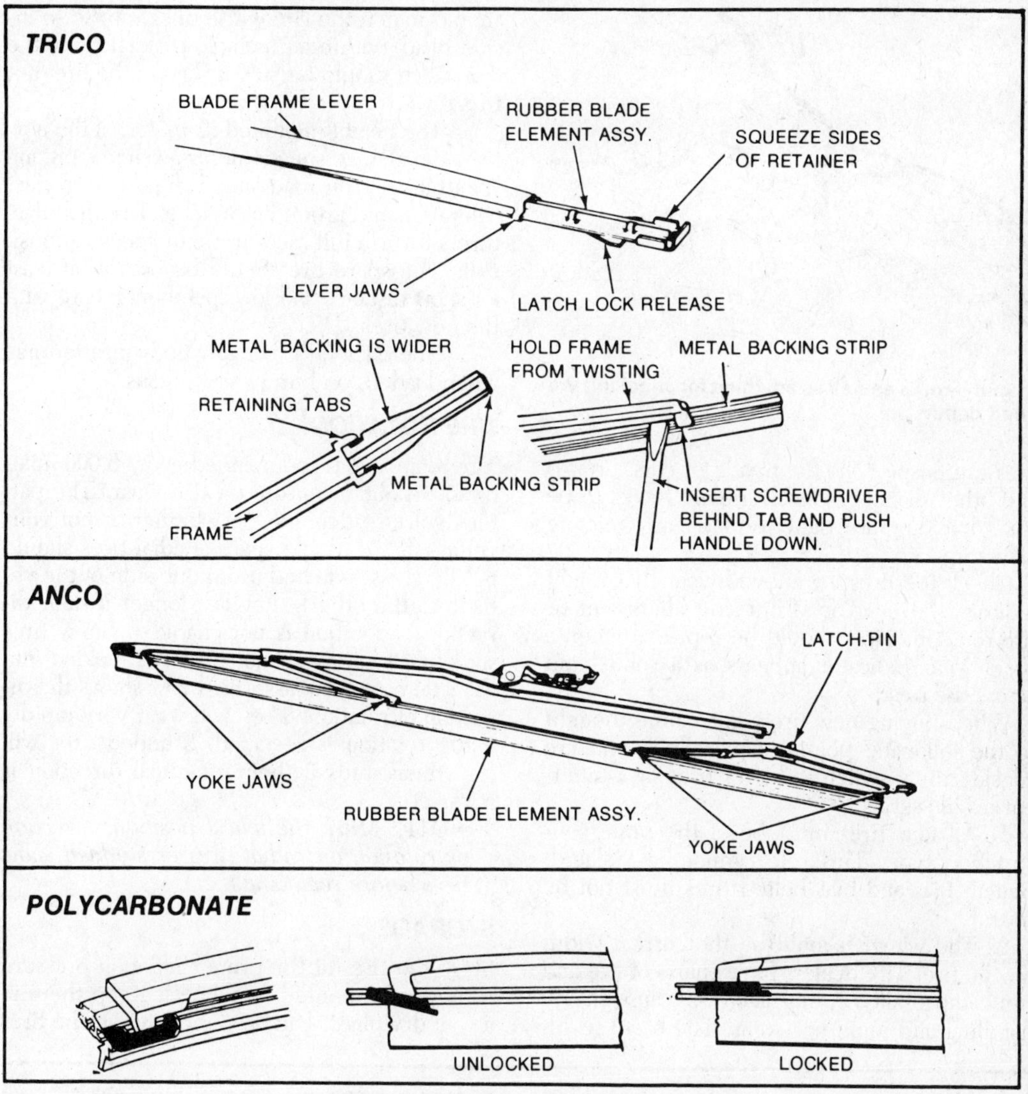

GENERAL INFORMATION AND MAINTENANCE

The three types of wiper element retention

Tread wear indicators will appear when the tire is worn out

cause not all gauges on service station air pumps can be trusted. When checking pressures, do not neglect the spare tire. Note that some spare tires require pressures considerably higher than those used in the other tires.

While you are about the task of checking air

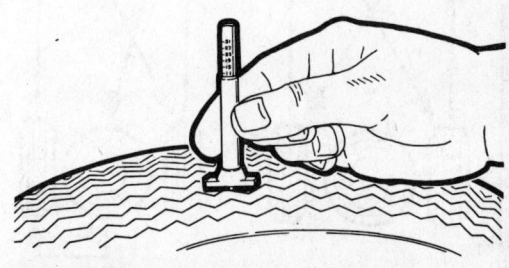

Tread depth can also be checked with an inexpensive gauge

GENERAL INFORMATION AND MAINTENANCE

A penny works as well as anything for checking tire tread depth

pressure, inspect the tire treads for cuts, bruises and other damage. Check the air valves to be sure that they are tight. Replace any missing valve caps.

Check the tires for uneven wear that might indicate the need for front end alignment or tire rotation. Tires should be replaced when a tread wear indicator appears as a solid band across the tread.

When buying new tires, give some thought to the following points, especially if you are considering a switch to larger tires or a different profile series.

1. All four tires must be of the same construction type. This rule cannot be violated. Radial, bias and bias belted tires must not be mixed.
2. The wheels should be the correct width for the tire. Tire dealers have charts of tire and rim compatibility. A mismatch will cause sloppy handling and rapid tire wear. The tread width should match the rim width (inside bead to inside bead) within an inch. For radial tires, the rim width should be 80% or less of the tire (not tread) width.
3. The height (mounted diameter) of the new tires can change speedometer accuracy, engine speed at a given road speed, fuel mileage, acceleration and ground clearance. Tire manufacturers furnish full measurement specifications.
4. The spare tire should be usable, at least for short distance and low speed operation, with the new tires.
5. There shouldn't be any body interference when loaded, on bumps or in turns.

TIRE ROTATION

Tire rotation is recommended every 6,000 miles or so, to obtain maximum tire wear. The pattern you use depends on whether or not your vehicle has a usable spare. Radial tires should not be cross switched (from one side of the vehicle to the other); they last longer if their direction of rotation is not changed. Snow tires sometimes have directional arrows molded into the side of the carcass; the arrow shows the direction of rotation. They will wear very rapidly if the rotation is reversed. Studded tires will lose their studs if their rotational direction is reversed.

NOTE: *Mark the wheel position, direction or rotation on radial tires or studded snow tires before removing them.*

STORAGE

Store the tires at the proper inflation pressure if they are mounted on wheels. Keep them in a cool dry place, laid on their sides. If the tires

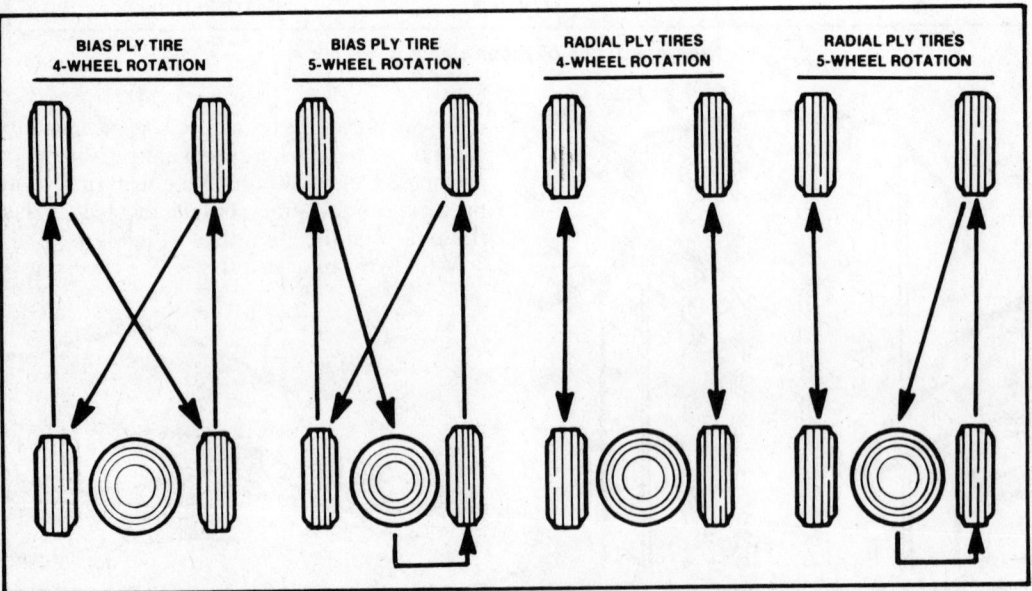

Tire rotation diagrams; note that radials should not be cross-switched

GENERAL INFORMATION AND MAINTENANCE

are stored in the garage or basement, DO NOT let them stand on a concrete floor; set them on strips of wood.

Fuel Filter

The fuel filter should be replaced every 2 years or 25,000 miles and ONLY when the engine is cold. Always place some absorbent cloths under the filter before disconnecting any lines, because some gas will spill from the bottom of the filter during removal.

REPLACEMENT

1970–73

The fuel filter is a clear plastic unit mounted in a clamp in the engine compartment.
1. Remove the filter from its clamp.
2. Disconnect the fuel lines from both ends of the filter.
3. Discard the old filter.
4. Install the fuel lines onto the replacement filter and tighten the clamps.
5. Replace the filter in the clamp.
6. Start the engine and check for leaks.

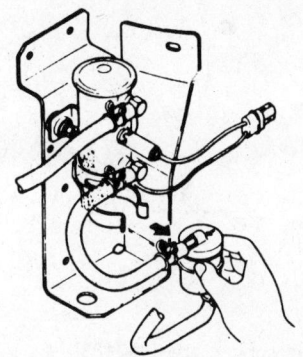

1974 fuel filter

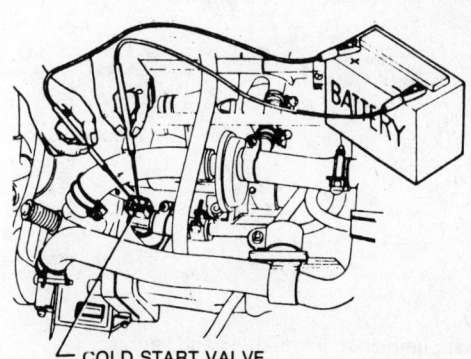

Energizing the cold start valve to release fuel system pressure on 1975–79 models

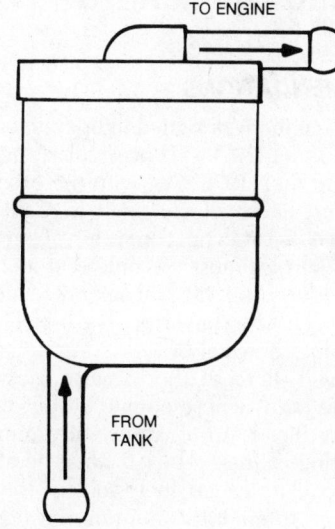

1970–73 fuel filter

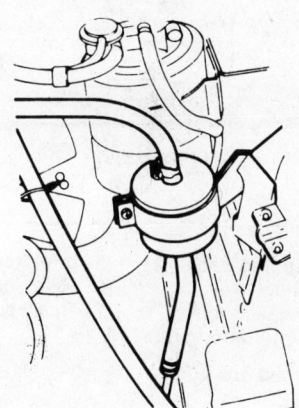

1975 and later fuel filter

1974

This filter is similar to the one used on earlier models but it is located near the rear axle along with the electric fuel pump. Raise the rear of the vehicle and support it on jackstands. Use the method given for earlier models to replace the filter.

1975–79

The fuel filter is retained by a bracket to the inner fender directly behind the evaporative canister. Before the filter can be replaced, the high pressure in the fuel system must be released.
1. Disconnect the negative battery cable.
2. Disconnect the cold start valve electrical connector. The cold start valve is located in the intake runner.
3. Use two jumper wires from the battery to connect to the terminals on the cold start valve.
   CAUTION: *Be careful not to short these against each other.*

GENERAL INFORMATION AND MAINTENANCE

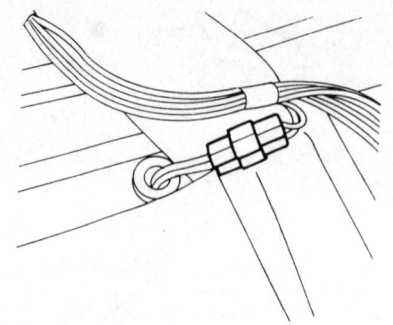

Fuel pump connector—1982–83

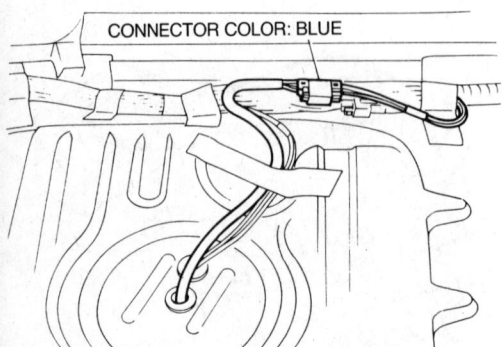

Fuel pump connector—1984 and later

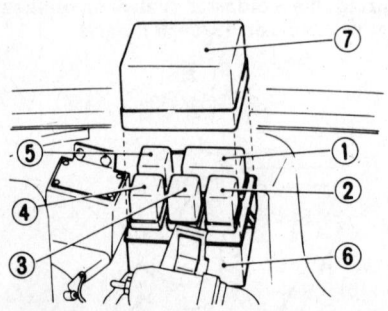

1. Fuel pump relay #2
2. Lighting relay
3. Bulb check relay
4. Air conditioning relay
5. Inhibitor relay
6. Relay box
7. Relay cover

Location of the fuel pump relay #2—1980–81

NOTE: *Hold the jumpers to the valve terminal for about 2–3 seconds. This will relieve the pressure in the fuel system.*

4. Remove the fuel lines from the fuel filter by loosening the clamps.

5. Remove the filter retaining bracket bolt and the filter.

6. To install, use a new filter and clamps, then reverse the removal procedures. Start the engine and check for leaks.

1980 and Later

The fuel filter is of the same type as that used on the other fuel injected models, but the method for discharging the fuel injection system is different.

1. Start the engine.
2. On the 1980–81 models, remove the fuel pump relay (No. 1 in the diagram) from the relay connector while the engine is running. The relay is located on the right-front fender in the engine compartment, just aft of the windshield washer reservoir. On 1982 and later models, lift the rear floor mat and disconnect the fuel pump electrical connector while the engine is running.
3. After the engine stalls, crank the engine 2–3 more times.
4. Turn the ignition switch OFF. Install the fuel pump relay (1980–81) or reconnect the connector (1982 and later).
5. Release the clamps securing the fuel hoses to the filter. Be careful not to spill fuel on the engine. Disconnect the hoses from the filter.
6. Remove the filter-to-bracket bolt and the filter.
7. Install the new filter. Connect the fuel hoses and secure them with new clamps.
8. Start the engine and check for leaks.

FUEL AND LUBRICANTS

Fuel

RECOMMENDATIONS

The Z-car engine is designed to operate on regular leaded fuel (1970–71) or regular, low lead or unleaded fuel (1972–79), with the exception of 1975 and later vehicles sold in California, which have a catalytic converter. Converter equipped vehicles must use unleaded fuel. This also applies to all 1980 and later ZX models, since they all have a converter. The use of leaded fuel will plug the catalyst rendering it inoperative and will increase the exhaust back pressure to the point where engine output will be severely reduced. In all cases, the minimum octane rating of the fuel used must be at least 91 RON. All unleaded fuels sold in the U.S. are required to meet this minimum octane rating.

Use of a fuel too low in octane (a measurement of anti-knock quality) will result in spark knock. Since many factors affect operating efficiency, such as altitude, terrain, air temperature and humidity, knocking may result even though the recommended fuel is being used. If persistent knocking occurs, it may be necessary to switch to a slightly higher grade of gasoline. Continuous or heavy knocking may result in engine damage.

NOTE: *Your engine's fuel requirement can change with time, mainly due to carbon buildup, which changes the compression ra-*

Capacities

Year	Model	Displacement cu in. (cc)	Engine Crankcase Qts (liters)		Transmission Pts (liters)		Drive Axle Pts (liters)	Gasoline Tank Gals (liters)	Cooling System Qts (liters)
			With Filter	Without Filter	Manual	Automatic			
1970–73	240-Z	146 (2393)	5 (4.7)	4.25 (4)	3⅛ (1.5)	11¾ (5.5)	2⅛ (1)	15⅞ (60)	10½ (9.9)
1974	260-Z	156.5 (2565)	5 (4.7)	4.25 (4)	3⅛ (1.5)	11¾ (5.5)	2⅛ (1)	15⅞ (60)	10 (9.4)
1975	280-Z	168 (2753)	5 (4.7)	4.25 (4)	3.13 (1.5)	11.75 (5.5)	2.75 (1.3)	17.25 (65)	10 (9.4)
1976	280-Z	168 (2753)	5 (4.7)	4.25 (4)	3.13 (1.5)	11.75 (5.5)	2.75 (1.3)	17.25 (65)	11 (10.4)
1977–78	280-Z	168 (2753)	5 (4.7)	4.25 (4)	3.63 (1.7)①	11.75 (5.5)	2.75 (1.3)②	17.25 (65)	11 (10.4)
1979–83	280-ZX	168 (2753)	4.75 (4.5)③	4.25 (4.0)④	3.63 (1.7)①	11.75 (5.5)	2.75 (1.3)②	21.12 (80)	11.12 (10.5)
1984–86	300 ZX	180.6 (2,960)	4.25 (4.0)	3.5 (3.3)	4 (1.9)	15.7 (7.0)	2.75 (1.3)	19 (72)	11.6 (11.0)

① For 4-speed; 5-speed capacity is 4.25 pts (2 liters)
② For rear axle used with manual transmissions; with automatic capacity is 2.13 pts (1 liter)
③ Turbocharged engines—5.5 qts.
④ Turbocharged engines—5.0 qts.

tio. If your engine pings, knocks or runs on, switch to a higher grade of fuel and check the ignition timing. If the engine requires unleaded fuel, sometimes changing brands will cure the problem. If it is necessary to retard the timing from specifications, don't change it more than a few degrees. Retarded timing will reduce power output and fuel mileage and will increase engine temperature.

Recommended Lubricants

Lubricant	Classification
Engine Oil	API SE or SF
Manual Transmission	API GL-4
Automatic Transmission	DEXRON® or DEXRON II®
Differential	API GL-5
Wheel Bearings	NLGI #2
Chassis Grease	NLGI #2
Driveshaft	NLGI #2
Brake Fluid	DOT 3
Clutch Fluid	DOT 3
Steering Gear: manual power	API GL-4 DEXRON® or DEXRON II®
Antifreeze	Ethylene Glycol

Engine

OIL RECOMMENDATION

The SAE (Society of Automotive Engineers) grade number indicates the viscosity of the engine oil and thus it's ability to lubricate at a given temperature. The lower the SAE grade number, the lighter the oil; the lower the viscosity, the easier it is to crank the engine in cold weather.

Oil viscosities should be chosen from those oils recommended for the lowest anticipated temperatures during the oil change interval.

Multi-viscosity oils (10W-30, 20W-50 and etc.) offer the important advantage of being adaptable to temperature extremes. They allow easy starting at low temperatures, yet give good protection at high speeds and engine temperatures. This is a decided advantage in changeable climates or in long distance touring.

The API (American Petroleum Institute) designation indicates the classification of engine oil for use under given operating conditions. Only oils designated for use Service SF should be used. Oils of the SF type perform a variety of functions inside the engine in addition to the basic function as a lubricant. Through a balanced system of metallic detergents and polymeric dispersants, the oil prevents the formation of high and low temperature deposits, plus keeping sludge and dirt particles in suspension. Acids, particularly sulfuric acid, as well

GENERAL INFORMATION AND MAINTENANCE

Maintenance Intervals Chart

Intervals are for numbers of months or thousands of miles, whichever comes first.

NOTE: *Heavy-duty operation (trailer towing, prolonged idling, severe stop and start driving, winter operation on salted roads) should be accompanied by a 50% increase in maintenance. Cut the interval in half for these conditions. Operation in extremely dusty conditions may require immediate changes of engine oil and all filters.*

Maintenance	1970–71	1972–73	1974	1975–78	1979	1980–86
Air cleaner (Replace)	24	24	24	24	24	24
PCV valve						
Check	12	12	12	12	12	12
Replace	12	12	12	24	24	①
Carbon canister filter (Replace)	—	—	24	24	24	①
Belt tension (Adjust)	6	6	12	12	12	12
Engine oil (Change)	3	3	4	6	6	6
Engine oil filter (Change)	6	6	8	6	6	6
Fuel filter (Replace)	24	24	24	24	24	24
Manual transmission						
Check	3	3	4	6	6	12
Change	30	30	36	24	24	48
Automatic transmission						
Check	—	3	4	6	6	12
Change	—	30	36	—	—	—
Differential						
Check	3	3	4	6	6	12
Change	30	30	36	24	48	48
Front wheel bearings (Clean and repack)	24	24	24	24	24	24
Engine coolant (Change)	24	24	24	24	24	24
Steering gear (Check)	6	6	12	12	12	12
Chassis lubrication Linkage and suspension ball joints	24	24	24	24	24	24
Axle shaft lubrication	30	30	36	24	24	24
Rotate tires	6	6	8	12	12	12
Valve lash ② (Check and adjust)	6	6	12	12	12	12
Brake and clutch fluid						
Check	3	3	4	6	6	12
Change ③	12	12	12	12	12	12
Air induction filter (Replace)	—	—	—	—	—	24
Oxygen sensor ④	—	—	—	—	—	30

① As necessary
② See Chapter 2
③ See Chapters 6 and 9
④ See Chapter 4

as other by products of combustion, are neutralized. Both the SAE grade number and the API designation can be found on the top of the oil can.

CAUTION: *Non-detergent or straight mineral oils must never be used.*

OIL LEVEL CHECK

At every stop for fuel, check the engine oil as follows:

1. Park the vehicle on the level.
2. The engine may be either hot or cold when

GENERAL INFORMATION AND MAINTENANCE

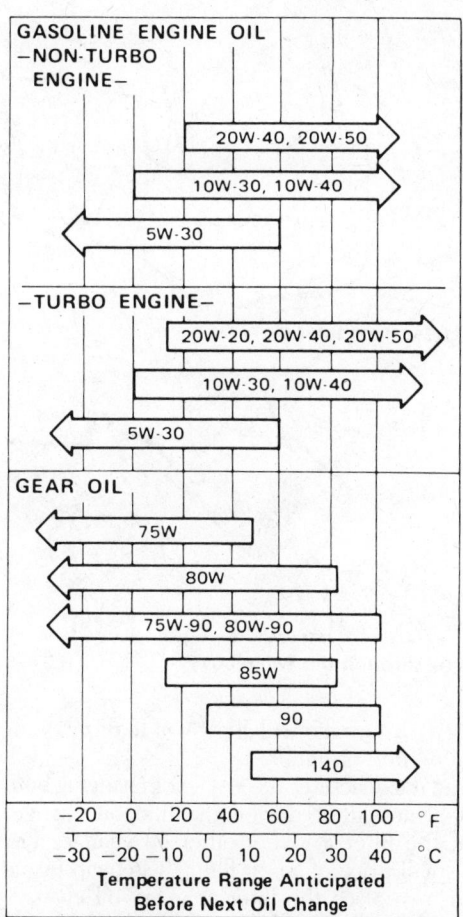

Oil viscosity chart

checking oil level. However, if it is hot, wait a few minutes after the engine has been shut off to allow the oil to drain back into the crankcase. If the engine is cold, do not start it before checking the oil level.

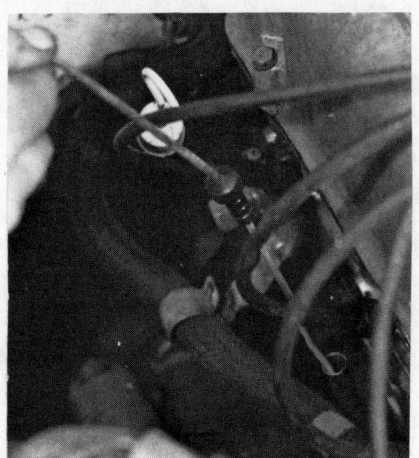

Oil level is checked with the dipstick located on the right side of the engine on 1970–83 models and on the left side on 1984 and later models

Add oil through the capped opening in the valve cover

3. Open the hood and locate the dipstick, which is on the right-side (passenger's side) of the engine. Pull the dipstick from its tube, wipe it clean and reinsert it.

4. Pull the dipstick again, then while holding it in a horizontal position, read the oil level. The oil should be between the H and L marks. If the oil is below the L mark, add oil of the proper viscosity through the capped opening in the front of the valve cover.

5. Replace the dipstick and check the level again after adding any oil. Be careful not to overfill the crankcase. Approximately one quart of oil will raise the level from L to H. Excess oil will generally be consumed at an accelerated rate even if no damage to the engine seal occurs.

CHANGING OIL AND FILTER

The mileage figures given in the Maintenance Intervals chart are the manufacturer's recommended intervals for oil and filter changes, assuming average driving. If your vehicle is being used under dusty, polluted or off-road conditions, change the oil and filter sooner than specified. The same thing goes for vehicles driven in stop-and-go traffic or only for short distances.

Always drain the oil after the engine has been running long enough to bring it to operating temperature. Hot oil will flow easier and more contaminants will be removed along with the oil than if it were drained cold. You will need a large capacity drain pan, which can be purchased at any store selling automotive parts. Another necessity is a container for the used oil; plastic bottles, such as those used for bleach or fabric softener, make excellent storage jugs. One ecologically desirable solution to the used oil disposal problem is to find a cooperative gas

26 GENERAL INFORMATION AND MAINTENANCE

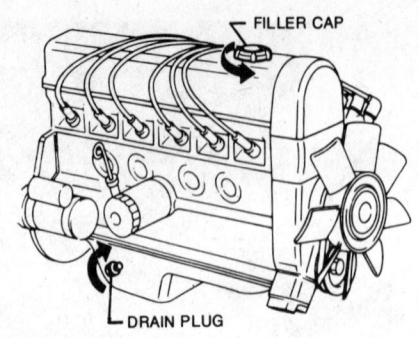
Oil drain plug location—1970–83

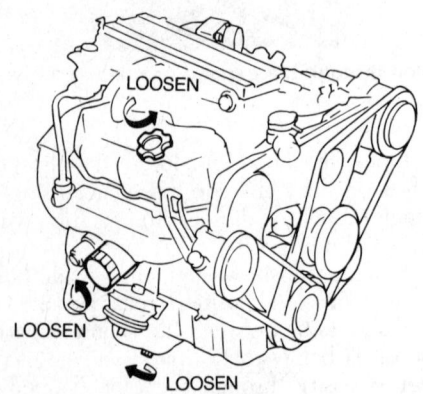
Oil drain plug location—V6 engine

Remove the oil filter with a strap wrench

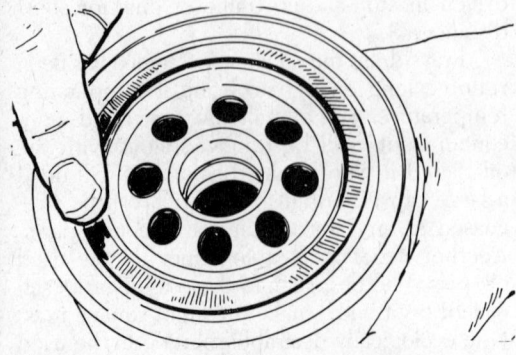
Coat the new oil filter gasket with clean oil

Install the new filter by hand

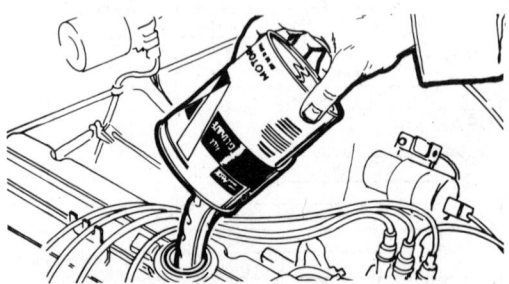
Add oil through the valve cover

station owner who will allow you to dump your used oil into his tank.

The manufacturer recommends changing both the oil and filter during the first oil change, then the filter at every other oil change. For the small price of an oil filter, it's cheap insurance to replace the filter at every oil change. One of the larger filter manufacturer's points out in its advertisements that not changing the filter leaves one quart of dirty oil in the engine. This claim is true and should be kept in mind when changing your oil. Change your oil as follows:

1. Run the engine until it reaches normal operating temperatures.
2. Raise the front of the vehicle and support it on jackstands.
3. Slide a drain pan, of at least 6 quarts capacity, under the oil pan.
4. Loosen the drain plug and turn the plug out by hand. By keeping an inward pressure on the plug as you unscrew it, oil won't escape past the threads and you can remove it without being burned by hot oil.
5. Allow the oil to drain completely, then install the drain plug. Don't overtighten the plug or you'll be buying a new pan or a trick replacement plug for stripped threads.
6. Using a strap wrench, remove the oil filter. Keep in mind that it's holding about one quart of dirty, hot oil.
7. Empty the old filter into the drain pan and dispose of the filter.
8. Using a clean rag, wipe off the filter adapter on the engine block. Be sure that the

GENERAL INFORMATION AND MAINTENANCE

rag doesn't leave any lint which could clog an oil passage.

9. Coat the rubber gasket on the filter with fresh oil. Spin it onto the engine by hand; when the gasket touches the adapter surface, give it another ½–¾ turn. No more or you'll squash the gasket and it will leak.

10. Refill the engine with the correct amount of fresh oil. See the Capacities chart.

11. Check the oil level on the dipstick. It is normal for the level to be a bit above the full mark. Start the engine and allow it to idle for a few minutes.

CAUTION: *DO NOT run the engine above idle speed until it has built up oil pressure, indicated when the oil light goes out.*

12. Turn OFF the engine and allow the oil to drain for a minute, then check the oil level. Check around the filter and drain plug for any leaks, then correct as necessary.

Transmission

FLUID RECOMMENDATION

For manual transmissions, there are a variety of fluids available (depending upon the outside temperature); be sure to use fluid with an API GL-4 rating.

For automatic transmissions, use Dexron® AFT (automatic transmission fluid).

LEVEL CHECK

Manual

Check the lubricant level at the interval specified in the maintenance chart.

1. With the vehicle parked on a level surface, remove the filler plug from the left-side of the transmission case. The filler plug has a square head.

2. If lubricant begins to trickle out the hole, there is enough. Otherwise, carefully insert a finger (watch out for sharp threads) and check to see if the oil is up to the edge of the hole.

3. If not, add lubricant through the hole to raise the level to the edge of the filler hole.

Most gear lubricants come in a plastic squeeze bottle with a nozzle, making additions easy. You can also use a squeeze bulb. Add API GL-4 gear oil of the proper viscosity (see the viscosity chart).

4. Replace the plug and check for leaks.

Automatic

Check the level of the automatic transmission fluid every 2,000 miles. There is a dipstick at the right-rear of the engine under the hood. The dipstick has H and L markings, which are accurate for level indications only when the transmission is hot (normal operating temperature). The transmission is considered hot after 15 miles of highway driving.

1. Park the vehicle on a level surface with the engine idling. Apply the parking brake.
2. Shift the transmission to Park.
3. Remove the dipstick, wipe it clean, then reinsert it firmly. Be certain that it has been pushed fully home. Remove the dipstick and check the fluid level while holding the dipstick

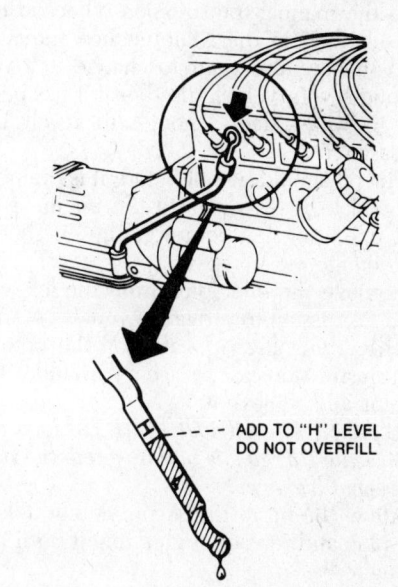

Automatic transmission dipstick—1970–83

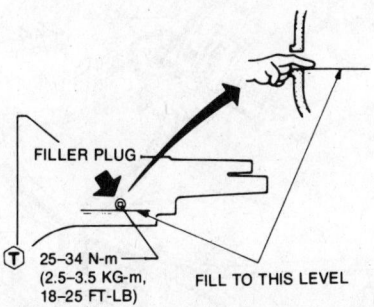

Remove the filler plug from the left side of the manual transmission to check the lubricant level

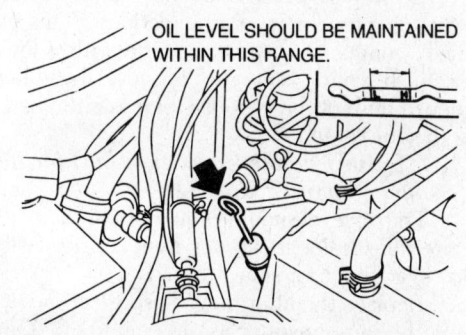

Automatic transmission dipstick—V6 engine

28 GENERAL INFORMATION AND MAINTENANCE

horizontally. The level should be at or near the H mark.

4. If the fluid level is below the L mark, add the DEXRON® type automatic transmission fluid through the dipstick tube. This is more easily accomplished with the aid of a funnel and hose. Check the level often between additions, being careful not to overfill the transmission. Overfilling will cause slippage, seal damage and overheating. Approximately one quart of fluid will raise the level from L to H.

NOTE: *The fluid on the dipstick should be a bright red color. If it is discolored (brown or black) or smells burnt, serious transmission troubles are present, probably due to overheating. The transmission should be inspected by a qualified mechanic to locate the cause of the burnt fluid.*

DRAIN AND REFILL
Manual

Change the manual transmission oil according to the schedule in the Maintenance Intervals chart. You may also want to change it if you have bought your vehicle used or if it has been driven in water deep enough to reach the transmission case.

1. The oil should be hot before it is drained. If the vehicle is driven until the engine is at normal operating temperature, the oil should be hot enough.
2. Remove the filler plug from the left-side of the transmission to provide a vent.
3. The drain plug is located on the bottom of the transmission case. Place a pan under the drain plug and remove it.

CAUTION: *The oil will be HOT. Push up against the threads as you unscrew the plug to prevent leakage.*

4. Allow the oil to drain completely. Clean off the plug and replace, tightening it until it is just snug.
5. Fill the transmission with gear oil through the filler plug hole. Use API service GL-4 gear oil of the proper viscosity (see the Viscosity Chart in this chapter for recommendations). This oil usually comes in a squeeze bottle with a long nozzle. If yours isn't you can use a rubber squeeze bulb of the type used for kitchen basting to squirt it in.

NOTE: *Refer to the Capacities chart for the amount of oil needed.*

6. The oil level should come right to the edge of the filler hole; stick your finger in to verify this. Watch out for sharp threads.
7. Replace the filler plug. Dispose of the old oil in the same manner as old engine oil. Take a drive in the vehicle, stop and check for leaks.

Automatic

The fluid should be changed according to the schedule in the Maintenance Intervals chart. If the vehicle is normally used in severe service, such as start-and-stop driving, trailer towing or the like, the interval should be halved. The fluid must be hot before it is drained; a 20 minute drive should accomplish this.

1. There is no drain plug; the transmission

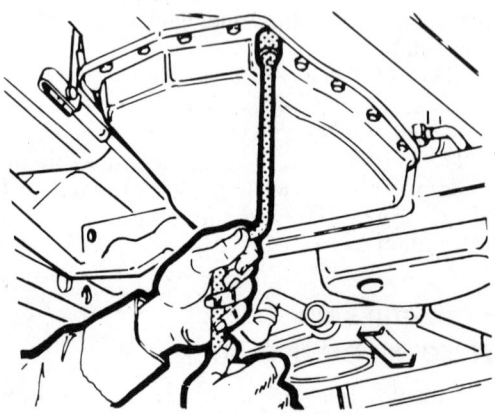

Remove the pan to drain the automatic transmission

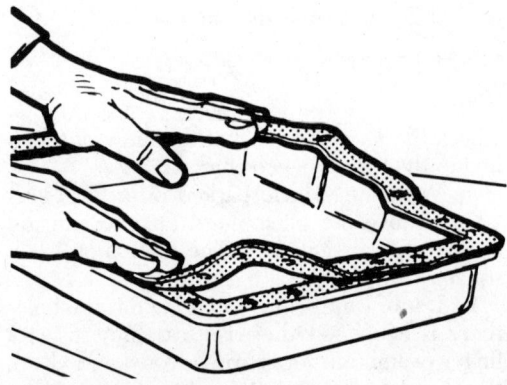

Install a new gasket

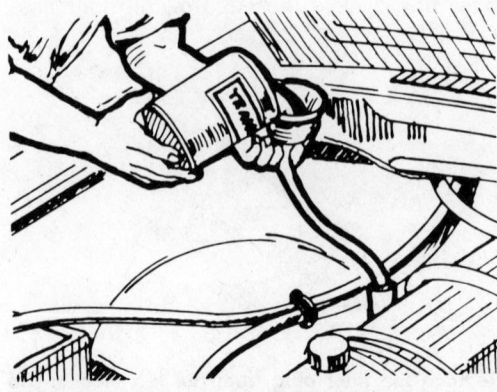

Add fluid through the dipstick tube

pan must be removed. Partially remove the pan screws until the pan can be pulled down at one corner. Place a container under the transmission, lower a rear corner of the pan and allow the fluid to drain.

2. After draining, remove the pan screws, the pan and the gasket.

3. Clean the pan thoroughly and allow it to air dry. If you wipe it out with a rag you risk leaving bits of lint in the pan which will clog the tiny hydraulic passages in the transmission.

4. To install, use a new gasket, sealant and reverse the removal procedures. Torque the pan screws evenly in rotation from the center outwards, to 3–5 ft.lbs.

CAUTION: *If sealer is used on the gasket, apply it only in a very thin bead running to the outside of the pan screw holes.*

NOTE: *It is a good idea to measure the amount of fluid drained to determine how much fresh fluid to add. This is because some parts of the transmission, such as the torque converter, will not drain completely and using the dry refill amount specified in the Capacities chart may lead to overfilling. Make sure that the funnel, hose or whatever you are using is completely clean and dry before pouring transmission fluid through it. Use DEXRON® or DEXRON® II automatic transmission fluid.*

5. Replace the dipstick after filling. Start the engine and allow it to idle. DO NOT race the engine.

6. After the engine has idled for a few minutes, shift the transmission slowly through the gears, then return the lever to Park. With the engine idling, check the fluid level on the dipstick. It should be between the H and L marks. If below L, add sufficient fluid to raise the level to between the marks.

7. Drive the vehicle until the transmission is at operating temperature. The fluid should be at the H mark. If not, add sufficient fluid until this is the case. Be careful not to overfill; overfilling causes slippage, overheating and seal damage.

NOTE: *If the drained fluid is discolored (brown or black), thick or smells burnt, serious transmission problems due to overheating should be suspected. Your vehicle's transmission should be inspected by a transmission specialist to determine the cause.*

Differential

FLUID RECOMMENDATION AND LEVEL CHECK

Check the differential fluid level at the interval specified in the maintenance chart. Park the

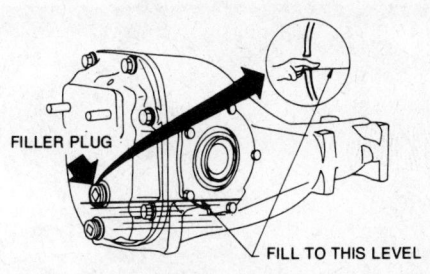

The differential fluid level is checked through the filler hole

vehicle on a level surface. Remove the filler plug in the rear center of the differential housing. The lubricant should be up to the level of the hole. You can check this with your finger (watch out for sharp threads). If the fluid is below the level of the hole, add API GL-5 gear oil of the proper viscosity through the hole to bring the lubricant up to the proper level.

NOTE: *Gear oil usually comes in a plastic squeeze bottle with a nozzle but you can use a squeeze bulb or a kitchen baster to squirt it in.*

DRAIN AND REFILL

The axle lubricant should be changed according to the schedule in the Maintenance Intervals chart; you may also want to change it if you have bought your vehicle used or if it has been driven in water deep enough to reach the axle.

1. Park the vehicle on a level surface. Place a pan of at least two quarts capacity underneath the drain plug. Remove the drain plug.

NOTE: *The drain plug is located on the center rear of the differential carrier, just below the filler plug.*

2. Allow the lubricant to drain completely.

3. Install the drain plug. Tighten it so that it will not leak but do not overtighten. If you have a torque wrench, recommended torque is 29–43 ft.lbs.

4. Refill the differential housing with API GL-5 gear oil of the proper viscosity. The correct level is to the edge of the filler hole.

5. Install the filler plug. Tighten to 29–43 ft.lbs.

Coolant

FLUID RECOMMENDATION AND LEVEL CHECK

The manufacturer recommends checking the radiator coolant every time you stop for gas. Dealing with the cooling system can be a dangerous matter unless the proper precautions are

GENERAL INFORMATION AND MAINTENANCE

On models without a coolant overflow tank, the coolant level should be about one inch below the filler neck (engine cold)

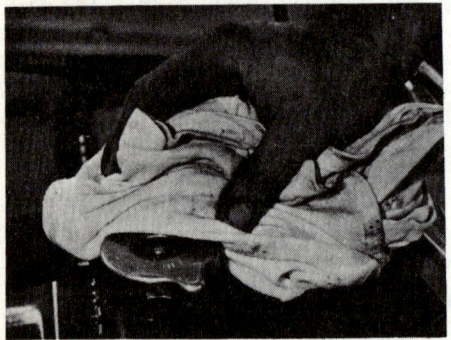

If the engine is hot, cover the radiator cap with a rag

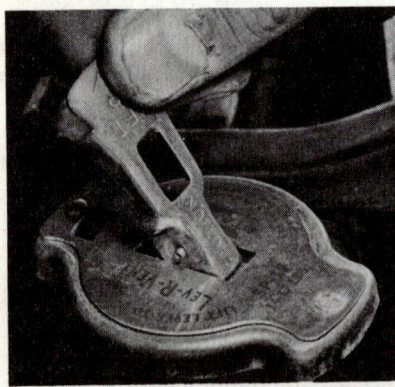

Some radiator caps have pressure release levers

observed. It is best to check the coolant level in the radiator when the engine is cold. This is done by removing the radiator cap and seeing that the coolant is within 2 in. of the bottom of the filler neck.

On 1976 and later models, the cooling system is equipped with an expansion tank. If coolant is visible above the MIN mark on the tank, the level is satisfactory. Always be certain that the filler caps on both the radiator and the reservoir are tightly closed.

In the event that the coolant level must be checked when the engine is warm on engines without the expansion tank, place a thick rag over the radiator cap and slowly turn the cap counterclockwise until it reaches the first detent. Allow all of the steam to escape. This will allow the pressure in the system to drop gradually, preventing an explosion of hot coolant. When the hissing noise stops, remove the cap the rest of the way.

If the coolant level is low, add equal amounts of ethylene glycol based antifreeze and clean water. On models without an expansion tank, add coolant through the radiator filled neck. Fill the expansion tank to the MAX level on vehicles with that system.

CAUTION: *Never add cold coolant to a hot engine unless the engine is running, to avoid cracking the engine block.*

The radiator hoses, clamps and the radiator cap should be checked at the same time as the coolant level. Hoses which are brittle, cracked or swollen should be replaced. Clamps should be checked for tightness (screwdriver tight only– DO NOT allow the clamp to cut into the hose or crush the fitting). The radiator cap gasket should be checked for any obvious tears, cracks, swelling or any signs of incorrect seating in the radiator neck.

DRAIN SYSTEM, FLUSH AND REFILL

Once every 24 months or 24,000 miles, the cooling system should be drained, thoroughly flushed and refilled. This should be done with the engine cold.

1. Remove the radiator cap.
2. There are two drain plugs in the cooling system; one at the bottom of the radiator and one at the rear of the driver's side of the engine. Both should be loosened to allow the coolant to drain.
3. Turn on the heater control to it's hottest

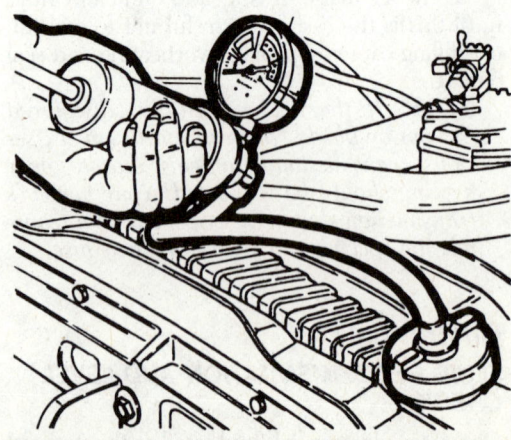

Pressurize the cooling system with the special tool shown to check for leaks

GENERAL INFORMATION AND MAINTENANCE

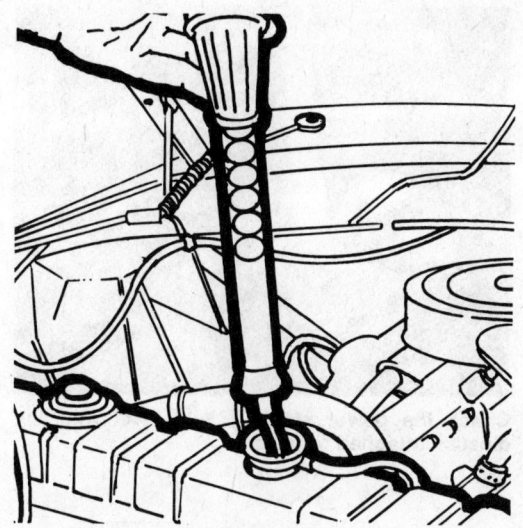

Coolant protection quality can be checked with an inexpensive float-type tester

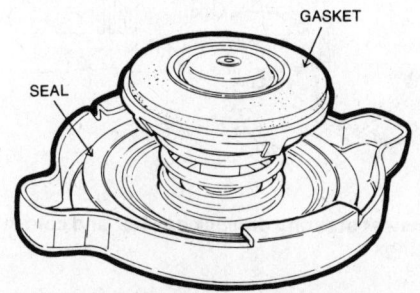

Check the radiator cap seal and gasket condition

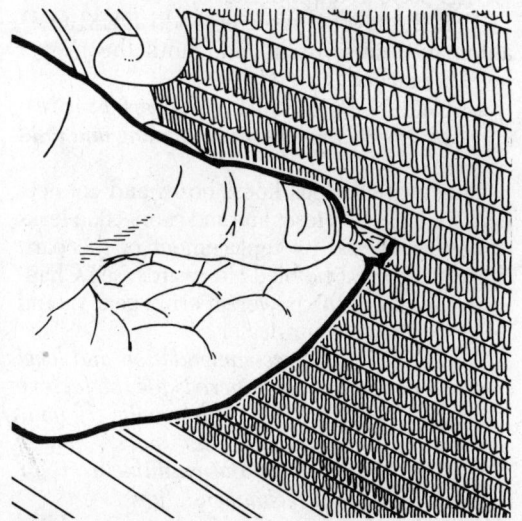

Clean the radiator fins of any debris which impedes air flow

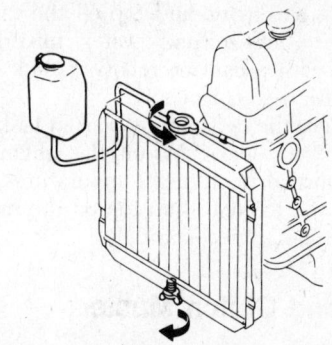

Open the radiator cap and radiator drain petcock to change the coolant

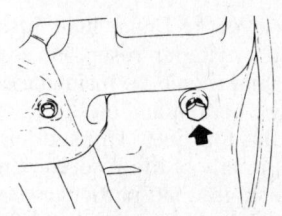

The engine block coolant drain plug is located at the left rear of the engine

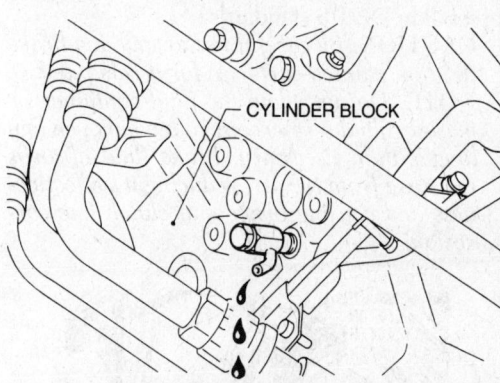

The engine block coolant drain plug is located on the right side—1984 and later

position. This ensures that the heater core is flushed out completely. Flush the system thoroughly by refilling it with clean water; flush it through the radiator opening as it escapes from the two drain cocks. Continue until the water running out is clear. Be sure to clean out the coolant recovery tank as well if equipped.

4. If the system is badly contaminated with rust or scale, use a commercial flushing solution to clear it; follow the manufacturer's instructions. Some causes of rust are air in the system, caused by a leaky radiator cap or an insufficiently filled or leaking system; failure to change the coolant regularly; use of excessively hard or soft water and failure to use a proper mix of antifreeze and water.

5. When the system is clear, allow all the water to drain, then close the drain plugs. Fill the system, through the radiator neck, with a 50/50 mix of ethylene glycol type antifreeze and water.

32 GENERAL INFORMATION AND MAINTENANCE

6. Start the engine and top off the radiator with the antifreeze and water mixture. If equipped with a coolant recovery tank, fill it half full with the coolant mix.

7. Replace the radiator and coolant tank caps, then check for leaks. When the engine has reached normal operating temperatures, shut it off, allow it to cool, then top off the radiator or coolant tank as necessary.

Brake and Clutch Master Cylinders

FLUID RECOMMENDATION AND LEVEL CHECK

Check the levels of brake fluid in brake and clutch master cylinder reservoirs every 3,000 miles. The fluid should be maintained to a level not below the bottom line on the reservoirs and not above the top line. Any sudden decrease in the level in any of the reservoirs indicates a probable leak in that particular system and should be checked out immediately.

When making additions of fluid, use only fresh, uncontaminated brake fluid, meeting or exceeding DOT 3 standards.

CAUTION: *Be careful not to spill any brake fluid on painted surfaces, for it eats paint.*

NOTE: *Do not allow the fluid container or master cylinder reservoirs to remain open any longer than necessary; brake fluid absorbs moisture from the air, reducing it's effectiveness and causing brake and clutch line corrosion.*

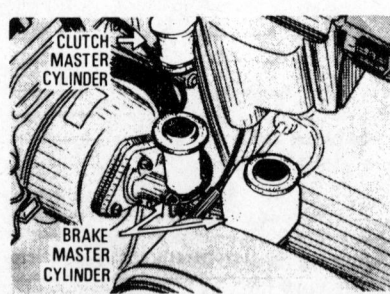

Check the fluid levels in the brake and clutch master cylinders

Power Steering Pump

FLUID RECOMMENDATION AND LEVEL CHECK

The ZX power steering gear reservoir is equipped with a level dipstick, attached to the filler cap. The dipstick has a scale on each side, one for cold and the other for hot.

1. The level is checked with the engine off and wheels pointed straight ahead.

Check the power steering fluid level with the dipstick attached to the cap

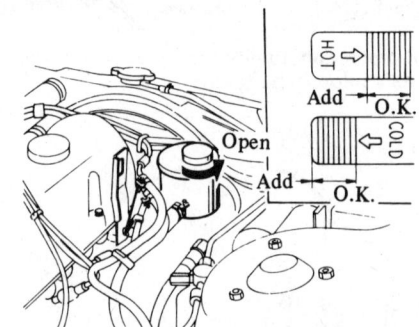

The power steering dipstick has hot and cold level markings

2. Remove the fluid reservoir cap and check the level on the dipstick. Use the HOT or COLD scale as appropriate.

3. If the level is incorrect, add DEXRON® automatic transmission fluid until the proper level is reached.

CAUTION: *Be careful not to overfill the reservoir; overfilling will cause foaming and fluid loss.*

Check the various lines, hoses and connections for leakage. Hose, line and connection leaks can be corrected by replacement of the part; the system must be bled afterwards (see Chapter 8). Leaks in the power steering gear should be corrected by your dealer.

NOTE: *The fluid recommendation and level check procedure given here is for the factory installed unit on ZX models only. If your 1970–78 Z-car has an after market power steering unit, consult the manufacturer for fluid checks and recommendations.*

Manual Steering Gear

FLUID RECOMMENDATION AND LEVEL CHECK

The manual rack and pinion steering gear should be inspected for leaks or seepage every 30,000

GENERAL INFORMATION AND MAINTENANCE

miles. The factory recommends inspection of the lubricant level at the same time. However, there is no filler plug on the gear housing. Consequently, level checks require removal of the backlash adjusting screw and locknut and resetting of the backlash adjustment afterwards. In general, if no leakage is evident, the fluid level can be assumed to be satisfactory.

Windshield Washer

FLUID RECOMMENDATION AND LEVEL CHECK

Check the fluid level in the windshield washer tank at every oil level check.

NOTE: *The ZX rear wiper/washer unit shares the tank with the front washer system.*

The fluid can be mixed in a 50% solution with water if desired, as long as temperatures remain above freezing. Below freezing, the fluid should be used full strength.

CAUTION: *Never add engine coolant antifreeze to the washer fluid, because it will damage the vehicle's paint.*

Headlight Washer

FLUID RECOMMENDATION AND LEVEL CHECK

The headlight washer tank is located in the left-front of the engine compartment. Use the same washing fluid as that used in the windshield washer tank. As with the windshield washer, the fluid should be used full strength in freezing weather.

Carburetor Damper Oil

On 1970–74 models, every 3,000 miles, check the level of the carburetor damper oil by removing the oil cap nut. If the oil level is below the lower line, add SAE 20 to restore it to the proper level. Do not use SAE 30!

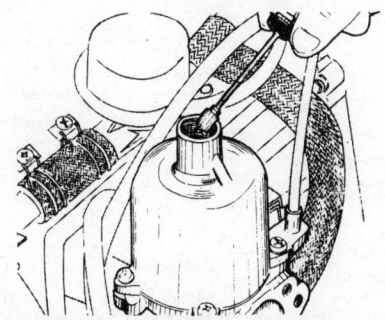

Check the carburetor damper oil level on the cap nut dipstick

Chassis Greasing

The manufacturer doesn't install lubrication fittings in lube points on the steering linkage or suspension. You can buy metric threaded fittings to grease these points or use a pointed, rubber tip end on your grease gun. Lubricate all joints equipped with a plug, every 24,000 miles, with NLGI No. 2 (Lithium base) grease. Replace the plugs after lubrication.

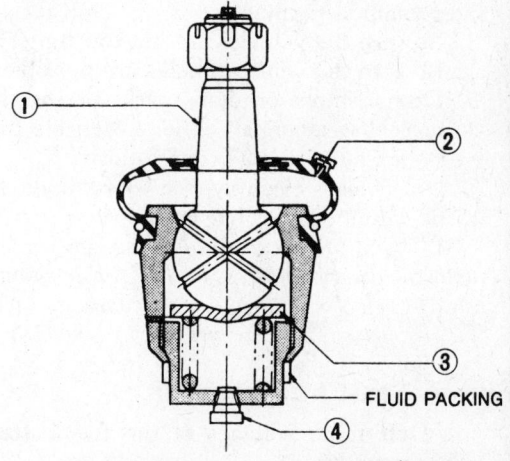

1. Ball stud
2. Grease bleeder
3. Spring seat
4. Plug

Cross-section of a suspension ball joint

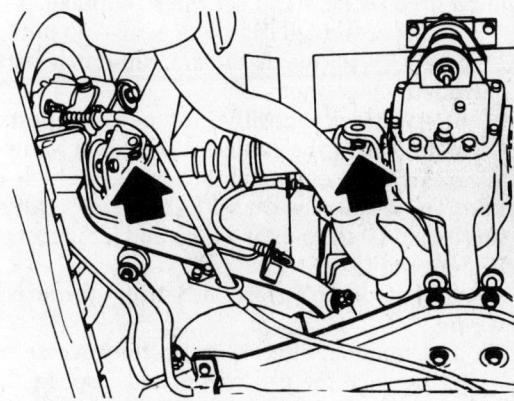

Axle shaft greasing locations

Body Lubrication

Lubricate all locks and hinges with multipurpose grease every 6,000 miles.

Wheel Bearings

Refer to the Wheel Bearings Packing procedure, in the Brakes section. Clean and repack wheel bearings every 30,000 miles.

34 GENERAL INFORMATION AND MAINTENANCE

JUMP STARTING A DEAD BATTERY

The chemical reaction in a battery produces explosive hydrogen gas. This is the safe way to jump start a dead battery, reducing the chances of an accidental spark that could cause an explosion.

Jump Starting Precautions

1. Be sure both batteries are of the same voltage.
2. Be sure both batteries are of the same polarity (have the same grounded terminal).
3. Be sure the vehicles are not touching.
4. Be sure the vent cap holes are not obstructed.
5. Do not smoke or allow sparks around the battery.
6. In cold weather, check for frozen electrolyte in the battery. Do not jump start a frozen battery.
7. Do not allow electrolyte on your skin or clothing.
8. Be sure the electrolyte is not frozen.

CAUTION: *Make certain that the ignition key, in the vehicle with the dead battery, is in the OFF position. Connecting cables to vehicles with on-board computers will result in computer destruction if the key is not in the OFF position.*

Jump Starting Procedure

1. Determine voltages of the two batteries; they must be the same.
2. Bring the starting vehicle close (they must not touch) so that the batteries can be reached easily.
3. Turn off all accessories and both engines. Put both cars in Neutral or Park and set the handbrake.
4. Cover the cell caps with a rag—do not cover terminals.
5. If the terminals on the run-down battery are heavily corroded, clean them.
6. Identify the positive and negative posts on both batteries and connect the cables in the order shown.
7. Start the engine of the starting vehicle and run it at fast idle. Try to start the car with the dead battery. Crank it for no more than 10 seconds at a time and let it cool off for 20 seconds in between tries.
8. If it doesn't start in 3 tries, there is something else wrong.
9. Disconnect the cables in the reverse order.
10. Replace the cell covers and dispose of the rags.

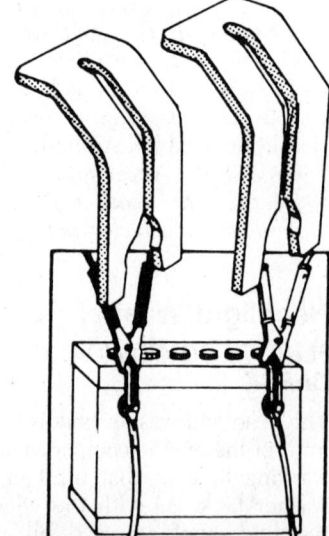

Side terminal batteries occasionally pose a problem when connecting jumper cables. There frequently isn't enough room to clamp the cables without touching sheet metal. Side terminal adaptors are available to alleviate this problem and should be removed after use.

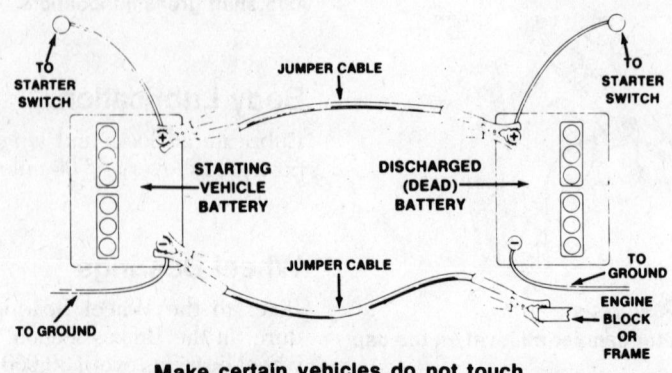

Make certain vehicles do not touch
This hook-up for negative ground cars only

GENERAL INFORMATION AND MAINTENANCE

TOWING

Manual Transmission

Tow forward using the hooks shown in the illustration. It may be necessary to remove the front apron on some earlier models.

CAUTION: *DO NOT attempt to tow the vehicle by the front suspension. Tow the vehicle so as to avoid a sudden impact on the hook.*

Automatic Transmission

If the distance to be traveled is six miles or less, the vehicle may be towed with the front wheels off the ground. The speed must not exceed 20 mph under these conditions.

If the transmission is not operating properly, greater distance is involved or higher speeds are required, tow the vehicle with the rear wheels off the ground and the steering wheel secured in a straight ahead position. The ignition key should be left in the lock in the OFF position. If the vehicle is towed on the front wheels with the ignition key removed (steering column locked), damage to the steering column or lock will result.

JUMP STARTING

Jump starting is the favored method of starting a vehicle with a dead battery. Make sure that the cables are properly connected, negative-to-negative and positive-to-positive or you stand a chance of damaging the electrical systems of both vehicles.

JACKING AND HOISTING

The vehicle is supplied with a scissors jack for emergency road repairs. The scissors jack may be used to raise the vehicle via the notches on either side, at the front and rear of the doors.

CAUTION: *DO NOT attempt to use the jack in any other places.*

Always block the diagonally opposite wheel when using a jack. When using a garage jack, support the vehicle at the center of the front suspension member or at the differential carrier.

CAUTION: *DO NOT attempt to jack the vehicle at the front suspension transverse link. Block both wheels at the opposite end of the vehicle.*

When using jackstands, use the side members at the front and the differential front mounting crossmember at the back for placement points.

Whenever working under the vehicle you must support it with jackstands or ramps.

CAUTION: *Never use cinder blocks or stacks of wood to support the vehicle, even if you're only going to be under it for a few minutes. Never crawl under the vehicle when it is supported only by a tire changing jack.*

Small hydraulic, screw or scissors jacks are satisfactory for raising the vehicle. Drive-on

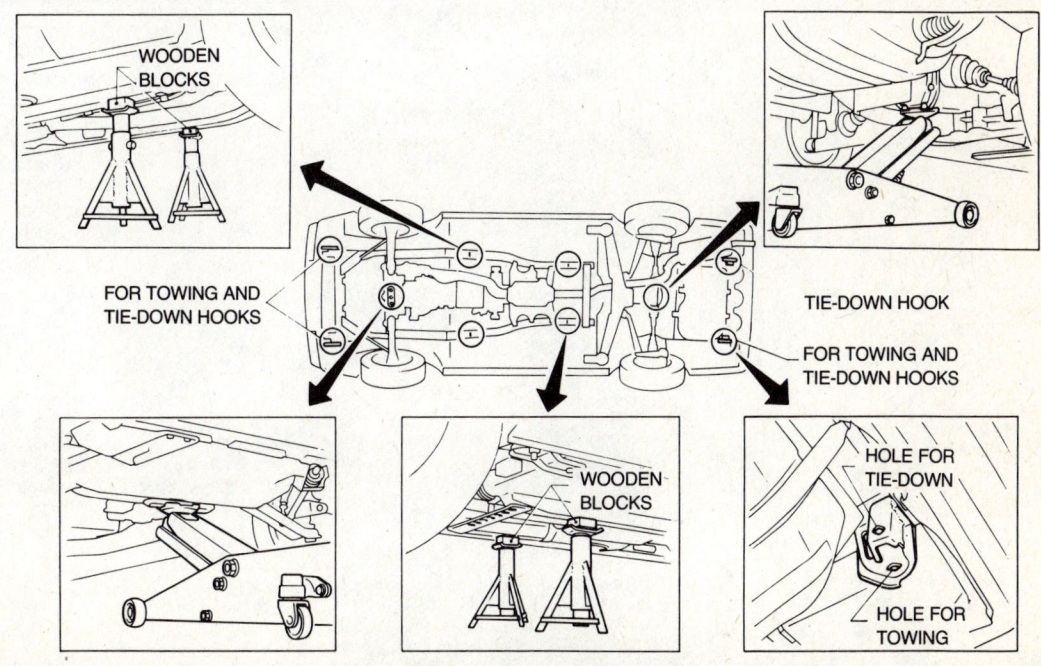

Lifting and towing locations—typical

GENERAL INFORMATION AND MAINTENANCE

trestles or ramps are also a handy and safe way to both raise and support the vehicle on jackstands. These can be bought or constructed from wood or steel.

If the vehicle is to be raised with a hoist such as the type used in service stations, the pads of the hoist should be positioned on the frame rails or at the points indicated for jackstand support in the illustration. Never support the vehicle on any suspension member or underbody panel.

Tune-Up and Performance Maintenance

2

TUNE-UP PROCEDURES

In order to extract the full measure of performance and economy from your engine it is essential that it be properly tuned at regular intervals. A regular tune-up will keep your engine running smoothly and will prevent the annoying minor breakdowns and poor performance associated with an untuned engine.

NOTE: *All Z-cars (1970–73) use a conventional breaker points ignition system. All models (1970–73) equipped with an automatic transmission, use a dual point system for emission control purposes; all models (1970–73) with manual transmission have single breaker points. All 1974 and later models use a fully transistorized ignition system. The 1974 automatic transmission models and all 1975–76 49 States and Canada models have dual pick-ups. The 1975–76 California models have only one pick-up. All 1977 and later models have single pick-up electronic ignition.*

A complete tune-up should be performed every 12,000 miles or twelve months, whichever comes first. This interval should be halved if the car is operated under severe conditions, such as trailer towing, prolonged idling, continual stop and start driving or if starting and running problems are noticed. It is assumed that the routine maintenance described in Chapter 1 has been kept up, as this will have a decided effect on the results of a tune-up. All of the applicable steps of a tune-up should be followed in order, as the result is a cumulative one.

If the specifications on the tune-up sticker in the engine compartment of your vehicle disagree with the Tune-Up Specifications chart in this chapter, the figures on the sticker must be used. The sticker often reflects changes made during the production run.

Spark Plugs

The spark plugs ignite the air and fuel mixture in the cylinder as the piston reaches the top of the compression stroke. The controlled explosion that results forces the piston down, turning the crankshaft and the drive train.

The average life of a spark plug is 12,000 miles (1979–80) or 30,000 miles (1981 and later). This is, however, dependent on a number of factors: the mechanical condition of the engine, the type of fuel, the drive conditions and the driver.

NOTE: *The tips of the late model spark plugs are platinum coated, which extends the life of the plugs.*

When you remove the spark plugs, check their condition. They are a good indicator of the condition of the engine. It is a good idea to remove the spark plugs every 6,000 miles to keep an eye on the mechanical state of the engine.

A small deposit of light tan or gray material (or rust red with unleaded fuel) on a spark plug that has been used for any period of time is to be considered normal. Any other color or abnormal amounts of deposit, indicates there is something wrong in the engine.

The gap between the center electrode and the side or ground electrode can be expected to increase not more than 0.001 in. every 1,000 miles under normal conditions.

When a spark plug is functioning normally or (more accurately) when the plug is installed in an engine that is functioning properly, the plugs can be taken out, cleaned, regapped and reinstalled in the engine without doing the engine any harm.

When and/or if a plug fouls (begins to misfire), investigate and correct the cause of the fouling; either clean or replace the plug.

There are several reasons why a spark plug will foul and you can learn which is at fault by

TUNE-UP AND PERFORMANCE MAINTENANCE

Tune-Up Specifications

Year	Engine Displacement cu in. (cc)	Spark Plugs Type	Spark Plugs Gap (in.) (mm)	Distributor Point Dwell (deg)	Distributor Point Gap (in.) (mm)	Ignition Timing (deg) MT	Ignition Timing (deg) AT	Compression Pressure (psi) (kg/cm²)	Idle Speed (rpm) MT	Idle Speed (rpm) AT	Hot Valve Clearance In	Hot Valve Clearance Ex
1970–71	146 (2393)	BP6E	.031–.035 (.8–.9)	35–41	.016–.019 (.4–.5)	5B	—	171–185 (12–13)	750	—	.010 (.25)	.012 (.30)
1972	146 (2393)	BP6ES	.031–.035 (.8–.9)	35–41	.016–.019 (.4–.5)	5B	TDC ②	171–185 (12–13)	750	600	.010 (.25)	.012 (.30)
1973	146 (2393)	BP6ES	.031–.035 (.8–.9)	35–41	.018–.021 (.45–.55)	7B	5B ③	171–185 (12–13)	750	600	.010 (.25)	.012 (.30)
1974	156 (2565)	BP6ES	.031–.035 (.8–.9)	—	.012–.016 ① (.3–.4)	8B	8B ③	171–185 (12–13)	750	600	.010 (.25)	.012 (.30)
1975	168 (2753)	BP6ES	.028–.031 (.7–.8)	—	.008–.016 ① (.2–.4)	7B ④⑤	7B ④⑤	164–178 (11.5–12.5)	800	700	.010 (.25)	.012 (.30)
1976	168 (2753)	BP6ES	.028–.031 (.7–.8)	—	.008–.016 ① (.2–.4)	7B ④⑤	7B ④⑤	164–178 (11.5–12.5)	800	700	.010 (.25)	.012 (.30)
1977	168 (2753)	BP6ES-11 ⑥	.039–.043 ⑦ (1.0–1.1)	—	.008–.016 ① (.2–.4)	10B	10B	164–178 (11.5–12.5)	800	700	.010 (.25)	.012 (.30)
1978	168 (2753)	BP6ES-11 ⑥	.039–.043 ⑦ (1.0–1.1)	—	.008–.016 ① (.2–.4)	10B	10B	164–178 (11.5–12.5)	800	700	.010 (.25)	.012 (.30)
1979	168 (2753)	B6ES-11 ⑧	.039–.043 (1.0–1.1)	—	.012–.020 ① (.3–.5)	10B	10B	171 (12)	800 ⑨	700	.010 (.25)	.012 (.30)
1980	168 (2753)	BP6ES-11 ⑩	.039–.043 (1.0–1.1)	—	.012–.020 ① (.3–.5)	10B	10B	171 (12)	700	700	.010 (.25)	.012 (.30)

TUNE-UP AND PERFORMANCE MAINTENANCE

Year	Displacement cu. in. (cc)	Spark Plug Type	Gap (in.)	Point Gap (in.)	Ign. Timing MT	Ign. Timing AT	Compression (psi)	Idle Speed MT	Idle Speed AT	Valve Clearance Intake (in./mm)	Valve Clearance Exhaust (in./mm)
1981	168 (2753)	BPR6ES-11	.039–.043 (1.0–1.1)	—	8B①	8B①	171 (12)	700	700	.010 (.25)	.012 (.30)
1981 (turbo)	168 (2753)	BPR6ES-11	.039–.043 (1.0–1.1)	.012–.020① (.3–.5)	20B	20B	141 (10)	650	650	.010 (.25)	.012 (.30)
1982	168 (2753)	BPR6ES-11	.039–.043 (1.0–1.1)	.012–.020① (.3–.5)	8B	8B	171 (12)	700	700	.010 (.25)	.012 (.30)
1982 (turbo)	168 (2753)	BPR6ES-11	.039–.043 (1.0–1.1)	.012–.020① (.3–.5)	20B	20B	141 (10)	700	650	.010 (.25)	.012 (.30)
1983	168 (2753)	BPR6ES-11	.039–.043 (1.0–1.1)	.012–.020① (.3–.5)	8B	8B	171 (12)	700	700	.010 (.25)	.012 (.30)
1983 (turbo)	168 (2753)	BPR6ES-11	.039–.043 (1.0–1.1)	.012–.020① (.3–.5)	24B	24B	141 (10)	700	650	.010 (.25)	.012 (.30)
1984–86	180.6 (2960)	BCPR6ES-11	.039–.043 (1.0–1.1)	NA	20B	20B	173 (12.2)	700	650	⑫	⑫
1984–86 (turbo)	180.6 (2960)	BCPR6E-11	.039–.043 (1.0–1.1)	NA	20B	20B	165 (11.6)	700	650	⑫	⑫

Part numbers in this chart are not recommendations by Chilton for any product by brand name.
— Not Applicable
NA — Not available
① Refers to air gap — electronic ignition
② 10B @ 600 below 30°F
③ 15B @ 600 advance
④ 10B on California models
⑤ 13B with engine cold on dual reluctor models
⑥ BR6ES — Canada
⑦ .028–.031 (.7–.8) — Canada
⑧ BR6ES-11 — Canada
⑨ 700 — Non-California models with catalytic converter
⑩ BPR6ES-11 — Canada
⑪ Canada — 10B
⑫ Hydraulic — no adjustment necessary

TUNE-UP AND PERFORMANCE MAINTENANCE

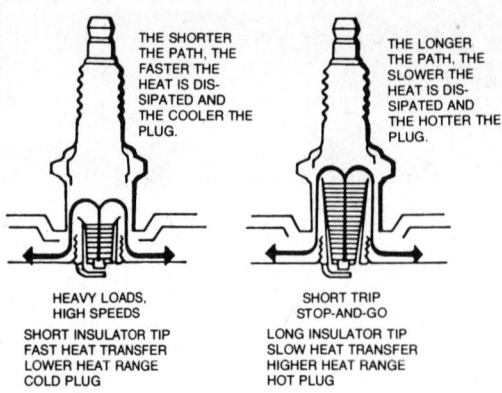

Spark plug heat range

just looking at the tip of the plug. A few of the most common reasons for plug fouling and a description of the fouled plug's appearance, are listed in the color section, which also offers solutions to the problems.

The spark plugs suitable for use in your vehicles's engine are offered in a number of different heat ranges. The amount of heat which the plug absorbs is determined by the length of the lower insulator. The longer the insulator, the hotter the plug will operate; the shorter the insulator, the cooler it will operate. A spark plug that absorbs (retains) little heat and remains too cool will accumulate deposits of lead, oil and carbon, because it is not hot enough to burn them off. This leads to fouling and consequent misfiring. A spark plug that absorbs too much heat will have no deposits but the electrodes will burn away quickly and (in some cases) preignition may result. Preignition occurs when the spark plug tips get so hot that they ignite the fuel/air mixture before the actual spark fires. This premature ignition will usually cause a pinging sound under conditions of low speed and heavy load. In severe cases, the heat may become high enough to start the fuel/air mixture burning throughout the combustion chamber rather than just to the front of the plug. In this case, the resultant explosion will be strong enough to damage pistons, rings and valves.

In most cases, the factory recommended heat range is correct; it is chosen to perform well under a wide range of operating conditions. However, if most of your driving is long distance, high speed travel, install a spark plug one step colder than standard. If most driving is of the short trip variety, when the engine may not always reach operating temperature, a hotter plug may help burn off the deposits normally accumulated under these conditions.

REMOVAL

1. Number the wires so that you won't cross them when you replace them.

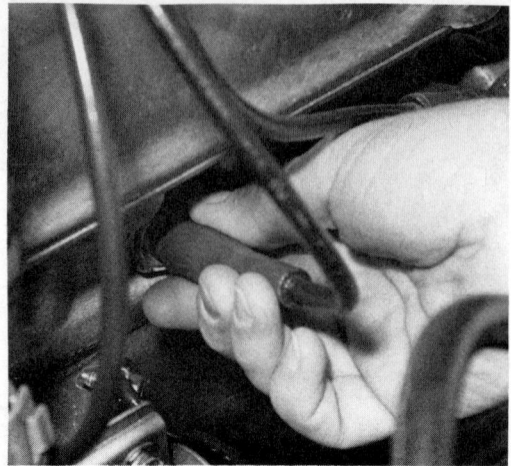

Pull on the spark plug boot, not on the wire

2. Remove the wire from the end of the spark plug by grasping the wire by the rubber boot. If the boot sticks to the plug, remove it by twisting and pulling it at the same time. DO NOT pull the wire itself for it will damage the core.

3. Use a $^{13}/_{16}$ in. spark plug socket to loosen all of the plugs about two turns.

NOTE: *The cylinder head is cast from aluminum. Remove the spark plugs when the engine is COLD (if possible) to prevent damage to the threads. If removal of the plugs is difficult, apply a few drops of penetrating oil or silicone spray to the area around the base of the plug and allow it a few minutes to work.*

4. If compressed air is available, apply it to the area around the spark plug holes. Otherwise, use a rag or a brush to clean the area. Be careful not to allow foreign material to drop into the spark plug holes.

5. Remove the plugs by unscrewing them from the engine.

INSPECTION

Check the plugs for deposits and wear. If they are not going to be replaced, clean the plugs thoroughly. Remember that any kind of de-

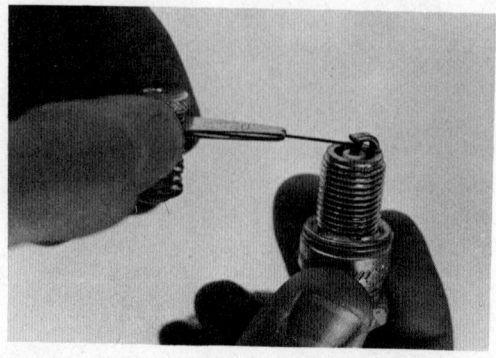

Check the spark plug gap with a wire gauge

TUNE-UP AND PERFORMANCE MAINTENANCE

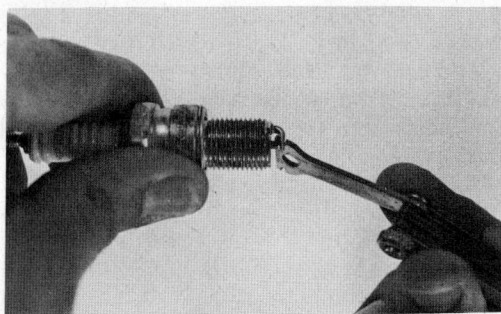

Bend the side electrode to adjust the gap

posit will decrease the efficiency of the plug. The plugs can be cleaned on a spark plug cleaning machine, which can sometimes be found in service stations or you can do an acceptable job of cleaning with a stiff brush. If the plugs are cleaned, the electrodes must be filed flat. Use an ignition points file, not an emery board or the like, which will leave deposits. The electrodes must be filed perfectly flat with sharp edges; rounded edges reduce the spark plug voltage by as much as 50%.

Check the spark plug gap before installation. The ground electrode must be parallel to the center electrode and the specified size wire gauge should pass through the gap with a slight drag. Always check the gap on new plugs; they are not always correctly set at the factory. Do not use a flat feeler gauge when measuring the gap, because the reading will be inaccurate. Wire gapping tools usually have a bending tool attached. Use that to adjust the side electrode until the proper distance is obtained. Absolutely never bend the center electrode. Also, be careful not to bend the side electrode too far or too often; it may weaken and break off within the engine, requiring removal of the cylinder head to retrieve it.

INSTALLATION

1. Lubricate the threads of the spark plugs with a drop of oil. Install the plugs and tighten them hand tight. Take care not to crossthread them.
2. Tighten the spark plugs with the socket. Do not apply the same amount of force you would use for a bolt; just snug them in. If a torque wrench is available, tighten to 11–15 ft.lb.
3. Install the wires on their respective plugs. Make sure the wires are firmly connected. You will be able to feel them click into place.

Spark Plug Wires

At every tune-up, visually inspect the spark plug cables for burns, cuts or breaks in the insulation. Check the boots and the nipples on the distributor cap and coil. Replace any damaged wiring.

About every 36,000 miles, the resistance of the wires should be checked with an ohmmeter. Wires with excessive resistance will cause misfiring and may make the engine difficult to start in damp weather. Generally, the useful life of the cables is 36,000–50,000 miles.

To check the resistance, remove the distributor cap, leaving the wires attached. Connect one lead of an ohmmeter to an electrode within the cap; connect the other lead to the corresponding spark plug terminal (remove it from the plug for this test). Replace any wire which shows a resistance over 50,000 Ω. Generally speaking, however, resistance should not be over 30,000 Ω and 50,000 Ω must be considered the outer limit of acceptability. Test the high tension lead from the coil by connecting the ohmmeter between the center contact in the distributor cap and either of the primary terminals of the coil. If resistance is more than 25,000 Ω, remove the cable from the coil and check the resistance of the cable alone. Anything over 15,000 Ω is cause for replacement. It should be remembered that resistance is also a function of length; the longer the cable, the greater the resistance. Thus, if the cables on your car are longer than the factory originals, resistance will be higher, quite possibly outside these limits.

When installing new cables, replace them one at a time to avoid mixups. Start by replacing the longest one first. Install the boot firmly over the spark plug. Route the wire over the same path as the original. Insert the nipple firmly into the tower on the cap or the coil.

FIRING ORDERS

NOTE: *To avoid confusion, remove and tag the wires one at a time.*

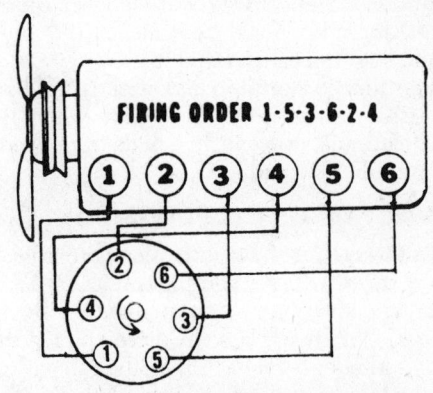

L24, L26 and L28 engine firing order: 1-5-3-6-2-4

42 TUNE-UP AND PERFORMANCE MAINTENANCE

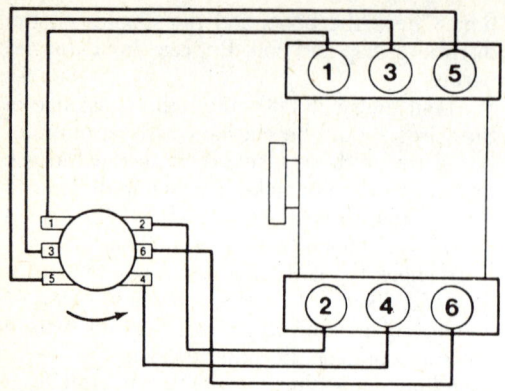

VG30E and VG30ET engine firing order: 1-2-3-4-5-6

Breaker Points and Condenser

The points function as a circuit breaker for the primary circuit of the ignition system. The ignition coil must boost the 12 volts of electrical pressure supplied by the battery to as much as 25,000 volts in order to fire the plugs. To do this, the coil depends on the points and the condenser to make a clean break in the primary circuit.

The coil has both a primary and a secondary circuit. When the ignition is turned ON, the battery voltage is directed through the coil and to the points. The points are connected to ground, completing the primary circuit. As the current passes through the coil, a magnetic field is created in the iron center core of the coil. When the cam in the distributor turns, the points open, breaking the primary circuit. The magnetic field in the primary circuit of the coil then collapses and cuts through the secondary circuit windings around the iron core. Because of the physical principle called electromagnetic induction, the battery voltage is increased to a level sufficient to fire the spark plugs.

When the points open, the electrical charge in the primary circuit tries to jump the gap created between the open contacts of the points. If this electrical charge were not transferred elsewhere, the metal contacts of the points would start to change rapidly.

The function of the condenser is to absorb excessive voltage from the points when they open and thus prevent the points from becoming pitted or burned.

INSPECTION OF THE POINTS

1. Disconnect the high tension wire from the top of the distributor and the coil.
2. The distributor cap is retained by two spring clips. Insert a screwdriver under their ends and release them. Lift off the cap with the spark plug wires attached. Inspect the inside of the cap. Wipe it clean (with a rag) and check for burned contacts, cracks and carbon tracks. A carbon track shows as a dark line running from one terminal to another. It cannot be successfully removed, so replace the cap if it has one of these. Generally, a cap and rotor will last 36,000 miles.

3. Remove the rotor from the distributor shaft by pulling it straight up. Examine the condition of the rotor. If it is cracked or the metal tip is excessively worn or burned, it should be replaced. Clean the metal tip with a clean cloth but don't file it.

4. Pry open the contacts of the points with a screwdriver and check the condition of the contacts. If they are excessively worn, burned or pitted, they should be replaced.

5. If the points are in good condition, adjust them, then replace the rotor and the distributor cap. If the points need to be replaced, follow the replacement procedure given next.

REPLACEMENT OF THE BREAKER POINTS AND CONDENSER

1. Remove the cap and rotor as outlined in Steps 1–3 of the preceding section.

On dual point distributors, #1 and #2 are the mounting screws. Do not loosen #3, the phase adjusting screw

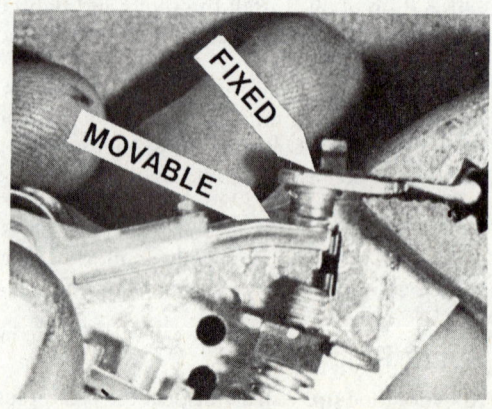

Bend the fixed point until the faces are square

TUNE-UP AND PERFORMANCE MAINTENANCE

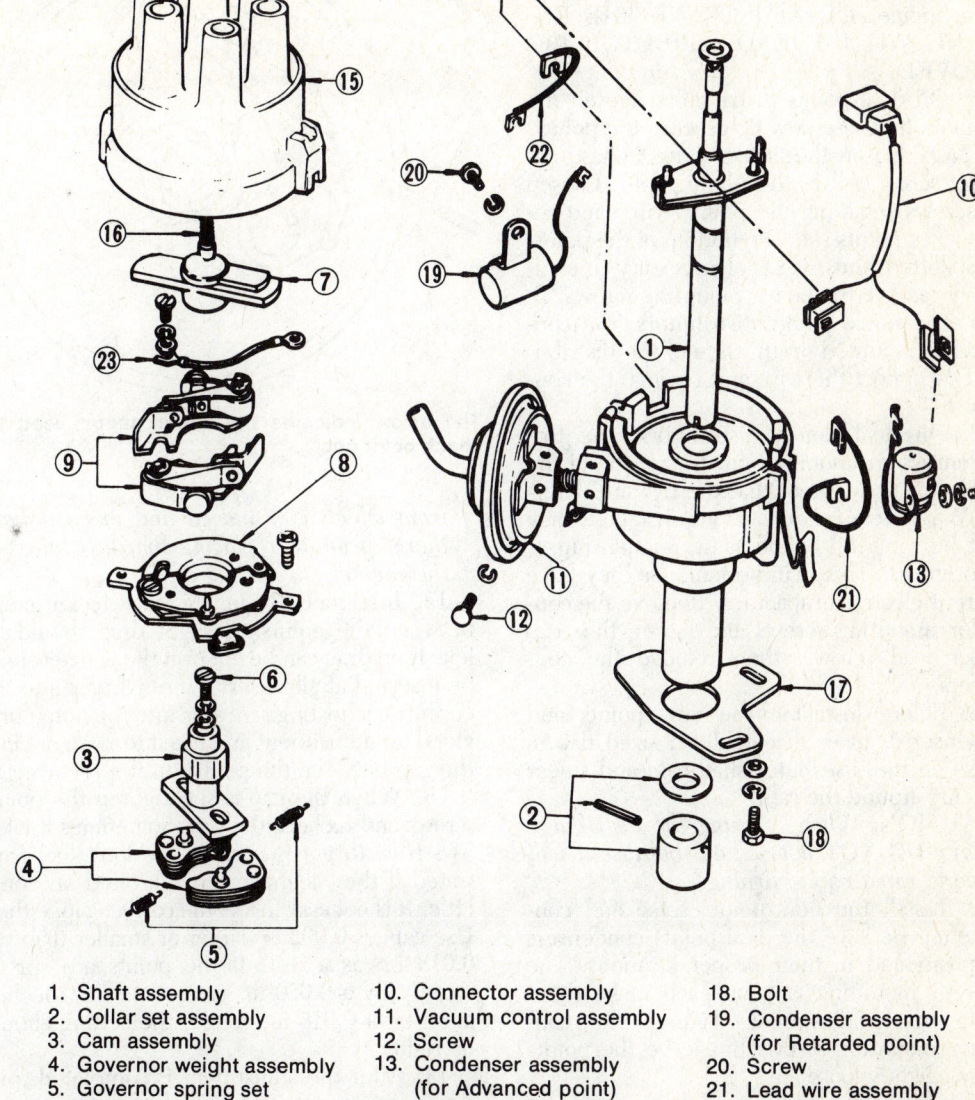

1. Shaft assembly
2. Collar set assembly
3. Cam assembly
4. Governor weight assembly
5. Governor spring set
7. Screw
7. Rotor head assembly
8. Breaker assembly
9. Contact set
10. Connector assembly
11. Vacuum control assembly
12. Screw
13. Condenser assembly (for Advanced point)
14. Screw
15. Distributor cap assembly
16. Carbon point assembly
17. Fixing plate
18. Bolt
19. Condenser assembly (for Retarded point)
20. Screw
21. Lead wire assembly (for Advanced point)
22. Lead wire assembly (for Retarded point)
23. Ground wire assembly

Exploded view of the dual point distributor

2. On single point distributors, loosen the two screws securing the points. Use a magnetic screwdriver to avoid losing a screw down the distributor. Loosen the point wire screw on the side of the distributor and slip the wire out. Remove the point set.

3. On dual points distributors, decide if the tools available to you will enable you to remove the two condensers on the outside of the distributor body. If you have a flexible screwdriver or one bent at a 90° angle, you should be able to get at them. Otherwise, it may be best to remove the distributor from the engine for points and condenser replacement.

4. To remove the distributor, perform the following procedure:

a. Using a scribing tool, mark the distributor-to-engine position on the hold down plate at the front of the distributor.

b. Mark the position of the rotor in relation to the distributor body. Do this by simply replacing the rotor on the distributor shaft and marking the spot on the distributor body where the rotor is pointing.

TUNE-UP AND PERFORMANCE MAINTENANCE

c. Remove the small bolt at the rear of the distributor and lift the distributor from the engine. DO NOT CRANK THE ENGINE WITH THE DISTRIBUTOR REMOVED.

5. On dual points distributors, loosen the two mounting screws which secure the points. DO NOT loosen the factory preset phase adjusting screw (#3 in the photograph). Loosen the screws retaining the points wires and remove each points set. The bottom of the points set is slotted; thus, it is not necessary to completely remove the points mounting screws.

6. On single points distributors, the condenser is mounted on the side of the distributor. Disconnect the wire and remove the condenser.

7. On dual points distributors, the two condensers are mounted on the outside of the distributor body. Note that the two are different. When new condensers are installed, they must be replaced in the same relationship as the originals. This is important, for they have different electrical capacities. Remove the condenser mounting screws and loosen the condenser lead screws, then remove the condensers.

8. Before installing the new points and condenser(s), place a matchhead sized dab of grease on the distributor shaft cam and smear it evenly around the cam.

CAUTION: *When greasing the distributor shaft, DO NOT not use oil, because it will lead to rapid point burning.*

9. Install the new points set(s) and condenser(s). Be sure the dual points condensers are positioned in their proper locations. The different mounting ears on each make them pretty much idiot-proof. Tighten the condenser mounting screws but leave the points screws slightly loose.

10. Check that the faces of the points meet squarely. If not, the fixed mount can be bent slightly with gentle force, using a pair of needlenose pliers. DO NOT bend the movable contact.

11. The point gap must be adjusted next. The gap is adjusted with the rubbing block of the points resting on one of the six high spots of the distributor cam. To get it there, the engine can be rotated by bumping the starter with the ignition key or turning the crankshaft, with a wrench on the crankshaft pulley bolt; this is easier to do with the spark plugs removed.

NOTE: *If the distributor is removed (dual points) the distributor shaft can be rotated until the points blocks are resting on the high spots of the cam. It won't matter if you move the distributor shaft; it can only go back into the engine one way. Just note the position*

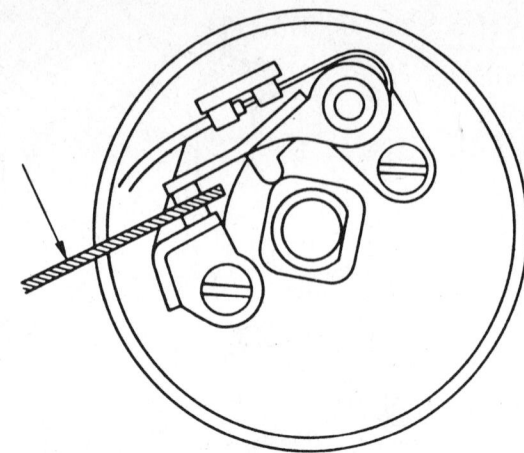

The arrow indicates the feeler gauge used to check point gap

from which it is moved and move it back there, prior to replacing the distributor in the engine.

12. Insert a 0.018 in. thick flat feeler gauge between the points. A slight drag should be felt. If no drag can be felt or if the gauge cannot be inserted at all, insert a screwdriver into the eccentric adjusting screw or into the notch provided for adjustment and use it to open or close the gap between the points until it is correct.

13. When the gap is set, tighten the points screws and recheck the gap. Sometimes it takes 3–4 tries to get it correct, so don't feel frustrated if they seem to move around on you a little. It is not easy to feel the correct gap, either. Use gauges 0.002 in. larger or smaller than the 0.018 in. as a test. If the points are spread slightly by a 0.020 in. gauge and not touched at all by a 0.016 in. gauge, the setting should be right.

14. After the adjustment is completed, pull a clean piece of tissue or a white business card between the points to clear any bits of grit.

15. On dual points distributors, if the distributor was removed, reset the shaft and rotor to their original positions, then install the distributor. Note that the slot for the oil pump drive is tapered and will only fit one way. Be sure the marks you made earlier line up and tighten the distributor hold down bolt.

16. Replace the rotor and distributor cap, then snap on the clips. If you have a dwell meter (recommended) you should next set the dwell. Otherwise, go on to the ignition timing.

ADJUSTMENT OF THE BREAKER POINTS WITH A DWELL METER
Single Point Distributor

The dwell angle is the number of degrees of distributor cam rotation through which the

TUNE-UP AND PERFORMANCE MAINTENANCE

points remain closed (conducting electricity). Increasing the point gap decreases the dwell, while decreasing the gap increases the dwell.

The dwell angle may be checked with the distributor cap and rotor installed plus the engine running or with the cap and rotor removed plus the engine cranking at starter speed. The meter gives a constant reading with the engine running. With the engine cranking, the meter will fluctuate between zero degrees dwell and the maximum figure for that setting. Never attempt to adjust the points when the ignition is on or you may receive a shock.

1. Connect a meter as per the manufacturer's instructions (usually one lead to the distributor's terminal of the coil and the other lead to a ground). Zero the meter, if necessary.
2. Check the dwell by either the cranking method or with the engine running. If the setting is incorrect, the points must be adjusted.
CAUTION: *Keep your hands, hair and/or clothing clear of the engine fan and pulleys. Be sure the wires from the dwell meter are routed out of the way. If the engine is running, block the front wheels, place the transmission in Neutral and set the parking brake.*
3. To change the dwell angle, turn the ignition OFF, loosen the points hold down screw and adjust the point gap; increase the gap to decrease the dwell and vice-versa. Tighten the hold down screw and check the dwell angle with the engine cranking. If it seems to be correct, replace the cap and rotor, then check the dwell with the engine running. Readjust as necessary.
4. Run the engine speed up to about 2,500 rpm and let the speed drop abruptly; the dwell reading should not change. If it does, a worn distributor shaft, bushing, cam or breaker plate is indicated. The parts must be inspected and replaced, if necessary.
5. After adjusting the dwell angle, perform the Ignition Timing. Ignition timing must be checked after adjusting the point gap, as 1° increase in dwell results in an ignition timing retard of 2° and vice-versa.

Dual Point Distributor

Adjust the point gap of a dual point distributor with a dwell meter as follows:
1. Disconnect the wiring harness of the distributor from the engine wiring harness.
2. Using a jumper wire (a length of wire with an alligator clip at each end), connect the black wire of the harness (engine-side) to the black wire of the distributor-side of the harness (advance points).
3. Start the engine and observe the reading on the dwell meter. Turn the engine OFF and

Use the terminals provided (arrows) for jumper wire connection

adjust the points according to the single point distributors procedure.
4. Disconnect the jumper wire from the black wire of the wiring harness (distributor-side) and connect it to the yellow wire (retard points).
5. Adjust the point gap as necessary, in the same manner.
6. After the dwell of both sets of points is correct, remove the jumper wire and connect the engine-to-distributor wiring harness securely.

Electronic Ignition
Non Turbocharged Engines

All 1974 and later vehicles are equipped with electronic ignition as standard equipment. The 1974 models (with an automatic transmission), plus the 1975–76 49 States and Canada models have two pick-ups in the distributor. All 1975–76 California models, plus all 1977 and later models have only one pick-up.

The 1974 system has a different electronic module than later systems, which precludes troubleshooting of the system by the home mechanic. However, the pick-up air gap adjustments and the ignition timing adjustments can be performed in the same manner as for the 1975–78 models. The 1978 system differs slightly from the 1975–77 system; the 1979 and later electronic ignition is markedly different, although the operating principle is the same.

The elctronic ignition differs from its conventional counterpart only in the distributor component area. The secondary side of the ignition system is the same as a conventional breaker points system.

Located in the distributor, in addition to the normal ignition rotor, is a six spoke rotor (reluctor) which rests on the distributor shaft where the breaker point's cam is found on earlier systems. A pick-up coil, consisting of a magnet, a coil and wiring, rests on the breaker plate next to the reluctor. The system also uses a transistorized ignition unit, located on the right-side of the firewall in the passenger compartment (1970–78). The 1979–83 models have an integrated circuit (IC) ignition unit, which is mounted on the side of the distributor. In addition, 1979–83 models use a ring type pick-up coil, which surrounds the reluctor, rather than the arm type coil used on the 1970–78 models.

When a reluctor spoke is not aligned with the pick-up coil, it generates large lines of flux between itself, the magnet and the pick-up coil. This large flux variation generates in a high voltage in the pick-up coil, preventing the current from flowing to the pick-up coil. When a reluctor spoke lines up with the pick-up coil, the flux variation is low–thus, zero voltage is generated, allowing current to flow to the pick-up coil. Ignition primary current is then cut off by the electronic unit, allowing the field in the ignition coil to collapse, inducing high secondary voltage in the conventional manner. The high voltage then flows through the distributor to the spark plug, as usual.

Because no points or condenser are used and the dwell is determined by the electronic unit, no adjustments are necessary. The ignition timing is checked in the usual way but unless the distributor is disturbed it is not likely to ever change very much.

Service consists of inspection of the distributor cap, the rotor and the ignition wires, replacing them (when necessary). These parts can be expected to last for at least 40,000 miles. In addition, the reluctor air gap should be checked periodically.

1. The distributor cap is held on by two clips. Release them with a screwdriver, then lift the cap straight up and off, with the wires attached. Inspect the cap for cracks, carbon tracks or a worn center contact. Replace it (if necessary), transferring the wires (one at a time) from the old cap to the new.

2. Pull the ignition rotor (not the spoked reluctor) straight up to remove it. Replace it if it's contacts are worn, burned or pitted. DO NOT file the contacts. To replace the rotor, press it firmly onto the shaft. It only goes on one way, so be sure it is fully seated.

3. Before replacing the ignition rotor, check the reluctor air gap. Use a non-magnetic feeler gauge. Rotate the engine until a reluctor spoke is aligned with the pick-up coil (either bump the engine around with the starter or turn it using a wrench on the crankshaft pulley bolt). The gap should measure 0.012–0.016 in. (0.3–0.4 mm) for 1974, 0.008–0.016 in. (0.2–0.4 mm) for 1975–78 or 0.012–0.020 in. (0.3–0.5 mm)

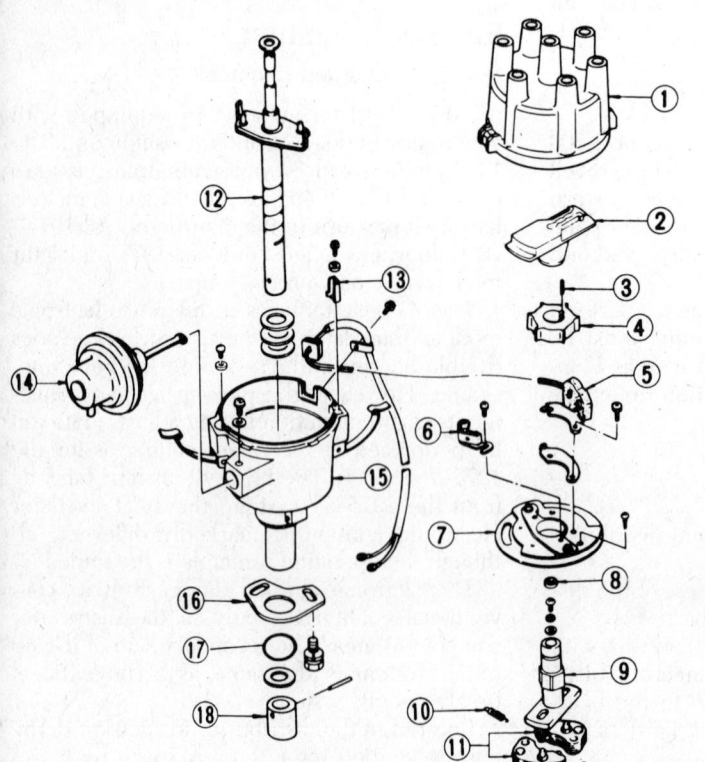

1. Cap assembly
2. Rotor head assembly
3. Roll pin
4. Reluctor
5. Pick-up coil
6. Contactor
7. Breaker plate assembly
8. Packing
9. Rotor shaft
10. Governor spring
11. Governor weight
12. Shaft assembly
13. Cap setter
14. Vacuum controller
15. Housing
16. Fixing plate
17. O-ring
18. Collar

Exploded view of the single pick-up electronic distributor (1975–78)—dual pick-up models are similar

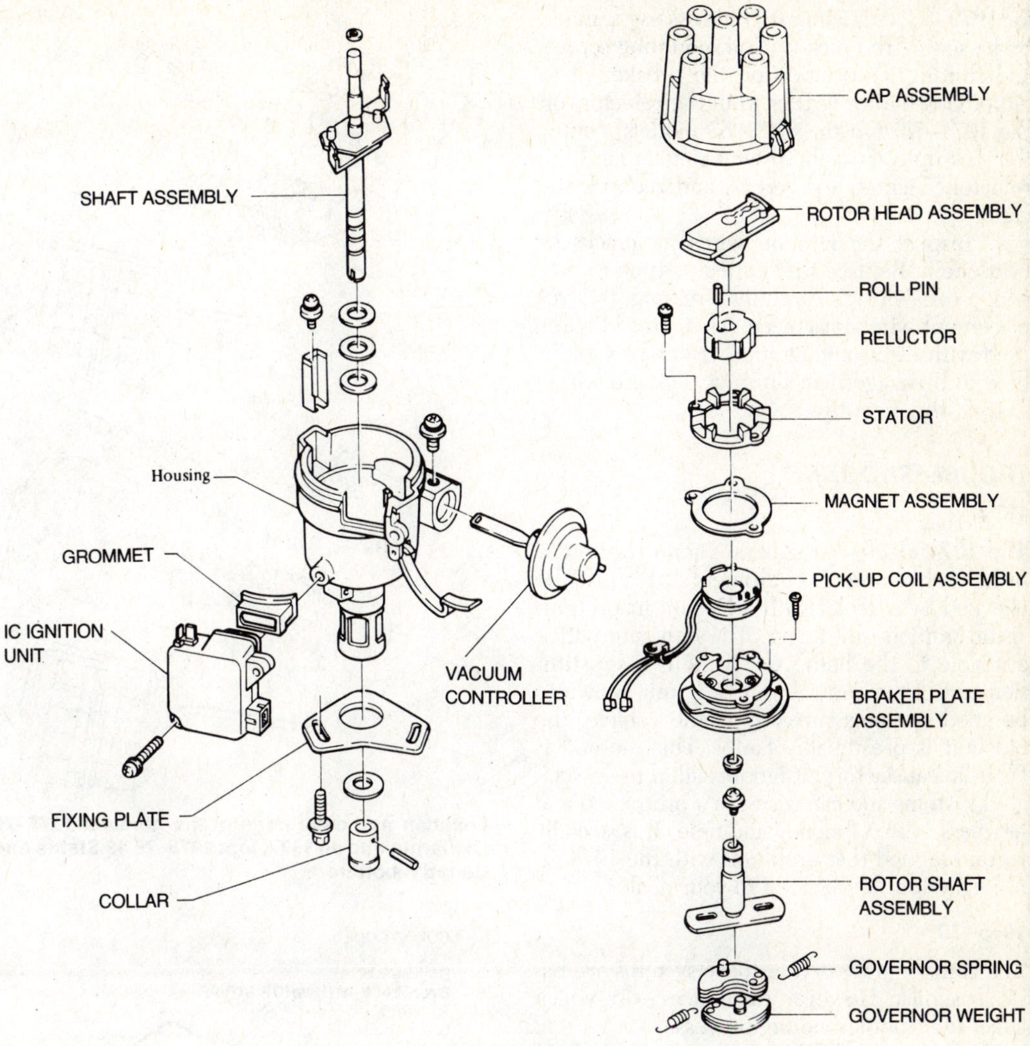

TUNE-UP AND PERFORMANCE MAINTENANCE

Exploded view of the non-turbo electronic distributor—1979–83

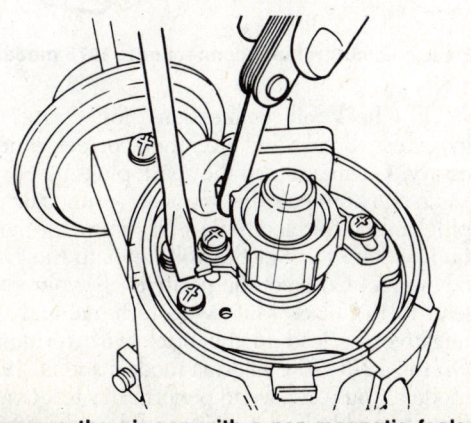

Measure the air gap with a non-magnetic feeler gauge

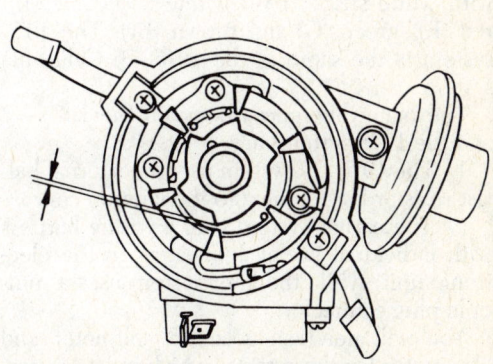

1979–83 air gap

48 TUNE-UP AND PERFORMANCE MAINTENANCE

for 1979–83. Adjustment (if necessary) is made by loosening the pick-up coil mounting screws and shifting it's position on the breaker plate either closer to or farther from the reluctor, on the 1974–78. On the 1979–83 models, center the pick-up coil (toothed stator ring) around the reluctor. Tighten the screws and recheck the gap.

4. Inspect the ignition wires for cracks or brittleness. Replace them one at a time to prevent cross-wiring, carefully pressing the replacement wires into place. The cores of wires used with electronic ignition are more susceptible to breakage than those of standard wires, so treat them gently.

TROUBLESHOOTING

1974

The 1974 electronic ignition cannot be tested using conventional equipment. It must be checked by a dealer with a Datsun made transistor ignition unit tester. The only alternative available to the home mechanic is a substitution test of the control unit. If a unit known to be good operates correctly in the vehicle, the old unit is presumably faulty. This method is far from satisfactory; it ignores all of the associated systems and can result in a protracted and needless waste of money and time. It is strongly recommended that problems with the 1974 ignition system be referred to your dealer.

1975–78

The components used in these systems are basically similar. However, differences exist, which affect the troubleshooting process.

There are two different systems used in 1975 and 1976. One is for Z-cars sold in California, which have one pick-up in the distributor. The wiring harness to the module is composed of six wires: one black (B), two black with white stripe (BW), one blue (L), one red (R) and one green (G). The 49 States and Canada models have seven wires in the harness: black (B), black with white stripe (BW), white (W), blue (L), red (R), green (G) and brown (Br). The 1977 system is the same as the 1975–76 California system.

The main differences between the 1975–77 and the 1978 systems are:

1. The 1975–77 system uses an external ballast resistor located next to the ignition coil.
2. The earlier system uses a wiring harness with individual eyelet connectors to the electronic unit, while the later system uses a multiple plug connector.

You will need an accurate voltmeter and ohmmeter for these tests, which must be performed in the order given:

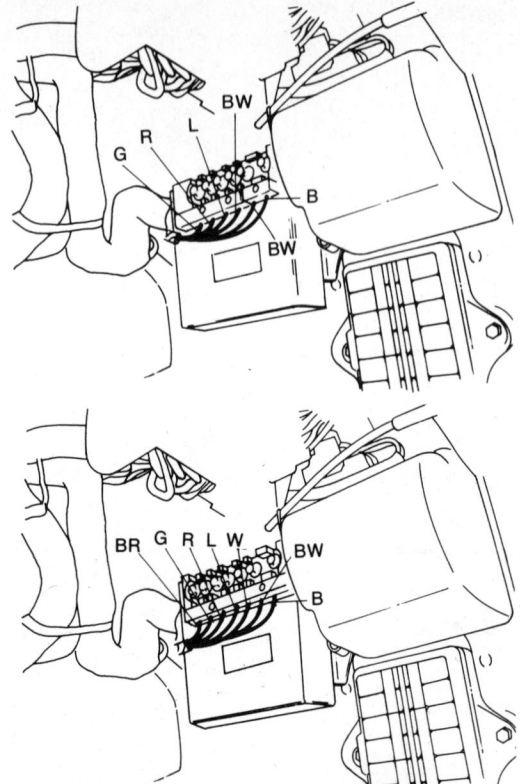

Location and color code of the module: 1975–76 California and all 1977, top; 1975–76 49 States and Canada, bottom

COLOR CODE

B :BLACK
BW :BLACK WITH WHITE STRIPE
R :RED
G :GREEN
L :BLUE

Electronic control unit connections, 1978 models

1. Check all connections for corrosion, looseness, breaks and etc., then correct, if necessary. Clean and gap the spark plugs.
2. Disconnect the harness (connector or plug) from the electronic unit. Turn the ignition swtich ON. Set the voltmeter to the DC, 50v range. Connect the positive (+) voltmeter lead to the black/white wire terminal and the negative (–) lead to the black wire terminal. On the 1975–76 California models and all 1977 models, you will have to perform this test twice, first at one black/white wire and then the other. Battery voltage should be obtained; if not, check

TUNE-UP AND PERFORMANCE MAINTENANCE

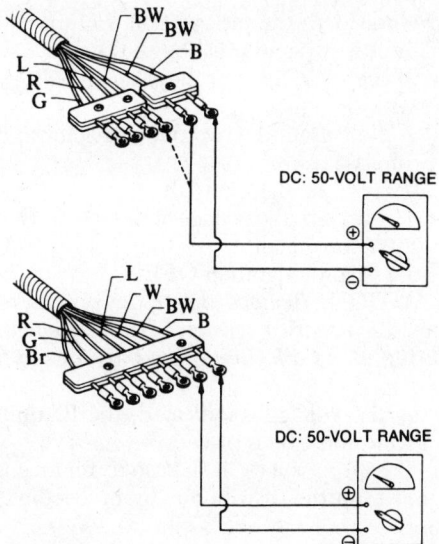

Check the power supply at the harness: 1975–76 California and all 1977, top; 1975–76 49 States and Canada, bottom

the black/white and black wires for continuity, the battery terminals for corrosion and the battery state of charge.

3. Connect the voltmeter positive lead to the blue wire and the negative lead to the black wire. Battery voltage should be obtained; if not, check the blue wire for continuity, the ignition coil terminals for corrosion or looseness and the coil for continuity. On the 1975–77 models, check the external ballast resistor connections.

4. On the 1975–77 models, disconnect the distributor harness wires from the ignition coil ballast resistor, leaving the ballast resistor-to-coil wires attached. On the 1978 models, disconnect the ignition coil wires. On the 1975–77 models, connect the leads of an ohmmeter to the ballast resistor outside terminals (at each end): resistance should be 1.6–2.0 Ω (1.6–1.8 Ω in 1975). On the 1978 models, connect the ohmmeter to the coil primary terminals: the resistance should be 0.0 Ω. If more than 1.8 Ω (1975), 2.0 Ω (1976–77) or 1.8 Ω (1978), replace the coil.

5. Disconnect the harness from the electronic control unit. Connect an ohmmeter to the red and green wire terminals; the resistance should be 720 Ω. If far more or far less, replace the distributor pick-up coil (retarded-side pick-up coil on 1975–76, 49 States and Canada models).

NOTE: *The following step is ONLY for 1975–76, 49 States and Canada models with two pick-up coils in the distributor. Skip this step if your vehicle has only one pick-up coil.*

6. Disconnect the brown wire from the control unit. Connect an ohmmeter between the brown and green wire terminals. The resistance should be approximately 720 Ω. If far more or far less, replace the advance side pick-up coil in the distributor.

7. Turn OFF the ignition. Disconnect the fuel injection wiring harness from the cold start valve. Connect a voltmeter to the red and green terminals of the electronic control harness. When the starter is cranked, the needle of the voltmeter should deflect slightly; if not, replace the distributor pick-up coil. This would be the retarded side coil, on models with two pick-up coils. Repeat the test between the brown and green terminals to check the advance-side pick-up coil (1975–76: 49 States and Canada models ONLY).

8. Reconnect the ignition coil and the electronic control unit harness. Disconnect the fuel injection wiring harness from the injectors and the cold start valve. Unplug the high tension lead (coil-to-distributor) from the distributor and hold it 1/8–1/4 in. from the cylinder head with a pair of insulated pliers and a heavy glove. When the engine is cranked, a spark should be observed. If not, check the lead and replace (if necessary). If still no spark, replace the electronic control unit.

CAUTION: *DO NOT make this test near the fuel injection wiring harness. Damage to the fuel injection control unit will result, if sparks travel to the harness.*

9. Reconnect all of the wires as follows.

   a. On the 1975–77 models: connect the voltmeter positive lead to the blue control unit wire terminal and the negative lead to the black wire terminal. The harness should be attached to the control unit.

   b. On the 1978 models: connect the voltmeter positive lead to the negative terminal of the ignition coil and the negative lead to a good ground.

10. As soon as the ignition switch is turned ON, the meter should indicate battery voltage. If not, replace the electronic control unit.

1978–83

1. Turn the ignition switch OFF. Disconnect the fusible link connector for the fuel injection wiring harness. Be sure the ignition is OFF before doing this. Disconnect the cold start valve wiring harness connector. Disconnect the high tension lead (coil-to-distributor) at the distributor and hold it 1/8–1/4 in. away from the cylinder head with a pair of insulated pliers and a heavy glove. When the engine is cranked, a spark should be observed. If not, check the lead and replace as necessary. If there is still no spark, go on with the following system checks.

2. Make a check of the power supply circuit. Turn the ignition OFF. Disconnect the

50 TUNE-UP AND PERFORMANCE MAINTENANCE

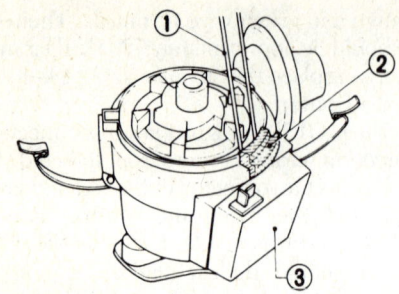

1 Tester probes 2 Grommet 3 IC ignition unit

Ohmmeter connection to the pick-up coil terminals, 1979–83

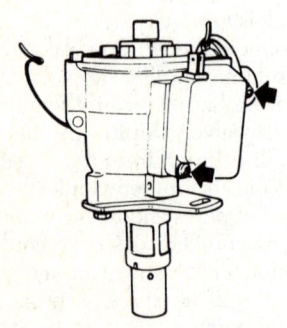

The arrows indicate the IC unit retaining screws, 1979–83

connector from the top of the IC unit. Turn the ignition ON. Measure the voltage at each terminal of the connector in turn by touching the probe of positive lead of the voltmeter to one of the terminals and touching the probe of the negative lead of the voltmeter to a ground, such as the engine. In each case, battery voltage should be indicated. If not, check all of the wiring, the ignition switch and all connectors for breaks, corrosion, discontinuity and etc., then repair as necessary.

3. Check the primary windings of the ignition coil. Turn the ignition OFF. Disconnect the harness connector from the negative coil terminal. Use an ohmmeter to measure the resistance between the positive and negative coil terminals. If resistance is 0.84–1.02 Ω, the coil is OK; replace it, if the reading is far from this range.

4. If the power supply, circuits, wiring and coil are in good shape, check the IC unit and pick-up coil as follows:
   a. Turn the ignition OFF.
   b. Remove the distributor cap and ignition rotor.
   c. Using an ohmmeter, measure the resistance between the two terminals of the pick-up coil, where they attach to the IC unit. Measure the resistance by reversing the polarity of the probes. If approximately 400 Ω are indicated, the pick-up coil is OK but the IC unit is bad and must be replaced.

5. If the resistance is other than 400 Ω, proceed with the following:
   a. Be certain the two pin connector to the IC unit is secure.
   b. Turn the ignition ON.
   c. Measure the voltage at the ignition coil's negative terminal.
   d. Turn the ignition OFF.

CAUTION: *Remove the tester probe from the coil negative terminal before switching the ignition OFF, to prevent burning out the tester.*

   e. If 0 voltage is indicated, the IC unit is bad and must be replaced.

6. If battery voltage is indicated, remove the IC unit from the distributor, by proceeding as follows:
   a. Disconnect the battery ground (negative) cable.
   b. Remove the distributor cap and ignition rotor.
   c. Disconnect the harness connector from the top of the IC unit.
   d. Remove the two screws securing the IC unit to the distributor.
   e. Disconnect the two pick-up coil wires from the IC unit.

CAUTION: *Pull the connectors free with a pair of needlenose pliers. DO NOT pull on the wires to detach the connectors.*

   f. Remove the IC unit.

7. Measure the resistance between the terminals of the pick-up coil. It should be approximately 400 Ω. If so, the pick-up coil is OK and the IC unit is bad. If the resistance is other than 400 Ω, the pick-up coil is bad and must be replaced.

1984 and Later

The 1984 and later distributor is checked by replacement ONLY.

PICK-UP COIL AND RELUCTOR REPLACEMENT

1974–78

The reluctor cannot be removed on some early 1974 models—it is an integral part of the distributor shaft. Non-removable reluctors can be distinguished by the absence of a roll pin (retaining pin) which locks the reluctor in place on the shaft.

PICK-UP COIL

1. Remove the distributor cap by releasing the two spring clips. Remove the ignition rotor by pulling it straight up and off the shaft.

TUNE-UP AND PERFORMANCE MAINTENANCE 51

2. Disconnect the distributor wiring harness at the terminal block.

3. Remove the pick-up coil mounting screws and the screws retaining the wiring harness to the distributor.

4. Remove the pick-up coil.

5. To replace the pick-up coil, reverse the removal procedures but leave the mounting screws slightly loose to facilitate air gap adjustment.

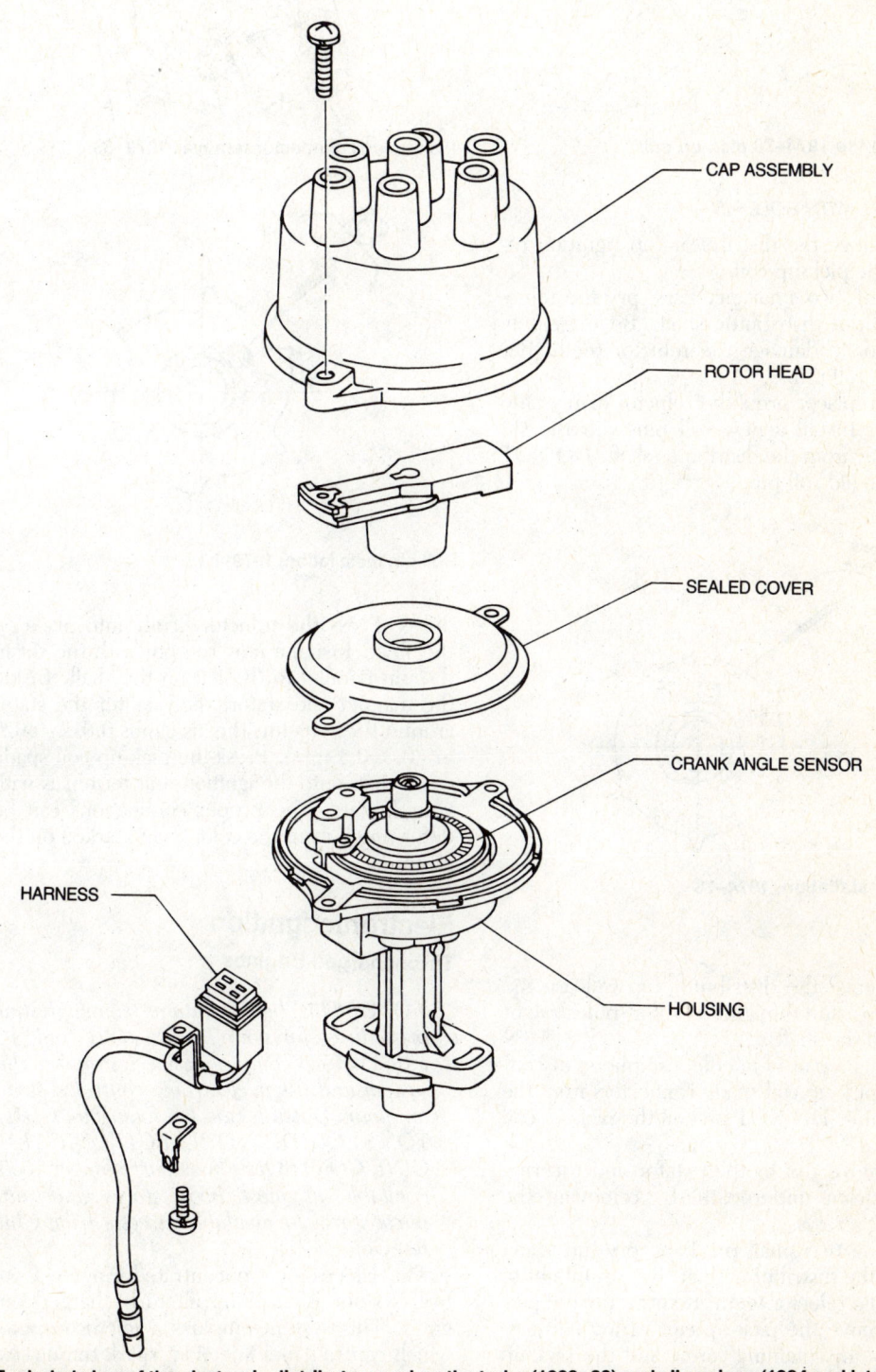

Exploded view of the electronic distributor used on the turbo (1982–83) and all engines (1984 and later), which are similar

TUNE-UP AND PERFORMANCE MAINTENANCE

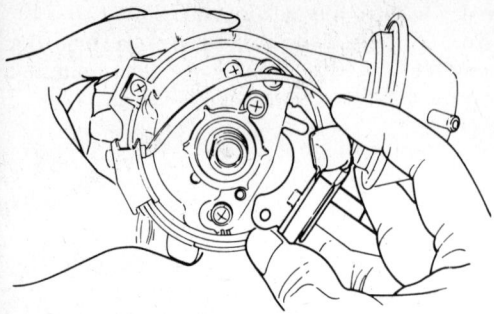

Removing the 1974–78 pick-up coil

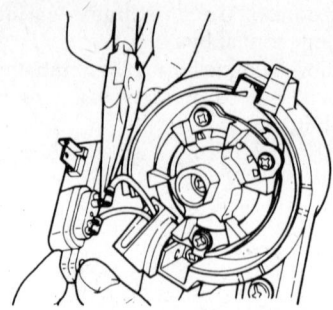

Pick-up coil connector removal, 1979–83

RELUCTOR—WITH ROLL PIN

1. Remove the distributor cap, ignition rotor and the pick-up coil.
2. Using two small pry bars, pry the reluctor from the distributor shaft. Be extremely careful not to damage the reluctor teeth. Remove the roll pin.
3. To replace, press the reluctor firmly onto the shaft. Install a new roll pin with the slit facing away from the distributor shaft. DO NOT re-use the old roll pin.

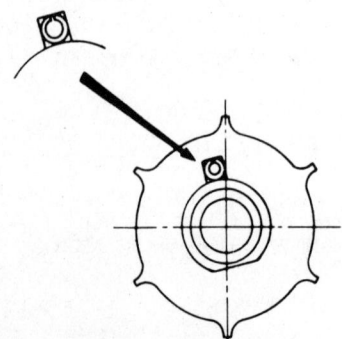

Roll pin installation, 1974–78

1979–83

1. Remove the distributor cap (release the spring clips) and the ignition rotor (pull straight up and off the shaft).
2. Using a pair of needlenose pliers, disconnect the pick-up coil spade connectors from the ignition unit. DO NOT pull on the pick-up coil wires.
3. Remove the toothed stator and the ring magnet (from underneath) by removing the mounting screws.
4. Using two small pry bars, pry the reluctor from the distributor shaft. Be careful not to damage the reluctor teeth. Remove the roll pin.
5. Remove the pick-up coil wiring harness-to-distributor retaining screw and the pick-up coil.
6. To install, reverse the removal proce-

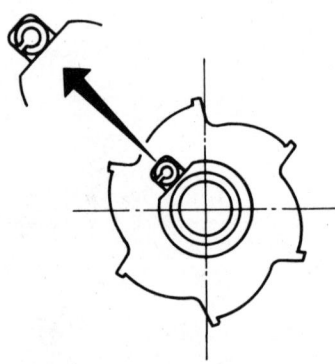

Roll pin installation, 1979–83

dures. Press the reluctor firmly into place on the shaft. Install a new roll pin with the slit in the pin parallel to the flat on the shaft. Install the magnet and stator, then center the stator around the reluctor; the air gap is 0.012–0.020 in. (0.3–0.4 mm). Press the pick-up coil spade connectors onto the ignition unit terminals with your fingers. The proper connections can be determined from the color code marked on the grommet.

Electronic Ignition

Turbocharged Engines

NOTE: *This book contains simple testing procedures for your Datsun's electronic ignition. More comprehensive testing on this system and other electronic control systems on your Datsun can be found in CHILTON'S GUIDE TO ELECTRONIC ENGINE CONTROLS, book part number 7535, available at most book stores and auto parts stores or available directly from Chilton Co.*

The Electronic Concentrated Engine Control System is used on all turbocharged engines. This system employs a microcomputer which controls fuel injection, spark timing, exhaust gas recirculation (EGR), idle speed, fuel pump operation and mixture ratio feedback.

TUNE-UP AND PERFORMANCE MAINTENANCE

Electrical signals from each sensor are fed into the computer and each actuator is controlled by an electrical pulse with a duration that is computed in the microcomputer. When engine malfunctions occur, the use of an ECCS analyzer is necessary to accurately diagnose the problem.

The ECCS analyzer monitors several input and output signals that are emitted in response to various engine operating and stopped conditions. Input signals are compared to computerized signal values stored in the Central Electronic Control Unit (CECU) while output signals are monitored to ensure they are properly attuned before they are emitted from the CECU unit to the actuators. In other words, this analyzer analyzes all electrical signals that are transmitted to and from the CECU unit.

Since this analyzer would be very expensive to purchase, any suspected malfunction of the engine cannot be corrected by an obvious visual inspection, this should be left to a qualified repair shop that contains this equipment.

Ignition Timing

Ignition timing is the measurement, in degrees of crankshaft rotation, of the point at which the spark plugs fire in each of the cylinders. It is measured in degrees before or after Top Dead Center (TDC) of the compression stroke.

Because it takes a fraction of a second for the spark plug to ignite the mixture in the cylinder, the spark plug must fire a little before the piston reaches TDC. Otherwise, the mixture will not be completely ignited as the piston passes TDC and the full power of the explosion will not be used by the engine.

The timing measurement is given in degrees of crankshaft rotation before the piston reaches TDC (BTDC). If the setting for the ignition timing is 5° BTDC, the spark plug must fire 5° before each piston reaches TDC. This only holds true, however, when the engine is at idle speed.

As the engine speed increases, the pistons go faster. The spark plugs have to ignite the fuel even sooner, if it is to be completely ignited when the piston reaches TDC. To do this, the distributor (1970–83) has two means of advancing the spark timing as the engine speed increases: a set of centrifugal weights within the distributor and a vacuum diaphragm, mounted on the side of the distributor.

If the ignition is set too far in advance (BTDC), the ignition and expansion of the fuel in the cylinder will occur too soon and tend to force the piston down while it is still traveling up; causing the engine to ping. If the ignition spark is set too far (retarded), after TDC (ATDC), the piston will have already passed TDC and started on it's way down, when the fuel is ignited. This will cause the piston to be forced down for only a portion of it's travel. This will result in poor engine performance and lack of power.

The timing marks consist of a notch on the rim of the crankshaft pulley and a scale of degrees attached to the front of the engine. The notch corresponds to the position of the piston in the No. 1 cylinder. A stroboscopic (dynamic) timing light is used, which is hooked into the circuit of the No. 1 cylinder spark plug. Every time the spark plug fires, the timing light flashes, making the mark on the pulley appear to be standing still. The proper timing is indicated when the notch is aligned with the correct number on the scale.

There are three basic types of timing light available:

1. The first type is a simple neon bulb with two wire connections (one for the spark plug and one for the plug wire, connecting the light in series). This type of light is quite dim and must be held closely to the marks to be seen; it is inexpensive.

2. The second type of light operates from the car battery. Two alligator clips connect to the battery terminals, while a third wire connects to a spark plug with an adapter. This type of light is more expensive and the xenon bulb provides a nice bright flash which can even be seen in sunlight.

3. The third type replaces the battery source with 110 volt house current. Some timing lights have other functions built into them, such as dwell meters, tachometers or remote starting switches. These are convenient, in that they reduce the tangle of wires under the hood but may duplicate the functions of tools you already have.

If your vehicle has an electronic ignition, use a timing light with an inductive pickup. This pickup simply clamps onto the No. 1 plug wire, eliminating the adapter. It is not susceptible to crossfiring or false triggering, which may occur with a conventional light, due to the greater voltages produced by electronic ignition.

IGNITION TIMING ADJUSTMENT

All Engines–Except Turbocharged (1982–83) and All (1984 and Later)

Refer to Chapter 4, Emission Controls and Fuel System, for the procedure to check and adjust the phase timing of the dual points or dual pickups in 1973–76 models.

NOTE: *If the underhood emissions decal differs from the information given below, always use the information on the decal as this reflects the latest changes made during production.*

TUNE-UP AND PERFORMANCE MAINTENANCE

1. On the 1970–73 models, set the dwell of the breaker points to the proper specification.
2. Locate the timing marks on the crankshaft pulley and the front of the engine.
3. Clean off the timing marks, so that you can see them.
4. Use chalk or white paint to color the mark on the crankshaft pulley and the mark on the scale which indicates the correct timing when aligned with the notch on the crankshaft pulley.
5. Attach a tachometer to the engine.
6. Attach a timing light to the engine, according to the manufacturer's instructions.
7. On the 1970–79 models, leave the vacuum hose connected to the distributor advance vacuum diaphragm.
8. On the 1980–81 models:
   a. Disconnect the throttle valve switch harness connector.
   b. Disconnect and plug the canister purge hose from the intake manifold.
   c. Plug the opening in the intake manifold.
   d. On the 1980, 49 States models, also disconnect the hose from the air induction pipe and cap the pipe, then disconnect and plug the vacuum advance hose at the distributor.

NOTE: *The disconnect and plug instructions, for the air induction pipe and the distributor vacuum advance, do not apply to 1980 models sold in California or Canada.*

9. On the 1982–83 models, disconnect and plug the distributor vacuum hose from the distributor vacuum controller. On the 1983 models, disconnect the grey harness connector from the distributor.
10. Check that all of the wires clear the fan, pulleys and belts, then start the engine. Allow the engine to reach normal operating temperature.

CAUTION: *Block the front wheels and set the parking brake. Shift the manual transmission into Neutral or the automatic transmission into Drive. DO NOT stand in front of the car when making adjustments!*

11. Adjust the idle to the correct setting. See the Idle Speed and Mixture section later in this chapter.
12. Aim the timing light at the timing marks. If the marks placed on the pulley and the engine are aligned when the light flashes, the timing is correct. Turn OFF the engine, then remove the tachometer and the timing light.
13. If the marks are not in alignment, proceed with the following steps:
   a. Turn OFF the engine.
   b. Loosen the distributor lockbolt just enough so that the distributor can be turned with a little effort.
   c. Start the engine. Keep the wires of the timing light clear of the fan.

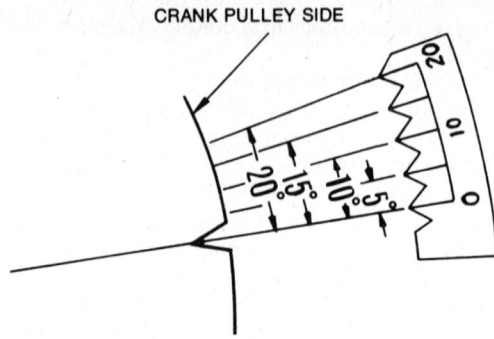

The crankshaft pulley and timing scale, 1973 240-Z

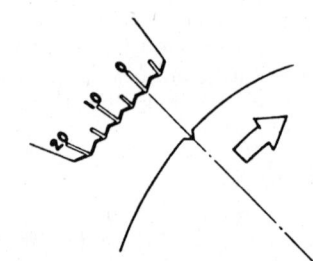

Timing scale—1974–83

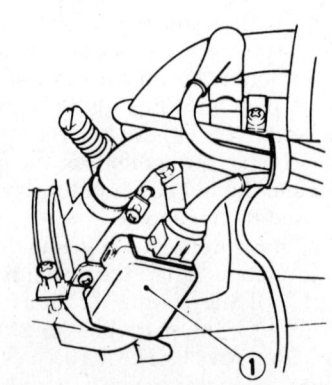

1980 throttle valve switch (1); others are similar

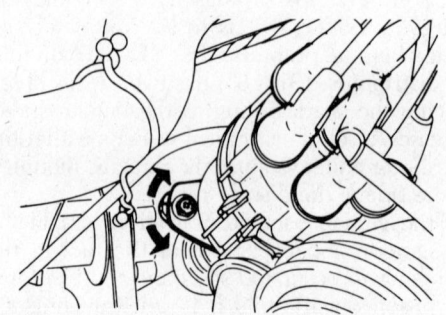

Loosen the distributor lockbolt and turn the distributor slightly to advance (upper arrow) or retard (lower arrow) the timing

TUNE-UP AND PERFORMANCE MAINTENANCE

d. With the timing light aimed at the pulley and the marks on the engine, turn the distributor in the direction of rotor rotation to retard the spark or in the opposite direction of rotor rotation to advance the spark. Align the marks on the pulley and the engine with the flashes of the timing light.

e. Tighten the distributor lockbolt and recheck the timing.

14. Reconnect all hoses and connectors.

Turbocharged (1982–83) and All (1984 and Later) Engines

The ignition timing is controlled by the Central Electronic Control Unit (CECU) adjusting to the engine operating conditions: that is, as the best ignition timing in each driving condition has been memorized in the unit, the ignition timing is determined by the electric signal calculated in the unit.

The signals used for determining the ignition timing are: cylinder head temperature, engine rpm, engine load, engine crank angle, detonation sensor and etc.

Then, the signal from the CECU is transmitted to the power transistor of the ignition coil and controls the ignition timing. If there is engine knocking, a detonation sensor monitors it's condition and the signal is transmitted to the CECU. After receiving it, the control unit controls the ignition timing to avoid the knocking condition.

The ignition timing is automatically controlled by the control unit and it is usually unnecessary to adjust it. However, the ignition timing can go wrong if the crank angle sensor must be adjusted.

This adjustment should be left to a qualified technician since it should be preceded by a system test using an ECCS analyzer. (See the explanation given under Electronic Ignition–Turbocharged Engines).

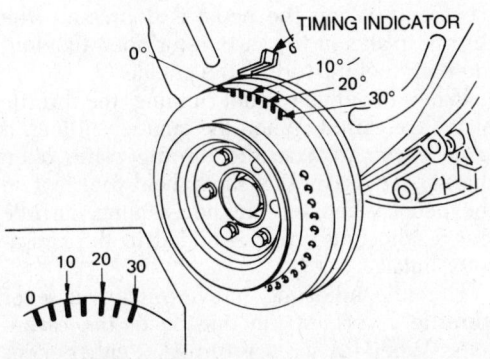

1984 and later timing marks

Valve Lash

1970–83

Valve adjustment determines how far the valves enter the cylinder and how long they stay open and closed.

If the valve clearance is too large, part of the lift of the camshaft will be used in removing the excessive clearance. Consequently, the valve will not be opening for as long as it should. This condition has two effects:

1. The valve train components will emit a tapping sound as they take up the excessive clearance.

2. The engine will perform poorly because the valves don't open fully to allow the proper amount of gases to flow through the engine.

If the valve clearance is too small, the intake and the exhaust valves will open too far and will not fully seat on the cylinder head when they close. When a valve seats itself on the cylinder head, it does two things:

1. It seals the combustion chamber so that none of the gases in the cylinder escape.

2. It cools itself by transferring some of the heat it absorbs from the combustion in the cylinder to the cylinder head and to the engine's cooling system.

If the valve clearance is too small, the engine will run poorly because of the gases escaping from the combustion chamber. The valves will also become overheated and will warp, since they cannot transfer heat unless they are touching the valve seat in the cylinder head.

NOTE: *While the valve adjustments must be made as accurately as possible, it is better to have the valve adjustment slightly loose rather than tight, as a burned valve may result from overly tight adjustments.*

1984 and Later

The 1984 and later models have hydraulic valve lifters. Periodic adjustment is not necessary.

ADJUSTMENT

NOTE: *The valves are adjusted with the engine at normal operating temperatures. The oil temperature and the resultant parts expansion are much more important than water temperature.*

1. Run the engine for at least fifteen minutes to ensure that all the parts have reached their full expansion. After the engine is warmed up, shut it off.

2. Purchase either a new gasket or some silicone gasket sealant before removing the camshaft cover. Note the location of any wires and hoses which may interfere with the cam cover removal, disconnect and move them aside. Remove the cam cover bolts and the cover.

TUNE-UP AND PERFORMANCE MAINTENANCE

3. Place a wrench on the crankshaft pulley bolt and rotate the engine until the valves for No. 1 cylinder are closed. When both cam lobes are pointing up, the valves are closed.

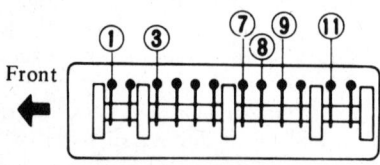

Valve arrangement as seen from the left side of the engine (E = exhaust; I = intake)

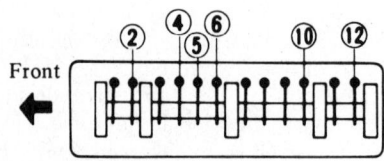

Adjust valves—1, 3, 7, 8, 9, and 11

Adjust valves—2, 4, 5, 6, 10 and 12

NOTE: *If you have not done this before, it is a good idea to turn the engine over slowly several times and watch the valve action until you have a clear idea of just when the valve is closed.*

4. Adjust the clearance of only half of the valves. Adjust only 1, 3, 7, 8, 9 and 11 valves.

5. Using a feeler gauge, measure the clearance between the cam lobe and the valve rocker. The valve clearance should be (hot) intake–(3, 8 and 11) 0.010 in. (0.25 mm), exhaust–(1, 7 and 9) 0.012 in. (0.30 mm).

6. If the clearance is not the specified value, loosen the pivot lock nut and turn the valve rocker pivot to provide proper clearance. The feeler gauge should move with a very slight drag when rechecked.

7. Turn the crankshaft (again) so that the high point of the No. 1 cam lobe points down. Adjust the clearance of the other half of the valves 2, 4, 5, 6, 10 and 12, using the same procedure as in step 6. The valve clearance should be (hot) intake–(2, 5 and 10) 0.010 in. (0.25 mm) and exhaust–(4, 6 and 12) 0.012 in. (0.30 mm).

8. Install the cam cover gasket, the cam cover, then any wires and hoses which were removed.

Carburetor

This section contains only tune-up adjustment procedures for carburetors. Descriptions, adjustments and overhaul procedures for carburetors can be found in the Fuel System section.

When the engine is running, the air/fuel mixture from the carburetor is being drawn into the engine by a partial vacuum which is created by the movement of the pistons downward on the intake stroke. The amount of air/fuel mixture that enters the engine is controlled by the throttle plates at the bottom of the carburetor. When the engine is not running the throttle plates are closed, completely blocking off the bottom of the carburetor. The throttle plates are connected by the throttle linkage to the accelerator pedal in the passenger compartment. When the pedal is depressed, the throttle plates in the carburetor open to admit more air/fuel mixture to the engine.

When the engine is not running, the throttle plates are closed. When the engine is idling, it is necessary to have the throttle plates open slightly. To prevent having to hold your foot on the pedal when the engine is idling, an idle speed adjusting screw is added to the carburetor linkage.

The idle adjusting screw contacts a lever (throttle lever) on the outside of the carburetor. When the screw is turned, it either opens or closes the throttle plates of the carburetor,

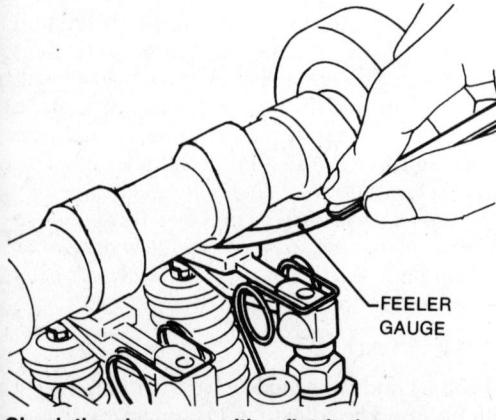

Check the clearance with a flat feeler gauge

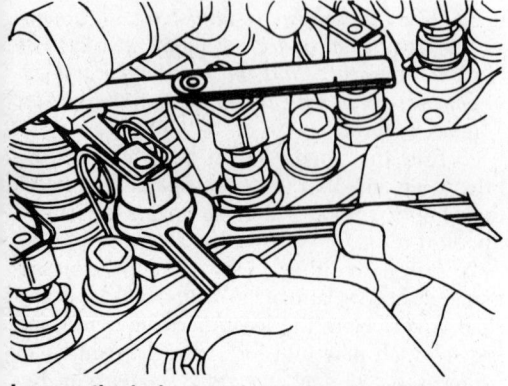

Loosen the locknut and turn the pivot adjuster to change the clearance

TUNE-UP AND PERFORMANCE MAINTENANCE

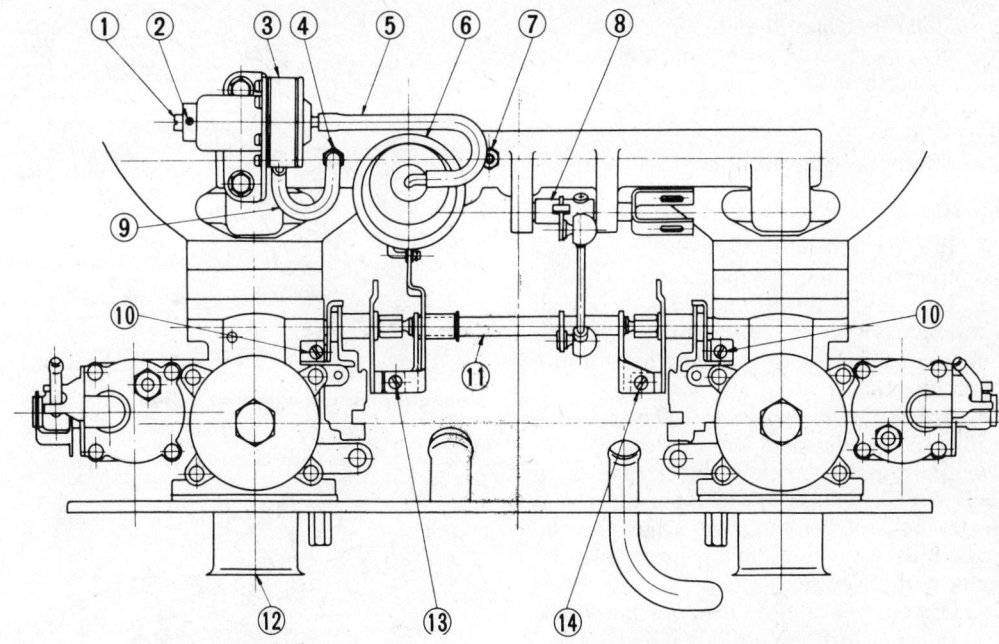

1. Vacuum adjusting screw
2. Lockscrew
3. Throttle control valve
4. Control valve manifold connection
5. Servo diaphragm vacuum tube
6. Servo diaphragm
7. A. B. valve connector
8. Auxiliary throttle shaft
9. Control valve vacuum tube
10. Throttle adjusting screw
11. Throttle shaft
12. Airhorn
13. Opener adjusting screw
14. Balance screw

Location of the throttle linkage and carburetor components on the 1970–72 models

raising or lowering the idle speed of the engine. This screw is called the curb idle adjusting screw.

A special mixture circuit is incorporated into the carburetor to enable the engine to run smoothly at idle. The circuit is controlled by the mixture screw, which determines the amount of fuel admitted at idle.

IDLE SPEED AND MIXTURE ADJUSTMENT
1970–72

1. Run the engine until it reaches operating temperature. Remove the air cleaner.
2. Adjust the idle speed to 750 rpm. Apply an air flow meter for 1–2 seconds to one of the carburetor air horns, holding it vertically. Then, check the flow of the other carburetor. Adjust the throttle adjusting screws so that the airflow is equal at 750 rpm.
3. Disconnect the control vacuum tube from the manifold connector and connect the servo diaphragm vacuum tube in it's place, in order to apply full vacuum to the diaphragm.
4. Adjust the opener adjusting screw to 1,200 rpm.
5. Using the flow meter as described above, adjust the balance screw so that the airflow is equal for the carburetors.
6. Disconnect and then reconnect the servo diaphragm vacuum tube where it is connected to the manifold. Check the rpm and flow rates, then, if necessary, readjust as in Steps 4 and 5.
7. Return the vacuum hoses to their original positions, disconnect the diaphragm tube from the manifold and reconnect it to the control valve, then reconnect the control valve hose to the manifold connection.
8. If a CO meter is available, adjust CO as follows:

   a. Disconnect the air pump belt so that the pump will be inoperative.

Idle mixture adjusting nut, 1970–72

TUNE-UP AND PERFORMANCE MAINTENANCE

b. Gently tighten the idle mixture adjusting nuts, located under the carburetors, until they hit their stops.

c. Turn both nuts equally outward until the CO is 5–7%.

d. Reconnect the air pump belt.

1973–74

1. Run the engine until it reaches operating temperature. Remove the air cleaner.
2. Loosen the throttle adjusting screw all the way. Except on the 1974 equipped with an automatic transmission, loosen the throttle opener adjusting screw all the way.
3. Adjust the idle speed to 750 rpm, using the idle speed adjusting screw. On the automatic transmission models, block the drive wheels, securely apply the parking brake and place the transmission in Drive. Adjust the idle speed adjusting screw to 600 rpm. Return the selector to the Neutral position.

NOTE: *On the 260-Z, with an automatic transmission, proceed to Step 6 as these vehicles do not employ a throttle opener control valve.*

4. Disconnect the vacuum control valve-to-servo diaphragm hose and the control valve-to-intake manifold hose.

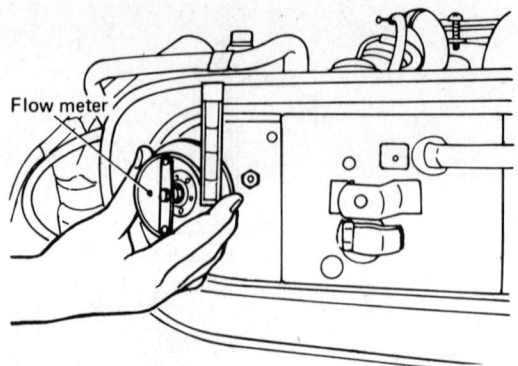

Measuring airflow with flow meter

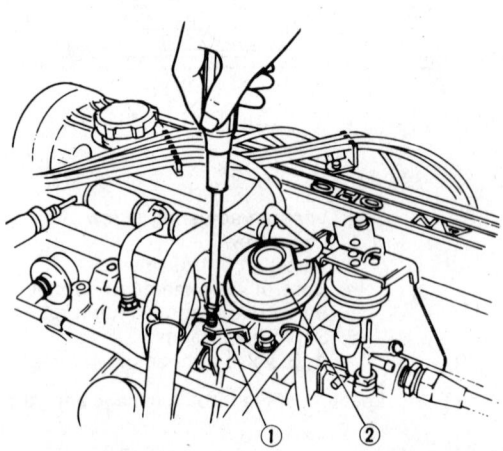

1. Fast idle screw   2. E.G.R. valve

Location of the fast idle screw on 1974 automatic transmission models

5. Connect a longer hose of the same diameter between the servo diaphragm-to-manifold connector.
6. On all models, except the 1974, 260-Z equipped with an automatic transmission, adjust the throttle opener adjusting screw to 1,400 rpm. On the 260-Zs, equipped with an automatic transmission, do the same with the fast idle adjusting screw.
7. Apply a flow meter briefly to the front carburetor intake. Turn the adjusting screw on the flow meter and align the upper end of the float with the scale. Then, tighten the screw.
8. Apply the meter to the rear carburetor air intake and adjust the balance adjusting screw, until the float in the meter is aligned with the scale.
9. Reinstall the air cleaner, connecting the vacuum motor to the temperature sensor with the vacuum hose.
10. Readjust the engine speed to 1,400 rpm as in Step 6.
11. Raise the engine speed briefly to 3,000 rpm. Then, raise it to 1,700 rpm with the

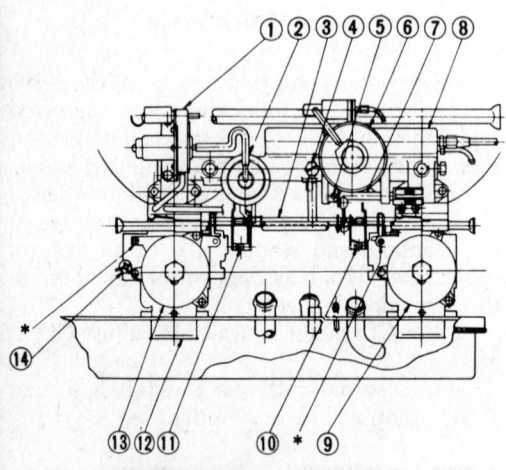

1. Throttle opener control valve
2. Servo diaphragm
3. Throttle shaft
4. Idle speed adjusting screw
5. Fast idle screw
6. E.G.R. valve
7. Auxiliary throttle shaft
8. Balance tube
9. Rear carburetor
10. Balance adjusting screw
11. Throttle opener adjusting screw
12. Airhorn
13. Front carburetor
14. Idle mixture adjusting screw

Throttle linkage and carburetor components on 1973–74 models

TUNE-UP AND PERFORMANCE MAINTENANCE

throttle opener or fast idle screw (depending on the model as specified above). Finally, gradually lower the speed down to 1,400 rpm.

12. Disconnect the air pump check valve hose and plug the check valve.

13. With a CO meter, adjust the CO to 1.0–1.6% for a manual transmission or 0.6–1.2% for automatics (in Neutral). This adjustment is made at the idle mixture adjusting screw.

14. On all vehicles, except the 260-Z (equipped with an AT), disconnect the servo diaphragm vacuum for 2–3 seconds and then reconnect it. Make sure that the rpm returns to 1,400; if not, readjust it at the throttle opener adjusting screw.

15. On all models, except the 1974 260-Z, remove the long vacuum hose and reconnect the hoses, so that one runs from the manifold-to-throttle opener control valve and the other from the control valve-to-servo. On the later model automatics, turn the fast idle screw out until there is a clearance of 0.078 in. (2 mm) between the lever and the tip of the screw.

16. Race the engine several times to verify that the idle speed is correct. Readjust it if necessary.

17. Unplug the check valve and reconnect the hose.

18. Measure the CO percentage and make sure that it is below 2.7%.

Fuel Injection

The 1975 and later models have electronic fuel injection as standard equipment. The only regular tune-up maintenance required with this system is an idle speed check and on the 1975–79 manual transmission models, a dashpot adjustment. The idle mixture is not adjustable during 1975–76. The idle mixture can be adjusted on 1977 and later models but it requires the use of a CO meter.

NOTE: *It is unlikely you will ever have need to adjust the mixture and because of the expense of a CO meter, it is suggested that any mixture adjustments be referred to your dealer or a qualified mechanic with access to the proper equipment.*

Idle Speed

ADJUSTMENT

1975–83

1. Warm the engine to normal operating temperature, either by driving the car or allowing it to idle.

2. When warm, continue to run the engine with the hood open for about five minutes at 2,000 rpm. If the car has air conditioning, it should be OFF.

3. Turn OFF the engine, then disconnect and plug the vacuum hose at the distributor vacuum controller.

NOTE: *On the 1982–83 models, disconnect the gray electrical harness from the distributor.*

4. Start the engine and race it 2–3 times under no load, then allow it to run at idle.

5. Set the parking brake and block the front wheels. Shift the manual transmissions into Neutral or the automatic transmissions into Drive.

6. Adjust the idle speed to specifications by turning the idle speed screw, which is located in the throttle chamber, next to the distributor.

Idle speed screw—1975–80

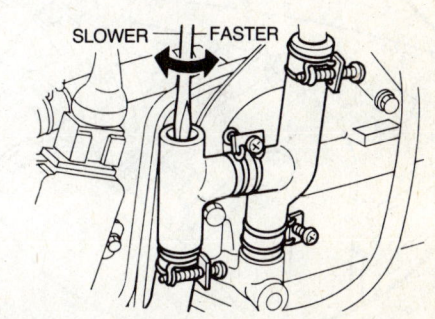

1981–82 idle speed screw

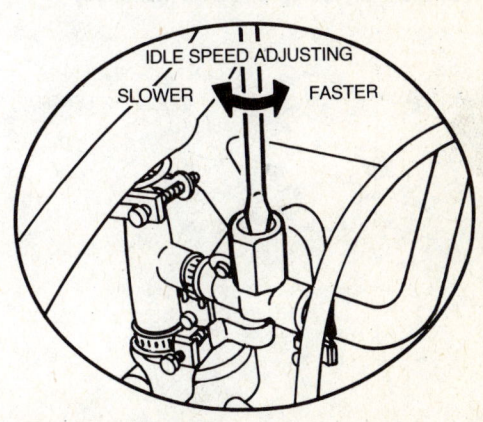

1983 idle speed screw

TUNE-UP AND PERFORMANCE MAINTENANCE

NOTE: *The idle speed for both transmissions should be 550–750 rpm.*

7. Using a timing light, check and/or adjust the ignition timing to 6–10° BTDC.

8. Operate the engine at 2,000 rpm for 2 minutes under no-load.

NOTE: *Make sure the inspection lamp on the control unit goes ON and OFF more than 5 times in 10 seconds.*

9. Turn the engine OFF and reconnect the vacuum hose

NOTE: *On the 1982–83 models, reconnect the grey harness to the distributor.*

10. Start the engine and race it 2–3 times, then allow it to idle.

11. Check and/or adjust the idle speed to 600–800 rpm.

1984 and Later

1. Start the engine and run it until it reaches normal operating temperature. The water temperature indicator should point to the middle of the gauge. Make sure that all of the accessories are turned OFF.

NOTE: *The checking and adjustment of the idle speed is made with the automatic trans-*

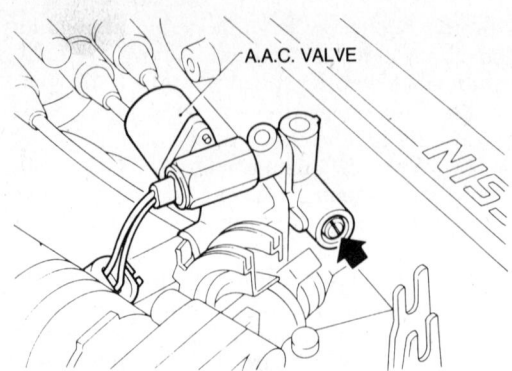

Location of the idle adjusting screw and the AAC valve—turbocharged engine

mission in the Drive position, so make sure the parking brake is fully engaged and both the front and rear wheels are blocked with wheel chocks.

2. If not equipped with a turbocharger, stop the engine. Disconnect the idle-up solenoid valve harness connector.

3. Start the engine and race it 2–3 times, under no-load, then return it to idle speed.

4. Check and adjust the idle speed as necessary by turning the idle speed adjusting screw. (Automatic transmission in Drive and the manual transmission in Neutral).

NOTE: *If not equipped with a turbocharger, set the idle speed to 650–750 rpm at sea level or 600–700 rpm at high altitude. If equipped with a turbocharger, set the idle speed to 650–750 rpm (M/T) or 600–700 (A/T).*

5. If equipped with a turbocharger, perform the following:

    a. Stop the engine and disconnect the AAC valve harness connector.
    b. Start the engine.
    c. Adjust the engine speed by turning the idle speed screw. The idle speed should be 650 rpm (M/T) or 600 rpm (A/T).
    d. Stop the engine.
    e. Reconnect the AAC valve harness connector and start the engine.

6. If not equipped with a turbocharger, stop the engine and reconnect the idle-up solenoid harness connector.

7. Using a timing light, start the engine and check the timing; it should be 18–22° BTDC. If not adjust the distributor.

8. If the timing adjustment was performed, recheck the idle speed.

DASHPOT AND ADJUSTMENT

1975–79 With Manual Transmission

1. Start the engine and run it at 2,000 rpm, under no load. If equipped with air conditioning, turn it OFF.

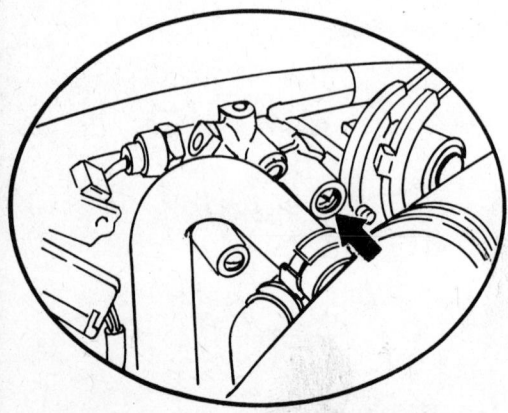

1984 and later, idle speed screw (nonturbo)

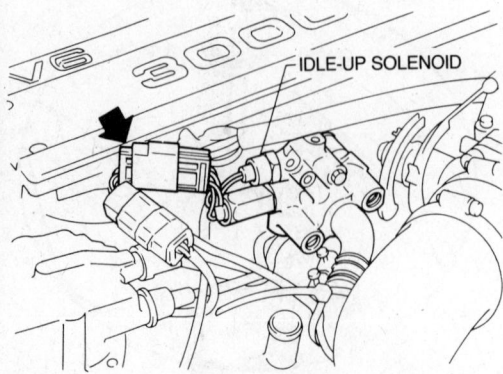

1984 and later, idle up solenoid (nonturbo)

TUNE-UP AND PERFORMANCE MAINTENANCE

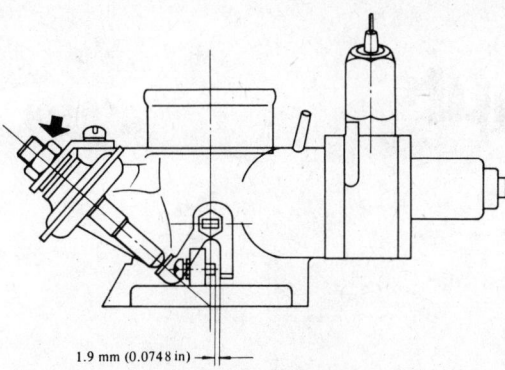

Dashpot measurement (1970–78), adjust at the locknut (arrow)

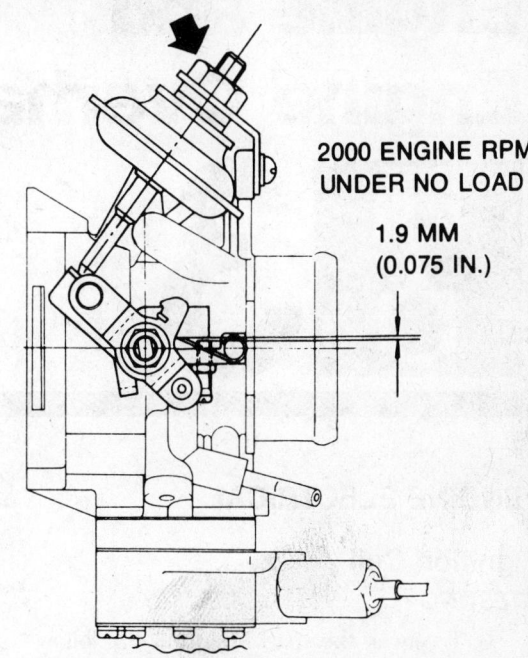

1979 dashpot measurement—adjustment is made at the locknut (arrow)

2. The clearance between the idle setscrew (preset at the factory) and the throttle lever should be exactly 0.075 in. (1.9 mm).

3. The dashpot plunger, when fully extended, should be in contact with the throttle lever.

4. If adjustment is necessary, loosen the dashpot mounting nut and turn the dashpot assembly until the clearance is correct. Tighten the nut and recheck the clearance.

Engine and Engine Overhaul

3

ENGINE ELECTRICAL

Ignition Coil

TESTING

1. To check the spark, perform the following:
   a. Disconnect the coil wire from the distributor cap.
   NOTE: *On Electronic Fuel Injection systems, disconnect the EFI fusible link connector and the cold start valve harness connector.*
   b. Using a pair of insulated pliers, hold the coil wire about a ¼ in. away from the engine block.
   c. Have an assistant turn the ignition switch to the Start position. With the engine rotating, spark should occur across the wire gap; if not, further inspection of the coil is necessary.
2. To check the coil's primary circuit, perform the following:
   a. Make sure that the ignition switch is turned OFF.
   b. Remove the primary wires from the (+) positive and the (−) negative terminals of the coil.
   c. Using an ohmmeter, set it to the 1.0 Ω range, then connect the probes to the primary terminals. The resistance should be 0.84–1.02 Ω's; if not, replace the ignition coil.
3. To check the coil's secondary circuit, perform the following:
   a. Make sure that the ignition switch is turned OFF.
   b. Remove the coil wire from the center terminal of the coil.
   c. Using an ohmmeter, set it to the 15,000 Ω range, then connect the one probe to the center terminal and the other to the (−) negative terminal. The resistance should be 8,200–12,400 Ω's; if not, replace the ignition coil.

REMOVAL AND INSTALLATION

1. Make sure that the ignition switch is in the OFF position.
2. Remove the coil wires from the primary and center terminals.
3. Loosen the coil bracket clamp and slide the coil from the bracket.
4. To install, reverse the removal procedures.

Distributor

REMOVAL

1. Remove the high-tension wires from the distributor cap terminal towers, noting their positions to assure correct reassembly. Number the wires with pieces of adhesive tape if they are not already numbered.
2. Disconnect the distributor wiring harness.
3. Disconnect the vacuum line(s).
4. Unlatch the two distributor cap retaining clips or screws and remove the distributor cap.
5. Note the position of the rotor in relation to the base. Scribe a mark on the base of the distributor and on the engine block to facilitate reinstallation. Align the marks with the direction the metal tip of the rotor is pointing.
6. Remove the distributor-to-engine bolt and hold-down plate.
7. Lift the distributor assembly from the engine.

INSTALLATION

Undisturbed Engine

1. Insert the distributor shaft and assembly into the engine. Line up the mark on the distributor and the one on the engine with the metal tip of the rotor.
   NOTE: *Make sure that the vacuum advance diaphragm is pointed in the same direction as it was pointed originally. This will be done*

ENGINE AND ENGINE OVERHAUL

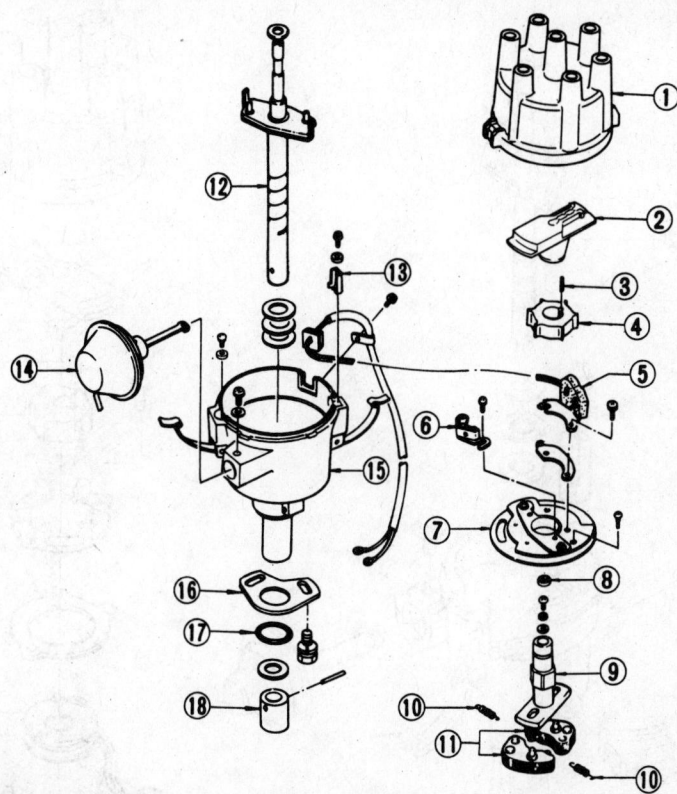

1. Cap assembly
2. Rotor head assembly
3. Roll pin
4. Reluctor
5. Pick-up coil
6. Contactor
7. Breaker plate assembly
8. Packing
9. Rotor shaft
10. Governor spring
11. Governor weight
12. Shaft assembly
13. Cap setter
14. Vacuum controller
15. Housing
16. Fixing plate
17. O-ring
18. Collar

Exploded view of the single pick-up electronic ignition distributor, 1974–78

automatically if the marks on the engine and the distributor are lined up with the rotor.

2. Install the distributor hold-down bolt and clamp. Leave the screw loose enough so that the distributor can be moved with heavy hand pressure.

3. Connect the distributor wiring harness. Install the distributor cap on the distributor housing. Secure the distributor cap with the spring clips or screws.

4. Install the spark plug wires. Make sure that the wires are pressed all the way into the top of the distributor cap and firmly onto the spark plug.

5. Adjust the point dwell (if equipped with points) and set the ignition timing.

Disturbed Engine

1. It is necessary to place the No. 1 cylinder in the firing position to correctly install the distributor. To locate this position, use the ignition timing marks on the crankshaft front pulley.

2. Remove the No. 1 cylinder spark plug. Turn the crankshaft until the piston in the No. 1 cylinder is moving up on the compression stroke. Stop turning the crankshaft when the timing marks are aligned.

NOTE: *To determine TDC of the compression stroke, place your thumb over the spark plug hole to feel the air being forced out of the cylinder.*

3. Oil the distributor housing lightly where the distributor bears on the cylinder block.

4. Install the distributor so that the rotor points toward the No. 1 spark plug terminal tower position when the cap is installed. Of course you won't be able to see the direction in which the rotor is pointing if the cap is on the distributor. Set the cap on the top of the distributor and make a mark on the side of the distributor housing just below the No. 1 spark plug terminal. Make sure that the rotor points toward that mark when you install the distributor.

5. When the distributor shaft has reached

64 ENGINE AND ENGINE OVERHAUL

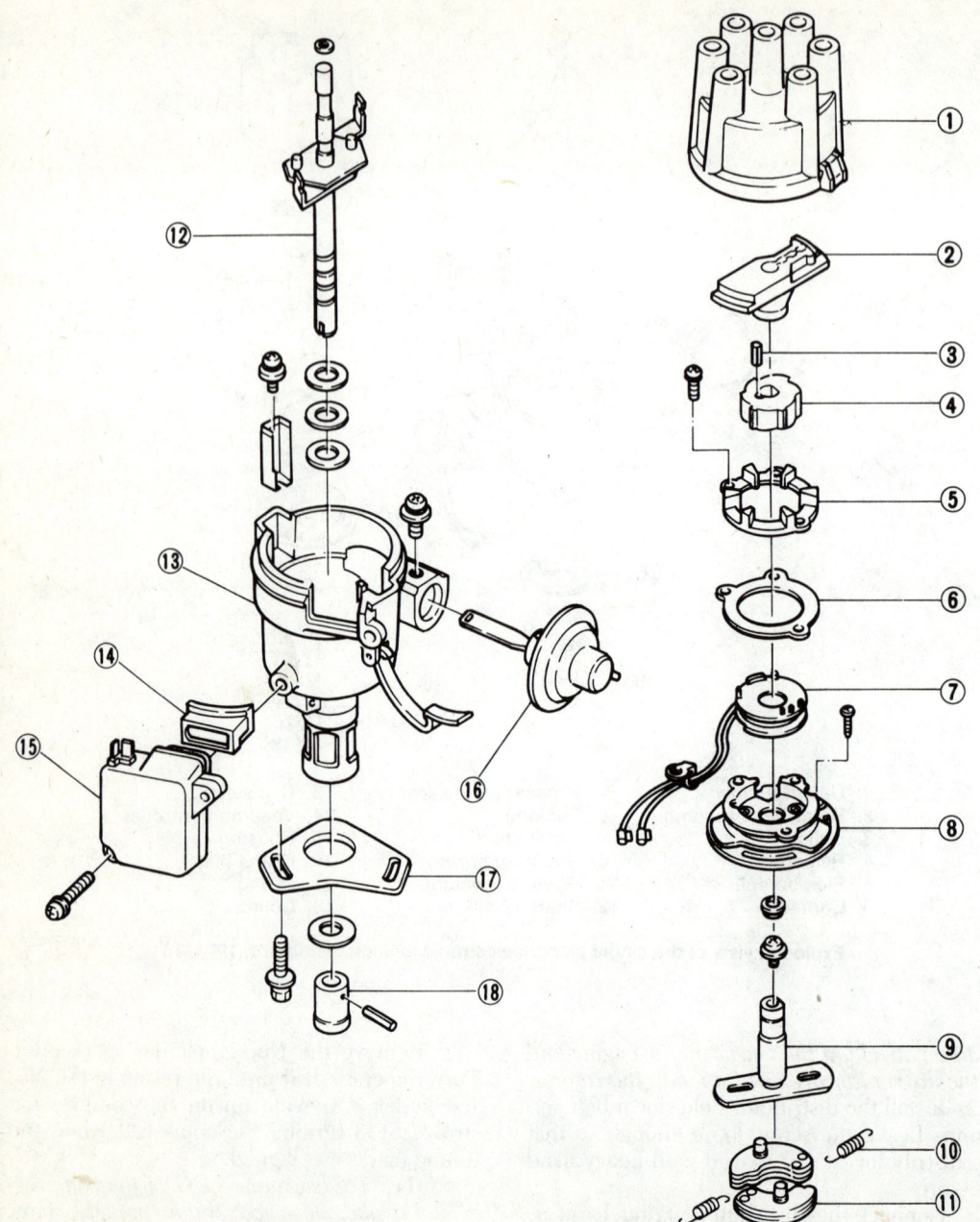

1. Cap assembly
2. Rotor head assembly
3. Roll pin
4. Reluctor
5. Stator
6. Magnet assembly
7. Pick-up coil assembly
8. Breaker plate assembly
9. Rotor shaft assembly
10. Governor spring
11. Governor weight
12. Shaft assembly
13. Housing
14. Grommet
15. IC ignition unit
16. Vacuum controller
17. Fixing plate
18. Collar

Distributor exploded view except engines with turbocharger—1979–83

ENGINE AND ENGINE OVERHAUL 65

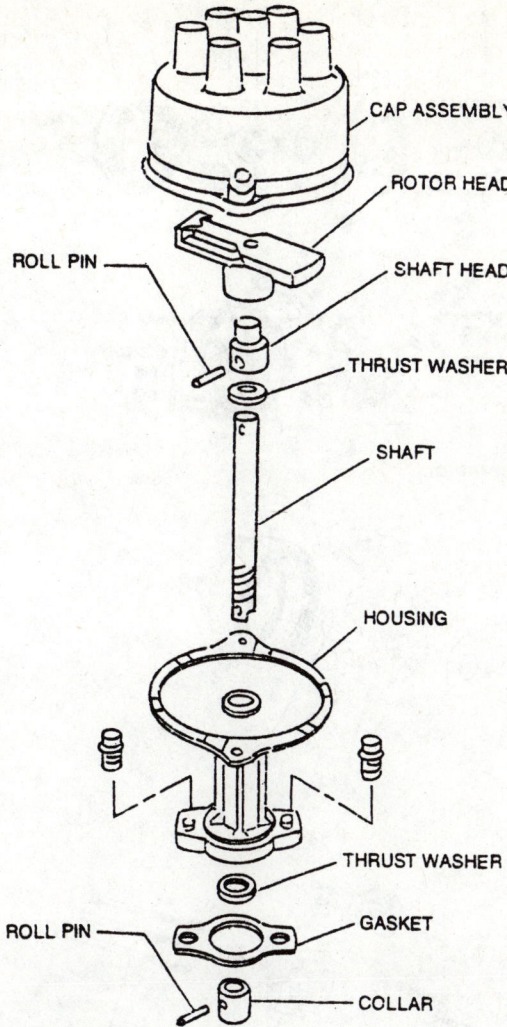

Exploded view of the distributor (turbocharged engines), 1982–83

the bottom of the hole, move the rotor back and forth slightly until the driving lug on the end of the oil pump shaft enters the slots cut in the end of the distributor shaft and the distributor assembly slides down into place.

6. When the distributor is correctly installed, the breaker points (conventional engines) should be in such a position that they are just ready to break contact with each other, the reluctor teeth (electronic ignition engines) should be aligned with the pick-up coil or on the Light Emitting Diode (LED) type, align the rotor with the No. 1 spark plug terminal. This can be accomplished by rotating the distributor body after it has been installed in the engine. Once again, line up the marks that you made before the distributor was removed.

7. Install the distributor hold-down bolt.
8. Install the spark plug into the No. 1 cyl-

inder and continue from Step 3 of the installation procedure, engine undisturbed.

Alternator

The Z and ZX-vehicles use 12 volt alternators, with amperage ratings varying according to year and model. The 1970–77 models use an electro-mechanical, adjustable voltage regulator. The 1978-83 models have a transistorized, non-adjustable regulator integral with the alternator. The 1984 and later models use two different model alternators: the Mitsubishi and the Hitachi.

ALTERNATOR PRECAUTIONS

To prevent damage to the alternator and regulator, the following precautionary measures must be taken when working with the electrical system.
• NEVER reverse the battery connections. Always check the battery polarity visually. This is to be done before any connections are made to ensure that all of the connections correspond to the battery ground polarity of the vehicle.
• Booster batteries must be connected properly. Make sure the positive cable of the booster battery is connected to the positive terminal of the battery which is getting the boost.
• Disconnect the battery cables before using a fast charger; the charger has a tendency to force current through the diodes in the opposite direction for which they were designed.
• NEVER use a fast charger as a booster for starting the vehicle.
• NEVER disconnect the voltage regulator while the engine is running, unless as noted for testing purposes.
• DO NOT ground the alternator output terminal.
• DO NOT operate the alternator on an open circuit with the field energized.
• DO NOT attempt to polarize the alternator.
• Disconnect the battery cables and remove the alternator before using an electric arc welder on the vehicle.
• Protect the alternator from excessive moisture. If the engine is to be steam cleaned, cover or remove the alternator.

REMOVAL

1. Disconnect the negative (−) battery terminal. Failure to do this may damage the electrical system.
2. Disconnect the plug connecting the alternator to the wiring harness. Disconnect and label the two lead wires.

NOTE: *On the 1984 and later models, re-*

66 ENGINE AND ENGINE OVERHAUL

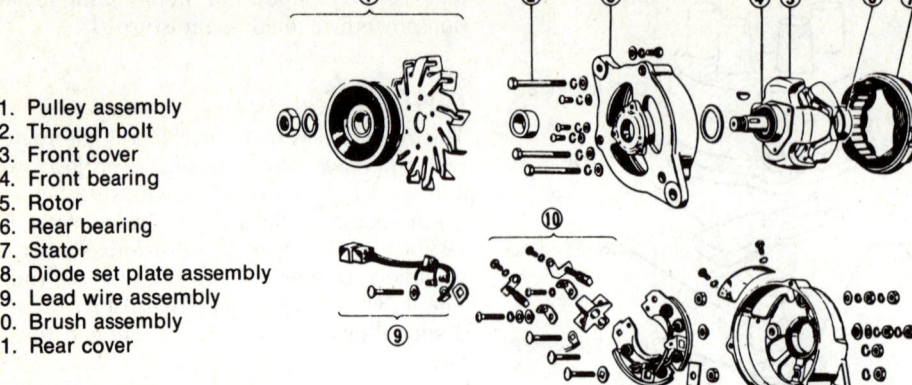

1. Pulley assembly
2. Through bolt
3. Front cover
4. Front bearing
5. Rotor
6. Rear bearing
7. Stator
8. Diode set plate assembly
9. Lead wire assembly
10. Brush assembly
11. Rear cover

1970–71 alternator

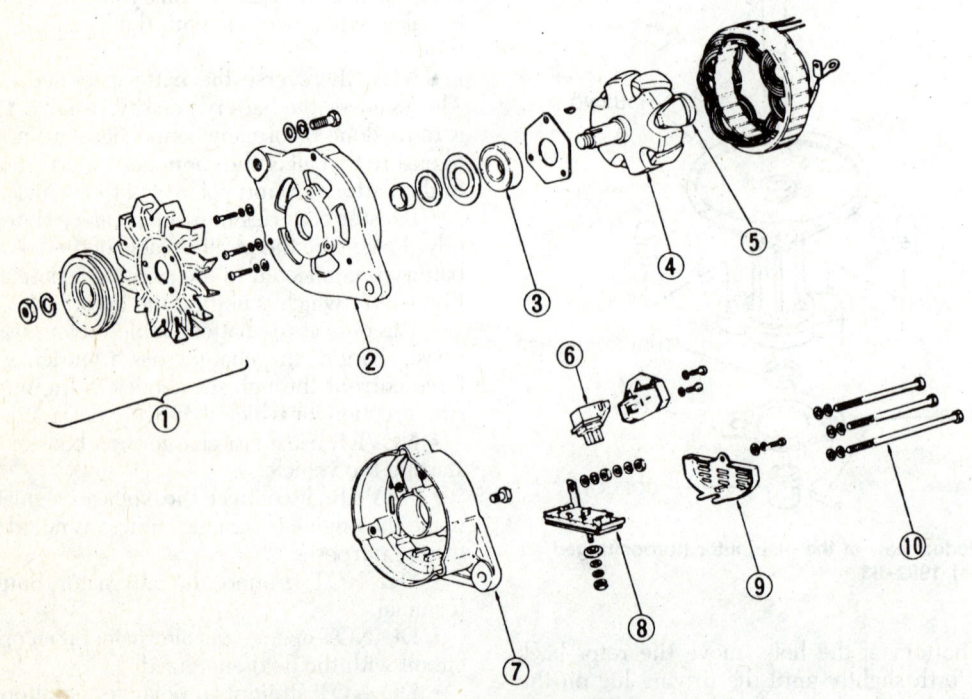

1. Pulley assembly
2. Front cover
3. Front bearing
4. Rotor
5. Rear bearing
6. Brush assembly
7. Rear cover
8. Diode (and plate) assembly
9. Diode cover
10. Through-bolts

1972–77 alternator

move the stabilizer clamp bolts and move the stabilizer down out of the way.

3. Remove the alternator adjusting bolt and move the alternator toward the crankshaft pulley, then remove the belt from the alternator pulley.

4. Remove the nut at the rear end of the lower mounting bolt and then slide the bolt out from the front while supporting the alternator.

5. Pull the alternator out of the engine compartment.

NOTE: *On the 1984 and later models, remove the alternator from the bottom of the vehicle.*

INSTALLATION

1. Place the alternator into position, lining up the two hinges with the bolt hole. Insert the

ENGINE AND ENGINE OVERHAUL 67

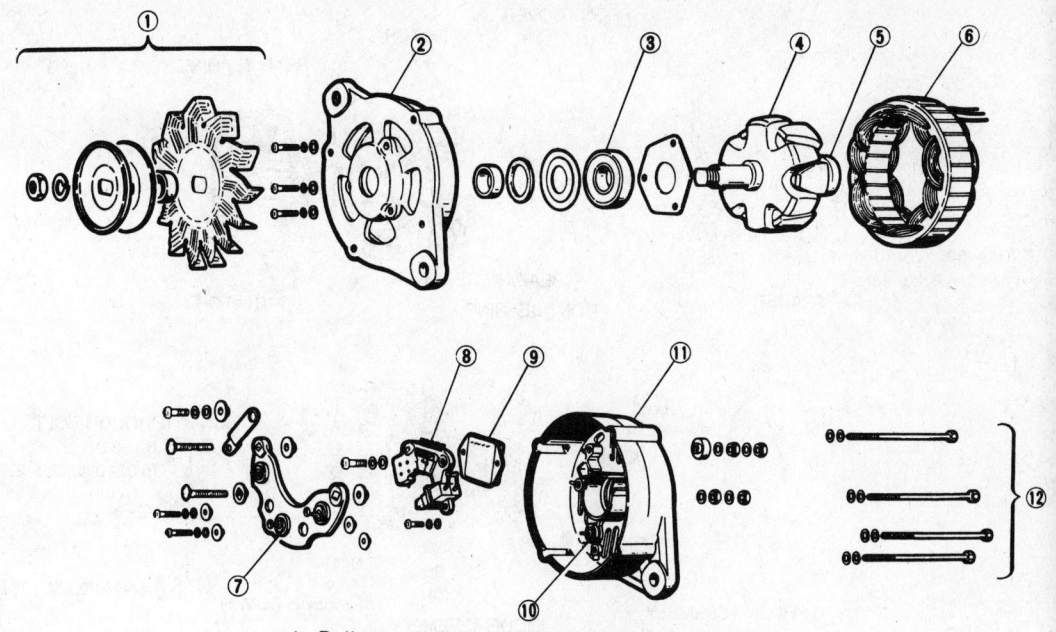

1. Pulley assembly
2. Front cover
3. Front bearing
4. Rotor
5. Rear bearing
6. Stator
7. Diode (Set plate assembly)
8. Brush assembly
9. IC voltage regulator
10. Diode
11. Rear cover
12. Through bolt

1978 alternator shown, others through 1983 similar

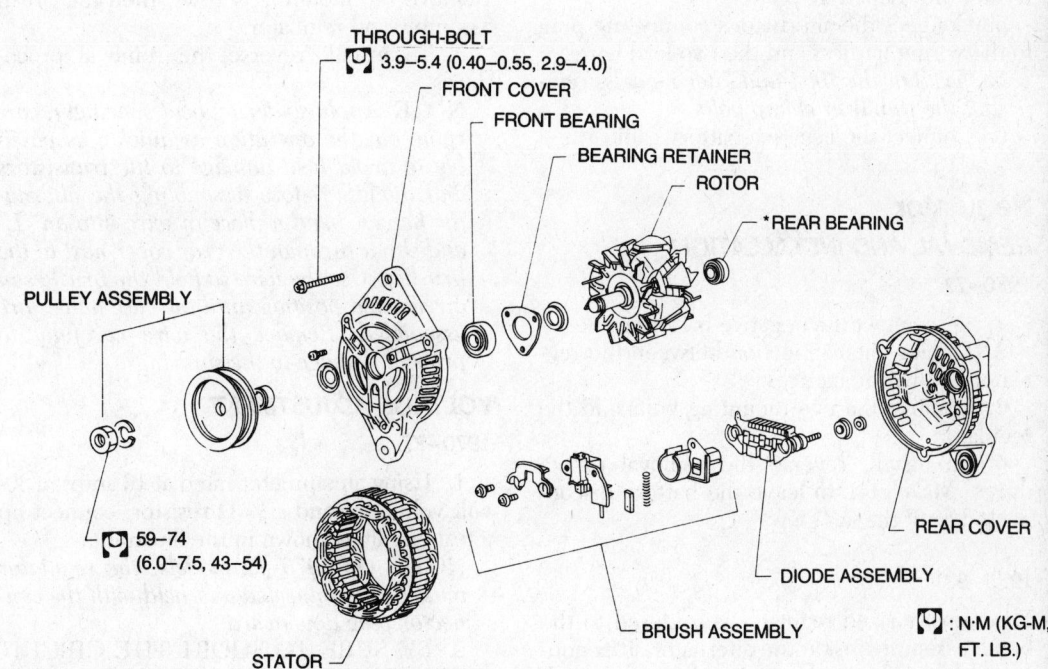

*Rear bearing

Mitsubishi alternator, exploded view—1984 and later

68 ENGINE AND ENGINE OVERHAUL

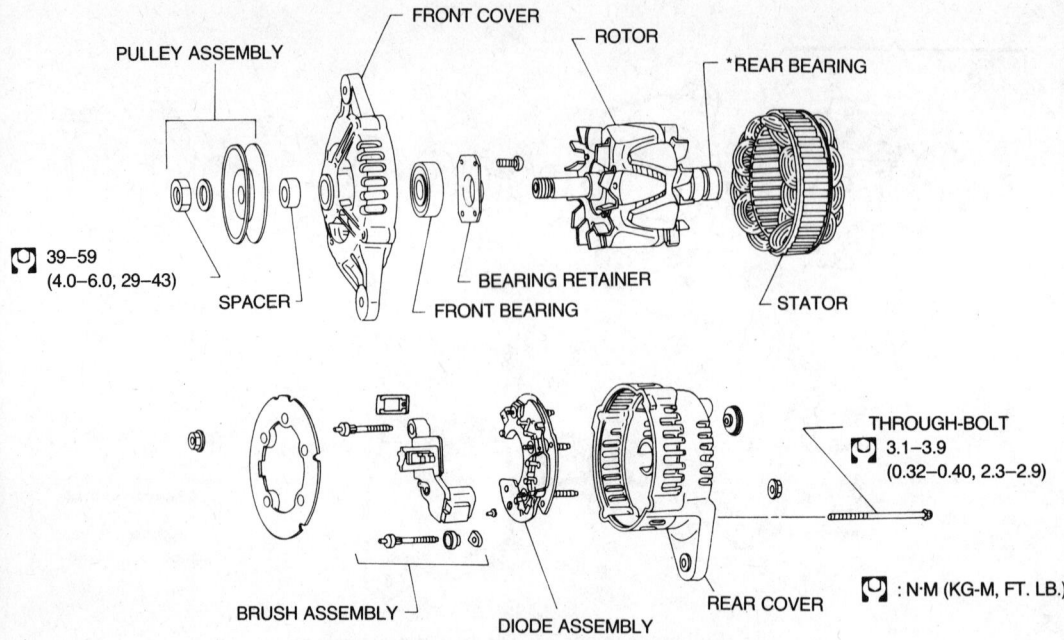

Hitachi alternator, exploded view—1984 and later

bolt through the hinges and bolt hole from the front.
2. Install the nut at the rear of the mounting bolt.
3. Tilt the alternator until the adjusting bolt can be installed and install it.
4. Install and tension the V-belt as described in Chapter 1.
5. Connect the alternator's connecting plug to the wiring harness and the two lead wires.
NOTE: *On the 1984 and later models, reinstall the stabilizer clamp bolts.*
6. Connect the negative battery cable.

Regulator

REMOVAL AND INSTALLATION

1970–77

1. Disconnect the negative battery cable.
2. Unplug the connection between the regulator and wiring harness.
3. Remove the two mounting bolts and the regulator.
4. To install, reverse the removal procedures. Make sure to leave the battery disconnected until the last step.

1978–83

The transistorized regulator is soldered to the brush assembly inside the alternator. It is non-adjustable and must be replaced together with the brush assembly if faulty.
1. Remove the alternator.

2. Remove the through bolts and separate the front cover from the stator housing.
3. Unsolder the stator lead wires from the diode terminals. Remove the screws securing the brush assembly. Remove the stator from the rear cover.
4. Unsolder the wires at the diode terminal. Remove the mounting screws, then the brush assembly and regulator.
5. To install, reverse the removal procedures.
NOTE: *Apply soldering heat sparingly, carrying out the operation as quickly as possible to avoid heat damage to the transistors and diodes. Before assembling the alternator halves, bend a piece of wire into an "L" and slip it through the rear cover next to the brushes. Use the wire to hold the brushes in a retracted position until the case halves are assembled. Remove the wire carefully to prevent damage to the slip rings.*

VOLTAGE ADJUSTMENT

1970–77

1. Using an ammeter rated at 10 amps, a 30-volt voltmeter and a ¼ Ω resistor, connect up a test circuit as shown in the illustrations.
NOTE: *On 1970–72 models, the regulator must be disconnected and held with the connector plug downward.*
2. BE SURE TO SHORT THE CIRCUIT BETWEEN THE FUSE BOX SIDE OF THE RESISTOR AND THE NEGATIVE TERMINAL OF THE AMMETER EVERY TIME

ENGINE AND ENGINE OVERHAUL

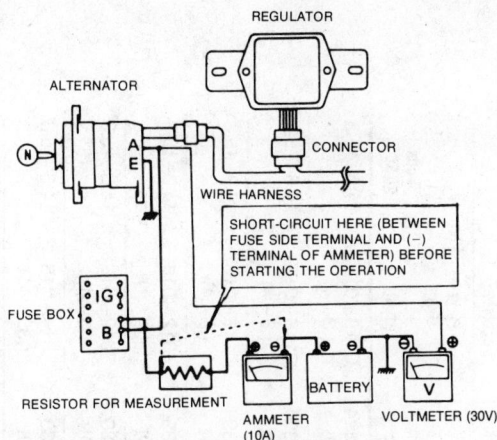

Hookup for voltage measurement

Temperature °C (°F)	Voltage V
−10(14)	14.75 to 15.25
0(32)	14.60 to 15.10
10(50)	14.45 to 14.95
20(68)	14.30 to 14.80
30(86)	14.15 to 14.65
40(104)	14.00 to 14.50

Temperature/Voltage Chart for 1975–77 models

Temperature °C (°F)	Voltage V
−10(14)	14.75 to 15.75
0(32)	14.60 to 15.60
10(50)	14.45 to 15.45
20(68)	14.30 to 15.30
30(86)	14.15 to 15.15
40(104)	14.00 to 15.00

Temperature/Voltage chart for 1975–77 models

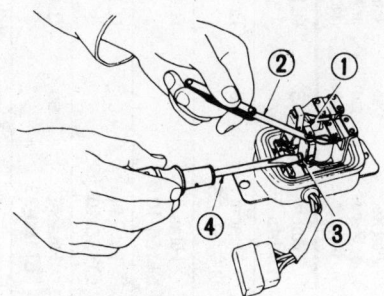

1. Contact set
2. Thickness gauge
3. 4 mm (0.1575 in.) dia. screw
4. Crosshead screwdriver

Voltage regulator core gap adjustment

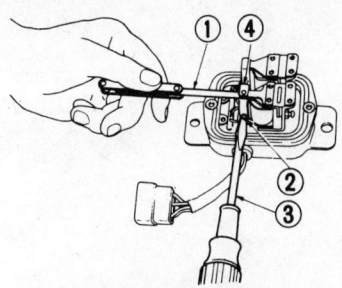

1. Thickness gauge
2. 3 mm (0.1181 in.) dia. screw
3. Crosshead screwdriver
4. Upper contact

Voltage regulator coil point gap adjustment

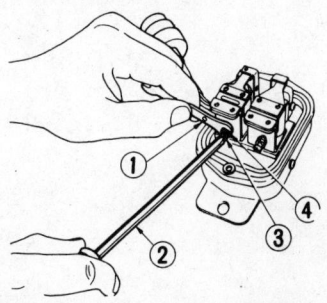

1. Wrench
2. Phillips screwdriver
3. Adjusting screw
4. Locknut

Regulated voltage adjustment

4. Make sure that the ammeter reading is below 5 amps. If not, the battery must be charged or another battery substituted so that the test may be made with the amperage within this range. Stop the engine.

5. Wait several minutes, then start the engine and slowly increase the speed to 2,500 rpm.

6. Compare the reading with the chart, allowing for the temperature around the regulator.

7. If the voltage is not within the specified range, adjust it as follows:

a. Adjust the voltage regulator core gap by loosening the screw which is used to secure the contact set on the yoke and move the contact up or down as necessary. Retighten the screw; the gap should be 0.024–0.039 in.

b. Adjust the point gap of the voltage regulator coil by loosening the screw used to secure the upper contact and move the upper contact up or down. The gap should be 0.012–0.016 in. (1970–75) or 0.014–0.018 in. (1976–77).

c. The core gap and point gap on the charge relay coil is or are adjusted in the same manner as previously outlined for the voltage regulator coil. The core gap is to be set

THE ENGINE IS STARTED. Then, disconnect the short circuit wire during testing.

3. Turn OFF all of the accessories. Operate the engine at 2,500 rpm for several minutes.

ENGINE AND ENGINE OVERHAUL

Alternator and Regulator Specifications

Year	Alternator Part No. or Manufacturer	Output (amps)	Part No. or Manufacturer	Charge Relay Core Gap in. (mm)	Charge Relay Point Gap in. (mm)	Regulator Volts to Close	Regulator Core Gap in. (mm)	Regulator Point Gap in. (mm)	Volts @ 68°F
1970–71	Hitachi LT145-35	45	TL1Z-37	.0315–.0394 (.8–1.0)	.0157–.0236 (.4–.6)	8–10 ①	.0236–.0394 (.6–1.0)	.0118–.0157 (.3–.4)	14.3–15.3
1972	Hitachi LT150-05	50	TL1Z-57	.0315–.0394 (.8–1.0)	.0157–.0236 (.4–.6)	4.2–5.2 ②	.0236–.0394 (.6–1.0)	.0118–.0157 (.3–.4)	14.3–15.3
1973	Hitachi LT150-10 ③	50 ③	TL1Z-57	.0315–.0394 (.8–1.0)	.0157–.0236 (.4–.6)	4.2–5.2 ②	.0236–.0394 (.6–1.0)	.0118–.0157 (.3–.4)	14.3–15.3
1974	Hitachi LT150-10 ③	50 ③	TL1Z-79	.0315–.0394 (.8–1.0)	.0157–.0236 (.4–.6)	4.2–5.2 ②	.024–.039 (.6–1.0)	.012–.016 (.3–.4)	14.3–15.3
1975	Hitachi LT160-23	60	TL1Z-85	.0315–.0394 (.8–1.0)	.0157–.0236 (.4–.6)	4.2–5.2 ②	.024–.039 (.6–1.0)	.012–.016 (.3–.4)	14.3–15.3
1976	Hitachi LT160-23	60	TL1Z-85B	.031–.039 (.8–1.0)	.016–.024 (.4–.6)	4.2–5.2 ②	.024–.039 (.6–1.0)	.014–.018 (.35–.45)	14.3–15.3

ENGINE AND ENGINE OVERHAUL

Year							
1977	Hitachi LT1Z-85C	60	TL1Z-85C	.031–.039 (.8–1.0)	.016–.024 (.4–.6)	4.2–5.2 ②	.024–.039 (.6–1.0)	.014–.018 (.35–.45)	14.3–15.3
1977	Hitachi LT160-23C	60							14.3–15.3
1978	Hitachi LR160-42	60	Integral			Non-Adjustable			14.4–15.0
1979–80	Hitachi LR160-42B	60	Integral			Non-Adjustable			14.4–15.0
1981–82	Hitachi LR160-82	60	Integral			Non-Adjustable			14.4–15.0
1983	Hitachi LR160-82B	60	Integral			Non-Adjustable			14.4–15.0
1983	Hitachi LR170-02B ④	70	Integral			Non-Adjustable			14.4–15.0
1984–86	Hitachi LR170-701B	70	Integral			Non-Adjustable			14.4–15.0
1984–86	Mitsubishi A2T48195 ④	70	Integral			Non-Adjustable			14.1–14.7

① At terminal A
② At terminal N
③ Lt160-23, 60 amps—Canada
④ Equipped with turbocharger

ENGINE AND ENGINE OVERHAUL

at 0.032–0.039 in. and the point gap adjusted to 0.016–0.024 in.

　d. The regulated voltage is adjusted by loosening the locknut and turning the adjusting screw clockwise to increase or counterclockwise to decrease the regulated voltage. The voltage should be between 14.3–15.3 volts at 68°F.

Battery
REMOVAL AND INSTALLATION

1. Disconnect the negative battery cable from the terminal and then the positive cable. Special pullers are available to remove the cable clamps.

　CAUTION: *To avoid sparks, always disconnect the ground cable first and connect it last.*

2. Remove the battery hold-down clamp.
3. Remove the battery, being careful not to spill the acid.

　NOTE: *Spilled acid can be neutralized with a baking soda/water solution. If you somehow get acid into your eyes, flush it out with lots of water and get to a doctor.*

4. Clean the battery posts thoroughly before reinstalling or when installing a new battery.
5. Clean the cable clamps, using a wire brush, both inside and out.
6. To install, reverse the removal procedures. Connect the positive and then the negative cables. DO NOT hammer them into place. The terminals should be coated lightly (externally) with grease to prevent corrosion. There are also felt washers impregnated with an anti-corrosion substance which are slipped over the battery posts before installing the cables; these are available in the auto parts stores.

　CAUTION: *Make absolutely sure that the battery is connected properly before you turn ON the ignition switch. Reversed polarity can burn out your alternator and regulator within a matter of seconds.*

ADJUSTMENTS

For maintenance procedures, refer to Battery in Chapter 1 for details.

Starter
REMOVAL AND INSTALLATION

1. Disconnect the negative battery cable.
　NOTE: *If equipped with the VG30E engine, raise and support the vehicle, then remove the starter from under the vehicle.*
2. Disconnect and label the wires from the solenoid terminals.
3. Remove the starter-to-flywheel housing bolts, then pull the starter forward and out.
4. To install, reverse the removal procedure.

BRUSH REPLACEMENT
1970–77

1. Remove the starter from the vehicle. On automatic transmission models, 1973–76 and all 1977 models, remove the dust cover, the E-ring and the two thrust washers from the rear cover. Remove the two brush holder set screws from the rear cover.
2. On all models, remove the two through bolts and the rear cover.
3. Remove the brushes from their holders by lifting the brush spring away from the brush; you can use a hook fabricated from wire to do this.
4. Unsolder the brush electrical connections.
5. Remove the brushes.
6. To install, insert the brushes into the holder, solder the brush electrical connections, raise the brushes far enough to permit installing the brush holder over the commutator and reverse the removal procedures.

1978 and Later

1. Remove the starter from the vehicle. Remove the solenoid from the starter.
2. Remove the through bolts and the rear cover. The cover can be pried off with a screwdriver but be careful not to damage the O-ring.
3. Remove the starter housing, the armature and the brush holder from the center housing; they can be removed as an assembly.
4. Remove the positive side brush from it's holder. The positive brush is insulated from the brush holder and it's lead wire is connected to the field coil.
5. Carefully lift the negative brush from the commutator and remove it from the holder.
6. Unsolder the brush electrical connections, then remove the brushes.
7. Install the new brushes and solder their wires to the connections. Install the brush holder, the armature and the starter housing to the center housing. Install the rear cover, the O-ring and the solenoid.

DRIVE REPLACEMENT
1970–77

1. Loosen the locknut and remove the connection going to the "M" terminal of the solenoid. Remove the securing screws and the solenoid.
2. On 1973–76 automatic transmission models and all 1977 models, remove the dust

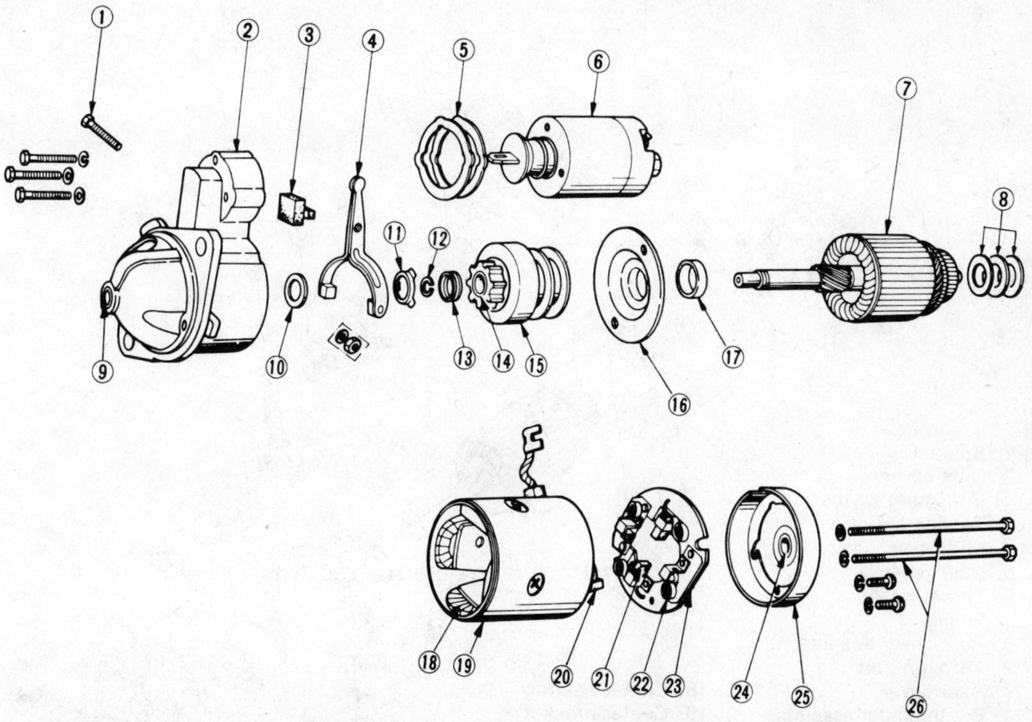

ENGINE AND ENGINE OVERHAUL 73

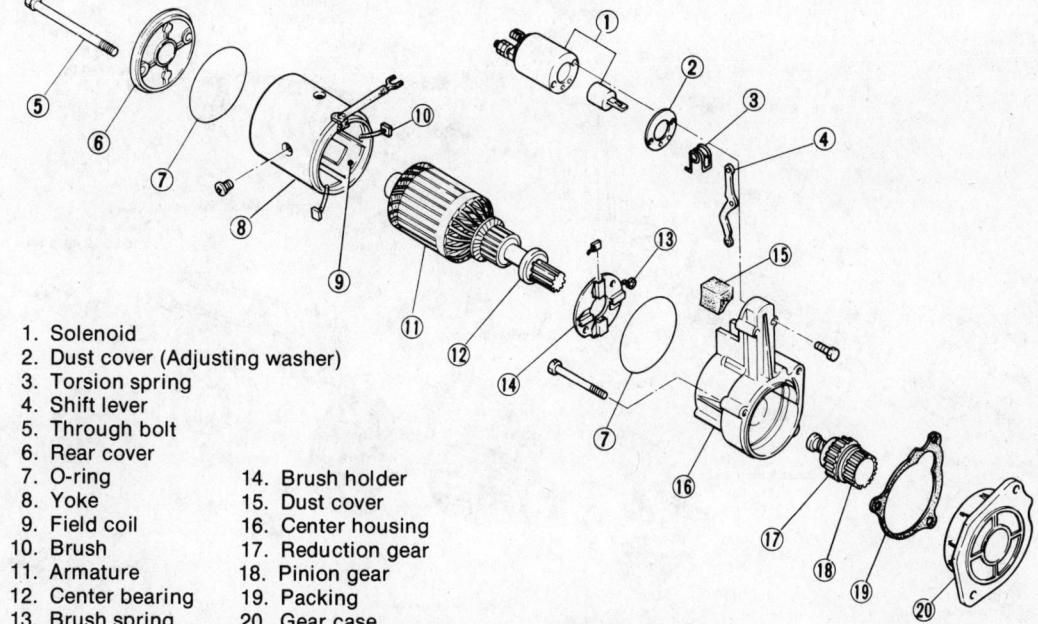

1. Shift lever pin
2. Gear case
3. Dust cover
4. Shift lever
5. Dust cover
6. Solenoid
7. Armature
8. Thrust washer
9. Bushing
10. Thrust washer
11. Stopper washer
12. Stopper clip
13. Pinion stopper
14. Pinion
15. Overrunning clutch
16. Center bracket
17. Center bearing
18. Field coil
19. Yoke
20. Brush (+)
21. Brush (−)
22. Brush spring
23. Brush holder assembly
24. Bushing
25. Rear cover
26. Through bolt

Exploded view of the starter used with manual transmission, 1970–76

1. Solenoid
2. Dust cover (Adjusting washer)
3. Torsion spring
4. Shift lever
5. Through bolt
6. Rear cover
7. O-ring
8. Yoke
9. Field coil
10. Brush
11. Armature
12. Center bearing
13. Brush spring
14. Brush holder
15. Dust cover
16. Center housing
17. Reduction gear
18. Pinion gear
19. Packing
20. Gear case

Reduction gear starter, 1978–83

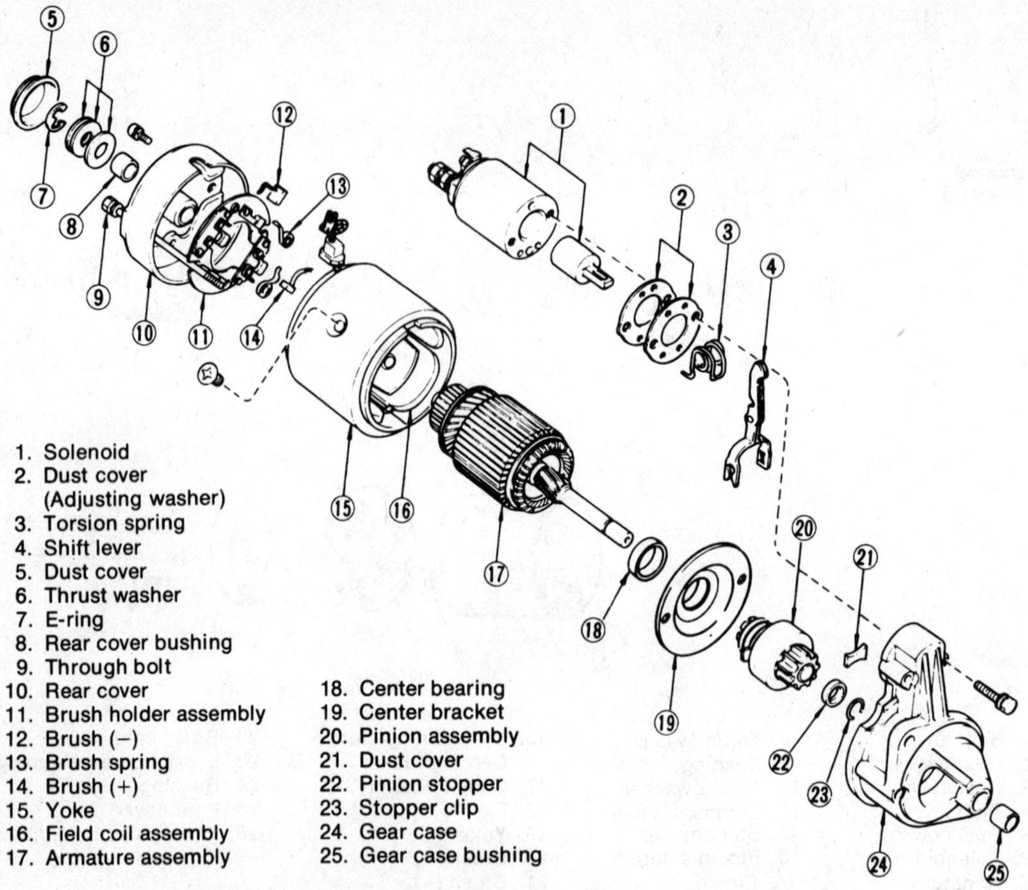

74 ENGINE AND ENGINE OVERHAUL

1. Solenoid
2. Dust cover (Adjusting washer)
3. Torsion spring
4. Shift lever
5. Dust cover
6. Thrust washer
7. E-ring
8. Rear cover bushing
9. Through bolt
10. Rear cover
11. Brush holder assembly
12. Brush (−)
13. Brush spring
14. Brush (+)
15. Yoke
16. Field coil assembly
17. Armature assembly
18. Center bearing
19. Center bracket
20. Pinion assembly
21. Dust cover
22. Pinion stopper
23. Stopper clip
24. Gear case
25. Gear case bushing

Exploded view of the starter used with automatic transmission, 1970–77

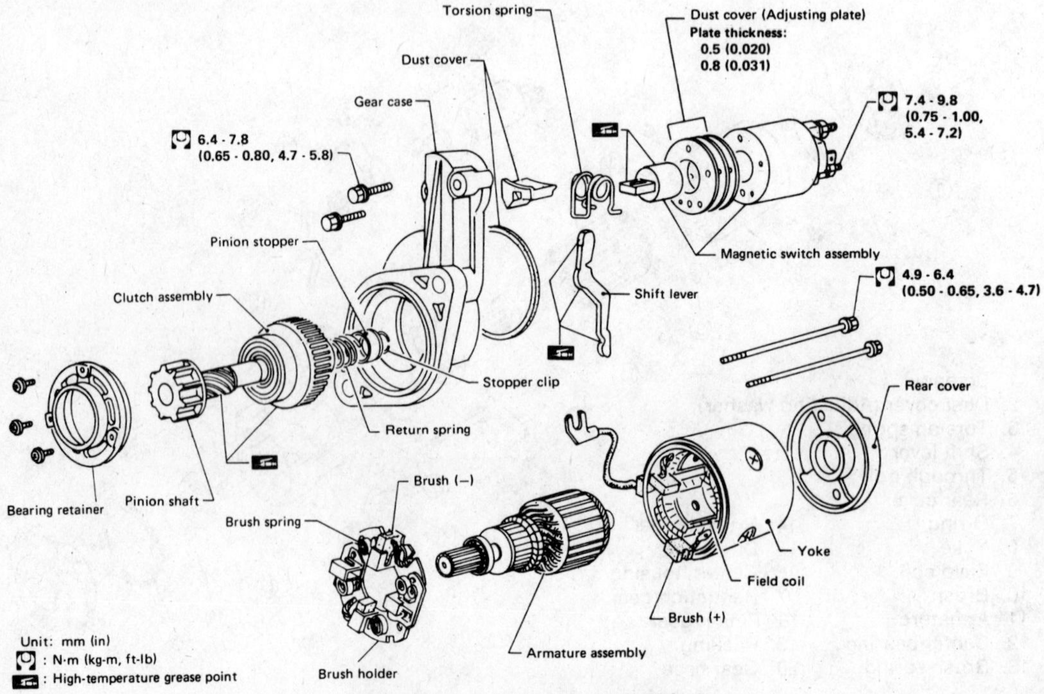

Torsion spring
Dust cover (Adjusting plate)
Plate thickness:
0.5 (0.020)
0.8 (0.031)

Dust cover
Gear case

6.4 - 7.8
(0.65 - 0.80, 4.7 - 5.8)

7.4 - 9.8
(0.75 - 1.00, 5.4 - 7.2)

Magnetic switch assembly

Pinion stopper
Clutch assembly
Shift lever

4.9 - 6.4
(0.50 - 0.65, 3.6 - 4.7)

Stopper clip
Return spring
Rear cover

Bearing retainer
Pinion shaft
Brush (−)
Brush spring
Yoke
Field coil
Brush (+)
Armature assembly
Brush holder

Unit: mm (in)
: N·m (kg-m, ft-lb)
: High-temperature grease point

1984 and later starter—exploded view

ENGINE AND ENGINE OVERHAUL

Battery and Starter Specifications

Year	Engine Displacement cu in. (cc)	Battery Ampere Hour Capacity	Volts	Terminal Grounded	Starter Lock Test Amps	Starter Lock Test Volts	Torque ft. lbs. (kg)	No-Load Test Amps	No-Load Test Volts	No-Load Test RPM	Brush Spring Tension lbs (kg)
1970–72	146 (2393)	60	12	Neg	460	6	10.1 (1.4)	60	12	5000	1.76 ① (0.8)
1973–74	146 (2393), 156 (2565)	60	12	Neg	460 ①	6 ②	10.1 (1.4)	60	12	5000 ③	3.53 (1.6)
1975–77	168 (2753)	65	12	Neg	Not Recommended			60	12	5000 ③	3.53 (1.6)
1978	168 (2753)	65	12	Neg	Not Recommended			100	12	4300	3.96 (1.8)
1979	168 (2753)	60 ④	12	Neg	Not Recommended			100	12	4300	3.96 (1.8)
1980–83	168 (2753)	60 ④	12	Neg	Not Recommended			100	11	3900	3.96 (1.8)
1984–86	180.6 (2960)	60 ④	12	Neg	Not Recommended			100	11	3900	3.96 (1.8)

① 3.52 (1.6)—1972
② Automatic—500 amps
③ Automatic—5 volts
④ 70 amps—Canada; optional, U.S.A.
⑤ 70 amps—Canada; optional, U.S.A.

cover, the E-ring, the thrust washers and the two screws retaining the brush holder assembly. Remove the brush cover through bolts and the cover assembly (all models).

3. Lift the brushes to free them from the commutator and remove the brush holder.

4. Tap the yoke assembly lightly with a wooden hammer and remove it from the field and the case.

5. Remove the nut and bolt which serve as a pin for the shift lever, carefully retaining the associated washers.

6. Remove the armature assembly and the shift lever.

7. Push the stop ring (located at the end of the armature shaft) toward the clutch, then remove the snap-ring and the stop ring.

8. Remove the clutch assembly from the armature shaft.

9. To install the drive, perform the following:

   a. Install the clutch assembly onto the armature shaft.

   b. Put the stop ring on and hold it toward the clutch while installing the snap-ring.

   c. Install the armature assembly and the shift lever into the yoke.

   d. Install the washers, the nut and bolt which serve as a shift lever pivot pin.

   e. Install the field back onto the yoke assembly.

   f. Lift the brushes and install the brush holder. Install the brush cover and through bolts.

NOTE: *On the 1973–76 automatic transmission models and all 1977 models, replace the brush holder set screws, the thrust washers, the E-ring and the dust cover.*

   g. Install the solenoid. Reconnect the wire to the "M" terminal of the solenoid.

1978 and Later

1. Remove the starter.
2. Remove the solenoid and the shift lever.
3. Remove the bolts securing the center housing to the front cover and separate the parts.
4. Remove the gears and the starter drive.
5. To install, reverse the removal procedures.

SOLENOID REPLACEMENT
All Models

1. Loosen the locknut and remove the connection going to the "M" terminal of the solenoid.

2. Remove the retaining screws and the solenoid.

3. To install, reverse the removal procedures.

ENGINE MECHANICAL

Description

From 1970–83 the L24, L26 and L28 engines were all single overhead camshaft, in-line 6 cyl power plants. The main difference between the three are varying bores and strokes to achieve the different displacements. The VG30E and the VG30ET, V6 engines were introduced in 1984.

Engine Overhaul

Most engine overhaul procedures are fairly standard. In addition to specific parts replacement procedures and complete specifications for your individual engine, this chapter also is a guide to acceptable rebuilding procedures. Examples of standard rebuilding practice are shown and should be used along with specific details concerning your particular engine.

Competent and accurate machine shop services will ensure maximum performance, reliability and engine life.

In most instances it is more profitable for the do-it-yourself mechanic to remove, clean and inspect the component, buy the necessary parts and deliver these to a shop for actual machine work.

On the other hand, much of the rebuilding work (crankshaft, block, bearings, piston rods and other components) is well within the scope of the do-it-yourself mechanic.

TOOLS

The tools required for an engine overhaul or parts replacement will depend on the depth of your involvement. With a few exceptions, they will be the tools found in a mechanic's tool kit (see Chapter 1). More in-depth work will require any or all of the following:
- a dial indicator (reading in thousandths) mounted on a universal base
- micrometers and telescope gauges
- jaw and screw-type pullers
- scraper
- valve spring compressor
- ring groove cleaner
- piston ring expander and compressor
- ridge reamer
- cylinder hone or glaze breaker
- Plastigage®
- engine stand

Use of most of these tools is illustrated in this chapter. Many can be rented for a one-time use from a local parts jobber or tool supply house specializing in automotive work.

Occasionally, the use of special tools are called for. See the information on Special Tools and Safety Notice in the front of this book before substituting another tool.

INSPECTION TECHNIQUES

Procedures and specifications are given in this chapter for inspecting, cleaning and assessing the wear limits of most major components. Other procedures such as Magnaflux® and Zyglo® can be used to locate material flaws and stress cracks. Magnaflux® is a magnetic process applicable only to ferrous materials. The Zyglo® process coats the material with a fluorescent dye penetrant and can be used on any material. Checks for suspected surface cracks can be more readily made using spot check dye. The dye is sprayed onto the suspected area, wiped off and the area sprayed with a developer. Cracks will show up brightly.

OVERHAUL TIPS

Aluminum has become extremely popular for use in engines, due to it's low weight. Observe the following precautions when handling aluminum parts:
- Never hot tank aluminum parts (the caustic hot tank solution will eat the aluminum.
- Remove all aluminum parts (identification tag, etc.) from engine parts prior to the tanking.
- Always coat threads lightly with engine oil or anti-seize compounds before installation, to prevent seizure.
- Never over-torque bolts or spark plugs especially in aluminum threads.

Stripped threads of any component can be repaired using any of several commercial repair kits (Heli-Coil®, Microdot®, Keenserts® and etc.).

When assembling the engine, any parts that will have frictional contact must be prelubed to provide lubrication at initial start-up. Any product specifically formulated for this purpose can be used but engine oil is not recommended as a prelube.

When semi-permanent (locked, but removable) installation of bolts or nuts are desired, clean and coat the threads with Loctite® or other similar, commercial non-hardening sealant.

REPAIRING DAMAGED THREADS

Several methods of repairing damaged threads are available: Heli-Coil® (shown here), Keenserts® and Microdot® are among the most widely used. All involve basically the same principle—drilling out stripped threads, tapping the hole and installing a prewound insert—making welding, plugging and oversize fasteners unnecessary.

Two types of thread repair inserts are usually supplied—a standard type for most Inch

ENGINE AND ENGINE OVERHAUL

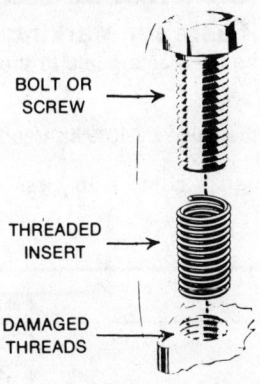

Damaged bolt holes can be repaired with thread repair inserts

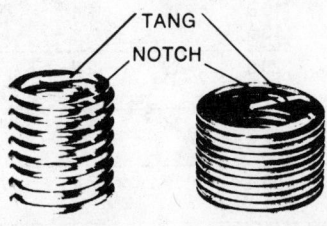

Standard thread repair insert (left) and spark plug thread insert (right)

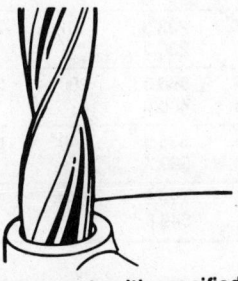

Drill out the damaged threads with specified drill. Drill completely through the hole or to the bottom of a blind hole

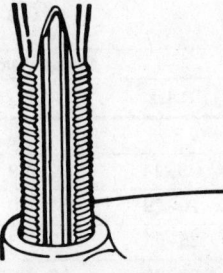

With the tap supplied, tap the hole to receive the thread insert. Keep the tap well oiled and back it out frequently to avoid clogging the threads

Coarse, Inch Fine, Metric Course and Metric Fine thread sizes and a spark plug type to fit most spark plug port sizes. Consult the individual manufacturer's catalog to determine exact

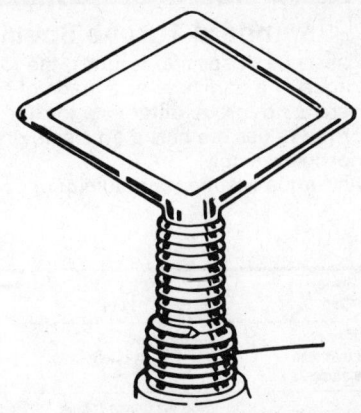

Screw the threaded insert onto the installation tool until the tang engages the slot. Screw the insert into the tapped hole until it is ¼–½ turn below the top surface. After installation break off the tang with a hammer and punch

applications. Typical thread repair kits will contain a selection of prewound threaded inserts, a tap (corresponding to the outside diameter threads of the insert) and an installation tool. Spark plug inserts usually differ because they require a tap equipped with pilot threads and a combined reamer/tap section. Most manufacturers also supply blister-packed thread repair inserts separately in addition to a master kit containing a variety of taps and inserts plus installation tools.

Before effecting a repair to a threaded hole, remove any snapped, broken or damaged bolts or studs. Penetrating oil can be used to free frozen threads; the offending item can be removed with locking pliers, a screwdriver or stud extractor. After the hole is clear, the thread can be repaired, as follows:

Checking Engine Compression

A noticeable lack of engine power, excessive oil consumption and/or poor fuel mileage measured over an extended period are all indicators of internal engine wear. Worn piston rings, scored or worn cylinder bores, blown head gaskets, sticking or burnt valves and worn valve seats are all possible culprits here. A check of each cylinder's compression will help you locate the problems.

As mentioned in the Tools and Equipment section of Chapter 1, a screw-in type compression gauge is more accurate than the type you simply hold against the spark plug hole, although it takes slightly longer to use. To obtain a more accurate reading, perform the following procedures:

1. Warm up the engine to normal operating temperatures.

ENGINE AND ENGINE OVERHAUL

Standard Torque Specifications and Fastener Markings

In the absence of specific torques, the following chart can be used as a guide to the maximum safe torque of a particular size/grade of fastener.
- There is no torque difference for fine or coarse threads.
- Torque values are based on clean, dry threads. Reduce the value by 10% if threads are oiled prior to assembly.
- The torque required for aluminum components or fasteners is considerably less.

U.S. Bolts

SAE Grade Number	1 or 2			5			6 or 7		
Number of lines always 2 less than the grade number.									
Bolt Size (Inches)—(Thread)	Maximum Torque			Maximum Torque			Maximum Torque		
	Ft./Lbs.	Kgm	Nm	Ft./Lbs.	Kgm	Nm	Ft./Lbs.	Kgm	Nm
¼—20	5	0.7	6.8	8	1.1	10.8	10	1.4	13.5
—28	6	0.8	8.1	10	1.4	13.6			
5/16—18	11	1.5	14.9	17	2.3	23.0	19	2.6	25.8
—24	13	1.8	17.6	19	2.6	25.7			
3/8—16	18	2.5	24.4	31	4.3	42.0	34	4.7	46.0
—24	20	2.75	27.1	35	4.8	47.5			
7/16—14	28	3.8	37.0	49	6.8	66.4	55	7.6	74.5
—20	30	4.2	40.7	55	7.6	74.5			
½—13	39	5.4	52.8	75	10.4	101.7	85	11.75	115.2
—20	41	5.7	55.6	85	11.7	115.2			
9/16—12	51	7.0	69.2	110	15.2	149.1	120	16.6	162.7
—18	55	7.6	74.5	120	16.6	162.7			
5/8—11	83	11.5	112.5	150	20.7	203.3	167	23.0	226.5
—18	95	13.1	128.8	170	23.5	230.5			
¾—10	105	14.5	142.3	270	37.3	366.0	280	38.7	379.6
—16	115	15.9	155.9	295	40.8	400.0			
7/8—9	160	22.1	216.9	395	54.6	535.5	440	60.9	596.5
—14	175	24.2	237.2	435	60.1	589.7			
1—8	236	32.5	318.6	590	81.6	799.9	660	91.3	894.8
—14	250	34.6	338.9	660	91.3	849.8			

Metric Bolts

Relative Strength Marking	4.6, 4.8			8.8		
Bolt Markings						
Bolt Size Thread Size x Pitch (mm)	Maximum Torque			Maximum Torque		
	Ft./Lbs.	Kgm	Nm	Ft./Lbs.	Kgm	Nm
6 x 1.0	2–3	.2–.4	3–4	3–6	.4–.8	5–8
8 x 1.25	6–8	.8–1	8–12	9–14	1.2–1.9	13–19
10 x 1.25	12–17	1.5–2.3	16–23	20–29	2.7–4.0	27–39
12 x 1.25	21–32	2.9–4.4	29–43	35–53	4.8–7.3	47–72
14 x 1.5	35–52	4.8–7.1	48–70	57–85	7.8–11.7	77–110
16 x 1.5	51–77	7.0–10.6	67–100	90–120	12.4–16.5	130–160
18 x 1.5	74–110	10.2–15.1	100–150	130–170	17.9–23.4	180–230
20 x 1.5	110–140	15.1–19.3	150–190	190–240	26.2–46.9	160–320
22 x 1.5	150–190	22.0–26.2	200–260	250–320	34.5–44.1	340–430
24 x 1.5	190–240	26.2–46.9	260–320	310–410	42.7–56.5	420–550

ENGINE AND ENGINE OVERHAUL

2. Remove all spark plugs.
3. Disconnect the high tension lead from the ignition coil.
4. On carbureted vehicles, fully open the throttle either by operating the carburetor throttle linkage by hand or by having an assistant floor the accelerator pedal. On fuel injected vehicles, disconnect the cold start valve and all the injector connections.
5. Screw the compression gauge into the No.1 spark plug hole until the fitting is snug.
NOTE: *Be careful not to cross-thread the plug hole. On aluminum cylinder heads use extra care, as the threads in these heads are easily ruined.*
6. Ask an assistant to depress the accelerator pedal fully on both carbureted and fuel injected vehicles. Then, while reading the compression gauge, ask the assistant to crank the engine 2–3 times in short bursts using the ignition switch.
7. Read the compression gauge at the end of each series of cranks and record the highest of these readings. Repeat this procedure for each of the engine's cylinders. Compare the highest reading of each cylinder to the compression pressure specification in the Tune-Up Specifications chart in Chapter 2. The specs in this chart are maximum values.
NOTE: *A cylinder's compression pressure is usually acceptable if it is not less than 80% of maximum. The difference between each cylinder should be no more than 12–14 pounds.*

8. If a cylinder is unusually low, pour a tablespoon of clean engine oil into the cylinder through the spark plug hole and repeat the compression test. If the compression comes up after adding the oil, it appears that the cylinder's piston rings or bore are damaged or worn. If the pressure remains low, the valves may not be seating properly (a valve job is needed) or the head gasket may be blown near that cylinder. If the compression in any two adjacent cylinders is low and the addition of oil doesn't increase the compression, there is leakage past the head gasket. Oil and coolant water in the combustion chamber can result from this problem. There may be evidence of water droplets on the engine dipstick when a head gasket has blown.

Engine

REMOVAL AND INSTALLATION

1970–83

The instructions below provide for removal of the engine and transmission as a unit, as this makes the operation easier and faster; the transmission removal is easier after the engine is out of the vehicle.

All operations involving hoisting the engine-transmission unit should be done with extreme care and should be carefully planned before hand. Read the procedure through before beginning. It is best to use fender covers so that

General Engine Specifications

Year	Engine Displacement cu in. (cc)	Carburetor Type	Horsepower @ rpm (Gross)	Torque @ rpm (ft. lbs.)	Bore x Stroke in. (mm)	Compression Ratio	Oil Pressure (psi)
1970–73	146 (2393)	Twin SU	151 @ 5600	146 @ 4400	3.27 (83) x 2.90 (74)	8.8:1	50–57
1974	156 (2565)	Twin SU	162 @ 5600	154 @ 4400	3.26 (83) x 3.11 (79)	8.8:1	50–57
1975–78	168 (2753)	Fuel Injection	170 @ 5600	177 @ 4400	3.39 (86) x 3.11 (79)	8.3:1	50–57
1979	168 (2753)	Fuel Injection	135 @ 5200 ①	144 @ 4400	3.39 (86) x 3.11 (79)	8.3:1	50–57
1980	168 (2753)	Fuel Injection	132 @ 5200 ①	144 @ 4000	3.39 (86) x 3.11 (79)	8.3:1	50–57
1981–83	168 (2753)	Fuel Injection	145 @ 5200	156 @ 4000	3.39 (86) x 3.11 (79)	8.8:1	50–57
1981–83 (Turbo)	168 (2753)	Fuel Injection	180 @ 5600	202 @ 2800	3.39 (86) x 3.11 (79)	7.4:1	—
1984–86	180.6 (2960)	Fuel Injection	160 @ 5200	173 @ 4000	3.43 (87) x 3.27 (83)	9.0:1	43 ②
1984–86 (Turbo)	180.6 (2960)	Fuel Injection	200 @ 5200	227 @ 3600	3.43 (87) x 3.27 (83)	7.8:1	43 ②

① Net horsepower ② 2000 rpm

ENGINE AND ENGINE OVERHAUL

Valve Specifications

Year	Engine Displacement cu in. (cc)	Seat Angle (deg)	Spring Test Pressure lbs @ in. (kg @ mm)	Spring Installed Height in. (mm)	Stem To Guide ① Clearance in. (mm) Intake	Stem To Guide ① Clearance in. (mm) Exhaust	Stem Diameter in. (mm) Intake	Stem Diameter in. (mm) Exhaust
1970–83	All	45 ④	108 @ 1.16 ② (49 @ 29.5)	1.575 ③ (40.0)	.0008–.0021 (.020–.053)	.0016–.0029 (.040–.073)	.3136–.3142 (7.965–7.980)	.3128–.3134 (7.945–7.960)
1984–86	180.6 (2960)	45°30′	118 @ 1.18 ② (53.4 @ 30)	1.575 ③ (40.0)	.0008–.0021 (.020–.053)	.0016–.0029 (.040–.073)	.2742–.2748 (6.965–6.980)	.3128–.3134 (7.945–7.960) ⑤

① Guides are replaceable
② Inner spring—56.2 @ 0.965 (25.5 @ 24.5)
③ Inner spring—27.1 @ 1,378 (12.3 @ 35.0)
④ 1979 and later—45°30′
⑤ 1985 and later: .3136–0.3138 (7.965–7.970)

Torque Specifications
All readings in ft. lbs. (kg-m)

Year	Engine Displacement cu in. (cc)	Cylinder Head Bolts	Rod Bearing Bolts	Main Bearing Bolts	Crankshaft Pulley Bolt	Flywheel To Crankshaft Bolts	Manifolds	Camshaft Sprocket Bolt
1970–72	146 (2393)	47 ①② (6.5)	19.5–23.9 (2.7–3.3)	33–40 (4.5–5.5)	115–130 (16–18)	101 (14)	5.8–8.7 (0.8–1.2)	36–43 (5–6)
1973	146 (2393)	47–61 ③ (6.5–8.5)	33–40 (4.5–5.5)	33–40 (4.5–5.5)	87–116 (12–16)	101–116 (14–16)	5.8–8.7 (0.8–1.2)	86–116 (12–16)
1974	156 (2565)	54–61 ③ (7.5–8.5)	27–31 (3.7–4.3)	33–40 (4.5–5.5)	94–108 (13–15)	94–108 (13–15)	5.8–8.7 (0.8–1.2)	94–108 (13–15)
1975–83	168 (2753)	54–61 ③ (7.5–8.5)	33–40 (4.5–5.5)	33–40 (4.5–5.5)	94–108 ④ (13–15)	94–108 (13–15)	⑤	94–108 (13–15)
1984–86	180.6 (2960)	40–47 (5.5–6.5)	33–40 (4.5–5.5)	67–74 (9.2–10.2)	90–98 (12.5–13.5)	72–80 (10–11)	⑥	58–65 (8.0–9.0)

① Tighten in two steps: 1st, 33(4.5); 2nd, 47(6.5)
② 1972: tighten in two steps: 1st, 47(6.5); 2nd, 55(7.5)
③ Tighten in three steps: 1st, 30(4.0); 2nd, 44(6.0); 3rd, 54–61(7.5–8.5)
④ 1977–78: 87–116(12–16); 1979–82: 101–116(14–16)
⑤ Small bolts (8M): 1975–78 10–13(1.4–1.8); 1979–82 11–18(1.5–2.5) large bolts (10M): 1975–78 25–36(3.5–5.0) 1979–82 25–33(3.5–4.5)
⑥ Intake bolt—12–14 (1.6–2.0), Intake nut—17–20 (2.4–2.8) Exhaust—13–16 (1.8–2.2)

the fenders will not be damaged during removal or installation.

1. On fuel injected models, the fuel system should be bleed before the battery is disconnected. See the procedure for changing the fuel filter, given in Chapter 1. Disconnect the battery cables; the negative cable first.
2. Using a scribing tool, mark the location of each hood hinge on the hood to facilitate reinstallation.
3. Carefully support the hood so that it's weight will not be resting on the hinge bolts. Then, remove the bolts.
4. Remove the hood with the help of an assistant.
5. Remove the air cleaner.
6. Drain the cooling system and the engine crankcase.
7. On automatic transmission models, remove the splash shield. Disconnect and plug the transmission cooler lines at the radiator. Disconnect the vacuum modulator hose at the intake manifold.
8. Disconnect the radiator hoses at the radiator. Remove the radiator mounting bolts, the radiator and the shroud.
9. On models with air conditioning, loosen the compressor mounting bolts and remove the drive belt. Unbolt the compressor and move it aside but DO NOT disconnect any of the refrigerant lines. If there is not enough slack in the lines (this may be the case on some earlier

ENGINE AND ENGINE OVERHAUL 81

Camshaft Specifications
(All measurements in inches)

| Year | Engine | Journal Diameter | | | | | Bearing Clearance | Lobe Lift | | Camshaft End Play |
		1	2	3	4	5		Intake	Exhaust	
1970–83	L24, L26, L28	1.8878–1.8883	1.8878–1.8883	1.8878–1.8883	1.8878–1.8883	1.8878–1.8883	0.0015–0.0026	0.276	0.276	0.0031–0.0150
1984 and Later	VG30E, VG30ET	1.8478–1.8486	1.8478–1.8486	1.8478–1.8486	1.8478–1.8486	1.8478–1.8486	0.0018–0.0035	N.A.	N.A.	0.0012–0.0024

ENGINE AND ENGINE OVERHAUL

Crankshaft and Connecting Rod Specifications
All measurements are given in inches (mm)

Year	Engine Displacement cu in. (cc)	Crankshaft					Connecting Rod		
		Main Brg Journal Dia	Main Brg Oil Clearance	Shaft End-Play	Thrust on No.	Journal Diameter	Oil Clearance	Side Clearance
1970–72	146 (2393)	2.1631–2.1636 (54.942–54.955)	.0008–.0028 (.020–.072)	.0020–.0071 (.05–.18)	4	1.9670–1.9675 (49.961–49.974)	.0006–.0022 (.014–.066)	.0079–.0118 (.20–.30)
1973–78	146 (2393), 156 (2565), 168 (2753)	2.1631–2.1636 (54.942–54.955)	.0008–.0028 (.020–.072)	.0020–.0071 (.05–.18)	4	1.9670–1.9675 (49.961–49.974)	.0010–.0022 (.025–.055)	.0079–.0118 (.20–.30)
1979–83	168 (2753)	2.1631–2.1636 (54.942–54.955)	.0008–.0026 (.020–.066)	.0020–.0071 (.05–.18)	4	1.9670–1.9675 (49.961–49.974)	.0009–.0026 (.024–.066)	.0079–.0118 (.20–.30)
1984–86	180.6 (2960)	2.4790–2.4793 (62.967–62.975)	.0011–.0022 (.028–.055)	.0020–.0067 (.05–.17)	4	1.9670–1.9675 (49.961–49.974)	.0004–.0020 (.010–.052)	.0079–.0138 (.20–.35)

ENGINE AND ENGINE OVERHAUL

Piston and Ring Specifications
All measurements in inches (mm)

Year	Engine Displacement cu in. (cc)	Piston Clearance	Ring Gap			Ring Side Clearance		
			Top Compression	Bottom Compression	Oil Control	Top Compression	Bottom Compression	Oil Control
1970–72	146 (2393)	.0010–.0018 (.025–.045)	.0091–.0150 (.23–.38)	.0059–.0118 (.15–.30)	.0059–.0118 (.15–.30)	.0018–.0031 (.45–.080)	.0012–.0025 (.030–.063)	.0010–.0025 (.025–.063)
1973–76	146 (2393), 156 (2565), 168 (2753)	.0010–.0018 (.025–.045)	.0091–.0150 (.23–.38)	.0059–.0118 (.15–.30)	.0059–.0118 (.15–.30)	.0018–.0031 (.045–.080)	.0012–.0028 (.030–.070)	0
1977–78	168 (2753)	.0010–.0018 (.025–.045)	.0098–.0157 (.25–.40)	.0118–.0197 (.30–.50)	.0118–.0354 (.30–.90)	.0016–.0029 (.040–.073)	.0012–.0028 (.030–.070)	0
1979–80	168 (2753)	.0010–.0018 (.025–.045)	.0098–.0157 (.25–.40)	.0118–.0197 (.30–.50)	.0118–.0354 (.30–.90)	.0016–.0029 (.040–.073)	.0012–.0025 (.030–.063)	0
1981–83	168 (2753)	.0010–.0018 (.025–.045)	.0098–.0157 (.25–.40)	.0059–.0118 (.15–.30)	.012–.035 (.3–.9)	.0016–.0029 (.040–.073)	.012–.025 (.030–.063)	.0009–.0028 (.023–.070)
1981–83 (Turbo)	168 (2753)	.0010–.0018 (.025–.045)	.0075–.0130 (.19–.33)	.0059–.0118 (.15–.30)	.012–.035 (.3–.9)	.0016–.0029 (.040–.073)	.012–.025 (.030–.063)	.0009–.0028 (.023–.070)
1984–86	180.6 (2960)	.0010–.0018 (.025–.045)	.0083–.0173 (.21–.44)	.0071–.0173 (.18–.44)	.0079–.0299 (.20–.76)	.0016–.0029 (.040–.073)	.012–.025 (.030–.063)	.0006–.0075 (.015–.190)

84 ENGINE AND ENGINE OVERHAUL

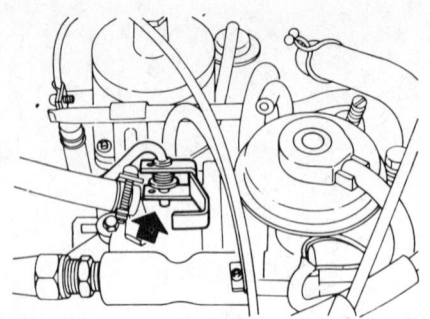

Disconnecting the accelerator linkage (through 1974)

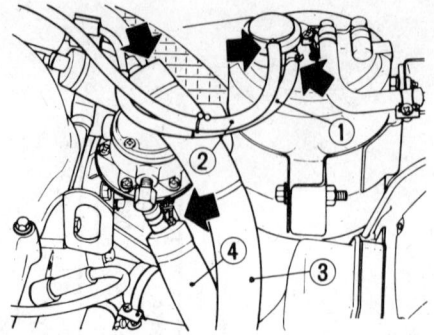

Remove: canister purge hose (1), vacuum signal hose (2), fuel return hose (3), and fuel charge hose (4); 1974 shown, later models similar

models), the system will have to be discharged and the lines disconnected. Unless you are thoroughly familiar with air conditioning systems, this job should be referred to a specialist with proper training.

CAUTION: *If it is necessary to disconnect the refrigerant lines from the compressor, BE CAREFUL of the escaping refrigerant, for it is extremely dangerous.*

10. On models with power steering, loosen the pump mounting bolts and remove the drive belt. Remove the mounting bolts and move the pump away from the engine. DO NOT disconnect the power steering hoses.

11. On carbureted models, disconnect the accelerator linkage (see the illustration).

12. Disconnect and label the following:
    a. Battery ground cable from the engine.
    b. Starter wiring.
    c. Coil-to-distributor high-tension cable.
    d. Primary wire to the distributor at the connection.
    e. Wire to the temperature senders.
    f. Wire to the water temperature switch at the connector.
    g. Alternator wires.
    h. Choke heat wires (1974) or linkage.
    i. Throttle solenoid wire (manual transmission) and throttle linkage.
    j. EGR solenoid wire at the connector, if equipped.
    k. Wire to the vacuum solenoid (manual transmission).
    l. Fuel lines(s) (two for 1974 models); on fuel injected models be sure to relieve fuel line pressure as outlined in fuel filter replacement in Chapter 1 and to disconnect all electrical wiring to the fuel injection.
    m. Heater hoses.
    n. Vacuum line to the brake cylinder at the manifold.
    o. Wires for the back-up lights, the neutral safety switch and to the detecting switch.
    p. Inhibitor switch and kick-down solenoid wires (automatic only).

13. Remove the clutch master cylinder (manual transmission only).

14. Disconnect the speedometer cable where it enters the rear extension housing of the transmission.

15. Disconnect the transmission control linkage.

16. Remove the shift lever (M/T) or disconnect the range selector (A/T).

17. Disconnect the exhaust tube from the manifold.

18. Mark the companion flange and the driveshaft for installation in the same place, then disconnect the shaft at the rear by removing the four bolts. Remove the shaft from the rear of the transmission and seal the opening.

19. Support the transmission carefully to remove all weight from the rear mounts. Remove the bolts which secure the rear mounts to the body.

20. Connect an adequate cable or chain between the two lifting hooks on the engine. Hook a cable or chain to a hoist and apply just enough lift to take the weight off the front mounts.

21. Remove the engine support-to-front mounting insulator bolts.

22. Working carefully to avoid damaging the engine or body parts, tilt the engine, lowering the transmission jack as necessary, until it can be pulled up and out of the engine compartment, front first.

23. Remove the transmission from the engine and mount the engine on a secure stand.

NOTE: *When reinstalling the engine, first carefully inspect the engine mounts. If any part of the mount is damaged or if the bonded surface is deteriorated or separated, replace the mount. The front mounts are identical but are installed in different positions on the right and left. The rear mount must also be installed in the proper direction.*

24. To install, reverse the removal procedures. Make sure that all engine mounts are

ENGINE AND ENGINE OVERHAUL 85

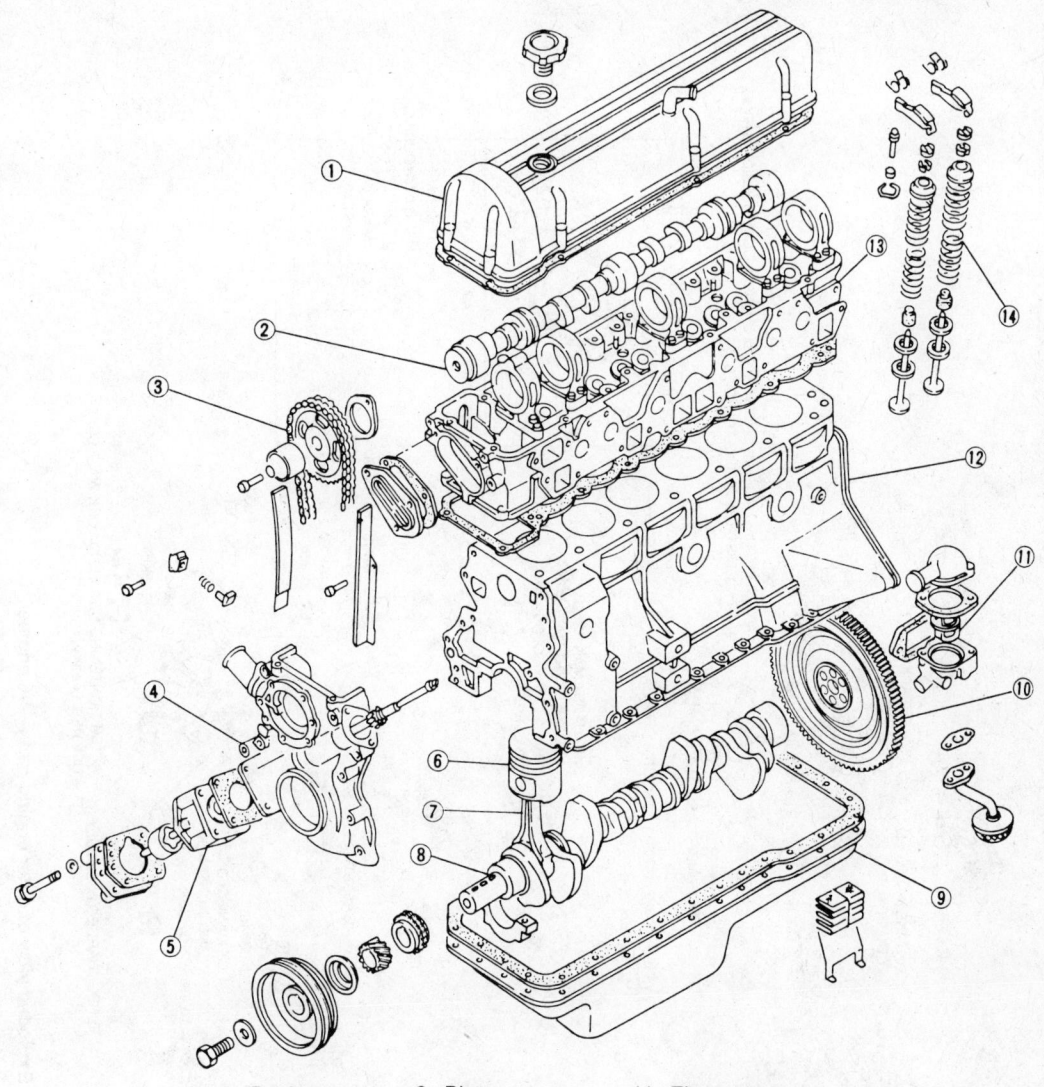

1. Rocker cover
2. Camshaft
3. Timing gear
4. Front cover
5. Oil pump
6. Piston
7. Connecting rod
8. Crankshaft
9. Oil pan
10. Flywheel
11. Thermostat
12. Cylinder block
13. Cylinder head
14. Valve mechanism

Exploded view of the engine—typical 1970-83

properly assembled and tight before removing the support.

1984 and Later

1. Using a scribing tool, mark the hood hinges to the hood, then remove the hood.
2. With the engine running, remove the rear luggage mat and disconnect the fuel pump harness connector. After the engine stalls, crank the engine 2–3 times, then turn the engine OFF and reconnect the fuel pump harness connector.
3. Disconnect and remove the battery.
4. If equipped with power steering and/or air conditioning, remove the power steering pump and/or the A/C compressor.

NOTE: *When removing the power steering pump and/or the A/C compressor, DO NOT disconnect the hoses, simply move the item aside and suspend it on a wire to avoid damaging the hoses.*

5. Drain the cooling system and the engine oil.
6. Remove the air cleaner and the radiator hoses.
7. Disconnect the fuel lines and the emission control canister hoses. Remove the emission control canister

86 ENGINE AND ENGINE OVERHAUL

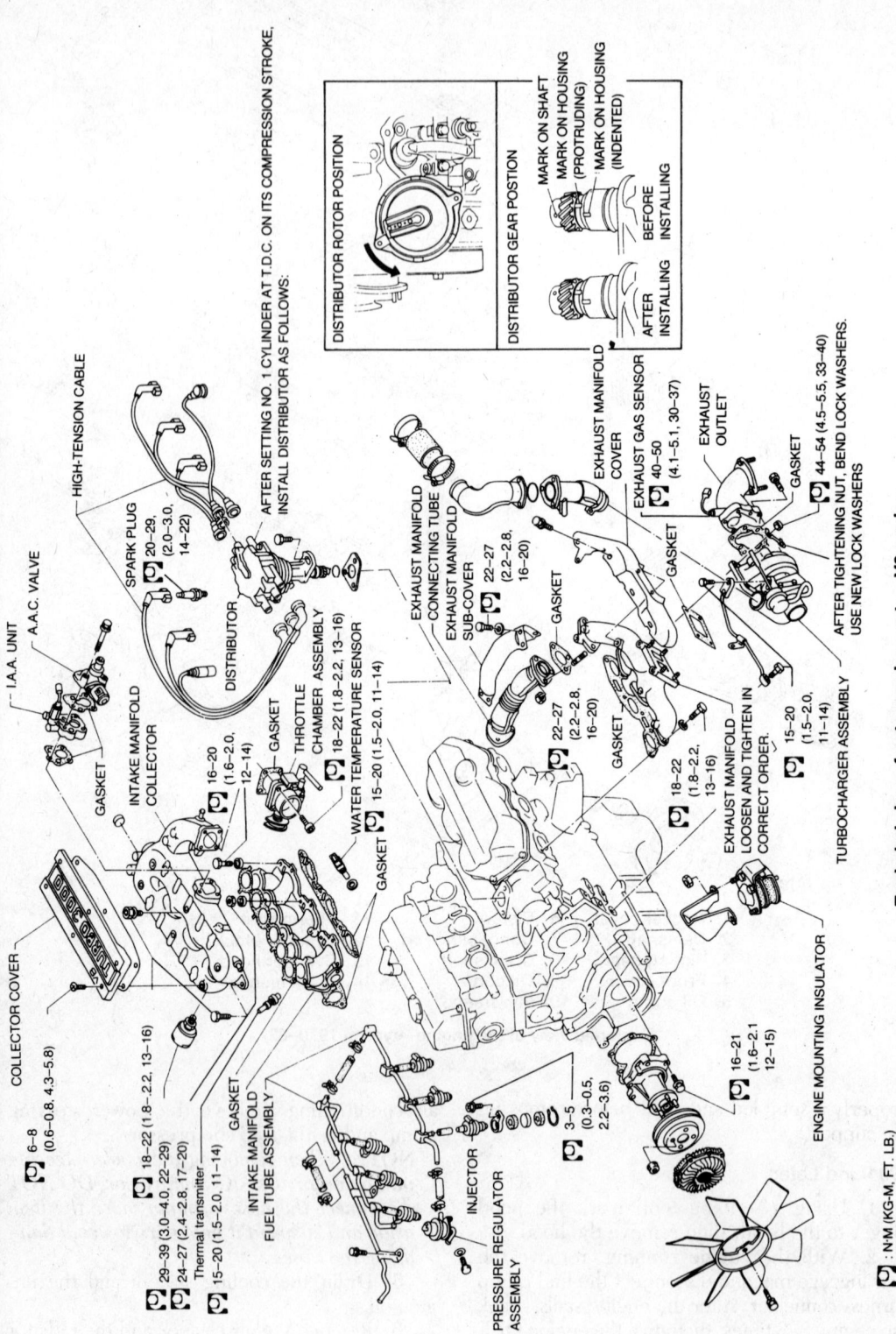

Exploded view of outer engine parts—V6 engine

ENGINE AND ENGINE OVERHAUL 87

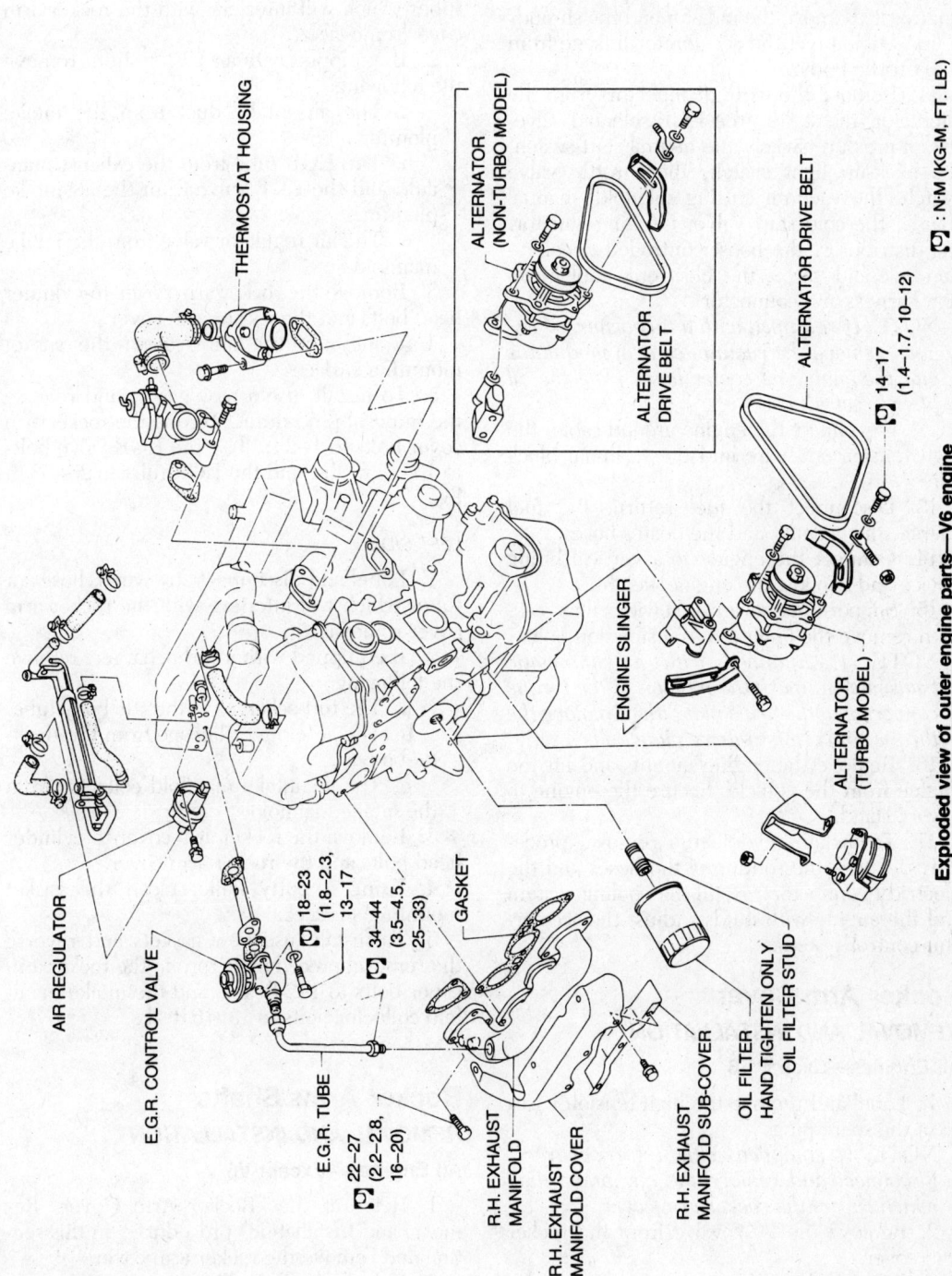

Exploded view of outer engine parts—V6 engine

ENGINE AND ENGINE OVERHAUL

8. If equipped with an Automatic Transmission, disconnect and plug the oil cooler lines from the radiator.

9. If equipped with a lower splash guard, remove it. Remove the radiator and the shroud.

10. Disconnect the accelerator linkage from the throttle body.

11. Remove the wiring connectors from the alternator, the starter, the EGR solenoid valve, the oil pressure switch, the neutral start switch, the back-up light switch, the throttle valve switch, the vacuum cutting solenoid (manual trans.), the cold start valve, the air regulator, the distributor, the boost controlled deceleration solenoid valve, the electronic fuel injection harness and connector.

NOTE: *If equipped with a turbocharged engine, remove the vacuum control modulator and the engine oil cooler hoses from the oil filter bracket.*

12. Disconnect the engine ground cable, the high tension coil wire and the terminal block wire.

13. Disconnect the fuel return, the fuel charge, the vacuum and the heater hoses.

14. Connect the engine to a vertical lifting device and support the engine weight.

15. Support the transmission with a floor jack, then remove the engine-to-transmission bolts.

NOTE: *If equipped with an automatic transmission, mark the position of the torque converter to the drive plate, then remove the torque convertor-to-drive plate bolts.*

16. Remove the engine mounts and lift the engine from the vehicle. Secure the engine to a work stand.

17. To install, reverse the removal procedures. Check the routing of the hoses and the electrical connectors. Refill the cooling system and the engine with fluids. Adjust the accelerator control system.

Rocker Arm Cover

REMOVAL AND INSTALLATION

All Engines—Except V6

1. Label and remove the high tension wires from the spark plugs.

NOTE: *If equipped with a turbocharger, disconnect and remove the air intake duct which covers the rocker arm cover.*

2. Remove the PCV valve from the rocker arm cover.

3. Remove the rocker arm cover-to-cylinder head bolts and the rocker arm cover.

4. Using a putty knife, clean the gasket mounting surfaces.

5. To install, use a new gasket and reverse the removal procedures. Torque the rocker arm cover bolts to 7–12 ft. lbs.

V6 Engines

RIGHT-SIDE

1. Label and disconnect any wires, hoses or tubes which will interfere with the rocker arm cover removal.

2. If equipped with an EFI system, remove the following:

   a. The air intake duct from the intake plenum.

   b. The EGR tube from the exhaust manifold and the EGR valve from the air intake plenum.

   c. The air regulator valve from the intake manifold.

3. Remove the rocker arm cover-to-cylinder head bolts and the rocker arm cover.

4. Using a putty knife, clean the gasket mounting surfaces.

5. To install, use a new gasket and reverse the removal procedures. Torque the rocker arm cover bolts to 1–2 ft. lbs., the EGR valve bolts to 13–17 ft. lbs. and the EGR tube to 25–33 ft. lbs.

LEFT-SIDE

1. Label and disconnect any wires, hoses or tubes which will interfere with the rocker arm cover removal.

2. If equipped with a turbocharger, remove the following:

   a. The turbocharger-to-throttle body tube.

   b. The accelerator linkage from the throttle body.

   c. The air intake manifold collector from the intake manifold.

3. Remove the rocker arm cover-to-cylinder head bolts and the rocker arm cover.

4. Using a putty knife, clean the gasket mounting surfaces.

5. To install, use new gaskets and reverse the removal procedures. Torque the rocker arm cover bolts to 1–2 ft. lbs. and the intake manifold collector bolts to 13–16 ft. lbs.

Rocker Arms/Shafts

REMOVAL AND INSTALLATION

All Engines—Except V6

1. Refer to the "Rocker Arm Cover, Removal and Installation" procedures, in this section and remove the rocker arm cover.

2. Using a small pry bar, compress the valve spring(s) and remove the rocker arm(s) from the valve(s) and the valve rocker pivot(s).

NOTE: *If necessary to remove the rocker arm pivots, loosen the locknut, then unscrew the pivot from the cylinder head.*

3. Inspect the rocker arms, the rocker piv-

ENGINE AND ENGINE OVERHAUL

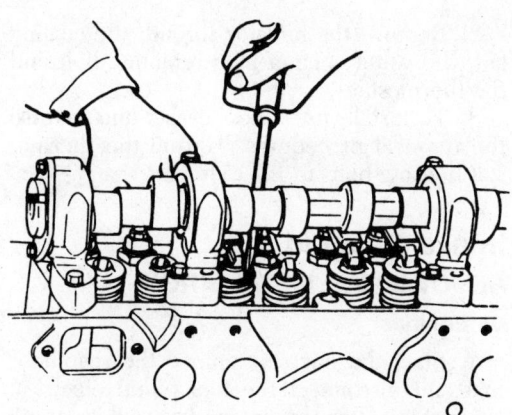

Installing the rocker arms—except V6 engines

ots and the camshaft for wear and/or damage; if necessary, replace the damaged parts.

4. To install, reverse the removal procedures.

V6 Engines

1. Refer to the "Rocker Arm Cover, Removal and Installation" procedures, in this section and remove the rocker arm cover.
2. Remove the rocker arm shaft-to-cylinder head bolts and lift the rocker arm/shaft assembly from the cylinder head.

3. Separate the rocker arms from the shaft.

NOTE: *When separating the rocker arms from the rocker arm shafts, be sure to keep the parts in order for reinstallation purposes.*

4. Check the rocker arms, the shafts, the valves and the valve lifter for damage. If necessary, replace the damaged components.

CAUTION: *When installing the rocker arm shafts, be certain that they are installed in their original positions.*

5. To install, reverse the removal procedures. Torque the rocker arm shaft bolts to 13–16 ft. lbs.

Thermostat

REMOVAL AND INSTALLATION

1970–83

1. Drain the radiator coolant through the lower drain cock.
2. Disconnect the upper radiator hose at the water outlet.
3. Loosen the mounting bolts, then remove the water outlet, the gasket and the thermostat.
4. To install, use a new gasket, sealant and reverse the removal procedures. Refill the cooling system.

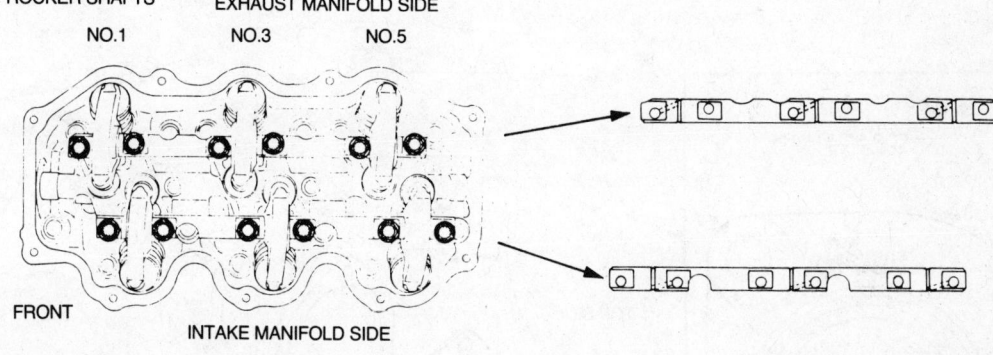

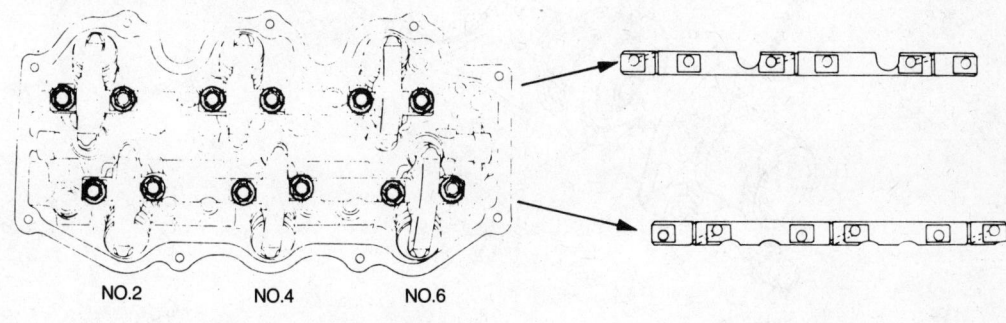

Determining the direction and position of the rocker arm shafts—V6 engine

90 ENGINE AND ENGINE OVERHAUL

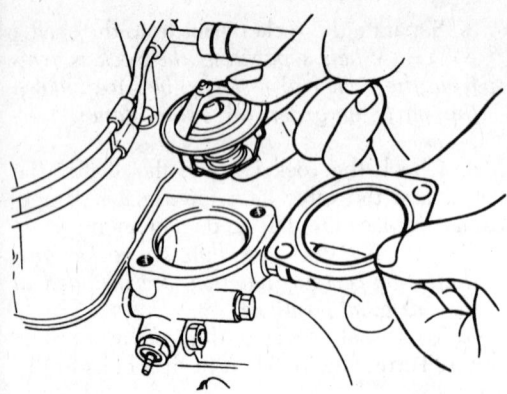

Thermostat installation, all except V6 engine

NOTE: *Install the thermostat with the wax pellet downward and use a new water outlet gasket coated with sealer. On the 1979 and later models use a thermostat with an air bleed hole in the flange. The thermostat should be installed with the hole facing the left-side of the engine. If it is necessary to replace the thermostat, be sure the new one has a bleed hole.*

1984 and Later

1. Drain the coolant from the drain cocks on the cylinder block and radiator.

2. Remove the radiator shroud, the cooling fan, the water suction pipe retaining bolt and the thermostat.

3. To install, use a new gasket and reverse the removal procedures. Torque the thermostat housing bolts to 12–15 ft. lbs.

Intake Manifold

REMOVAL AND INSTALLATION

V6 Engines

1. Start the engine, remove the rear floor mat and disconnect the fuel pump electrical connector. After the engine has stalled, crank the engine 2–3 times, then turn OFF the ignition switch and reconnect the fuel pump electrical connector.

2. Disconnect the negative battery cable. Drain the cooling system.

3. Disconnect the accelerator linkage from the throttle body.

4. Remove the collector cover and the collector.

5. Disconnect the fuel lines from the fuel injector assembly.

6. Remove the intake manifold-to-engine bolts and the intake manifold with the fuel injector lines as an assembly.

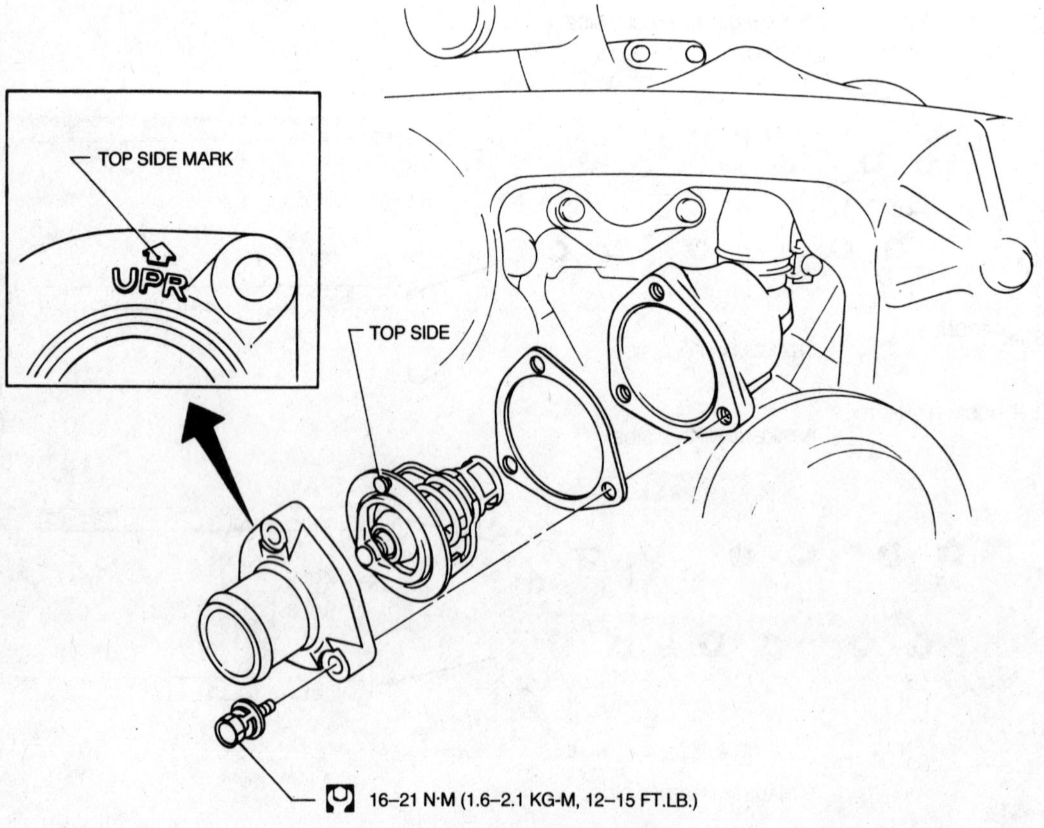

Thermostat installation—V6 engine

ENGINE AND ENGINE OVERHAUL

7. Using a putty knife, clean the gasket mounting surfaces.
8. To install, use new gaskets and reverse the removal procedures. Torque the intake manifold-to-engine nut/bolts to 17–20 ft. lbs. Refill the cooling system.

Exhaust Manifold
REMOVAL AND INSTALLATION
V6 Engines

1. Remove the exhaust manifold covers.
2. Disconnect the exhaust manifold crossover tube from the exhaust manifolds at the rear of the engine.
3. Disconnect the exhaust pipe from the left exhaust manifold.
4. If equipped with a turbocharger, perform the following:
   a. Disconnect the oil passage tube from the turbocharger.
   b. Remove the turbocharger-to-throttle body air intake tube.
   c. Remove the turbocharger from the exhaust manifold.
5. Remove the exhaust manifold-to-engine bolts and the manifolds from the engine.
6. Using a putty knife, clean the gasket mounting surfaces.
7. To install, use new gaskets and reverse the removal procedures. Torque the exhaust manifold-to-engine bolts to 13–16 ft. lbs., the crossover tube-to-exhaust manifold nuts to 16–20 ft. lbs. and the turbocharger-to-exhaust manifold nuts to 33–40 ft. lbs.

Combination Manifold
REMOVAL AND INSTALLATION
All Engines Except V6

NOTE: *It is important to replace the gasket whenever either manifold is removed. Because the manifolds share a common gasket, it is necessary to remove both manifolds for access to the gasket. Be sure to get the correct replacement gasket for your vehicle. The 1979–83 models have square exhaust ports, instead of the round ports used on 1970–78 models; the gaskets are not interchangeable.*

1. Disconnect the battery negative cable.
2. Disconnect the air and vacuum hoses from the air cleaner and the air cleaner (if necessary).
3. On the carbureted models, perform the following:
   a. Disconnect the hose linking the balance tube and the temperature sensor at the balance tube end.
   b. Drain enough coolant from the bottom of the radiator so the top radiator hose may be removed without losing coolant.
   c. Disconnect the coolant, the air, the vacuum and the fuel hoses from the intake manifold and carburetor(s).
   d. Remove the carburetor(s) from the intake manifold.
   e. Disconnect the rear coolant inlet pipe and the exhaust gas inlet tube from the intake manifold.
   f. Remove the air conditioner fast idle mechanism and bracket from the manifold (if equipped).
   g. Remove the securing nut and disconnect the coolant tube from the balance tube.
4. On fuel injected models, perform the following:
   a. Refer to the "Fuel Filter, Replacement" procedures, in Chapter 1 and release the fuel pressure.
   b. Disconnect the fuel injection wiring harness connector.
   c. Disconnect the rocker arm cover-to-

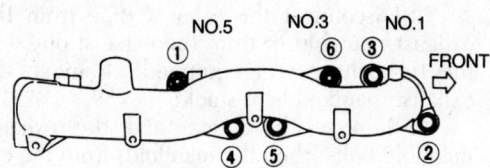

L.H. exhaust manifold

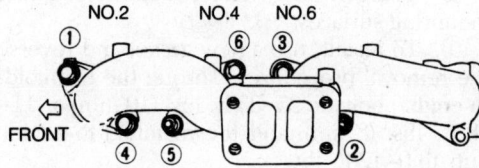

Exhaust manifold bolt removal sequence—V6 engine

R.H. exhaust manifold

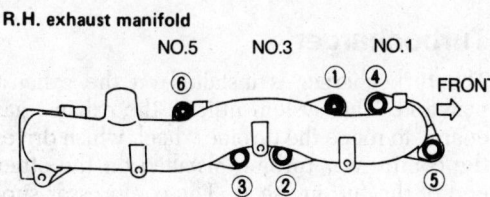

L.H. exhaust manifold

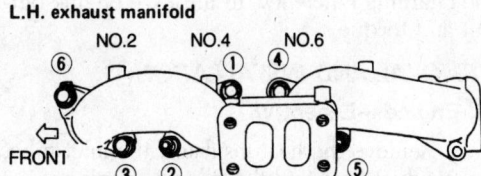

TIGHTEN IN NUMERICAL ORDER.
Exhaust manifold torque sequence—V6 engine

92 ENGINE AND ENGINE OVERHAUL

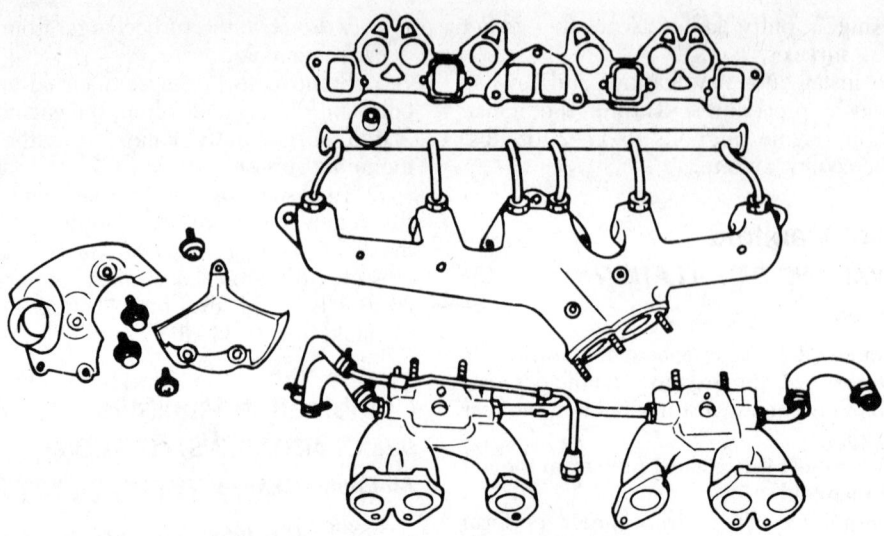

Intake and exhaust manifolds—carbureted models

throttle body hose from the rocker arm cover.

   d. Drain the cooling system into a clean container.

   e. Disconnect the heater-to-coolant inlet hose from the inlet.

   f. Remove the coolant pipe/fuel pipe-to-cylinder head bolt.

   g. Remove the heater-to-thermostat housing tube.

   h. Disconnect the fuel lines from the injector rail.

5. Disconnect the vacuum hose from the EGR valve and the EGR tube from the exhaust manifold.

6. If equipped with an air pump, disconnect the air injection hose from the air injection gallery on the exhaust manifold at the check valve.

7. Disconnect the exhaust pipe from the exhaust manifold or from the exhaust outlet of the turbocharger (if equipped). Remove the exhaust manifold heat shield.

8. Remove the intake and the exhaust manifold bolts, then the manifolds from the engine.

9. Using a putty knife, clean the gasket mounting surfaces.

10. To install, use a new gasket and reverse the removal procedures. Torque the manifold-to-engine bolts to 25–33 ft. lbs. (10 mm) or 11–18 ft. lbs. (8 mm) and the manifold-to-engine nuts to 9–12 ft. lbs.

   NOTE: *When torquing the manifold bolts, work from the center outwards, in two progressive steps, to the proper torque.*

Turbocharger

The turbocharger is installed on the exhaust manifold. This system utilizes the exhaust gas energy to rotate the turbine wheel, which drives the compressor turbine installed on the other end of the turbine shaft. The compressor supplies compressed air to the engine (to increase the charging efficiency) to improve engine output and torque.

REMOVAL AND INSTALLATION

All Engines–Except V6

1. Remove the heat insulator, the inlet tube, the air duct hose and the suction air pipe.

2. Disconnect the exhaust gas sensor harness connector, the front tube, the oil delivery tube and the oil drain pipe.

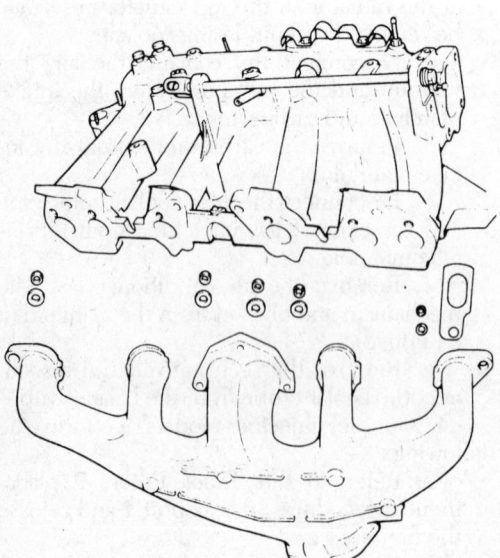

View of the intake and exhaust manifolds for fuel injected engines—except V6

ENGINE AND ENGINE OVERHAUL

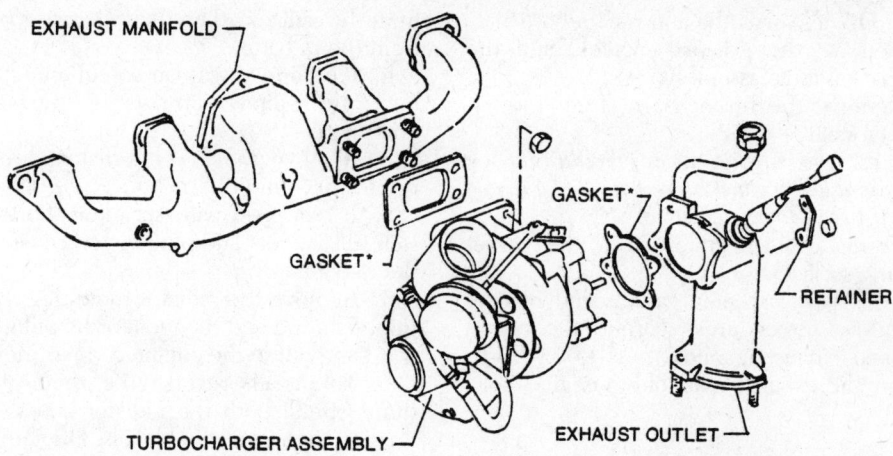

Turbocharger assembly—typical through 1983

3. Remove the turbocharger-to-exhaust manifold nuts and the turbocharger.

NOTE: *The turbocharger should not be disassembled; it must be replaced as a whole unit if found to be defective.*

4. Using a putty knife, clean the gasket mounting surfaces.

5. To install, reverse the removal procedures. Torque the turbocharger-to-exhaust manifold nuts to 33–40 ft. lbs.

1984 and Later V6 Engines

1. Remove the following:
   a. Compressor and compressor bracket.
   b. Exhaust front tube.
   c. Center cable.
   d. Heat insulator for the brake master cylinder.
   e. Air duct and hoses.
   f. Exhaust manifold connecting tube and heat shield plate.

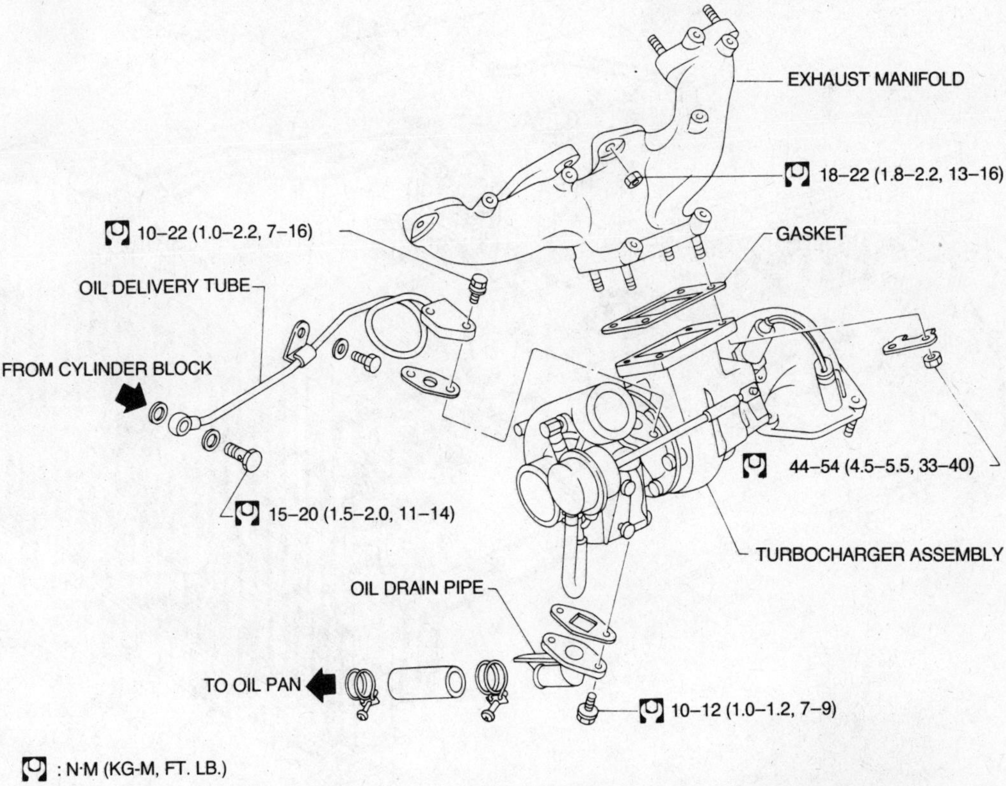

Turbocharger assembly, removal and installation—V6 engine

94 ENGINE AND ENGINE OVERHAUL

g. Oil delivery tube and return hose.

2. Remove the exhaust manifold and the turbocharger as an assembly.

3. Remove the turbocharger from the exhaust manifold.

NOTE: *The turbocharger should not be disassembled; it must be replaced as a whole unit if found to be defective.*

4. Using a putty knife, clean the gasket mounting surfaces.

5. To install, use new gaskets and reverse the removal procedures. Torque the turbocharger-to-exhaust manifold nuts to 33–40 ft. lbs. and the exhaust manifold-to-engine bolts to 13–16 ft. lbs.

Radiator

REMOVAL AND INSTALLATION

1970–83

1. Drain the cooling system by opening the drain cock at the bottom of the radiator.

NOTE: *Removing the pressure cap will speed the draining of the cooling system.*

2. If equipped with an undercover, remove it.

3. Disconnect the upper and lower hoses from the radiator, then the water reservoir hose from the radiator.

4. If equipped with air conditioning, disconnect the pipe clip screw (turbocharger equipped).

5. Remove the lower radiator shroud and remove it from underneath.

6. If equipped with an automatic transmission, disconnect and plug the oil cooler lines at the radiator.

7. Remove the radiator mounting bolts, the upper shroud and the radiator by pulling it upward and out of the engine compartment.

8. To install, reverse the removal procedures. Refill both the radiator and the transmission to the specified levels. Operate the engine and continue filling radiator (to the proper level) until all of the air bubbles are removed.

1984 and Later

1. Remove the front bumper assembly.

2. Drain the cooling system by opening the drain cock at the bottom of the radiator.

NOTE: *Removing the pressure cap will speed the draining of the cooling system.*

3. Disconnect the upper and lower hoses at the radiator, then the water reservoir hose from the radiator.

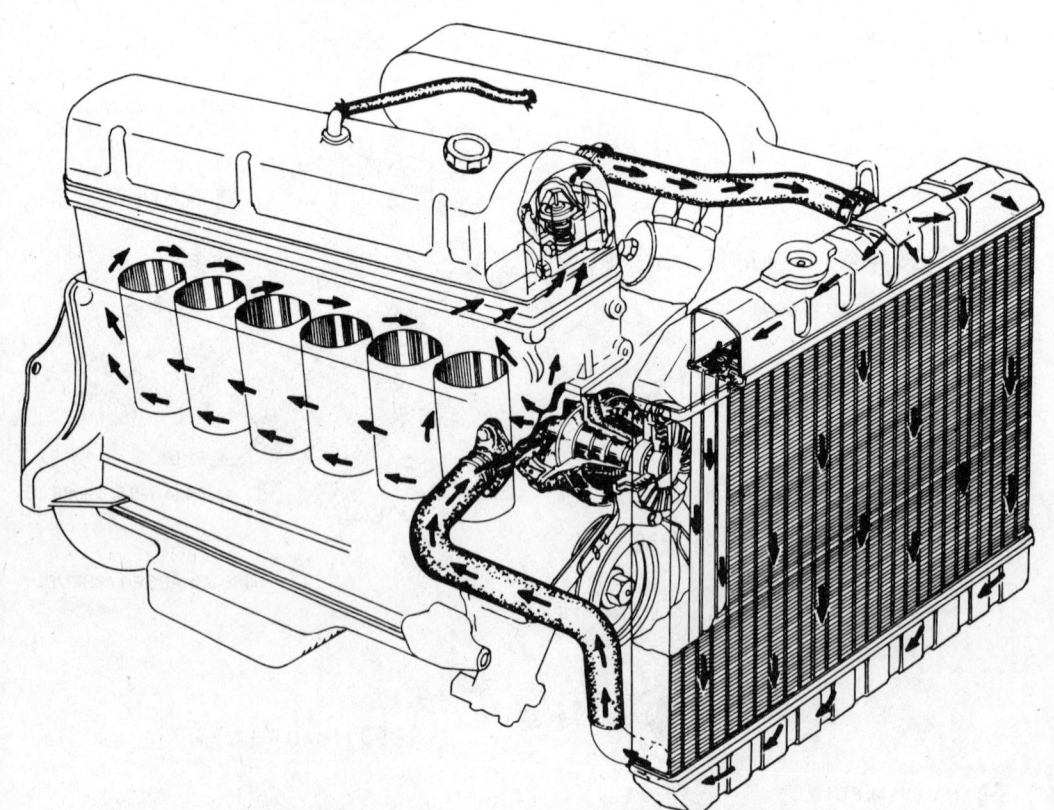

Cooling system flow diagram—260-Z; others similar

ENGINE AND ENGINE OVERHAUL 95

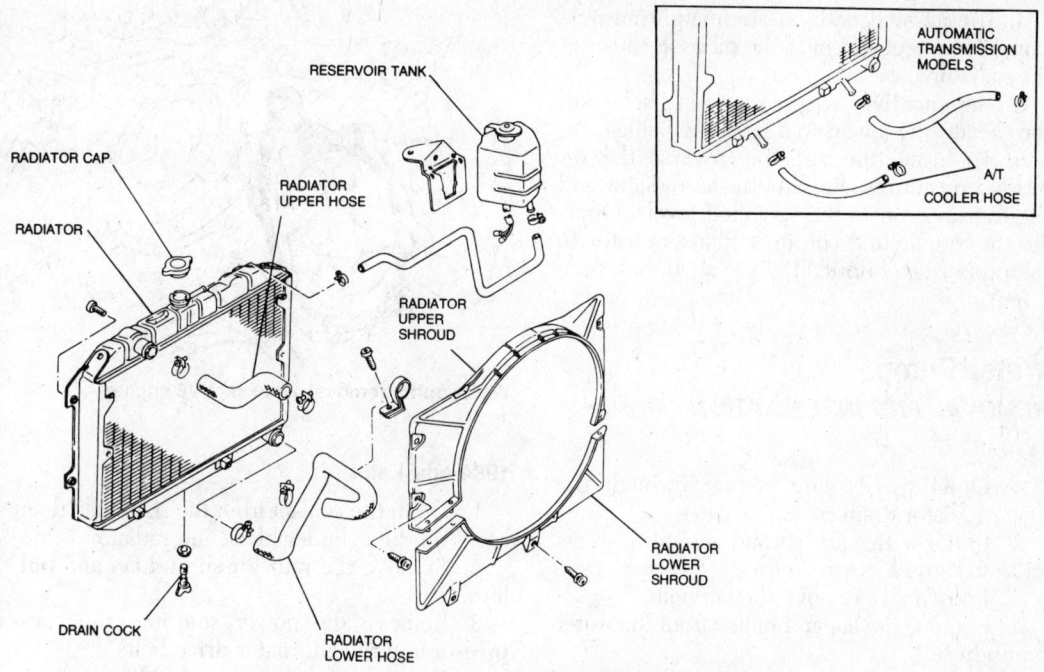

Radiator installation details—typical through 1983

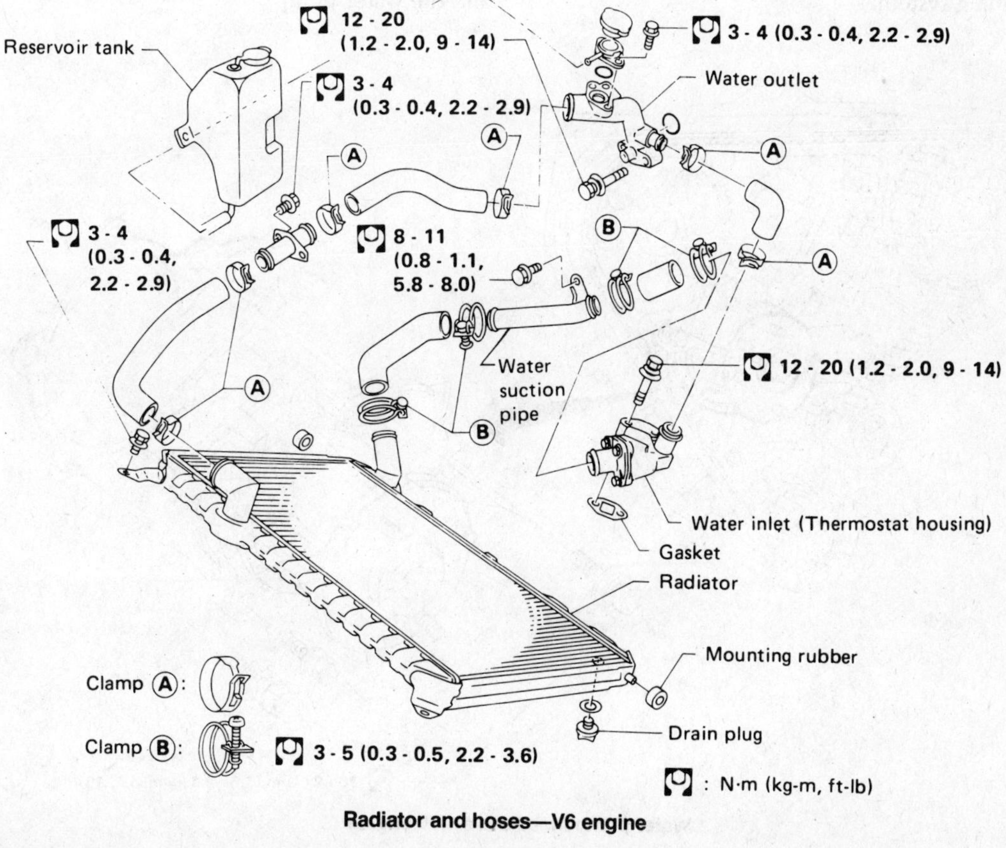

Radiator and hoses—V6 engine

96 ENGINE AND ENGINE OVERHAUL

4. If equipped with an automatic transmission, disconnect and plug the oil cooler lines at the radiator.
5. Remove the radiator mounting bolts and the radiator by lowering it from the vehicle.
6. To install the radiator, reverse the removal procedures. Refill both the radiator and the transmission to the specified levels. Operate the engine and continue filling radiator to the proper level until all of the air bubbles are removed.

Water Pump

REMOVAL AND INSTALLATION

1970–83

1. Drain the cooling system through the lower radiator drain cock.
2. Remove the fan shroud mounting bolts and the shroud.
3. Loosen and remove the fan belt.
4. Remove the fan and pulley from the water pump hub.
5. Remove the water pump-to-front cover bolts and water pump.
6. Using a putty knife, clean the gasket mounting surfaces.
7. To install, use a new gasket, sealant and reverse the removal procedures. Refill the cooling system.

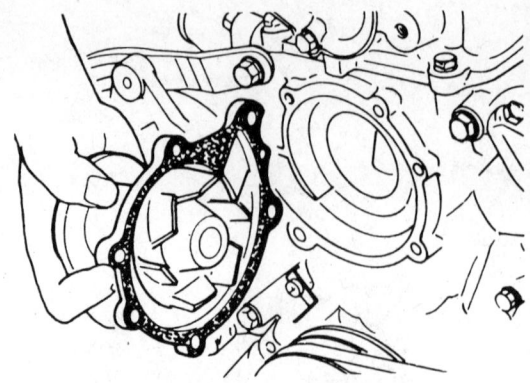

Water pump removal, all except V6 engine

1984 and Later

1. Drain the coolant from the right-side drain cocks on the cylinder block and radiator.
2. Remove the radiator shroud fan and pulleys.
3. Remove the power steering, the compressor and the alternator drive belts.
4. Disconnect the water pump hose.
5. Remove the upper and lower timing covers.

NOTE: *Be careful not to get coolant on the timing belt.*

6. Remove the water pump retaining bolts and the water pump.

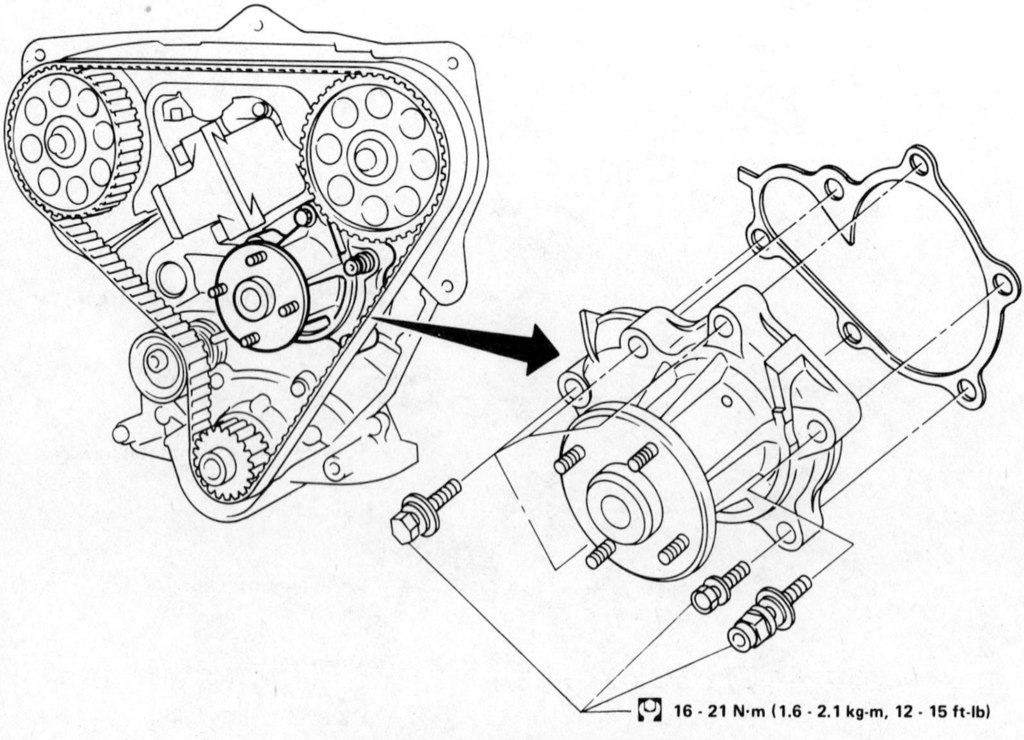

Water pump installation—V6 engine

16 - 21 N·m (1.6 - 2.1 kg-m, 12 - 15 ft-lb)

ENGINE AND ENGINE OVERHAUL

7. To install, reverse the removal procedures. Torque the bolts to 12–15 ft. lbs. Refill the cooling system.

Cylinder Head

REMOVAL

All Engines Except V6

1. Crank the engine until the No. 1 cylinder is at TDC of the compression stroke.
2. Disconnect the negative battery cable, drain the coolant, then remove the air cleaner and the attending hoses.
3. Remove the upper radiator hose, the heater hoses, the thermostat housing (coolant outlet elbow) and the thermostat. Label the electrical connectors.

NOTE: *When removing the thermostat housing, the thermo-time switch (fuel injected models), the temperature switch(s) and the vacuum switching valve can be removed as an assembly.*

4. If equipped with power steering, unbolt the pump and move it aside; DO NOT disconnect the lines. If necessary, remove the alternator, on some models.
5. Label and disconnect the spark plug wires, then remove the spark plugs.
6. Disconnect the fuel line(s).

NOTE: *On fuel injected models, be sure to relieve fuel line pressure as outlined in fuel filter replacement in Chapter 1; label and disconnect all of the electrical wiring to the fuel injection.*

7. On 1970–74 models, disconnect the water, the air, the vacuum and the fuel hoses or lines from the carburetors, then remove the fuel pump.
8. On fuel injected models, the fuel injection assembly will be removed intact with the intake manifold. Disconnect the hose from the rocker cover which runs to the throttle chamber. Remove the coolant pipe/fuel pipe retaining bolt from the cylinder head.
9. If equipped, disconnect and remove the EGR control tube and the EGR valve.
10. Disconnect the coolant piping and the exhaust gas inlet tube from the intake manifold.
11. Most 1979 and later models have an auxiliary coolant fan on the right-side of the engine, with ducting which runs over the rocker cover to the intake manifold. Remove this ducting, if equipped.
12. Remove the rocker arm cover.
13. Remove the air conditioner fast idle mechanism and bracket, if equipped.
14. Remove the coolant tube from the balance tube of the manifold, then remove the balance tube, if equipped.
15. Remove the exhaust heat shield plate,

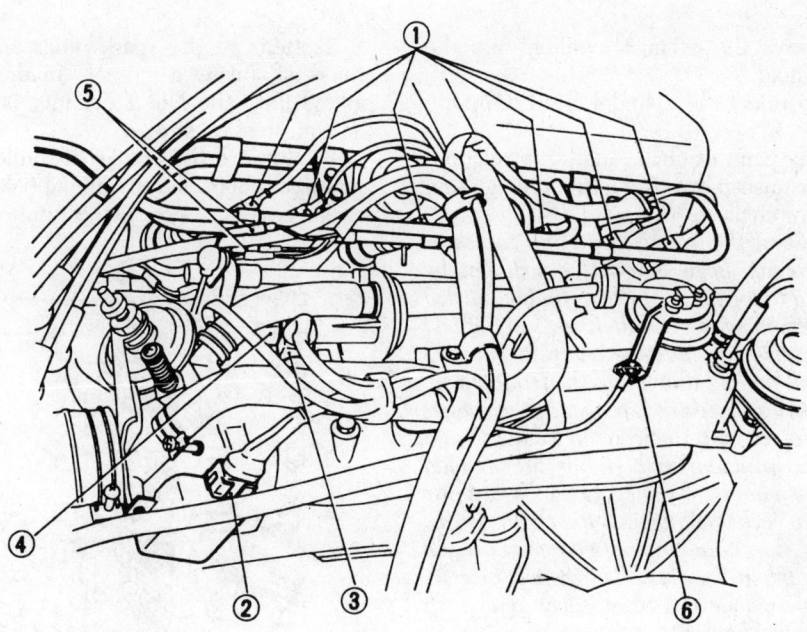

1. Injector connector
2. Throttle valve switch connector
3. Cold start valve connector
4. Air regulator connector
5. E.F.I. sub-harness connector
6. Engine ground

Removing the EFI harness—except V6 engines

98 ENGINE AND ENGINE OVERHAUL

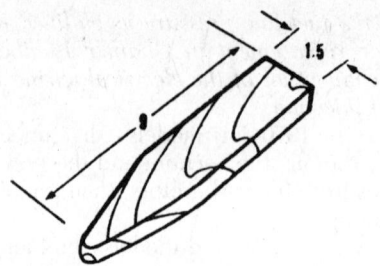

Dimensions for fabricating the wooden wedge used to support the timing chain

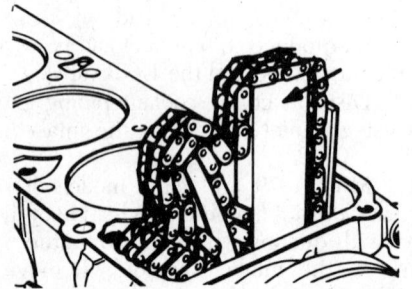

Supporting the timing chain with a wedge—except V6 engines

then disconnect the exhaust pipe from the exhaust manifold or from the turbocharger exhaust outlet (if equipped). Disconnect the EGR tube from the exhaust manifold.

16. If equipped with air injection, remove the air pump hose from the air injection gallery pipe.

17. Remove the exhaust manifold and the intake manifold.

18. Disconnect the cylinder head temperature sender.

19. Using paint or chalk, mark the relationship of the camshaft sprocket to the timing chain with paint or chalk.

NOTE: *Once the timing chain and camshaft sprocket have been marked, it will not be necessary to locate the factory timing marks. Before removing the camshaft sprocket, it will be necessary to wedge the chain in place so that it will not fall down into the front cover. The factory procedure is to wedge the timing chain in place with the wooden wedge shown here. The problem with this is that it may allow the chain tensioner to move out far enough to cock itself against the chain. If this happens, the chain may not go back over the sprocket when it is installed; it will be necessary to remove the front cover and push the tensioner back.*

20. After installing the wedge, unbolt and remove the camshaft sprocket.

21. If equipped, remove the valve train oil gallery pipe.

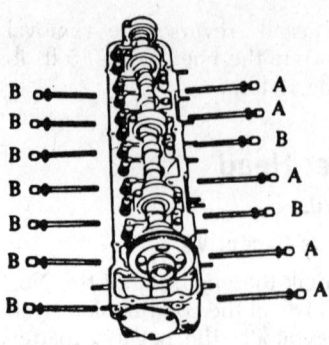

Note the use and position of different length bolts, labeled A or B—except V6 engines

NOTE: *The cylinder head bolts are of two different lengths, be sure to install them in their correct positions.*

22. Using a 10 mm Allen wrench, loosen and remove the cylinder head bolts in the reverse order of the tightening sequence to prevent head warpage. Keep the bolts in order, for they are of different lengths. Lift the cylinder head from the engine; this may require an assistant.

V6 Engine—1984 and Later

NOTE: *This procedure includes the camshaft, the intake manifold, the exhaust manifold and the rocker arm shaft removal procedures.*

1. Refer to the "Engine, Removal and Installation" procedures, in this section, then remove the engine and support it on an engine stand.

2. Remove the spark plugs and turn the crankshaft (using a wrench on the crankshaft pulley) until the No. 1 cylinder is at TDC of the compression stroke.

3. Remove the crankshaft pulley bolt, the crankshaft pulley and the timing belt (upper and lower) covers. Loosen the timing belt ten-

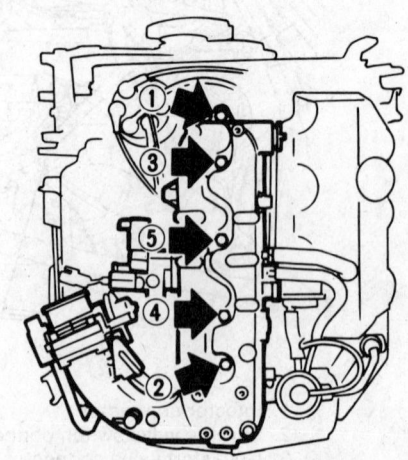

Intake manifold collector cover bolt removal sequence—V6 engine

ENGINE AND ENGINE OVERHAUL

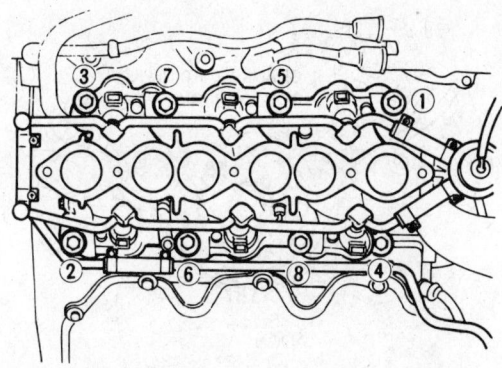

Intake manifold bolt removal sequence—V6 engine

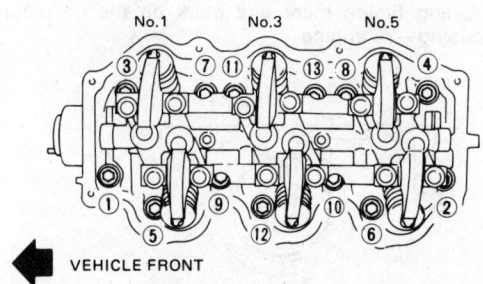

Cylinder head bolt removal sequence—V6 engine

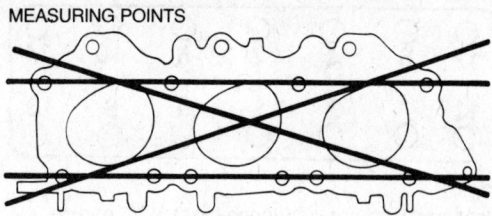

Cylinder head measuring points—V6 engine

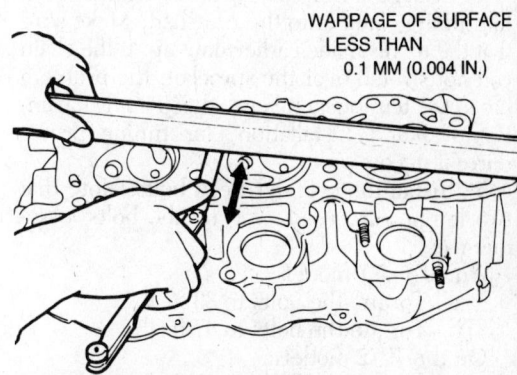

Using a straight edge and feeler gauge to measure cylinder head distortion—V6 engine

sioner pulley, then remove the timing belt (mark the direction of rotation).

NOTE: *Before removing the timing belt, be sure to mark the belt with the relationship of the camshaft sprockets and the crankshaft sprocket.*

4. Remove the camshaft sprocket bolts, the sprockets and the rear timing belt cover.
5. Remove the coolant drain cocks from the cylinder block and drain the coolant from the block.
6. Remove the collector cover and collector.
7. Remove the intake manifold with fuel tube assembly.
8. Remove the power steering pump bracket.
9. Remove the exhaust manifold stay, then disconnect the exhaust manifold connecting tube.
10. Remove the compressor, the compressor bracket and the valve covers.
11. Remove the cylinder head with the exhaust manifold.

CLEANING AND INSPECTION

Using a putty knife, clean the gasket surface of the cylinder head. Using a wire brush, clean the carbon from the piston head depressions and the valves in the cylinder head.

Inspect the cylinder head for cracks and other flaws. Using a straightedge and a feeler gauge, measure the warpage of the cylinder head-to-block mating surface. If warpage exceeds 0.004 in. (0.1 mm) or there is other damage, repair or replace the head, as required.

RESURFACING

If the cylinder head warpage is significant, requiring the head to be machined, submit it to a reputable automotive machine shop.

NOTE: *Before resurfacing, the cylinder head must be disassembled. Refer to the "Camshaft, Removal and Installation" procedures, in this section and disassemble the cylinder head.*

INSTALLATION

All Engines–Except V6

1. With the crankshaft turned so that the No. 1 cylinder is at TDC of the compression stroke (if not already done so), make sure that the camshaft sprocket timing mark and the oblong groove in the camshaft retaining plate are aligned.
2. Place the cylinder head in position on the block, being careful not to allow any of the valves to contact any of the pistons.

NOTE: *DO NOT rotate the crankshaft or camshaft separately because of possible damage which might occur to the valves.*

3. Temporarily install and tighten the two center (right and left) cylinder head bolts to 14.5 ft. lbs.

100 ENGINE AND ENGINE OVERHAUL

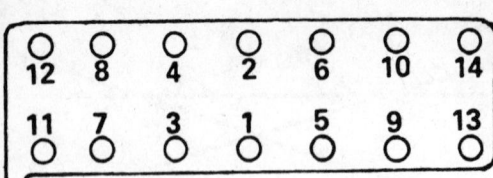

Head bolt torquing sequence—except V6 engine

4. Install the camshaft sprocket together with the timing chain onto the camshaft. Make sure that the marks made earlier, line up. If the chain will not stretch over the sprocket, the problem lies in the tensioner. Refer to the "Timing Chain, Removal and Installation" for timing procedure, if necessary.
5. Install the cylinder head bolts. Note that two lengths are used. Torque the bolts in sequence.
  On 1970–71 models:
   a. Torque the bolts to 33 ft. lbs.
   b. Torque the bolts to 47 ft. lbs.
  On the 1972 models:
   a. Torque the bolts to 47 ft. lbs.
   b. Torque the bolts to 55 ft. lbs.
  On 1973–83 models:
   a. Torque the bolts to 30 ft. lbs.
   b. Torque the bolts to 44 ft. lbs.
   c. Torque the bolts to 54–61 ft. lbs.
6. To complete the installation, reverse the removal procedures. Adjust the valves to a preliminary COLD clearance of 0.008 in. for the intake and 0.010 in. for the exhaust. Operate the engine until it is at normal operating temperature, retorque the head bolts (loosen them slightly and retighten to the final torque figure) and adjust the valves to the HOT clearance specifications.

V6 Engine

1. Make sure the No. 1 cylinder is set at TDC on its compression stroke as follows:
   a. Align the crankshaft timing sprocket mark with the mark on the oil pump housing.
   b. The knock pin in the front end of the camshaft should be facing upward.
   NOTE: *DO NOT rotate the crankshaft or the camshaft separately because the valves will hit the piston head.*
2. Using a new cylinder head gasket, install the cylinder head.
   NOTE: *Before installing the cylinder head bolts, apply oil to the thread and the seat portions.*
3. Torque the cylinder head bolts in five steps, using the numerical sequence, by performing the following procedures:
   a. Torque the bolts to 22 ft. lbs. (29 Nm).

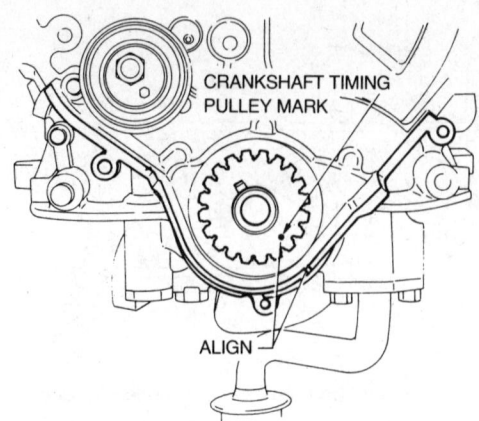

Aligning timing mark and mark on the oil pump housing—V6 engine

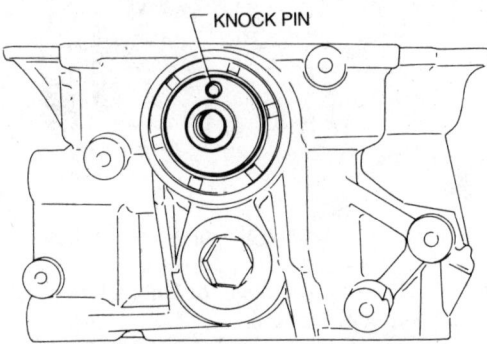

Knockpin of camshaft facing upward—V6 engine

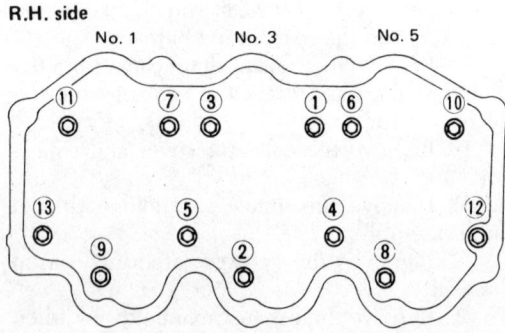

Cylinder head torque sequence—V6 engine

ENGINE AND ENGINE OVERHAUL

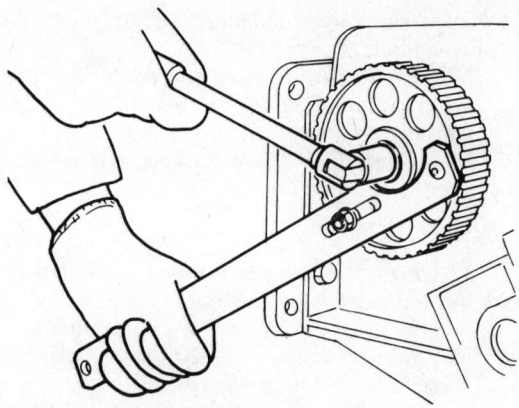

Installing camshaft pulley—V6 engine

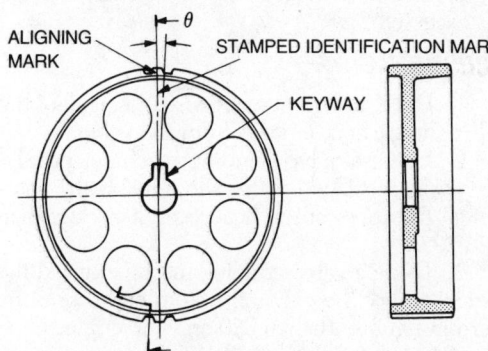

Camshaft pulley alignment marks—V6 engine

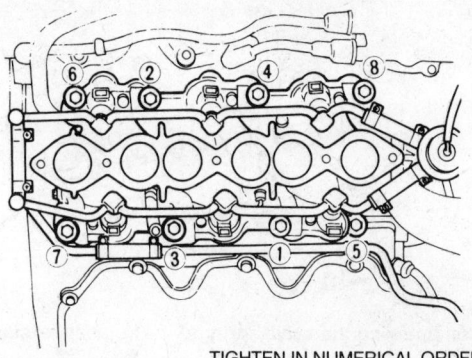

Intake manifold torque sequence—V6 engine

b. Torque the bolts to 43 ft. lbs. (59 Nm).
c. Loosen the bolts completely.
d. Torque the bolts to 22 ft. lbs. (29 Nm).
e. Torque the bolts to 40–47 ft. lbs. (54–64 Nm) or if using an angle wrench, turn the bolts 60–65° clockwise.
4. Tighten the rear timing cover.
5. Install the camshaft pulley and torque the bolt to 58–65 ft. lbs.

NOTE: *The right-hand and the left-hand camshaft pulleys are different parts. Install them in the correct positions. The right-hand pulley has an R3 identification mark and the left-hand has an L3.*

6. Install the timing belt and adjust the tension.
7. Install the front upper and lower belt covers.
8. Install the valve lifters and lifter guide. Hold all valve lifters with a wire as was done during disassembly and install to their original position.
9. Install the rocker shafts with the rocker arms and tighten the rocker shaft bolts to 13–16 ft. lbs., in two or three stages.
10. Install the rocker cover.
11. Install the intake manifold and fuel tube; torque the bolts in two or three stages, in numerical order:
Nuts:
   a. Torque the nuts to 2.2–3.6 ft. lbs. (3–5 Nm).
   b. Torque the nuts to 17–20 ft. lbs. (24–27 Nm).
Bolts:
   a. Torque the bolts to 2.2–3.6 ft. lbs. (3–5 Nm).
   b. Torque the bolts to 12–14 ft. lbs. (16–20 Nm).
12. Install the exhaust manifolds and connecting tube, then torque the fasteners in sequence to 13–16 ft. lbs. Tighten the connector tube to 16–20 ft. lbs.
13. To complete the installation, reverse the removal procedures.

Valves

REMOVAL AND INSTALLATION

All Engines–Except V6

1. Refer to the "Cylinder Head, Removal and Installation" procedures, in this section and remove the cylinder head, then place it on a workbench.
2. Using a medium size pry bar (as a lever) and the camshaft (as the pivot point), compress the valve springs and remove the rocker arms.

NOTE: *If the rocker arms are difficult to remove, it may be necessary to loosen the rocker arm pivot lock nut and screw the pivot down to make clearance. After removing the rocker arms, be careful not to loosen the valve rocker guide.*

3. Remove the camshaft sprocket and the camshaft thrust plate, then remove the camshaft by pulling it through the rear of the cylinder head.

CAUTION: *When removing the camshaft, be careful not to damage the camshaft lobes.*

4. Using the Valve Spring Compressor tool

ENGINE AND ENGINE OVERHAUL

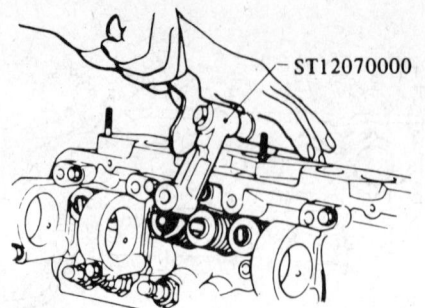

Compressing the valve springs—all engines, except V6

No. ST12070000, compress the valve springs and remove the valve collets.

5. Carefully release the spring pressure, then remove the valve retainers, the springs, the valve and etc.

NOTE: *Be sure to keep the parts in order for installation purposes. Install new valve oil seals.*

6. To install, use new gaskets and reverse the removal procedures.

NOTE: *If the rocker arm pivot lock nut was loosened, the valve clearance must be adjusted.*

V6 Engine

1. Refer to the "Cylinder Head, Removal and Installation" procedures, in this section and remove the cylinder head, then place it on a workbench.

2. Remove the rocker arm assemblies with the valve lifter guide and valve lifter.

NOTE: *When removing the rocker arm assemblies and the valve lifter guide, be sure to keep the parts in order, for they are not interchangeable.*

3. Using the Valve Spring Compressor tool No. KV10110600, mount it on the cylinder head and compress the valve springs, then remove the valve collets.

4. Carefully release the spring pressure, then remove the valves retainers, the springs, the valve and etc.

NOTE: *Be sure to keep the parts in order for installation purposes. Install new valve oil seals.*

5. To install, use new gaskets and reverse the removal procedures.

INSPECTION

1. Check the valves for worn, damaged or deformed valve head or stem.

NOTE: *If the valve head is worn down to a marginal thickness of 0.020 in., replace the valve. The grinding allowance for the valve stem is 0.020 in. (all engines–except V6) or 0.008 in (V6), otherwise replace the valve.*

2. Reface or replace the valve if the damage is excessive.

RESURFACING

1. Using a wire power brush, clean all of the dirt and carbon deposits from the valve.

2. Using a valve grinding machine, grind a new mating face on the valve head; the marginal thickness of the head cannot be less than 0.020 in.

3. Using a valve grinding machine, grind the stem end of the valve; the stem end cannot be ground more than 0.020 in. (all engines–except V6) or 0.008 in. (V6).

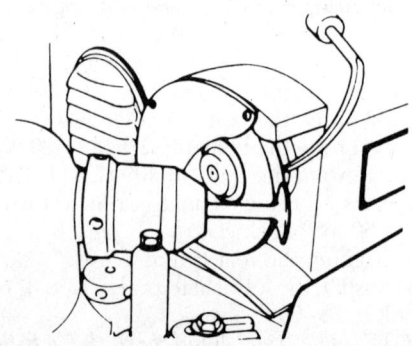

Resurfacing the valve face using a valve grinding machine

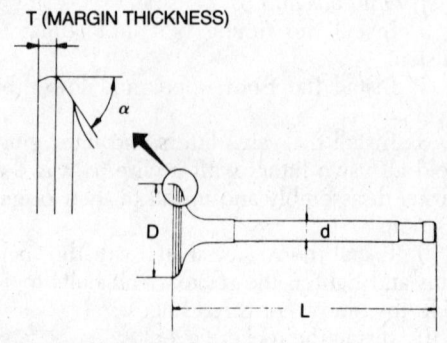

Compressing the valve springs—V6 engine

View of the valve

ENGINE AND ENGINE OVERHAUL

Valve Springs

REMOVAL AND INSTALLATION

Refer to the "Valve, Removal and Installation" procedures, in this section and remove the valve and the springs.

INSPECTION

1. Place the spring(s) on a surface plate and check the squareness, using a steel square.

NOTE: *If the outer spring is out of square more than 0.087 in., replace it. If the inner spring is out of square more than 0.047 in. (all engines–except V6) or 0.075 in., replace it.*

2. Measure the free length of the spring; the outer spring should be 2.00 in., the inner spring should be 1.76 in.

3. Using a spring pressure tester, measure the spring tension; the outer spring should be 1.16 in. @ 108 lbs. (all engines–except V6) or 1.18 in. @ 117.7 lbs. (V6), the inner spring should be 0.96 in. @ 56.2 lbs.

Valve Seats

REMOVAL AND INSTALLATION

1. Check the valve seat inserts for pitting where the valve contacts them and recut the seat or replace it as necessary.

2. Bore the old seat until it collapses, setting the machine depth stop so boring cannot affect the bottom of the insert recess.

3. Select a standard or 0.020 in. (0.5 mm) oversize seat as determined by measuring the cylinder head recess. Machine the recess to the proper size concentric with the valve guide center, according to a measurement of the outside diameter of the seat. Do this at room temperature.

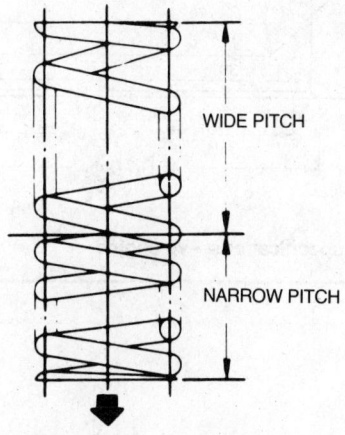

Valve spring assembly—V6 engine

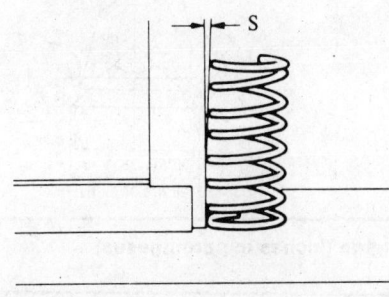

Checking the valve spring for squareness

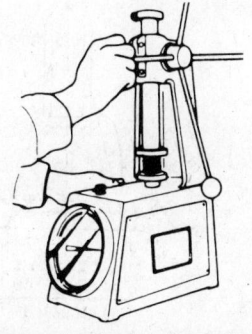

Using a pressure tester to check the valve spring tension

Valve Seat Interference Fit—in. (mm)

Year	Intake	Exhaust
1970–73	0.0031–0.0043 (0.08–0.11)	0.0024–0.0039 (0.06–0.10)
1974–82	0.0032–0.0044 (0.081–0.113)	0.0025–0.0038 (0.064–0.096)

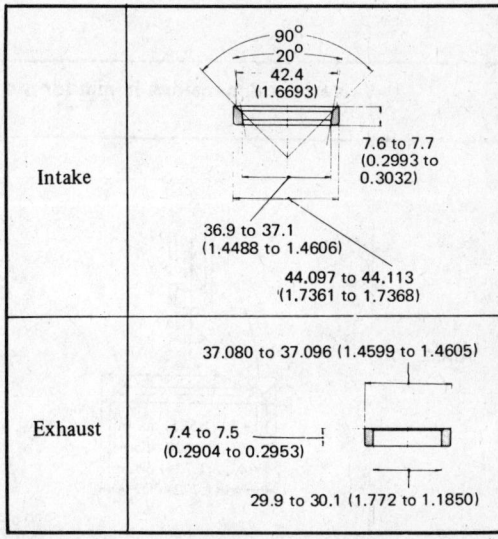

Valve seat dimensions in mm for 1973 engines (inches in parentheses)

104 ENGINE AND ENGINE OVERHAUL

4. Heat the cylinder head to a temperature of 302–320°F (150–160°C).
5. Press fit the insert until it seats on the bottom and caulk more than 4 points.
6. Using a valve seat cutting tool, cut or grind the valve inserts to specifications.

Cylinder Head Recess Diameter—in. (mm)

Year-Type	Intake	Exhaust
1970–72	1.791–1.7918 (45.5–45.52)	1.476–1.4768 (37.5–37.52)
1973		
Standard	1.732–1.734 (43.987–44.003)	1.456–1.458 (36.980–37.036)
Service	1.749–1.751 (44.433–44.487)	1.476–1.478 (37.480–37.536)
1974–82		
Standard	1.7323–1.7329 ① (44.0–44.016)	1.4567–1.4573 (37.0–37.016)
Service	1.7520–1.7526 ② (44.5–44.516)	1.4764–1.4770 (37.5–37.516)

① For 1975–80 1.7717–1.7723 (45.000–45.016)
② For 1977–80 1.7913–1.7920 (45.50–45.516)

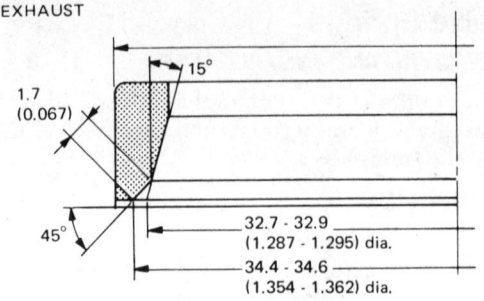
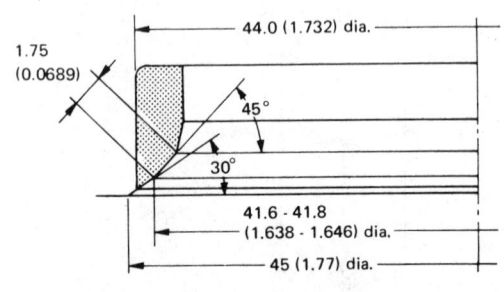

Valve seat specifications—V6 engine

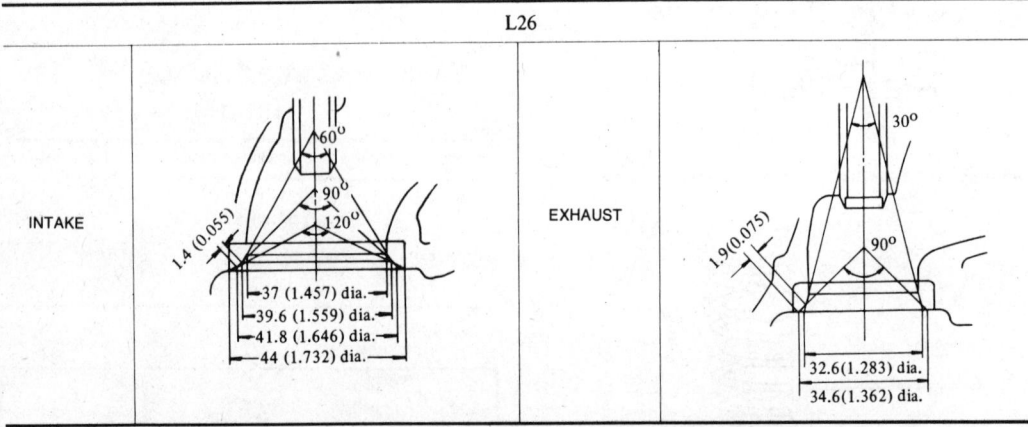

Valve seat dimensions in mm for the 2600 cc engine (inches in parentheses)

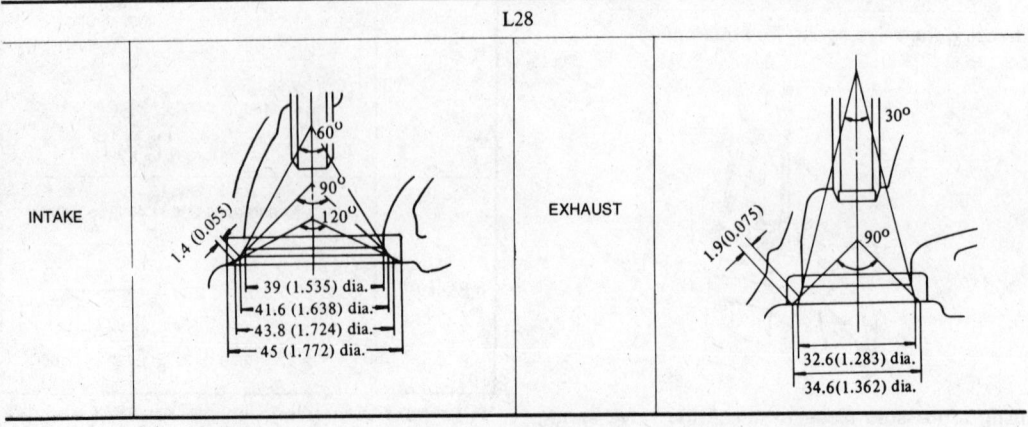

Valve seat dimensions in mm for the 2800 cc engine (inches in parentheses)

ENGINE AND ENGINE OVERHAUL

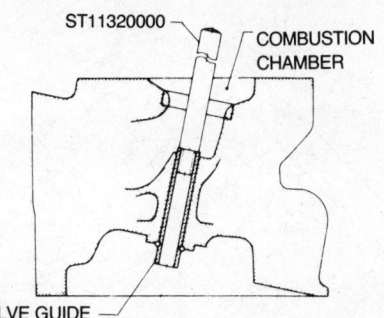

Removing the valve guide from the cylinder head

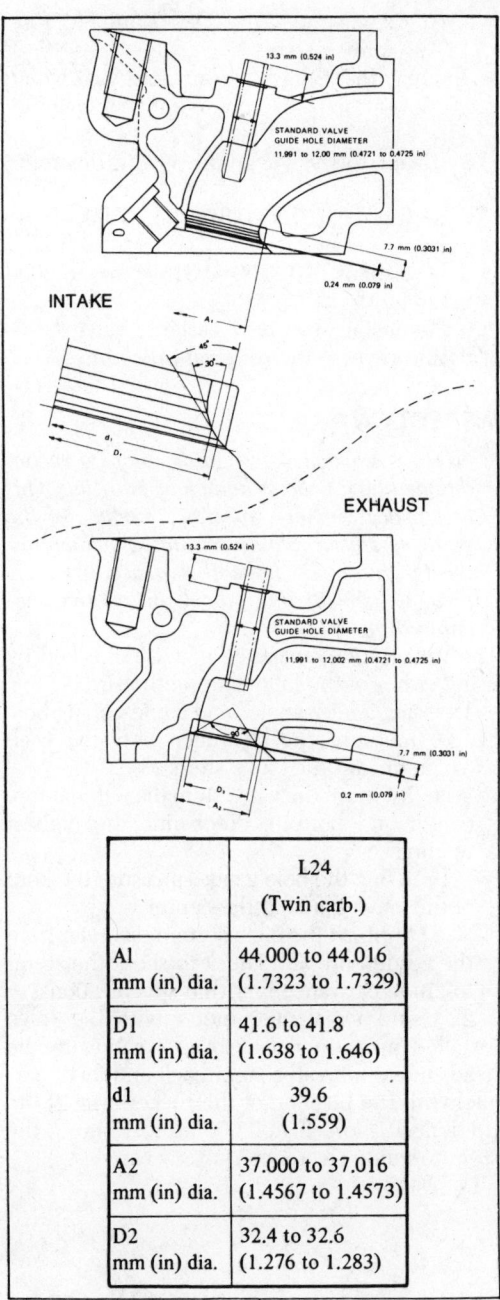

Valve seat dimensions for 1970–72 engines

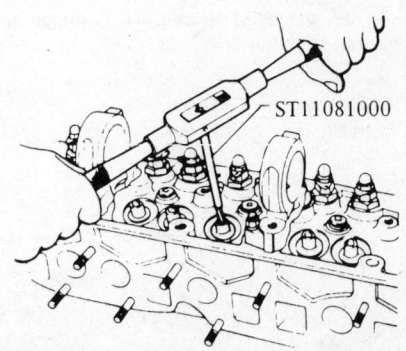

Reaming the valve guide bore—all engines, except V6

	L24 (Twin carb.)
A1 mm (in) dia.	44.000 to 44.016 (1.7323 to 1.7329)
D1 mm (in) dia.	41.6 to 41.8 (1.638 to 1.646)
d1 mm (in) dia.	39.6 (1.559)
A2 mm (in) dia.	37.000 to 37.016 (1.4567 to 1.4573)
D2 mm (in) dia.	32.4 to 32.6 (1.276 to 1.283)

7. After cutting, lap the valve inserts with a lapping compound.

Valve Guides

REMOVAL AND INSTALLATION

All Engines—Except V6

1. Refer to the "Valve Springs, Removal and Installation" procedures, in this section and remove the valve springs.

2. Using an hydraulic press and the Valve Guide Removal tool No. ST11320000, remove the guides that are excessively worn. This requires a press with about two tons of pressure; press toward the rocker arm cover side.

NOTE: *Removing the valve guides is easier to perform if the cylinder head is heated before attempting it.*

3. If using heat, allow the head to cool to room temperature and ream the guide hole to 0.4794–0.4802 in. (12.185–12.196 mm).

4. Heat the cylinder head to 302–392°F (150–200°C), then press 0.008 in. (0.2 mm) oversize guides into the head. Interference fit of the guide should be 0.0011–0.0019 in. (0.027–0.049 mm).

5. Using the Valve Guide Reamer tool No. ST11081000, ream the bore of the new guides to 0.3150–0.3157 in. (8.000–8.018 mm).

6. Correct the valve seat surface as described under "Valve Seat, Removal and Installation" if a new seat is not required.

7. To install, use new gaskets, valve guide seals and reverse the removal procedures.

V6 Engine

1. Refer to the "Valve Springs, Removal and Installation" procedures, in this section and remove the valve springs.

2. Heat the cylinder head to at least 320°F, then drive out the guide using an arbor press or a hammer and drift punch.

106 ENGINE AND ENGINE OVERHAUL

Removing the valve guide using a hammer and a suitable tool—V6 engine

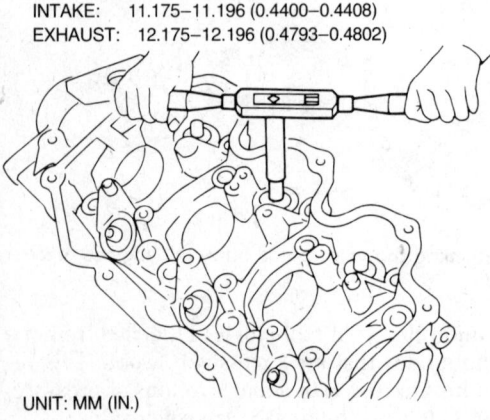

Reaming the valve guide hole—V6 engine

Installation of the service valve guide onto the cylinder head—V6 engine

NOTE: *Drive the valve guides toward the rocker arm cover side of the cylinder head.*

3. With the valve guides removed, ream the cylinder head valve guide hole (inside diameter) to:

    a. Intake: 0.4400–0.4408 in. (11.175–11.196 mm)

    b. Exhaust: 0.4793–0.4802 in. (12.175–12.196 mm)

4. Heat the cylinder to at least 320°F and press the service valve guide onto the cylinder head.

5. Ream the valve guide (inside diameter) to:

    a. Intake: 0.2756–0.2763 in. (7.000–7.018 mm)

    b. Exhaust: 0.3150–0.3157 in. (8.000–8.018 mm)

6. To install, use new gaskets, valve guide seals and reverse the removal procedures.

INSPECTION

NOTE: *A worn valve guide may be reconditioned by a process known as knurling: This is a process where the inner surface of the guide is raised, thus creating a smaller diameter bore. To have this procedure performed, consult your local automotive machine shop.*

The valve guide clearance may be checked by using either of the following methods:

1. Using a micrometer and a telescoping hole gauge, measure the clearance between each valve guide and the valve stem.

    a. Measure the valve stem diameter at top, center and bottom; determine the highest reading.

    b. Using the hole gauge, measure the bore of the valve guide at the center.

    c. Subtract the highest stem diameter from the guide bore and check to see if the stem-to-guide clearance is within specifications.

2. Using a dial micrometer with the valve installed in it's normal closed position in the head, move the valve stem back-and-forth parallel with the position of the rocker arm. If the tip deflects more than 0.008 in. (0.19 mm), the stem-to-guide clearance is excessive.

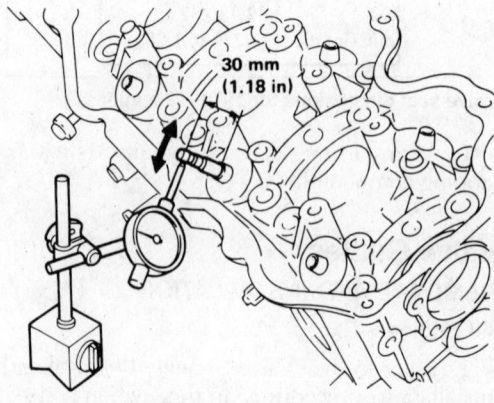

Using a dial gauge to measure valve guide clearance—V6 engine

ENGINE AND ENGINE OVERHAUL

Oil Pan

REMOVAL AND INSTALLATION

All Engines—Except V6

1. If the engine is in the vehicle, attach a lift, support the engine and remove the engine mounting bolts as described in the "Engine, Removal and Installation" procedures.
2. Raise the engine slightly, watching to make sure that the hoses or wires are not damaged.
3. Drain the engine oil.
4. Remove the oil pan bolts and slide the pan out to the rear.
5. Using a putty knife, clean the gasket mounting surfaces.
6. To install, use a new oil pan gasket (coat both sides with silicone sealant). Torque the pan bolts to 4–7 ft. lbs., in a circular pattern from the center to the ends. Over-tightening will distort the pan lip, causing leakage. Refill the oil pan with new oil.

NOTE: *Before installing the oil pan, apply a thin bead of silicone sealant to the engine block at the junctions of the block-to-front cover and the block-to-main bearing cap.*

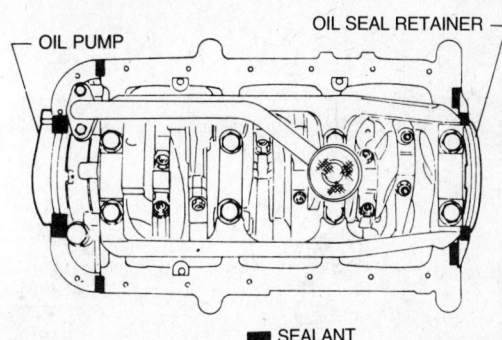

Apply sealant to these areas before installing the oil pan gasket—V6 engine

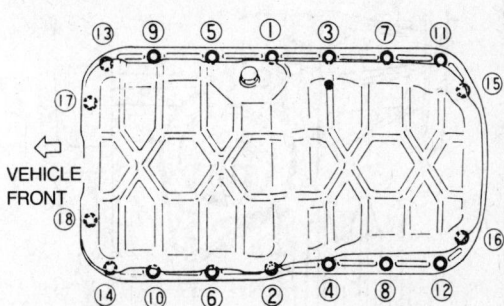

Oil pan bolt tightening sequence—V6 engine

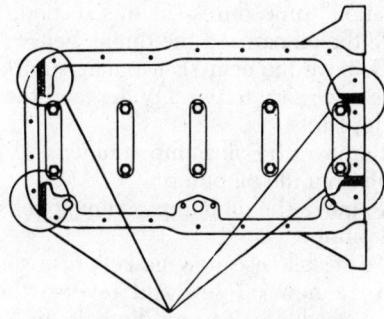

Apply sealant to these areas before installing the pan gasket on the block—all except V6 engine

V6 Engine

1. Drain the engine oil.
2. Raise and support the vehicle on jack stands.
3. Remove the front stabilizer bar retaining nuts and bolts from the suspension crossmember.
4. Remove the steering column shaft from the gear housing.
5. Remove the tension rod retaining nuts from the transverse link.
6. Using a vertical lifting device, raise and support the engine.
7. Remove the rear plate cover from the transmission case.
8. Remove the oil pan retaining bolts.
9. Remove the suspension crossmember retaining bolts.
10. Remove the strut mounting insulator retaining nuts.
11. Remove the screws retaining the refrigerant lines and power steering tubes to the suspension crossmember.
12. Lower the suspension crossmember.
13. Remove the oil pan from the rear-side.
14. Using a putty knife, clean the gasket mounting surfaces.
15. To install, use a new oil pan gasket (coat both sides with silicone sealant) and reverse the removal procedures. Torque the pan retaining bolts to 3.5–5.1 ft. lbs., in numerical order. Refill the crankcase with new oil.

NOTE: *Before installing the oil pan, apply sealant to the surface points indicated in the illustration.*

Oil Pump

REMOVAL AND INSTALLATION

1970–79

1. Rotate the crankshaft until the No. 1 cylinder is at the TDC on the compression stroke.
2. Drain the crankcase oil. Remove the splash shield, if equipped.
3. Remove the high-tension wires and the distributor.

ENGINE AND ENGINE OVERHAUL

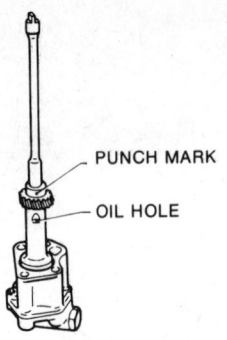

Lining up the marks on the oil pump and the distributor drive spindle—in-line 6 cyl engine

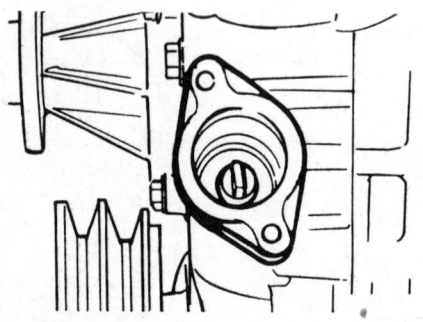

Proper alignment of the distributor drive spindle—in-line 6 cyl engine

4. Remove the oil pump bolts and pull the pump out.
5. To install, use a new oil pump gasket and perform the following:
   a. Fill the oil pump housing with clean engine oil.
   b. Align the drive pump hole and spindle mark by turning the spindle. Then, turn the spindle one gear tooth to the right.
   c. Install the pump and torque the mounting bolts to 8.0–10.8 ft. lbs.
   d. The projection on top of the spindle should now be at the 11:25 o'clock position, with the smaller half of the spindle facing forward.
   e. Reinstall the splash shield. Refill the crankcase with new oil.
   f. Reinstall the distributor and the hold-down bolt, carefully rotating the rotor back-and-forth until the bottom of the distributor shaft engages the projection on top of the oil pump spindle.

1980–83

1. Drain the crankcase oil.
2. Turn the crankshaft so that the No. 1 piston is at TDC of the compression stroke.
3. Remove the distributor cap and mark the position of the distributor rotor in relation to the distributor base with a piece of chalk.
4. If equipped, remove the front stabilizer bar. Remove the splash shield.
5. Remove the oil pump body with the drive spindle assembly.
6. To install, fill the pump housing with engine oil, align the punch mark on the spindle with the hole in the oil pump. The No. 1 piston should be at TDC of the compression stroke.
7. Install a new gasket (placed over the drive spindle), the oil pump and the drive spindle assembly, making sure the tip of the drive spindle fits into the distributor shaft notch securely. The distributor rotor should align with the chalk mark made earlier.
NOTE: *Great care must be taken not to disturb the distributor rotor while installing the oil pump or the ignition timing may be wrong.*
8. To complete the installation procedures, reverse the removal procedures.

1984 and Later

1. Refer to the "Oil Pan, Removal and Installation" and the "Timing Belt, Removal and Installation" procedures, in this section, then remove the oil pan and the timing belt.
2. Remove the crankshaft timing sprocket (it may be necessary to use a puller) and the timing belt plate.
3. Remove the oil pump strainer and pick-up tube from the oil pump.
4. Remove the oil pump retaining bolts and the oil pump.
5. To install, use new gaskets (use silicone sealant), a new oil seal and reverse the removal procedures. Torque the bolts to 4–5 ft. lbs. (6 mm) or to 9–12 ft. lbs. (8 mm). Refill the crankcase.
NOTE: *Before installing the oil pump, be sure to pack the pump's cavity with petroleum jelly, then make sure the O-ring is properly fitted.*

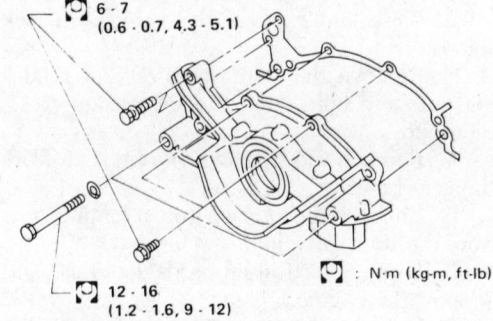

Oil pump installation—V6 engine

ENGINE AND ENGINE OVERHAUL

Timing Belt/Chain Cover and Seal
REMOVAL AND INSTALLATION

All Engines—Except V6

1. Disconnect the negative battery cable and drain the coolant. Remove the radiator hoses, the automatic transmission cooler lines (if equipped), the radiator and the shroud.
2. If equipped with power steering, unbolt the pump and move it aside. DO NOT disconnect any of the hoses. Remove the pump mounting bracket from the engine. Remove the idler adjusting bracket from the engine.
3. If equipped with an air pump, remove the pump and bracket.
4. If equipped with air conditioning, remove the idler pulley bracket and the belt. Unbolt the two lower compressor mounting bolts and support the compressor, then remove the two upper bolts and the mounting bracket.

NOTE: *Support the compressor in such a way that stress will not be placed on the hoses. DO NOT disconnect any of the compressor hoses or lines.*

5. Remove the distributor.
6. Remove the oil pump attaching bolts, the pump and it's drive spindle. Refer to the "Engine Lubrication" section for details.
7. Remove the engine cooling fan and the pulley, together with the drive belt, then remove the water pump.
8. Remove the crankshaft pulley bolt and the pulley, lock-up the engine to do this. The best way is to remove the flywheel inspection cover between the engine and transmission, then lock the flywheel with a tool made for the purpose. These are available in auto parts stores.
9. Remove the front cover-to-cylinder block bolts, the four bolts retaining the oil pan to the front cover and the two bolts screwed down through the front of the cylinder head into the top of the front cover.
10. Carefully pry the front cover off the engine.
11. Cut the exposed front section of the oil pan gasket away from the oil pan. Do the same to the gasket at the top of the front cover. Remove the two side gaskets and clean all the mating surfaces thoroughly.
12. Cut the portions needed from a new oil pan gasket and top front cover gasket.
13. Apply sealant to all of the gaskets and position them on the engine in their proper places.
14. To replace the oil seal, perform the following:

   a. Using a pointed piece of plastic or wood, pry the old seal from the cover. DO NOT use a screwdriver or other metal tools, which will damage the sealing lip.

   b. Oil the lip of the new seal; DO NOT use grease. Press the seal into place, making sure the flat side faces forward and the lip faces the front of the engine. Use a seal driver made for the purpose (if possible) or a socket of the proper diameter.

   c. Oil the crankshaft and the newly installed seal, then install the front cover.

15. Carefully mount the front cover to the engine. Install the mounting bolts and torque the bolts to 7–12 ft. lbs. (8 mm) or to 3–6 ft. lbs. (6 mm) and the oil pan bolts to 4–7 ft. lbs.
16. Before installing the oil pump, place the gasket over the shaft and make sure that the mark on the drive spindle faces (aligns with) the oil pump hole. Install the oil pump so that the projection on the top of the shaft is located in the exact position as when it was removed or is in the 11:25 o'clock position with the piston in the No. 1 cylinder placed at TDC on the compression stroke (if the engine was disturbed). This will ensure proper distributor timing. Torque the oil pump bolts to 8–10 ft. lbs.

NOTE: *For further information on the oil*

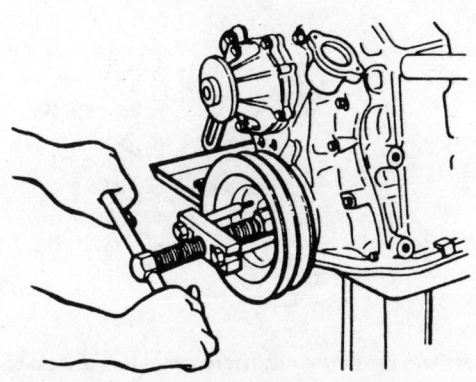

Removing the crankshaft pulley with a puller—except V6 engine

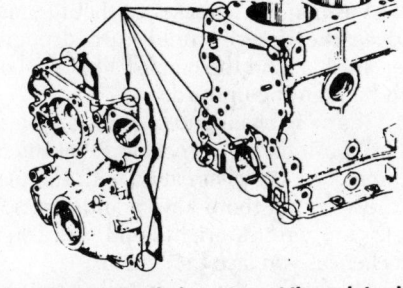

Apply sealant to the timing cover at the points shown—except V6 engine

110 ENGINE AND ENGINE OVERHAUL

pump, refer to the "Oil Pump, Removal and Installation" procedures, in this section.

17. To complete the installation, reverse the removal procedures.

V6 Engine

NOTE: *The front oil seal is a part of the oil pump assembly. To replace the oil pump seal, refer to the "Oil Pump, Removal and Installation" procedures, in this section and replace the oil seal.*

1. Remove the radiator shroud, the fan and the pulleys.
2. Drain the coolant from the radiator and remove the water pump hose.
3. Remove the power steering, compressor and alternator drive belts.
4. Remove the front upper and lower belt covers.
5. To install, reverse the removal procedures.

Timing Belt/Chain and Tensioner
REMOVAL AND INSTALLATION
All Engines–Except V6

1. Before beginning any disassembly procedures, position the No. 1 cylinder at TDC on the compression stroke.
2. Remove the front cover and the rocker arm cover.
3. With the No. 1 cylinder at TDC, the timing marks on the camshaft sprocket and the timing chain should be visible. Mark both of them with paint. Also mark the relationship of the camshaft sprocket to the camshaft. At this point you will see that there are three sets of timing marks and locating holes in the sprocket. They are for making adjustments to compensate for the timing chain stretch.

NOTE: *When adjusting the timing chain, refer to the "Timing Chain, Adjustment" procedures, in this section for details.*

4. With the timing marks on the cam sprocket clearly marked, locate and mark the timing marks on the crankshaft sprocket. Also mark the chain timing mark.
5. Unbolt the camshaft sprocket and remove the sprocket along with the chain. When removing the chain, hold it where the chain tensioner contacts it. When the chain is removed, the tensioner is going to come apart. Hold on to it and you won't lose any of the parts.

NOTE: *The crankshaft sprocket can be removed with a puller, if necessary. There is no need to remove the chain guide unless it is being replaced.*

6. To install the timing chain and the cam-

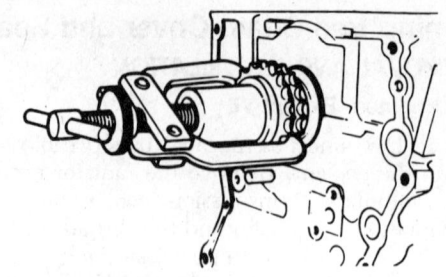

Removing the crankshaft sprocket with a puller–in-line 6 cyl engine

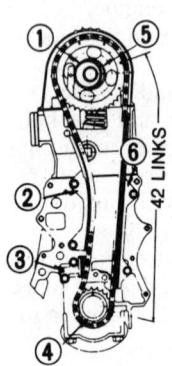

1. Fuel pump drive cam
2. Chain guide
3. Chain tensioner
4. Crank sprocket
5. Cam sprocket
6. Chain guide

Installing the timing chain. The number of "links" refers to the pins–in-line 6 cyl engine

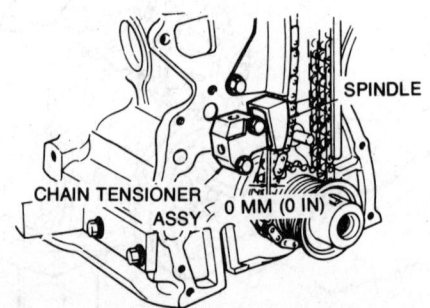

Installing the timing chain tensioner–in-line 6 cyl engine

shaft sprocket together, after first positioning the chain over the crankshaft sprocket, perform the following:

a. Position the sprocket so that the marks made earlier line up (undisturbed engine). The camshaft and the crankshaft keys should both be pointing upward.

b. If a new chain and/or gear is being installed, position the sprocket so that the timing marks on the chain align with the marks on the sprocket (both keys pointing up); the marks are on the right-hand side of the sprockets as you face the engine.

c. When the chain is installed correctly, there will be 42 links between the mating marks of the chain and sprockets (1970–78)

ENGINE AND ENGINE OVERHAUL

  d. The 1979–83 engines have two marked links which align with the marks on the sprockets, as an aid to proper timing.

  e. Count the links; this is an important step. If the exact number of links between the timing marks are not correct, the valve timing will be off and the engine will either not run at all or run very badly.

7. Install the chain tensioner. Adjust the protrusion of the chain tensioner spindle to zero clearance.

8. To complete the installation, use a new oil seal and reverse removal procedures.

V6 Engine

1. Refer to the "Timing Belt/Chain Cover and Seal, Removal and Installation" procedures, in this section and remove the timing belt covers.

2. Turn the crankshaft so that the No. 1 cylinder is at the TDC of the compression stroke.

3. Using chalk or paint, mark the relationship of the timing belt to the camshaft and the crankshaft sprockets; also, mark the timing belt's direction of rotation.

4. Loosen the timing belt tensioner and return spring, then remove the timing belt.

CAUTION: *Before installing the timing belt, confirm that the No. 1 cylinder is set at the TDC of the compression stroke.*

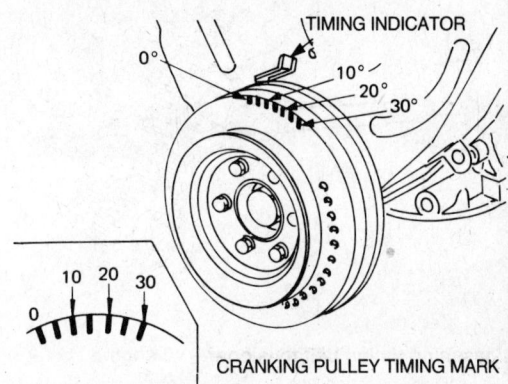

Crankshaft pulley timing mark—V6 engine

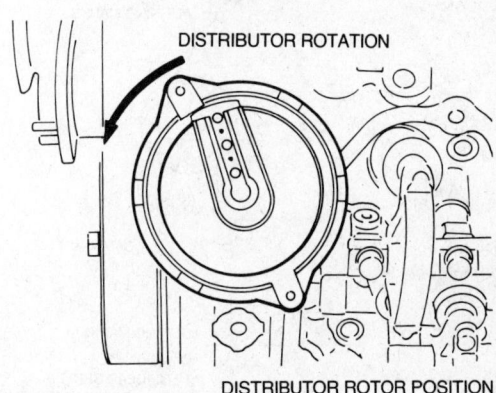

Distributor rotor position—V6 engine

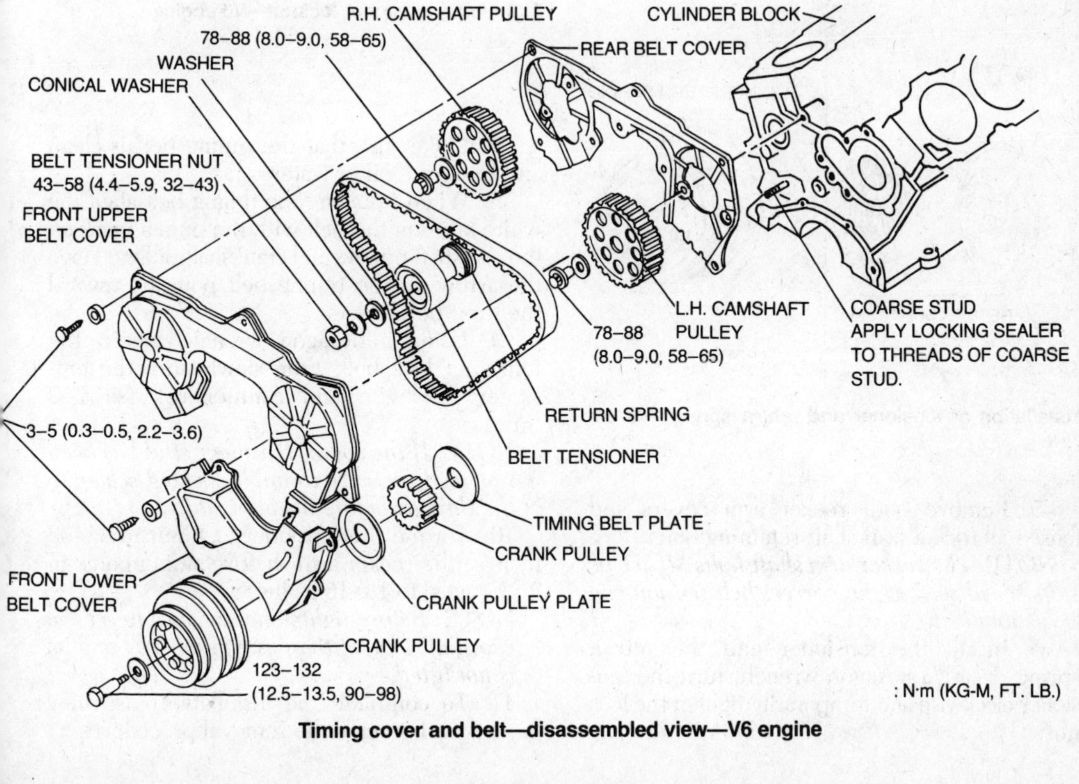

Timing cover and belt—disassembled view—V6 engine

112 ENGINE AND ENGINE OVERHAUL

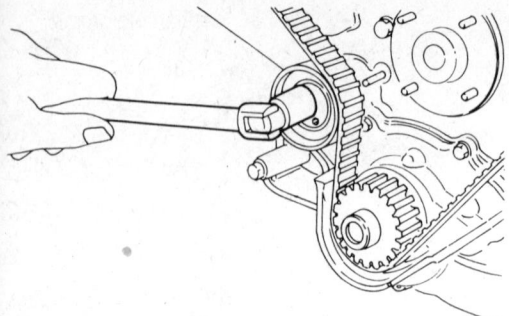

Loosening timing belt tensioner—V6 engine

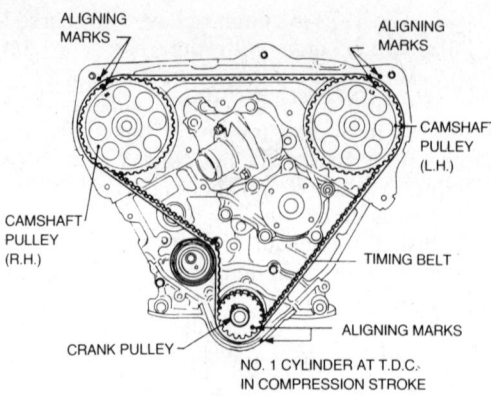

Aligning timing belt white lines with marks on camshaft and crankshaft pulleys—V6 engine

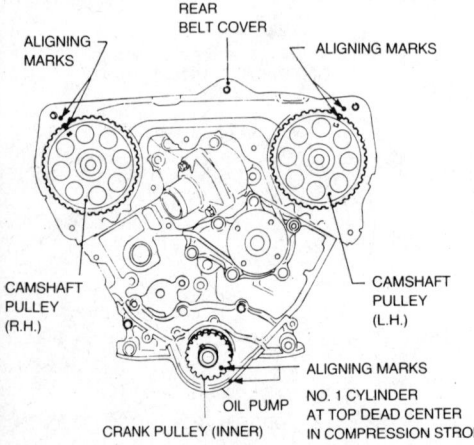

Align camshaft and crankshaft pulley marks—V6 engine

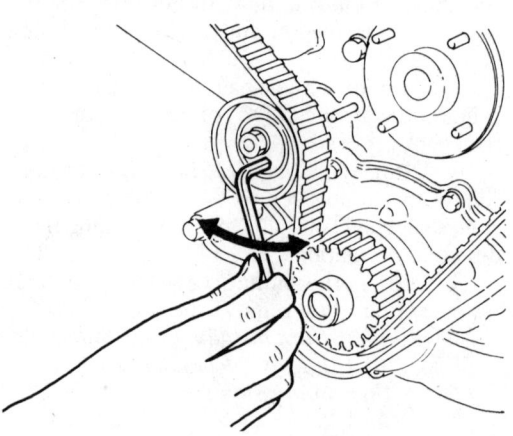

Tightening tensioner locknut—V6 engine

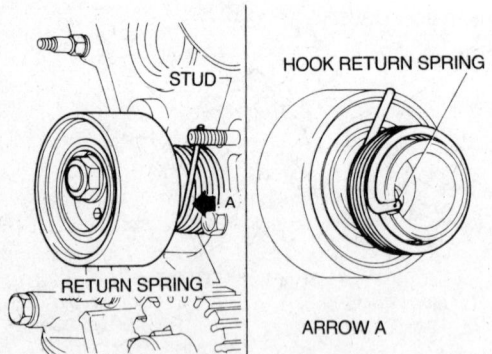

Installation of tensioner and return spring—V6 engine

5. Remove both rocker arm covers and loosen all rocker arm shaft retaining bolts.
NOTE: *The rocker arm shaft bolts MUST be loosened so that the correct belt tension can be obtained.*
6. Install the tensioner and the return spring. Using a hexagon wrench, turn the tensioner clockwise and temporarily tighten the lock nut.

7. Make sure that the timing belt is clean and free from oil or water.
8. When installing the timing belt align the white lines on the belt with the punch mark on the camshaft pulleys and crankshaft pulley. Have the arrow on the timing belt pointing toward the front belt covers.
9. Using a hexagon wrench, loosen the tensioner lock bolt, then slowly turn the tensioner clockwise and counterclockwise 2–3 times.
NOTE: *If the coarse tensioner stud has been removed, be sure to apply locking sealer to the threads before installing it.*
10. Torque the tensioner lock nut to 32–43 ft. lbs., the rocker arm shaft retaining bolts (in 2–3 stages) to 13–16 ft. lbs.
NOTE: *Before tightening, be sure to set the camshaft lobe at the position where the lobe is not lifted.*
11. To complete the installation, use new gaskets and reverse the removal procedures.

ENGINE AND ENGINE OVERHAUL

TIMING CHAIN ADJUSTMENT
All Engines—Except V6

When the timing chain stretches excessively, the valve timing will be incorrect. There are three sets of holes and timing marks on the camshaft sprocket which are provided to correct the valve timing.

If the stretch of the chain roller links is excessive, adjust the camshaft sprocket location by transferring the camshaft set position of the camshaft sprocket from the factory position of No. 1 to No. 2 or 3 as follows:

1. Turn the crankshaft until the No. 1 cylinder is at TDC of the compression stroke. Check to see if the camshaft sprocket locating notch is to the left of the oblong groove on the camshaft retaining plate.

NOTE: *If the notch is to the left of the groove in the retaining plate, then the chain is stretched and needs to be adjusted.*

2. Remove the camshaft sprocket together with the chain and install the sprocket and chain with the locating dowel on the camshaft inserted into either of the other two holes in the sprocket. Use the No. 2 or No. 3 hole, depending on how badly the chain is stretched.

NOTE: *If the chain stretch could be corrected by moving the sprocket to the No. 2 position, then the locating dowel on the camshaft would be inserted into the No. 2 hole of the sprocket and the timing mark on the chain would be aligned with the No. 2 mark on the sprocket. The amount of modification for each location is 4° of crankshaft rotation.*

3. Recheck the valve timing as outlined in Step 1 of this procedure. The notch in the sprocket should be to the right of the groove in the camshaft retaining plate.

4. If or when the notch cannot be brought to the right of the groove with the sprocket installed in the No. 3 hole, the timing chain must be replaced to gain the proper valve timing.

Camshaft Sprocket/Pulleys
REMOVAL AND INSTALLATION
All Engines—Except V6

1. Refer to the "Timing Belt/Chain and tensioner, Removal and Installation" procedures, in this section and remove the timing chain with the camshaft sprocket.

NOTE: *The engines are designed so that the camshaft sprocket MUST be removed at the same time that the timing chain is removed.*

2. To install, use new gaskets and reverse the removal procedures. If necessary, adjust the timing chain.

V6 Engine

1. Refer to the "Timing Belt/Chain and tensioner, Removal and Installation" procedures, in this section and remove the timing belt.

2. Using an adjustable spanner wrench (to hold the camshaft pulley) and a socket wrench, remove the camshaft pulley bolt and washer.

3. Pull the camshaft pulley(s) from the camshaft(s). Be careful not to lose the woodruff key.

NOTE: *The R.H. and L.H. camshaft pulleys are different parts. Install them in their correct positions. The R.H. pulley has an R3 identification mark and the L.H. has an L3.*

4. To install the camshaft pulleys, perform the following:

   a. Remove the rocker arm covers.
   b. Loosen the rocker arm shaft assembly bolts.
   c. Remove the spark plugs.
   d. Install the camshaft pulleys by reversing the removal procedures.

5. Install and adjust the timing belt.

6. To complete the installation, reverse the removal procedures.

Camshaft And Bearings
REMOVAL AND INSTALLATION
All Engines—Except V6

1. Refer to the "Cylinder Head, Removal and Installation" procedures, in this section and remove the cylinder head.

2. To remove the valve rocker arms, perform the following:

   a. Remove the valve rocker spring.
   b. Loosen the rocker arm pivot locknut; loosen the adjustment as far as possible. Using a medium pry bar, depress the valve spring and remove the rocker arm.

3. Remove the camshaft locating plate.

4. Pull the camshaft slowly out toward the rear of the head, being especially careful to avoid damaging the lobes and bearings.

5. To install the camshaft, perform the following:

   a. Coat the camshaft bearings and the cam

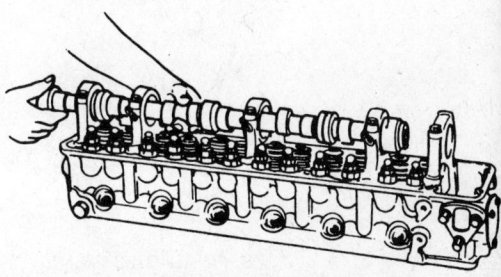

Installing the camshaft—all except V6 engine

ENGINE AND ENGINE OVERHAUL

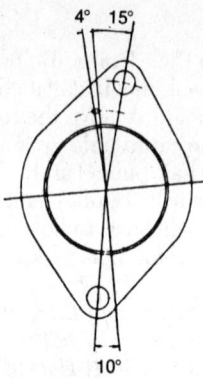

The camshaft locating plate—all except V6 engine

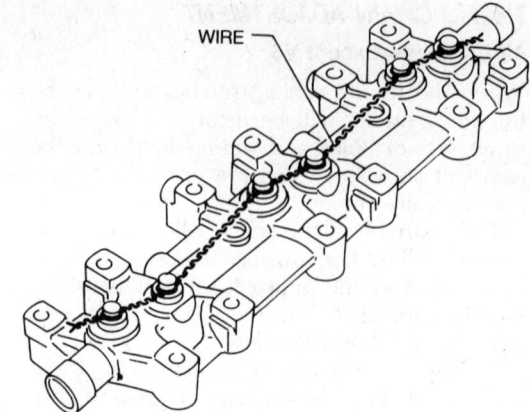

Hold the valve lifters with wire—V6 engine

lobes with clean motor oil. Carefully slide the camshaft in place in the camshaft carrier.

b. Install the camshaft locating plate with the groove in the upward position.

6. To complete the installation, use new gaskets and reverse the removal procedures. Adjust the timing chain (if necessary) and the valve rocker arm pivots.

V6 Engine

1. Refer to the "Cylinder Head, Removal and Installation" procedures, in this section and remove the cylinder head.
2. Remove the rocker shafts with the rocker arms; loosen the bolts in two or three stages.
3. Remove the hydraulic valve lifters and lifter guide.

NOTE: *Hold the valve lifters with wire so that they will not drop from the lifter guide. Put an identification mark on the lifters to avoid mixing them up.*

4. At the rear of the cylinder head, remove the cylinder head rear cover, the camshaft bolt and the locating plate.

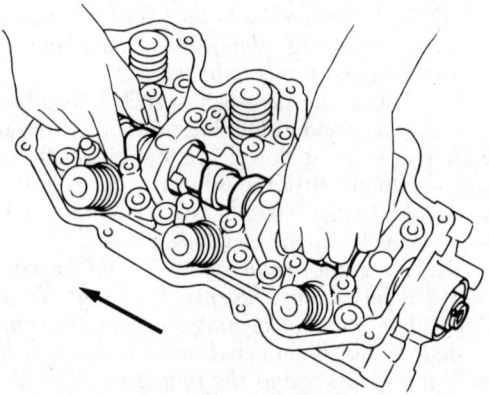

Remove the camshaft in direction of arrow—V6 engine

5. Remove the camshaft and the camshaft oil seal through the front of the cylinder head.
6. Using a putty knife, clean the gasket mounting surfaces.

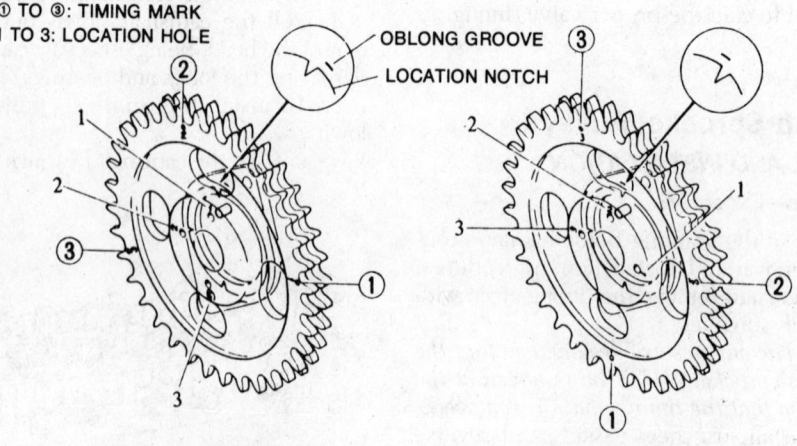

Camshaft sprocket adjustment location—all except V6 engine

ENGINE AND ENGINE OVERHAUL 115

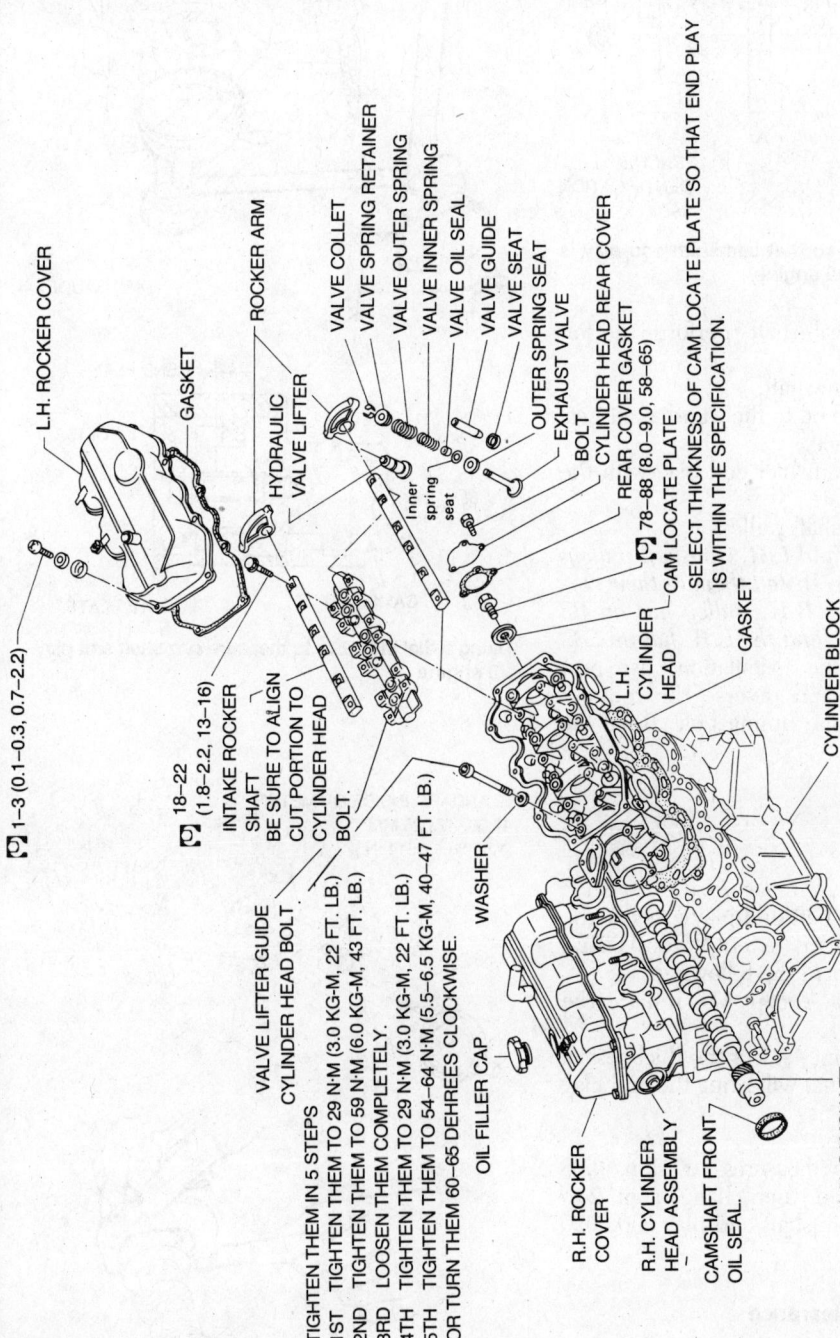

Exploded view of cylinder head and block—V6 engine

116 ENGINE AND ENGINE OVERHAUL

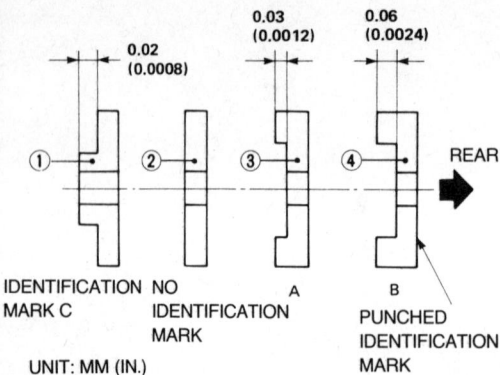

Select shim thickness so that camshaft end play is within specification—V6 engine

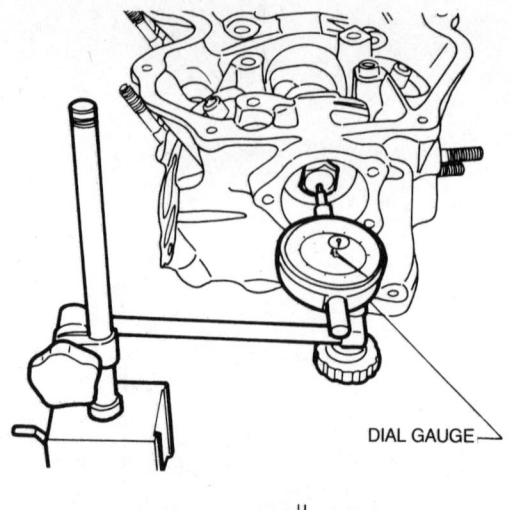

DIAL GAUGE

7. To install the camshaft, perform the following:
   a. Install the camshaft.
   b. Apply engine oil to the camshaft oil seal and install it in place.
   c. Adjust the camshaft end play with the correct locating plate.
8. Install the camshaft pulleys.
NOTE: *The R.H. and L.H. camshaft pulleys are different parts. Install them in their correct positions. The R.H. pulley has an R3 identification mark and the L.H. has an L3.*
9. To complete the installation, use new gaskets, an oil seal and reverse the removal procedures. Adjust the timing belt. Refill the cooling system.

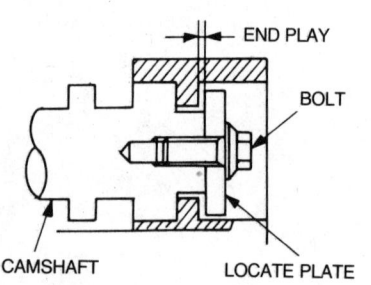

Using a dial indicator to measure camshaft end play—V6 engine

INSPECTION

Camshaft End Play

Using a dial indicator, measure the camshaft end play. If the camshaft end play exceeds the limit of 0.0031–0.0150 in. (except V6) or 0.0012–0.0024 in. (V6), perform the following:

1. On all engines—except V6, replace the thrust plate.
2. On the V6 engine, select the thickness of a cam locating plate that will bring the end play within specifications.
   Example:
   If camshaft end play measures 0.0031 in. (0.08 mm) with shim 2 used, then change shim 2 to shim 3 so that the camshaft end play is 0.0020 in. (0.05 mm).

Camshaft Journal Clearance

Using an internal dial indicator, measure the inside diameter of the camshaft bearings in the head; using a micrometer, measure the diameter of the camshaft journals.
   Standard Inside Diameter:
   • 1.8898–1.8904 in. (48.000–48.016 mm), for all engines—except V6.

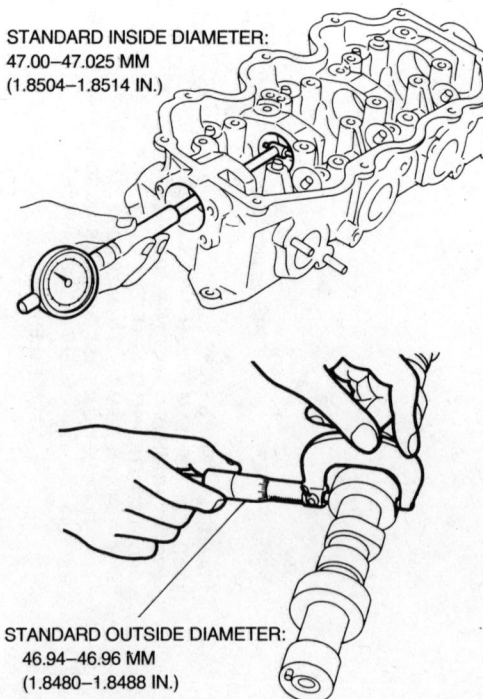

Measuring the camshaft journal clearance—V6 engine

ENGINE AND ENGINE OVERHAUL

- 1.8504–1.8514 in. (47.00–47.025 mm), for V6 engines.

Standard Outside Diameter:
- 1.8878–1.8883 in. (47.949–47.962 mm), for all engines—except V6.
- 1.8478–1.8486 in. (46.94–46.96 mm), for V6 engines.
- Wear limit: 0.0059 in. (0.15 mm).

Camshaft Runout

1. Place the camshaft (using the camshaft journals) onto a set of V-blocks.
2. Using a dial indicator, place it so that it rides on the camshaft journal.
3. Turn the camshaft and measure the runout of the camshaft journals.
4. The maximum runout is 0.004 in. (0.1 mm).

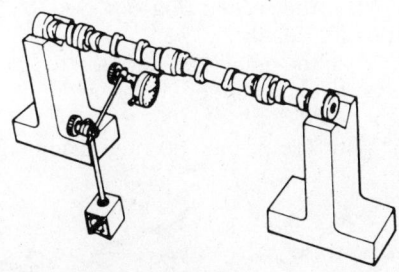

Checking the camshaft runout

Pistons and Connecting Rods

REMOVAL AND INSTALLATION

1. Refer the "Engine, Removal and Installation" procedures, in this section, then remove the engine and secure it to a workstand.
2. Remove the cylinder head and the oil pan.
3. Using a ridge reamer tool, remove any carbon buildup from the cylinder wall at the top end of the piston travel.
4. Position the piston to be removed at the bottom of it's stroke so that the connecting rod bearing cap can be reached easily from under the engine.
5. Unscrew the connecting rod bearing cap,

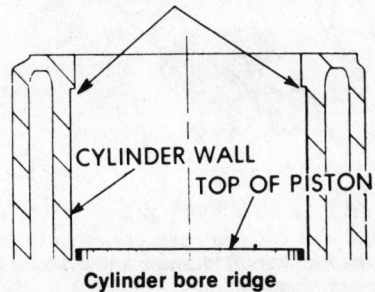

Cylinder bore ridge

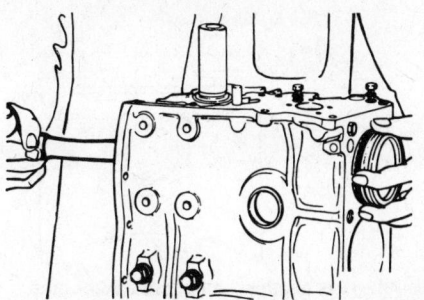

Removing the piston and connecting rod assembly from the cylinder block

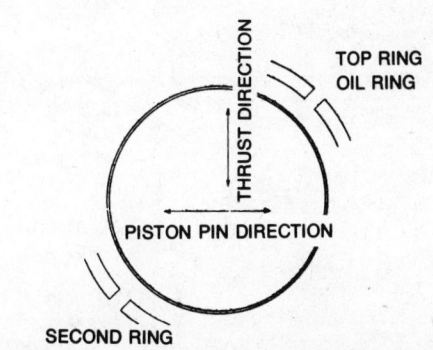

Arrangement of the piston ring gaps around the piston, 1970–78

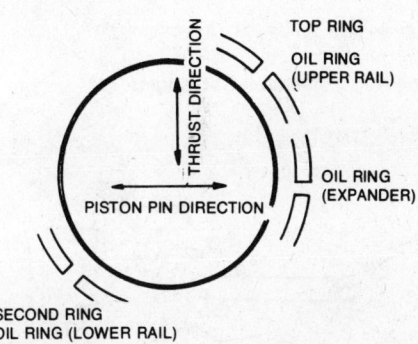

Arrangement of the piston ring gaps around the piston, 1979–83

then remove the cap and lower half of the bearing.

NOTE: *It is advisable to number the pistons, connecting rods and bearing caps in some manner so that they can be reinstalled in the same cylinder, facing the same direction, from which they are removed.*

6. Push the piston/connecting rod assembly up and out of the cylinder block with a length of wood. Use care not to scratch the cylinder wall with the connecting rod or the wooden tool.
7. Keep all of the components from each cylinder together and install them in the cylinder from which they were removed.

118 ENGINE AND ENGINE OVERHAUL

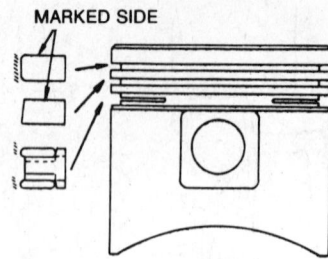

Piston ring installation—all except V6 engine

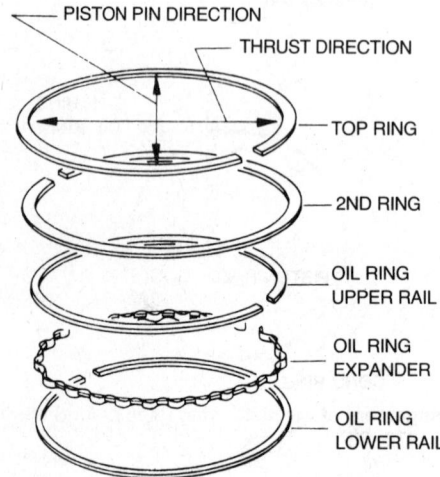

MARK SHOULD BE FACING UPWARD.

Piston ring installation—V6 engine

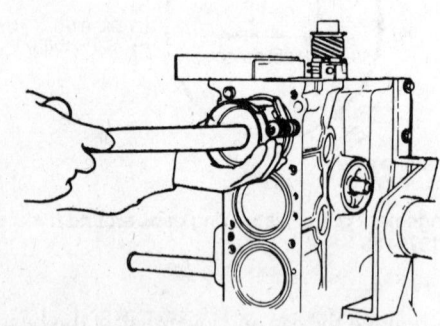

Installing piston and connecting rod—typical

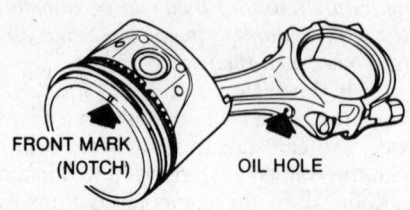

Piston and connecting rod identification and positioning—typical

8. Coat the bearing face of the connecting rod and the outer face of the pistons with engine oil.

9. When installing the piston, align them according to the following procedure:

    a. On the 1970–78 engines, turn the top compression ring to bring it's gap to about the 1:30 o'clock position. Set the remaining rings so that their gaps are positioned 180° apart around the piston. The oil ring gap will be directly under the top compression ring gap.

    b. On 1979 and later engines, set the top ring gap at the 1:00 o'clock position. Position the second ring gap 180° opposite the top ring gap. The top oil ring rail gap should then be placed under the top ring gap, the expander ring should be at the 3:00 o'clock position and the bottom oil ring rail gap should be under the second ring gap. See the illustration for details.

10. Turn the crankshaft until the rod journal of the particular cylinder you are working on is brought to TDC.

11. With the piston and rings clamped in a

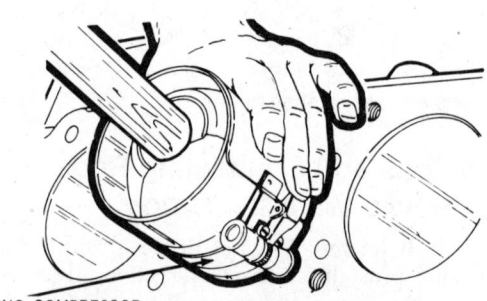

Install the piston using a ring compressor

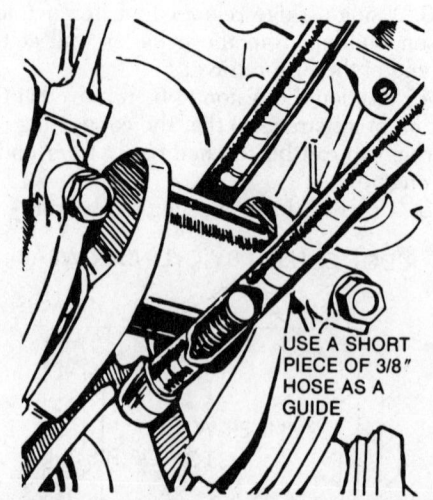

Use lengths of vacuum hose or rubber tubing to protect the crankshaft journals and cylinder walls during piston installation

ENGINE AND ENGINE OVERHAUL

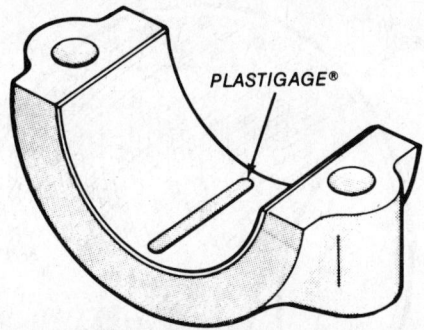

Plastigage® installed on the lower bearing shell

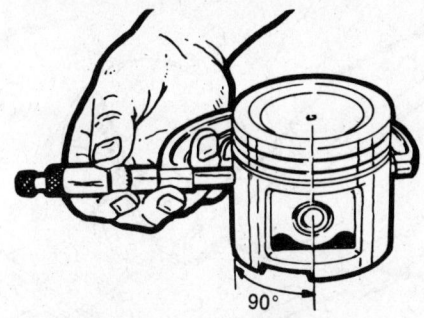

Measure the piston prior to fitting

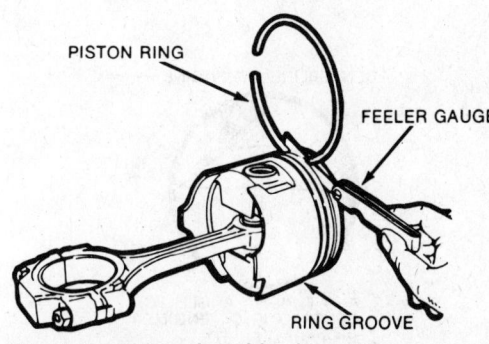

Check the piston ring side clearance

ring compressor, the notched mark on the head of the piston toward the front of the engine and the oil hole side of the connecting rod toward the right-side (except V6) or facing the crankshaft (V6) of the engine, push the piston and connecting rod assembly into the cylinder bore until the big bearing end of the connecting rod contacts and is seated on the rod journal of the crankshaft. Use care not to scratch the cylinder wall with the connecting rod.

12. Push down farther on the piston and turn the crankshaft while the connecting rod rides around on the crankshaft rod journal. Turn the crankshaft until the crankshaft rod journal is at BDC (bottom dead center).

13. Align the mark on the connecting rod bearing cap with that on the connecting rod and tighten the bearing cap bolts to the specified torque.

14. Install the piston/connecting rod assemblies in the manner outlined above, use the plastigage® method of checking the connecting rod-to-crankshaft bearing tolerances.

15. To complete the installation, reverse the removal procedures.

CLEANING AND INSPECTION
Pistons

NOTE: *For the following operations, the piston should be disassembled from the connecting rod.*

1. Using a wooden scraper, clean the carbon from the outer surface of the pistons.

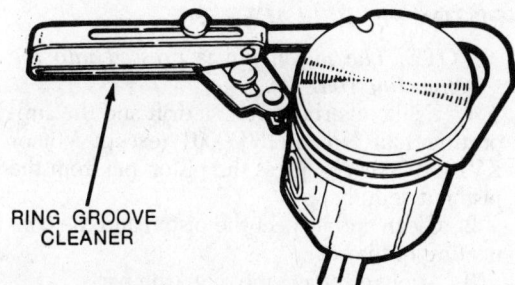

Clean the piston ring grooves

2. Using a piston ring land area cleaning or a piece of an old piston ring, scrape the carbon from the piston's ring land area.

CAUTION: *When cleaning the piston's ring land area, be careful not to remove any metal from the piston.*

3. Flush the piston in solvent to remove any oil and loose debris.

4. Inspect the piston for damage or wear (especially at the skirt area) and make sure that the piston pin slides easily into the piston bore.

5. Using the new piston rings and a feeler gauge, check the piston ring land areas for the ring side clearance, it must not be greater than 0.004 in. (0.1 mm).

Connecting Rods

1. Disassemble the connecting rod from the piston.

2. Clean the connecting rod in solvent to remove the oil and loose debris.

3. Using an internal dial micrometer, check the diameter of the piston pin and the crankshaft bore.

4. Using the Magnaflux® process, inspect the connecting rod for damage, stress cracks or wear; replace it (if necessary).

Engine Block

1. Using solvent an a clean rag, wipe the cylinder bores clean of the oil and loose debris.

2. Using an internal dial micrometer or telescoping gauges and a micrometer, measure

ENGINE AND ENGINE OVERHAUL

Measure the cylinder bore with a dial gauge

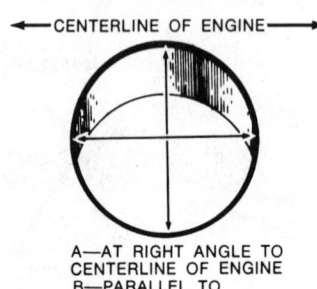
Cylinder bore measuring points

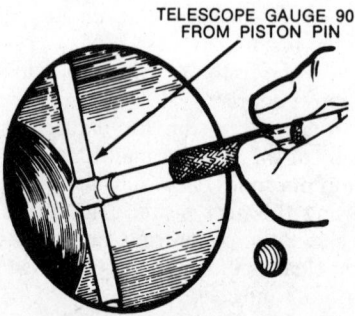
Measure the cylinder bore with a telescope gauge

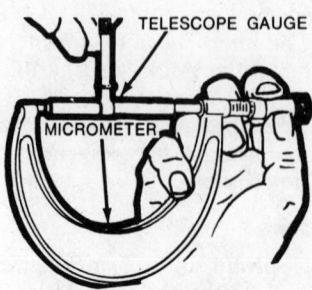
Measure the telescope gauge with a micrometer to determine the cylinder bore

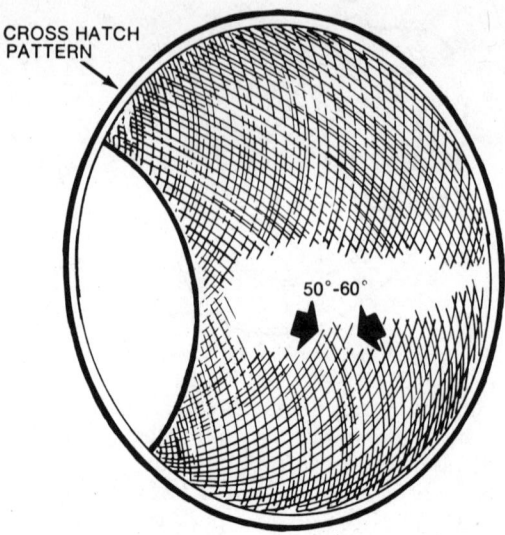
Finish hone the cylinders:

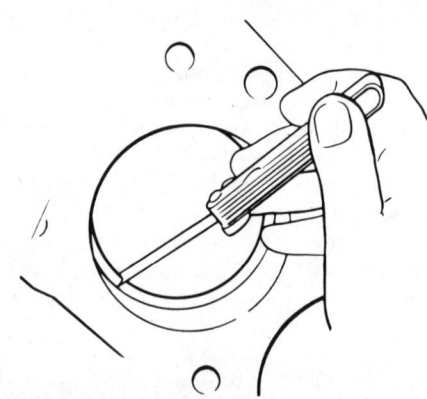
Check the piston ring end gap

the cylinder bore at the top, middle and bottom. When measuring the cylinder bore, be sure to make a measurement at 90° to the initial one.

3. Using a honing tool and some clean engine oil, hone the cylinder walls (to break the glaze). The cylinder bore MUST BE the same diameter throughout the length of the bore.

4. Place the new piston rings into the cylinder bore, then using a feeler gauge, check the ring end gap.

PISTON PIN REPLACEMENT

NOTE: *The piston pin is pressed into the connecting rod.*

1. Using an arbor press, a drift and the supporting tool No. ST13030001 (except V6) or KV10110300 (V6), press the piston pin from the piston assembly.

2. Clean and inspect the piston and the connecting rod bores.

3. Apply clean engine oil to the parts.

4. To install the piston pin, press the pin into

ENGINE AND ENGINE OVERHAUL

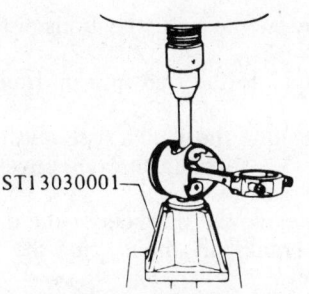

Removing the piston pin from the piston assembly—except V6 engine which is similar

the piston assembly until the pin is flush with the piston.

PISTON RING REPLACEMENT

1. Using a ring expander tool, remove the rings from the piston.
2. Clean and inspect the piston's ring land area for damage or wear, replace the piston (if necessary).
NOTE: *The contact edges of the rings used on the turbocharged engines are not as sharply machined as the ones used on the nonturbocharged engines.*
3. Place the new rings into the cylinder bore and check them with a feeler gauge to make sure that the end gap is correct; the maximum end gap is 0.04 in. (1.0 mm).
NOTE: *To identify the top of the rings, look for a marking on the top or a beveled edge.*
CAUTION: *When using the ring expander, be careful not to break the rings.*
4. Using new rings and a ring expander tool, install the new rings onto the piston; start with the bottom ring and work toward the top compression ring.

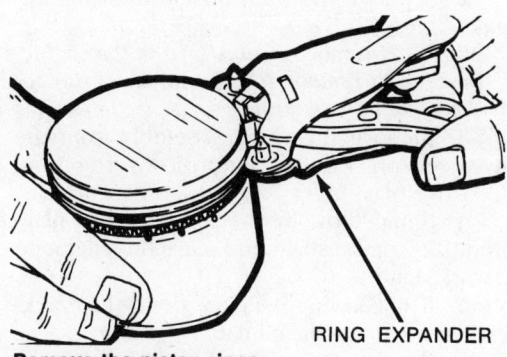

Remove the piston rings

ROD BEARING REPLACEMENT

The connecting rod-to-crankshaft bearings are two piece, they are held into the rod and the rod bearing cap by tabs. When replacing the bearings, be sure that the oil hole in the rod aligns with the oil hole in the bearing.

Rear Main Oil Seal
REMOVAL AND INSTALLATION
All Engines—Except V6

1. Refer to the "Engine, Removal and Installation" procedures, in this section and remove the engine with the transmission from the vehicle.
2. Separate the transmission from the engine.
3. Remove the clutch assembly from the flywheel (M/T) or the torque converter from the drive plate (A/T).
4. Remove the flywheel or the drive plate from the crankshaft, then secure the engine to a workstand.
5. If not having done so, drain the crankcase, then remove the oil pan.
6. Remove the rear main bearing cap using the special tool No. KV101041S0. Remove the bearing cap side seals.
7. Remove the rear main oil seal from around the crankshaft.
8. Using a putty knife, clean the gasket mounting surfaces.
9. Apply oil to the sealing lip of the new oil seal and install it around the crankshaft, using the Oil Seal Installation tool No. KV10105500 or ST15310000.
10. Apply sealer to the rear main bearing

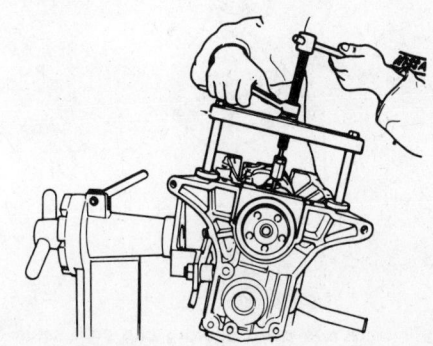

Removing the rear main bearing cap with a puller-in-line 6 cyl engine

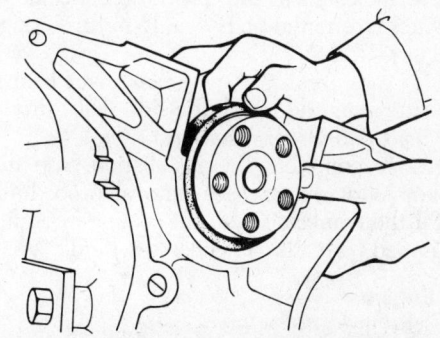

Removing the rear main seal—in-line 6 cyl engine

122 ENGINE AND ENGINE OVERHAUL

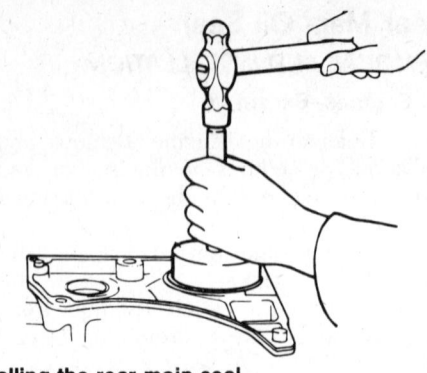

Installing the rear main seal

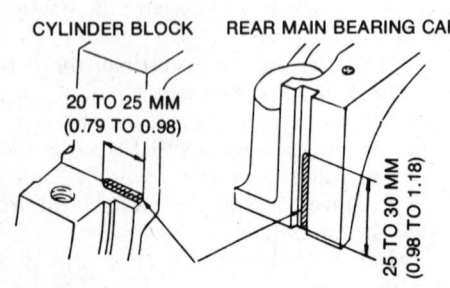

Application of sealer to the rear main bearing cap—in-line 6 cyl engine

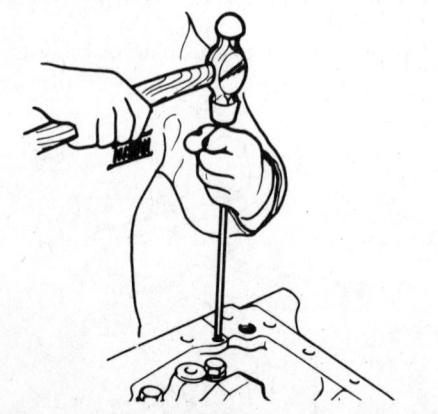

Installing the rear main bearing cap side seals—in-line 6 cyl engine

cap as indicated in the illustration. Install the cap and torque the bolts evenly in three stages to 33–40 ft. lbs.

11. Apply sealant to the rear main bearing cap side seals and install the side seals, driving the seals into place with a drift.

12. To complete the installation, use new gaskets and reverse the removal procedures. Refill the crankcase and the cooling system; if equipped with an A/T, check the fluid.

V6 Engine

1. Refer to the "Engine, Removal and Installation" procedures, in this section and re-

move the engine with the transmission from the vehicle.

2. Separate the transmission from the engine.

3. Remove the clutch assembly from the flywheel (M/T) or the torque converter from the drive plate (A/T).

4. Remove the flywheel or the drive plate from the crankshaft, then secure the engine to a workstand.

5. If not having done so, drain the oil from the crankcase, then remove the oil pan.

6. Remove the rear oil seal retainer from the rear of the engine.

7. Using a medium pry bar, pry the oil seal from the oil seal retainer.

8. Using a putty knife, clean the gasket mounting surfaces.

9. Apply oil to the sealing lip and the mounting surface of the new oil seal, then press the seal into the oil seal retainer. Install the oil seal retainer/seal around the crankshaft.

10. To complete the installation, use new gaskets and reverse the removal procedures. Refill the crankcase and the cooling system; if equipped with an A/T, check the fluid.

Crankshaft And Main Bearings
REMOVAL AND INSTALLATION
All Engines—Except V6

1. Refer to the "Engine, Removal and Installation" and the "Timing Belt/Chain and Tensioner, Removal and Installation" procedures, in this section, then remove the engine with the transmission from the vehicle and the timing chain from the engine.

2. Separate the transmission from the engine.

NOTE: *If removing an A/T from the engine, be sure to remove the torque convertor-to-drive plate bolts, first.*

3. Remove the clutch assembly from the flywheel (M/T) or the torque converter from the drive plate (A/T).

4. Remove the flywheel or the drive plate from the crankshaft, then secure the engine to a work stand.

5. If not having done so, drain the crankcase and remove the oil pan.

6. Remove the connecting rod bearing cap bolts and the bearing caps, then push the connecting rods away from the crankshaft.

NOTE: *The connecting rod bearing caps are numbered, be sure to keep the parts in order for installation purposes. Be sure to slip short pieces of hose over the connecting rod studs, to prevent damaging the crankshaft bearing surfaces.*

ENGINE AND ENGINE OVERHAUL

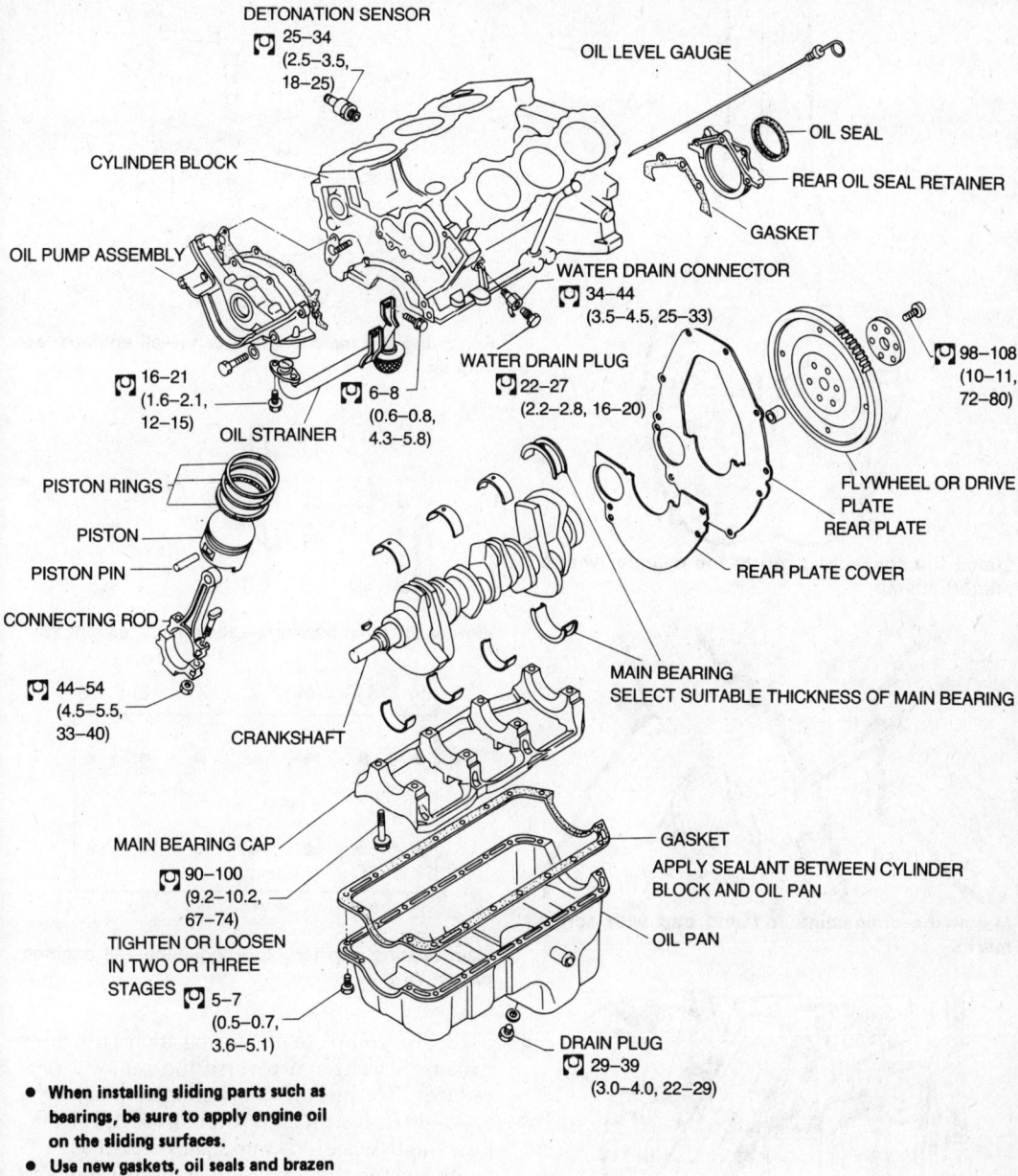

Exploded view of the V6 engine block

7. Remove the main bearing cap bolts, then using the special tool No. KV101041S0, remove the main bearing caps. Remove the rear main bearing cap side seals.

NOTE: *When removing the main bearing caps, be sure to keep the parts in order for installation purposes.*

8. Remove the rear main oil seal from around the crankshaft.

9. Remove the crankshaft, then lift the main bearings from the engine block.

10. Using a putty knife, clean the gasket mounting surfaces. Clean and inspect the engine parts.

11. To install, use new bearings (apply sealant to the rear main bearing caps) and oil seals, then the main bearing caps. Torque the main bearing cap bolts (evenly, in three stages) to 33–40 ft. lbs.

CAUTION: *After torquing each of the main or connecting rod bearing caps, turn the crankshaft to make sure that the crankshaft turns and the engine is not locked.*

12. Apply sealant to the rear main bearing

124 ENGINE AND ENGINE OVERHAUL

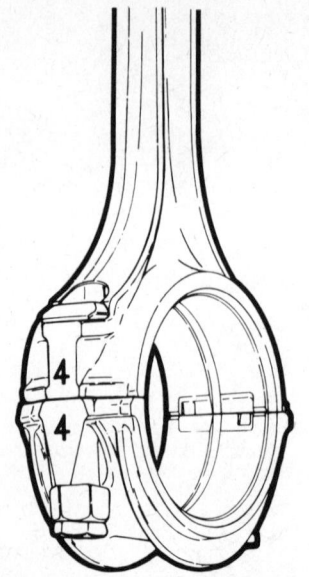

Match the connecting rod to the cylinder with a number stamp

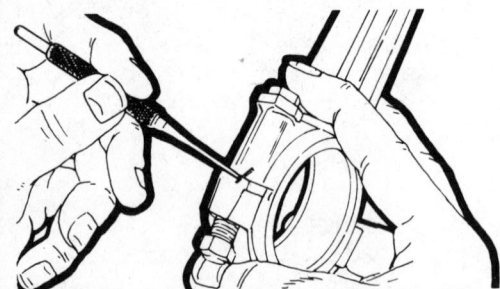

Match the connecting rod and cap with scribe marks

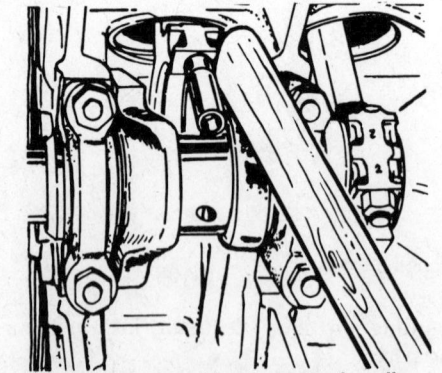

Push the piston out with a hammer handle

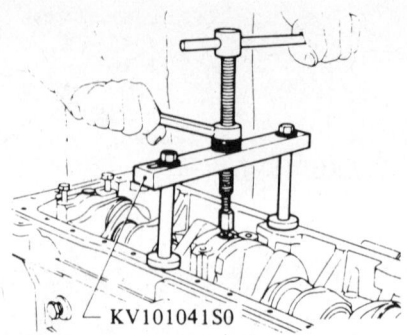

Removing the main bearing caps—all engines, except V6

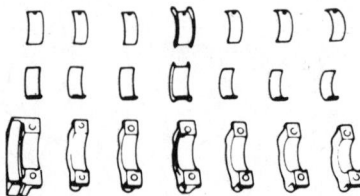

View of the main bearings—all engines, except V6

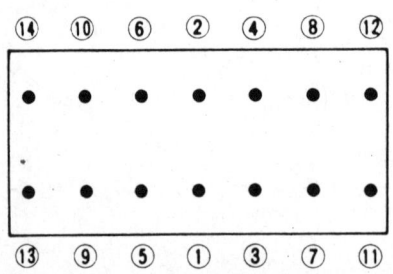

Main bearing cap torquing sequence—all engines, except V6

cap side seals and install the side seals, driving the seals into place with a drift.

NOTE: *When installing the new main or connecting rod bearings, be sure that the bearings surfaces are clean (free of dirt), lubricated, the oil holes are aligned and the bearings are seated with the aligning notches in their respective slots.*

13. To complete the installation, use new gaskets, sealant and reverse the removal procedures. Torque the connecting rod cap bolts to 33–40 ft. lbs., the oil pan bolts to 4.3–7.2 ft. lbs., the flywheel-to-crankshaft bolts to 94–108 ft. lbs. or the drive plate-to-crankshaft bolts to 94–108 ft. lbs. Refill the crankcase and the cooling system; if equipped with an A/T, check the fluid. Start the engine and adjust the timing.

V6 Engine

1. Refer to the "Engine, Removal and Installation" procedures, in this section, then remove the engine with the transmission from the vehicle. Separate the transmission from engine and mount the engine on a workstand.

NOTE: *If removing an A/T from the engine, be sure to remove the torque convertor-to-drive plate bolts, first.*

2. Remove the clutch assembly from the

ENGINE AND ENGINE OVERHAUL

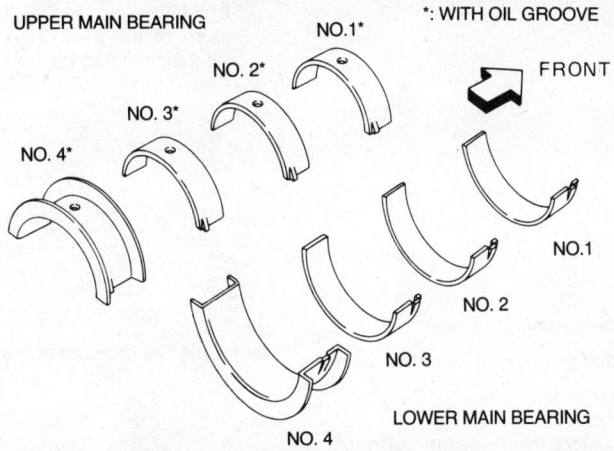

View of the main bearings—V6 engine

flywheel (M/T) or the torque converter from the drive plate (A/T).

3. Remove the flywheel or the drive plate from the crankshaft, then secure the engine to a work stand.

4. Refer to the "Oil Pump, Removal and Installation" procedures, in this section and remove the oil pump from the engine.

5. Remove the connecting rod bearing cap bolts and the bearing caps, then push the connecting rods away from the crankshaft.

NOTE: *The connecting rod bearing caps are numbered, be sure to keep the parts in order for installation purposes. Be sure to slip short pieces of hose over the connecting rod studs, to prevent damaging the crankshaft bearing surfaces.*

6. Remove the main bearing cap bolts and the main bearing caps. Remove the rear oil seal retainer.

NOTE: *When removing the main bearing caps, be sure to keep the parts in order for installation purposes.*

7. Remove the crankshaft, then lift the main bearings from the engine block.

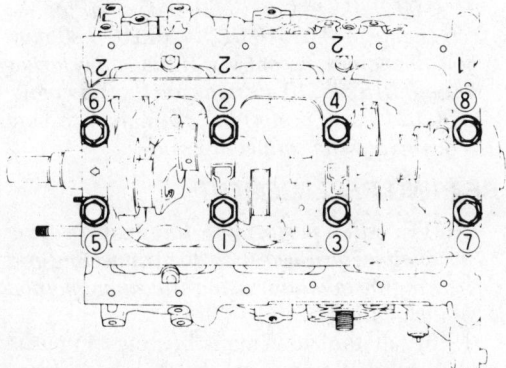

Main bearing torquing sequence—V6 engine

8. Using a putty knife, clean the gasket mounting surfaces. Clean and inspect the engine parts.

9. To install, use new main bearings and oil seals, then the main bearing caps. Torque the main bearing cap bolts (evenly, in three stages) to 67–74 ft. lbs.

CAUTION: *After torquing each of the main or connecting rod bearing caps, turn the crankshaft to make sure that the crankshaft turns and the engine is not locked.*

NOTE: *When installing the new main or connecting rod bearings, be sure that the bearings surfaces are clean (free of dirt), lubricated, the oil holes are aligned and the bearings are seated with the aligning notches in their respective slots.*

10. To complete the installation, use new gaskets, sealant and reverse the removal procedures. Torque the connecting rod cap bolts to 33–40 ft. lbs., the oil pan bolts to 3.6–5.1 ft. lbs., the flywheel-to-crankshaft bolts to 72–80 ft. lbs. or the drive plate-to-crankshaft bolts to 72–80 ft. lbs. Refill the crankcase and the cooling system; if equipped with an A/T, check the fluid. Start the engine and adjust the timing.

CLEANING AND INSPECTION

Crankshaft

1. Using solvent clean the crankshaft of debris and oil.

2. Inspect the crankshaft for scoring, wear or cracks.

3. Using an outside micrometer, check the crankshaft's connecting rod journals for taper and out-of-round conditions:

   a. To measure the journal's taper, make a measurement at each end of the connecting rod journal.

   b. Make a second measurement at 90° to

ENGINE AND ENGINE OVERHAUL

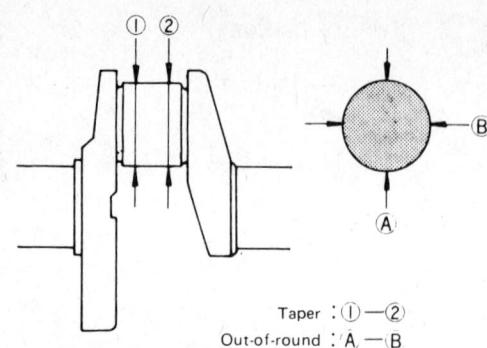

Measuring the connecting rod journal for out-of-round and taper conditions

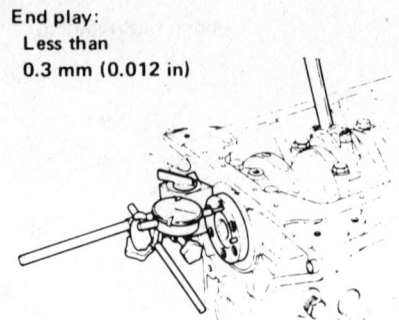

Measuring the crankshaft end play

the first two measurements, then compare the measurements for an out-of-round condition. If the out-of-round measurement difference is greater than 0.0002 in., the connecting rod journals must be reground.

   c. Compare the measurements at each end of the connecting rod journals for taper conditions. If the taper measurement difference is greater than 0.0002 in. (0.005 mm), the connecting rod journals must be reground.

4. Position the crankshaft between two V-blocks, then position a dial indicator so that it will ride on a main bearing journal.

   a. Turn the crankshaft and check the journal runout.

   b. If the runout is greater than 0.0039 in. (0.10 mm), regrind the main bearing journals.

5. Once the main bearings have been installed, check the crankshaft end play:

   a. Push the crankshaft (in one direction) all of the way until it stops.

   b. Using a dial indicator, place the indicator against the end of the crankshaft and zero the dial.

   c. Using a feeler gauge, measure the gap between the thrust bearing and the crankshaft.

NOTE: *The crankshaft end play should be 0.0020–0.0067 in. (0.05–0.17 mm); if it is greater than 0.012 in. (0.30 mm), replace the thrust bearing with a thicker one.*

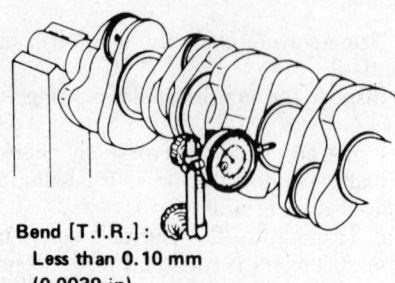

Measuring the crankshaft main bearing journal

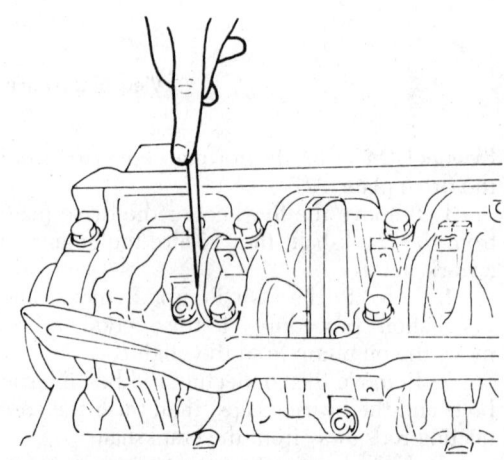

Checking the connecting rod side clearance

   d. Push the crankshaft (all the way) in the opposite direction. Using the dial indicator, measure the difference of the crankshaft (end direction) movement.

6. To check the connecting rod-to-crankshaft side clearance, perform the following:

   a. Push the connecting rod to the extreme side of the crankshaft pin.

   b. Using a feeler gauge, insert it into the connecting rod-to-crankshaft gap and check the side clearance.

NOTE: *The connecting rod clearance should be 0.0079–0.0138 in. (0.20–0.35 mm) for the V6 engine or 0.008–0.012 in. (0.20–0.30 mm) for all engines, except V6. If the gap is larger than 0.0157 in. (0.40 mm) for the V6 engine or 0.024 in. (0.6 mm) for all engines, except V6, replace the connecting rod.*

BEARING REPLACEMENT

NOTE: *After performing the main bearing installation, proceed with the connecting rod bearing installation, using the same method of installation.*

1. Install the new main bearings into the engine block. Make sure that the bearing oil holes align with the engine block oil holes and

ENGINE AND ENGINE OVERHAUL   127

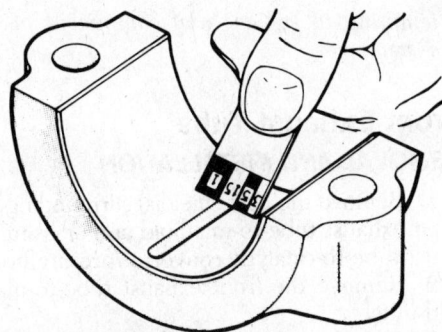

Measure Plastigage® to determine main bearing clearance

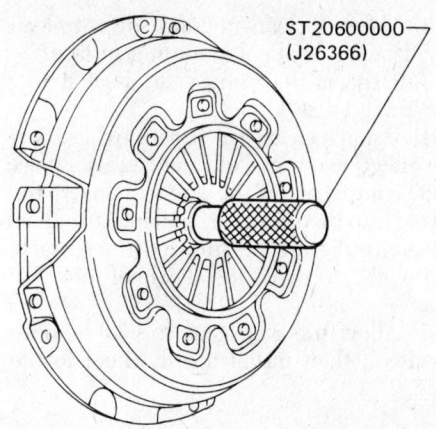

Installing the clutch disc supporting tool—V6 engine, other models are similar

that the bearing tabs are seated into the journal notches.

2. Install the other half of the main bearing into the bearing caps, making sure that the bearing tabs are seated into the bearing cap notches.

3. Install the crankshaft into the engine block.

4. Using the Plastigage® method of checking the bearing clearance, place a piece of Plastigage® onto each main bearing surface.

5. Install the main bearing caps and torque to specifications.

6. After all of the main bearings have been torqued to specifications, remove the main bearing caps.

7. Using the width gauge (supplied with each Plastigage® kit), compare the gauge with the squashed Plastigage® strip.

NOTE: *The width of the squashed plastigage® will relate to the bearing clearance. If necessary, replace the bearing(s) to acquire the correct bearing clearance.*

8. With the bearing correct, remove the Plastigage® material, oil the bearing surface, install the bearing cap and torque it to specifications.

Flywheel and Ring Gear

NOTE: *Always use new bolts when installing the flywheel. Inspect the clutch shaft pilot bushing in the crankshaft. If the bushing is excessively worn, remove it with an expanding puller and a slide hammer, then tap a new bushing into place.*

REMOVAL AND INSTALLATION

1. Refer to the "Manual Transmission, Removal and Installation" or "Automatic Transmission, Removal and Installation" procedures, in Chapter 6, then remove the transmission from the engine.

NOTE: *Before removing the pressure plate from the flywheel or torque convertor from the drive plate, be sure to mark the relationship to one another.*

2. If equipped with a manual transmission, perform the following:

  a. Using the Clutch Disc Alignment tool No. KV30100100 (except V6) or ST20600000 (V6), support the clutch assembly.

  b. Loosen the pressure plate-to-flywheel bolts, evenly, a little at a time, in a crisscross fashion, until the spring pressure is released.

  c. Remove the pressure plate, the clutch disc and the alignment tool.

3. If equipped with an automatic transmission, perform the following:

  a. Remove the torque convertor cover plate.

  b. Remove the torque convertor-to-drive plate bolts.

  c. Slide the torque convertor back into the transmission and tie it into place.

4. Remove the flywheel-to-crankshaft bolts and the flywheel.

5. To install, reverse the removal procedures. Torque the flywheel/drive plate-to-crankshaft bolts to 72–80 ft. lbs. (98–108 Nm) for V6 or 94–108 ft. lbs. (127–147 Nm) for all other engines, the pressure plate/torque convertor-to-flywheel bolts 15–22 ft. lbs. (21–29 Nm).

RING GEAR REPLACEMENT

1. To remove the ring gear from the flywheel, perform the following:

  a. Secure the flywheel so that the ring gear may be removed without damaging it.

  b. Using a cold chisel and a hammer, cut through the ring gear. Remove the ring gear from the flywheel.

CAUTION: *When cutting through the ring gear, be careful not to damage the flywheel.*

ENGINE AND ENGINE OVERHAUL

2. Using a clean rag and solvent clean the ring gear-to-flywheel mounting surface.

3. Using a new ring gear, heat it to 356–428°F (180–220°C).

4. Using a clean, flat surface (which heat will not affect) and a mallet (if necessary), place the HOT ring gear on the surface. Insert the flywheel into the ring gear, making sure that both items are flat on the surface; if necessary, use the mallet to drive the flywheel into the ring gear.

5. Allow the ring gear to COOL onto the flywheel, then install the flywheel to the engine.

EXHAUST SYSTEM

The Exhaust systems vary slightly from year-to-year or model-to-model. From 1970–78, the 49-State models DO NOT use a catalytic converter, while the California models DO; the 49-State models use a pre-muffler in place of the catalytic converter. The 1979 and later models use a catalytic converter. Since the catalytic converter produces extreme heat, it is encased in a 2-piece heat shield.

The catalytic converter is constructed of a stainless steel shell and internal precious metals, such as: Platinum, Palladium and Rhodium; the internal metals act as a catalyst to convert the HC and the NOx (of the engine exhaust) into H_2O and CO_2. The average life of a converter is 50,000 miles but under ideal operating conditions the life can be extended.

The 1979–81 models utilize a tail pipe tube, which runs from the muffler at the left-rear to the right-rear of the vehicle. On most exhaust systems, the components are encased in removable heat shields.

Normally, when one component of the exhaust system becomes deteriorated, the entire system is (or soon will be) in need of repair. It is recommended that when repairing the exhaust system, replace the entire system, except for the catalytic convertor (which may be salvageable).

CAUTION: *Before working on the exhaust system, make sure that the system has had time to cool down.*
NOTE: *To work on the exhaust system, the vehicle MUST BE raised and supported on jackstands. Since the exhaust system is subjected to extreme heat conditions, the nuts, bolts and tube connections may be welded together. If the components cannot be separated, use a hacksaw, a cutting torch or a metal cutting saw to remove the system or components. Be sure to acquire adequate clamps, bolts, studs and nuts before attempting to replace any component of the system.*

Front Exhaust Tube
REMOVAL AND INSTALLATION

1. Remove the heat shield(s) surrounding the front exhaust tube-to-manifold and/or front exhaust tube-to-catalytic converter/pre-muffler.

2. Remove the front exhaust tube-to-manifold nuts.
NOTE: *To remove the exhaust tube-to-manifold nuts, it may be necessary to run a die over the stud threads (to remove the rust) and soak the studs/nuts with a rust penetrating substance (to dissolve the rust).*
CAUTION: *If the studs break off, when removing the nuts, it will be necessary to drill out the studs, tap a new hole and replace the studs or drill out the studs, then insert a bolt and nut.*

3. Remove the front exhaust tube-to-converter/pre-muffler bolts, then remove the front exhaust tube.

4. Using a putty knife, clean the mounting surfaces.

5. To install, use a new front exhaust tube, gasket(s), bolts, nuts and reverse the removal procedures.

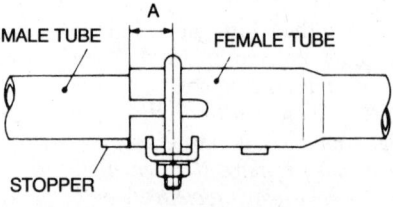

Connecting the exhaust system

Catalytic Converter/Pre-Muffler

CAUTION: *When handling the catalytic converter, be careful not to damage it or have it come in contact with oil, water or other fluids.*

REMOVAL AND INSTALLATION

1. Remove the heat shield(s) surrounding the front exhaust tube-to-manifold, the extension tube and the front exhaust tube-to-catalytic converter/pre-muffler.

2. Remove the front exhaust tube-to-manifold nuts.
NOTE: *To remove the exhaust tube-to-manifold nuts, it may be necessary to run a die over the stud threads (to remove the rust) and soak the studs/nuts with a rust penetrating substance (to dissolve the rust).*
CAUTION: *If the studs break off, when removing the nuts, it will be necessary to drill*

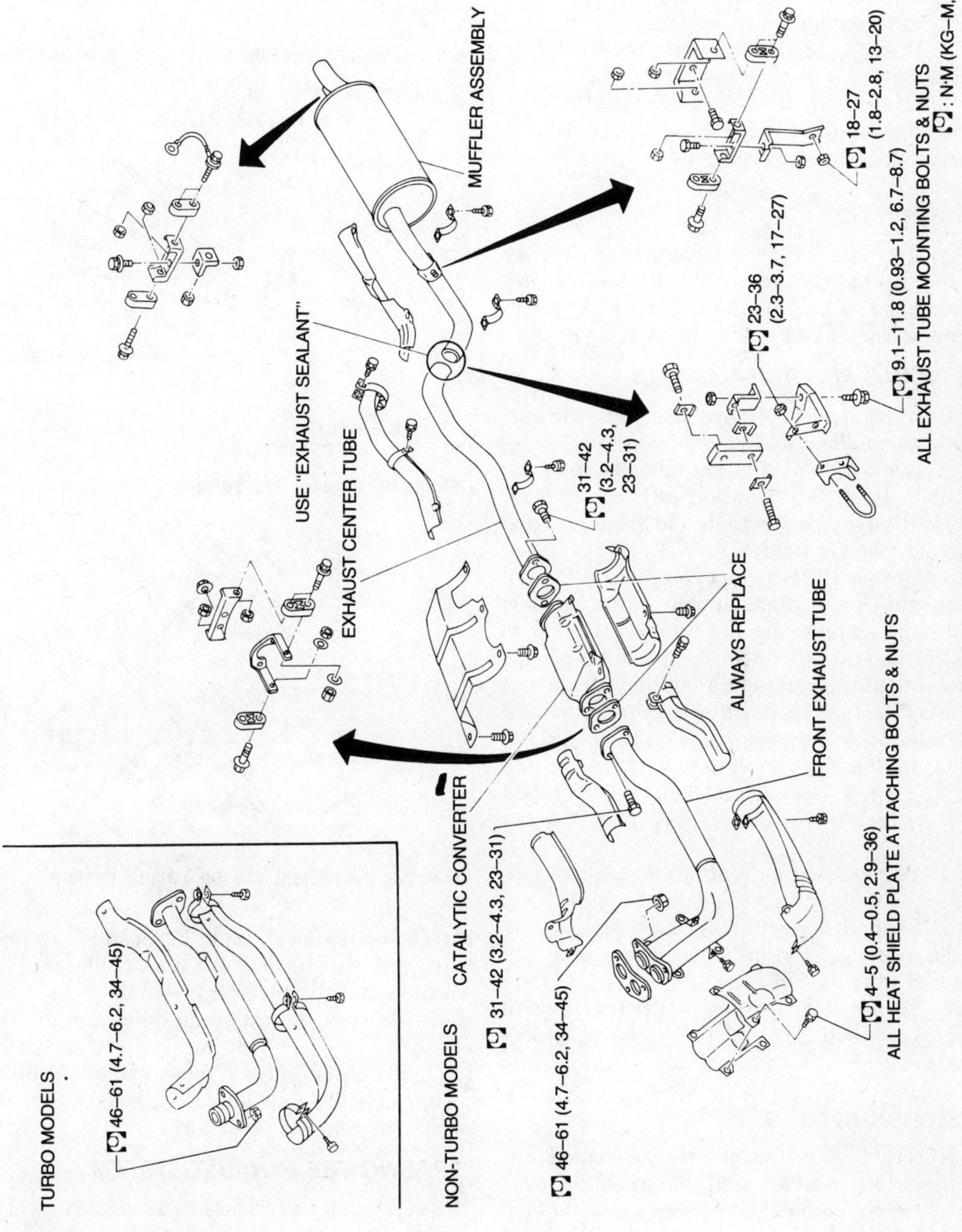

ENGINE AND ENGINE OVERHAUL

Exploded view of the exhaust system—300 ZX, other models are similar

out the studs, tap a new hole and replace the studs or drill out the studs, then insert a bolt and nut.

3. Remove the front exhaust tube-to-converter/pre-muffler bolts, then remove the front exhaust tube.

4. Support the catalytic converter/pre-muffler, then remove the converter/pre-muffler-to-extension tube bolts and the catalytic converter/pre-muffler.

5. Using a putty knife, clean the mounting surfaces.

6. To install, use a new catalytic converter/pre-muffler, gasket(s), bolts, nuts and reverse the removal procedures.

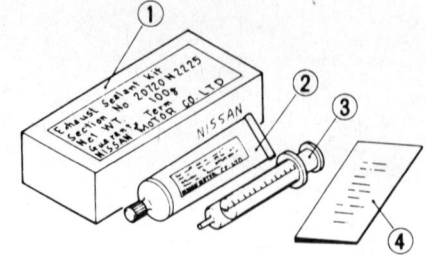

1. Case
2. Sealant tube (polyethylene)
3. Injector
4. Instruction sheet

The exhaust sealant kit

Muffler

NOTE: *The muffler is located at the rear of the exhaust system. Some mufflers are clamped to the extension tube, while others are welded to the extension tube.*

REMOVAL AND INSTALLATION

1. If equipped, remove the heat shield(s) from the muffler and the extension tube.

2. Remove the extension tube clamp at the muffler or at the extension tube intersection (welded tube type); separate the extension tube from the hanger bracket.

3. On the 1979–81 models, remove the tail tube and clamps from the rear of the muffler. Using a hammer, rap the tube connection to loosen the rust. Remove the tail tube hanger brackets and the tail tube from the vehicle.

NOTE: *If the tube will not separate, drive a cold chisel between the mating surface to loosen the tube or cut the muffler tube from the muffler (without damaging the tail tube), then remove the cutoff piece from the tail tube.*

4. Working at the front of the muffler, separate the muffler from the extension tube.

5. Support the muffler, then remove the muffler-to-hanger bracket bolt/nut and the muffler from the vehicle.

6. To install, use a new muffler, clamps (if necessary) and reverse the removal procedures.

Extension Tube

NOTE: *The extension tube is located between the muffler and the catalytic converter/pre-muffler. To remove it, the muffler or the catalytic converter/pre-muffler must be removed, which ever is easier.*

REMOVAL AND INSTALLATION

1. Refer to the "Muffler, Removal and Installation" or the "Catalytic Converter/Pre-

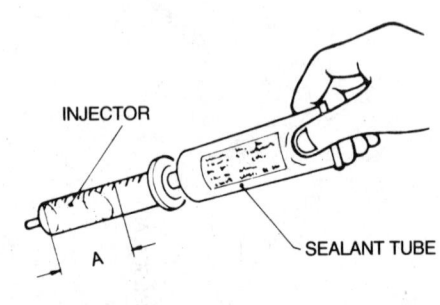

A: 5 TO 6 CC
(0.31 TO 0.37 CU IN)

Filling the injector with sealant

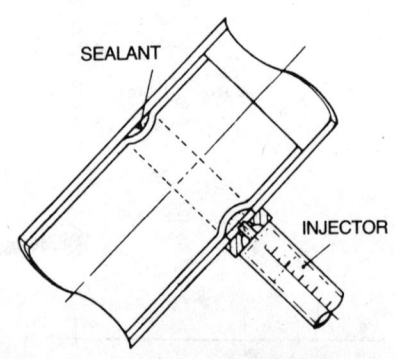

Injecting the sealant into the exhaust system

Muffler, Removal and Installation" procedures, in this section and remove the muffler or the catalytic converter/pre-muffler.

2. Remove the extension tube from the vehicle.

3. To install, use a new extension tube, clamps, bolts, nuts and/or gasket(s), then reverse the removal procedures.

SEALING THE EXHAUST SYSTEM

Nissan supplies an exhaust system sealant, which can be installed when the exhaust system is new or the components are clean (bare metal). The Exhaust Sealant Kit No. 20720-N2225, is used to eliminate gas leakage past the joints.

1. Wipe all of the joint contact surfaces clean and allow them to dry.

ENGINE AND ENGINE OVERHAUL

2. Mount the exhaust system onto the vehicle.
3. Torque the U-bolts to 16–22 ft. lbs.

CAUTION: *If you get exhaust sealant on your skin, it may cause a rash; wash it off thoroughly with water.*

4. For each joint, squeeze 0.31–0.37 cu. in. (5–6 cc) of sealant into the injector from the sealant tube.

CAUTION: *Be sure to replace the cap on the sealant tube, for the sealant will dry out.*

5. Position the injector nozzle to the tube guide and squeeze firmly; the sealant will flow into the guide. When the sealant flows out of the slit of the tube, no further sealant is necessary.

CAUTION: *Be careful not to use too much sealant, for it will clog the tube. When finished, be sure to wash the injector thoroughly in water.*

6. Start the engine and allow it to idle for 10 minutes, to harden the sealant.
7. Before driving the vehicle, check the condition of the sealant. DO NOT accelerate the engine sharply for 20–30 minutes, after the operation.

Emission Controls and Fuel Systems

EMISSION CONTROLS

Due to the complex nature of the modern electronic engine control systems, comprehensive diagnosis and testing procedures fall outside of the confines of this repair manual. For complete information on the diagnosis, testing and repair procedures concerning all modern engine and emission control systems, please refer to *Chilton's Guide To Electronic Engine Controls*.

There are three sources of automotive pollutants: crankcase fumes, exhaust gases and gasoline evaporation. The pollutants formed from these substances fall into three categories: unburnt hydrocarbons (HC), carbon monoxide (CO) and oxides of nitrogen (NOx). The equipment used to limit these pollutants is called emission control equipment.

Due to varying state, federal and provincial regulations, specific emission control equipment has been devised for each. The U.S. emission equipment is divided into two categories: California and 49 States. In this section, the term "California" applies only to vehicles originally built to be sold in California. California emissions equipment is generally not shared with equipment installed on vehicles built to be sold in the other 49 States. Models built to be sold in Canada also have specific emissions equipment, although in most years 49 State and Canadian equipment is the same.

Crankcase Ventilation System
OPERATION

A closed, positive crankcase ventilation system is employed on all vehicles. This system cycles incompletely burned fuel, which works it's way past the piston rings, back into the intake manifold for reburning with an fuel/air mixture. The oil filler cap is sealed and air is drawn from the top of the crankcase into the intake manifold through a valve with a variable orifice.

The valve (commonly known as the PCV valve) employs spring pressure and a sliding plunger to regulate the flow of air into the manifold according to the amount of manifold vacuum. When the throttle plate(s) are open fairly wide, this valve opens to maximize the flow. However, at idle speed, when manifold vacuum is at maximum, the PCV valve throttles the flow in order not to unnecessarily affect the small volume of mixture passing into the engine.

A ventilating line connects the valve cover with the air cleaner (carburetor) or the intake manifold (throttle body). During most driving conditions, manifold vacuum is high and the vapor from the crankcase, plus a small amount of excess air, is drawn into the manifold through the PCV. However, at full-throttle, the increase in the volume of blow-by and the decrease in manifold vacuum make the flow through the PCV inadequate. Under these conditions, excess vapors are drawn into the air cleaner and pass through the carburetor and into the engine.

SERVICE CHECKS

After every 12,000 miles or every year, perform the following services:
1. Check the condition of the hoses and the connectors to ensure that there is no leakage; replace the parts, if necessary.
2. Disconnect the hoses and blow them clean with compressed air. Where extreme clogging is encountered, replace the hose.
3. Check the PCV valve as follows:
   a. Start the engine and allow it to idle.
   b. Disconnect the ventilating hose from the PCV valve, allowing fresh air to be drawn into the manifold through the valve.
   NOTE The flow of air should produce an au-

EMISSION CONTROLS AND FUEL SYSTEM

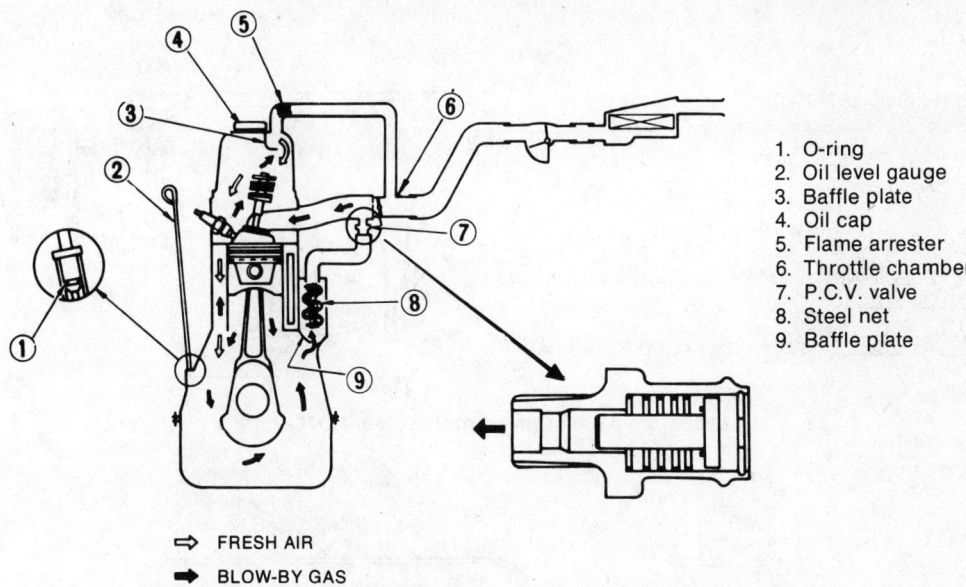

1. O-ring
2. Oil level gauge
3. Baffle plate
4. Oil cap
5. Flame arrester
6. Throttle chamber
7. P.C.V. valve
8. Steel net
9. Baffle plate

Crankcase emission control system, except turbocharged engines

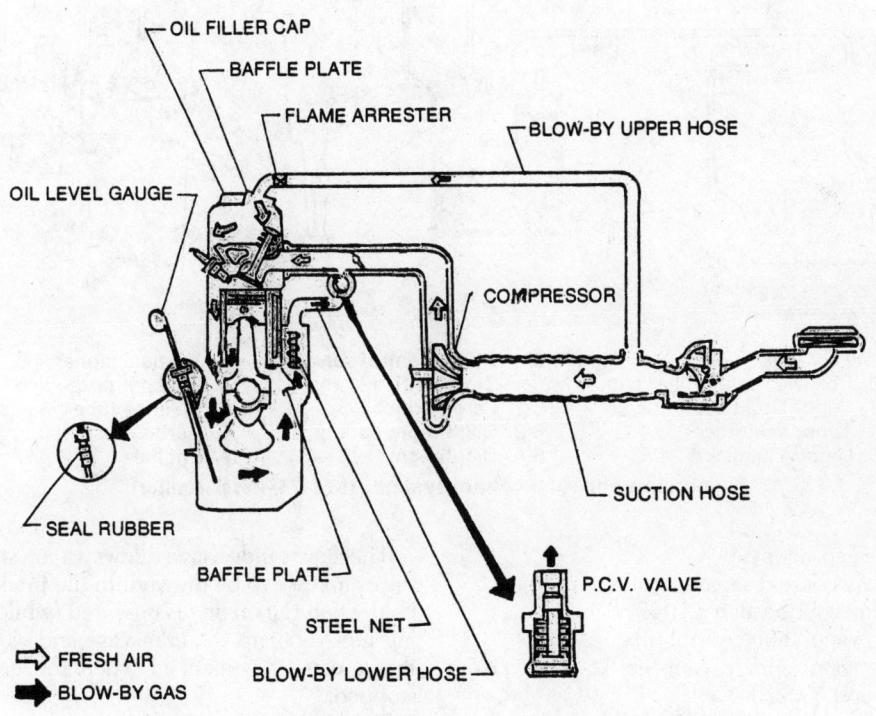

Crankcase emission control system, turbocharged engines

dible "hiss" and it should be possible to feel a strong vacuum when placing a finger over the valve inlet.

c. If the valve is clogged, replace it as it is not serviceable. Replace the valve every two years.

Evaporative Emission Control System
OPERATION

The Evaporative Emission Control System employs:

134 EMISSION CONTROLS AND FUEL SYSTEM

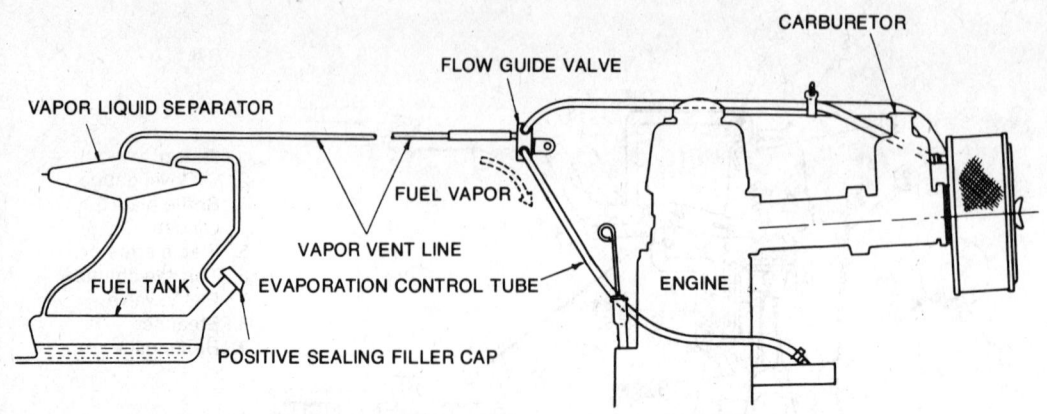

Evaporative emission control system (1970–73)

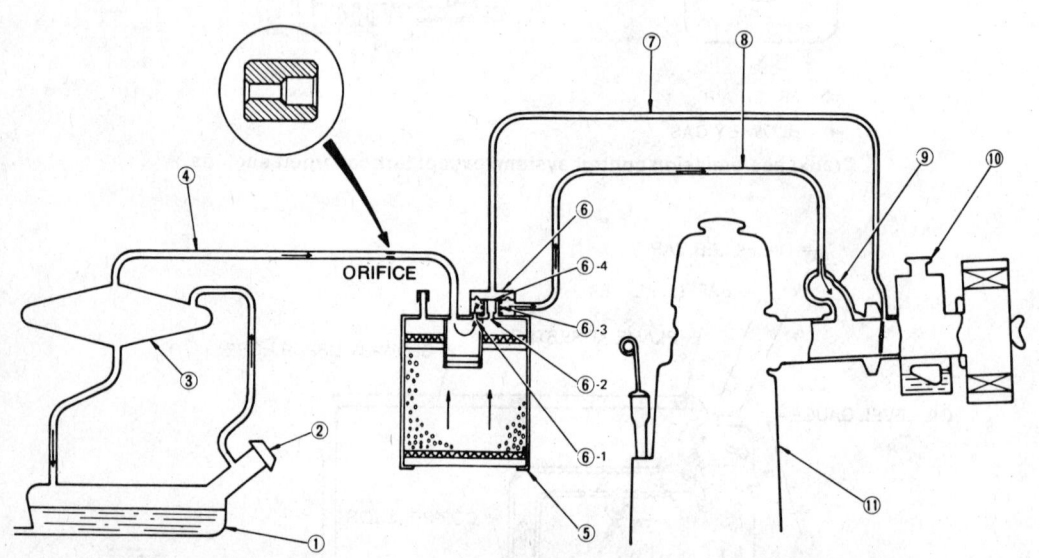

1. Fuel tank	6. Purge control valve	7. Vacuum signal line
2. Positive sealing filler cap	6-1. Small orifice	8. Canister purge line
3. Vapor liquid separator	6-2. Large orifice	9. Balance tube
4. Vapor vent line	6-3. Diaphragm spring	10. Carburetor
5. Carbon canister	6-4. Diaphragm	11. Engine

Evaporative emission control system (1974–75—later similar)

- A sealed filler cap.
- A vapor-liquid separator and vent line.
- A flow guide valve (240-Z).
- An evaporation control tube (240-Z).
- A carbon storage canister (260-Z, 280-Z, 280-ZX and 300ZX).
- A fuel check valve (1976 and later models).

The sealed filler cap allows vacuum (created as the fuel pump empties the tank) to draw air into the tank to replace the used fuel. This avoids damaging the tank or starving the fuel system. It will not, however, allow fuel vapor to escape.

The vapor-liquid separator allows a vent line to collect the vapor formed in the gas tank and store it in the crankcase or in a carbon canister but prohibits liquid fuel from passing into the vent line.

The flow guide valve allows vapor stored in the crankcase to be drawn into the intake manifold when the engine is operated, while shunting fuel vapor to the crankcase and closing off the line to the manifold when the engine is stopped.

The evaporation control tube carries the fuel vapor from the crankcase when the engine is stopped.

The carbon canister stores the fuel vapor from the tank when the engine is not running. When the engine starts, vacuum carried by a vacuum signal line opens a purge valve on the top of the canister. Air is then drawn through a filter on the bottom of the canister, through the charcoal, a nozzle in the purge valve and into the manifold.

The fuel check valve, installed in the vapor

EMISSION CONTROLS AND FUEL SYSTEM

line between the fuel tank and the carbon canister, allows air flow into the fuel tank but prevents vapor flow to the canister except under high vacuum.

CHECKING FUEL TANK, FILLER CAP AND VENT LINE

1. Periodically inspect the hoses and the fuel tank filler cap for poor conditions, cracks or other deficiencies and replace the parts, as necessary. When inspecting the filler cap, pull the pressure relief valve outward to check for free, smooth operation. Check that it seals effectively. Replace the defective parts as necessary.

2. Disconnect the vapor vent line at the canister or the flow guide valve. Install a "T," connecting a source of air pressure and a pressure gauge which reads in inches of water.

3. Slowly apply pressure until the pressure gauge reads 14.5 inches. Close off the air supply and wait 2½ minutes.

4. Check the reading on the gauge. It should not have dropped below 13.5 inches.

5. Remove the filler cap. The pressure should drop to zero in a few seconds. If not, the vent line is clogged.

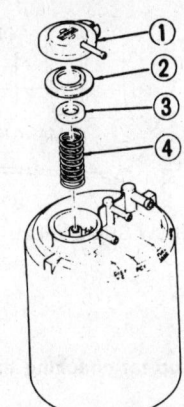

1. Cover
2. Diaphragm
3. Retainer
4. Diaphragm spring

Exploded view of the carbon canister purge valve

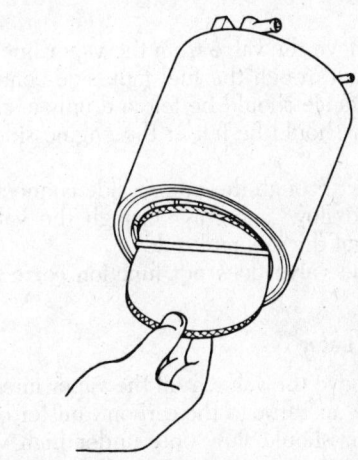

Replacing the canister filter

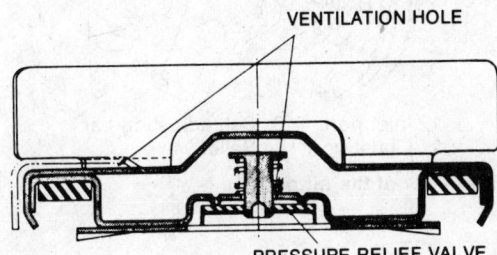

Fuel filler cap

CHECKING THE CARBON CANISTER PURGE VALVE

1. Disconnect the rubber hose which runs between the manifold and canister at the T-connector.

2. Blow into the open end of the hose and listen for leaks.

3. If there are leaks, remove the top cover of the purge valve and check for a dislocated or cracked diaphragm; replace the parts, as necessary.

4. At this time the filter on the bottom of the canister should be inspected. If the filter is clogged, replace it. Inspection and replacement can be accomplished without removing the canister.

CHECKING THE FLOW GUIDE VALVE

1. Disconnect the hoses to the valve.
2. Force low pressure air into the fuel tank

vent connection. Air should flow from the crankcase side.

3. Force air into the air cleaner connection. Air should flow from the fuel tank and/or crankcase vent connection.

4. Force air into the crankcase vent line connection. There should be no leakage.

5. If the valve fails any of these tests, replace it.

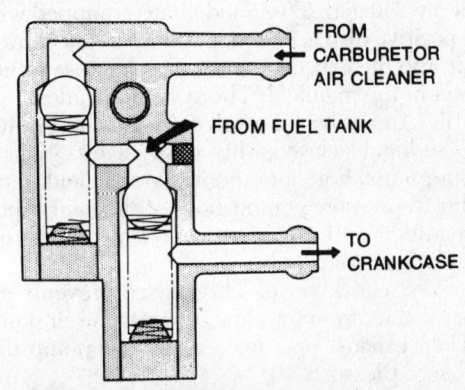

The flow guide valve (1970–73 models only)

136 EMISSION CONTROLS AND FUEL SYSTEM

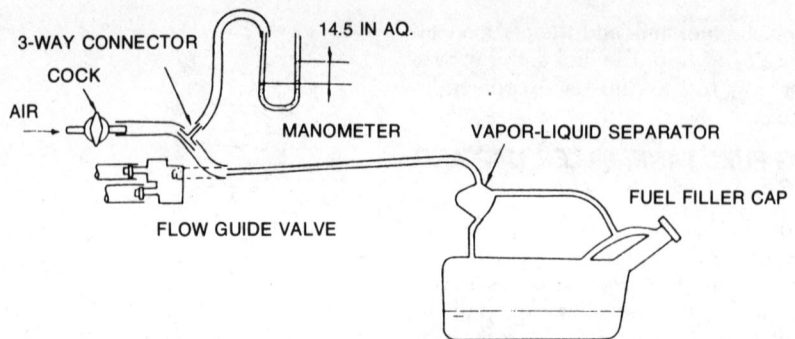

Gauge hook-up for checking the evaporative emission control system

CHECKING THE FUEL CHECK VALVE

1976–78

1. Remove the valve from the vapor line.
2. Blow through the fuel tank side connector. Resistance should be felt and only a small flow of air should be felt at the engine side of the valve.
3. Blow through the engine side connector. Air should flow smoothly through the valve, emerging at the fuel tank side.
4. If the valve does not function correctly, replace it.

1979 and Later

1. Remove the valve from the vapor line.
2. Suck air through the carbon canister connector. Air should flow only under high vacuum.
3. Suck air through the fuel tank side of the valve. Air should flow only under high vacuum.
4. Repeat Step 3 while closing off the carbon canister connector with your finger. Air should flow only under extremely high vacuum.
5. If the valve does not function correctly, replace it.

Air Injection Reactor

Some 240 and 260-Z models are equipped with a positive displacement air pump to inject fresh air into the exhaust ports to accelerate combustion in the manifold. The system includes:

1. An antibackfire valve. When the throttle is suddenly closed, this valve diverts the air pump discharge into the intake manifold in order to promote combustion in the combustion chambers and minimize combustion in the exhaust manifold.
2. A check valve. This device prevents exhaust gases from traveling back into the air pump when exhaust pressure exceeds air pump discharge pressure.

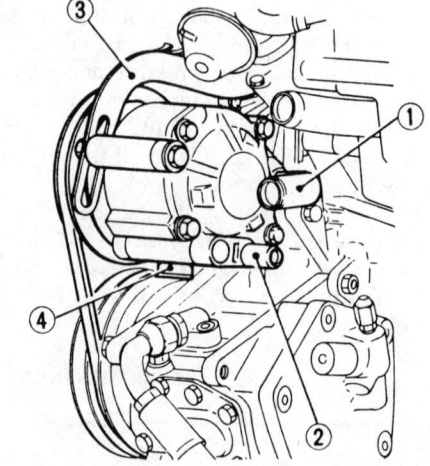

1. Inlet port   3. Belt adjusting bar
2. Outlet port   4. Relief valve

Rear view of the air pump

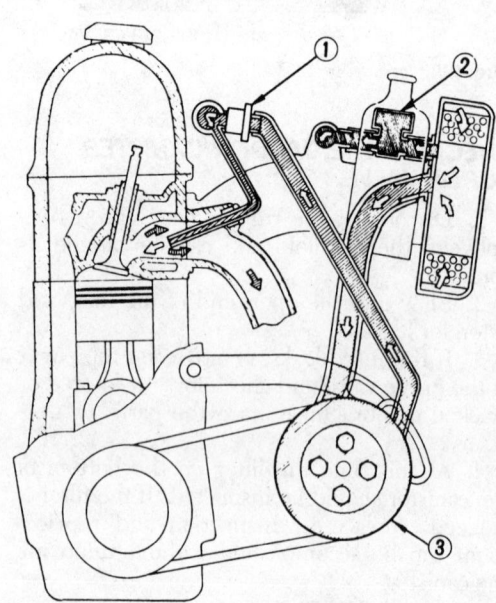

1. Check valve   2. Antibackfire valve   3. Air pump

The air injection system

EMISSION CONTROLS AND FUEL SYSTEM

3. An air pump relief valve. This valve controls the air pump discharge pressure in order to protect the pump from excessive pressure.

TESTING THE AIR PUMP AND VALVES

1. Operate the engine until it reaches operating temperature.
2. Inspect the hoses and connections, replace any damaged hoses or clamps and retighten connections as necessary.
3. Check the air pump belt tension and adjust, as necessary.
4. Disconnect the air supply hose from the check valve.
5. Insert the open end of a special Air Pump Test Gauge Adapter into the air supply hose and clamp it securely. This adapter is required because it provides a relief port of critical size.
6. Operate the engine at 1,500 rpm and read the test gauge. The pressure should be 0.63 in. Hg. or more.
7. With the engine still at 1,500 rpm, close the relief port in the gauge adapter and listen for leaks. If there is any leakage from the relief valve, it is faulty.
8. If the system fails the pressure test, the pump must be replaced unless the problem is in the relief valve.
9. Stop the engine. Inspect the check valve plate position. The plate should be lightly in contact with the seat away from the air manifold.
10. Insert a small screwdriver into the valve connection, depress the valve plate and release it. It should return to the seat freely.
11. Start the engine and slowly bring it's speed to 1,500 rpm. There should be no leakage of exhaust gas from the check valve although a slight fluttering at idle is normal.
12. If the check valve fails any of the tests, replace it.
13. Reconnect the air supply hose and remove the air cleaner cover.
14. Lightly position a finger over the inlet hole for the anti-backfire valve. DO NOT shut the hole off entirely.
15. Increase the engine speed to 3,000–3,500 rpm, then suddenly release the linkage. There should be a sudden flow of air during deceleration. If there is no outflow or if outflow exists under other than deceleration conditions, replace the valve.

AIR PUMP REMOVAL AND INSTALLATION

1. Disconnect the hoses from the housing.
2. Remove the bolt used to position the pump on the belt adjusting bar. Remove the pump-to-mounting bracket bolts.
3. Remove the drive belt and the pump.

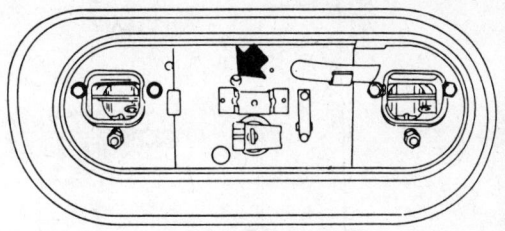

The antibackfire valve air inlet hole

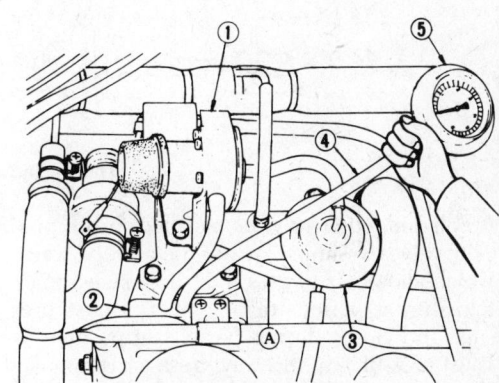

1. Throttle opener control valve
2. Intake manifold
3. Servo diaphragm
4. Vacuum gauge hose
5. Vacuum gauge

Connecting the vacuum gauge to the manifold

4. To install the pump, reverse the removal procedures. Adjust the drive belt tension.

ANTIBACKFIRE VALVE REPLACEMENT

No special instructions are required except that the valve must be replaced with its diaphragm chamber upward. Never attempt to disassemble and repair the valve.

CHECK VALVE REMOVAL AND INSTALLATION

1. Disconnect the air supply hose.
2. While removing the valve, put opposing pressure on the flange of the air manifold with a wrench.
3. To install, reverse the removal procedures, again putting pressure in opposition to installation torque on the air manifold flange. Never attempt to disassemble and repair the valve.

Air Induction System

The 1980, 49 State models have an Air Induction System to supply fresh air to the exhaust manifold. The system is not used on models sold in California or Canada.

The components include an air pipe connecting the air cleaner to the exhaust manifold.

138 EMISSION CONTROLS AND FUEL SYSTEM

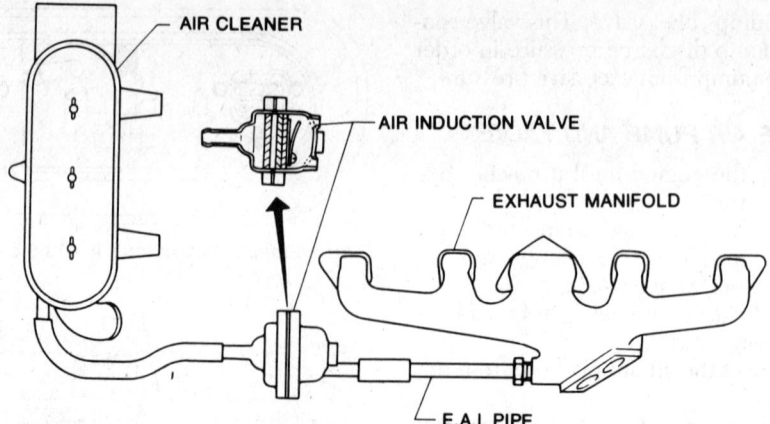

The air induction system

An air induction valve is installed in the pipe. The valve is simply a four petal reed valve, which allows air to pass into the exhaust manifold during periods of negative exhaust pressure and closes during periods of positive exhaust pressure. In this way, fresh air is siphoned into the exhaust manifold without the need for an air pump. The fresh air promotes burning of hot HC and CO gases which otherwise would escape the combustion process.

SERVICE

The only periodic maintenance required is replacement of the air induction filter at 24,000 mile or 30 month intervals. This procedure is covered in Chapter 1.

Throttle Opener

All 1970–73 models and 1974 models, equipped with a manual transmission, have a throttle

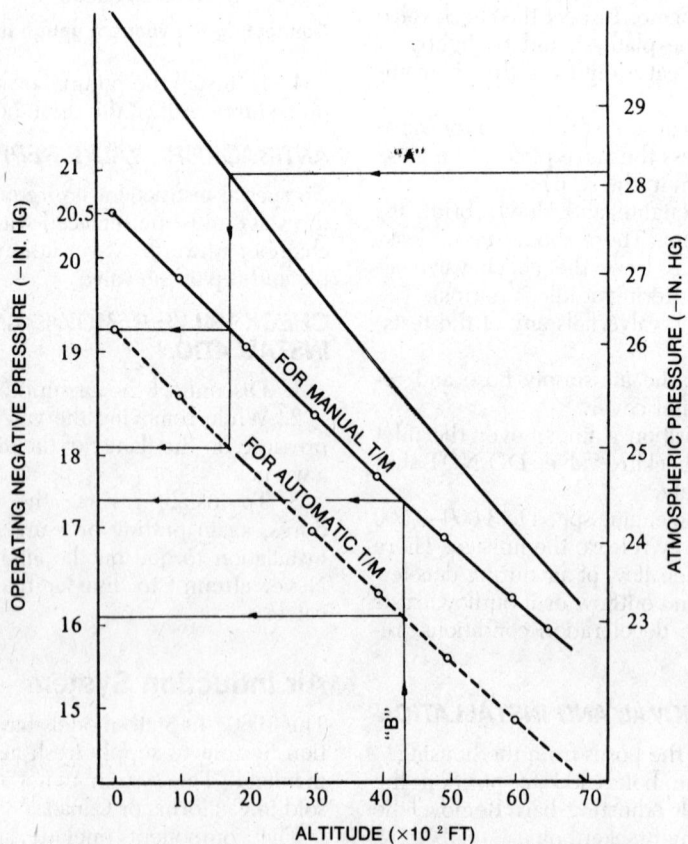

Operating pressure of the throttle opener—1972 and earlier

EMISSION CONTROLS AND FUEL SYSTEM

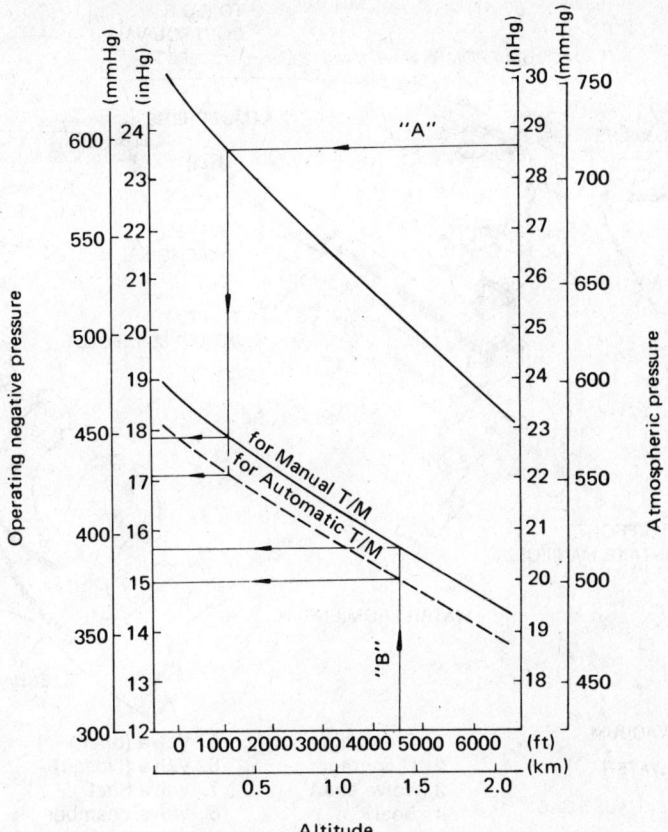

Operating pressure of the throttle opener—1973 and later

opener to reduce emissions during deceleration.

ADJUSTMENT

1. Bring the engine to operating temperature.
2. Disconnect the vacuum hose at point "A." Connect a vacuum gauge which gives quick response where the hose was removed.
3. On 1973 and later models, disconnect the throttle opener solenoid harness.
4. Rev the engine to approximately 3,000 rpm and release the throttle. Note the reading on the pressure gauge between the time that the throttle actuator begins to work and the time that the throttle reaches normal idle position. The reading should be constant between these two points.
5. Compare the reading with the appropriate chart, using the altitude or barometric pressure.
6. Loosen the vacuum adjusting screw locknut and adjust the pressure as necessary. If the pressure is too low, adjust the screw clockwise. It is too high, turn the screw counterclockwise.
7. Tighten the locknut and recheck the adjustment.
8. If the throttle actuator holds the throttle open all the time (engine does not drop to idle speed), it will be necessary to rig the gauge so that it can be read with the vehicle decelerating from about 50 mph in High gear. Adjust the screw as necessary on the basis of this test.

Exhaust Gas Recirculation (EGR) System

Oxides of nitrogen (NOx) are formed in the engine under conditions of high temperature and pressure. Elimination of one of these two conditions reduces the formation of NOx. Exhaust gas recirculation is used to reduce combustion temperatures in the engine.

ALL EXCEPT TURBOCHARGED ENGINES

All 1973–74 models have an EGR. Only the 1975–76 models sold in California have an EGR. All 1977–79 models and all 1980 models (except California) use an EGR system. All 1981 and later models have an EGR system.

An EGR valve is mounted on the intake manifold. The exhaust gas is drawn from the exhaust manifold, through the EGR valve and into the intake manifold. The EGR valve is

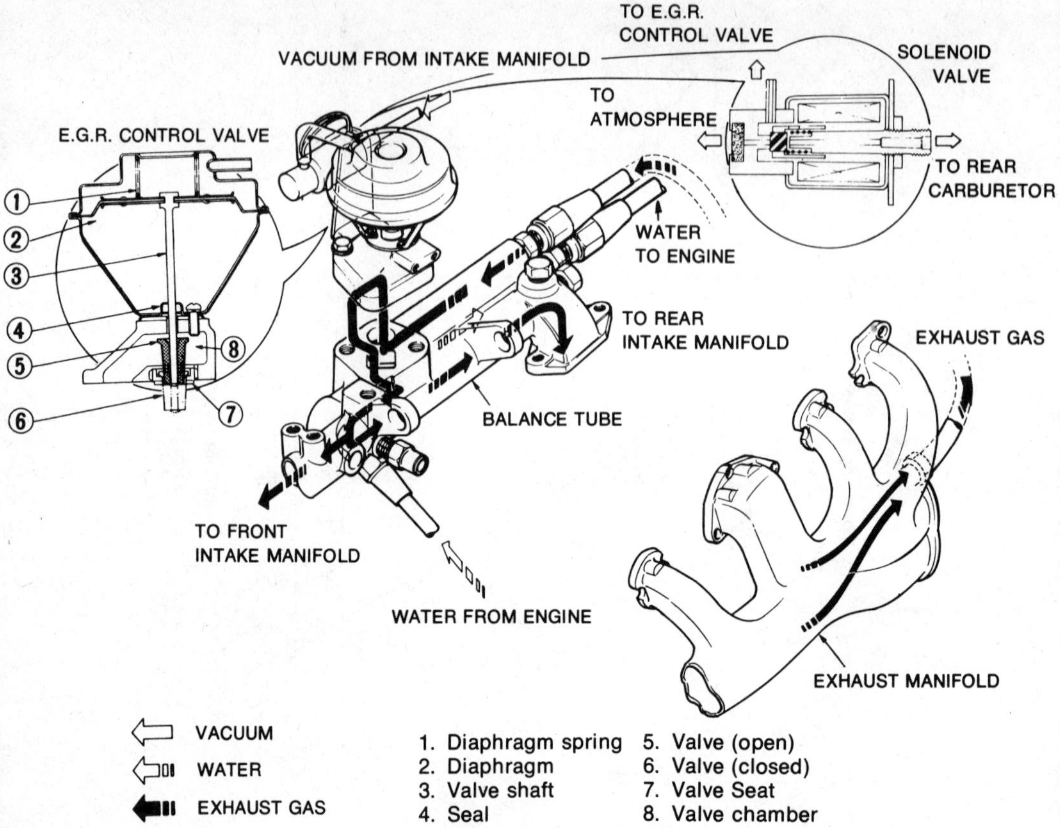

140 EMISSION CONTROLS AND FUEL SYSTEM

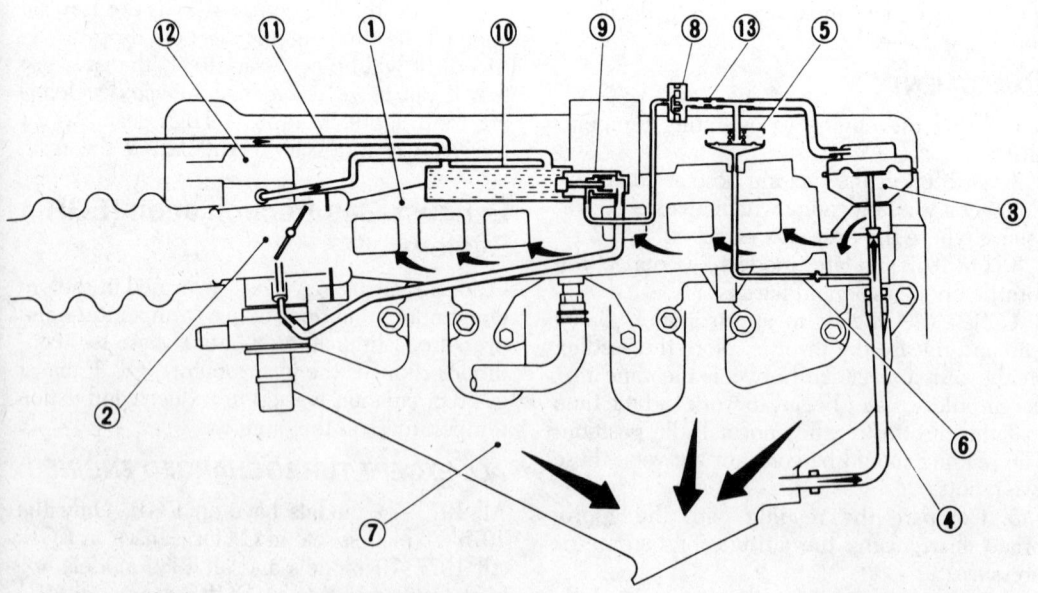

1. Diaphragm spring
2. Diaphragm
3. Valve shaft
4. Seal
5. Valve (open)
6. Valve (closed)
7. Valve Seat
8. Valve chamber

The 1973–74 exhaust gas recirculation system

1. Intake manifold
2. Throttle chamber
3. E.G.R. control valve
4. E.G.R. tube
5. B.P.T. valve
6. B.P.T. valve control tube
7. Exhaust manifold
8. Vacuum delay valve (Models equipped with catalytic converter)
9. Thermal vacuum valve
10. Heater housing
11. Water return tube
12. Thermostat housing
13. Vacuum orifice

EGR system schematic, typical of all 1975–83 models (1979 shown)

EMISSION CONTROLS AND FUEL SYSTEM

closed when the engine is idling; exhaust gas recirculation would cause a rough idle. As the throttle is opened, vacuum is applied to the EGR valve vacuum diaphragm. When the vacuum reaches about 2 inches of mercury (Hg) the diaphragm moves against spring pressure and is fully open at 8 in. Hg. of vacuum. As the diaphragm moves up, it pulls the EGR valve pintle from its seat, allowing exhaust gas to be pulled into the intake manifold by intake vacuum. The valve closes at full throttle, when EGR is not needed, as a means of improving fuel economy.

The 1973–74 models have an electrically operated solenoid valve mounted on the EGR valve. The vacuum signal to the EGR valve must travel through the solenoid valve. The solenoid valve prevents EGR when the engine is cold. Temperature signals to the solenoid valve are sent by a passenger compartment temperature sensor in 1973; as long as the temperature inside the vehicle is below freezing, the solenoid valve blocks vacuum to the EGR valve, preventing exhaust recirculation. The 1974–76 models use a temperature switch installed in the engine coolant outlet housing; as long as engine coolant temperatures remain below approximately 106°F (41°C) for 1974 or below approximately 122°F (50°C), 1975–76, the solenoid valve blocks the vacuum to the EGR valve. When the temperature of the engine coolant or in the passenger compartment, reaches normal operating temperature, the solenoid is deactivated, then the intake manifold vacuum is allowed to act upon the EGR valve diaphragm and exhaust gas recirculation takes place.

On 1977 and later models, a Thermal Vacuum Valve (TVV) controls the application of vacuum to the EGR valve. When the engine coolant reaches a predetermined temperature, the TVV opens and allows vacuum to be routed to the EGR valve. Below the predetermined temperature, the TVV closes and blocks vacuum to the EGR valve.

The 1977–79 models and all 1980, 49 State U.S. models have a Back Pressure Transducer (BPT) valve installed between the EGR valve and the thermal vacuum valve. The BPT valve has a diaphragm raised or lowered by exhaust back pressure. The diaphragm opens or closes an air bleed, which is connected into the EGR vacuum line. High pressure results in higher levels of EGR, because the BPT diaphragm is raised, closing off the air bleed, which allows more vacuum to reach and open the EGR valve. Thus, the amount of recirculated exhaust gas varies with exhaust pressure.

The 1977–78 (California) models, the 1979 (catalytic converter) models and the 1980 (49 State) models have a Vacuum Delay Valve (VDV) installed in the line between the thermal vacuum valve and the EGR valve. The valve delays rapid drops in vacuum in the EGR signal line, thus effecting a longer EGR time.

TURBOCHARGED ENGINES

The EGR is controlled by the central electronic control unit adjusting to the engine operating conditions.

The cylinder head temperature, the engine rpm, the engine load, the air temperature and the barometric pressure are used for determining the amount of the EGR.

These signals are transmitted to the control unit where optimum EGR quantities are recorded. To obtain the optimum EGR quantity that corresponds to the engine operating conditions at the time, an electric signal is sent to the Vacuum Control Modulator (VCM). The vacuum control modulator transforms the electric signal to a vacuum signal, which in turn controls the EGR valve.

A one-way valve is utilized for the purpose of preventing the VCM from applying positive pressure in high speed conditions.

This valve is installed in the vacuum line leading to the VCM.

Inspection

1973–76

1. Visually inspect the entire EGR control system. Clean the mechanism of any oil or dirt. Replace the rubber hoses found to be cracked or broken. On the 1973 models, check the vacuum tube which runs from the solenoid to the carburetor; if deformed, replace it. Torque for this tube is 3.0 ft. lbs. (4.0 Nm).
2. Check the solenoid electrical connections for corrosion, breaks in the insulation or etc. and correct as necessary.
3. Start the engine and allow it to reach normal operating temperature. On the 1973 models, the temperature in the passenger compartment must be over 60°F. Increase the engine speed to 3,000–3,500 rpm. The plate of the EGR control diaphragm and the valve shaft should move upward. This can be more easily seen with a mirror placed under the EGR valve.
4. Disconnect the EGR solenoid electrical leads and connect them directly to the vehicle battery with a pair of jumper cables. Race the engine again with the solenoid connected to the battery. The EGR valve diaphragm should remain stationary.
5. With the engine running at idle, reach up under the EGR valve and raise the diaphragm by pushing it upwards with your fin-

gers. Wear a heavy glove to protect your hand from the hot engine. When the diaphragm is raised, the idle should become rough, indicating that exhaust gases are recirculating. If the roughness does not occur, the EGR passages are blocked.

Inspect the individual components as follows:

1. Remove the EGR valve from the intake manifold.
2. Apply 6.0 in. Hg of vacuum to the EGR valve vacuum connection. The valve should open. Pinch off the connection with the vacuum still applied. The valve should remain in the raised position for at least 30 seconds.
3. Inspect the EGR valve for any signs of warpage or damage and replace as necessary.
4. Clean the EGR valve seat with a brush and compressed air.
5. Connect the solenoid to a 12 volt DC power source. The solenoid should click when power is applied. If the valve clicks, it is considered to be working properly.
6. Check the 1974–76 temperature switch by removing it from the engine (drain the engine coolant first) and placing it in a container of water together with a thermometer. Connect a self-powered test light to the temperature switch electrical leads. Heat the water. The switch should conduct current when the water temperature is below 77°F (25°C) on 1974 models or below 122°F (50°C) on 1975–76 models. The switch should stop conduction somewhere between 88–106°F (31–41°C) on 1974 models or between 134–145°F (57–63°C) on 1975–76 models. Replace the switch if it behaves otherwise.

1977 AND LATER

1. Remove the EGR valve. Apply enough vacuum to the EGR valve vacuum connection to raise the diaphragm and open the valve. Pinch off the vacuum connection. The valve should remain open for at least 30 seconds. If not, the diaphragm is leaking and the valve must be replaced.
2. Check the valve for damage, warpage, cracks or etc. and replace as necessary.
3. Clean the valve seat with a wire brush and compressed air.
4. Install the EGR valve on the engine. Start the engine and allow it to idle. With the engine idling, reach up under the EGR valve and raise the diaphragm by pushing it upwards with your fingers. Wear a glove to protect your hand if the engine is hot. When the diaphragm is raised, the engine idle should become rough, indicating that exhaust gases are recirculating. If the roughness does not occur, the EGR passages are blocked.
5. To check the operation of the thermal vacuum valve, drain the engine coolant and remove the valve. Connect two lengths of vacuum hose to the two TVV vacuum connections. Place the valve in a container of water together with a thermostat, with the vacuum hoses above the level of the water. DO NOT allow water to get into the valve. When the temperature is below 177°F (47°C), the vacuum passage should be closed. Check this by sucking on one of the vacuum hoses.
6. Heat the water. On 1977 models, the valve should open (conduct vacuum) when the water temperature reaches 117–127°F (47–53°C). On

EGR valve (left) and BPT valve (right)

EMISSION CONTROLS AND FUEL SYSTEM

1978–80 models, the valve should open at about 122°F (50°C) and remain open until the water temperature reaches about 203°F (95°C). On 1978 and later models only, the valve should close again when water temperature reaches about 208°F (98°C). Replace the valve if it behaves otherwise.

7. To test the BPT valve installed on some 1977 and later models, disconnect the two vacuum hoses on the valve. Plug one of the ports. While applying pressure to the bottom of the valve, apply vacuum to the unplugged port and check for leakage. If any exists, replace the valve.

8. To check the delay valve installed on some 1977 and later models, remove the valve and blow into the side which connects to the EGR or BPT valve. Air should flow. When air is applied to the other side, air flow resistance should be greater. If not, replace the valve.

EGR VALVE AND BALANCE TUBE REMOVAL AND INSTALLATION

1. Disconnect the vacuum line from the EGR valve.
2. Remove the two valve mounting bolts and the valve.
3. To remove the balance tube on 1973–74 models, disconnect:
   a. The fuel hose to the rear carburetor.
   b. The hose between the air cleaner and rocker cover.
   c. The hose between the anti-backfire valve and balance tube.
   d. The vacuum lines between the balance tube-to-air cleaner, intake manifold-to-throttle opener valve and throttle opener valve-to-air cleaner.
4. Remove the throttle opener valve and servo.
5. Disconnect the water tube between the thermostat housing and balance tube.
6. Remove the exhaust gas return tube and water outlet hose.
7. Disconnect the throttle linkage at the joint.
8. Remove the mounting bolts and pull the balance tube from the engine. Disconnect the idle screw block-to-air/fuel by-pass tube hose.
9. To install, reverse the removal procedures.

Automatic Temperature Control (ATC) Air Cleaner (1970–74)

This system is designed to stabilize the temperature of air going to the carburetors in order to permit smooth operation with leaner fuel/air mixtures. It incorporates a temperature sensor which feeds a vacuum motor varying amounts of vacuum according to the temperature of the air in the air cleaner. The vacuum motor controls an air door which in turn controls the amount of air to pass over the exhaust manifold on its way to the air cleaner.

ATC SYSTEM TEST

1. Allow the engine to cool until the engine compartment is below 86°F (30°C). Make sure that the air door is open.
2. Start the engine and operate it at idle. If the air door closes right away, it and the vacuum motor are in good condition.
3. Watch the air door to ensure that it opens gradually. In hot weather, it will eventually open all the way; in cold weather, it will open only slightly.
4. If there is doubt about the operation of the system, tape a small thermometer to the inside of the air cleaner cover, as close as possible to the sensor. Then operate the engine until the thermometer has had time to reach a stable reading. Finally, open the air cleaner and read the thermometer. It should read between 100–130°F (38–55°C).
5. If the system is faulty, the vacuum motor may be tested by removing it's vacuum supply hose from the temperature sensor and connecting it directly to the manifold. If the valve closes with the engine operating at idle speed, the problem must be in the temperature sensor or the hoses.

Manifold Heat Control Thermostat

This device is installed on 1970–72 models, to heat the manifold during engine warmup. En-

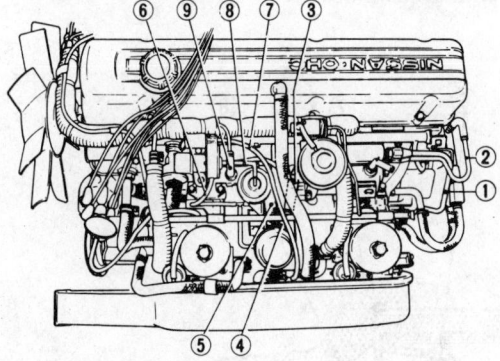

1. Exhaust gas return tube
2. Water outlet tube
3. ISS hose
4. Crankcase ventilation hose
5. Antibackfire valve hose
6. Throttle opener vacuum signal hose
7. Throttle opener hose (throttle opener to air cleaner)
8. Throttle opener hose (throttle opener to servo diaphragm)
9. Canister purge hose

EGR connections, 1970–74

144 EMISSION CONTROLS AND FUEL SYSTEM

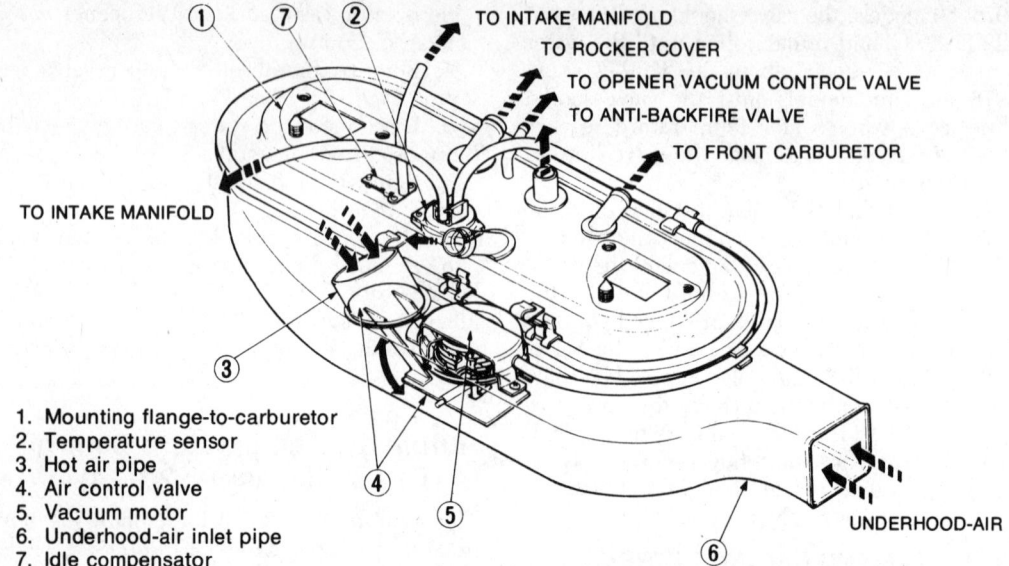

1. Mounting flange-to-carburetor
2. Temperature sensor
3. Hot air pipe
4. Air control valve
5. Vacuum motor
6. Underhood-air inlet pipe
7. Idle compensator

The ATC air cleaner

gine coolant passes through passages in the manifold until a temperature of about 150°F exists. At this point, the thermostat closes off the flow of coolant through the manifold.

To test the thermostat, remove it and attach a length of rubber hose to the inlet end. Then immerse the thermostat in water heated to 175°F. After the thermostat has had a minute or so to reach the temperature of the water, force air at low pressure into the hose. If bubbles come out the other end of the thermostat, replace it.

Boost Controlled Deceleration Device

This unit is used on all 1975 and later models (except turbocharged engines), to perform the same function as the throttle opener used on earlier models, to reduce emissions of HC during deceleration. The device is a part of the throttle chamber and is located at the bottom. If the throttle hangs open for long periods during deceleration, it's a sign that the BCDD requires adjustment. This should be referred to your Datsun dealer.

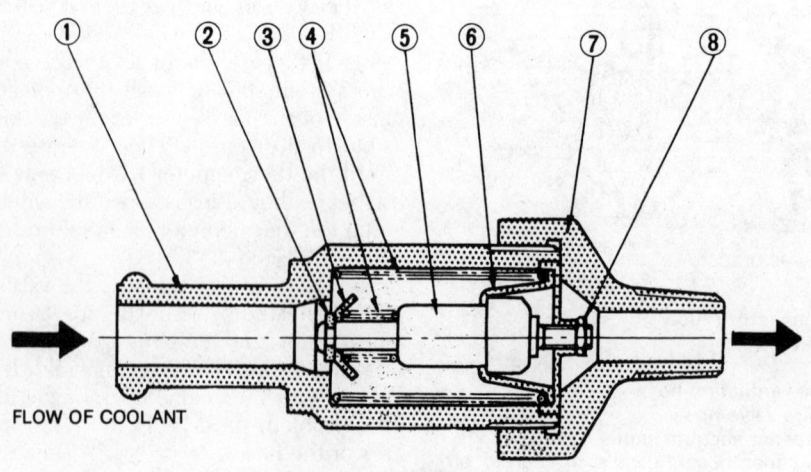

1. Case
2. E-ring
3. Valve
4. Spring
5. Pellet
6. Supporting case
7. Adjusting nut
8. Case cover

The manifold heat control thermostat

EMISSION CONTROLS AND FUEL SYSTEM

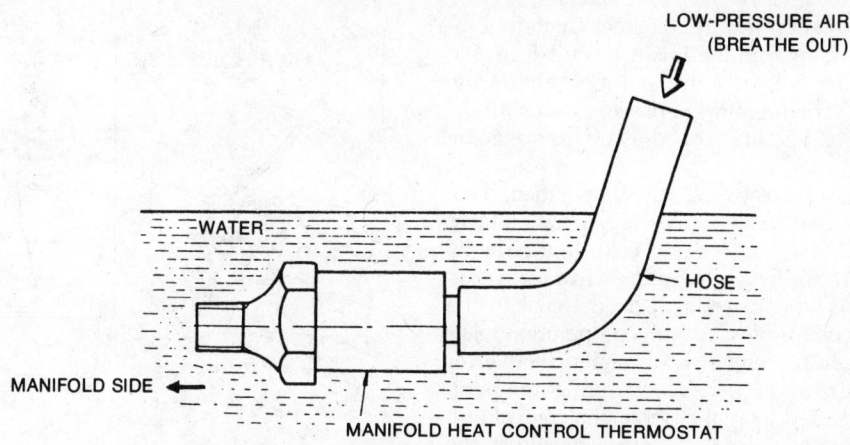

Checking the manifold heat control thermostat

Catalytic Converter

All 1975 and later (California) models, some 1979 (49 States) models and all 1980 and later (U.S. and Canada) models, have a catalytic converter, which is a muffler-shaped device installed in the exhaust system. The converter is filled with a monolithic substrate coated with small amounts of platinum and palladium. Through catalytic action, a chemical change converts carbon monoxide and hydrocarbons into carbon dioxide and water. The 1980 (California) models and all 1981 and later models, have a three-way catalytic converter. Platinum, palladium and rhodium are used in an oxidation-reduction process which acts on all three major constituents of exhaust pollution; HC and CO are oxidized in the usual manner into H_2O and CO_2, plus oxides of nitrogen are reduced to free oxygen and nitrogen (O_2 and N_2 respectively).

The 1975–78 (California) models have a floor temperature warning system, consisting of a temperature sensor installed onto the floor of the vehicle above the converter; a relay, located under the passenger seat and a light, installed on the instrument panel. The lamp illuminates when floor temperatures become abnormally high, due to converter or engine malfunction. The light also comes ON when the ignition switch is turned to Start, to check it's operation. The 1979 and later models do not have the warning system.

The 1980 (California) models and all 1981 and later models have an oxygen sensor warning light on the dashboard, which illuminates at the first 30,000 mile interval, signaling the need for oxygen sensor replacement. The oxygen sensor is part of the Mixture Ratio Feedback System, described later in this section. The Feedback System uses the three-way converter as one of its major components.

No regular maintenance is required for the catalytic converter system, except for periodic replacement of the Air Induction System filter on 1980 (49 State) models. The Air Induction System is described earlier in this chapter; filter replacement procedures are in Chapter 1. The Air Induction System is used to supply the catalytic converter with fresh air; oxygen present in the air is used in the oxidation process.

Mixture Ratio Feedback System

The need for better fuel economy coupled to increasingly strict emission control regulations dictates a more exact control of the engine air/fuel mixture. Datsun has developed a Mixture Ratio Feedback System in response to these needs. The system is installed on all 1980 (California) models and all 1981 and later models.

The principle of the system is to control the air/fuel mixture, so that more complete combustion can occur in the engine, more thorough oxidation and reduction of the exhaust gases can occur in the catalytic converter. The object is to maintain a stoichiometric air/fuel mixture, which is chemically correct for theoretically complete combustion. The stoichiometric ratio is 14.7:1 (air to fuel). At that point, the converter's efficiency is greatest in oxidizing and reducing HC, CO and NOx into CO_2, H_2O, O_2, and N_2.

Components used in the system include an oxygen sensor (installed in the exhaust manifold upstream of the converter), a three-way oxidation-reduction catalytic converter, an electronic control unit (part of the electronic fuel injection control unit) and the fuel injection system.

The oxygen sensor reads the oxygen content of the exhaust gases. It generates an electrical signal which is sent to the control unit. The control unit then decides how to adjust the

146 EMISSION CONTROLS AND FUEL SYSTEM

mixture to keep it at the correct air-to-fuel ratio. For example, if the mixture is too lean, the control unit increases the fuel metering to the injectors. The monitoring process is a continual one, so that fine mixture adjustments are going on at all times.

The system has two modes of operation: open loop and closed loop. Open loop operation takes place when the engine is still cold. In this mode, the control unit ignores signals from the oxygen sensor and provides a fixed signal to the fuel injection unit. Closed loop operation takes place when the engine and catalytic converter have warmed to normal operating temperature. In closed loop operation, the control unit uses the oxygen sensor signals to adjust the mixture; the burned mixture's oxygen content is read by the oxygen sensor, which continues to signal the control unit and etc. Thus, the closed loop mode is an interdependent system of information feedback.

Mixture is, of course, not readily adjustable in this system. All system adjustments require the use of a CO meter; thus, this should be entrusted to a qualified dealer with access to the equipment and special training in the system's repair. The only regularly scheduled maintenance is replacement of the oxygen sensor at 30,000 mile intervals. This procedure is covered in the following section.

It should be noted that proper operation of the system is entirely dependent on the oxygen sensor. Thus, if the sensor is not replaced at the correct interval or if the sensor fails during normal operation, the engine fuel mixture will be incorrect, resulting in poor fuel economy, starting problems, stumbling and stalling of the engine when warm.

Oxygen Sensor

An exhaust gas sensor warning light will illuminate on the instrument panel when the vehicle has reached 30,000 miles. This is a signal that the oxygen sensor must be replaced.

Note that the warning light is not part of a repeating system; that is, after the first 30,000 mile service, the warning light will not illuminate again. However, it is important to replace the oxygen sensor every 30,000 miles, to ensure proper monitoring and control of the engine air/fuel mixture.

INSPECTION

1. Start the engine and allow it to reach normal operating temperature.
2. Run the engine at approximately 2,000 rpm under no load. Block the front wheels and set the parking brake.
3. An inspection lamp has been provided on

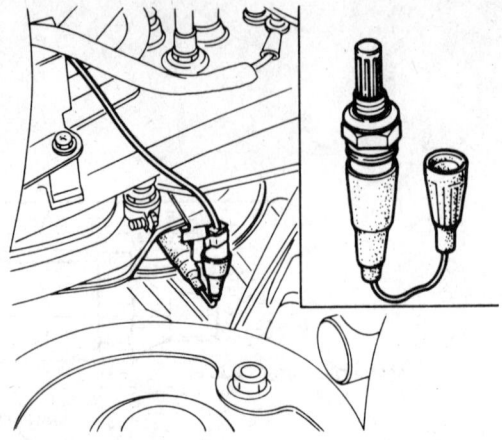

Oxygen sensor

the bottom of the control unit, which is located in the passenger compartment on the driver's side kick panel, next to the clutch or brake pedal. If the oxygen sensor is operating correctly, the inspection lamp will go on and off more than 5 times in 10 seconds. The inspection lamp can be more easily seen with the aid of a mirror.

4. If the lamp does not go on and off as specified, the system is not operating correctly. Check the battery, the ignition system, the engine oil, the coolant levels, the fuses, the fuel injection wiring harness connectors, the vacuum hoses, the oil filler cap and dipstick for proper seating, the valve clearance and the engine compression. If all of these parts are in good working order and the inspection lamp still does not function correctly, the oxygen sensor is probably faulty. However, the possibility exists that the malfunction could be in the fuel injection control unit. The system should be tested by a qualified dealer with specific training in the Mixture Ratio Feedback System.

REMOVAL AND INSTALLATION

1. Disconnect the negative battery cable.
2. Disconnect the sensor electrical lead. Unscrew the sensor from the exhaust manifold.
3. Coat the threads of the replacement sensor with a nickel base anti-seize compound. DO NOT use other types of compounds, since they may electrically insulate the sensor.
4. To install the sensor into the manifold, reverse the removal procedures. Torque the sensor is 29–36 ft. lbs. (40–50 Nm).

CAUTION: *Be careful handling the electrical lead; it is easily damaged.*

NOTE: *After the first 30,000 mile replacement, the warning lamp harness connector should be unplugged to extinguish the lamp. The connector is located under the right-side*

EMISSION CONTROLS AND FUEL SYSTEM

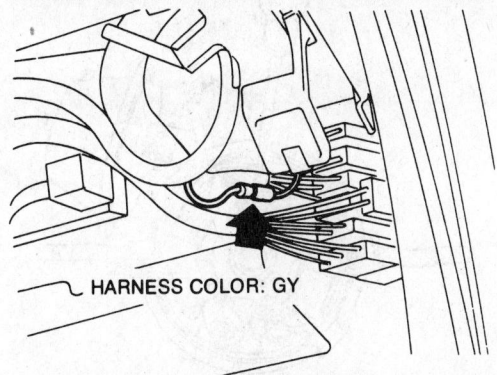

UNDER THE RIGHT SIDE OF INSTRUMENT PANEL
HARNESS COLOR: GY

Oxygen sensor warning lamp harness connector

of the instrument panel; the harness wire color is green with a yellow stripe.

Spark Timing Control System (1970–76)

Retardation of the ignition timing can be used to control the emission of oxides of nitrogen and hydrocarbons. The 1970–73 (A/T) models have a dual point distributor to provide advanced and retarded distributor characteristics. The 1974 (A/T) models and 1975–76 (49 States and Canada) models use a distributor with dual pick-ups for the same purpose.

The distributor has two sets of breaker points or two electronic ignition pick-ups which operate independently of each other and are positioned with a relative phase angle of 10° (1970–73), 7° (1974) or 6° (1975–76) apart. This makes one set the advanced set and the other the retarded set.

The two sets are connected in parallel to the primary side of the ignition circuit. One set of points or pick-ups controls the firing of the spark plugs and hence the ignition timing, depending on whether or not the retarded set is energized.

When both sets are electrically energized, the first set to open has no control over breaking the ignition coil primary circuit because the retarded set is still closed and maintaining a complete circuit to ground. When the retarded set opens, the advanced set is still open and the primary circuit is broken causing the electromagnetic field in the ignition coil to collapse and the ignition spark to be produced.

When the retarded set is removed from the primary ignition circuit through the operation of a distributor relay inserted into the retarded circuit, the advanced set controls the primary circuit.

PHASE DIFFERENCE ADJUSTMENT

1. On 1970–73 models, disconnect the distributor wiring harness from the engine harness. Connect the black wire of the engine harness to the black wire of the distributor harness using a jumper wire. This connects the advanced set of points. On 1974 models, disconnect the engine harness from the coolant temperature switch. This activates the advanced pick-up. On 1975–76 models, disconnect the red engine harness wire from the coolant temperature switch. Ground the engine harness wire to the engine block (use a jumper wire if necessary).

2. With the engine at normal operating temperature and idling at the specified idling speed, adjust the engine timing to the advanced specification.

3. On 1970–73 models, disconnect the jumper wire from the black wire of the distributor harness and connect it to the yellow wire of the distributor harness. This connects the retarded set of points. To connect the retarded pick-ups on the 1974 models, use a jumper wire to short circuit the engine harness wire disconnected from the temperature switch in Step 1. This will short circuit the advance control relay. On the 1975–76 models, remove the ground

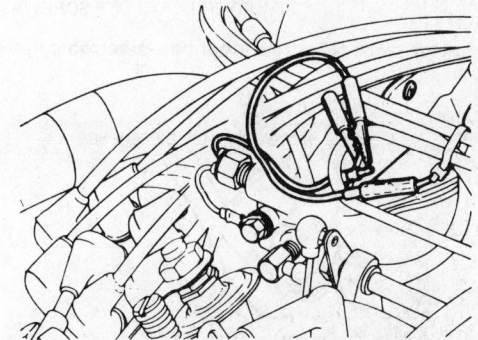

Ground the engine harness wire (1975–76)

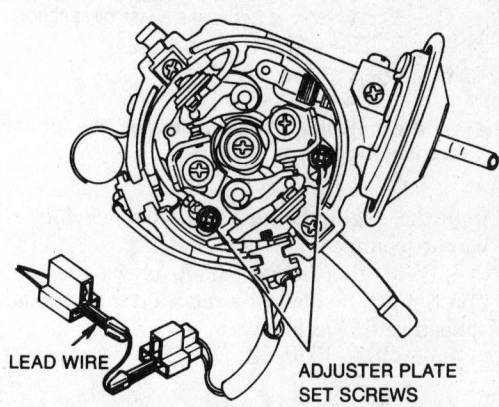

LEAD WIRE — ADJUSTER PLATE SET SCREWS

Adjuster plate set screw location—1970–73

148 EMISSION CONTROLS AND FUEL SYSTEM

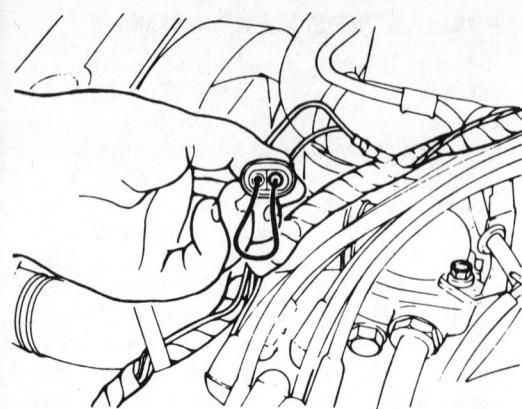

Jumper wire connection to the engine harness (1974)

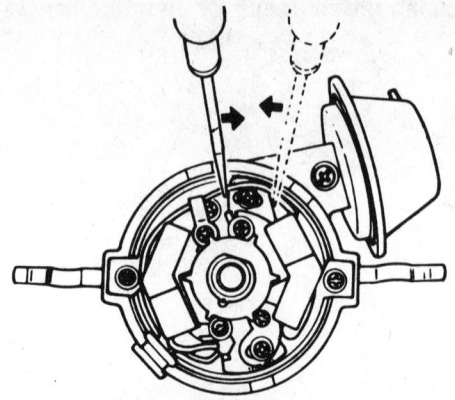

Phase difference adjustment on electronic ignition models

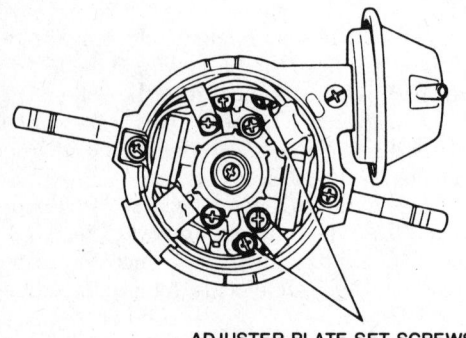

Adjuster plate set screw location—electronic ignition

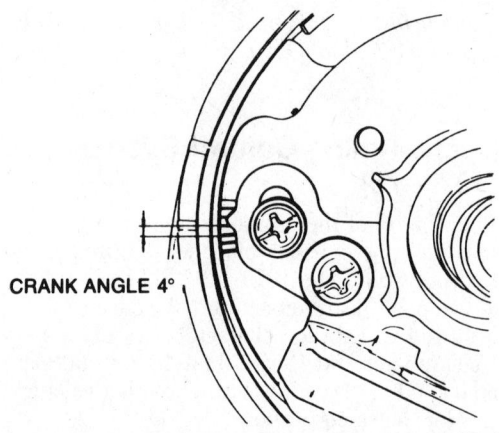

The graduations on the adjuster plate equal 4° of crankshaft rotation

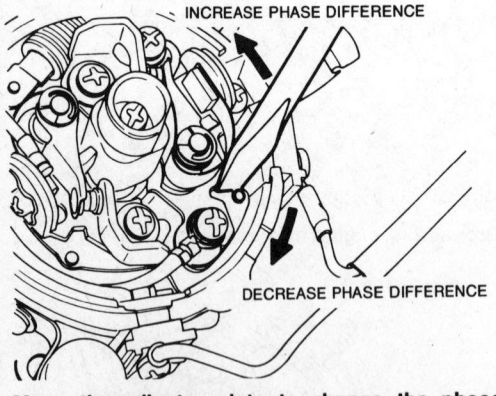

Move the adjuster plate to change the phase difference—point type models

from the engine harness red wire, leaving the wire disconnected.

4. With the engine idling, check the ignition timing. It should be retarded from the advanced setting as follows:
 • 10°—1970–73
 • 7°—1974
 • 6°—1975–76

5. To adjust the phase angle of the ignition timing, loosen the adjuster plate set screws on the same side as the retarded point or pick-up set.

6. Place the blade of a screwdriver in the adjusting notch of the adjuster plate and move the adjuster plate as required to obtain the correct retarded ignition timing specification. The timing is retarded when the adjuster plate is turned counterclockwise. There are graduations on the plate to make the adjustment easier: one graduation is equal to 4° of crankshaft rotation.

7. Replace the distributor cap, start the engine and check the ignition timing with the retarded side activated (as in Step 3).

8. Repeat Steps 6 and 7 as necessary to properly set the retarded ignition timing.

Transmission Controlled Spark Advance (1975–76)

This system is used on all 1975–76 (M/T) models, except those delivered in California. The system consists of a transmission mounted electri-

EMISSION CONTROLS AND FUEL SYSTEM

cal switch and a vacuum switching valve. The switch functions to limit vacuum advance to operation in 4th gear only. The vacuum switching valve is energized in all gears except 4th and vents vacuum from the throttle chamber into the atmosphere. When the transmission is shifted into 4th gear, the switch breaks the circuit and the vacuum valve is deenergized and vacuum reaches the advance unit on the distributor.

Spark Timing Control System

Two different systems are used in 1979–80 but both are given the name of Spark Timing Control System. Basically, both systems are designed to control distributor vacuum advance.

1979

All U.S. models with a catalytic converter and all models sold in Canada have this system. It is designed to control distributor vacuum advance during acceleration to limit emissions of HC and NOx.

The system simply consists of a vacuum delay valve spliced into the distributor vacuum advance hose. During acceleration, the valve restricts the amount of air flow in the vacuum hose. Inside the valve are a metering disc and a one-way umbrella valve. Air flows freely past the umbrella valve, from the throttle to the distributor. The metering valve restricts air flow in the opposite direction, from the distributor to the throttle.

1980 and Later

This system is slightly more complicated than the 1979 system. Spark timing is controlled by a single Thermal Vacuum Valve (TVV) on the California and Canada models. The 1980 (California) models and all 1981 and later (USA) models have a TVV installed in the engine thermostat housing. The valve has two vacuum connections: one for fresh air from the vacuum connector, the other to the distributor vacuum advance. The 1980 and later (Canadian) models have a TVV installed in the intake manifold heater housing. The valve has three vacuum connections: one for fresh air, one to the EGR valve and one to the distributor vacuum advance.

The USA models have two TVVs and a one-way valve. One TVV is installed in the intake manifold in the same manner as the Canadian TVV; it has the same connections as the Canadian TVV. The other TVV is installed in the thermostat housing and also has three vacuum connections: one to the one-way valve, one to the distributor vacuum advance unit and one to a vacuum source on the throttle chamber. The one-way valve is installed in the line between the vacuum connector and the TVV installed in the thermostat housing.

INSPECTION

1979

1. Remove the valve from the distributor vacuum hose.
2. Blow through the valve from the throttle side. This is the black side of the valve. Air should flow through freely.
3. Blow through the distributor side of the valve. This is the brown side. There should be resistance to the air flow.
4. If the valve does not perform correctly, replace it. When installing the valve, be sure the brown side is connected to the distributor hose and the black side is connected to the throttle hose.

1980 and Later

This inspection procedure applies to the entire system, regardless of the specific components used.

1. Check all vacuum hoses for leaks, kinks, breaks, improper connections or etc., then correct, as necessary.
2. Check that the distributor vacuum advance unit is working properly.
3. Connect a timing light to the engine.
4. Check the TVV as follows:
   a. Start the engine; it must be cold. Check and record the ignition timing.
   b. As the engine warms up, check and record the ignition timing. The timing should be retarded from it's cold setting.
   c. Allow the engine to warm up to normal operating temperature. The timing should advance to it's normal setting.
5. If the timing does not change as specified, replace the TVV (both TVVs on USA State models).
6. The one-way valve installed on USA models can be inspected as follows:
   a. Remove the one-way valve.
   b. Blow air through the vacuum connector side of the valve (black side). Air should flow through freely.
   c. Blow air through the TVV side of the valve (white side); there should be resistance to the air flow.
   d. If the valve does not perform correctly, replace it. When installing the valve, be sure that the black side is connected to the vacuum connector hose and the white side is connected to the TVV hose.

150 EMISSION CONTROLS AND FUEL SYSTEM

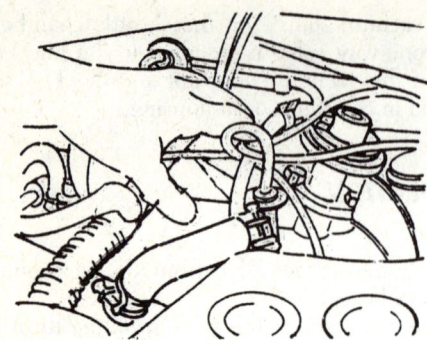

Checking the vacuum control valve

Deceleration Control System

VACUUM CONTROL VALVE

This system is used on 1981 and later (turbocharged) models and is designed to control the intake manifold vacuum under decelerating driving conditions so as to reduce oil consumption. Air is directed from a 3-way connector through an air hose and vacuum control valve. To keep oil consumption low, as the air enters, the intake manifold vacuum will be maintained at less than the specified level. To check the operation of the vacuum control valve proceed as follows:

1. Disconnect one end (Air Regulator side) of the air hose connecting the 3-way connector to the control valve.
2. Make sure that the vacuum control valve operates when the engine speed is decreased from 3,500–4,000 rpm to idle.
3. Place fingers on the hose end to check for valve operation. If the intake vacuum is not present at the end of the air hose, replace the vacuum control valve.

NOTE: *The above procedure is not accurate at altitudes above 2,300–4,000 ft. range.*

CARBURETED FUEL SYSTEM

Mechanical Fuel Pump (1970–74)

REMOVAL AND INSTALLATION

1. Disconnect the inlet and outlet lines from the pump.
2. Remove the mounting bolts.
3. Remove the pump and discard the gasket.
4. Lubricate the rocker arm, rocker arm pin and lever pin of the pump.
5. Put a new gasket into position and bolt the pump in place.
6. Connect the fuel lines.

1. Gasket
2. Inlet pipe
3. Fuel return connector
4. Outlet pipe
5. Valve ass'y
6. Valve gasket
7. Valve retainer
8. Diaphragm
9. Diaphragm spring
10. Spacer
11. Gasket
12. Rocker arm spring

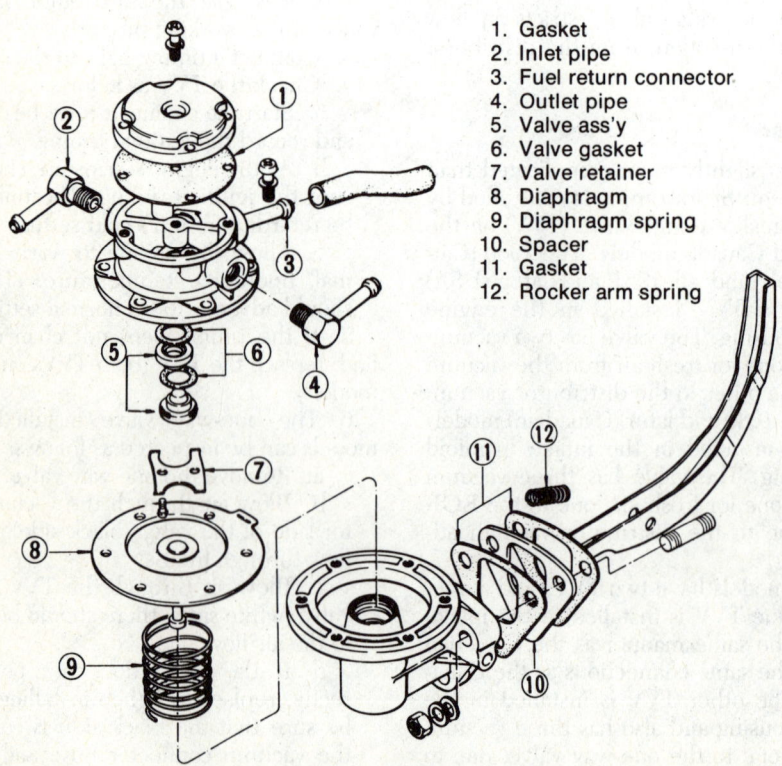

The mechanical fuel pump

EMISSION CONTROLS AND FUEL SYSTEM 151

TESTING

1. Disconnect the fuel pump-to-carburetor hose from the pump.
2. Tee in a pressure gauge going as close to the carburetor as possible.
3. Start the engine and operate it at various speeds. The fuel pump pressure should be 3.4–4.25 psi.

Pressure below these specifications indicates excessive wear, while high pressure indicates a faulty spring or diaphragm. In either case, the pump requires removal and disassembly for replacement of faulty parts. If the pump passes the pressure test but if there is still a question that it's performance may not be adequate, proceed with the capacity test below.

1. Disconnect the pressure gauge from the tee and position a large container under the open end.
2. Start the engine and operate it at 1,000

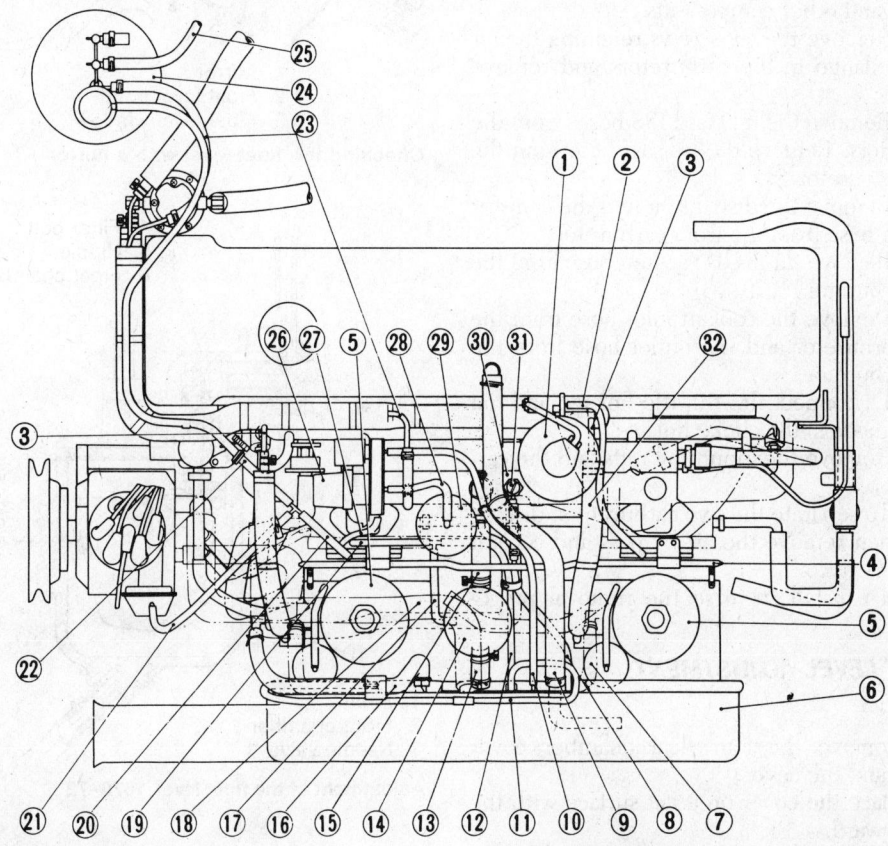

1. E.G.R. control valve
2. E.G.R. vacuum signal hose
3. Fuel inlet hose
4. I.S.S. tube
5. Carburetor
6. Air cleaner
7. Air by-pass hose
8. Idle compensator hose
9. Crankcase ventilation hose
10. Throttle opener hose (from throttle opener solenoid to air cleaner)
11. Temp. sensor hose (from temp. sensor to vacuum motor)
12. Temp. sensor hose (from temp. sensor to intake manifold)
13. A. B. valve hose (from air cleaner to A. B. valve)
14. Antibackfire (A. B.) valve
15. A. B. valve hose (from A. B. valve to balance tube)
16. Air by-pass hose (from air cleaner to front carburetor)
17. A. B. valve vacuum signal hose
18. Air pump inlet hose
19. A. B. valve and temp. sensor vacuum signal hose
20. Distributor and canister vacuum signal hose
21. Distributor vacuum signal hose
22. Canister vacuum signal hose
23. Canister purge hose
24. Carbon canister
25. Vapor vent hose
26. Throttle opener control valve
27. Throttle opener vacuum signal hose
28. Throttle opener servo diaphragm hose
29. Throttle opener servo diaphragm
30. Balance tube
31. Idle speed adjusting screw
32. Heat shield material

Carburetor and air cleaner piping

152 EMISSION CONTROLS AND FUEL SYSTEM

rpm for 15 seconds. The pump should deliver at least 0.42 qts (400 cc) of fuel in this time.
NOTE: *Failure of this test indicates a faulty pump or clogged suction line.*

Carburetors

REMOVAL AND INSTALLATION

1. Remove the three thumb screws and detach the air cleaner cover.
2. Disconnect all of the hoses between air cleaner and other components.
3. Remove the six screws retaining the air cleaner flange to the carburetors and remove it.
4. Remove the fuel and ISS hoses from the carburetors. Remove the by-pass hose from the front carburetor.
5. Remove the distributor and the canister vacuum hose from the front carburetor.
6. Remove the EGR vacuum hose from the rear carburetor (1970–73).
7. Remove the coolant inlet hose from the front carburetor and the outlet hose from the rear carburetor.
8. Disconnect the throttle linkage and (on earlier models) the choke linkage.
9. Remove the mounting nuts and the carburetors.
10. To separate the two carburetors, disconnect, then remove the air by-pass and coolant hoses.
11. To install, reverse the removal procedures.

FLOAT LEVEL ADJUSTMENT

1970–72

1. Remove the four float chamber cover screws and the cover.
2. Place the cover on a flat surface with the float upward.
3. Lift the float up until the needle valve is open and then lower it just until the needle valve contacts the seat.
4. See the illustration and measure the distance between fuel level and the top of the float chamber. It should be 0.5512–0.5906 in. (14–15 mm).
5. If necessary, correct the dimension by bending the float lever.
6. Replace the float chamber cover.

1973

1. Remove the carburetor from the engine. Remove the float chamber cover.
2. Measure the distance between the portion of the float lever which contacts the needle valve and the float chamber cover. It should be 0.598 in. (15.2 mm).

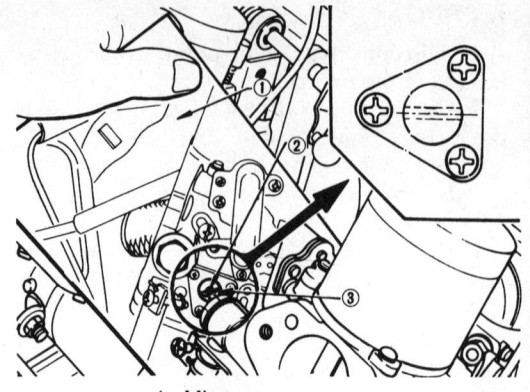

1. Mirror
2. Float level point
3. Float level window

Checking the float level with a mirror

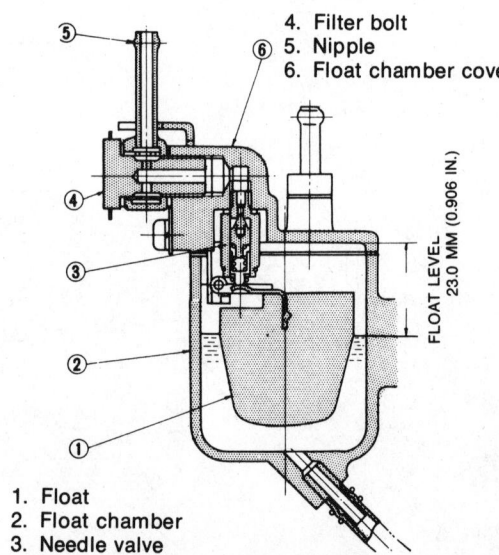

4. Filter bolt
5. Nipple
6. Float chamber cover

1. Float
2. Float chamber
3. Needle valve

Adjustment of the float level, 1970–72

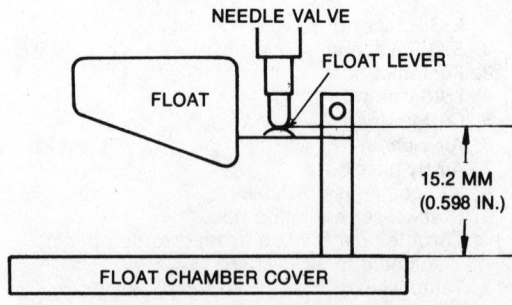

Where to check float level height—1973 models

3. If necessary, bend the float lever to adjust the dimension. Recheck to make sure that the dimension is to specification.
4. Install the float chamber cover and reinstall the carburetor on the engine.

EMISSION CONTROLS AND FUEL SYSTEM

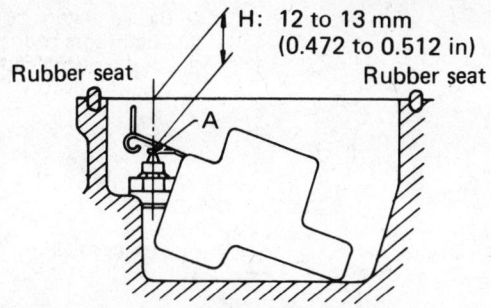

Measuring dimension "H"

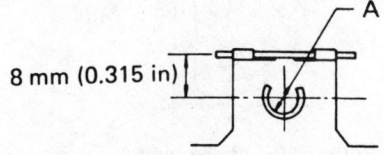

The location of point "A"

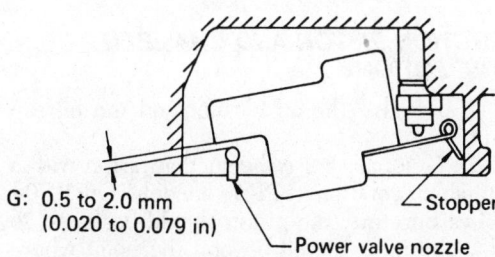

The location of dimension "G"

5. Check float level by operating the engine and checking that the fuel level is in the center of the float level window.

1974

1. Remove the carburetor from the intake manifold. Remove the seven attaching screws and remove the float chamber cover.
2. Turn the carburetor upside down to check the position of the float lever. Both floats should touch the inner wall of the carburetor.
3. Measure dimension "H" between the end face of the float chamber and the float lever tongue which contacts the needle valve (point "A"). It should be 0.472–0.512 in. (12–13 mm).
4. If necessary, bend the float lever near the float to bring the dimension to within specifications.
5. Turn the carburetor right side up. Measure the gap "G" between the power valve nozzle and float. It should be 0.020–0.079 in. (0.5–2.0 mm).
6. Adjust the gap, as necessary, by bending the stop as required; then, recheck dimension "H."
7. Install the float chamber cover and install the carburetor on the engine.
8. When the engine is operating, the fuel level should be even with the center line of the float level window.

FAST IDLE ADJUSTMENT
1970–72

1. Measure the clearance between the throttle valve and bore when the choke lever is out all the way. The clearance should be 0.232–0.271 in. (0.59–0.69 mm).
2. Correct the clearance by bending the connecting rod.

NOTE: *Making the rod longer increases the clearance.*

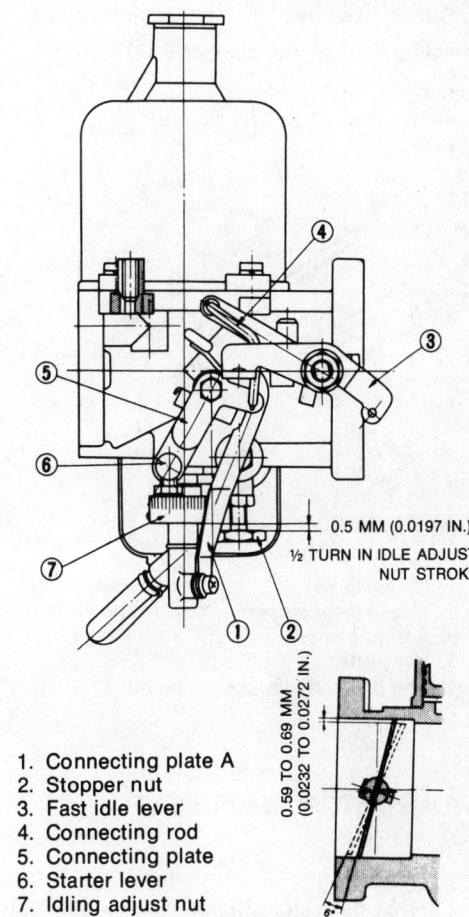

1. Connecting plate A
2. Stopper nut
3. Fast idle lever
4. Connecting rod
5. Connecting plate
6. Starter lever
7. Idling adjust nut

Adjusting the fast idle opening—1970–72

1973–74

1. Place the fast idle screw on the first step of the fast idle cam.
2. Adjust the screw so that the clearance between the throttle valve and the lower throttle bore is 0.023–0.025 in. (0.59–0.64 mm).

154 EMISSION CONTROLS AND FUEL SYSTEM

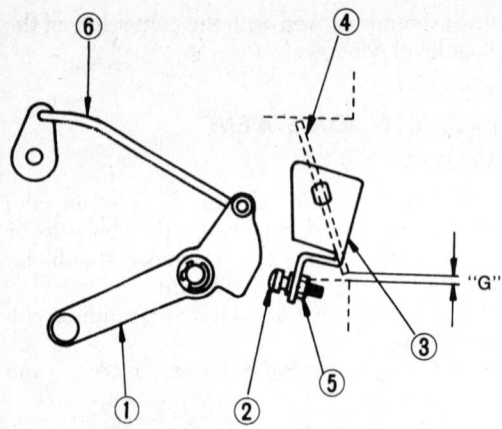

1. Choke lever
2. Fast idle screw
3. Fast idle lever
4. Throttle valve
5. Locknut
6. Connecting rod

Adjusting the fast idle opening—1973 models

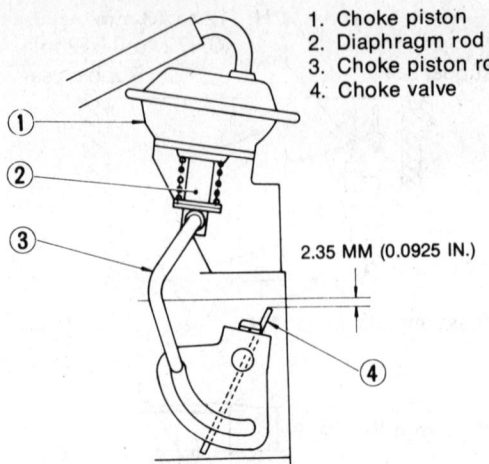

1. Choke piston
2. Diaphragm rod
3. Choke piston rod
4. Choke valve

2.35 MM (0.0925 IN.)

Adjusting the 260-Z choke piston

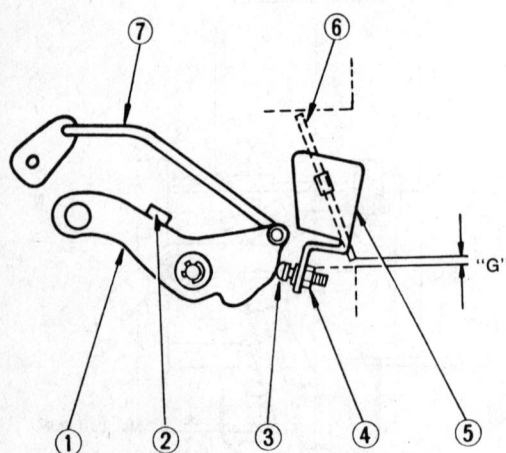

1. Choke lever
2. Choke lever stopper
3. Fast idle screw
4. Locknut
5. Fast idle lever
6. Throttle valve
7. Connecting rod

Adjusting the fast idle opening—260-Z

CHOKE PISTON ADJUSTMENT
1974

1. Close the choke valve all the way.
2. Hold the valve shut by stretching a rubber band between the lever connected to the choke wire and the carburetor.
3. Using a pair of pliers, gently grip the diaphragm rod and pull it all the way out.
4. Hold the rod in this position, then check the gap between the choke valve and carburetor body. The gap should be 0.0925 in. (2.35 mm).
5. Bend the choke piston rod as necessary to secure the proper adjustment.

SUCTION PISTON AND CHAMBER INSPECTION

1. Remove the air cleaner and the oil cap nut.
2. Gradually raise the suction piston with a suitable probe on 1973–74 models. On 1970–72 carburetors, the piston should be raised so that the lifter is well beyond the point where the lifter head contacts the suction piston.
3. Release the piston. The piston should drop smoothly and a sucking sound should be audible.
4. Install the oil cap nut. Raise the suction with your finger, going in through the throttle bore and then let it drop. The piston should resist rising due to damper operation and it should return to the bottom of it's travel smoothly. Otherwise, the piston and chamber require cleaning.

OVERHAUL
1973–74

On 1973–74 models, the factory does not recommend overhaul, except as described below, because of the extreme precision with which carburetors are calibrated at the factory.

FLOAT CHAMBER
1973

1. Loosen the mounting screws and remove the float chamber cover.
2. Remove the clip and the needle valve parts. DO NOT touch the needle jet setting nut or bend the float stopper.
3. Reassemble the needle valve parts. Adjust the float level as described above.
4. Install the float chamber cover.

EMISSION CONTROLS AND FUEL SYSTEM

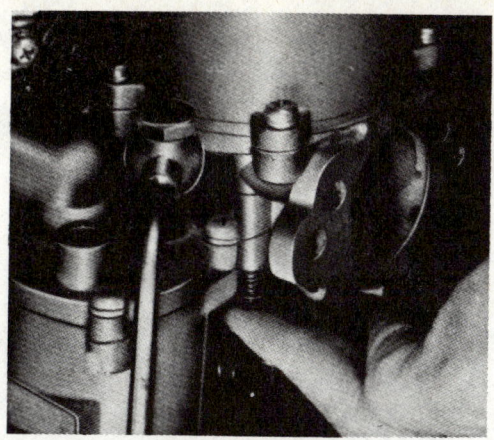
Location of the suction piston lifter

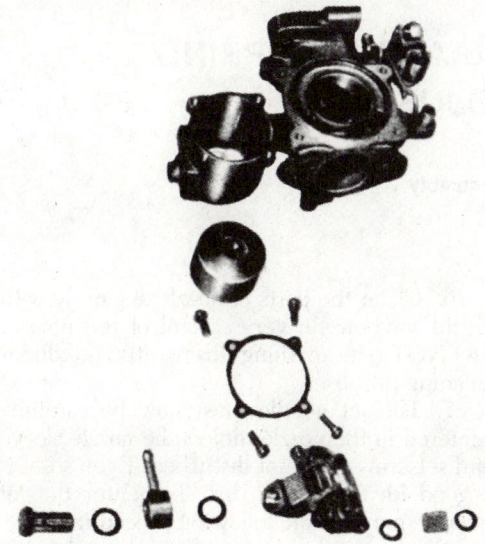
The float bowl assembly

diaphragm and replace it, if necessary. Reassemble and install the valve.

OVERHAUL
1970–72

To disassemble the carburetors:
1. Remove screws and suction chamber.
2. Remove suction spring, nylon packing and suction piston from chamber. Be extremely careful not to bend the jet needle.
3. DO NOT remove the jet needle from the suction piston unless it must be replaced. To remove, loosen jet needle setscrew. Hold the needle with pliers at a point no more than 0.10 in. from the piston. Remove the needle by pulling and turning it slowly. Replace the needle with the shoulder portion flush with the piston surface. Check this with a straightedge. Tighten the setscrew.
4. Clean the parts of suction chamber as-

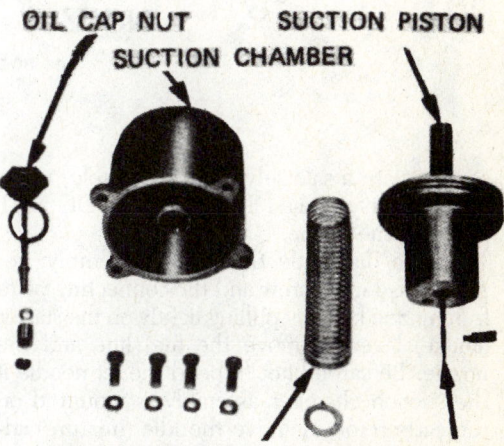
The suction chamber assembly

1974

1. Remove the float chamber cover mounting screws and the cover.
CAUTION: *DO NOT attempt to remove the float and needle valve parts.*
2. Adjust the float (see "Float Level Adjustment").
3. To assemble, reverse the removal procedures.

POWER VALVE
1973–74

If the carbon monoxide (CO) emissions in the exhaust are abnormally high and there is no obvious reason, check the power valve. Remove the mounting screws and the valve from the carburetor. Remove the other screws and disassemble the valve. Carefully inspect the

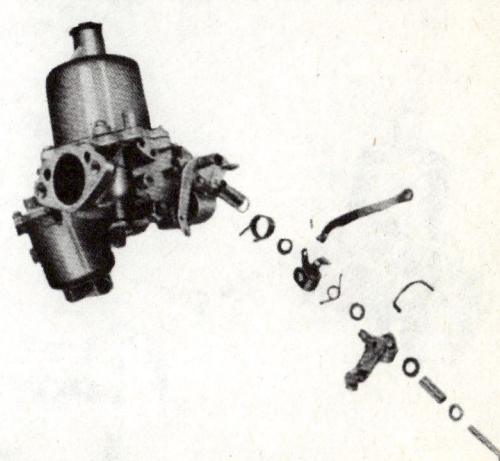
Choke linkage—exploded view

EMISSION CONTROLS AND FUEL SYSTEM

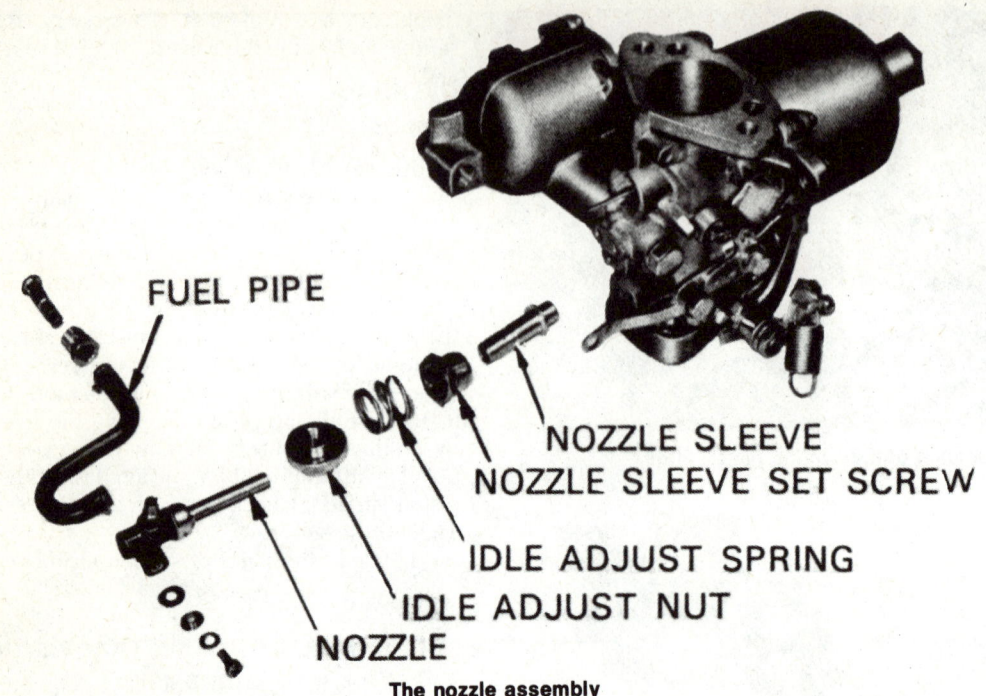

The nozzle assembly

sembly with a safe solvent. Reassemble, using all new parts supplied in overhaul kit. DO NOT lubricate the piston.

5. To dismantle the nozzle assembly, remove the 4 mm screw and the connecting plate from nozzle head by pulling lightly on the starter (choke) lever. Remove the fuel line and the nozzle. Be careful not to bend the jet needle if the suction chamber assembly is mounted on the carburetor. Remove the idle (mixture) adjusting nut and spring. DO NOT remove the nozzle sleeve unless absolutely necessary. Special care is required to replace this part. Remove the nozzle sleeve setscrew and the nozzle sleeve.

6. Clean the parts of nozzle assembly with a safe solvent. Be very careful of the nozzle. DO NOT pass anything through the nozzle for cleaning purposes.

7. The jet needle must now be carefully centered in the nozzle, unless the nozzle sleeve and setscrew were not disturbed. Even so, it is a good idea to check this. To center the jet needle, perform the following procedures:

 a. Insert the nozzle sleeve into the carburetor body with the setscrew loose.
 b. Carefully install the suction piston assembly without the plunger rod.
 c. Insert the nozzle without spring and mixture adjusting nut until the nozzle contacts the nozzle sleeve.
 d. Position the nozzle sleeve so that the jet needle is centered inside the sleeve and does not contact the sleeve.
 e. Test the centering by raising and releasing the suction piston. It should drop smoothly, making a metallic sound when it hits the stop.
 f. Tighten the nozzle sleeve setscrew when the needle is centered.

8. Reassemble the nozzle assembly. Replace the fuel line and the damper plunger rod.

9. Pull the starter lever slightly, then replace the connecting plate and the 4 mm screw.

10. Carburetor synchronization and mixture adjustments MUST BE performed after reinstalling carburetors.

linkage—exploded view

CHILTON'S
FUEL ECONOMY & TUNE-UP TIPS

Tune-up • Spark Plug Diagnosis • Emission Controls
Fuel System • Cooling System • Tires and Wheels
General Maintenance

55 WAYS TO IMPROVE FUEL ECONOMY

CHILTON'S FUEL ECONOMY & TUNE-UP TIPS

Fuel economy is important to everyone, no matter what kind of vehicle you drive. The maintenance-minded motorist can save both money and fuel using these tips and the periodic maintenance and tune-up procedures in this Repair and Tune-Up Guide.

There are more than 130,000,000 cars and trucks registered for private use in the United States. Each travels an average of 10-12,000 miles per year, and, and in total they consume close to 70 billion gallons of fuel each year. This represents nearly ⅔ of the oil imported by the United States each year. The Federal government's goal is to reduce consumption 10% by 1985. A variety of methods are either already in use or under serious consideration, and they all affect you driving and the cars you will drive. In addition to "down-sizing", the auto industry is using or investigating the use of electronic fuel delivery, electronic engine controls and alternative engines for use in smaller and lighter vehicles, among other alternatives to meet the federally mandated Corporate Average Fuel Economy (CAFE) of 27.5 mpg by 1985. The government, for its part, is considering rationing, mandatory driving curtailments and tax increases on motor vehicle fuel in an effort to reduce consumption. The government's goal of a 10% reduction could be realized — and further government regulation avoided — if every private vehicle could use just 1 less gallon of fuel per week.

How Much Can You Save?

Tests have proven that almost anyone can make at least a 10% reduction in fuel consumption through regular maintenance and tune-ups. When a major manufacturer of spark plugs sur-

TUNE-UP

1. Check the cylinder compression to be sure the engine will really benefit from a tune-up and that it is capable of producing good fuel economy. A tune-up will be wasted on an engine in poor mechanical condition.
2. Replace spark plugs regularly. New spark plugs alone can increase fuel economy 3%.
3. Be sure the spark plugs are the correct type (heat range) for your vehicle. See the Tune-Up Specifications.

Heat range refers to the spark plug's ability to conduct heat away from the firing end. It must conduct the heat away in an even pattern to avoid becoming a source of pre-ignition, yet it must also operate hot enough to burn off conductive deposits that could cause misfiring.

The heat range is usually indicated by a number on the spark plug, part of the manufacturer's designation for each individual spark plug. The numbers in bold-face indicate the heat range in each manufacturer's identification system.

Manufacturer	Typical Designation
AC	R **45** TS
Bosch (old)	WA **145** T30
Bosch (new)	HR **8** Y
Champion	RBL **15** Y
Fram/Autolite	**415**
Mopar	P-**62** PR
Motorcraft	BRF-**42**
NGK	BP **5** ES-15
Nippondenso	W **16** EP
Prestolite	14GR **5** 2A

Periodically, check the spark plugs to be sure they are firing efficiently. They are excellent indicators of the internal condition of your engine.

On AC, Bosch (new), Champion, Fram/Autolite, Mopar, Motorcraft and Prestolite, a higher number indicates a hotter plug. On Bosch (old), NGK and Nippondenso, a higher number indicates a colder plug.

4. Make sure the spark plugs are properly gapped. See the Tune-Up Specifications in this book.
5. Be sure the spark plugs are firing efficiently. The illustrations on the next 2 pages show you how to "read" the firing end of the spark plug.
6. Check the ignition timing and set it to specifications. Tests show that almost all cars have incorrect ignition timing by more than 2°.

veyed over 6,000 cars nationwide, they found that a tune-up, on cars that needed one, increased fuel economy over 11%. Replacing worn plugs alone, accounted for a 3% increase. The same test also revealed that 8 out of every 10 vehicles will have some maintenance deficiency that will directly affect fuel economy, emissions or performance. Most of this mileage-robbing neglect could be prevented with regular maintenance.

Modern engines require that all of the functioning systems operate properly for maximum efficiency. A malfunction anywhere wastes fuel. You can keep your vehicle running as efficiently and economically as possible, by being aware of your vehicle's operating and performance characteristics. If your vehicle suddenly develops performance or fuel economy problems it could be due to one or more of the following:

PROBLEM	POSSIBLE CAUSE
Engine Idles Rough	Ignition timing, idle mixture, vacuum leak or something amiss in the emission control system.
Hesitates on Acceleration	Dirty carburetor or fuel filter, improper accelerator pump setting, ignition timing or fouled spark plugs.
Starts Hard or Fails to Start	Worn spark plugs, improperly set automatic choke, ice (or water) in fuel system.
Stalls Frequently	Automatic choke improperly adjusted and possible dirty air filter or fuel filter.
Performs Sluggishly	Worn spark plugs, dirty fuel or air filter, ignition timing or automatic choke out of adjustment.

Check spark plug wires on conventional point type ignition for cracks by bending them in a loop around your finger.

Be sure that spark plug wires leading to adjacent cylinders do not run too close together. (Photo courtesy Champion Spark Plug Co.)

7. If your vehicle does not have electronic ignition, check the points, rotor and cap as specified.

8. Check the spark plug wires (used with conventional point-type ignitions) for cracks and burned or broken insulation by bending them in a loop around your finger. Cracked wires decrease fuel efficiency by failing to deliver full voltage to the spark plugs. One misfiring spark plug can cost you as much as 2 mpg.

9. Check the routing of the plug wires. Misfiring can be the result of spark plug leads to adjacent cylinders running parallel to each other and too close together. One wire tends to pick up voltage from the other causing it to fire "out of time".

10. Check all electrical and ignition circuits for voltage drop and resistance.

11. Check the distributor mechanical and/or vacuum advance mechanisms for proper functioning. The vacuum advance can be checked by twisting the distributor plate in the opposite direction of rotation. It should spring back when released.

12. Check and adjust the valve clearance on engines with mechanical lifters. The clearance should be slightly loose rather than too tight.

SPARK PLUG DIAGNOSIS

Normal

APPEARANCE: This plug is typical of one operating normally. The insulator nose varies from a light tan to grayish color with slight electrode wear. The presence of slight deposits is normal on used plugs and will have no adverse effect on engine performance. The spark plug heat range is correct for the engine and the engine is running normally.

CAUSE: Properly running engine.

RECOMMENDATION: Before reinstalling this plug, the electrodes should be cleaned and filed square. Set the gap to specifications. If the plug has been in service for more than 10-12,000 miles, the entire set should probably be replaced with a fresh set of the same heat range.

Oil Deposits

APPEARANCE: The firing end of the plug is covered with a wet, oily coating.

CAUSE: The problem is poor oil control. On high mileage engines, oil is leaking past the rings or valve guides into the combustion chamber. A common cause is also a plugged PCV valve, and a ruptured fuel pump diaphragm can also cause this condition. Oil fouled plugs such as these are often found in new or recently overhauled engines, before normal oil control is achieved, and can be cleaned and reinstalled.

RECOMMENDATION: A hotter spark plug may temporarily relieve the problem, but the engine is probably in need of work.

Incorrect Heat Range

APPEARANCE: The effects of high temperature on a spark plug are indicated by clean white, often blistered insulator. This can also be accompanied by excessive wear of the electrode, and the absence of deposits.

CAUSE: Check for the correct spark plug heat range. A plug which is too hot for the engine can result in overheating. A car operated mostly at high speeds can require a colder plug. Also check ignition timing, cooling system level, fuel mixture and leaking intake manifold.

RECOMMENDATION: If all ignition and engine adjustments are known to be correct, and no other malfunction exists, install spark plugs one heat range colder.

Carbon Deposits

APPEARANCE: Carbon fouling is easily identified by the presence of dry, soft, black, sooty deposits.

CAUSE: Changing the heat range can often lead to carbon fouling, as can prolonged slow, stop-and-start driving. If the heat range is correct, carbon fouling can be attributed to a rich fuel mixture, sticking choke, clogged air cleaner, worn breaker points, retarded timing or low compression. If only one or two plugs are carbon fouled, check for corroded or cracked wires on the affected plugs. Also look for cracks in the distributor cap between the towers of affected cylinders.

RECOMMENDATION: After the problem is corrected, these plugs can be cleaned and reinstalled if not worn severely.

Photos Courtesy Fram Corporation

MMT Fouled

APPEARANCE: Spark plugs fouled by MMT (Methycyclopentadienyl Maganese Tricarbonyl) have reddish, rusty appearance on the insulator and side electrode.
CAUSE: MMT is an anti-knock additive in gasoline used to replace lead. During the combustion process, the MMT leaves a reddish deposit on the insulator and side electrode.
RECOMMENDATION: No engine malfunction is indicated and the deposits will not affect plug performance any more than lead deposits (see Ash Deposits). MMT fouled plugs can be cleaned, regapped and reinstalled.

High Speed Glazing

APPEARANCE: Glazing appears as shiny coating on the plug, either yellow or tan in color.
CAUSE: During hard, fast acceleration, plug temperatures rise suddenly. Deposits from normal combustion have no chance to fluff-off; instead, they melt on the insulator forming an electrically conductive coating which causes misfiring.
RECOMMENDATION: Glazed plugs are not easily cleaned. They should be replaced with a fresh set of plugs of the correct heat range. If the condition recurs, using plugs with a heat range one step colder may cure the problem.

Ash (Lead) Deposits

APPEARANCE: Ash deposits are characterized by light brown or white colored deposits crusted on the side or center electrodes. In some cases it may give the plug a rusty appearance.
CAUSE: Ash deposits are normally derived from oil or fuel additives burned during normal combustion. Normally they are harmless, though excessive amounts can cause misfiring. If deposits are excessive in short mileage, the valve guides may be worn.
RECOMMENDATION: Ash-fouled plugs can be cleaned, gapped and reinstalled.

Detonation

APPEARANCE: Detonation is usually characterized by a broken plug insulator.
CAUSE: A portion of the fuel charge will begin to burn spontaneously, from the increased heat following ignition. The explosion that results applies extreme pressure to engine components, frequently damaging spark plugs and pistons.
  Detonation can result by over-advanced ignition timing, inferior gasoline (low octane) lean air/fuel mixture, poor carburetion, engine lugging or an increase in compression ratio due to combustion chamber deposits or engine modification.
RECOMMENDATION: Replace the plugs after correcting the problem.

Photos Courtesy Champion Spark Plug Co.

EMISSION CONTROLS

13. Be aware of the general condition of the emission control system. It contributes to reduced pollution and should be serviced regularly to maintain efficient engine operation.

14. Check all vacuum lines for dried, cracked or brittle conditions. Something as simple as a leaking vacuum hose can cause poor performance and loss of economy.

15. Avoid tampering with the emission control system. Attempting to improve fuel econ-

FUEL SYSTEM

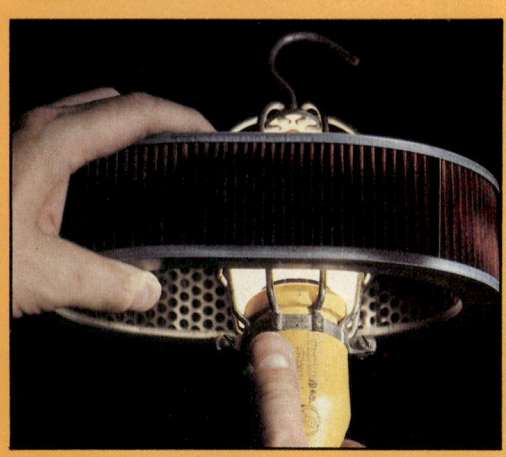

Check the air filter with a light behind it. If you can see light through the filter it can be reused.

Extremely clogged filters should be discarded and replaced with a new one.

18. Replace the air filter regularly. A dirty air filter richens the air/fuel mixture and can increase fuel consumption as much as 10%. Tests show that ⅓ of all vehicles have air filters in need of replacement.

19. Replace the fuel filter at least as often as recommended.

20. Set the idle speed and carburetor mixture to specifications.

21. Check the automatic choke. A sticking or malfunctioning choke wastes gas.

22. During the summer months, adjust the automatic choke for a leaner mixture which will produce faster engine warm-ups.

COOLING SYSTEM

29. Be sure all accessory drive belts are in good condition. Check for cracks or wear.

30. Adjust all accessory drive belts to proper tension.

31. Check all hoses for swollen areas, worn spots, or loose clamps.

32. Check coolant level in the radiator or expansion tank.

33. Be sure the thermostat is operating properly. A stuck thermostat delays engine warm-up and a cold engine uses nearly twice as much fuel as a warm engine.

34. Drain and replace the engine coolant at least as often as recommended. Rust and scale

TIRES & WHEELS

38. Check the tire pressure often with a pencil type gauge. Tests by a major tire manufacturer show that 90% of all vehicles have at least 1 tire improperly inflated. Better mileage can be achieved by over-inflating tires, but never exceed the maximum inflation pressure on the side of the tire.

39. If possible, install radial tires. Radial tires deliver as much as ½ mpg more than bias belted tires.

40. Avoid installing super-wide tires. They only create extra rolling resistance and decrease fuel mileage. Stick to the manufacturer's recommendations.

41. Have the wheels properly balanced.

omy by tampering with emission controls is more likely to worsen fuel economy than improve it. Emission control changes on modern engines are not readily reversible.

16. Clean (or replace) the EGR valve and lines as recommended.

17. Be sure that all vacuum lines and hoses are reconnected properly after working under the hood. An unconnected or misrouted vacuum line can wreak havoc with engine performance.

---

23. Check for fuel leaks at the carburetor, fuel pump, fuel lines and fuel tank. Be sure all lines and connections are tight.

24. Periodically check the tightness of the carburetor and intake manifold attaching nuts and bolts. These are a common place for vacuum leaks to occur.

25. Clean the carburetor periodically and lubricate the linkage.

26. The condition of the tailpipe can be an excellent indicator of proper engine combustion. After a long drive at highway speeds, the inside of the tailpipe should be a light grey in color. Black or soot on the insides indicates an overly rich mixture.

27. Check the fuel pump pressure. The fuel pump may be supplying more fuel than the engine needs.

28. Use the proper grade of gasoline for your engine. Don't try to compensate for knocking or "pinging" by advancing the ignition timing. This practice will only increase plug temperature and the chances of detonation or pre-ignition with relatively little performance gain.

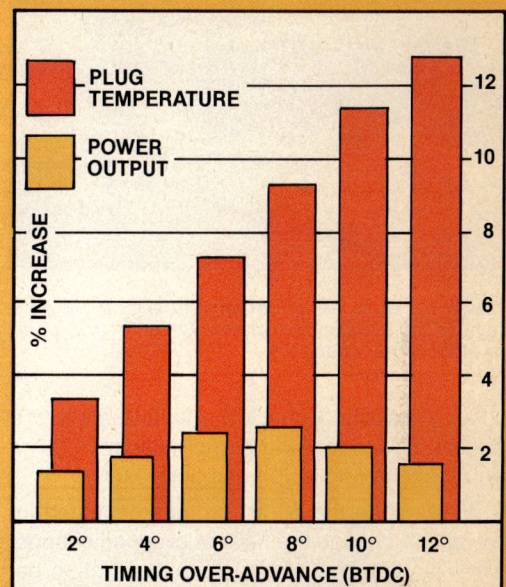

Increasing ignition timing past the specified setting results in a drastic increase in spark plug temperature with increased chance of detonation or preignition. Performance increase is considerably less. (Photo courtesy Champion Spark Plug Co.)

---

that form in the engine should be flushed out to allow the engine to operate at peak efficiency.

35. Clean the radiator of debris that can decrease cooling efficiency.

36. Install a flex-type or electric cooling fan, if you don't have a clutch type fan. Flex fans use curved plastic blades to push more air at low speeds when more cooling is needed; at high speeds the blades flatten out for less resistance. Electric fans only run when the engine temperature reaches a predetermined level.

37. Check the radiator cap for a worn or cracked gasket. If the cap does not seal properly, the cooling system will not function properly.

---

42. Be sure the front end is correctly aligned. A misaligned front end actually has wheels going in differed directions. The increased drag can reduce fuel economy by .3 mpg.

43. Correctly adjust the wheel bearings. Wheel bearings that are adjusted too tight increase rolling resistance.

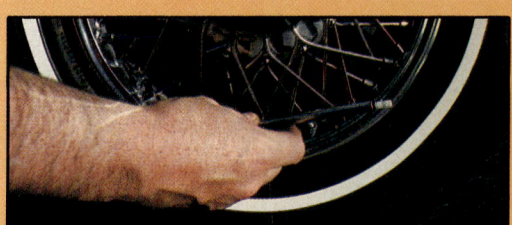

Check tire pressures regularly with a reliable pocket type gauge. Be sure to check the pressure on a cold tire.

GENERAL MAINTENANCE

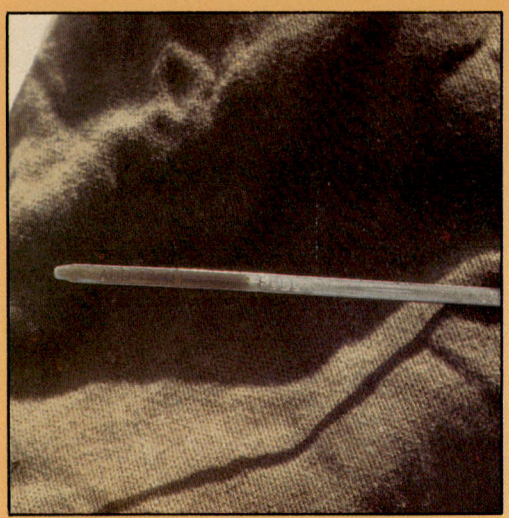

Check the fluid levels (particularly engine oil) on a regular basis. Be sure to check the oil for grit, water or other contamination.

A vacuum gauge is another excellent indicator of internal engine condition and can also be installed in the dash as a mileage indicator.

44. Periodically check the fluid levels in the engine, power steering pump, master cylinder, automatic transmission and drive axle.

45. Change the oil at the recommended interval and change the filter at every oil change. Dirty oil is thick and causes extra friction between moving parts, cutting efficiency and increasing wear. A worn engine requires more frequent tune-ups and gets progressively worse fuel economy. In general, use the lightest viscosity oil for the driving conditions you will encounter.

46. Use the recommended viscosity fluids in the transmission and axle.

47. Be sure the battery is fully charged for fast starts. A slow starting engine wastes fuel.

48. Be sure battery terminals are clean and tight.

49. Check the battery electrolyte level and add distilled water if necessary.

50. Check the exhaust system for crushed pipes, blockages and leaks.

51. Adjust the brakes. Dragging brakes or brakes that are not releasing create increased drag on the engine.

52. Install a vacuum gauge or miles-per-gallon gauge. These gauges visually indicate engine vacuum in the intake manifold. High vacuum = good mileage and low vacuum = poorer mileage. The gauge can also be an excellent indicator of internal engine conditions.

53. Be sure the clutch is properly adjusted. A slipping clutch wastes fuel.

54. Check and periodically lubricate the heat control valve in the exhaust manifold. A sticking or inoperative valve prevents engine warm-up and wastes gas.

55. Keep accurate records to check fuel economy over a period of time. A sudden drop in fuel economy may signal a need for tune-up or other maintenance.

© 1980 Chilton Book Company, Radnor, PA 19089

EMISSION CONTROLS AND FUEL SYSTEM 157

Carburetor Specifications
in. (mm)

Engine and Year	Make and Type	Bore Dia	Venturi Dia	Fuel Pressure psi (kg/cm²)	Needle Valve Dia	Nozzle No.	Power Jet No.	Jet Needle No.	Suction Spring No.	Suction Hole Dia	Fast Idle Throttle Opening	Damper Plunger Dia
L24 1970–72	Hitachi HJG46W-3A	1.811 (46)	1.339 (34)	3.4 (.24)	.0787 (2.0)	A	—	N-27	23	—	—	—
L24 1973	Hitachi HMB46W-1	1.811 (46)	1.654 (42)	3.4 (.24)	—	—	40	N-62	50	.295 (7.5)	.0232–.0252 (.59–.64)	.349 (8.86)
L26 1974	Hitachi HMB46W-4	1.811 (46)	1.654 (42)	4.6 (.32)	—	—	40	—	50	.295 (7.5)	.0232–.0252 (.59–.64)	.349 (8.86)

EMISSION CONTROLS AND FUEL SYSTEM

GASOLINE FUEL INJECTION SYSTEM

The 1975 and later models are equipped with electronic fuel injection built under Bosch patents. The Bosch L-Jetronic system precisely controls the fuel injection to match the engine requirements, reducing the emissions and increasing driveability.

NOTE: *This book contains simple testing and service procedures for your Datsun's fuel injection system. More comprehensive testing and diagnosis procedures may be found in CHILTON'S GUIDE TO FUEL INJECTION AND FEEDBACK CARBURETORS, book part number 7488, available at most book stores and auto parts stores or available directly from Chilton Co.*

The electric fuel pump, pumps fuel through a damper and a filter to the pressure regulator. The six fuel injectors are electric solenoid valves which open and close by signals from the control unit.

The control unit receives input from various sensors to determine engine operating condition.

1. Air flow meter–measures the amount of intake air.
2. Ignition coil–engine rpm.
3. Throttle valve switch–amount of throttle opening.
4. Water temperature sensor or cylinder head temperature sensor–temperature of coolant or engine.
5. Air temperature sensor–temperature of intake air (ambient temperature).
6. Thermotime switch–signal used to control cold start valve fuel enrichment when the engine is cold.
7. Starting switch–signals that the starter is operating.
8. Altitude switch–used on 1977–78 (California) models to signal changes in atmospheric pressure.
9. Exhaust gas sensor–used in 1980 (California) models and all 1981 and later models to measure the oxygen content of the exhaust gas.

NOTE: *The sensors provide the input to the control unit, which determines the amount of fuel to be injected by it's preset program. The L-Jetronic fuel injection system is a highly complex unit. All repair or adjustment should be left to an expert Datsun technician.*

Electric Fuel Pump (1974 and Later)

The electric pump used on 260-Z models is a transistorized plunger type which force feeds the conventional mechanical fuel pump in order to minimize the chances of vapor lock or other fuel deficiency problems. The pump is located in the corner where the differential mounting member intersects the side member. The 1975–83 models are equipped with one electric fuel pump mounted near the fuel tank and the right-rear wheel. On the 1984 and later models, the fuel pump is mounted in the gas tank.

REMOVAL AND INSTALLATION

1974

1. Disconnect the negative battery cable.
2. Remove the inlet hose at the fuel strainer. Remove the outlet hose at the pump and drain the remaining fuel into a suitable container.
3. Disconnect both electrical connections at the pump.
4. Remove the mounting bolts and the pump from the bracket.
5. To install, reverse the removal procedures.

1975–79

1. Disconnect the negative battery cable.
2. Disconnect the wiring harness to the cold start valve.
3. Using two jumper wires from the battery, energize the cold start valve for 2–3 seconds to relieve pressure in the fuel system.

CAUTION: *Be careful not to short the two jumpers together.*

4. Raise and support the rear of the vehicle on jackstands. Have a can and a rag handy to catch any spilled fuel.
5. Clamp the hose between the fuel tank and the fuel pump.
6. Loosen the hose clamps on the fuel lines at both ends of the pump and remove the lines from the pump.
7. Remove the retaining screws and the fuel pump bracket.
8. Disconnect the fuel pump harness connector. On the 280-Z models, roll back the carpet behind the passenger seat to reach the connector. On 280-Z, 2+2 models, remove the rear seat and the harness cover. Disconnect the wiring. On ZX models, remove the mat in the luggage compartment and disconnect the harness connector at the rear of the compartment.
9. Pull the harness through the rubber grommet in the floor and remove the fuel pump.
10. To install the fuel pump, reverse the removal procedures.

1980–83

1. To reduce the fuel line pressure to zero, perform the following:

EMISSION CONTROLS AND FUEL SYSTEM 159

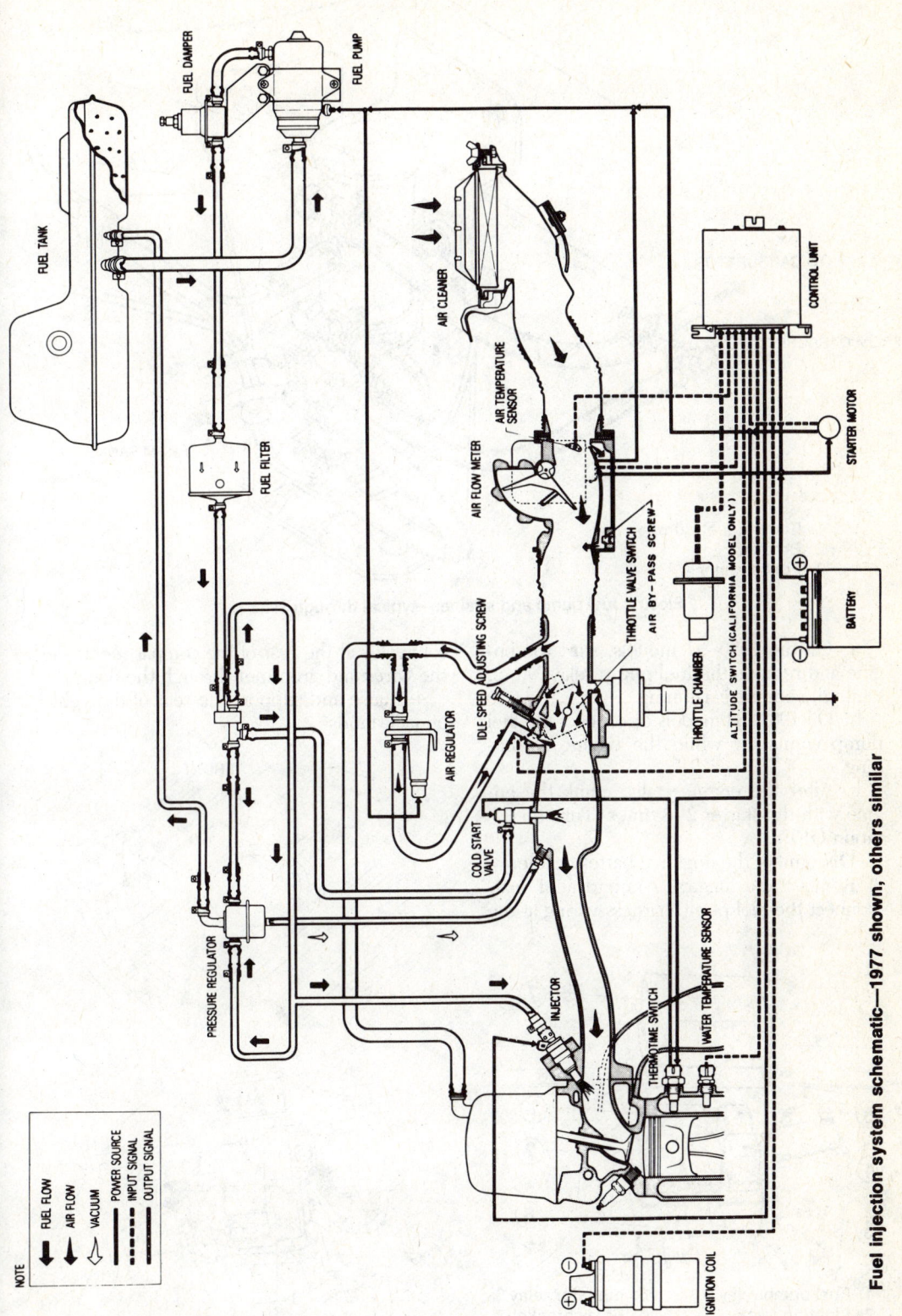

Fuel injection system schematic—1977 shown, others similar

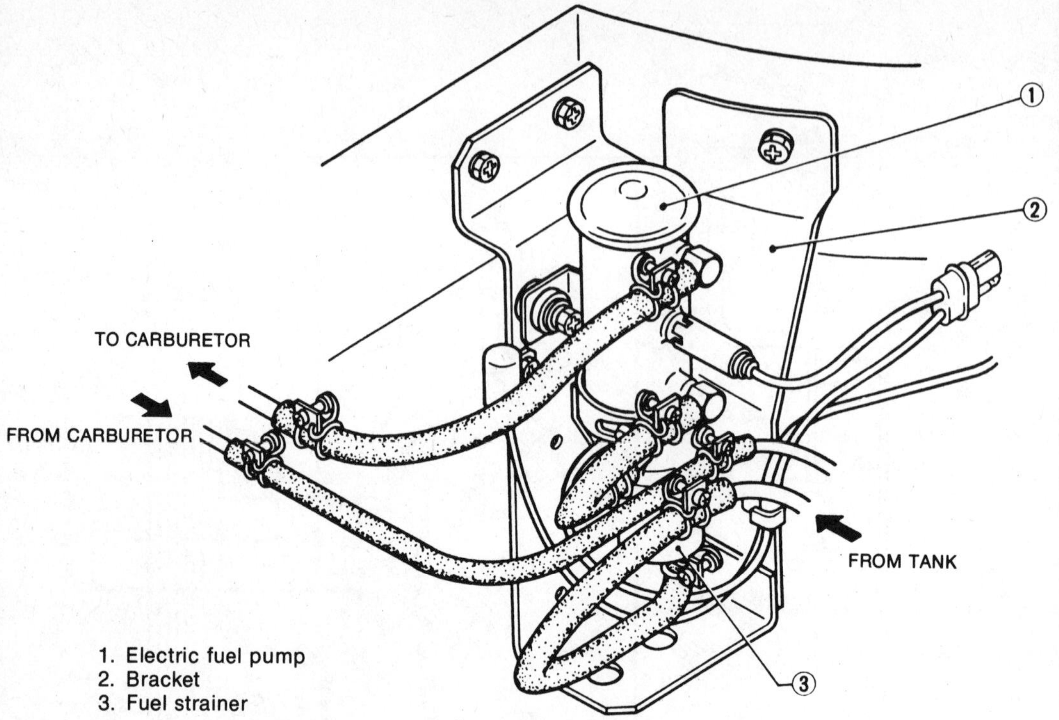

160 EMISSION CONTROLS AND FUEL SYSTEM

1. Electric fuel pump
2. Bracket
3. Fuel strainer

Electric fuel pump and strainer—typical through 1983

a. On the 1980–81 models, start the engine and remove the fuel pump relay No. 2, while the engine is running.

b. On 1982–83 models disconnect the fuel pump connector while the engine is running.

c. After the engine stalls, crank the engine with the starter 2–3 times. Turn the ignition OFF.

2. Disconnect the negative battery cable.

3. Remove the luggage compartment mat. Disconnect the fuel pump harness wiring at the connector at the rear of the compartment. Push the wires and grommet through the floor.

4. Raise and support the rear of the vehicle on jackstands.

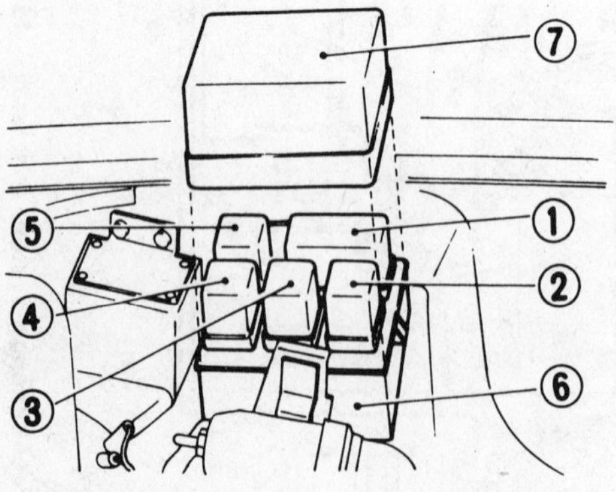

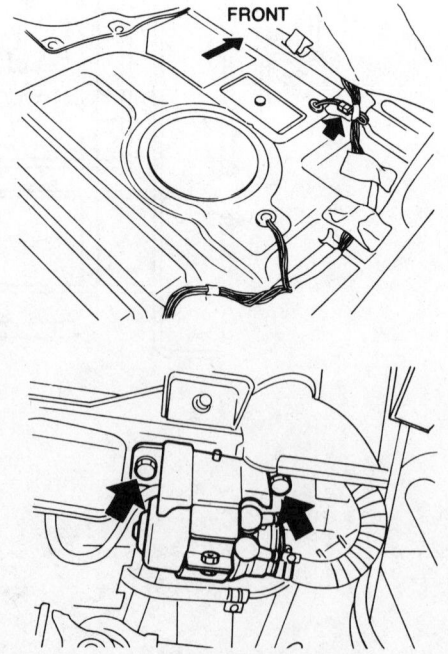

1. Fuel pump relay #2
2. Lighting relay
3. Bulb check relay
4. Air conditioner relay
5. Inhibitor relay
6. Relay bracket
7. Relay cover

Fuel pump relay No. 2—1980–81

1980–81 fuel pump installation; the upper diagram shows the location of the harness wiring connector (arrow), and the lower diagram shows the pump installation bolts (Arrow)

EMISSION CONTROLS AND FUEL SYSTEM

5. Clamp the hose between the fuel tank and the pump.
6. Loosen the fuel line clamps and disconnect the hoses from the pump.
   NOTE: *Have a metal container ready to catch the fuel which will spill from the lines.*
7. Remove the pump bracket-to-body bolts and the pump.
8. To install, reverse the removal procedures.

1984 and Later

1. Refer to the "Fuel Tank, Removal and Installation" procedures, in this section and remove the fuel tank.
2. Using a brass drift and a mallet, loosen the retaining ring at the top of the fuel tank.
3. Lift the fuel pump assembly from the fuel tank.
4. Separate the fuel pump from the assembly.
5. To install, reverse the removal procedures. Run the engine and check for leaks. DO NOT overtighten hose clamps and damage the hoses.

ELECTRIC FUEL PUMP TEST

1974

1. Disconnect the fuel pump outlet hose.
2. Connect a hose with an inside diameter of 0.236 in. (6 mm) to the pump outlet. DO NOT use a hose of a smaller diameter. Raise the end of the hose above the level of the pump.
3. Start the engine and allow it to run for a minute. Capacity should be 85.5 cu. in. (1,400 cc) in one minute or less. There is normally enough fuel in the carburetor float bowls to perform this test.
4. If capacity is sufficient but there is still some doubt about the pump's performance, connect a pressure gauge to the pump outlet with a hose of the same diameter as used in Step 2. Pressure should be 4.6 psi.

1975-78

FUNCTIONAL TEST

1. Disconnect the cable from the "S" terminal of the starter motor solenoid.
2. Unplug the cold start valve wiring harness connector.
3. Turn the ignition key to Start. You should be able to hear the fuel pump running. If not, check the wiring circuits and fuses. If the circuits and fuses are in order, replace the pump.

PRESSURE TEST

1. Reduce the fuel line pressure to zero, following Steps 1-3 of the pump removal and installation procedure.
2. Connect a pressure gauge into the fuel line in the engine compartment between the fuel tube and the fuel filter outlet hose.
3. Disconnect the wire from the "S" terminal of the starter motor solenoid.
4. Connect the negative battery cable.
5. Turn the ignition key to Start.
6. Pressure should be approximately 36.3 psi.
7. If not, replace the pressure regulator and repeat the tests. If the pressure is still not correct, check all fuel lines for kinks or blockage, then replace the pump, as necessary.

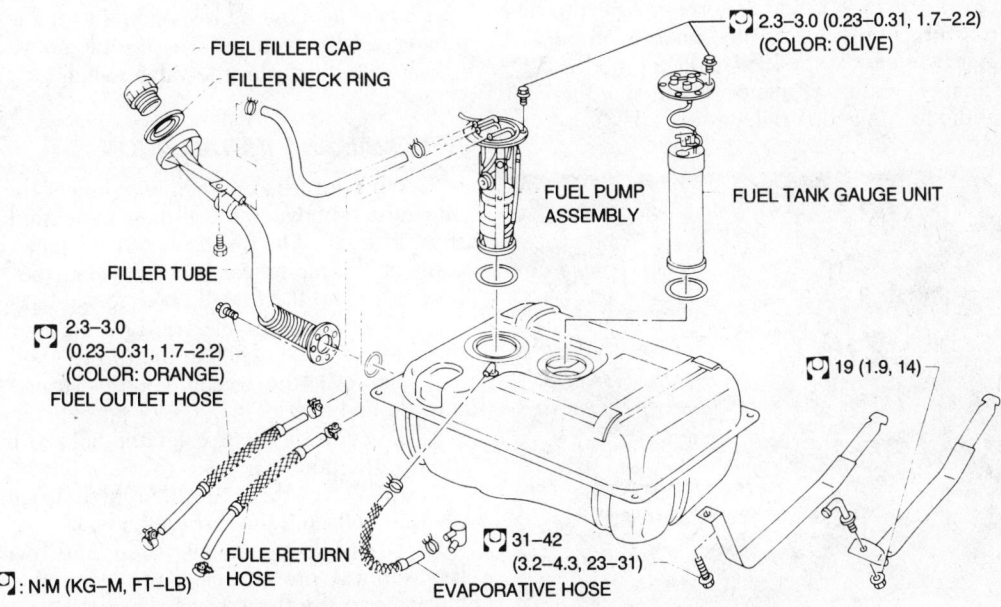

Removing the fuel pump from the fuel tank—1984 and later

162 EMISSION CONTROLS AND FUEL SYSTEM

1979 and Later

FUNCTIONAL TEST

1. Disconnect either the wire to the alternator "L" terminal or the oil pressure switch connector.
2. Turn the ignition key to Start. You should be able to hear the fuel pump running. If not, check the wiring circuits and fuses; if they are in order, replace the fuel pump.

PRESSURE TEST

1. Reduce the fuel pressure to zero.
NOTE: *For the 1979 models, follow Steps 1–3 of the 1975–79 fuel pump replacement procedure. For the 1980 and later models, follow Step 1 of the 1980–83 fuel pump replacement procedure.*
2. On the 1979 models, connect the negative battery cable.
3. Connect a fuel pressure gauge into the fuel line in the engine compartment between the fuel pipe and the fuel filter outlet hose.
4. Start the engine and read the fuel pressure. It should be approximately 30 psi at idle and approximately 37 psi (except turbo) or 44 psi (turbo) at any speed above idle.
5. If the pressure is incorrect, replace the pressure regulator, following the replacement procedure given later in this chapter. After replacement of the regulator, repeat the pressure test. If still incorrect, check the fuel lines for kinks or blockage and replace the pump as necessary.

Fuel Pressure Regulator

On the 1975–83 models (except V6), the fuel pressure regulator is located midway on the fuel injection rail. On the 1984 and later models (V6), the fuel pressure regulator is located at the front of the fuel injection rail.

Fuel pressure regulator

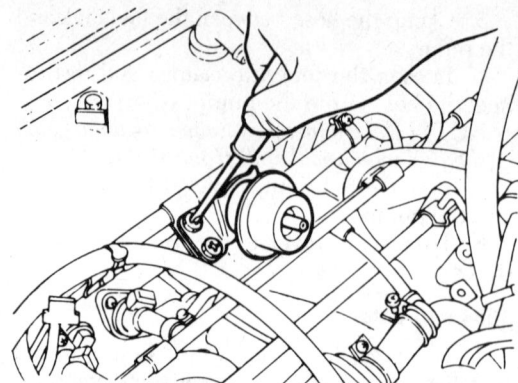

Fuel pressure regulator removal

REMOVAL AND INSTALLATION

1975 and Later

1. Reduce the fuel line pressure to zero, using the appropriate procedure given under the fuel pump replacement instructions.
2. Disconnect the vacuum hose from the pressure regulator.
3. Remove the regulator attaching screws.
4. Place a rag under the regulator to catch the fuel which will spill when the fuel lines are disconnected. Loosen the hose clamps and remove the fuel lines from the regulator.
5. To install, reverse the removal procedures.

Throttle Body

The throttle body is located between the air flow meter and the intake manifold. It controls the intake air flow by responding to the accelerator pedal movement. The throttle body shaft is connected to a throttle valve switch.

REMOVAL AND INSTALLATION

1. On nonturbo engines, disconnect the air intake tube between the air flow meter and the throttle body. On turbocharged engines, disconnect the air intake tube between the turbocharger and the throttle body.
2. Disconnect the electrical connector from the throttle valve switch at the throttle body.
3. Remove the vacuum hoses from the throttle body.
4. Disconnect the accelerator linkage from the throttle body.
5. Remove the throttle body-to-intake plenum bolts and the throttle body.
6. To install, use a new gasket and reverse the removal procedures. Adjust the throttle linkage and the throttle valve switch (if necessary).

EMISSION CONTROLS AND FUEL SYSTEM

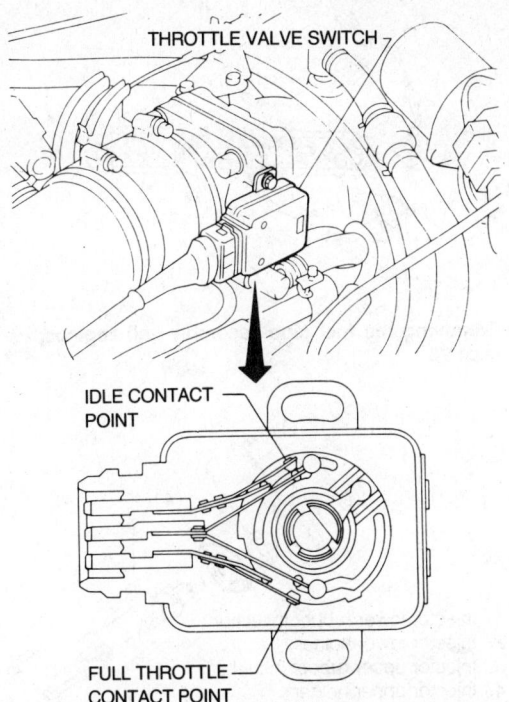

View of the throttle body with the throttle valve switch

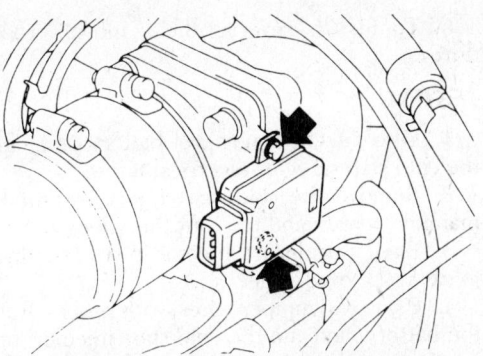

Adjusting the throttle valve switch—V6 engine

ADJUSTMENTS

Throttle Valve Switch

1. Remove the electrical harness connector from the throttle valve switch.

2. Using an ohmmeter (set on the 1 ohm position), connect the leads to the No. 2 and 18 pins (1975–78), No. 29 and 30 pins (1979–81), No. 18 and 25 pins (1982 and later); there should be continuity, if not, proceed to the next step.

3. Loosen the throttle valve switch-to-throttle body bolts.

NOTE: *On the 1984 and later, turbocharged models, disconnect the Auxiliary Air Control (AAC) Valve's electrical connector.*

4. Start and idle the engine, by opening the throttle valve (by hand), to 1,400 rpm (1975–79), to 900 rpm (1980–83), to 850–950 rpm (1984 and later, without turbo) or 800–900 rpm (1984 and later, with turbo), then adjust the throttle valve switch to turn from ON to OFF.

NOTE: *If the throttle valve switch cannot be adjusted, replace it.*

5. Tighten the throttle valve switch-to-throttle body bolts and reconnect the electrical connector.

NOTE: *On the 1984 and later, turbocharged models, connect the Auxiliary Air Control (AAC) Valve's electrical connector.*

Cold Start Injector

REMOVAL AND INSTALLATION

All Engines—Except V6

1. Disconnect the negative battery cable and the cold start injector electrical harness.

2. Using two jumper wires (with probes) from the battery, activate the cold start injector for 2–3 seconds to release the fuel pressure.

CAUTION: *Be sure to keep the jumper wires separated to avoid a short circuit.*

3. Remove the cold start injector-to-intake manifold screws and pull out the injector.

4. Remove the fuel hose clamp and disengage the cold start injector from the fuel hose.

NOTE: *When removing the cold start injector, place a container under the fuel hose to catch the excess fuel from the hose.*

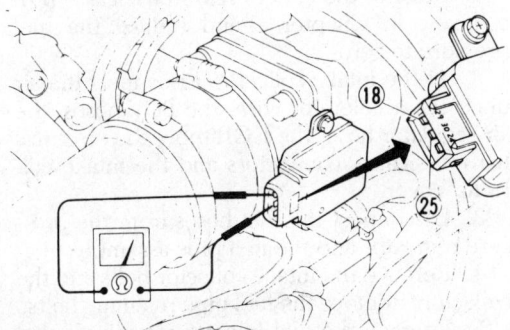

Using an ohmmeter to check the throttle valve switch's continuity—V6 engine

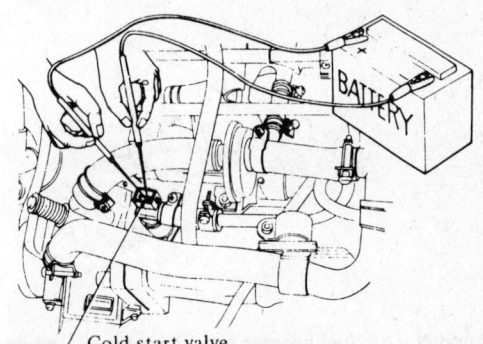

Activating the cold start injector

164 EMISSION CONTROLS AND FUEL SYSTEM

5. To install, reverse the removal procedures.

TESTING

1. Disconnect the negative battery cable and the cold start injector electrical harness.
2. Remove the cold start injector-to-intake manifold screws and pull out the injector.
3. Place a cold start injector into a container to catch the excess fuel.
4. Using two jumper wires (with probes) from the battery, activate the cold start injector; operation of the injector will be indicated by the fuel spray.
CAUTION: *Be sure to keep the jumper wires separated to avoid a short circuit.*
5. To install, reverse the removal procedures.

Fuel Injectors

REMOVAL AND INSTALLATION

All Engines-Except V6

1. Refer to the "Fuel Pressure Release" procedures, in Chapter 1 and reduce the fuel pressure.
2. Disconnect the electrical connector(s) from the fuel injector(s), then disengage the harness from the fuel pipe wiring clamp.
3. Disconnect the PCV hose from the rocker cover.
4. Disconnect the pressure regulator-to-intake manifold vacuum hose from the pressure regulator.
5. Remove the air regulator pipe.
6. Disconnect the fuel feed and the fuel return hoses from the fuel pipe.
CAUTION: *When removing the fuel hoses from the fuel pipe, place a rag under the connections to catch the excess fuel.*
7. Remove the fuel pipe bolts and the fuel injector-to-engine retaining screws, then pull out the fuel pipe, the injectors and the pressure regulator as an assembly.
8. Loosen the fuel injector(s)-to-fuel pipe hose

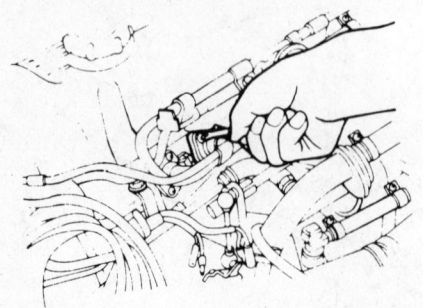

Removing the fuel injector retaining screws—all engines, except V6

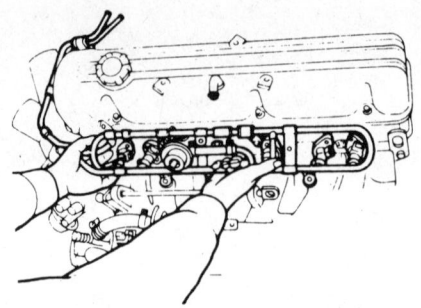

Removing the fuel pipe assembly—all engines, except V6

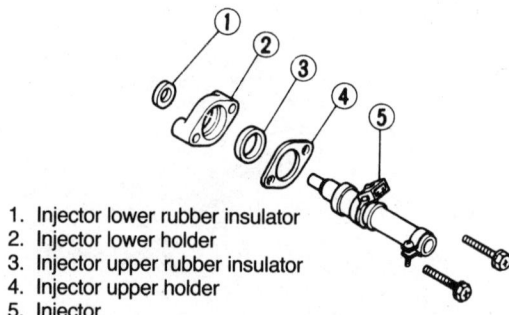

1. Injector lower rubber insulator
2. Injector lower holder
3. Injector upper rubber insulator
4. Injector upper holder
5. Injector

Exploded view of the fuel injector assembly—all engines, except V6

clamp(s) and pull the fuel injector(s) from the fuel pipe.
CAUTION: *When removing the fuel injector(s) from the fuel pipe, place a rag under the connections to catch the excess fuel.*
9. To install the fuel pipe assembly, use new upper/lower injector insulator washers and reverse the removal procedures. Start the engine and check for fuel leaks.
NOTE: *When installing the injectors, make sure that there are no scratches or abrasions at the lower rubber insulator and securely install them so that they are air tight.*

V6 Engine

1. Refer to the "Fuel Pressure Release" procedures, in Chapter 1 and reduce the fuel pressure to zero.
2. At the intake collector, disconnect the air duct, the accelerator wire, the PCV hoses, the air regulator hose, the EGR tube, the electrical harness clamps/connectors and the intake collector cover.
3. Disconnect the fuel hoses from the pressure regulator and the fuel pipe assembly.
4. Remove the intake collector bolts and the collector. Remove the fuel pipe retaining bolts.
5. Remove the fuel injector retaining bolts, then injectors, the fuel pipe and the pressure regulator as an assembly.

EMISSION CONTROLS AND FUEL SYSTEM

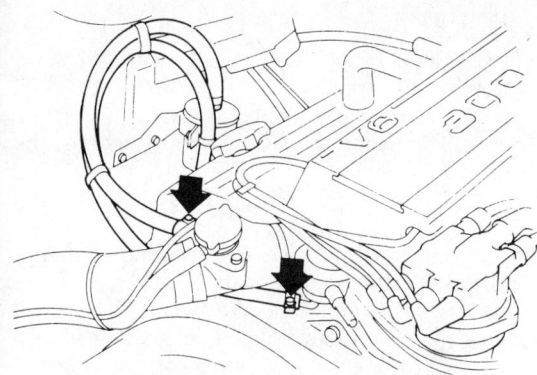

Disconnecting the fuel hoses—V6 Engine

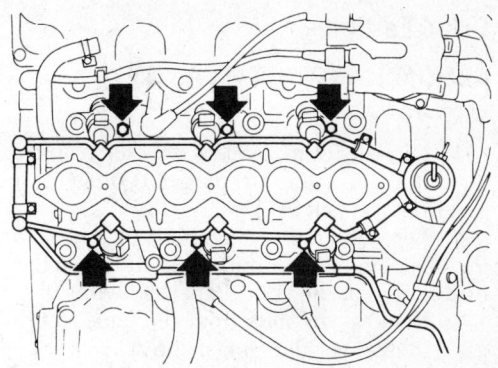

Removing the fuel injector hold down bolts—V6 Engine

Removing the intake collector—V6 Engine

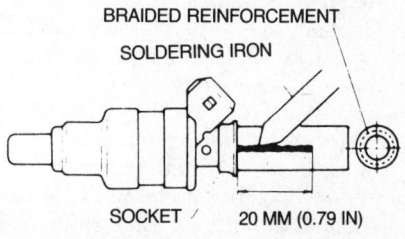

Removing the rubber hose from the fuel injector

a. On the rubber hose of the injector, measure a point approx. 0.79 in. (20 mm) from the socket end.
b. Using a 150 watt soldering iron, cut into the braided reinforcement from the mark to the socket end; DO NOT allow the soldering iron to touch the injector tail piece or the plastic electrical connector.
c. Pull the rubber hose from the injector.
3. To install a new rubber hose onto the fuel injector, perform the following:
a. Clean the exterior tail piece of the fuel injector and wet the interior of the new hose with fuel.
b. Push the new rubber hose (with hose socket) onto the injector's tail piece (by hand) as far as it will go; it is not necessary to clamp the hose to the injector.
c. Install the injector(s) onto the fuel pipe and secure with a clamp.

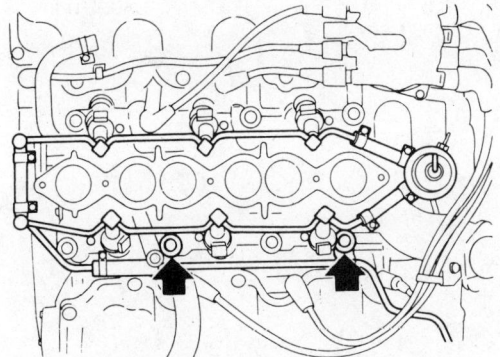

Removing the fuel pipe retaining bolts—V6 Engine

6. To install, use new O-rings on the injectors and reverse the removal procedures. Start the engine and check for fuel leaks.

FUEL INJECTOR HOSE REPLACEMENT

1. Refer to the "Fuel Injector, Removal and Installation" procedures, in this section and remove the fuel injector(s) from the fuel pipe.
2. To remove the rubber hose from the fuel injector, perform the following:

TESTING

1. With the engine operating, place a screwdriver (firmly) onto the injector(s) and feel it operating.
2. If the operation of an injector is questionable, remove each injector's electrical connector (one at a time) to notice the rough operating conditions of the engine.
3. When the faulty injector is located, replace it.

EMISSION CONTROLS AND FUEL SYSTEM

Fuel Tank

REMOVAL AND INSTALLATION

1970–78

1. Disconnect the negative battery cable.
2. Remove the drain plug and drain all the fuel from the tank.
3. Disconnect the gauge unit electrical wiring. Disconnect the outlet or outlets and return hose(s) at the tank. Label the wires.
4. Remove the nuts from the tank securing bands and lower the tank slightly.
5. Disconnect and label the three ventilation hoses used on models with evaporative emission control. Disconnect the fuel tank filler pipe. Remove the tank.
6. The tank should be checked carefully for dents or cracks which might cause leaks. Replace the tank as necessary.
7. To install, reverse the removal procedures. Be sure to connect the filler hose after the tank has been mounted, to prevent leakage at the connection. Be careful not to kink hoses or overtighten the fittings when reconnecting.

1979–83

1. Reduce the fuel line pressure to zero. Follow the appropriate steps under the fuel pump removal procedure.
2. The tank has no drain plug. Fuel must be drained as follows:
   a. Disconnect the fuel outlet hose from the fuel pipe.
   b. Place the hose into a metal container and seal the opening with a rag.
   c. Disconnect the alternator "L" terminal or the oil pressure switch electrical lead.
   d. Connect the negative battery cable.
   e. Turn the ignition switch to ON.
   f. Allow the fuel pump to empty the tank into the container.

CAUTION: *Stop the fuel pump before the tank is completely empty to prevent damage to the pump. Disconnect the negative battery cable after emptying the tank.*

3. Remove the fuel filler pipe protector inside the right-rear wheel opening. Disconnect the filler hose and the evaporative emission control hose. Plug the hose openings.

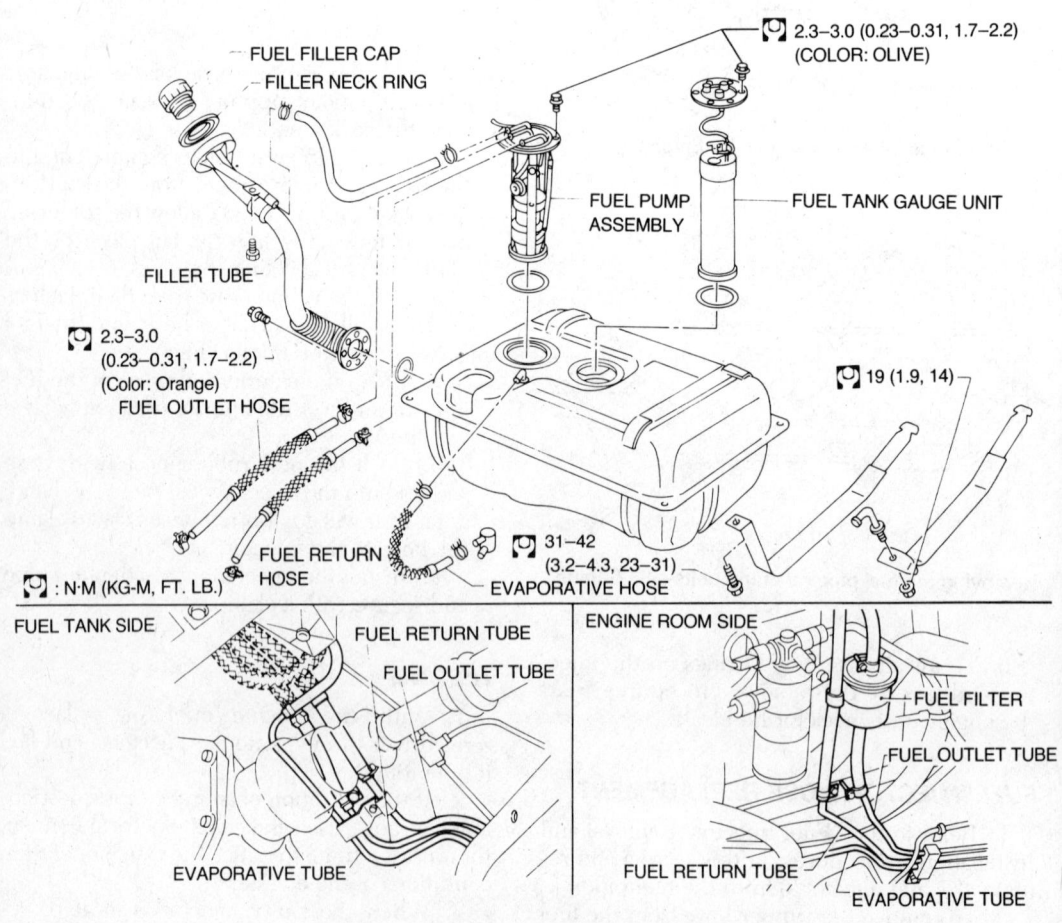

Fuel tank, pump and gauges—300 ZX

EMISSION CONTROLS AND FUEL SYSTEM

4. Remove the luggage compartment mat. Remove the cover over the tank sending unit and hose connections. Disconnect the gauge electrical harness, the ventilation, the fuel feed and the fuel return hoses.
5. Remove the fuel tank retaining straps/nuts and the tank.
6. To install, reverse the removal procedures. Be careful not to twist or kink any of the hoses.

1984 and Later

NOTE: *Before disconnecting any fuel lines the fuel pressure must be released.*
1. Release the fuel pressure as follows.
   a. Start the engine.
   b. Remove the luggage floor mat and disconnect the fuel pump connector with the engine running.
   c. After the engine stalls crank the engine 2–3 times to make sure the pressure is released.
   d. Turn the ignition switch OFF and connect the fuel pump connector.
2. Disconnect the negative battery cable.
3. Disconnect the harness connectors of the fuel tank gauge unit and the electric fuel pump in the luggage compartment.
4. Siphon or pump fuel from the filler opening of the fuel tank into a suitable container.

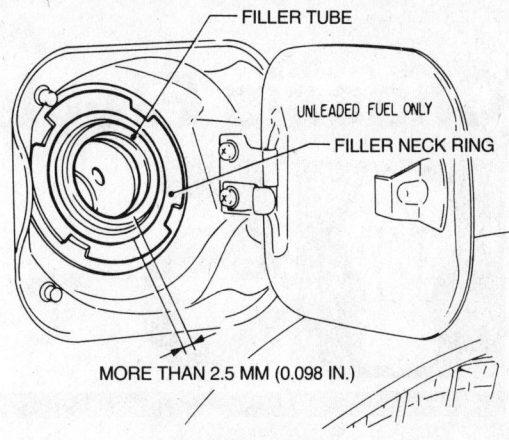

Filler neck ring installation—300 ZX

5. Remove the fuel filler neck ring.
6. Remove the right-side wheel.
7. Remove the fuel filler tube protectors and disconnect the ventilation hose.
8. Disconnect the fuel hoses and the evaporative hose on the fuel tube side.
9. Loosen the bolt and nut on the fuel tank retaining straps, then remove the fuel tank with the filler tube.

NOTE: *DO NOT separate the tank from the filler tube unless replacement is necessary.*

10. To install, reverse the removal procedures. Tighten the filler ring.

Chassis Electrical

UNDERSTANDING BASIC ELECTRICITY

For any electrical system to operate, it must make a complete circuit. This simply means that the power flow from the battery must make a complete circle. When an electrical component is operating, power flows from the battery to the component, passes through the component causing it to perform it's function (lighting a light bulb, for example) and then returns to the battery through the ground of the circuit. This ground is usually (but not always) the metal parts of the vehicle on which the electrical component is mounted.

Perhaps the easiest way to visualize this is to think of a light bulb with two wires attached to the vehicles battery. The battery has two posts (negative and positive). If one of the two wires is attached to the negative post and the other to the positive post, the circuit will be completed. Current from the positive battery post will flow to the light bulb, causing it to light. It would then leave the light bulb, travel through the other wire and return to negative battery post.

The normal automotive circuit differs from this simple example in two ways. First, instead of having a return wire from the bulb to the battery, the light bulb returns the current to the battery through the chassis of the vehicle. Since the negative battery cable is attached to the chassis and the chassis is made of electrically conductive metal, the chassis of the vehicle can serve as a ground wire to complete the circuit. Secondly, most automotive circuits contain switches to turn components ON and OFF as required.

There are many types of switches but the most common simply serves to prevent the passage of current when it is turned OFF. Since the switch is a part of the circle necessary for a complete circuit, it serves to leave an opening in the circuit and thus an incomplete or open circuit, when it is turned OFF.

Some electrical components which require a large amount of current to operate also have a relay in their circuit. Since these circuits carry a large amount of current, the thickness of the wire (gauge size) in the circuit is also greater. If this large wire were connected from the component, a voltage drop would occur in the circuit. To prevent this potential drop in voltage, an electromagnetic switch (relay) is used. The large wires in the circuit are connected from the battery to one side of the relay and from the opposite side of the relay to the component. The relay is normally OPEN, preventing current from passing through the circuit. An additional, smaller, wire is connected from the relay to the control switch for the circuit. When the control switch is turned ON, it grounds the smaller wire from the relay and completes the circuit. This closes the relay and allows current to flow from the battery to the component. The horn, headlight and starter circuits are three which use relays.

You have probably noticed that the instrument panel lights get brighter the faster the engine rev's. This happens because the alternator (which supplies the battery) puts out more current at speeds above idle; this is normal. However, it is possible for larger surges of current to pass through the electrical system of the vehicle. If this surge of current were to reach an electrical component, it could burn the component out. To prevent this from happening, fuses are connected in the current supply wires of most of the major electrical systems on the vehicle; the fuse serves to head off the surge. When an electrical current of excessive power passes through the component's fuse, the fuse blows out and breaks the circuit, saving it from destruction.

The fuse also protects the component from damage if the power supply wire to the component is grounded before the current reaches the component.

There is another important rule to the complete circle circuit. *Every complete circuit from a power source MUST include a component which is using the power from the power source.* If you were to disconnect the light bulb (from the previous example of a light bulb being connected to the battery by two wires together (take our word for it–DO NOT try it) the result would literally be shocking. A similar thing happens (on a smaller scale) when the power supply wire to a component or the electrical component (itself) becomes grounded before the normal ground connection for the circuit. To prevent damage to the system, the fuse for the circuit blows to interrupt the circuit–protecting the components from damage. Because grounding a wire from a power source makes a complete circuit–less the required component to use the power–this phenomenon is called a short circuit. The most common causes of short circuits are: the rubber insulation on a wire breaking or rubbing through to expose the current carrying core of the wire to a metal part of the vehicle or a short switch.

Some electrical systems on the vehicle are protected by a circuit breaker which is basically, a self-repairing fuse. When either of the above-described events takes place in a system which is protected by a circuit breaker, the circuit breaker opens the circuit the same way a fuse does. However, when either the short is removed from the circuit or the surge subsides, the circuit breaker resets itself and does not have to be replaced as a fuse does.

The final protective device in the chassis electrical system is a fuse link. A fuse link is a wire that acts as a fuse. It is connected between the starter relay and the main wiring harness of the vehicle. This connection is under the hood, very near a similar fuse link which protects all the chassis electrical components. It is the probable cause of trouble when none of the electrical components function, unless the battery is disconnected or dead.

Electrical problems generally fall into one of three areas:
1. The component that is not functioning is not receiving current.
2. The component (itself) is not functioning.
3. The component is not properly grounded.

Problems that fall into the first category are by far the most complicated. It is the current supply system to the component which contains all the switches, relays, fuses, etc.

The electrical system can be checked with a test light and a jumper wire. A test light is a device that looks like a pointed screwdriver with a wire attached to it. It has a light bulb in it's handle. A jumper wire is a piece of insulated wire with an alligator clip attached to each end.

If a light bulb is not working, you must follow a systematic plan to determine which of the three causes is the villian.
1. Turn ON the switch that controls the defective bulb.
2. Disconnect the power supply wire from the bulb.
3. Attach the ground wire of the test light to a good metallic ground.
4. Touch the probe end of the test light to the end of the power supply wire that was disconnected from the bulb. If the bulb is receiving current, the test light will turn ON.

NOTE: *If the bulb is one which works ONLY when the ignition switch is turned ON (turn signal), make sure the switch is turned ON.*

If the test light does not turn ON, then the problem is in the circuit between the battery and the bulb. As mentioned before, this includes all the switches, fuses and relays in the system. The problem is an open circuit between the battery and the bulb. If the fuse is blown and when replaced, immediately blows again, there is a short circuit in the system which must be located and repaired. If there is a switch in the system, bypass it with a jumper wire. This is done by connecting one end of the jumper wire to the power supply wire into the switch and the other end of the jumper wire to the wire coming out of the switch. If the test light turns ON with the jumper wire installed the switch or whatever was bypassed, is defective.

NOTE: *Never substitute the jumper wire for the bulb, as the bulb is the component required to use the power from the power source.*

5. If the bulb of the test light turns ON, then the current is getting to the bulb that is not working on the vehicle. This eliminates the first of the three possible causes. Connect the power supply wire and connect a jumper wire from the bulb to a good metal ground. Do this with the switch (which controls the bulb) turned ON and/or the ignition switch turned ON, if it is required to make the light work. If the bulb works with the jumper wire installed, then it has a bad ground. This is usually caused by the metallic area, on which the bulb mounts to the vehicle, being coated with some type of foreign matter or rust.

6. If neither test located the source of the trouble, then the light bulb is defective.

The above test procedure can be applied to any of the components of the chassis electrical system by substituting the component that is not working for the light bulb. Remember that

170 CHASSIS ELECTRICAL

for any electrical system to work, all connections must be clean and tight.

HEATER

Blower Motor (without A/C)
REMOVAL AND INSTALLATION
1970–78

1. Disconnect the negative battery cable.
2. Remove the clamp at the air intake duct so as to disconnect the air intake box control cable.
3. Disconnect the blower and the resistor wires at the connectors.
4. Remove the retaining screws and the blower unit.
5. The motor and fan may be separated from the blower unit by removing the mounting screws. Be careful to retain the washers and spacers.
6. To install, reverse the removal procedures.

NOTE: *When reassembling the control cable for the air intake door, set the AIR lever in the OFF position and position the wire in the clamp so that the door will just be closed.*

1979 and Later

1. Disconnect the negative battery cable.
2. Remove the lower instrument panel cover and the glove box.
3. Remove the floor nozzle, the defroster duct and the side defroster duct on the right-side.
4. Remove the heater duct.
5. Disconnect the blower motor wiring harness.
6. Disconnect the control cable at the blower assembly by removing the clip.
7. Remove the blower assembly-to-firewall bolts and the blower assembly.
8. The motor and fan can be removed by removing the motor retaining screws.

NOTE: *The fan simply bolts onto the motor shaft.*

9. To install, reverse the removal procedures.

The motor and fan can also be removed without removing the entire blower housing assembly:

1. Disconnect the negative battery cable.
2. Remove the lower instrument panel cover and the floor nozzle on the right-side.
3. Disconnect the blower motor wiring harness.
4. Remove the mounting screws, then the motor and fan as a unit from the blower housing.

Blower Motor (with A/C)
REMOVAL AND INSTALLATION
1970–78

1. Disconnect the negative battery cable. Disconnect the vacuum hose at the intake door actuator.
2. Remove the defroster duct which is located near the passenger seat.
3. Disconnect the connectors at the blower motor and at the resistor.

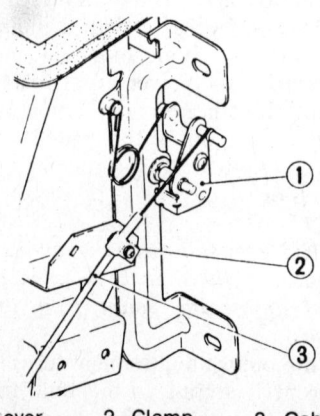

1. Lever   2. Clamp   3. Cable

Disconnecting the intake door control cable (1970–78)

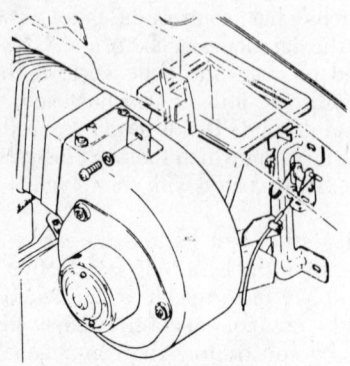

Removing the blower housing, 1970–78

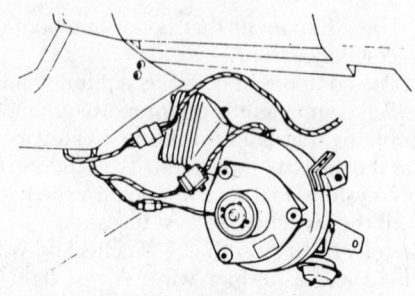

Removing the blower housing with air conditioning, 1970–78

CHASSIS ELECTRICAL 171

duct and the side defroster duct on the passenger's side.

4. Disconnect the blower motor electrical harness.
5. Disconnect and label the two vacuum hoses.
6. Remove the mounting bolts and the blower assembly.
7. To install, reverse the removal procedures.

The motor can be removed without removing the blower assembly:

1. Disconnect the negative battery cable.
2. Remove the instrument panel lower cover and the floor nozzle on the right-side.
3. Disconnect the blower motor electrical harness.
4. Remove the mounting screws, then the motor and fan as an assembly from the blower housing.
5. To install, reverse the removal procedures.

Heater Core (Without A/C)
REMOVAL AND INSTALLATION
1970–78

NOTE: *The entire heater unit MUST BE removed for access to the heater core.*

1. Disconnect the negative battery cable and drain the engine coolant.
2. Remove the floor console.
3. Remove the finish panel around the heater control retaining screws and pull the panel out slightly. Disconnect the wires and remove the panel.
4. Remove the duct-to-instrument panel bracket screws and the brackets screws, then the brackets. Disconnect the ventilator duct hose from the ventilator outlet, then remove the outlet from the center panel.

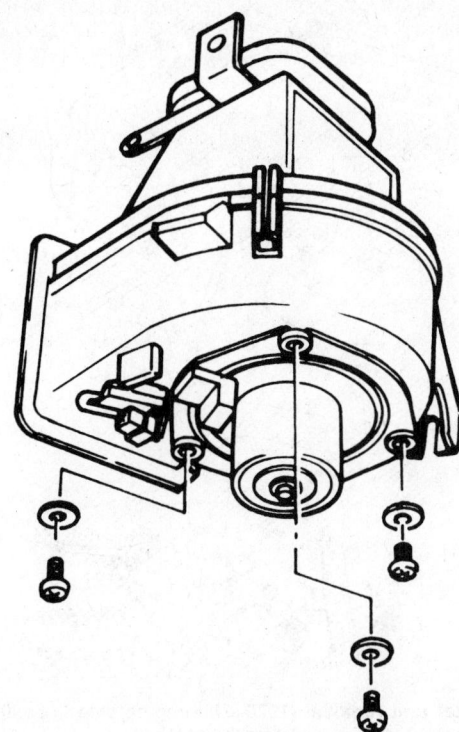

ZX blower motor and fan removal

4. Remove the mounting bolts and the housing.
5. The motor may be removed by removing the bolts and pulling it out. Be careful to retain the washers and spacers.
6. To install, reverse the removal procedures.

1979 and Later

1. Disconnect the negative battery cable.
2. Remove the instrument panel lower cover on the right-side. Remove the glove box.
3. Remove the floor nozzle, the defroster

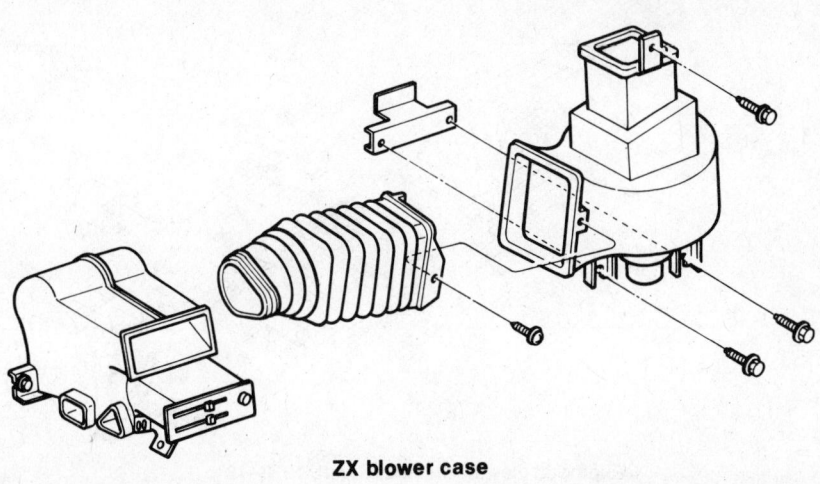

ZX blower case

172 CHASSIS ELECTRICAL

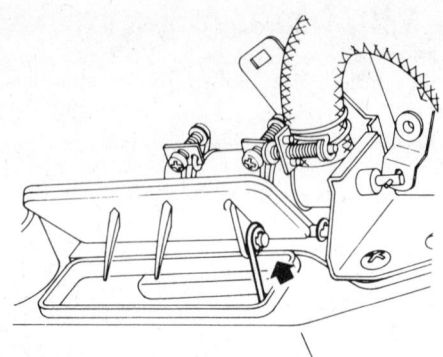

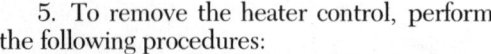
Disconnecting the heater door rod, 1970–78

5. To remove the heater control, perform the following procedures:
   a. Remove the control cables at the air intake duct, the heat control valve and the floor heater door, then disconnect the door control rod.
   b. Disconnect the wires from the heater control to the heater harness at the connectors.
   c. Remove the control assembly-to-instrument panel screws.
   d. Remove the heater control panel reinforcement-to-instrument panel screws and the reinforcement.
   e. Remove the heater control-to-heater unit screws.
6. Disconnect the defroster ducts from the heater unit. Remove the heater inlet and outlet clamps and hoses, then the hoses from the tubes.
7. Remove the duct adapter-to-heater unit screws.
8. Remove the heater unit-to-firewall nuts/screws. The nuts are on the engine side of the firewall; the screws are under the heater control unit.
9. Pull the heater out slightly and turn it

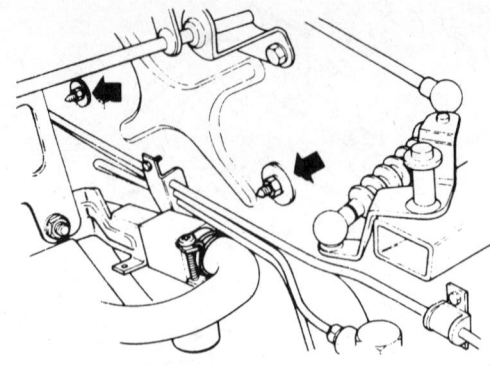

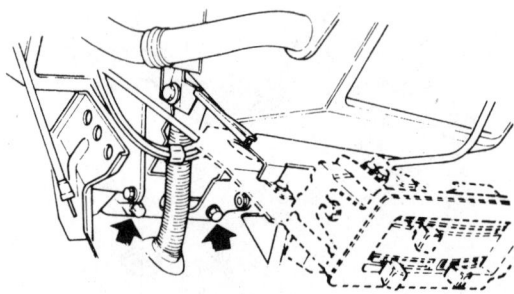
Heater unit removal (1970–78)—engine side firewall nuts (top) and inside bolts (bottom)

90° to the left. Remove the heater unit from the instrument panel.
10. Loosen the hose clamps on the heat control valve and disconnect the hoses.
11. Remove the two screws retaining the valve to it's bracket.
12. Remove the heater bracket screws (from the unit) and the bracket.
13. Remove the capillary tube bracket-to-unit screws and the capillary tube from the unit. Remove the valve at the same time.
CAUTION: *Be careful not to bend or twist the tube too much. If the tube must be bent slightly, be sure the valve is open to prevent*

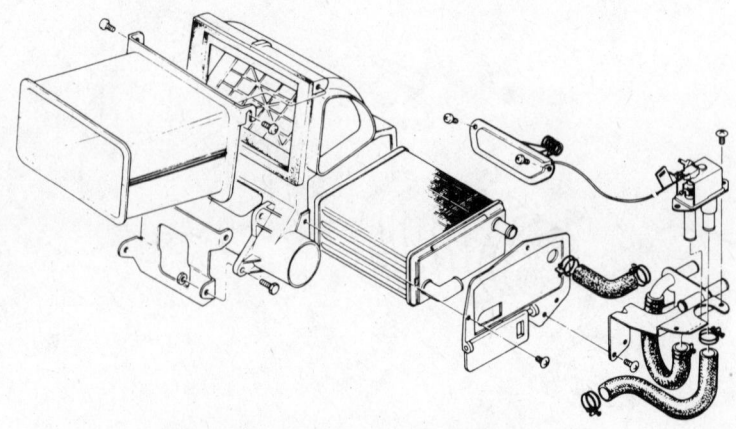
Exploded view of the heater unit, 1970–78

CHASSIS ELECTRICAL

any change in the operating characteristics of the capillary tube.

14. Remove the heat control valve bracket-to-unit screws and the hose connector from the unit.
15. Loosen the hose clamps from the heater core tubes and disconnect the hoses from the core tubes. Remove the heat control valve bracket and the hose connector.
16. Disconnect the floor door operating rod from the door.
17. Remove the side cover from the unit.
18. Open the floor door to prevent scratching the heater core and remove the core from the unit.
19. To assemble and install, reverse the removal procedures. Adjust the air intake door, the mode door, the floor door and the heat control valve cables so that:
   a. When the AIR lever is OFF, the air intake door is closed.
   b. When the AIR lever is on HEAT, the mode door lever is moved toward the firewall.
   c. When the AIR lever is on DEF, the floor door lever is pushed forward toward the firewall to the defrost position.
   d. When the TEMP lever is on HOT, the heat control valve is open (pulled towards you).

1979 and Later

NOTE: *The heater unit MUST BE removed for access to the heater core.*

1. Disconnect the negative battery cable.
2. Set the TEMP lever to HOT and drain the coolant.
3. Remove the instrument panel lower covers, the floor nozzles, the defroster ducts, the instrument console and the center ventilator.
4. Remove the glove box and the heater duct.
5. Remove the control cables and rod from the heater unit. Remove the heater control assembly attaching screws and the control assembly.
6. Disconnect the heater inlet and outlet hoses inside the passenger compartment.
7. Remove the blower assembly. Refer to the procedure earlier in this chapter.
8. Remove the heater unit-to-firewall bolts and the unit. All the bolts are on the passenger compartment side of the firewall and are accessible through the center of the instrument panel opening.
9. Remove the heat control valve.
10. Remove the clips from the heater case seam and separate the case. Remove the core.
11. To assemble and install, reverse the removal procedures.

Heater Core (With A/C)
REMOVAL AND INSTALLATION
1970–78

1. Disconnect the negative battery cable.
2. Drain the engine coolant.
3. Working in the engine compartment, loosen the heater hose clamps and pull the hoses from the tubes.
4. Remove the blower housing, using the procedure given earlier in this chapter.
5. To remove the heater control valve, perform the following procedures:
   a. Move the TEMP lever to HOT.
   b. Remove the hoses from the valve.
   c. Remove the valve-to-bracket screws. Be careful not to twist or bend the capillary tube excessively.
   d. Remove the vacuum valve-to-heater core outlet hose.
   e. Remove the vacuum valve and the heater valve bracket screws.
   f. Remove the vacuum hose, then the vacuum valve and heater valve bracket as an assembly.
6. Disengage the control cable from the heater door and remove the rod from the door.
7. Remove the heater core cover screws and the cover. Pull the core from the housing. Keep the heater door open when doing this to prevent damage to the core.
8. To assemble and install, reverse the removal procedures.

1979 and Later

CAUTION: *This procedure requires evacuation of the air conditioning refrigerant. DO NOT attempt to discharge the system unless you are thoroughly familiar with air conditioning systems. Escaping refrigerant will freeze any surface it contacts. If you do not*

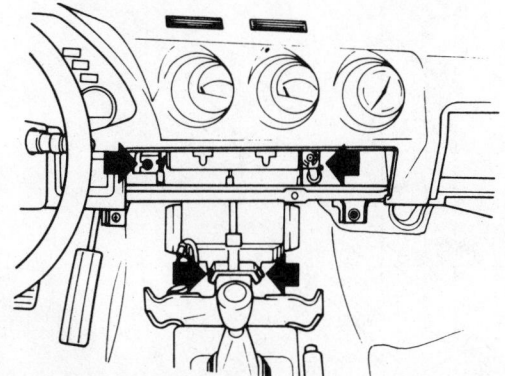

ZX heater unit removal

174 CHASSIS ELECTRICAL

have proper training, have the system discharged and recharged by a professional.

1. Disconnect the negative battery cable. Set the TEMP lever to HOT and drain the coolant.
2. Remove the blower unit using the procedure given earlier in this chapter.
3. To remove the cooling unit, perform the following procedures:
    a. Discharge the cooling system.
    b. Loosen the flare nuts at each of the inlet and outlet pipe connections at the evaporator. Plug the openings immediately to prevent the entry of moisture or dirt.
    c. Remove the passenger side defroster duct.
    d. Remove the mounting bolts and the cooling unit from beneath the instrument panel.
4. To remove the heater controls, perform the following procedures:
    a. Remove the lower instrument panel trim covers.
    b. Remove the console.
    c. Remove the ventilator and the duct from the center of the instrument panel.
    d. Disconnect the cable from the heat control valve.
    e. Disconnect the wiring connector. Disconnect and label the vacuum hoses or the connections of the vacuum selector.
    f. Remove the attaching screws and the control assembly.
5. Remove the instrument panel lower cover and the floor nozzle on the driver's side.
6. Disconnect the heater inlet and outlet hoses.
7. Remove the heater unit-to-firewall bolts and the unit.
8. Remove the heat control valve.
9. Remove the clips from the heater case seam and separate the two halves of the case.
10. Remove the heater core.
11. To assemble and install, reverse the removal procedures. Adjust the heat control cables.

RADIO

REMOVAL AND INSTALLATION
240-Z

1. Disconnect the negative battery cable.
2. Remove the instrument console finish panel screws and the panel.
3. Pull off the radio knobs and remove the retaining nuts behind them. Disconnect the power and speaker wiring, then the antenna cable at the connectors.
4. Remove the radio.
5. To install, reverse the removal procedures.

260-Z and 280-Z

1. Disconnect the negative battery cable.
2. Remove the floor console mounting screws.
3. Remove the choke control wire and the wiring harness connector from the console, then the console.
4. Disconnect the radio power and antenna switch wires at the connectors. Remove the feeder cable.
5. Pull off the knobs and remove the escutcheon nuts.
6. Remove the radio-to-console box screws and remove it.
7. To install, reverse the removal procedures.

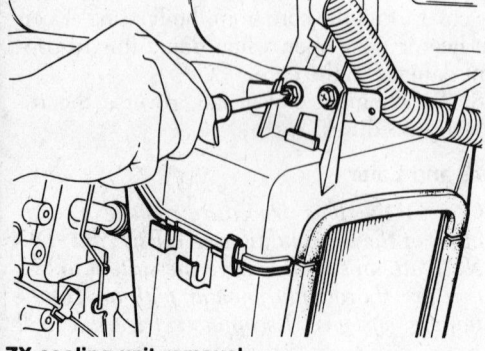

ZX cooling unit removal

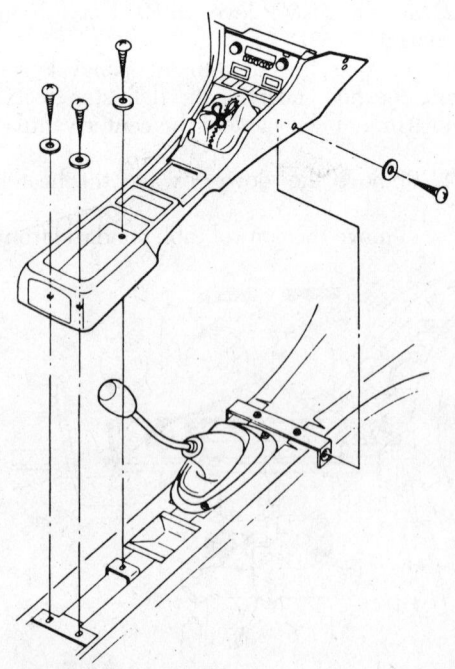

Console removal, 1970–78

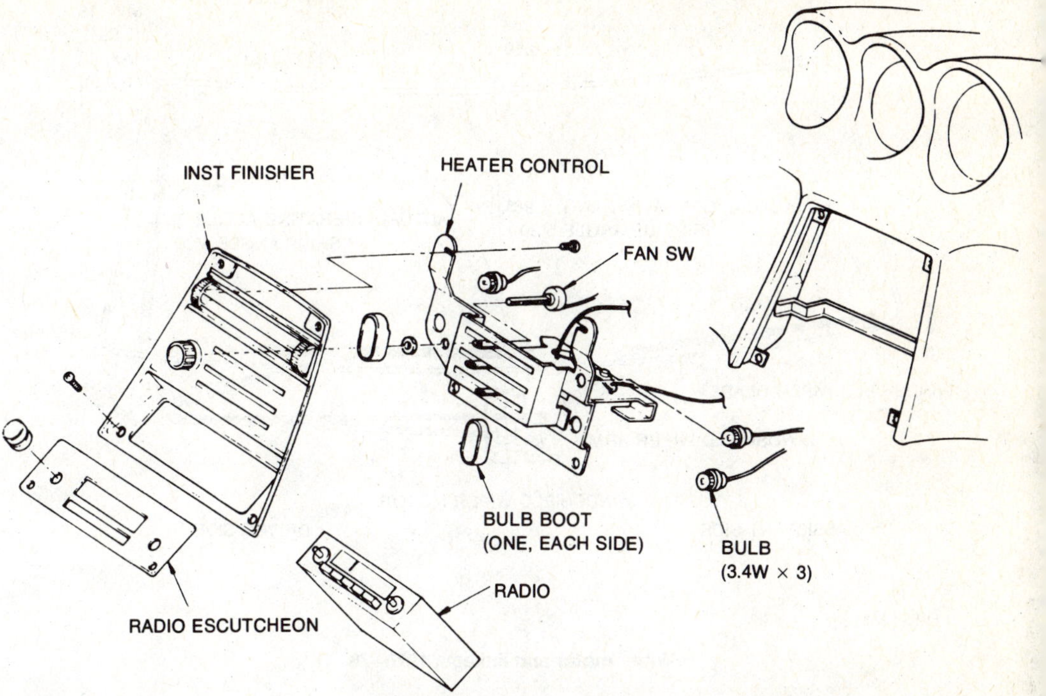

CHASSIS ELECTRICAL 175

Removing the radio, 1970–78

280-ZX and 300-ZX

1. Disconnect the negative battery cable.
2. Remove the lower instrument panel cover.
3. Remove the console.
4. Pull the radio knobs off the shafts. Remove the nuts from the shafts.
5. Disconnect the power, the speaker and the antenna wiring from the rear of the radio.
6. Remove the radio bolts (at the bottom) and the radio from behind the instrument panel.
7. To install, reverse the removal procedures.

WINDSHIELD WIPERS

Blade and Arm
REMOVAL AND INSTALLATION
240, 260 and 280-Z Models

1. Raise the wiper blade off the glass.
2. Unscrew the retaining nut on the shaft and pull the arm from the shaft.

NOTE: *Before installing the arm, be sure the motor is in the Park position.*

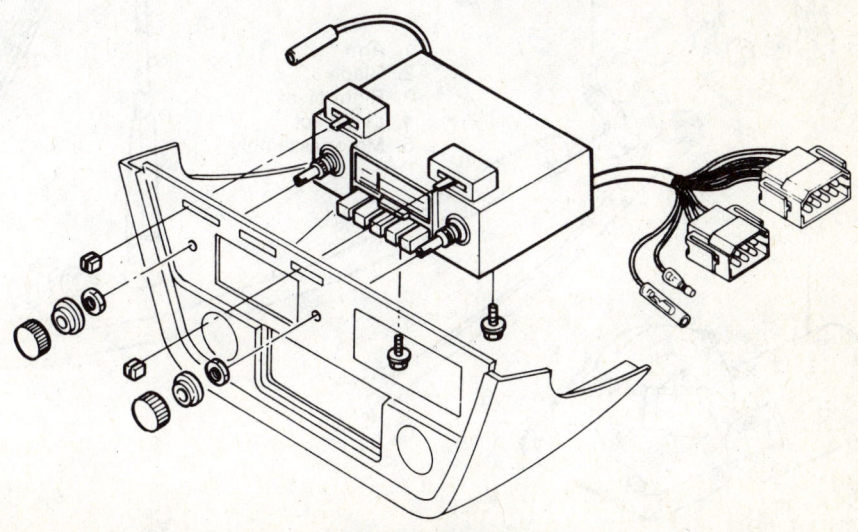

ZX radio removal

176 CHASSIS ELECTRICAL

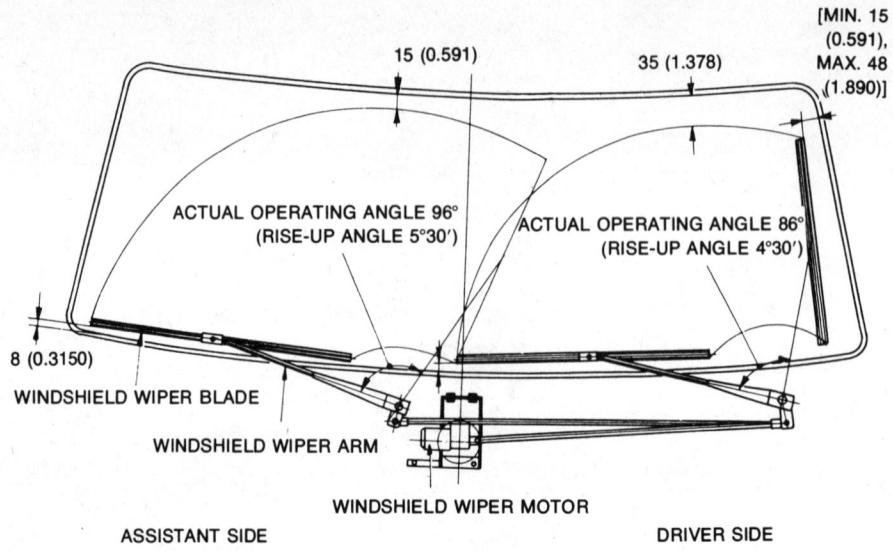

Wiper motor and linkage, 1970–78

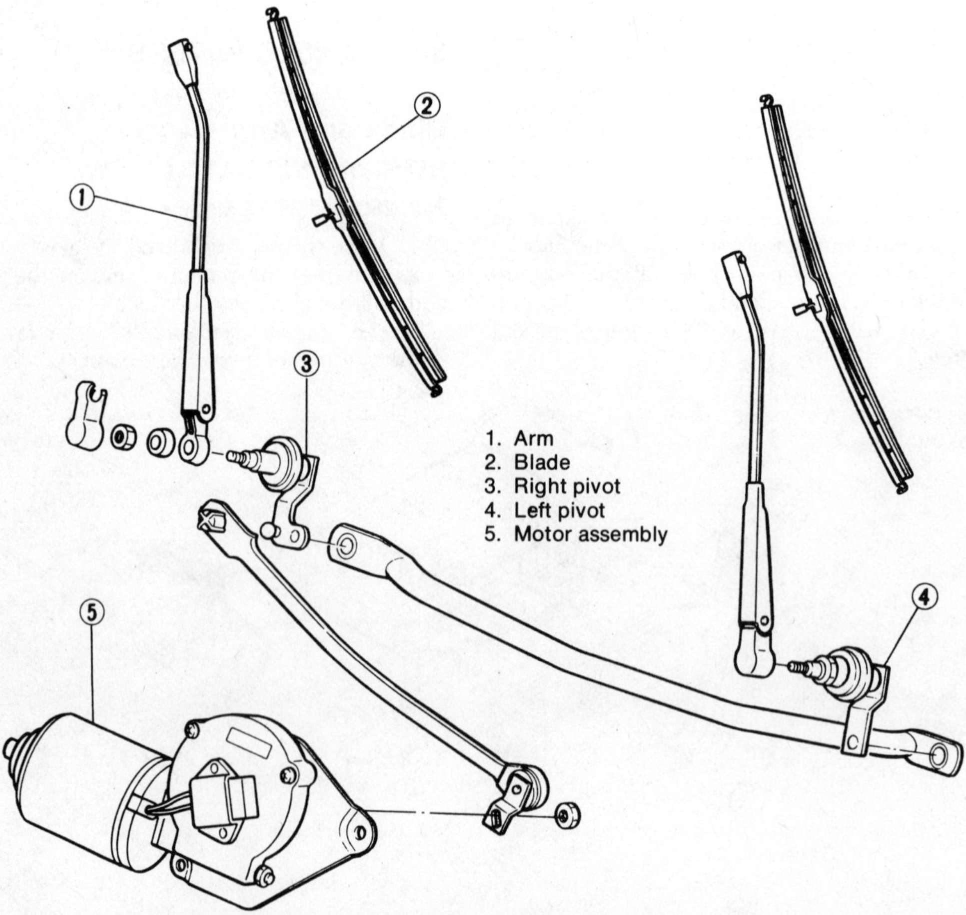

1. Arm
2. Blade
3. Right pivot
4. Left pivot
5. Motor assembly

ZX wiper motor and linkage, 1979 and later

CHASSIS ELECTRICAL

3. Turn the ignition switch ON and cycle the motor a few times. Then turn OFF the wiper motor with the wiper switch, not the ignition switch.

4. Turn the ignition OFF and press the arm onto the shaft.

NOTE: *Proper arm installation figures are given in the illustration.*

280 and 300-ZX Models

1. Pry the cover upwards to expose the retaining nut.

2. Unscrew the nut and pull the arm from the shaft.

NOTE: *Before installing the arm, be sure the motor is in the Park position.*

3. Turn the ignition switch ON and cycle the motor a few times. Then turn OFF the wiper motor with the wiper switch, not the ignition switch.

4. Turn the ignition OFF and press the arm onto the shaft.

NOTE: *The blade should be parked approximately 0.315 in. (280-ZX) or 0.59–0.98 in. (300-ZX) from the bottom windshield molding.*

Motor and Linkage
REMOVAL AND INSTALLATION

1. Disconnect the negative battery cable. Remove the wiper arms.

2. Disconnect the wiper motor connector from under the hood.

3. Remove the cowl cover retaining screws and the cover.

4. Remove the wiper motor bracket retaining screws and the bracket.

5. If only the motor is to be removed, disconnect the linkage from the motor and remove the motor.

6. If the motor and linkage are to be removed, remove the screws which retain each pivot and the linkage.

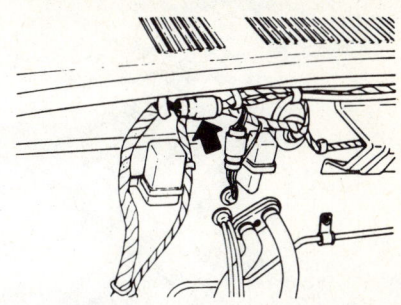
Arrow shows the wiper motor connector, 1970–78

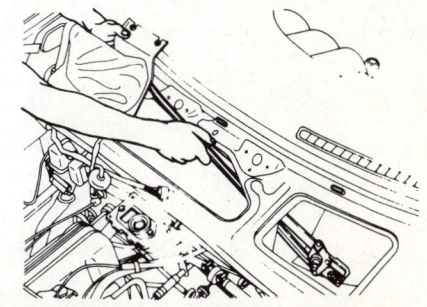
Removing the wiper linkage on Z models

7. To install, reverse the removal procedures.

Rear Window Wiper Motor
REMOVAL AND INSTALLATION
280 and 300-ZX Models

1. Disconnect the negative battery cable.

2. Remove the wiper arm from the rear window wiper motor.

3. Raise the rear door and remove the wiper motor cover plate.

4. Disconnect the rear wiper motor electrical connectors.

5. Remove the wiper motor mounting bolts and separate the linkage, then remove the motor from the rear door.

6. To install, reverse the removal procedures.

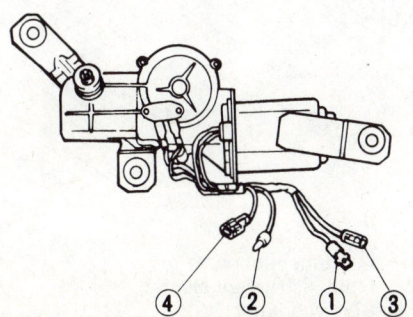
View of the rear wiper motor and circuitry—280 and 300-ZX

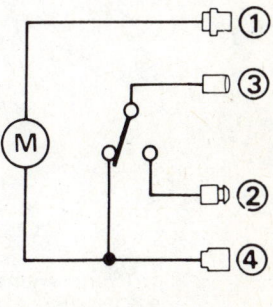

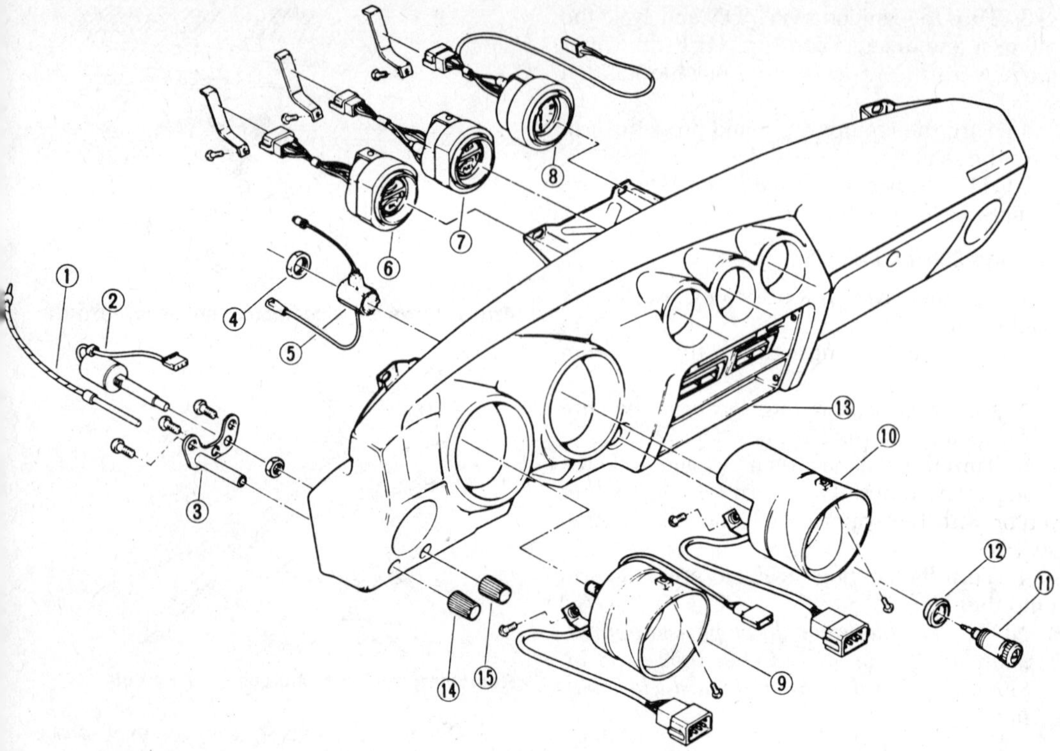

178 CHASSIS ELECTRICAL

1. Trip meter reset knob
2. Resistor (illumination control)
3. Bracket
4. Cigarette lighter retaining nut
5. Cigarette lighter housing
6. Oil-temp gauge
7. Amp-fuel gauge
8. Clock
9. Speedometer
10. Tachometer
11. Cigarette lighter
12. Escutcheon
13. Instrument finish panel
14. Knob (trip meter reset)
15. Knob (resistor)

Exploded view of the Z model instrument panel

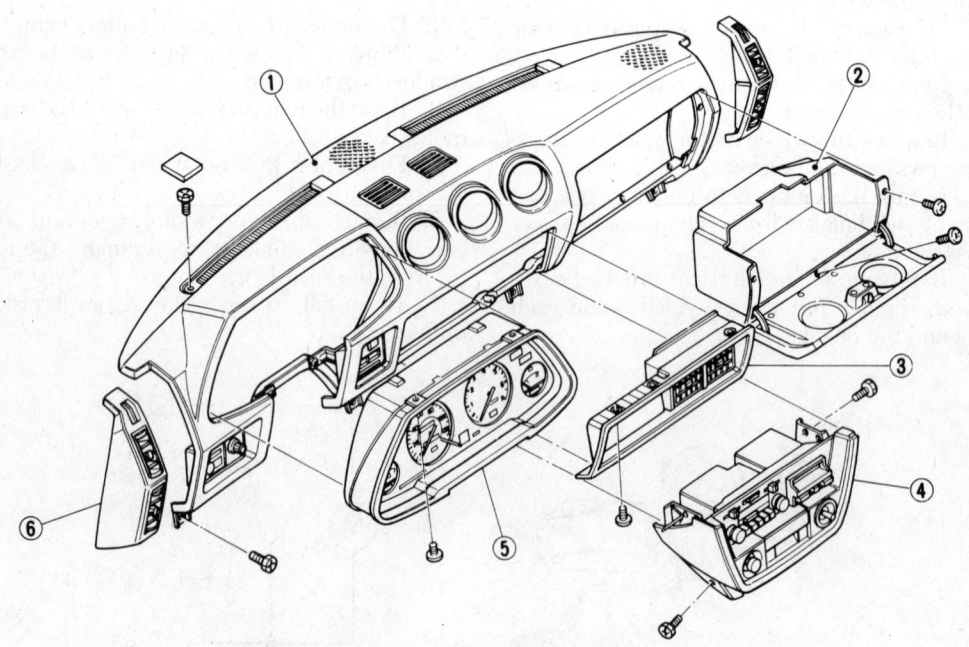

1. Instrument pad
2. Glove box
3. Center ventilator
4. Instrument console
5. Main instrument cluster
6. Side ventilator

Exploded view of the ZX instrument panel, 1979–83

CHASSIS ELECTRICAL 179

INSTRUMENT AND SWITCHES

Instrument Cluster
REMOVAL AND INSTALLATION

1. Refer to the "Steering Wheel, Removal and Installation" procedures, in Chapter 7 and remove the steering wheel.
2. Remove the steering column trim covers (shell).
3. Remove the lower instrument panel trim cover on the left-side.
4. Disconnect the speedometer cable at the connector inside the passenger compartment.
5. Remove the combination switch by performing the following procedures:

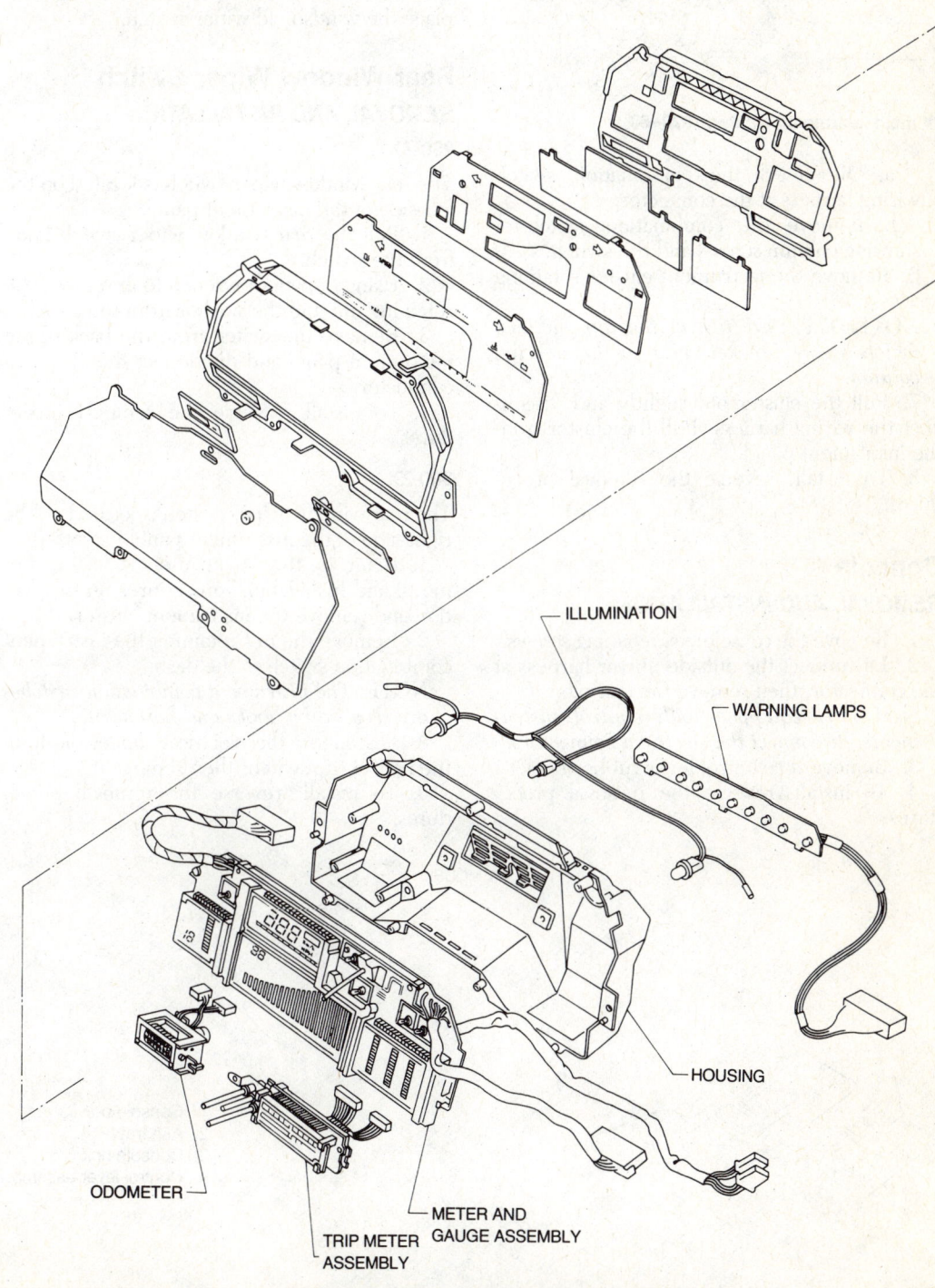

Exploded view of combination meter—300 ZX

180 CHASSIS ELECTRICAL

ZX main instrument cluster, 1979–83

a. Disconnect the combination switch wiring harness at the connector.
b. Remove the combination switch-to-steering column screws and the switch.
6. Remove the instrument cluster retaining screws.
NOTE: *There are two at the top and two which secure brackets next to the steering column.*
7. Pull the cluster out slightly and disconnect the wiring harness. Pull the cluster from the instrument panel.
8. To install, reverse the removal procedures.

Console
REMOVAL AND INSTALLATION

1. Remove the console box retaining screws.
2. Disconnect the outside mirror harness at the connector, then remove the console.
NOTE: *If equipped with control instruments, disconnect the electrical connectors.*
3. Remove the control lever rubber boot.
4. To install, reverse the removal procedures.

Windshield Wiper Switch

The windshield wiper switch is a part of the combination switch which is mounted on the steering column.

REMOVAL AND INSTALLATION

Refer to the "Combination Switch, Removal and Installation" procedures, in Chapter 7 and replace the windshield wiper switch.

Rear Window Wiper Switch
REMOVAL AND INSTALLATION
280-ZX

The rear window wiper switch is located on the left-side of the instrument panel.
1. Pull the rear window wiper switch knob from the switch.
2. Using a spanner wrench tool, remove the retaining nut and the washer from the switch.
3. Remove the switch from the back of the instrument panel and disconnect the electrical connector.
4. To install, reverse the removal procedures.

300-ZX

The rear window wiper switch is located on the right-side of the instrument panel.
1. Refer to the "Instrument Cluster, Removal and Installation" procedures, in this section and remove the instrument cluster.
2. Remove the nut retaining the instrument combination switch to the dash.
NOTE: *The instrument combination switches are secured by hooks and basements.*
3. Disconnect the electrical connectors from the rear of the switch, then remove it.
4. To install, reverse the removal procedures.

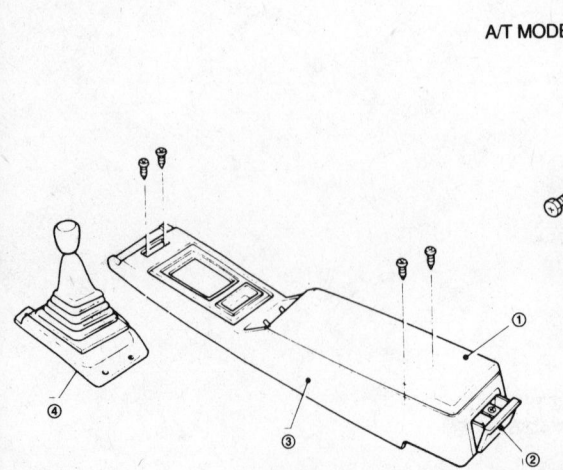

1. Console box lid
2. Ash tray
3. Console box
4. Control lever assembly

Removing the console—280-ZX, others are similar

CHASSIS ELECTRICAL 181

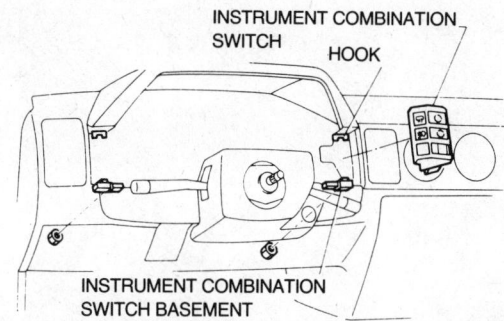

Removing the instrument combination switch—300-ZX

Headlight Switch
REMOVAL AND INSTALLATION
280 and 300-ZX

Since the headlight switch is a part of the combination switch, refer to the "Combination Switch, Removal and Installation" procedures, in Chapter 7, then remove the switch.

Speedometer Cable

The 300-ZX models use an electronic speed sensor; therefore, a mechanical speedometer cable is not used.

REMOVAL AND INSTALLATION

1. Reach up under the instrument panel and disconnect the cable housing from the back of the speedometer. It is attached by a knurled knob which simply unscrews.
2. On the 240, 260 and 280-Z models, remove the screw under the instrument panel, which retains the speedometer cable to a bracket. Pull the cable from the housing.
3. The 280-ZX models have an intermediate connection in the passenger compartment. Unscrew the intermediate connection and pull the two cables from the housings.
NOTE: *If the cable is broken, the other half of the cable will have to be removed from the transmission end.*
4. Unscrew the retaining knob and remove the cable from the transmission.
5. Lubricate the cable with graphite powder or speedometer cable lubricant and feed the cable into the housing.
NOTE: *It is best to start at the speedometer end and feed the cable down towards the transmission. It is also usually necessary to unscrew the transmission connection and install the cable end to the gear, then reconnect the housing to the transmission.*
6. To install, reverse the removal procedures.

Tachometer
REMOVAL AND INSTALLATION
260-Z and 280-Z

1. Remove the screw, located just above the tachometer face, which retains the tach at the top.
2. From under the instrument panel, remove the screw which holds the tach to the instrument panel bracket.
3. Pull the tach out, disconnect the instrument harness connector and fully remove the tach.
4. To install, reverse the removal procedures.

Speedometer
REMOVAL AND INSTALLATION
260-Z and 280-Z

1. Refer to the "Tachometer, Removal and Installation" procedures, in this section and remove the tachometer.
2. Disconnect the speedometer cable at the junction screw on the speedometer back.
3. Disconnect the trip meter reset cable, going in through the tachometer opening.
4. Disconnect the two retaining screws for the speedometer in the same way as the two tachometer retaining screws were removed. Disconnect the resistor lead wire from the connector while under the instrument panel.
5. Pull the speedometer out slightly, disconnect the instrument harness connector and remove the speedometer.
6. To install, reverse the removal procedures.

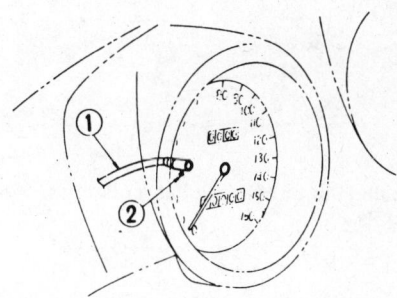

1. Trip meter reset cable   2. Retaining screw
Removing the reset cable on Z models

Speedometer or Tachometer
REMOVAL AND INSTALLATION
240-Z

1. Remove the heater air duct which passes behind the instruments.

182 CHASSIS ELECTRICAL

2. Remove the wing nuts and washers which retain the instrument to be removed from behind.
3. Pull the instrument down slightly, then remove the electrical connector(s) and the instrument.
NOTE: *If removing the speedometer, remove the speedometer cable.*
4. To install, reverse the removal procedures.

Temp-Oil and Volt-Fuel Gauges
REMOVAL AND INSTALLATION
260-Z and 280-Z

1. Remove the retaining screws for the instrument finish panel (located under the three small gauges) and pull it out slightly. Disconnect the electrical connectors and remove the finish panel.
2. Remove the three-way duct-to-instrument panel screws and the three-way duct-to-bracket screws.
3. Disconnect the duct hoses and remove the duct.
4. Remove the screw(s) retaining the gauge or gauges to be removed from the instrument panel.
5. Pull the gauge to the rear, disconnect the connector(s) and remove the gauge.
6. To install, reverse the removal procedures.

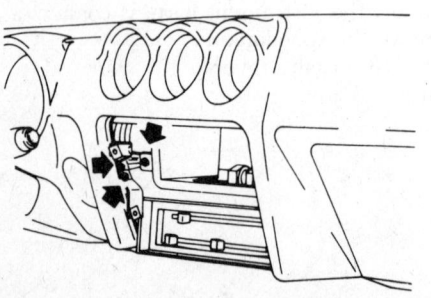
Removing the three-way duct retaining screws on Z models

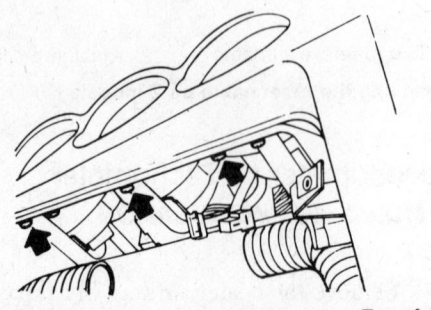
Removing the gauge retaining screws on Z models

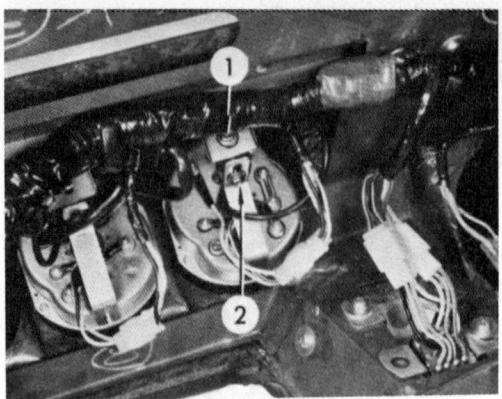
Removing the mounting screws for the temperature/oil pressure gauge on Z models

240-Z

1. Remove the instrument panel finish panel.
2. Go in where the panel was with a pair of pliers and carefully loosen the hex-head screws on the back of the instrument to be removed.
3. Pull the gauge to the rear, disconnect the connector(s) and remove it.
4. To install, reverse the removal procedures.

LIGHTING

Headlamp
REMOVAL AND INSTALLATION
1970–78

1. Disconnect the headlamp connector behind the front fender panel.
2. Go in through the wheel opening and remove the four headlamp housing retaining screws.
3. Pull the headlamp assembly out.
4. Loosen the retaining ring screws, rotate the ring and remove it.
5. Disconnect the connector and remove the sealed beam unit.
6. To install, reverse the removal procedures. Aim the new headlamp, if necessary.
NOTE: *Connect the wiring connector to the new sealed beam unit and position it so that the three location tabs fit the hollows in the mounting ring. The letters on the sealed beam must be in an upright position.*

1979–83

1. The headlights are accessible through the engine compartment. For access to the left headlight, remove the headlight cleaner reservoir tank, if equipped. For access to the right headlight, remove the coolant reservoir tank and the charcoal canister.

CHASSIS ELECTRICAL   183

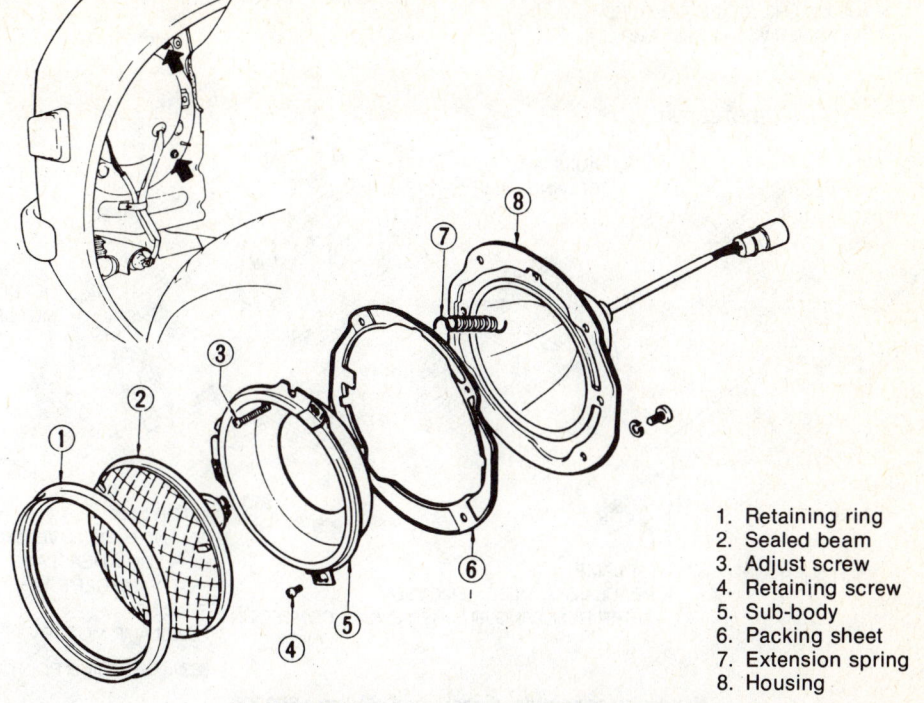

1. Retaining ring
2. Sealed beam
3. Adjust screw
4. Retaining screw
5. Sub-body
6. Packing sheet
7. Extension spring
8. Housing

Exploded view of the headlamp parts—Z models

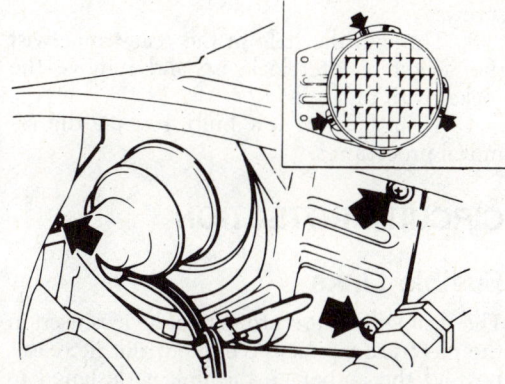

ZX headlamp removal—typical through 1983

2. Disconnect the headlamp wiring from the rear of the bulb.
3. Remove the bolts retaining the headlight bracket.
4. Pull the bracket back and remove the screws holding the headlight retaining ring. Remove the ring and the headlight. Be careful not to touch the headlight aiming screws, located at the top and the outside of the ring.
5. To install, reverse the removal procedures.

1984 and Later

1. Turn ON the headlamp switch and after the headlamps are open, disconnect the battery ground cable.

2. Remove the headlight trim finisher screws. Push down on the finisher and pull out on the upper part while pulling up on the headlight cover to remove it.

NOTE: *Be careful not to break the trim finisher when removing it.*

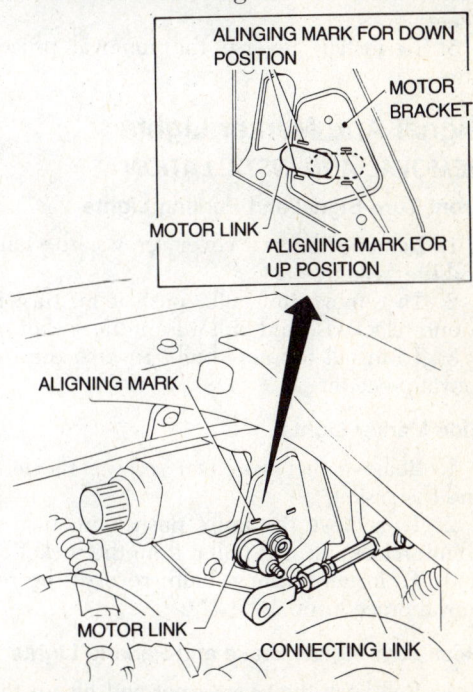

Headlamp link assembly installation—300 ZX

184 CHASSIS ELECTRICAL

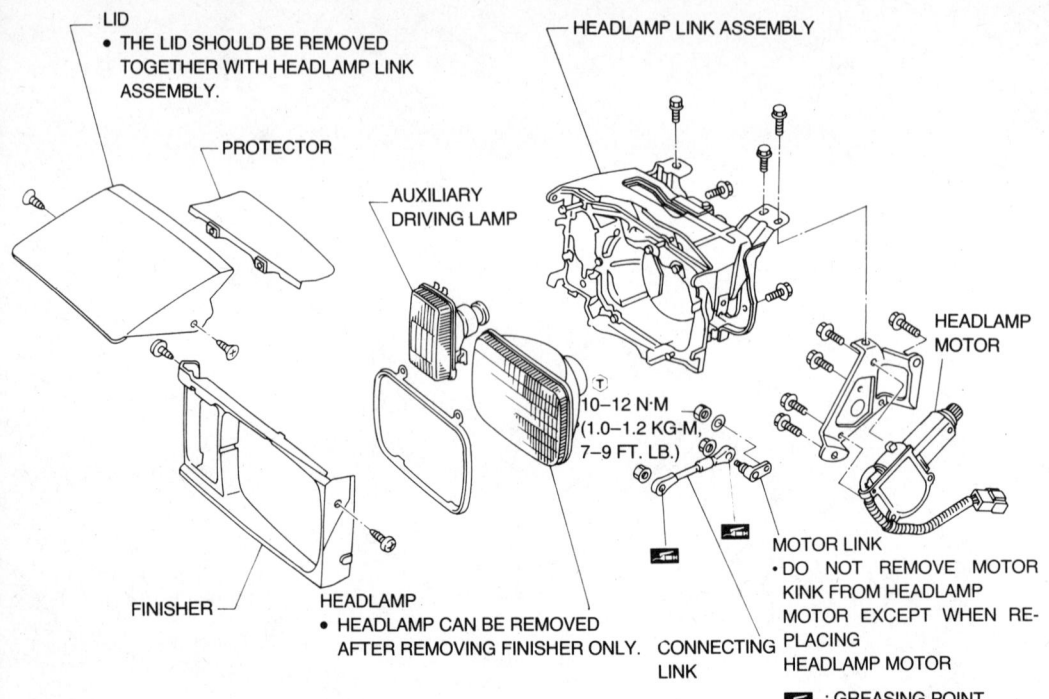

Headlamp assembly, disassembled view—300 ZX

3. Loosen the screws holding the headlight retaining ring and remove the headlight from the retaining ring.

NOTE: *DO NOT* disturb the headlight adjusting screws.

4. Disconnect the wiring connector from the back of the sealed beam and remove the sealed beam.

5. To install, reverse the removal procedures.

Signal And Marker Lights
REMOVAL AND INSTALLATION
Front Turn Signal and Parking Lights

1. Remove the two cover screws, the lens and the gasket.
2. To remove the bulb, push it in, turn it counterclockwise and pull it from the socket.
3. To install the new bulb, reverse the removal procedures.

Side Marker Lights

1. Remove the two cover screws, the lens and the gasket.
2. To remove the bulb, push it in, turn it counterclockwise and pull it from the socket.
3. To install the new bulb, reverse the removal procedures.

Rear Turn Signal, Brake and Parking Lights

1. Pull back the rear carpet and lift up the luggage floor center trim.

2. Remove the rear trim cover lid retaining screws.
3. Through the hole in the rear trim, twist the socket counterclockwise and remove the socket with the bulb.
4. To install the new bulb, reverse the removal procedures.

CIRCUIT PROTECTION

Fusible Links

The fusible links are protective devices used in the electrical circuits. When current increases beyond the amperage the link is designed to withstand, the fusible metal of the link melts, breaking the circuit and preventing further damage to other components and wiring. Whenever a fusible link has melted because of a short circuit, correct the cause before installing a new link.

CAUTION: *Always use replacements of the same electrical capacity as the original, available from your dealer. Replacements of a different electrical value will not provide adequate system protection.*

All 280 and 300-ZX models fusible links are located in a case next to the battery in the engine compartment. Circuits protected include the electronic fuel injection circuit, the ignition circuit, the ignition supply to the fuse box, the accessory supply to the fuse box and the headlight circuit.

CHASSIS ELECTRICAL 185

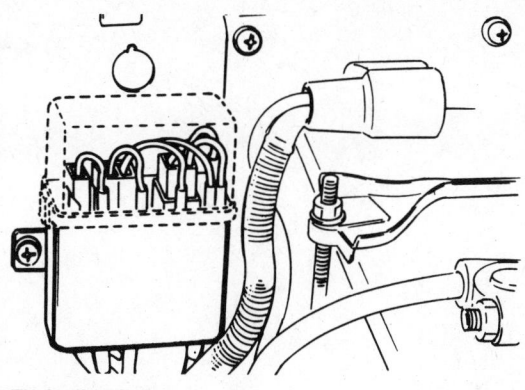

ZX fusible links

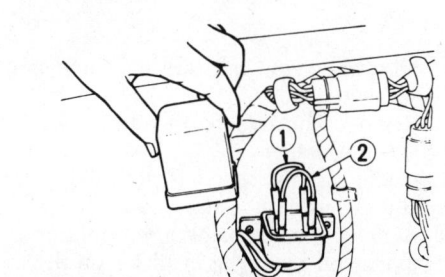

Fusible links—black (1) and green (2)—used in the 260-Z

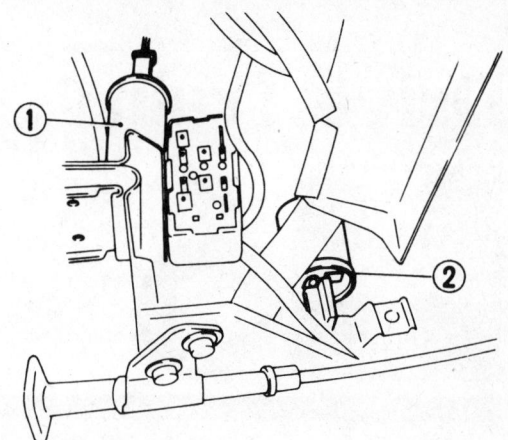

Hazard flasher (1) and turn signal flasher (2) locations—Z models

The 280-Z fusible links are located on the relay bracket on the inner right-fender in front of the battery. The fuel injection fusible link is connected between the battery positive cable and the fuel injection harness.

On the 260-Z, the fusible link box is located on the firewall on the right-side of the engine compartment. These links protect the alternator and the starter.

On the 240-Z, the links are located at the starter motor and alternator.

Fuses and Flashers

The turn signal and hazard warning flashers are located underneath the left-side of the instrument panel, next to the kick panel on all Z models. The two flasher units are under the instrument panel just to the left of the steering column on ZX models. In both cases, replacement is made by unplugging the old unit and plugging in a new one.

The 300-ZX fuse panel is located under the instrument panel on the left-side kick panel.

On 280-ZX models, the fuse box is under the instrument panel on the right-side kick panel. The fuse ratings and circuits they protect are marked on the lid of the box.

On 260-Z and 280-Z models, the fuse block is located at the right-side trim panel under the instrument panel.

On 240-Z models, the fuse block is in the console under the ash tray.

WIRING DIAGRAMS

Wiring diagrams have been omitted from this book. As vehicles have become virtually more complex, wiring diagrams have grown in size and complexity as well. It has become virtually impossible to provide a readable reproduction in a reasonable number of pages. Information on obtaining wiring diagrams from the manufacturer is available at your Datsun dealer.

Drive Train

MANUAL TRANSMISSION

The Datsun Z, 1970–71 models use a F4W71A, 4-speed transmission; the 1972–79 models use the F4W71B, 4-speed transmission; the 1977–83 models use the FS5W71B 5-speed transmission; the 1984 and later models use the Nissan FS5W71C 5-speed (non-turbo) or a Borg Warner BWT-5 (FS5R90A) 5-speed (turbo) models. All models use a single to rail shifter with internal linkage. No shift linkage adjustments are necessary or possible.

Transmission

REMOVAL AND INSTALLATION

1. Disconnect the battery negative cable and the accelerator linkage. Drain the transmission oil.
2. Remove the console screws. Disconnect the wiring harness and remove the console. Remove the shift lever boot.
   NOTE: *If equipped with a carburetor, remove the choke control wire from the console.*
3. Place the transmission in the Neutral position.
   NOTE: *On the 1970–83 models, remove the E-ring from the gearshift lever pin, then the pin and the gearshift lever. On the 1984 and later models, remove the gearshift lever internal snap ring (FS5W71C) or the gearshift lever plate BW T-5 (FS5R90A).*
4. Raise and support the vehicle on jackstands.
5. Disconnect the exhaust pipe from the exhaust manifold. Remove the exhaust pipe bracket from the extension housing. Support the pipe with a length of wire.
   NOTE: *On the 1984 and later models, remove the exhaust front tube, the catalytic converter and the exhaust manifold crossover tube.*
6. Disconnect the back-up light and neutral safety switch wires.
7. Remove the clutch operating cylinder from the transmission.
8. Disconnect the speedometer cable at the rear of the extension housing.
9. Remove the resonator and/or muffler insulator bolts and place the insulator on the exhaust pipe.
10. Using an awl, scribe matchmarks on the rear of the driveshaft and companion flanges.
11. Remove driveshaft flange bolts, then pull the rear down and draw the driveshaft sleeve yoke from the transmission. Withdraw the driveshaft carefully so as not to damage the oil seal, then plug the transmission opening with a clean rag.
12. Using a block of wood (between the jack and the oil pan) and a floor jack, support the engine under the oil pan.
13. Place a transmission jack under the transmission and support it; DO NOT place the jack under the drain plug.
14. Remove the nut attaching the transmission to the rear crossmember. Remove the crossmember-to-frame bolts and the crossmember.
15. Disconnect the starter wiring and remove the starter motor.
16. Remove the transmission-to-engine bolts, then slide the transmission rearward, downward and remove it from the vehicle.

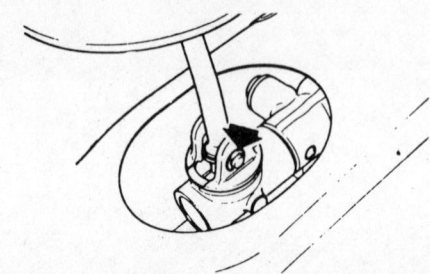

Disconnecting the gearshift lever E-clip, 1970–83

DRIVE TRAIN

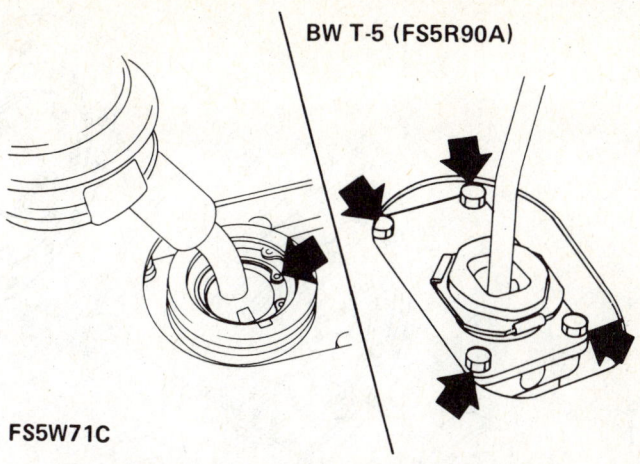

Removing the gearshift lever—1984 and later models

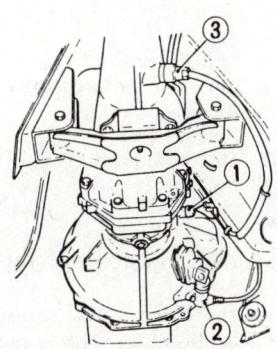

1. Neutral safety switch
2. Clutch slave cylinder
3. Speedometer

The underside of the transmission

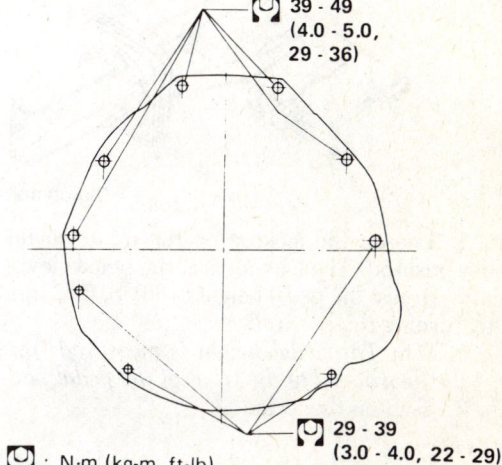

Transmission torquing sequence—1984 and later

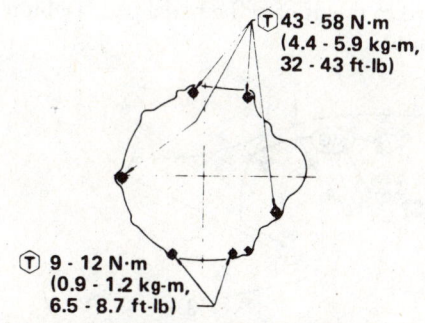

Transmission torquing sequence—1970–83

17. To install, perform the following:
    a. Clean the mating surfaces of the engine and transmission case.
    b. Lightly grease the clutch disc and mainshaft splines.
    c. To complete the installation, reverse removal procedures. Torque the engine-to-transmission bolts to 32–43 ft. lbs. (1970–83) or 29–36 ft. lbs. (1984 and later) for the upper bolts and 6.5–8.7 ft. lbs. (1970–83) or 22–29 ft. lbs. (1984 and later) for the bottom bolts. Refill the transmission to the level of the filler plug with the recommended oil.

CLUTCH

The clutch consists of a driven disc splined to the transmission mainshaft and a pressure plate which is bolted to the engine flywheel. When the clutch pedal is released, the pressure plate moves toward the flywheel and sandwiches the driven disc between itself and the flywheel, thus providing smooth engagement but a solid drive connection.

PEDAL HEIGHT AND FREE PLAY ADJUSTMENTS

1970–71

Pedal height is adjusted by varying the effective length of the master cylinder pushrod.

188 DRIVE TRAIN

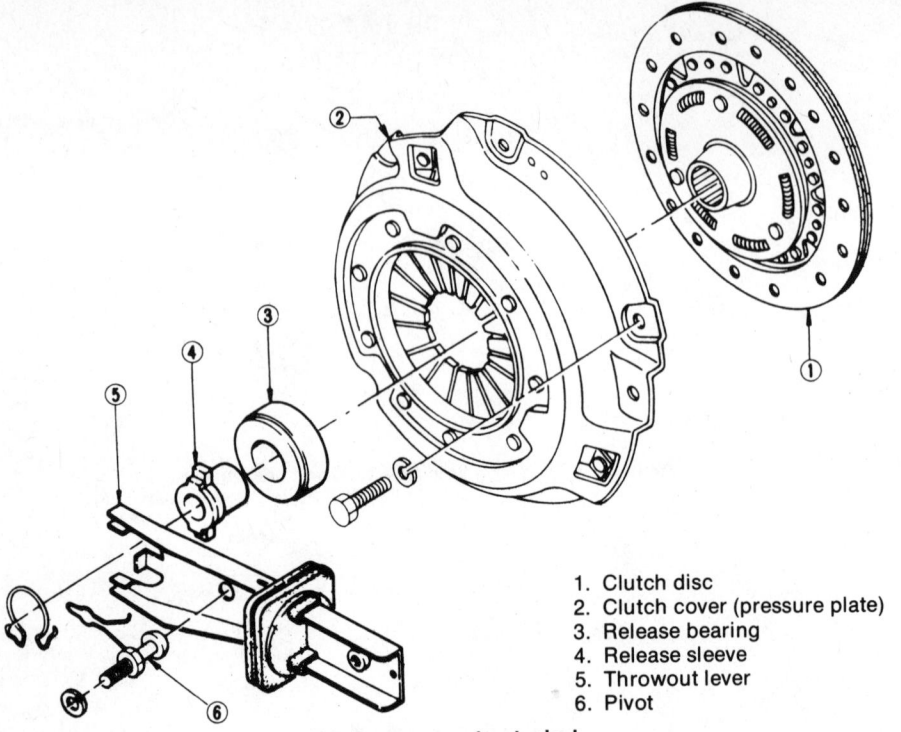

1. Clutch disc
2. Clutch cover (pressure plate)
3. Release bearing
4. Release sleeve
5. Throwout lever
6. Pivot

Clutch components—typical

1. Loosen the locknut on the master cylinder pushrod. The locknut is at the pedal clevis.
2. Adjust the pedal height to 8.0 in. (202 mm) by turning the pushrod.

NOTE: *The pedal height is measured from the floorboard to the front of the pedal pad.*

3. Tighten the locknut.

1972–75

The height is first adjusted by varying the effective length of the master cylinder pushrod. The height is then adjusted with the pedal stop bumper.

1. Loosen the locknut and screw the pedal stop in as far as it will go. The pedal should be free to move out as far as possible.
2. Loosen the master cylinder pushrod locknut; it is located at the pedal clevis. Adjust the rod so that the pedal height is 8.9 in. (226 mm). Pedal height is measured from the floorboard to the front of the pedal pad. Tighten the locknut.

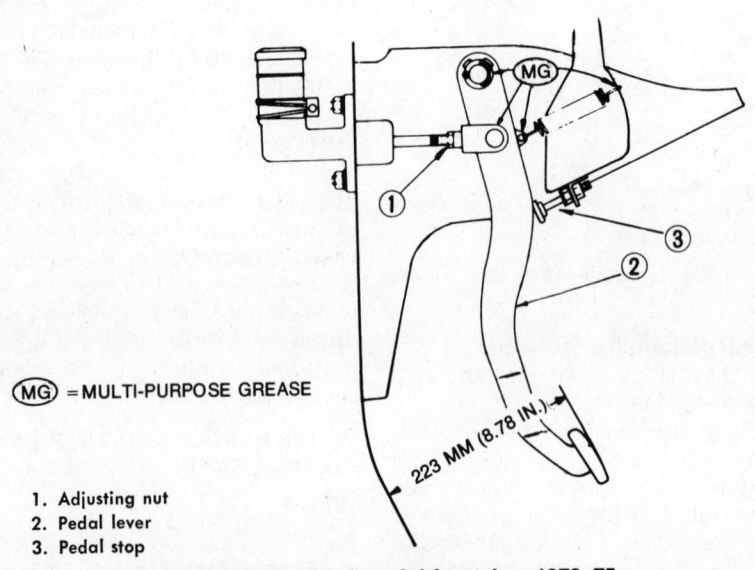

(MG) = MULTI-PURPOSE GREASE

1. Adjusting nut
2. Pedal lever
3. Pedal stop

Adjusting the clutch pedal free-play, 1972–75

DRIVE TRAIN

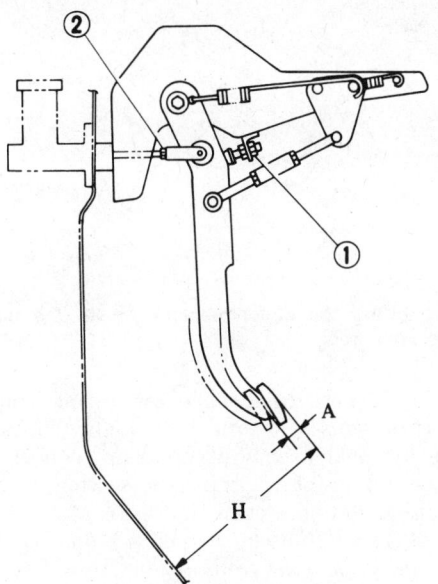

1. Pedal stop/clutch switch locknut
2. Pushrod locknut

1976-79 pedal height adjustment: "A" is the free-play; "H" is the pedal height

3. Screw the pedal stop back out until the pedal height is 8.78 in. (223 mm). Tighten the locknut.

1976-79

The pedal height is first adjusted with the pedal stop bumper or the clutch switch. Free play is then adjusted by varying the effective length of the master cylinder pushrod.

1. Loosen the locknut on the pedal stop bumper or clutch switch. Turn the bumper or switch in or out until the pedal height is 8.8 in. (223 mm), for 1976-78 or 7.87-8.11 in. (200-206 mm), for 1979. Tighten the locknut.
   NOTE: *The pedal height is measured from the floorboard to the front of the pedal pad.*
2. Loosen the master cylinder pushrod locknut. The locknut is at the pedal clevis.
3. Adjust the pedal free play by turning the pushrod. Free play should be 0.04-0.12 in. (1.0-3.0 mm) for 1976-77 or 0.04-0.20 in. (1.0-5.0 mm) for 1978-79. Tighten the locknut.

1980-83

Three adjustments are to be made. The first is to the adjusting rod, which connects the pedal arm to the return spring pivot. The second is made by varying the effective length of the master cylinder pushrod. The third is made by adjusting the clutch switch or pedal stop bumper.

1. Check the length of the adjusting rod. The distance between the center of each end should be 6.10 in. (155 mm). If not, loosen the locknuts and turn the adjuster until the length is correct. Tighten the locknuts.
2. Loosen the clutch switch or the pedal stop bumper locknut. Turn the switch or bumper all the way in so that the pedal arm does not make contact.
3. Loosen the master cylinder pushrod locknut (located at the pedal clevis). Adjust the pedal height by turning the master cylinder pushrod. Pedal height is measured from the floorboard to the front of the pedal pad. The height should be 8.11 in. (1980-82) or 8.03 in. (1983). Tighten the locknut.
4. Turn the clutch switch or the pedal stop until the pedal height measures 7.99 in. (1980-82) or 7.91 in. (1983). Tighten the locknut on the switch or stop.
5. Check the pedal free play. It should be 0.04-0.20 in. (1.0-5.0 mm). If incorrect, adjust with the master cylinder pushrod.

1984 and Later

Two adjustments are to be made. The first is made by adjusting the clutch switch or pedal stop bumper. The second is made by varying the effective length of the master cylinder pushrod.

1. Loosen the clutch switch or the pedal stop bumper locknut.
2. Turn the clutch switch or the pedal stop until the pedal height measures 7.68-8.07 in. (195-205 mm). Tighten the locknut on the switch or stop.
   NOTE: *Pedal height is measured from the floorboard to the front of the pedal pad.*
3. Loosen the master cylinder pushrod locknut (located at the pedal clevis). Adjust the

DRIVE TRAIN

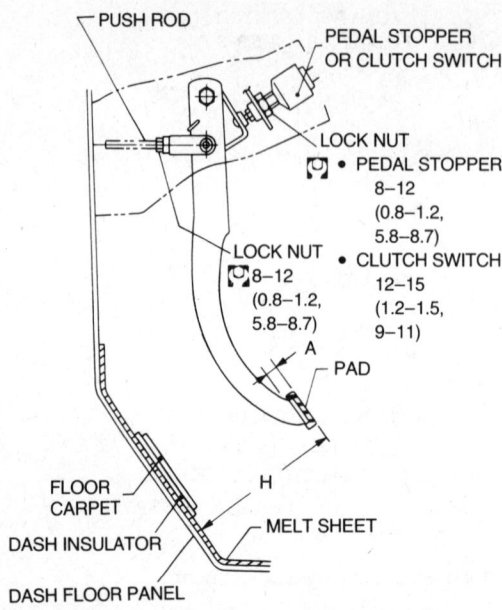

1984 and later pedal height adjustment

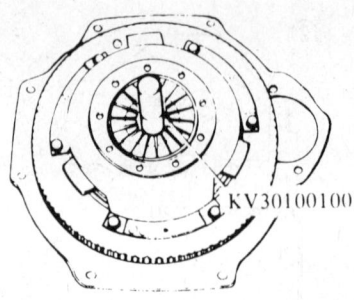

Supporting the clutch assembly with the clutch alignment tool

free play by turning the master cylinder pushrod. Tighten the locknut.

4. Check the pedal free play. It should be 0.04–0.20 in. (1.0–5.0 mm). If incorrect, adjust with the master cylinder pushrod.

Clutch Disc And Pressure Plate
REMOVAL AND INSTALLATION

CAUTION: *The clutch driven disc contains asbestos, which has been determined to be a cancer causing agent. Never clean clutch surfaces with compressed air! Avoid inhaling any dust from any clutch surface! When cleaning clutch surfaces, use a commercially available brake cleaning fluid.*

1. Refer to the "Transmission, Removal and Installation" procedures, in this section and remove the transmission.

2. Using the Clutch Aligning Bar tool No. KV30100100 (1970–84) or ST20600000 (1985 and later), insert it all the way into the clutch disc hub. Mark the clutch assembly-to-flywheel relationship with paint or a center punch so that the clutch assembly can be assembled in the same position from which it is removed.

NOTE: *Using the clutch aligning bar, support the weight of the clutch disc during removal.*

3. Loosen the pressure plate-to-flywheel bolts evenly, one turn at a time, until the spring pressure is released.

4. Remove the bolts and pull the pressure plate and disc from the flywheel.

5. Inspect the flywheel for scoring, roughness or signs of overheating. Light scoring of the flywheel may be cleaned up with emery cloth but any deep grooves or scoring warrant replacement or refacing (if possible).

NOTE: *If the clutch faces or flywheel are oily, inspect the transmission front cover oil seal, the pilot bushing and the engine rear seals for leakage, then correct the problem before replacing the clutch.*

6. If the pilot bushing in the crankshaft is worn, replace it. Install it using a soft hammer. The installation depth should be 0.18–0.20 in. (1970–77), 0.374 in. (1978) or 0.157 in. (1979 and later).

NOTE: *When installing the pilot bushing, the depth is measured from the end of the crankshaft flange to the transmission end. The factory-supplied part does not have to be oiled but check the procedure if you are using an aftermarket part.*

7. Inspect the clutch cover for wear or scoring, then replace if necessary. The pressure plate and spring cannot be disassembled; you must replace the clutch cover as an assembly.

8. Inspect the clutch release bearing; if it is rough or noisy, it should be replaced by performing the following procedures:

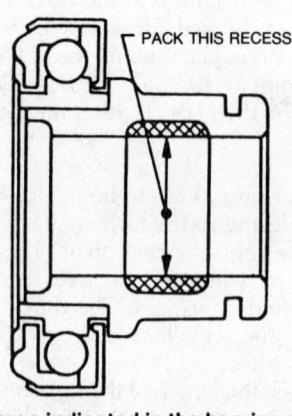

Coat the area indicated in the bearing sleeve with grease

DRIVE TRAIN

a. Using a puller, remove the bearing.
b. Using a press, install the new bearing.
c. After installation, coat the groove in the sleeve, the contact surfaces of the release lever, pivot pin and sleeve and the release bearing contact surfaces on the transmission front cover with a light coat of grease.
CAUTION: *When greasing the clutch release bearing, be careful not to use too much grease, it will run at high temperatures and get onto the clutch faces.*
d. Reinstall the release bearing on the lever.

9. Apply a thin coat of grease to the pressure plate wire ring, diaphragm spring, clutch cover grooves and the drive bosses on the pressure plate.
10. Apply a thin coat of Lubriplate® to the splines in the driven plate. Slide the clutch disc into the splines, then move it back and forth several times. Remove the disc and wipe off the excess lubricant. Be very careful not to get any grease on the clutch faces.
11. Assemble the clutch cover and the clutch plate on the clutch alignment tool.
12. Align the marks made on the clutch cover and the flywheel (if the old cover is being used) and install the clutch cover-to-flywheel bolts. Dowels are used to locate the clutch cover on the flywheel. Tighten the bolts in a criss-cross pattern, one turn at a time, to 12–15 ft. lbs. (1970–82) or 16–20 ft. lbs. (1983 and later). Remove the clutch alignment tool.
13. To complete the installation, reverse the removal procedures.

Clutch Master Cylinder

REMOVAL AND INSTALLATION

1. Remove the snap pin and the pushrod clevis pin from the master cylinder.
2. Disconnect the clutch tube from the master cylinder and drain the fluid.
   NOTE: *On some fuel injected models, it may be necessary to remove the windshield washer tank and the dropping resistor (out of the way), so that the clutch master cylinder may be removed.*
3. Remove the mounting bolts and the cylinder from the vehicle.
4. To install, reverse the removal procedures. Torque the master cylinder-to-dash nuts/bolts to 5.8–8.7 ft. lbs. Bleed the air from the clutch release system.

OVERHAUL

1. Remove the dust cover (discard it) and the stopper ring from the master cylinder body.
2. Remove the pushrod and the piston assembly.
3. Remove the piston cups (discard them), the spring seat from the piston and the supply valve (if necessary).
4. Using clean brake fluid, wash all of the parts.
5. Check the cylinder for uneven wear/or damage and measure the clearance between the piston and cylinder. The clearance should not be more than 0.0059 in. (0.15 mm). If defects are found, replace the master cylinder.

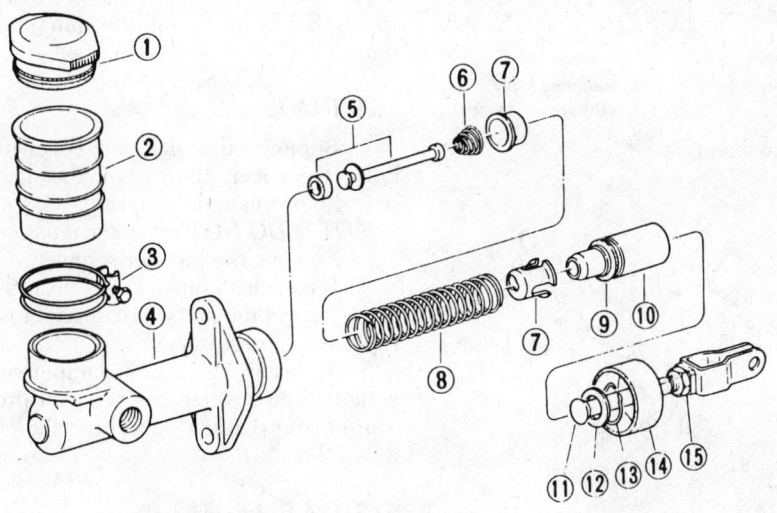

1. Reservoir cap
2. Reservoir
3. Reservoir band
4. Cylinder body
5. Valve assembly
6. Valve spring
7. Spring seat
8. Return spring
9. Piston cup
10. Piston
11. Pushrod
12. Stopper
13. Stopper ring
14. Dust cover
15. Nut

Exploded view of the clutch master cylinder—typical of all models

192 DRIVE TRAIN

6. Inspect the dust cover, the reservoir and the cap, then replace the parts as necessary.
7. Inspect the return valve springs and replace if broken or weak.
8. Inspect the hose and tube, then replace the parts as necessary.
9. To assemble, use a new piston cup, dip the parts in clean brake fluid, coat the piston and the cylinder with fluid, then reverse the disassembly procedures.

NOTE: *When installing the piston cup, make sure it is facing the right direction.*

Clutch Slave Cylinder

REMOVAL AND INSTALLATION

1. Remove the return spring. Detach the fluid line from the slave cylinder and drain the fluid.
2. Remove the mounting bolts and the slave cylinder.
3. To install, reverse the removal procedures. Torque the slave cylinder-to-clutch housing bolts to 18–22 ft. lbs. (1970–78) or 22–30 ft. lbs. (1979 and later). Bleed the clutch release system.

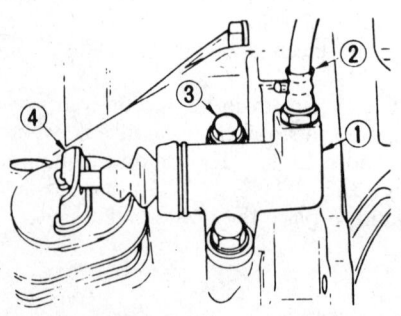

1. Clutch slave cylinder
2. Clutch hose
3. Mounting bolts
4. Withdrawal lever

Slave cylinder mounting

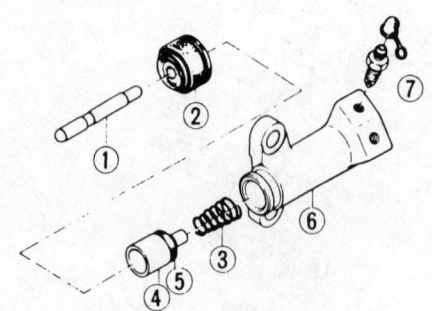

1. Pushrod
2. Dust cover
3. Piston spring
4. Piston
5. Piston cup
6. Operating cylinder
7. Bleeder screw

Exploded view of the clutch slave cylinder

OVERHAUL

1. Remove the pushrod and dust cover (discard it).
2. Remove the piston and piston cup as an assembly. Remove the spring.
3. Remove the bleeder screw.
4. Using clean brake fluid, wash all of the parts.
5. To inspect for damage, perform the following procedures:
   a. Check the piston and cylinder for excessive wear or scoring.
   b. Using a feeler gauge, check the clearance between the cylinder and the cylinder wall, it must not be more than 0.0059 in. (0.15 mm).
6. To assemble, dip the piston in clean brake fluid and coat the cylinder wall, then reverse the disassembly procedures.

NOTE: *When installing the new piston cup, be sure it is facing the right direction.*

Clutch Damper

The clutch damper is used to relieve the pressure shock within the clutch release system.

REMOVAL AND INSTALLATION
1984 and Later

1. Disconnect both fluid tubes from the clutch damper and drain the system.
2. Remove the clutch damper-to-frame bolts and the damper from the vehicle.
3. To install, reverse the removal procedures. Torque the clutch damper-to-frame bolts to 5.8–8.7 ft. lbs. Bleed the clutch release system.

OVERHAUL

1. Remove the damper cover-to-cylinder bolts, the cover, the gasket, the damper rubber, the piston and the spring.

NOTE: *DO NOT reuse the damper rubber.*

2. Remove the bleeder screw.
3. Using clean brake fluid, clean the parts.
4. Inspect the parts for damage or wear, then replace it (if necessary).
5. To install, use a new damper rubber and gasket, then reverse the removal procedures. Torque the damper cover-to-cylinder bolts to 2.2–4.3 ft. lbs.

SYSTEM BLEEDING

1. Fill the master cylinder with the recommended fluid to the proper level.
2. Clean any dirt from the bleeder screw(s) of the slave cylinder and the clutch damper (if equipped), then install a hose to the bleeder

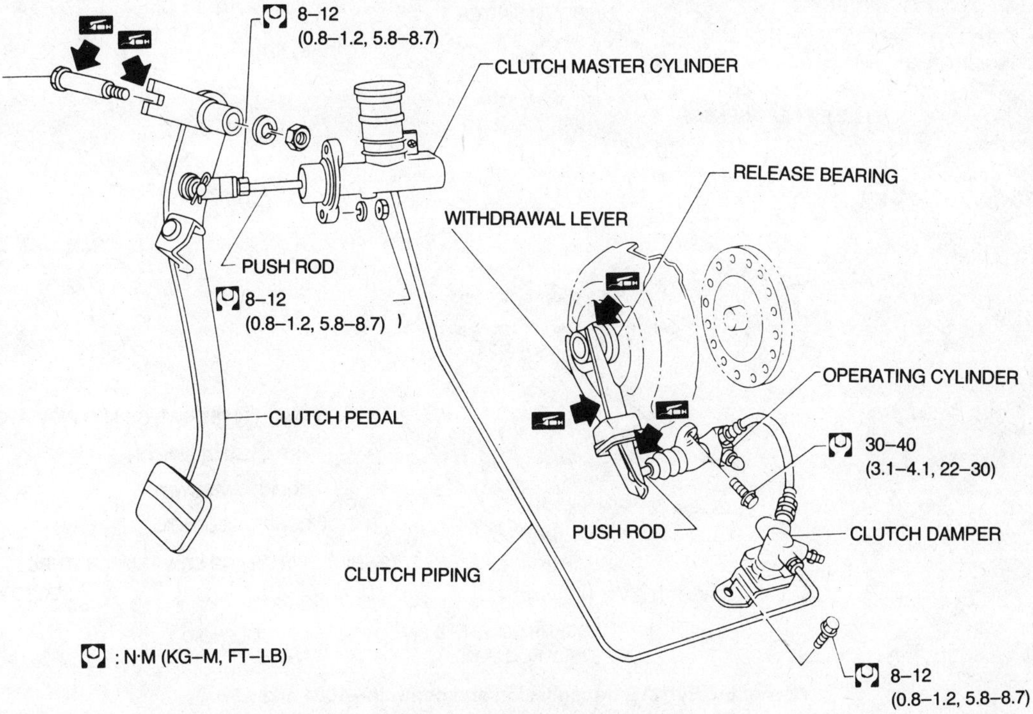

DRIVE TRAIN

View of the clutch release system—1984 and later

screw(s). Submerge the free end of the hose in a container of clean brake fluid.

3. Have an assistant depress the clutch pedal slowly. Loosen the bleeder screw as the pedal starts moving down and retighten it before the pedal stops moving downward.

NOTE: *On the 1984 and later models, bleed the clutch damper (first) and the slave cylinder (second).*

4. Have the assistant release the clutch pedal, then repeat Step 3 until the fluid in the bleed hose is bubble-free.

NOTE: *When bleeding the clutch release system, keep an eye on the fluid level and refill the reservoir with fresh fluid as necessary.*

5. When all the air is bled, refill the master cylinder, tighten the bleeder screw snugly and remove the bleeder hose.

AUTOMATIC TRANSMISSION

The optional automatic transmission is a JATCO (Japan Automatic Transmission Co., Ltd.) model 3N71A 1970–72; the 1973–82 models use the

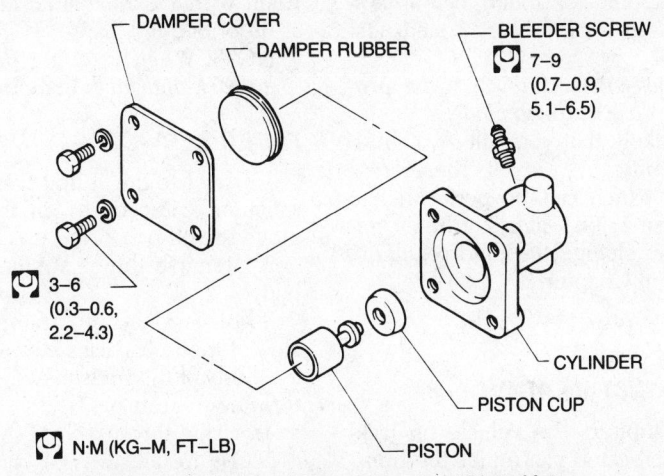

Exploded view of the clutch damper—1984 and later

194 DRIVE TRAIN

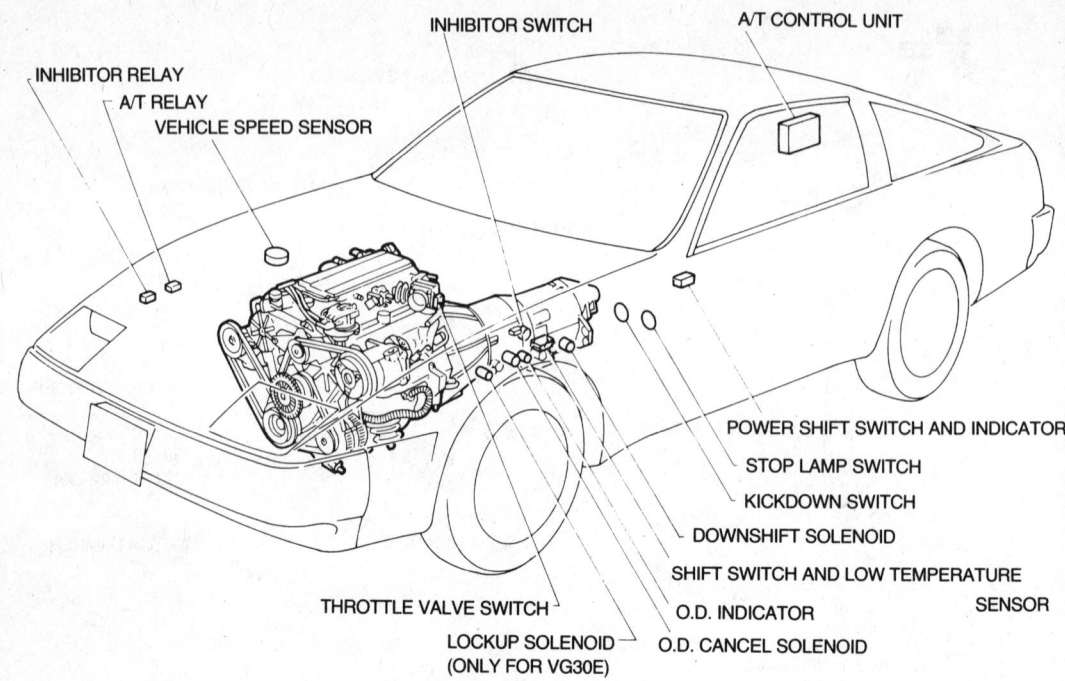

View of the E4N71B transmission and controls—1984 and later

JATCO 3N71B; the 1983 models use the JATCO L3N71B; the 1984 and later models use the JATCO E4N71B.

The 3N71A and 3N71B models are fully automatic units with a three element torque converter and two planetary gear sets. The L3N71B model incorporates a hydraulic lock-up torque convertor. The transmissions shift gears in response to signals of both engine speed and manifold vacuum.

The E4N71B model provides a shifting pattern of "Standard" or "Power" which is automatically selected by the microcomputer, depending upon the vehicle speed and the throttle position. The elecronic-controlled lock-up system permits lock-up of all forward speeds (1st thru 4th).

NOTE: *The lock-up mechanism is not provided with the VG30E turbo models.*

While it is unlikely that you will ever disassemble the transmission yourself, there are a few adjustments which can be performed to prolong the transmission's life. The most important thing is to change the fluid regularly, which is covered in Chapter 1.

Fluid Pan

REMOVAL AND INSTALLATION

1. Raise and support the vehicle on jackstands. Place an oil catch pan under the transmission.

2. Remove the oil pan-to-transmission mounting bolts.
3. Remove the pan slowly, keeping it level to avoid spilling fluid. Drain the fluid.

NOTE: *Inspect the oil pan for sludge and/or metal particles. If metal particles are present, further disassembly of the transmission is necessary to determine the cause.*

4. Using solvent, clean the pan.
5. Using a putty knife, clean the gasket mounting surfaces.
6. To install, use a new gasket and reverse the removal procedures. Torque the pan-to-transmission bolts to 3.6–5.1 ft. lbs. (5–7 Nm). Refill with Dexron® fluid and check the level as described in Chapter 1.

NOTE: *When torquing the mounting bolts, go back-and-forth in a criss-cross fashion.*

FILTER SERVICE

1. Refer to the "Fluid Pan, Removal and Installation" procedures, in this section and remove the oil pan.
2. Remove the oil strainer from the control body.
3. Inspect the oil strainer for metal particles. If metal particles are present, further disassembly of the transmission is necessary to determine the cause.
4. Using solvent, clean the oil strainer.
5. To install, reverse the removal procedures.

Adjustments

BRAKE BAND

1970–83

1. Refer to the "Fluid Pan, Removal and Installation" procedures, in this section and remove the fluid pan.
2. Loosen the locknut on the piston stem.
3. Tighten the piston stem to 9–11 ft. lbs. (12–15 Nm).
4. Loosen the piston stem exactly two turns (1970–83) or three turns (1984 and later).
   CAUTION: *When loosening the piston stem, DO NOT back it OFF too far, for the anchor block may fall out of place.*
5. Hold the stem and tighten the locknut to 14 ft. lbs. (20 Nm). If the stem turns when the locknut is tightened, loosen the locknut and repeat the adjustment.
6. Replace the fluid pan and refill the transmission.

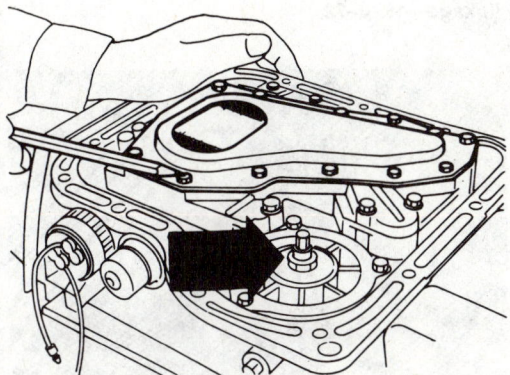

Brake band piston stem and locknut (arrow)

SECOND BRAKE BAND

The second brake band of the E4N71B transmission is located in the same position as the brake band of the 3N71B model.

1984 and Later

1. Refer to the "Fluid Pan, Removal and Installation" procedures, in this section and remove the fluid pan.
2. Loosen the locknut on the piston stem.
3. Tighten the piston stem to 9–11 ft. lbs. (12–15 Nm).
4. Loosen the piston stem exactly three turns.
   CAUTION: *When loosening the piston stem, DO NOT back it OFF too far, for the anchor block may fall out of place.*
5. Hold the stem and tighten the locknut to 14 ft. lbs. (20 Nm). If the stem turns when the locknut is tightened, loosen the locknut and repeat the adjustment.

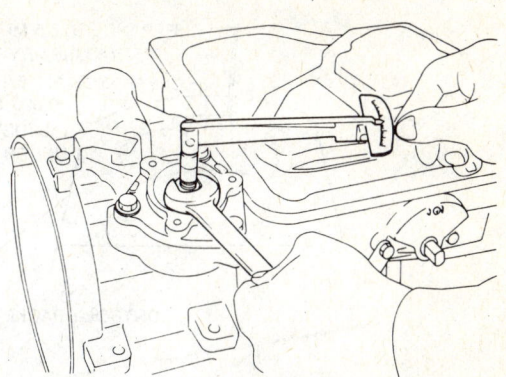

Adjusting the overdrive brake band—1984 and later

6. Replace the fluid pan and refill the transmission.

OVERDRIVE BRAKE BAND

The overdrive brake band is located at the underside of the overdrive unit, which is the section between the transmission case and the convertor housing.

1984 and Later

1. Raise and support the vehicle on jackstands.
2. At the overdrive section, remove the overdrive servo cover.
3. Loosen the overdrive piston stem locknut.
4. Tighten the overdrive piston stem to 5.1–7.2 ft. lbs. (7–10 Nm), then back it off exactly two turns.
5. Holding the piston stem in position, torque the locknut to 11–29 ft. lbs. (15–39 Nm).
6. Install the overdrive servo cover. Torque the cover-to-overdrive case to 7–11 ft. lbs. (10–15 Nm).

SHIFT LINKAGE

1970–72

1. Loosen the trunnion locknuts at the lower end of the control lever. Remove the selector lever knob and console.
2. Place the transmission selector in "N" and place the transmission shift lever in the Neutral position by pushing it all the way back, then moving it forward two stops.
3. Check the vertical clearance between the top of the shift lever pin and transmission control bracket ("A" in the illustration). It should be 0.020–0.059 in. (0.5–1.5 mm). Adjust the nut at the lower end of the selector lever compression rod, as necessary.
4. Check the horizontal clearance "B" between the shift lever pin and transmission control bracket. It should be 0.020 in. (0.5 mm).

196 DRIVE TRAIN

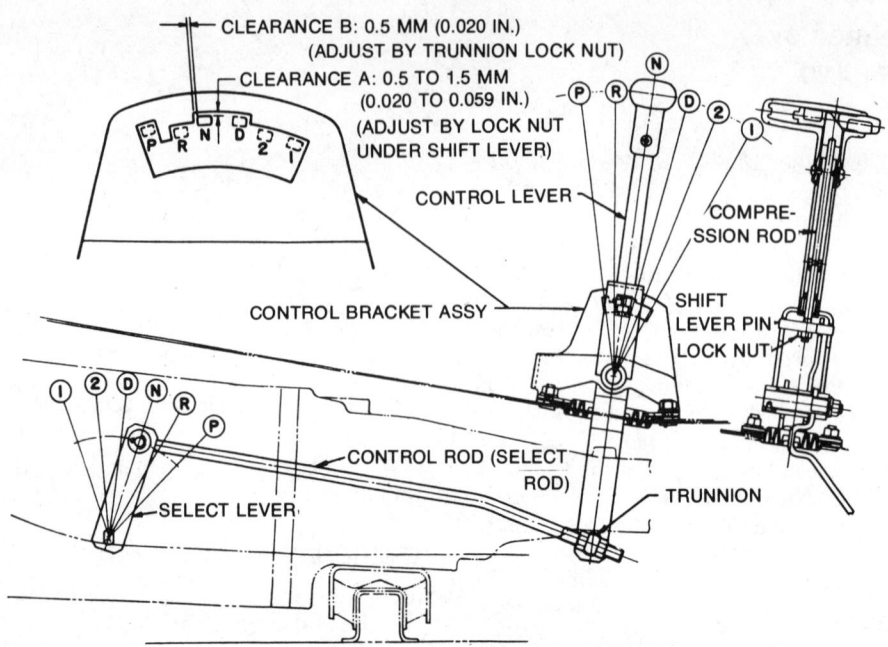

Transmission control linkage—1970–72

Adjust the trunnion locknuts as necessary to get this clearance.

5. Replace the console with the shift pointer correctly aligned. Install the shift knob.

1973–78

1. Loosen the adjusting nuts "B."
2. Set both the transmission control lever and the range selector lever in the "N" position.
3. Tighten the adjusting nuts so that they both just touch the trunnion "2."
4. Tighten the nuts. Test the shifter for proper operation.

1979–83

Adjustment is made at the locknuts at the base of the shifter, which control the length of the shift control rod.

1. Place the shift lever in "D."
2. Loosen the locknuts and move the shift lever until it is firmly in the "D" range, the pointer is aligned and the transmission is in "D" range.
3. Tighten the locknuts.
4. Check the adjustment. Start the vehicle and apply the parking brake. Shift through all the ranges, starting in "P." As the lever is moved from "P" to "1," you should be able to feel the detents in each range. If proper adjustment is not possible, the grommets are probably worn and should be replaced.

1984 and Later

If the detents cannot be felt or the pointer indicator is improperly aligned while shifting from

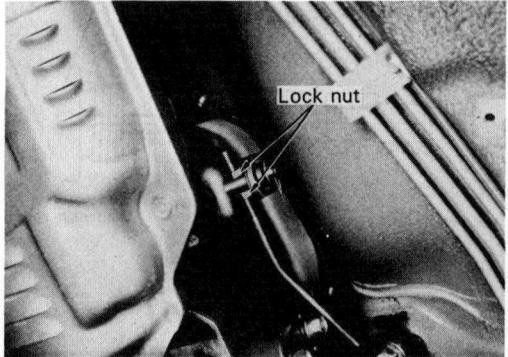

Loosen these locknuts for adjustment—1984 and later

the "P" range to range "1," the linkage should be adjusted.

1. Place the shifter in the "N" position.
2. Loosen the locknuts.
3. Move the range selector lever at the transmission to the "N" range.
4. Tighten the locknuts when the floor control lever is in the "N" range and pushed against the "P" range side.
5. Shift the control lever through the different ranges to make sure it shifts smoothly and without any sliding noises.

CHECKING KICK-DOWN SWITCH AND SOLENOID

1. Turn the key to the normal ON position and depress the accelerator all the way. The solenoid in the transmission should make an audible click.

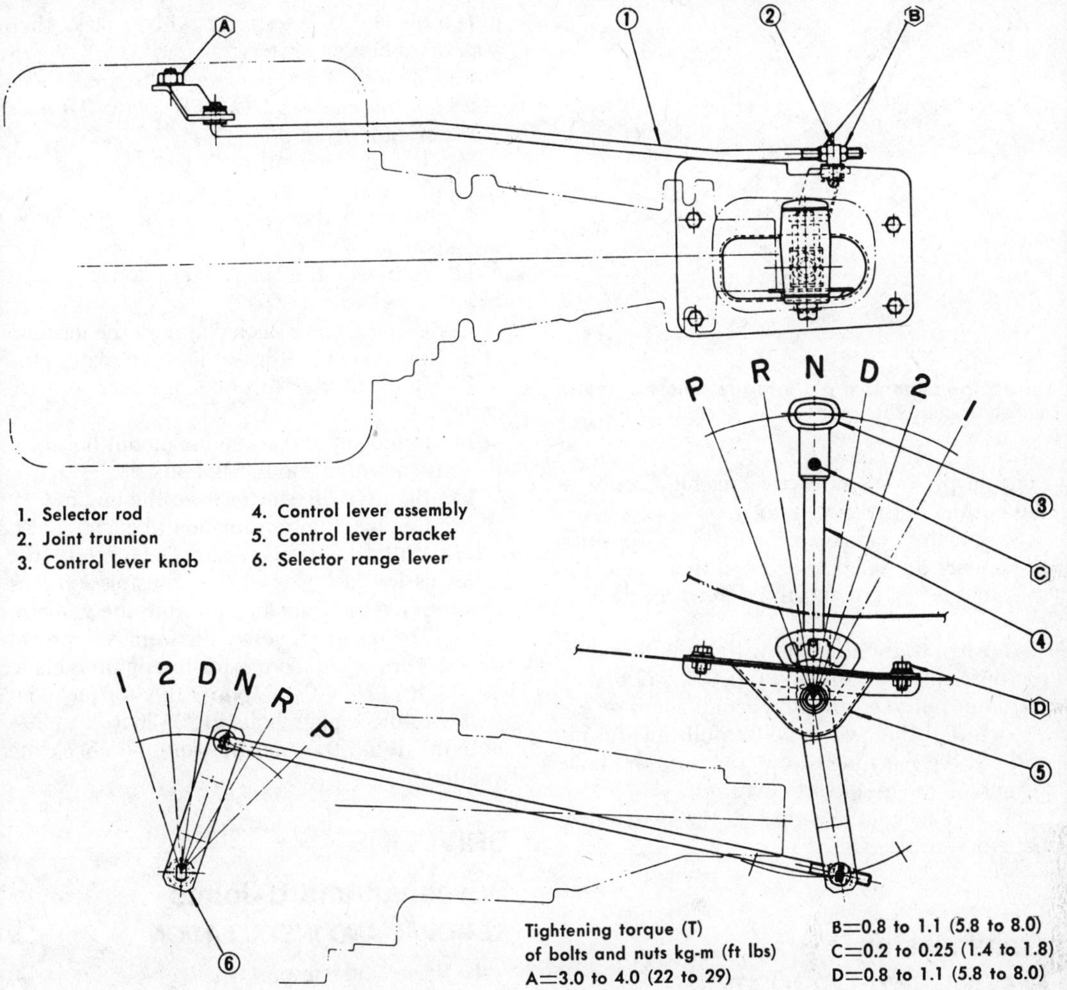

DRIVE TRAIN 197

1. Selector rod
2. Joint trunnion
3. Control lever knob
4. Control lever assembly
5. Control lever bracket
6. Selector range lever

Tightening torque (T) of bolts and nuts kg-m (ft lbs)
A=3.0 to 4.0 (22 to 29)
B=0.8 to 1.1 (5.8 to 8.0)
C=0.2 to 0.25 (1.4 to 1.8)
D=0.8 to 1.1 (5.8 to 8.0)

Transmission control linkage—1973–78

2. If the solenoid does not work, inspect the wiring and test it electrically to determine whether the problem is in the wiring, the kickdown switch or the solenoid.

3. If the solenoid requires replacement, drain a little over 2 pts (1 liter) of fluid from the transmission before removing it.

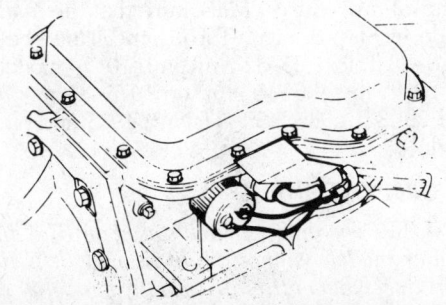

Location of the downshift solenoid

Neutral Safety Switch

REMOVAL AND INSTALLATION

1. Disconnect the neutral safety switch electrical connector.
2. Disconnect the shifting rod from the neutral safety switch.
3. Remove the safety switch-to-transmission screws and the switch.
4. To install, reverse the removal procedures. Adjust the neutral safety switch.

ADJUSTMENT

1. Apply the brakes and check to see that the starter works only in the "P" and "N" transmission ranges. If the starter works with the transmission in gear, adjust the switch as described below.
2. Remove the fastening nut of the range selector lever and the bolts which hold the switch

198 DRIVE TRAIN

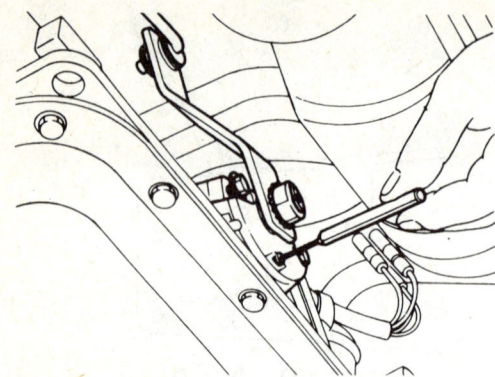

Insert the alignment pin into the hole for neutral safety switch alignment

body in place. Remove the machine screw at the bottom of the switch body.

3. Put the manual shaft in the "N" position by moving the selector lever so that the slot in the shaft is vertical and the detent mechanism clicks.

4. Align the screw hole with the internal rotor pin hole and insert a 0.079 in. (2.0 mm) diameter pin to ensure and retain alignment.

5. Install the switch bolts, pull out the pin and put the machine screw back into the hole. Install the range selector lever nut.

6. Test again as in Step 1. If the switch does not work, replace it.

Transmission

REMOVAL AND INSTALLATION

1. Disconnect the negative battery cable.
2. Raise and support the vehicle on jackstands.
3. Remove the drive shaft.
NOTE: *When the driveshaft is removed, plug the transmission opening to prevent oil from flowing from the opening.*
4. Disconnect the front exhaust tube, the selector range lever from the manual shaft and the inhibitor switch electrical connector.
5. Disconnect the vacuum tube from the vacuum diaphragm and the downshift solenoid electrical connector.
6. Disconnect the speedometer cable from the rear extension housing, the oil discharge pipe and the oil cooler tubes from the transmission.
NOTE: *When disconnecting the oil cooler lines from the transmission, be sure to plug the lines to prevent oil from draining from the lines.*
7. Disconnect the governor tube from the convertor housing and the transmission case.
8. Place a wooden block against the engine's oil pan and support with a jack, then support the engine.
CAUTION: *When placing the wooden block under the engine, DO NOT place it under the oil pan drain plug.*
9. Using a transmission jack, support the transmission.
10. Remove the engine-to-converter housing gussets.
11. Remove the converter housing dust cover.
12. Using a piece of chalk, mark the location of the torque converter to the drive plate.
13. Remove the torque converter-to-drive plate bolts.
14. Remove the rear engine mount bolts and the crossmember mounting bolts.
15. Remove the starter from the engine.
16. Remove the transmission-to-engine bolts.
17. With the transmission secured to the transmission jack, lower the transmission jack and remove the transmission from the vehicle.
18. To install, reverse the removal procedures. Torque the converter-to-engine bolts to 29–36 ft. lbs. (39–49 Nm), the torque converter-to-drive plate bolts to 29–36 ft. lbs. (39–49 Nm). Refill the transmission and check the shifting.

DRIVELINE

Driveshaft and U-Joints

REMOVAL AND INSTALLATION

1. Raise and support the vehicle on jackstands.
NOTE: *It may be necessary to move the exhaust pipe and insulator out of the way on some models.*
2. Scribe matchmarks on the rear of the driveshaft and the companion flange.
3. Remove the bolts and nuts from the companion flange.
4. Pull the rear of the driveshaft downward and pull the splined portion at the front out of the transmission. Plug the hole in the transmission extension housing.
5. To install, oil the splines and reverse the removal procedures. Make sure that the marks made in Step 3 align. Torque the flange bolts to 18–23 ft. lbs. (25–32 Nm) on 1970–74 models, 25–33 ft. lbs. (35–45 Nm) on 1975–84 models and 29–33 ft. lbs. (39–44 Nm) 1985 and later models.

U-JOINT OVERHAUL

NOTE: *The universal joints used on 1975 and later models cannot be disassembled. If defective, the entire driveshaft must be replaced as a unit.*

DRIVE TRAIN

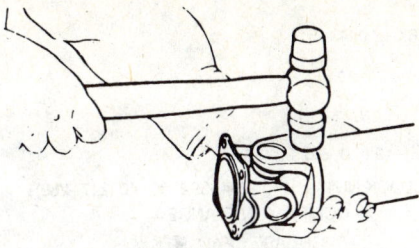

Removing the U-joint bearings

Snap-Rings

Thickness in. (mm)	Color
.0787 (2.0)	White
.0795 (2.02)	Yellow
.0803 (2.04)	Red
.0811 (2.06)	Green
.0819 (2.08)	Blue
.0827 (2.10)	Brown
.0835 (2.12)	Unpainted
.0843 (2.43)	Pink

1. Clean all the parts in a safe solvent.
2. Mark the driveshaft and joint so that they can be reassembled in exactly the same position.
3. Using a screwdriver, remove the snap-rings.
4. Using a soft hammer, lightly tap the base of the yoke and remove each bearing race.
5. Check the spider bearing journals for dents or brinell marks. Make sure that the yoke holes are not worn.
6. Check the snap-rings, bearings and seal rings, replace the parts (as necessary).
7. Check the shaft tube for dents or cracks, then replace (if necessary).
8. To assemble, reverse the disassembly procedures.

NOTE: *The needle rollers may be held in the races with grease. Reusable bearings should be carefully packed with grease.*

9. Install the snap-rings that are equal in thickness opposite each other. Choose the thickness so that play will not exceed 0.0008 in. (0.02 mm).
10. Check the frictional resistance of the joint, it should not exceed 9 in. lbs. (10 kg-cm) on the 240-Z models or 13 in. lbs. (15 kg-cm) on the 260-Z models.

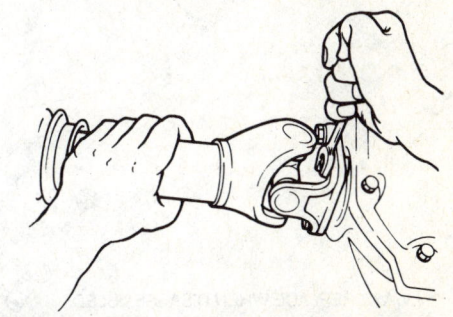

Removing the yoke flange bolts at the differential

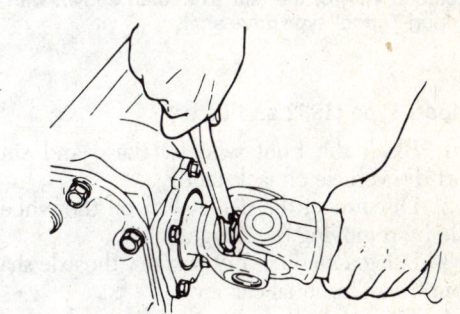

Removing the yoke flange center bolt at the differential

REAR AXLE

Identification

There are three types of rear axle shafts: Cardan (1974–83), Tripod (1982 and later) used on the turbo models and Double Offset-Birfield (1984 and later) used on the non-turbo models.

The Cardan type rear axle shaft employs two styles of differential mounts: Side Flange (M/T model) used with a R200 differential and Side Yoke (A/T model) used with a R180 differential.

During 1974–83, two types of differentials are used: R180 model used with an automatic transmission and R200 model used with a manual transmission. The 1984 and later models use an R200 differential only.

Axle Drive Shaft

REMOVAL AND INSTALLATION

Cardan Type (1974–83)

1. Block the front wheels. Raise and support the rear of the vehicle on jackstands.
2. Remove the U-joint yoke flange bolts at the wheel-side.
3. At the differential, remove the axle shaft side flange nuts (R200) or the center bolt (R180).
4. Remove the axle shaft.
5. To install, reverse the removal procedures. Torque the wheel-side flange bolts to 36–43 ft. lbs. (50–60 Nm), the differential-to-side flange nuts to 36–43 ft. lbs. (50–60 Nm) and the side yoke-to-differential bolt to 17–23 ft. lbs. (24–32 Nm) for 1974–77 models or 23–31 ft. lbs. (32–43 Nm) 1978–83 models.

200 DRIVE TRAIN

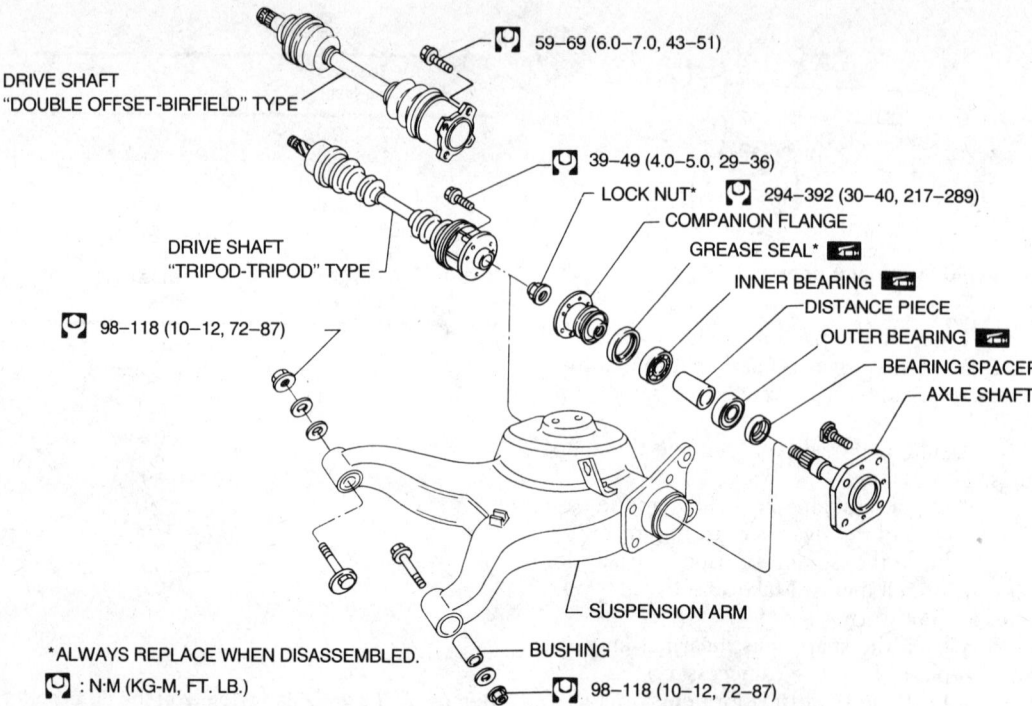

Exploded view of the rear axle shaft shown with either the "Double Offset Birfield" type drive shaft or the "Tripod-Tripod" type drive shaft

Tripod Type (1982 and Later)

1. Block the front wheels. Raise and support the vehicle on jackstands.
2. Disconnect the drive shaft on the wheel-side by removing the flange bolts.
3. Using a medium pry bar, pry the axle shaft from the differential carrier.
4. To install, reverse the removal procedures. Torque the companion flange bolts to 20–27 ft. lbs. (1982–83) or 29–36 ft. lbs. (1984 and later).

CAUTION: *When installing the axle shaft, be careful not to damage the oil seal at either end of the axle shaft.*

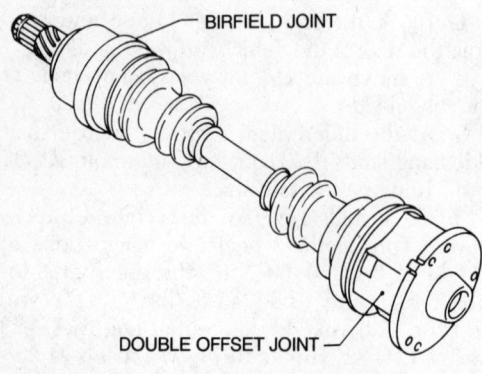

"Double Offset Birfield" type drive shaft

Double Offset-Birfield Type (1984 and Later)

1. Block the front wheels. Raise and support the vehicle on jackstands.
2. Disconnect the drive shaft on the wheel-side by removing the flange nuts/bolts.
3. Using a medium pry bar, pry the axle shaft from the differential carrier.
4. To install, reverse the removal procedures. Torque the companion flange nuts/bolts to 43–51 ft. lbs. (59–69 Nm).

CAUTION: *When installing the axle shaft, be careful not to damage the oil seal at either end of the axle shaft.*

INSPECTION

Cardan Type (1974–83)

1. Check the parts for wear or damage, replace the shaft as an assembly, if defects are found.
2. Extend and compress the axle shaft (full stroke). Check the action for smoothness.
3. Using a dial indicator, fully compress the shaft and check the play of the axle shaft. If the play exceeds 0.004 in. (0.1 mm) for 1970–78 models or 0.008 (0.2 mm) for 1979–83 models, the shaft must be replaced.

NOTE: *The sleeve yoke, balls, spacers and outer shaft are not available as service parts.*

4. Check the U-joints for smoothness. If the

DRIVE TRAIN 201

Measuring the play in the axle shaft

movement is notchy or loose, overhaul the U-joints.

5. Check the U-joint axial play, if it exceeds 0.0008 in. (0.02 mm), overhaul the U-joints.

Tripod Type (1982 and Later)

1. Thoroughly clean the parts in a cleaning solvent and dry with compressed air.
2. Check the parts for cracks, scratches or other damage. If necessary, replace the shaft as an assembly.
3. Always use new boots, boot bands and O-rings once they have been removed.

Double Offset-Birfield Type (1984 and Later)

1. Check the drive shaft for twists or cracks; if necessary, replace it.
2. Check the joint (wheel-side) assembly for burns, wear or excessive play; if necessary, replace it.
3. Check the slide joint (wheel-side) housing for cracks, wear or deformation; (if necessary) replace it.
4. Check the joint (differential-side) assembly for deformation or damage; if necessary (replace it).
5. Check the boot for fatigue, cracks or wear; (if necessary) replace it.

OVERHAUL

Cardan Type (1974–83)

1. Matchmark the parts of the U-joint journals and the sliding yoke (outer shaft-to-sleeve yoke).

NOTE: *The axle shaft is balanced as a unit and must be rebuilt as originally assembled.*

2. Remove the snap rings from the U-joints and disassemble them as outlined in the "U-joint Overhaul" procedure in this chapter.

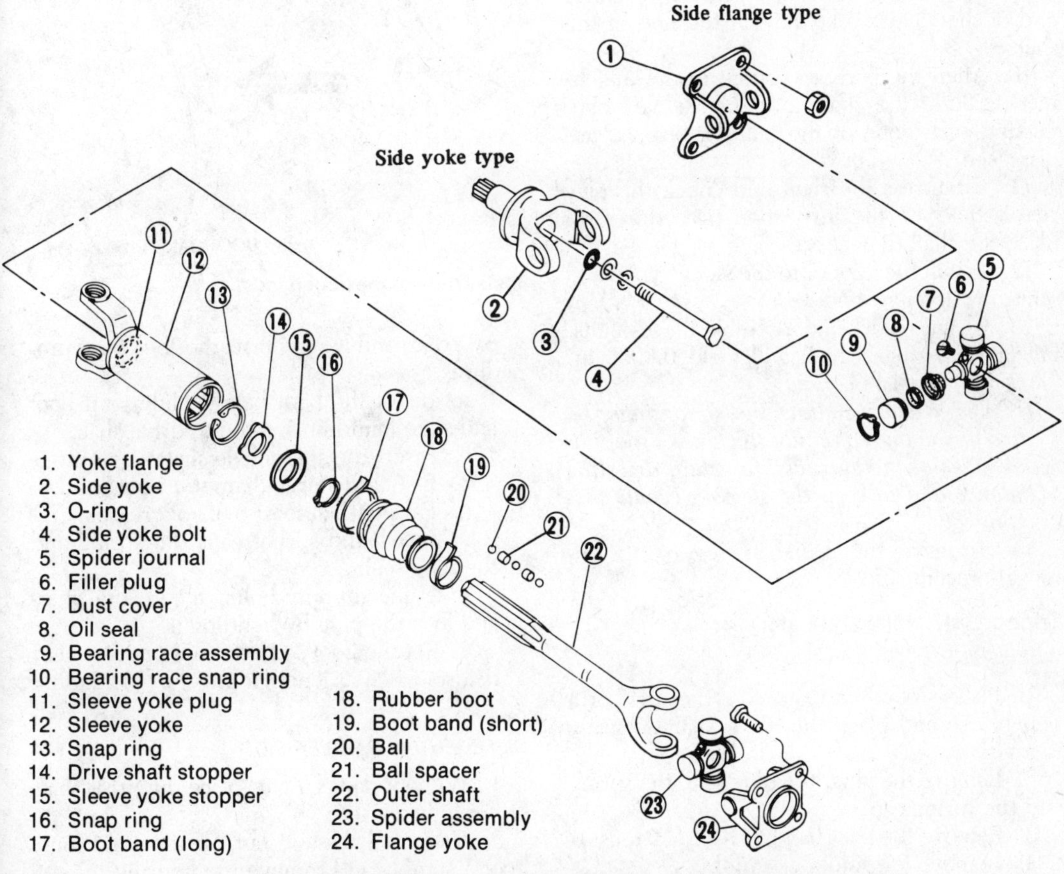

1. Yoke flange
2. Side yoke
3. O-ring
4. Side yoke bolt
5. Spider journal
6. Filler plug
7. Dust cover
8. Oil seal
9. Bearing race assembly
10. Bearing race snap ring
11. Sleeve yoke plug
12. Sleeve yoke
13. Snap ring
14. Drive shaft stopper
15. Sleeve yoke stopper
16. Snap ring
17. Boot band (long)
18. Rubber boot
19. Boot band (short)
20. Ball
21. Ball spacer
22. Outer shaft
23. Spider assembly
24. Flange yoke

Exploded view of the axle driveshaft–Cardan universal type, 1974–83

202 DRIVE TRAIN

3. Cut the boot band and remove the boot from the sleeve yoke.

4. Remove the snap rings from the sleeve yoke at the boot end.

5. Remove the outer shaft carefully; DO NOT lose the balls or spacers.

NOTE: *It is not necessary to remove the snap rings or the sleeve yoke plug at the differential end of the sleeve yoke, because the parts are not available for service. If any damage is present, the entire axle shaft MUST BE replaced.*

6. Clean the spacers, balls, sleeve yoke and outer shaft grooves in solvent. Check the parts for wear, brinelling, distortion, cracks, straightness or etc. If there is any question as to the integrity of the part, replace the axle shaft.

7. Check the snap ring, grease seal and dust seal for wear or damage. These parts are available for service and should be replaced as necessary.

8. Apply a fairly generous amount of grease to the yoke and shaft grooves. Install the balls and spacers onto the shaft. The grease will retain them. Be sure they are in the correct sequence.

9. Before assembling the shaft to the sleeve yoke, apply a large glob of grease to the inner end of the sleeve yoke and on the end of the shaft.

10. Align the parts according to the matchmarks. Slide the shaft into the sleeve yoke, making sure none of the balls or spacers are displaced.

11. Compress the shaft and check the play again. Refer to the inspection procedure; replace the shaft (if necessary).

12. Install the boot onto the sleeve yoke and secure with a new boot band.

13. Clean, repack and assemble the U-joints. Select snap rings which will yield 0.0008 in. (0.02 mm) of axial play.

NOTE: *When installing the snap rings, be sure to use ones of equal thickness on opposite sides of the journals, to retain driveline balance and to keep the stresses evenly distributed.*

14. To install the axle shaft, reverse the removal procedures.

Tripod Type (1982 and Later)
WHEEL-SIDE

1. Place something soft over the jaws of a bench vise and place the drive shaft securely in a vise.

2. Remove the plug, the plug seal, the spring and the spring cap.

3. Remove the boot bands (DO NOT reuse).

4. Remove the spider assembly.

5. Remove the slide joint boot.

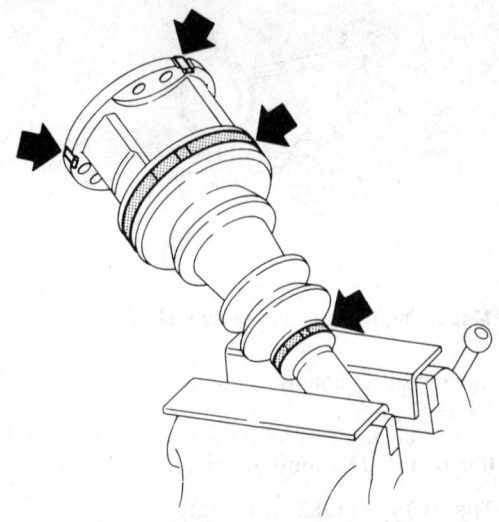

With the drive shaft in a vise remove the plug and boot bands

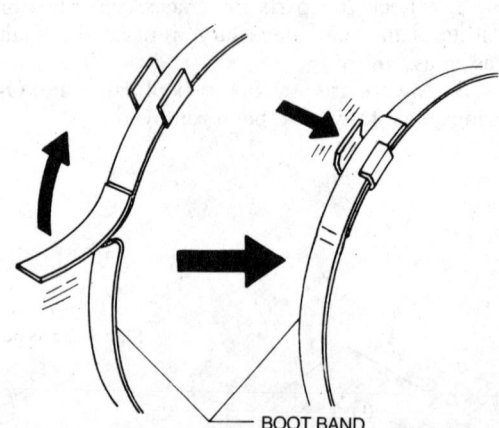

Installation of the boot bands

6. To assemble, perform the following procedures:

   a. Insert the boot bands, slide joint boot and slide joint housing to the drive shaft.
   b. Insert the spider/axle shaft assembly.
   c. Install the large diameter boot band.
   d. Pack with at least 6 oz. of grease.
   e. Install the spring cap, the spring and the plug seal.
   f. Using dummy bolts, secure the plugs and lock the plug by bending it.
   g. Set the boot so that it does not swell or deform when its length is 4.07 in. (103.5 mm).

DIFFERENTIAL CARRIER-SIDE

1. Without damaging it, place the drive shaft securely in a vise.

2. Using a hacksaw, cut off the hold joint boot assembly and remove the housing sub-assembly.

DRIVE TRAIN 203

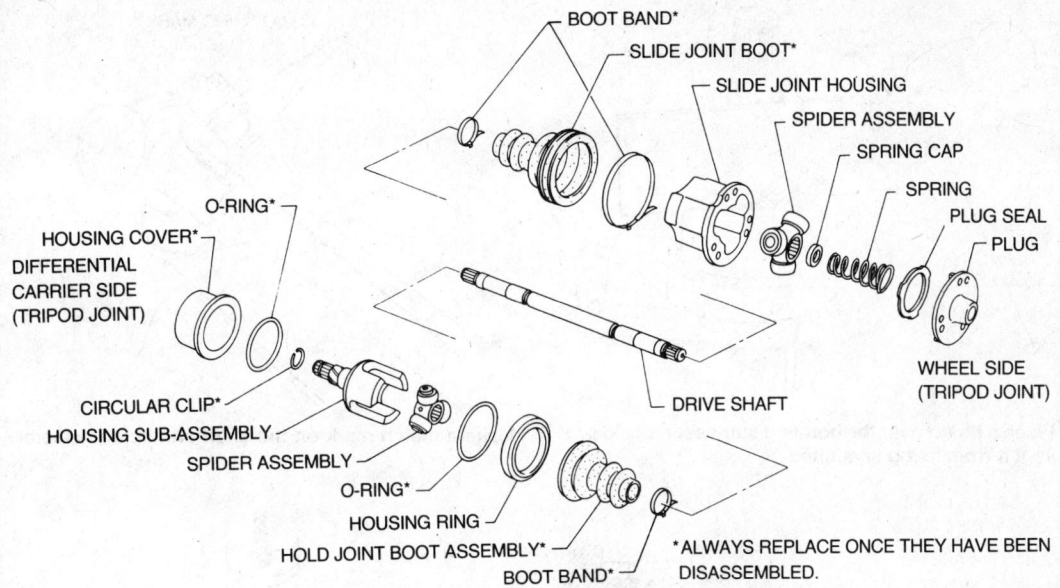

Exploded view of the "Tripod-Tripod" type drive shaft

NOTE: *To prevent the spider assembly from being scratched, make sure that the drive shaft is pushed into the housing sub-assembly while cutting off the hold joint boot assembly.*

3. Remove the boot band.

NOTE: *DO NOT reuse the boot band once it has been removed.*

4. Remove the spider assembly.

5. Using a hacksaw, cut off the remaining portion of the hold joint boot assembly and remove it from the housing sub-assembly.

NOTE: *Be careful not to scratch the housing ring or sub-assembly. The housing ring is selected to suit the outside diameter of the housing sub-assembly. DO NOT change the original combination when replacing parts.*

6. Remove the housing cover (DO NOT reuse once it has been removed).

7. Remove the O-ring (DO NOT reuse once it has been removed).

8. Remove the housing ring and pull out the hold joint boot.

9. To assemble the differential carrier-side, perform the following:

    a. Attach the housing ring, the O-ring, the housing sub-assembly and the housing cover to a new hold joint boot assembly, then place the assembled unit flange in a vise. Apply a coat of grease to the O-ring.

NOTE: *DO NOT place any other part of the assembled unit in a vise.*

    b. Bend the edge over along the entire circumference.

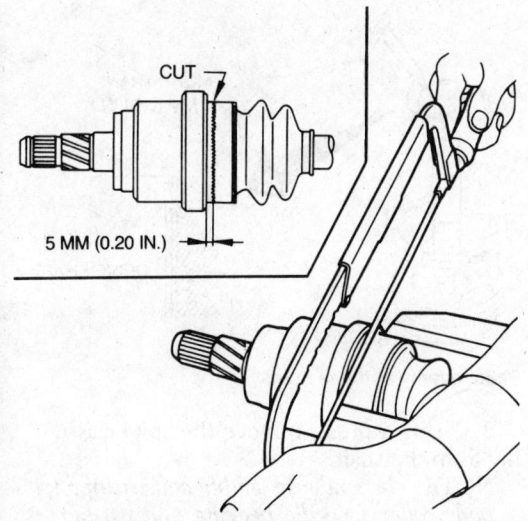

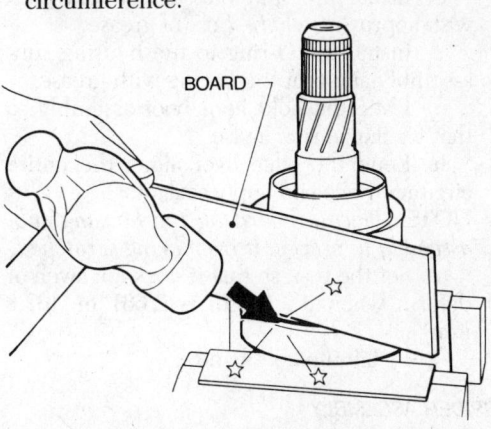

Place a board over the housing cover to prevent it from being scratched

204 DRIVE TRAIN

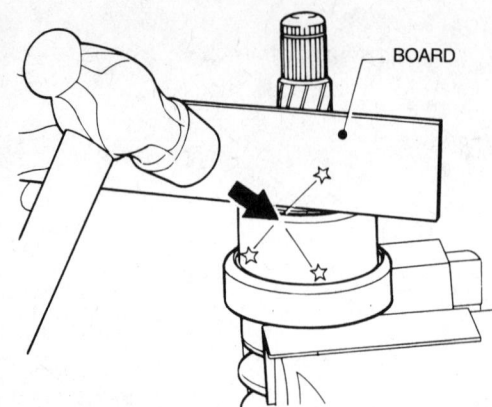

Place a board over the housing sub-assembly to prevent it from being scratched

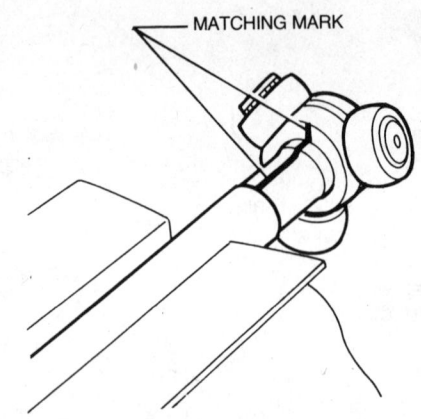

Make a match mark on the shaft and spider assembly

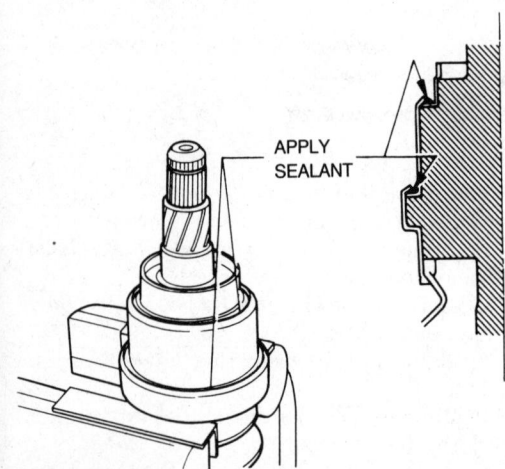

Apply sealant to these areas

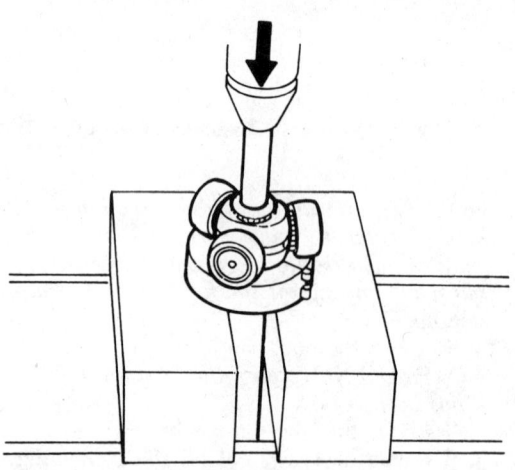

Removing the spider assembly using a press

NOTE: *Place a board on the housing cover to prevent it from being scratched.*

   c. Withdraw the housing sub-assembly.
   d. Install a new boot band and hold the joint boot assembly onto the drive shaft.
   e. Install the spider assembly and pack with approximately 6–7 oz. of grease.
   f. Install the O-ring to the housing sub-assembly and coat the O-ring with grease.
   g. Place the hold joint boot assembly so that it's flange is in a vise.
   h. Bend the edge over along the entire circumference and apply sealant.

NOTE: *Place a board on the housing sub-assembly to prevent it from being scratched.*

   i. Set the boot so that it does not swell or deform when it's length is 2.661 in. (67.6 mm).
   j. Install the boot band.

SPIDER ASSEMBLY

1. Match mark the shaft and the spider assembly.

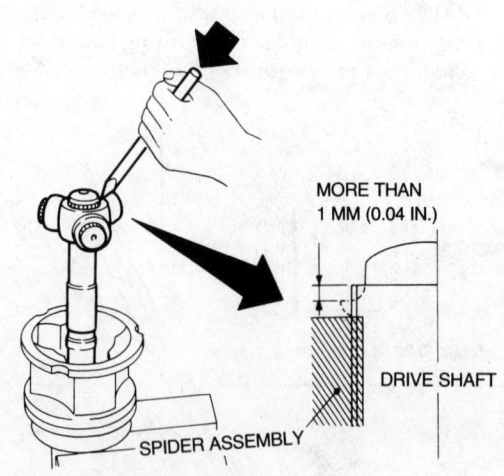

Stake evenly at these areas

2. Using a press, remove the spider assembly from the shaft.
NOTE: *The spider assembly consists of a tripod, rollers, needle bearing and washer; it is the non-disassembling type.*

DRIVE TRAIN 205

3. To assemble, perform the following procedures:

    a. Insert the spider assembly by placing the drive shaft in a vise and install the spider so that the marks are aligned.

NOTE: *If there is no mark, position both spider assemblies (one on the wheel-side and the other on the differential carrier-side) so that their phases are nearly 180°. Press-fit with the spider assembly serration chamfer facing shaft.*

    b. Stake the serration portion evenly at three places.

NOTE: *Always stake two or three teeth at a place where staked gap is more than 0.04 in (1.0 mm).*

Double Offset-Birfield Type (1984 and Later)

Axle shafts using the Double Offset and the Birfield Joints are of a nondisassembling design. If the joints are found to be defective, they must be replaced as an assembly.

DIFFERENTIAL CARRIER-SIDE

1. Place the axle shaft (center) in a soft jawed vise.
2. Remove the large boot band and push back on the boot.
3. Matchmark the axle shaft-to-joint assembly.

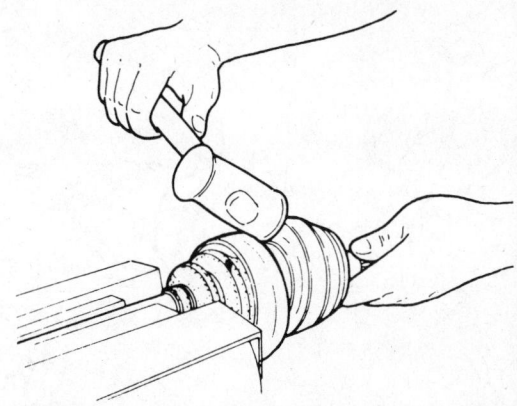

Removing the Birfield joint from the axle shaft—1984 and later

4. Using a soft hammer, tap the joint assembly away from the axle shaft.

NOTE: *The joint assembly is held onto the axle shaft by circlip.*

5. Using solvent, clean the parts of the joint, then using compressed air, blow the parts dry.
6. Install a new circlip "B" and boot onto the axle shaft.

NOTE: *If installing a new boot, be careful not to damage it, when sliding it onto the axle shaft.*

7. Pack the boot with about 5 oz. of grease.

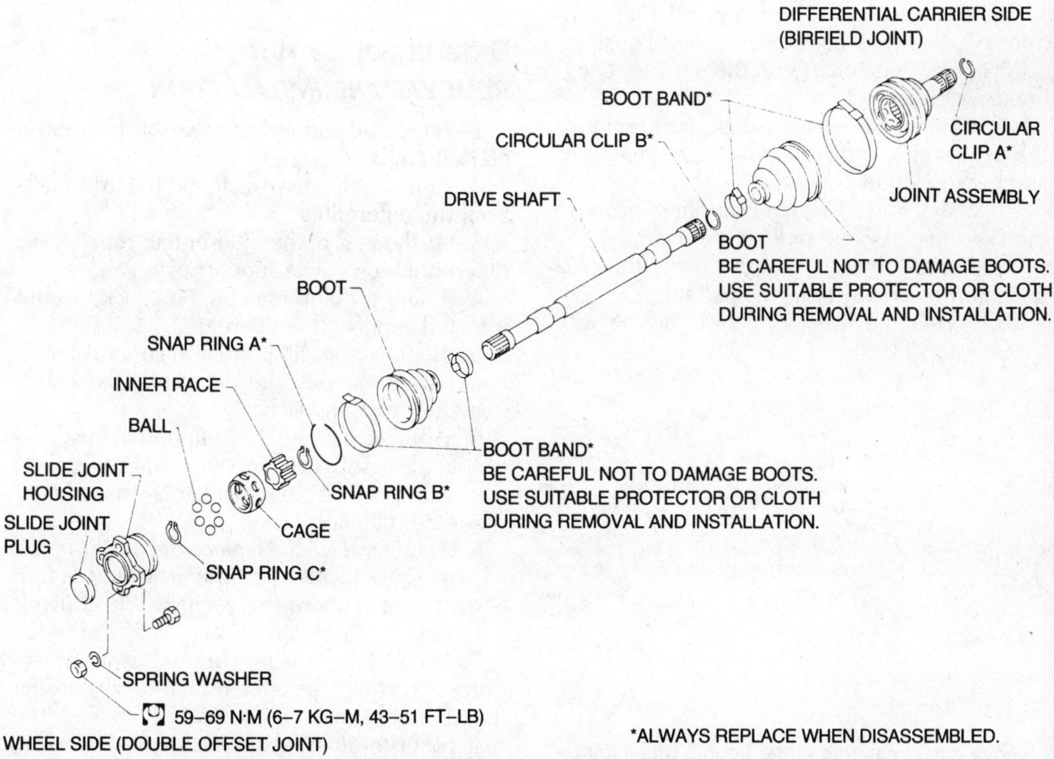

Exploded view of the Double Offset-Birfield type axle shaft—1984 and later

206 DRIVE TRAIN

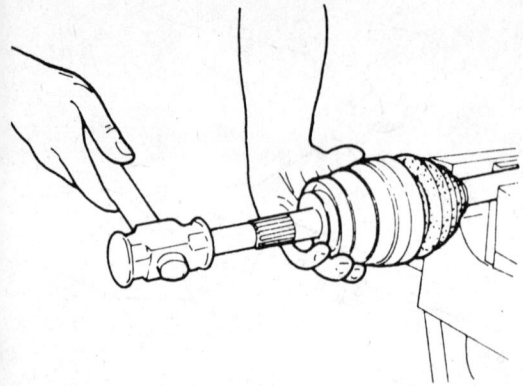

Installing the Birfield joint onto the axle shaft—1984 and later

8. Set the joint assembly onto the axle shaft and align the matchmarks, then tap it onto the circlip using a soft hammer.
9. Using a new boot lock band, secure the boot into place.
10. Set the boot so that it does not swell or deform when it's length is 3.58 in. (91 mm).

WHEEL-SIDE

1. Place the axle shaft (center) in a soft jawed vise.
2. Remove the boot bands and push back on the boot.
3. Place matchmarks on the slide joint housing and the inner race.
4. Using a screwdriver, pry off the snap-ring "A", then pull out the slide joint housing.
5. Place matchmarks on the inner race and the driveshaft.
6. Using a pair of snap-ring pliers, remove the snap-ring "C", then the ball cage, inner race and balls as a unit.
7. Using a pair of snap-ring pliers, remove the snap-ring "B" and pull off the boot.
8. Using solvent, clean the parts, then using compressed air, blow the parts dry.
9. Install the new boot and pack it with about 5 oz. of grease.

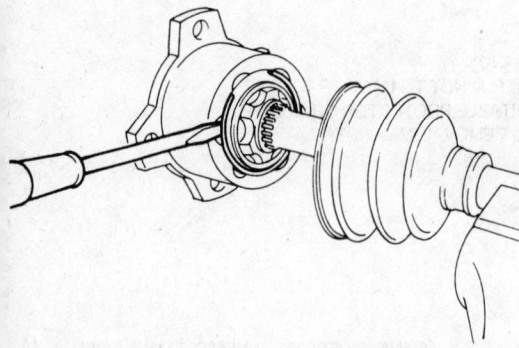

Removing the snap-ring of the Double Offset joint—1984 and later

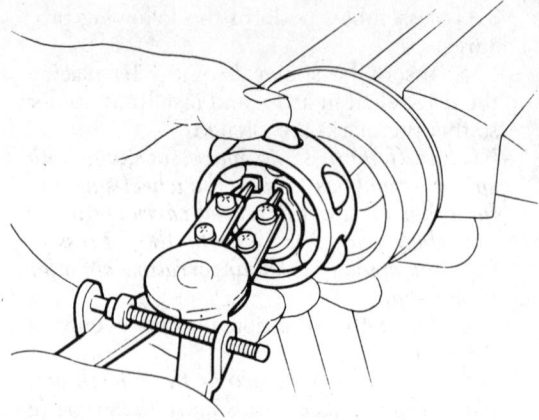

Removing the snap-ring "C" of the Double Offset joint—1984 and later

NOTE: *If installing a new boot, be careful not to damage it, when sliding it onto the axle shaft.*

10. To install, reverse the removal procedures.

NOTE: *When assembling, be sure to align the matchmarks.*

11. Using new boot lock bands, secure the boot into place.
12. Set the boot so that it does not swell or deform when it's length is 3.70 in. (94 mm).

Differential Carrier

REMOVAL AND INSTALLATION

1. Raise and support the rear of the vehicle on jackstands.
2. Remove the driveshaft and the axle shafts from the differential.
3. At the rear of the differential, remove the differential-to-vehicle support plate.
4. Using a differential support jack, secure it to and support the differential.
5. Remove the differential-to-support member bolts, then pull the differential backward (together) with the jack.
6. After removing the differential, use the jackstand to support the suspension member; this will prevent the insulators from being twisted or damaged.

CAUTION: *DO NOT place the center of the suspension member on the jackstand before the removal operation, for it will be difficult to remove the differential.*

7. To install, reverse the removal procedures. Torque the differential-to-suspension member bolts to 43–58 ft. lbs. (59–78 Nm), the rear cover-to-differential nuts to 43–58 ft. lbs. (59–78 Nm). Check the gear oil level.

DRIVE TRAIN

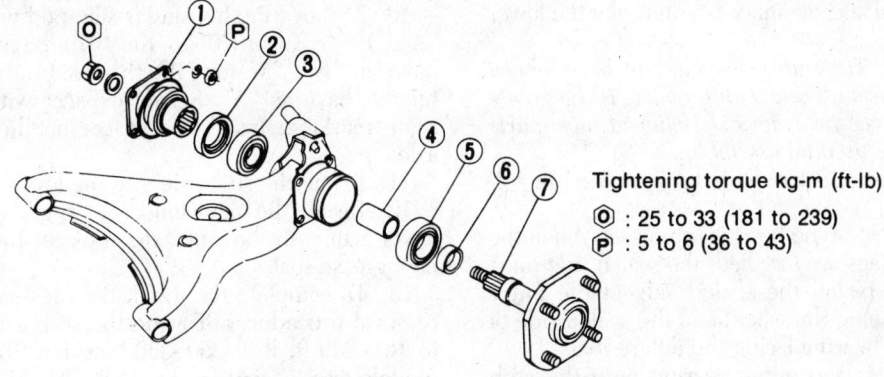

Tightening torque kg-m (ft-lb)
- Ⓞ : 25 to 33 (181 to 239)
- Ⓟ : 5 to 6 (36 to 43)

1. Companion flange
2. Grease seal
3. Inner wheel bearing
4. Spacer
5. Outer wheel bearing
6. Bearing spacer
7. Stub axle

Stub axle and rear wheel bearings, 1979–83 shown, other models similar

Stub Axle and Rear Wheel Bearings

REMOVAL AND INSTALLATION

All Models

1. Refer to the "Rear Disc or Drum Brake, Removal and Installation" procedures, in Chapter 8 and remove the disc or drum brakes.
2. Disconnect the axle shaft(s) from the stub shaft(s).
3. Using the Rear Axle Stand tool No. KV40101000 and a bar, remove the stub axle nut.
   NOTE: *Hold the stub axle at the outside while removing the nut from the stub shaft side. The nut will require a good deal of force to remove, be sure to hold the stub axle firmly.*
4. Using the Rear Axle Stand tool No.

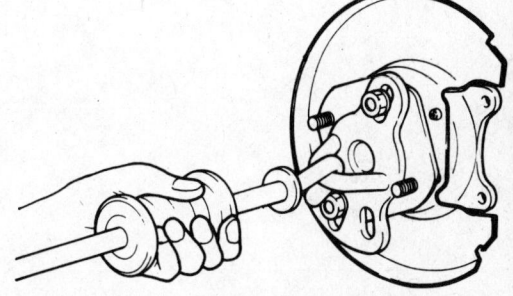

Remove the stub axle with a slide hammer

KV40101000 and a Slide Hammer Adapter tool No. ST36230000, remove the stub axle.
   NOTE: *The outer wheel bearing will come off with the stub axle.*

5. Remove the companion flange from the lower arm.
6. Using the Rear Axle Shaft Bearing Drift tool No. ST37750000, remove and discard the

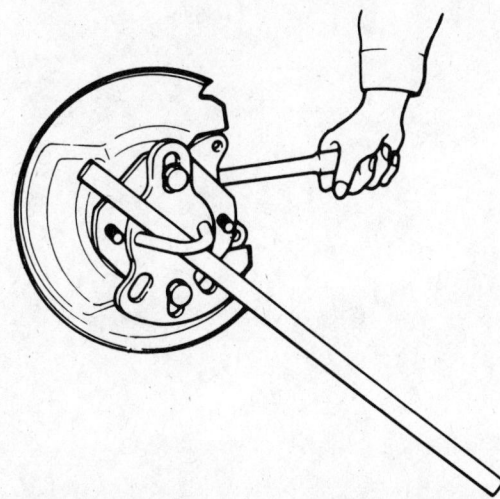

Hold the stub axle while removing the nut from the axle shaft side

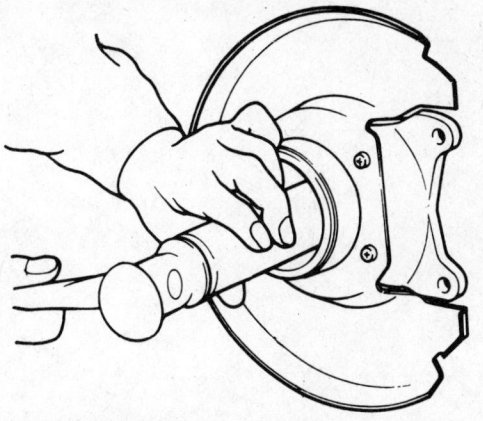

Remove the grease seal and inner bearing with a drift or driver

grease seal and the inner bearing from the lower arm.

NOTE: *The outer bearing can be removed from the stub axle with a puller. If the grease seal or the bearings are removed, new parts must be used on assembly.*

7. Clean all the parts to be reused in solvent.

8. Sealed-type bearings are used. When the new bearings are installed, the sealed side must face out. Install the sealed side of the outer bearing facing the wheel and the sealed side of the inner bearing facing the differential.

9. Press the outer bearing onto the stub axle.

10. The bearing housing is stamped with an "A", "B" or "C", 1970–78; the 1979–83 models have an "N", "M" or "P"; the 1984 and later models have an "A". Select a spacer with the same marking. Install the spacer on the stub axle.

11. Install the stub axle into the lower arm.

12. Install the new inner bearing into the lower arm with the stub axle in place. Install a new grease seal.

13. To complete the installation, reverse the removal procedures. Torque the stub axle nut to 181–239 ft. lbs. (250–330 Nm) for 1970–83 models or 217–289 ft. lbs. (294–392 Nm) for 1984 and later models.

Suspension and Steering

7

FRONT SUSPENSION

The front suspension system is of the Mac-Pherson strut type. The struts used (on either side) are a combination spring and shock absorber with the outer casing of the shock actually supporting the spring at the bottom and forming a major structural component of the suspension. The wheel spindle is welded to the bottom of the strut. A strut mounting thrust bearing at the top and a ball joint at the bottom allow the entire strut to rotate in cornering maneuvers.

A rubber-bushed transverse link (lower arm) connects the lower portion of the strut to the main front crossmember via the ball joint; the link thus allows for vertical movement. Compression rods, 1970–78, connect the outer ends of the transverse links to the chassis at points in back of the outer ends, thus preventing excessive fore-and-aft movement. From 1979 and later, the compression rods were replaced by tension rods, which mount to brackets at the front of the vehicle and run back to the transverse links, controlling the fore-and-aft movement.

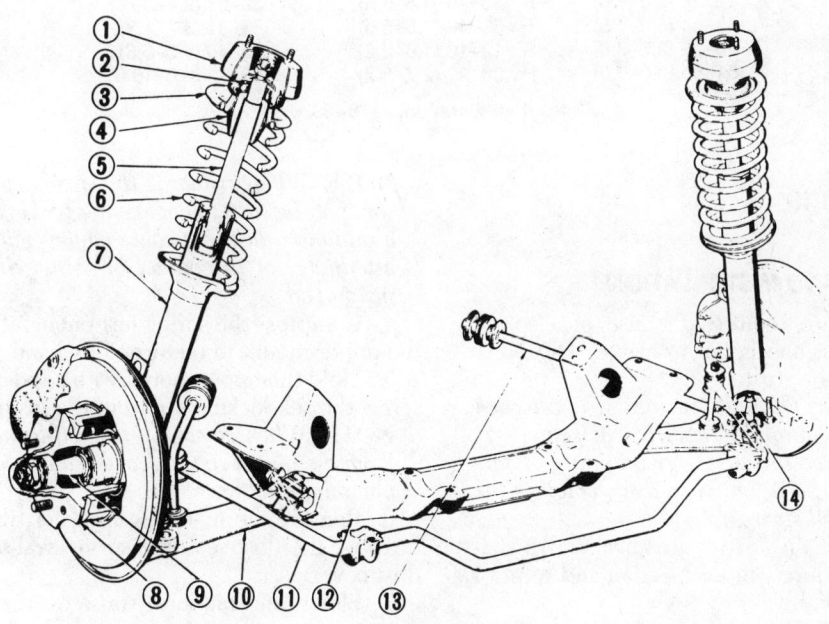

1. Strut mounting insulator
2. Strut mounting bearing
3. Upper spring seat
4. Bumper rubber
5. Piston rod
6. Front spring
7. Strut assembly
8. Hub assembly
9. Spindle
10. Transverse link
11. Stabilizer
12. Suspension member
13. Compression rod
14. Ball joint

Z model front suspension, 1970–78

210 SUSPENSION AND STEERING

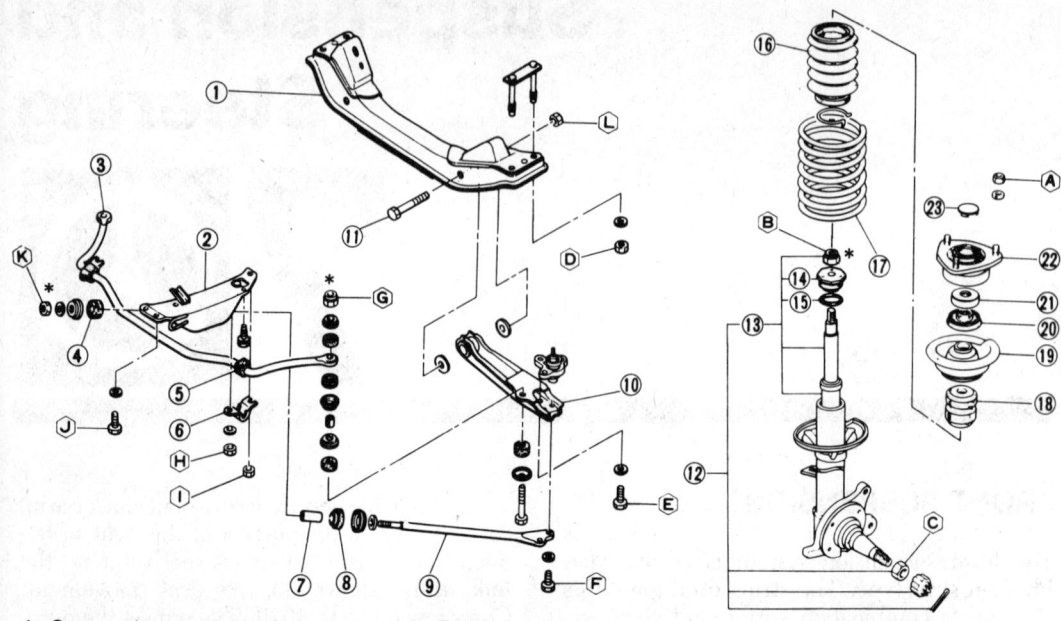

1. Suspension crossmember
2. Tension rod bracket
3. Stabilizer bar
4. Tension rod mounting bushing
5. Stabilizer bushing
6. Stabilizer bracket
7. Tension rod collar
8. Tension rod mounting bushing
9. Tension rod
10. Transverse link
11. Transverse link mounting bolt
12. Strut assembly
13. Shock absorber
14. Gland packing
15. O-ring
16. Dust cover
17. Front spring
18. Bound bumper
19. Front spring upper seat
20. Dust seal
21. Strut mounting bearing
22. Strut mounting insulator
23. Cap

*: Replace self-locking nut whenever strut is disassembled.

Tightening torque in ft. lbs. (kg-m)
A. 22–29 (3.0–4.0)
B. 43–54 (6.0–7.5)
C. 18–22 (2.5–3.0)
D. 51–65 (7.0–9.0)
E. 33–40 (4.5–5.5)
F. 33–40 (4.5–5.5)
G. 12–16 (1.6–2.2)
H. 20–27 (2.7–3.7)
I. 20–27 (2.7–3.7)
J. 23–31 (3.2–4.3)
K. 33–40 (4.5–5.5)
L. 58–72 (8.0–10.0)

ZX front suspension, 1979–83

Coil Springs

REMOVAL AND INSTALLATION

This procedure requires the use of a spring compressor; if one is not available, DO NOT disassemble the strut.

CAUTION: *The coil springs are retained under considerable pressure. They can exert enough force to cause serious injury. Exercise extreme caution when disassembling the strut for coil spring removal.*

1. Refer to the "Strut, Removal and Installation" procedures, in this section and remove the strut assembly.
2. Bolt the bottom of the strut to the Strut and Steering Gear Housing Attachment tool No. KV48100300 (1970–83) or No. ST35652000 (1984 and later) and secure the tool in a vise.
3. Install a Spring Compressor tool No. ST3565S001 (1970–83) or small compressor (1984 and later) onto the coil spring.

NOTE: *When installing the spring compressor tool, be sure to engage the tool evenly on a minimum of three coils, paying particular attention not to contact or stress the strut piston rod.*

4. Compress the spring just enough to allow the upper mount to be turned by hand.
5. Hold the upper mount with a rod and unscrew the self-locking nut from the piston rod.

NOTE: *When removing the self-locking nut from the piston rod, discard it and use a new one on assembly.*

6. Remove the mounting insulator, the strut bearing, the dust seal, the spring seat and the dust cover.
7. Slowly and cautiously unscrew the spring compressor until all of the spring tension is relieved. Remove the spring and the rubber bumper.

CAUTION: *DO NOT disassemble the shock absorber.*

8. To assemble, perform the following procedures:

SUSPENSION AND STEERING

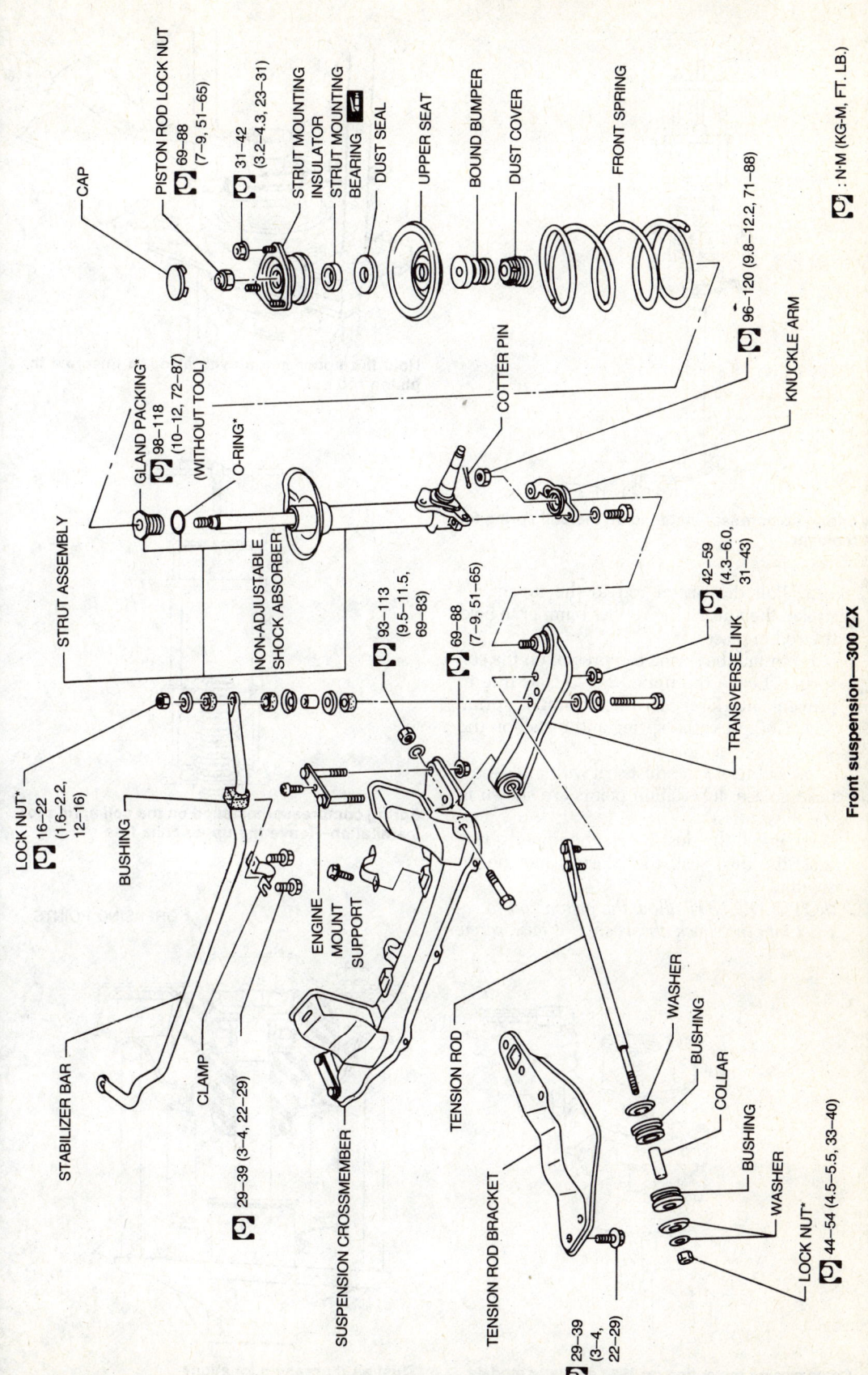

Front suspension—300 ZX

SUSPENSION AND STEERING

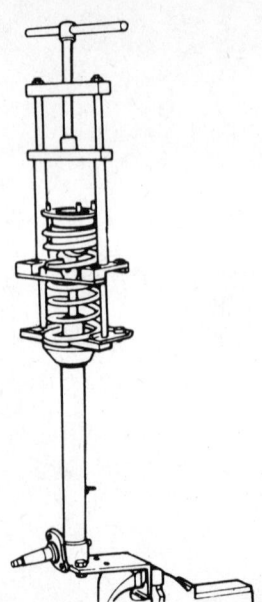

Spring compressor installed on the coil spring for removal

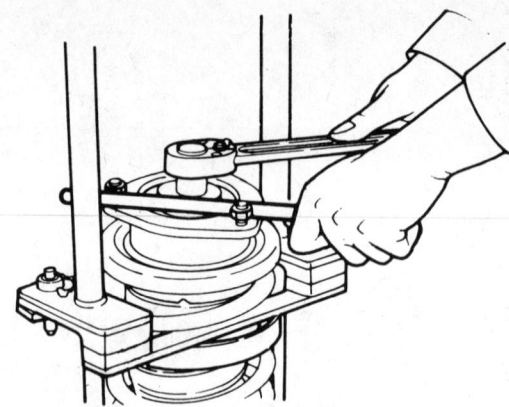

Hold the upper mount with a rod to unscrew the piston rod nut

a. Pull the piston rod to the top of it's stroke, then install the rubber bumper to hold the rod in place.

b. Install the spring compressor on the coil spring. Leave the upper 2½–3 coils free to prevent interference with the upper spring seat. Compress the spring and install on the strut.

c. Lubricate the dust seal with multi-purpose grease; lubrication points are shown in the illustration.

d. Install the dust cover, the upper spring seat, the dust seal, the bearing and the insulator.

NOTE: *DO NOT* allow the piston rod to retract into the shock absorber. If it falls, screw

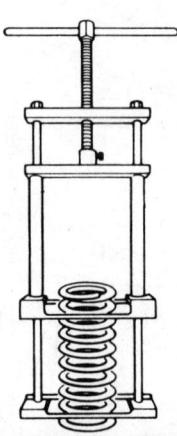

Spring compressor installed on the coil spring for installation—leave the upper coils free

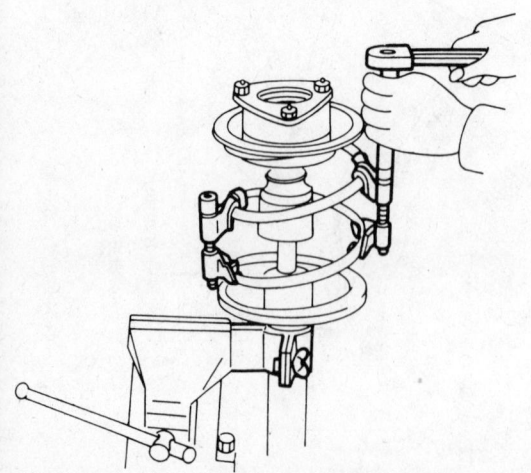

Compressing the spring on 1984 and later models

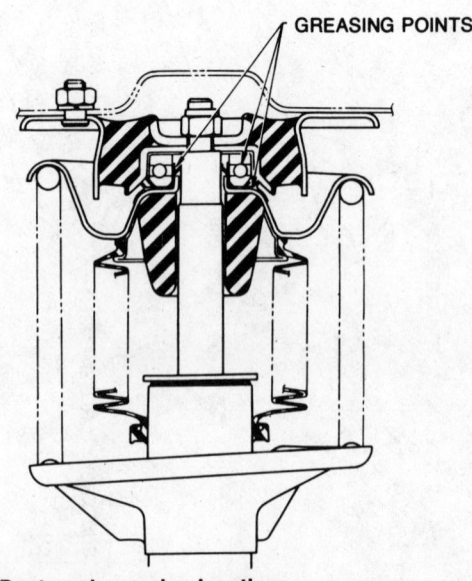

Dust seal greasing locations

SUSPENSION AND STEERING

a nut onto the rod and pull the rod out. DO NOT use pliers or the like to grip the rod, because they will damage it's surface, resulting in leaks, uneven operation and seal damage. Be extremely careful in all operations not to stress or contact the rod.

　e. Install a new self-locking nut on the piston rod. Tighten the nut temporarily to about 35 ft. lbs. (55 Nm).

　f. Place the spring in position between the upper and lower spring seats. Slowly and carefully unscrew the compressor until all spring tension is relieved, then remove the compressor.

　g. Raise the bound bumper to the upper spring seat.

9. To install the strut, reverse the removal procedures. After installation, torque the piston rod nut to 54–69 ft. lbs. (75–95 Nm) for 1970–78, 43–54 ft. lbs. (60–75 Nm) for 1979–83 or 51–65 ft. lbs. (69–88 Nm) for 1984 and later.

Tension Rod
REMOVAL AND INSTALLATION

1. Raise and support the front of the vehicle on jackstands.
2. Remove the splash board, if equipped.
3. Back off the tension rod retaining nut, then remove the nut, the washers and the rubber bushing.
4. Remove the tension rod-to-transverse link bolts and the tension rod.

NOTE: *The tension rods are designed with a left and a right direction, be sure to install each in it's correct position.*

5. To install, reverse the removal procedures. Torque the tension rod-to-transverse link to 44–51 ft. lbs. (61–71 Nm) for 1970–83 or 31–43 ft. lbs. (42–59 Nm) for 1984 and later; the tension rod-to-body nuts to 33–40 ft. lbs. (44–54 Nm).

NOTE: *Make sure that the tension rod bushings are facing the proper direction. After installation, make sure that the minimum clearances between the tension rods and the stabilizer bar are equal on both sides.*

MacPherson Struts
TESTING SHOCK ABSORBER ACTION

Shock absorbers require replacement if the vehicle fails to recover quickly after a large bump is encountered, if there is a tendency for the vehicle to sway, nose dive excessively or if the suspension is overly susceptible to vibration.

A good way to test the shocks is to intermittently apply downward pressure to one corner of the vehicle until it is moving up and down for almost the full suspension travel, then release it and watch the recovery. If the vehicle bounces slightly about one more time and then comes to rest, the shock absorbers are serviceable. If the vehicle goes on bouncing, the shocks require replacement.

REMOVAL AND INSTALLATION

The struts are precision parts and retain the springs under tremendous pressure even when removed from the vehicle. For these reasons, several expensive special tools and substantial specialized knowledge are required to safely and effectively work on these parts. It is recommended that if spring or shock absorber repair work is required, remove the strut(s) involved and take them to a repair facility which is fully equipped and familiar with the vehicle.

1. Raise and support the vehicle under the chassis with jackstands as shown in Chapter 1.
2. Remove the hub nuts and the wheel.
3. Remove the splash board, if necessary.
4. Loosen the brake hose connection. Remove the hose locking spring, pull the plate off and remove the hose from the strut assembly bracket.
5. Remove the brake caliper retaining bolts and the caliper assembly.

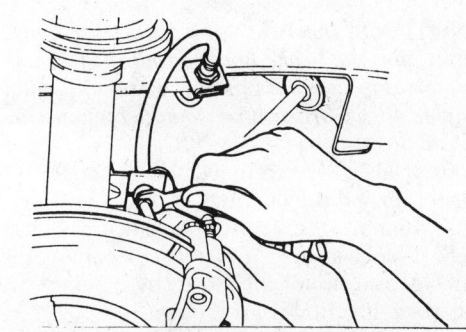
Brake hose disconnection—Z model shown

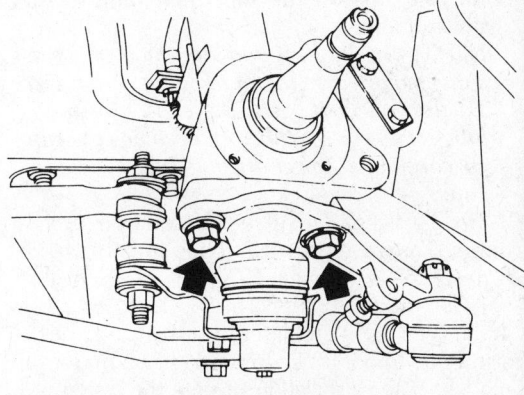
Knuckle arm to strut bolts—280 ZX shown

214 SUSPENSION AND STEERING

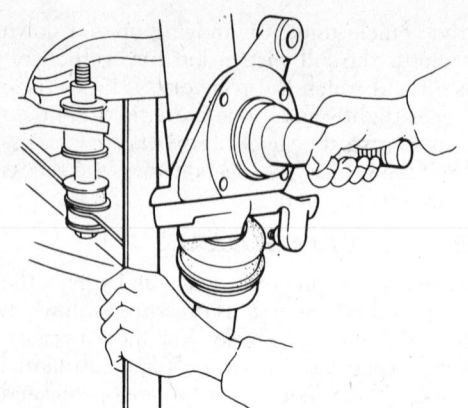
Separate the knuckle arm from the strut with a bar

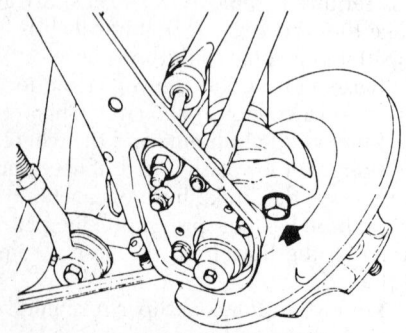
Knuckle arm bolts—Z models

NOTE: *On the 1970–83 models, disconnect and plug the brake hose so that dust cannot enter the system. On the 1984 and later models, the brake hose should remain connected.*

6. If necessary, remove the hub nut, the wheel hub and the bearings.
7. Remove the strut-to-knuckle arm bolts.
8. Using a long pry bar, separate the knuckle arm from the strut by forcing the transverse link (lower arm) down.
9. Support the strut assembly. Remove the three nuts inside the engine compartment which retain the strut at the top, then remove the strut assembly.

NOTE: *On the 1984 and later models, a sensor is mounted on top of the strut piston rod. To disconnect it, grip the caps protruding lobes, squeeze the lobes and remove the cap. Be careful not to get dirt and/or water in the cap.*

10. To install, reverse the removal procedures. Torque the strut-to-body nuts to 18–25 ft. lbs. (25–35 Nm) for 1970–78, 22–29 ft. lbs. (29–39 Nm) for 1979–83 or 23–31 ft. lbs. (31–42 Nm) for 1984 and later; the strut-to-knuckle arm bolts to 53–72 ft. lbs. (73–100 Nm) for all models. After installation, torque the piston rod nut to 54–69 ft. lbs. (75–95 Nm) for 1970–78, 43–54 ft. lbs. (60–75 Nm) for 1979–83 or 51–65 ft. lbs. (69–88 Nm) for 1984 and later.

OVERHAUL

1. Refer to the "Coil Spring, Removal and Installation" procedures, in this section and remove the coil spring.
2. Using the Gland Packing Wrench tool No. ST35500001 (1970–83) or No. ST35490000 (1984 and later), remove the gland packing from the strut.
3. Slowly withdraw the piston rod from the cylinder.
4. The metallic parts should be washed in solvent and blown dry. The nonmetallic parts should be blown clean with compressed air.
5. Inspect the parts for damage, cracks or deformation; if necessary, replace the parts of the complete strut.
6. Install the piston rod assembly.
7. Using high quality strut fluid, fill the strut cylinder with 20.7 cu. in. (340 cc) for 1970–78, 16.78 cu. in. (275 cc) for 1979–80, 9.3 fl. oz. (275 ml) for 1981–83 or 9.1 fl. oz. (270 ml) for 1984 and later.
8. Wrap tape around the piston rod threaded end to prevent damage to the new gland packing. Slide the gland packing over the piston rod.
9. Assemble the gland packing. Torque the gland packing (adjustable, 1984 and later ONLY) to 87–108 ft. lbs. (118–147 Nm) or (non-adjustable) to 72–94 ft. lbs. (98–127 Nm).
10. To complete the assembly, reverse the removal procedures. Bleed the air from the strut, by pulling the piston rod upward, then invert the strut and push the piston rod inward; perform this procedure several times.

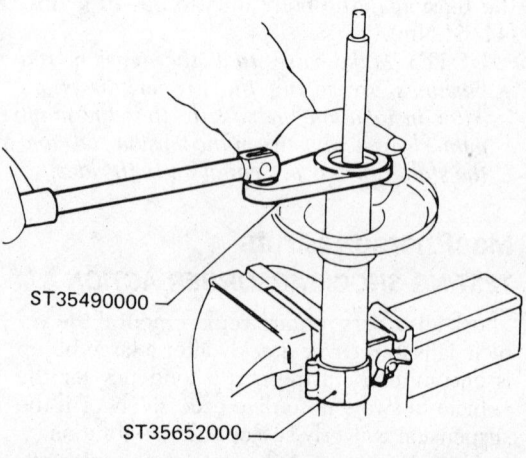
Removing the gland packing from the strut, 1984 and later

SUSPENSION AND STEERING 215

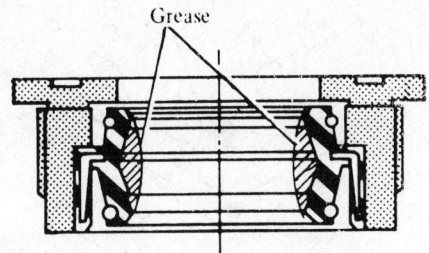

View of the gland packing used as the strut seal

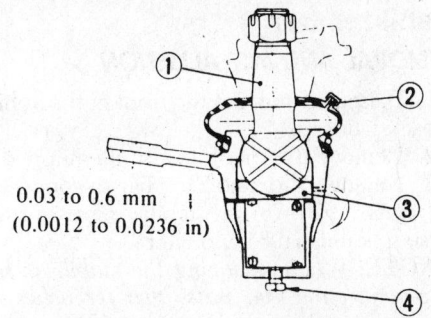

1. Ball stud 3. Spring seat
2. Grease bleeder 4. Plug

Cross section of ball joint—typical

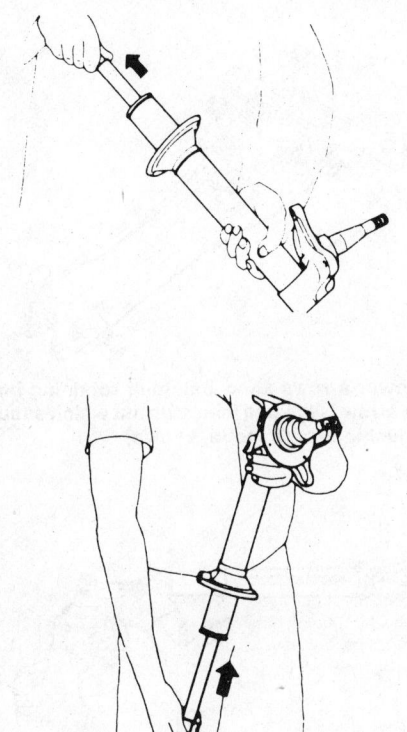

Bleeding the air from the strut

Ball Joint

INSPECTION

1. Put the vehicle on a lift so that all weight is removed from both front wheels.
2. Apply downward and upward pressure to the outer end of the transverse link, avoid any compression of the spring.
3. Measure the play between the link and the bottom of the strut which effectively is the axial play in the ball joint. If play exceeds 0.0236 in. (0.6 mm), replace the ball joint as later described.

REMOVAL AND INSTALLATION

On the 1984 and later models, the ball joint is a part of the transverse link and cannot be re-

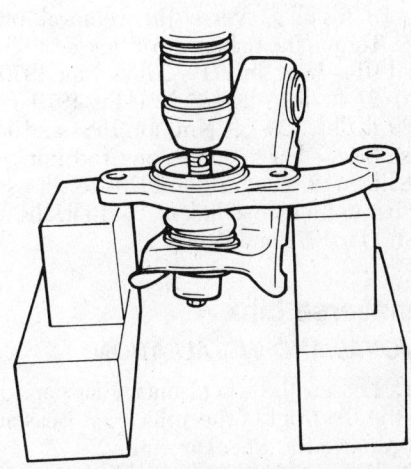

Separating the knuckle arm from the ball joint

placed; therefore, the ball joint must be replaced with the transverse link as an assembly.

1. Refer to the "Transverse link, Removal and Installation" procedures, in this section and remove the transverse link from the vehicle.
2. On the 1970–83 models, place the transverse link in a vise, then remove the ball joint-to-transverse link bolt and the ball joint/knuckle arm assembly.
3. Remove the cotter pin and the castle nut from the ball joint stud.
4. Using an arbor press, place the knuckle arm/ball joint assembly (1970–83) or transverse link/knuckle arm assembly (1984 and later) on blocks and press the ball joint from the knuckle arm.
5. To install, reverse the removal procedures. Torque the ball joint-to-knuckle arm nut to 40–55 ft. lbs. (55–76 Nm) for 1970–78 or 71–88 ft. lbs. (96–120 Nm) for 1979 and later; the ball joint-to-transverse link bolt to 14–18 ft. lbs. (19–25 Nm) for 1970–78 or 33–40 ft. lbs. (44–54 Nm) for 1979–83.

216 SUSPENSION AND STEERING

Stabilizer Bar

REMOVAL AND INSTALLATION

1. Raise and support the front of the vehicle on jackstands.
2. Remove the splash board, if equipped.
3. Remove the stabilizer bar-to-connecting rod nuts (1970–78) or stabilizer bar-to-transverse link nuts (1984 and later).
   NOTE: *When removing the stabilizer bar-to-connecting rod nuts, two wrenches are necessary.*
4. Remove the stabilizer bar bracket-to-frame bolts and the stabilizer bar.
   NOTE: *Final torquing of the stabilizer bar fasteners should be performed with the wheels on the ground.*
5. To install, reverse the removal procedures. Torque the stabilizer bar bracket-to-frame bolts to 14–18 ft. lbs. (19–25 Nm) for 1970–78 or 20–27 ft. lbs. (26–36 Nm) for 1979–83 or 22–29 ft. lbs. (29–39 Nm) for 1984 and later; the stabilizer bar-to-connecting rod nut to 9–20 ft. lbs. (12–27 Nm) for 1970–78; the stabilizer bar-to-transverse link to 12–16 ft. lbs. (16–22 Nm) for 1979 and later.

Transverse Link

REMOVAL AND INSTALLATION

1. Loosen the wheel nuts. Raise and support the the front of the vehicle on jackstands, then remove the wheel assembly.
2. Remove the splash shield.
3. Remove the cotter pin and the castle nut from the steering linkage ball joint at the steering knuckle.
4. Using the Ball Joint Removal tool No. HT2520000, separate the steering linkage from the knuckle.
5. Remove the knuckle arm-to-MacPherson strut bolts. Using a long pry bar, separate the knuckle from the strut.

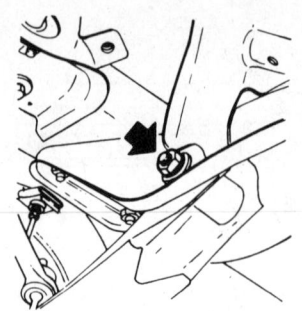

Transverse link mounting bolt

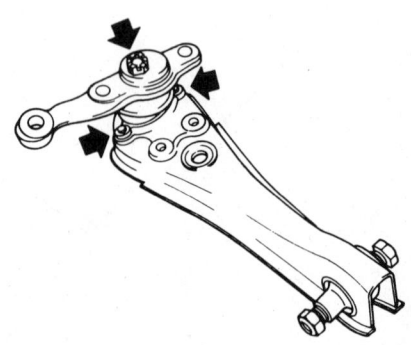

Two lower arrows show ball joint retaining bolts; upper arrow is the ball joint stud nut which secures the knuckle arm (Z model shown)

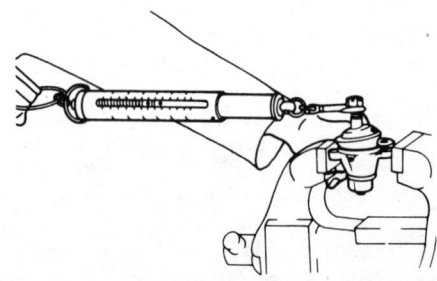

Measuring the ball joint axial play

6. Remove the compression rod (1970–78) or the tension rod (1979 and later) and the stabilizer bar from the transverse link.
7. Remove the transverse link (lower arm) mounting bolt and the link from the vehicle, complete with the knuckle and ball joint.
8. To inspect the ball joint, perform the following:
   a. On the 1970–74 models, check the ball joint axial play. Hook a spring scale onto the ball joint stud and measure the amount of force necessary to move it. It should be 0.28–1.25 in. oz. (20–90 gr-cm).
   b. On the 1975 and later models, measure the ball joint turning torque. Hook a spring scale into the cotter pin hole and measure the amount of force necessary to turn the ball joint. The torque figures are: 35 in.

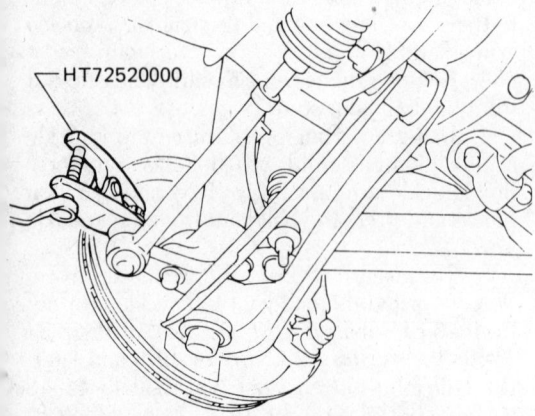

Separating the tie rod from the knuckle arm

lbs. (40 kg-cm) for 1975; more than 43 in. lbs. (50 kg-cm) for 1976–78; more than 13 in. lbs. (15 kg-cm) for 1979–83; more than 9 in. lbs. (10 kg-cm) for 1984 and later.

NOTE: *The ball joint turning force figures are for used parts. New part turning torques will be considerably higher. In all cases, these are the minimum figures; replace the ball joint if the turning torque is less than specified.*

9. To inspect the transverse link bushing, perform the following:

   a. Check the bushing for melted or cracked areas where it adheres to the inner or outer tubes.

   b. Check for cracks inside the bushing.

   c. If damage is found, the bushing must be pressed from the link. This will require a driver or a length of pipe of the same outer diameter as the bushing and a spacer to be placed under the link, through which the bushing can pass as it is pressed from the link. The new bushing must be pressed into the link, using the driver used for removal.

10. To install the parts, perform the following procedures:

   a. Remove the bolt from the bottom of the ball joint and install a grease nipple. Pump multi-purpose grease (NLGI No. 2 lithium soap base) into the ball joint until all old grease is expelled and the joint is full. Do not allow new grease to be forced past the clamped portion of the joint. Remove the grease nipple and install the plug.

   b. Install the parts in the reverse order of removal. Torque the ball joint stud nut (castle nut) to 40–54 ft. lbs. (55–75 Nm) for 1970–78; 71–88 ft. lbs. (98–122 Nm) for 1979 and later. Install a new cotter pin after installation.

   c. Torque the ball joint-to-transverse link bolt to 35–45 ft. lbs. (49–63 Nm) for 1970–73; 44–51 ft. lbs. (61–71 Nm) for 1974; 14–18 ft. lbs. (19–25 Nm) for 1975–78 or 33–40 ft. lbs. (45–55 Nm) for 1979–83.

   d. When installing the transverse link, install the pivot bolt and tighten it enough to hold it in place. When assembly is complete, lower the vehicle and torque (with the weight of the vehicle on its wheels) the transverse link-to-suspension crossmember bolt/nut to 80–94 ft. lbs. (110–130 Nm) for 1970–73, 80–101 ft. lbs. (111–140 Nm) for 1974–78, 58–80 ft. lbs. (80–110 Nm) for 1979–83 or 69–83 ft. lbs. (93–113 Nm) for 1984 and later.

Knuckle And Spindle

The steering knuckle and wheel spindle are a part of the MacPherson strut assembly. If necessary to remove them, refer to the "MacPherson Strut, Removal and Installation" procedures, in this section and remove the strut.

Front End Alignment

Alignment should be performed after it has been verified that all parts of the steering and suspension systems are in good condition. Tire pressures must be correct with tires cold.

Camber and caster angles are determined by the basic geometry of the suspension and cannot be adjusted except through repair of faulty or bent components. Ride height also is non-adjustable and if the vehicle is not level, a replacement spring of appropriate length must be substituted for a weak one.

Toe

Toe is the amount, measured in a fraction of an inch, that the front wheels are closer together at one end than the other. Toe-in means that the front wheels are closer together at the front of the tire than at the rear of the tire; toe-out means that the rear of the tires are closer together than the front. The Z and ZX are designed to have a slight amount of toe-in. Toe-in compensates for the tendency of the front wheels to be forced outwards when the vehicle is moving forward.

Toe-in is adjusted by turning the tie-rods, which have right-hand threads on one side and left-hand threads on the other. You can make this adjustment if you make very careful measurements, although it is recommended that the adjustment be made by your dealer or a qualified shop. The wheels must be dead straight ahead. The vehicle must have a full tank of gas, all fluids must be at their proper levels, the wheel bearings must be properly adjusted and the tires must be properly inflated to their cold specification.

ADJUSTMENT

1. Raise the front of the vehicle, then mark a base line across the left and the right wheels.

NOTE: *If the tread pattern on your vehicle's tires makes this impossible, measure between the edges of the wheel rims but be sure to move the vehicle forward and measure in a couple of places to avoid errors caused by bent rims or wheel runout.*

2. With the wheels in the straight ahead position, lower the vehicle.

NOTE: *After lowering the vehicle, move it up and down to eliminate the friction.*

3. If the measurement is not within specification, loosen the locknuts at both tie-rods for all models (except, 1979–81 power steering) or

SUSPENSION AND STEERING

Wheel Alignment

Year	Model	Caster Range (deg)	Camber Range (deg)	Toe-in① Inches (mm)	Steering Axis Inclination (deg)	Wheel Pivot Ratio (deg) Inner Wheel	Wheel Pivot Ratio (deg) Outer Wheel
1970–73	240-Z	2°55' ± 30'	50' ± 30'	0–0.12 (0–3)②	12°10' ± 30'	33° ± 30'	31.7° ± 30'
1974	260-Z	2°54' ± 45'	46' ± 45'	0–0.12 (0–3)②	12°10' ± 30'	33° ± 30'	31.7° ± 30'
1975–78	280-Z	2°3'–3°33'	18'–1°48'	0–0.12 (0–3)	11°14'–12°44'	33°54'–34°54'	32°6'–34°6'
	280-Z 2+2	2°3'–3°33'	21'–1°51'	0–0.12 (0–3)	11°14'–12°44'	36°18'–37°18'	34°24'–36°24'
1979–83	280-ZX	4°10'–5°40'	–35'–+55'	0.04–0.12 (1–3)	8°35'–10°5'	33°30'–37°30'③	29°–33°④
1984–86	300-ZX	5°50'–7°20'	–35'–+55'	0.04–0.12 (1–3)	12°15'–13°45'	35°–39°	27°–31°

① Car fully laden—see text
② Car laden plus two 150 pound passengers
③ 32°–36° with power steering
④ 24°30'–28°30' with power steering

SUSPENSION AND STEERING 219

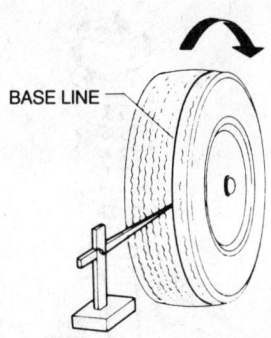
Marking the wheel for alignment purposes

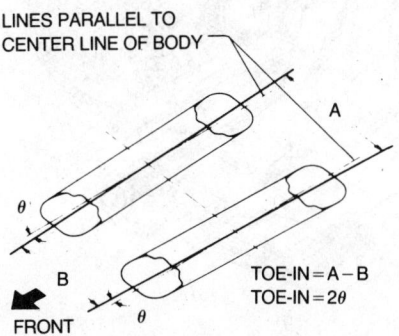
Checking the wheel alignment

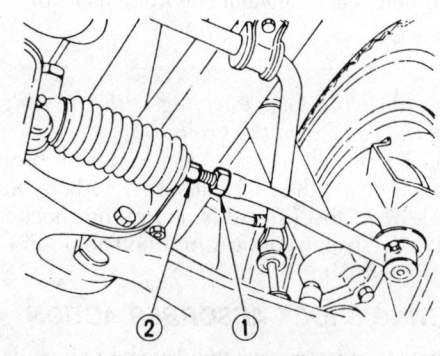
Location of locknut (1) and adjusting nut (2) for toe-in

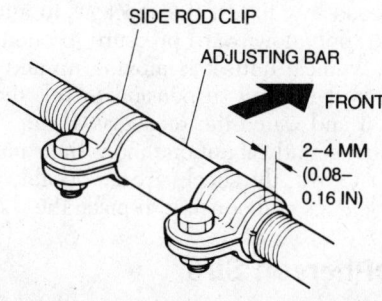
Adjusting the side rod clip for 1979–81 power steering models

loosen the clamp nuts for 1979–81 (power steering models).

4. Turn the tie-rods or the adjusting sleeve on power steering models (1979–81), equally in opposite directions until toe-in is correct.

5. Measure the toe-in and make the necessary adjustments. The toe-in is equal to the distance at the rear minus the distance at the front; it should be 0.04–0.12 in. (1–3 mm) or 6′–16′ (on both sides).

6. Tighten the locknuts or clamp nuts and recheck the adjustment.

NOTE: *After the adjustment is made, be sure that the tie-rod threads are engaged into the steering rack ends to a depth of at least 0.98 in. (25 mm) for all models (except, 1979–81 power steering) or 1.38 in. (35 mm) for 1979–81 (power steering). On the 1979–81 power steering models, the side rod clip should be held within 0.08–0.16 in. (2–4 mm) from the end of the adjusting bar and the side rod clamp bolts MUST face toward the rear of the vehicle.*

REAR SUSPENSION

Coil Springs

REMOVAL AND INSTALLATION

1970–83 Models

Since these models use a MacPherson type strut, with an integral coil spring, refer to the "MacPherson Strut, Removal and Installation" procedures in this section and remove the strut.

Refer to the "Coil Spring, Removal and Installation" procedures, in the Front Suspension section and remove the coil spring from the strut.

1984 and Later

1. Raise and support the rear of the vehicle on jackstands at each wheel.
2. Attach a spring compressor to the coil spring and compress the spring.
3. Disconnect the lower end of the shock absorber at the side which the spring is to be removed.
4. Raise the vehicle, allowing the suspension arm assembly to swing down.
5. Remove the coil spring with the compressor.
6. Inspect the coil spring for yield, deformation or cracks; replace it (if necessary). Check the upper and lower spring seat rubbers for wear, cracks or damage; replace them (if necessary).

NOTE: *When installing the shock absorber,*

220 SUSPENSION AND STEERING

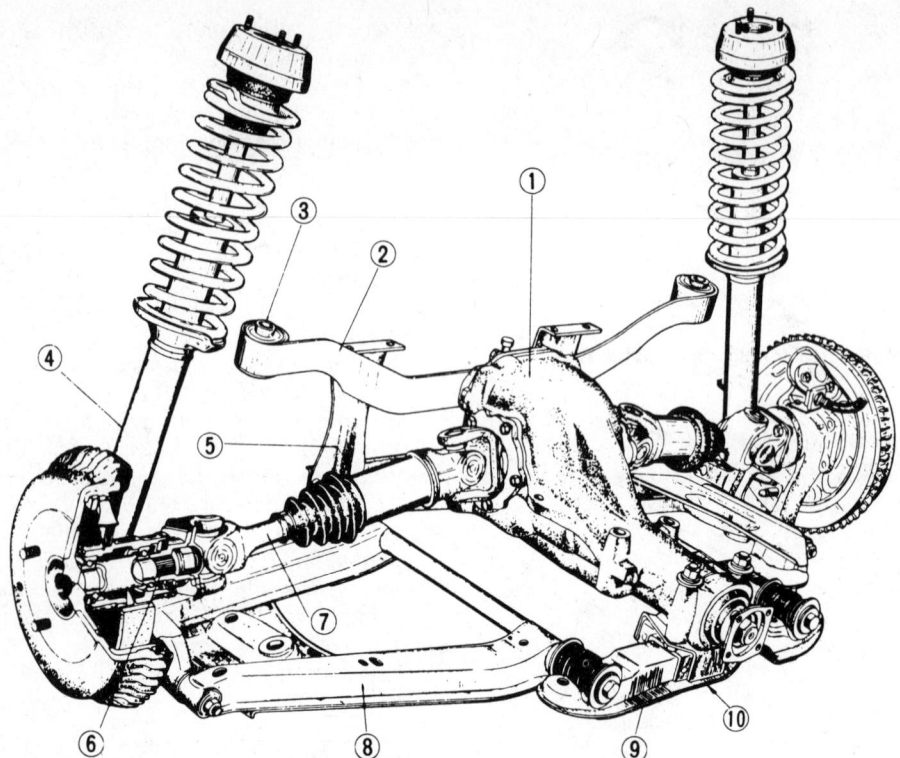

1. Gear carrier
2. Differential case mounting rear member
3. Differential case mounting rear insulator
4. Strut assembly
5. Link mounting brace
6. Rear axle shaft
7. Driveshaft
8. Transverse link
9. Differential case mounting front member
10. Differential case mounting front insulator

Z model rear suspension

perform the final torquing with the weight of the vehicle on the ground.

7. To install, reverse the removal procedures. Torque the lower shock absorber-to-suspension arm nut/bolt to 43–58 ft. lbs. (59–78 Nm).

Shock Absorbers

REMOVAL AND INSTALLATION

1984 and Later

1. Raise and support the rear of the vehicle with jackstands, under the suspension arms.
2. Working inside the luggage compartment, remove the shock absorber-to-body nuts.
3. Disconnect the lower shock absorber-to-suspension arm bolt.
4. Compress the shock absorber and remove it from the vehicle.
5. Check the shock absorber for leakage, cracks, deformation or other damage; (if necessary) replace it. Check the rubber parts for wear, cracks or other damage; (if necessary) replace them.

NOTE: *When installing the shock absorber,*

perform the final torquing with the weight of the vehicle on the ground.

6. To install, reverse the removal procedures. Torque the shock absorber-to-body nuts to 23–31 ft. lbs. (31–42 Nm) and the shock absorber-to-suspension arm nut/bolt to 43–58 ft. lbs. (59–78 Nm).

TESTING SHOCK ABSORBER ACTION

Shocks require replacement if the vehicle fails to recover quickly after hitting a large bump or if the vehicle sways excessively with a change in steering wheel position.

A good way to test the shocks is to intermittently apply downward pressure to one corner of the vehicle until it is moving up and down for almost the full suspension travel, then release it and watch the recovery. If the vehicle bounces slightly about one more time and then comes to rest, the shocks are serviceable. If the vehicle goes on bouncing, replace the shocks.

MacPherson Strut

The struts are precision parts and retain the springs under tremendous pressure even when

SUSPENSION AND STEERING

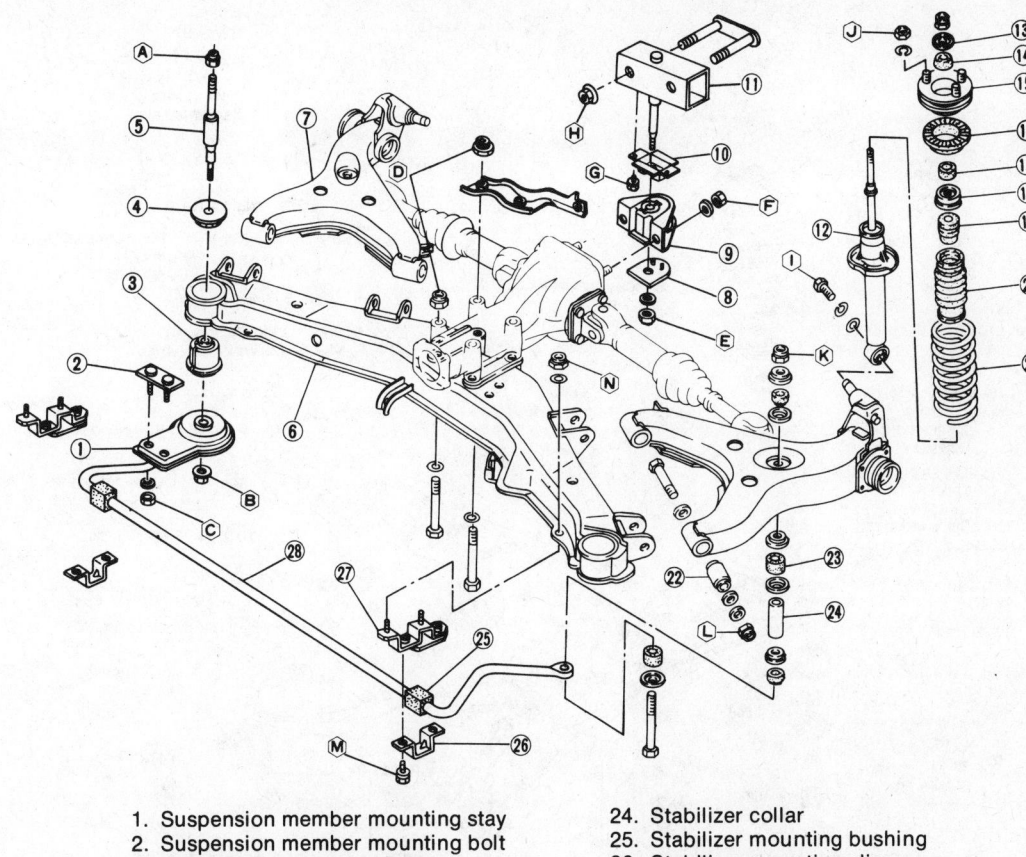

1. Suspension member mounting stay
2. Suspension member mounting bolt
3. Member mounting insulator
4. Member mounting upper stopper
5. Suspension mounting bolt
6. Suspension member assembly
7. Suspension arm assembly
8. Differential mounting plate
9. Differential mounting insulator
10. Differential mounting adapter plate
11. Differential mounting bracket
12. Shock absorber assembly
13. Special washer
14. Shock absorber mounting bushing A
15. Shock absorber mounting insulator
16. Spring seat rubber
17. Shock absorber mounting bushing B
18. Bound bumper cover
19. Bound bumper
20. Dust cover
21. Coil spring
22. Suspension arm bushing
23. Stabilizer bushing
24. Stabilizer collar
25. Stabilizer mounting bushing
26. Stabilizer mounting clip
27. Stabilizer mounting bracket
28. Rear stabilizer

Tightening torque in ft. lbs. (kg-m)
A. 87–116 (12–16)
B. 58–72 (8–10)
C. 14–19 (2.0–2.6)
D. 43–58 (6.0–8.0)
E. 87–108 (12–15)
F. 65–87 (9–12)—R200 differential
   43–58 (6–8)—R180 differential
G. 23–31 (3.2–4.3)
H. 43–58 (6–8)
I. 43–58 (6–8)
J. 22–29 (3–4)
K. 12–15 (1.6–2.1)
L. 58–72 (8–10)
M. 12–15 (1.6–2.1)
N. 12–15 (1.6–2.1)

Exploded view of the ZX rear suspension, 1979–83

removed from the vehicle. For these reasons, several expensive special tools and substantial specialized knowledge are required to safely and effectively work on these parts. We recommend that if a spring or shock absorber repair is required, you remove the strut(s) involved and take them to a repair facility which is fully equipped and familiar with the vehicle.

REMOVAL AND INSTALLATION
1970–78

This procedure can be used to remove the strut, the wheel bearing housing, the bearings, the stub axle and the rear brake assembly as a unit. If you wish to remove the stub axle first, refer to Chapter 6. In any case, it is easiest to re-

222 SUSPENSION AND STEERING

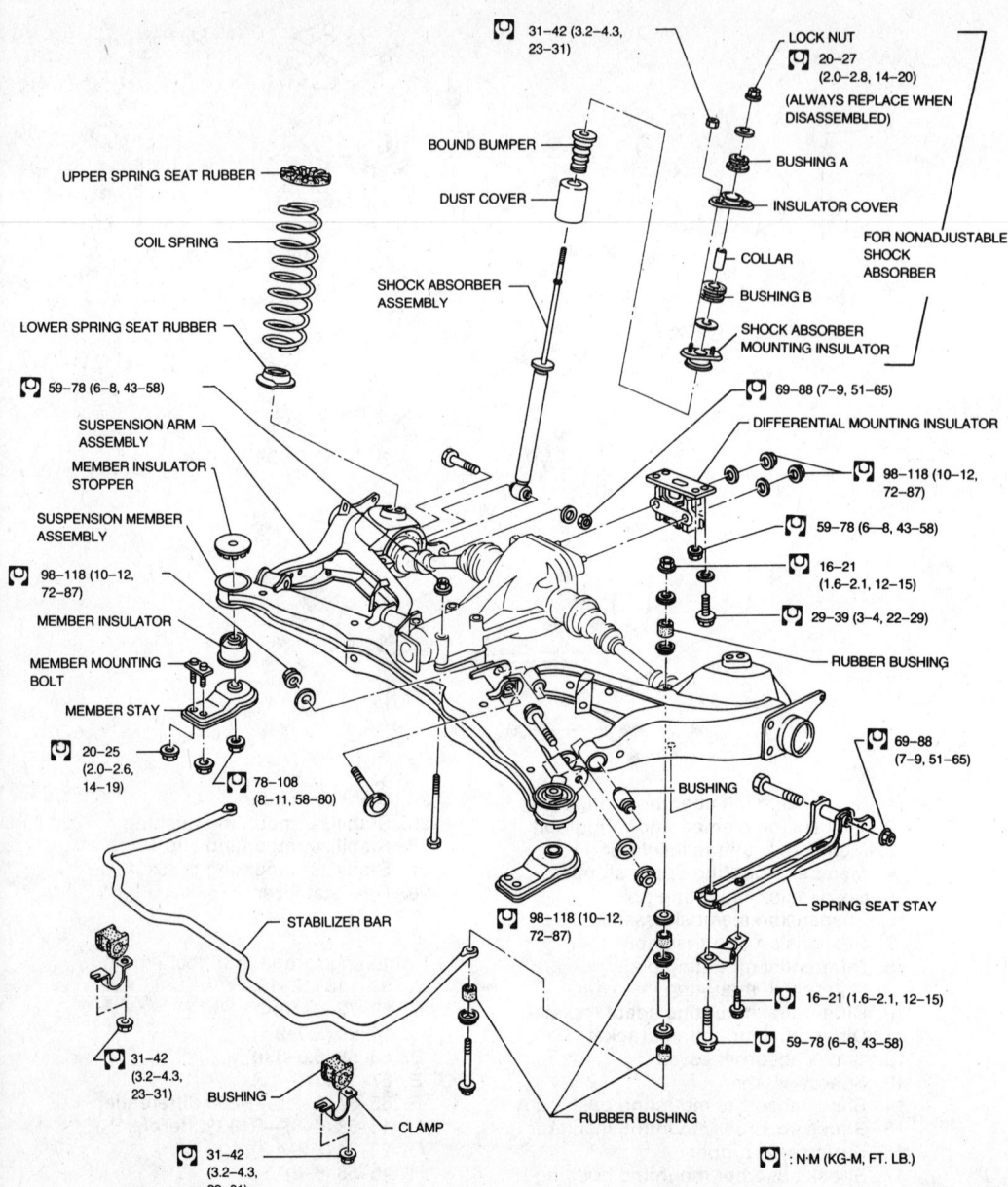

Rear suspension, exploded view—300 ZX

move the brake with the strut and disassemble the parts after removal from the vehicle.

1. Loosen the wheel nuts. Raise and support the vehicle on jackstands as shown in Chapter 1.
2. Remove the wheel nuts and wheels. Disconnect the brake hose at (1) and the linkage at (2).
3. Disconnect the stabilizer bar at the crossmember and the transverse link.
4. Remove the transverse link outer spindle self-locking nuts (2) and the spindle bolt (1). Pull the spindle out and separate the transverse link and strut.
5. Disconnect the driveshaft at the outer end.
6. Place a jack under the lower end of the strut. Remove the strut installation nuts from inside the passenger compartment. Lower the strut carefully with the jack.
7. Inspect all of the bushings and replace as necessary.
8. To install, reverse the removal procedures.

NOTE: *Install the spindle so that the shorter length, when measured from the locking bolt notch, is toward the front.*

9. Use the following torquing figures:
   • Axle shaft flange bolts at the differ-

SUSPENSION AND STEERING

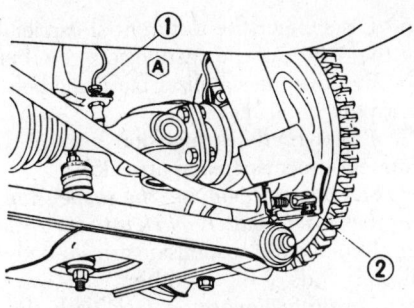

TIGHTENING TORQUE:
Ⓐ: 1.5 TO 1.8 KG-M (11 TO 13 FT-LB)

Disconnect the brake line at (1) and the side linkage at (2)—Z models

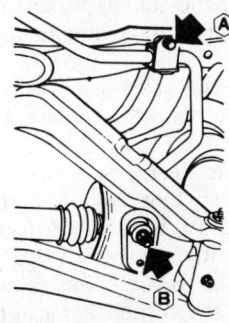

TIGHTENING TORQUE:
Ⓐ: 1.0 TO 1.2 KG-M (7.2 TO 8.7 FT-LB)
Ⓑ: 1.2 TO 1.7 KG-M (8.7 TO 12.3 FT-LB)

Arrows show stabilizer bar retaining bolts—Z models

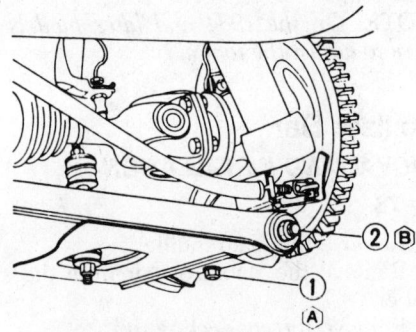

TIGHTENING TORQUE:
Ⓐ: 1.0 TO 1.2 KG-M (7.2 TO 8.7 FT-LB)
Ⓑ: 7.5 TO 9.5 KG-M (54 TO 69 FT-LB)

Transverse link lockbolt (1) and nuts (2)—Z models

ential side to 36–43 ft. lbs. (50–60 Nm) for 1970–72; 23–31 ft. lbs. (32–43 Nm) for 1973–74 and 1978 or 17–23 ft. lbs. (24–43 Nm) for 1977.
- Axle shaft flange bolts at the wheel side to 36–43 ft. lbs. (50–60 Nm).
- Strut installation nuts to 12–15 ft. lbs. (16–21 Nm) for 1970–72 or 18–25 ft. lbs. (25–35 Nm), 1973–78.
- Link spindle locknuts to 54–69 ft. lbs. (75–95 Nm).
- Link spindle lock bolt to 7.2–8.7 ft. lbs. (10–12 Nm).
- Stabilizer bar at the link to 8.7–12.3 ft. lbs. (12–17 Nm).
- Stabilizer bar at the crossmember to 7.2–8.7 ft. lbs. (10–12 Nm).
- Brake line connector to 11–13 ft. lbs. (15–18 Nm).

10. Fill and bleed brake system.

1979–83

1. Block the front wheels.
2. Raise and support the rear of the vehicle on jackstands.

NOTE: *The vehicle should be far enough off the ground so that the rear spring does not support any weight.*

3. Working inside the luggage compartment, turn and remove the caps above the strut mounts. Remove the three strut mounting nuts.
4. Remove the mounting bolt for the strut at the lower arm (transverse link) and remove the strut.
5. To install, reverse the removal procedures. Install the top end first and secure with the nuts snugged down but not tightened to the final torque figure. Attach the lower end of the strut to the lower arm, then torque the top mounting nuts to 22–29 ft. lbs. (30–40 Nm). Torque the strut bolt at the lower arm to 43–58 ft. lbs. (60–80 Nm).

Transverse Link

REMOVAL AND INSTALLATION

1970–78

NOTE: *If necessary to remove the rear axle, refer to the "Rear Axle Shaft, Removal and Installation" procedures, in Chapter 6 and remove the rear axle.*

1. Chock the front wheels.
2. Loosen the rear wheel nuts. Raise and support the rear of the vehicle on jackstands, under the frame.
3. Remove the wheel nuts and the wheels.
4. Remove the stabilizer bar from the transverse link.
5. Separate the transverse link from the strut.
6. Position a jack under the differential and raise it.
7. Loosen the transverse link inner bolts and damper plate bolts.
8. Remove the differential mount front insulator nut.
9. Remove the differential mounting front

224 SUSPENSION AND STEERING

member nuts and the differential front member.

10. Remove the transverse link rear mounting bracket and the transverse link.

11. Using the Rear Transverse Link Bushing Replacer tool No. ST38800000 (if necessary), remove the outer bushing from the transverse link.

12. Inspect the transverse link for cracks, deformation or damage; replace it, if necessary.

13. To install, reverse the removal procedures. Torque the transverse link inner bolt to 101–106 ft. lbs. (140–160 Nm), the rear link mounting bracket bolt to 23–31 ft. lbs. (32–43 Nm) and the transverse link outer lock nut to 54–69 ft. lbs. (75–95 Nm).

Suspension Arm

REMOVAL AND INSTALLATION

1979 and Later

1. Block the front wheels.
2. Raise the rear of the vehicle and support it on jackstands under the body member on both sides.
3. Using a floor jack, place it under and support the differential carrier.
4. Disconnect and plug the brake tube (1). Disconnect hand brake cable (2) from the suspension arm and member, be careful not to twist it.

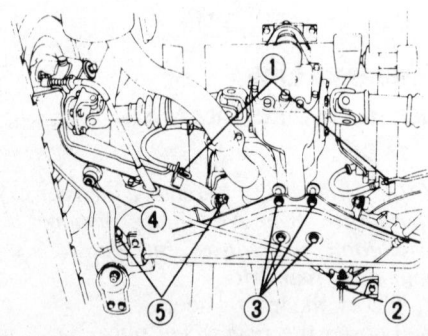

Disconnecting the suspension members, 1979–83

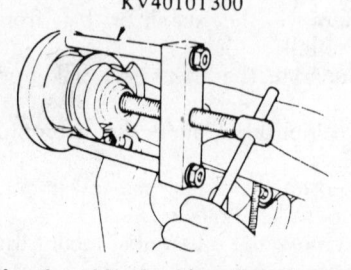

Removing the rubber bushings from the suspension member

5. Disconnect the differential carrier bolts (3) at the center of the suspension member.
6. Remove the stabilizer bar fixing bolt from the suspension arm (4).
7. Remove the suspension arm pins and disconnect the suspension arms (5).

NOTE: *Before removing the suspension arm pin, be sure to match mark it to the bracket.*

8. Remove the suspension arm-to-body nuts from both ends of the member.
9. Carefully lower the jack with the suspension arm member, together with the stabilizer and remove it.

NOTE: *When removing the suspension member assembly, be careful that it does not tilt and fall off of the jack.*

10. Remove the stabilizer bar from the suspension member by removing the mounting clip bolts.
11. Inspect the suspension arm for cracks, deformation or damage; replace it (if necessary).
12. Using the Rear Suspension Member Insulator Replacer tool No. KV40101300, remove (if necessary) the rubber insulators from the suspension member.
13. To install, reverse the removal procedures. Torque the suspension arm pin nut and lock nut to 58–72 ft. lbs. (78–98 Nm), the differential carrier nut to 43–58 ft. lbs. (59–78 Nm), the suspension member stay nut to 14–19 ft. lbs. (20–25 Nm) and the stabilizer bar fixing bolt, clip bolt and bracket nut to 12–15 ft. lbs. (16–21 Nm).

NOTE: *On the 1984 and later models, be sure to adjust the toe-in.*

Stabilizer Bar

REMOVAL AND INSTALLATION

1970–78

1. Remove the main muffler.
2. Remove the stabilizer bar from the side member.
3. Remove the connecting rod.
4. Inspect the stabilizer bar and the bushings for damage; replace (if necessary).
5. To install, reverse the removal procedures.

1979 and Later

To remove the stabilizer bar, refer to the "Suspension Arm, Removal and Installation" procedures, in this section.

Rear Suspension Adjustments

On 1970–83 models the rear suspension is not adjustable for wheel alignment. However,

SUSPENSION AND STEERING 225

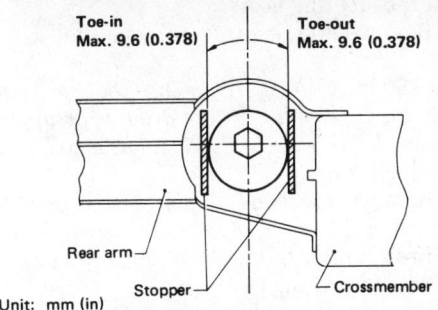

Rear wheel alignment—300 ZX

alignment should be checked periodically and repairs made to defective or bent parts, as necessary.

On 1984 and later models the toe-in can be adjusted by the inside of the rear arm bushing pins. When performing toe adjustment, always set the cams in the same position on the right and left rear arm bushing pins.

STEERING

Steering Wheel

REMOVAL AND INSTALLATION

1. Disconnect the battery negative terminal.
2. On models 1970–78, depress the horn pad, turn it counterclockwise and remove it. On 1979 and later, ZX models, pull the horn pad off.
3. Remove the steering wheel nut.
4. Using the Steering Wheel Puller tool No. ST27180001, thread the anchor screws into the holes provided for this purpose in the wheel, then remove the steering wheel.

CAUTION: *DO NOT hammer on the end of the steering shaft. Striking the shaft will damage the bearing or impair the collapsibility of the column.*

5. To install, perform the following procedures:

   a. Apply grease to all portions which will slide together during installation.
   b. Place the punch mark on the top of the column shaft and install the wheel in a straight-ahead position.
   c. Torque the steering wheel nut to 36–51 ft. lbs. (50–70 Nm) on 1970–76 models; 29–36 ft. lbs. (39–49 Nm) on 1977–83 models; 36–43 ft. lbs. (49–59 Nm) on 1984 and later models.

6. Turn the wheel through the whole range of the steering system and make sure that it does not grab.
7. Install the horn pad, reconnect the battery and test the horn.

Combination Switch

REMOVAL AND INSTALLATION

The combination switch operates the lights, wipers, windshield washer, turn signals and the dimmer switch 1970–78. To the 1979 and later combination switch, an automatic speed control has been added.

1970–78

1. Disconnect the negative battery terminal.
2. Remove the screws which hold the shell cover halves together and the covers from the column jacket.
3. Disconnect all six (five on 1977 and later models) electrical connectors.
4. Remove the two screws which hold the switch to the column jacket.
5. Separate the switch halves (without disconnecting the connector which connects the two halves electrically) and remove the switch.
6. To install, reverse the removal procedures, ensuring that the location tab inside the turn signal switch lines up with the hole in the jacket of the steering column.

1979–83

1. Disconnect the negative battery cable.
2. Remove the horn pad.

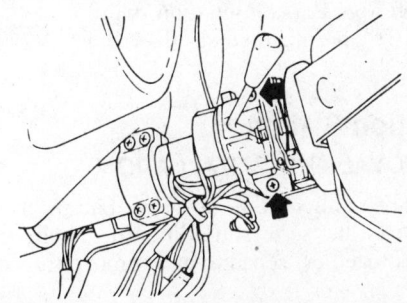

Combination switch retaining screws (arrows)—Z models

SUSPENSION AND STEERING

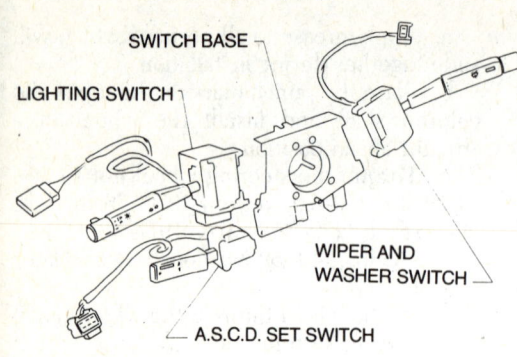

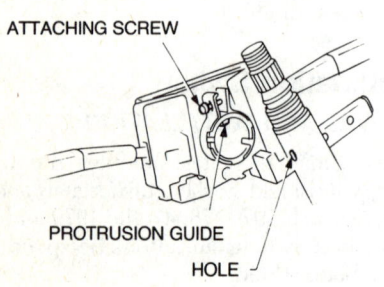

Combination switch—300 ZX

3. Remove the steering wheel.
4. Remove the steering column cover.
5. Unplug the combination switch wires at the electrical connector.
6. Remove the retaining screws and the combination switch assembly.
7. To install, reverse the removal procedures.

1984 and Later

The wiper switch can be removed without removing the combination switch from the steering column.
1. Remove the steering column cover.
2. Disconnect the wiper switch electrical connector.
3. Remove the wiper switch electrical connector.
4. Remove the wiper switch-to-combination switch retaining screws, then pull the wiper switch from the combination switch.
5. To install, reverse the removal procedures.

Ignition Switch
REMOVAL AND INSTALLATION

1. Disconnect the negative battery cable. Remove the screws holding the shell cover halves together, separate and remove the cover halves.
2. Disconnect the lead wires at the connector located at the bottom of the steering lock.
3. Remove the screw which holds the switch to the steering lock and remove the switch.
4. To install, reverse the removal procedures.

Steering Column
REMOVAL AND INSTALLATION

1. Refer to the "Steering Wheel, Removal and Installation" procedures in this section and remove the steering wheel.
2. Remove the lower joint-to-rubber coupling (1970–83) or lower joint (1984 and later) bolt at the steering gear.
3. Remove the steering column shell covers.

CAUTION: *When removing the steering column, be careful not to strike it or apply too much pressure to it, for it has a collapsible type column.*

4. Remove the combination switch assembly.
5. From under the dash, remove the jacket tube bracket and the cover.
6. Remove the column mounting bracket bolts and the bracket.
7. Pull the steering column out from the driver's side.
8. To install, reverse the removal procedures. Torque the column mounting bracket bolts to 5.8–8.0 ft. lbs. (8–11 Nm) for 1970–78; 9–13 ft. lbs. (13–18 Nm) for 1979–83 or 6.5–10.1 ft. lbs. (9–14 Nm) for 1984 and later; the lower joint-to-coupling bolt to 29–36 ft. lbs. (40–50 Nm) for 1970–78, 17–20 ft. lbs. (23–36 Nm) for 1979–83 or 24–28 ft. lbs. (32–38 Nm) for 1984 and later.

Tie-rod and Steering Ball Joint
REMOVAL AND INSTALLATION

Manual Steering (All Models)
and Power Steering (1982 and Later)

1. Raise and support the vehicle on jackstands, then remove the front wheel(s).
2. Remove the splash board, if necessary.
3. Remove the cotter pins and nuts which hold the ball studs to the knuckle arms.
4. Using the Steering Ball Joint Removal tool No. HT2520000, separate the ball joint from the steering knuckle arm.
5. Loosen the tie-rod locknut and unscrew the rod from the steering gear.
6. To install, reverse the removal procedure, torque the ball joint stud nut (castle nut) to 40–55 ft. lbs. (55–76 Nm) for 1970–78 or 40–72 ft. lbs. (54–98 Nm) for 1979 and later; the tie-rod-to-steering gear nut to 58–72 ft. lbs. (78–98 Nm). Install a new cotter pin. Tighten

SUSPENSION AND STEERING

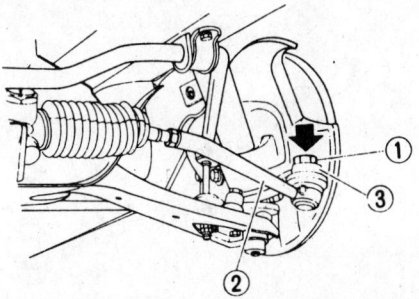

Arrow shows the location of the outer ball stud nut (1). (2) indicates the tie-rod, and (3) the knuckle arm—Z model shown

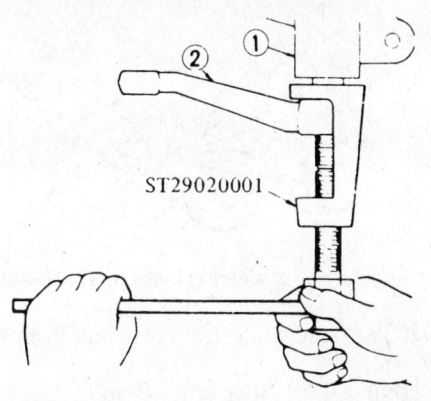

Removing the pitman from the power steering pump, 1979–81

the castle nut to align the cotter pin holes but do not loosen it. Check and adjust the toe-in.

Power Steering Linkage (1979–81)
REMOVAL AND INSTALLATION
Pitman Arm

1. Block the rear wheels.
2. Raise and support the front of the vehicle on jackstands.
3. Remove the cross link-to-pitman arm cotter pin and the castle nut.
4. Using the Ball Joint Removal tool No. HT72520000, separate the cross link from the pitman arm.
5. Remove the pitman arm nut and washer from the power steering pump.

6. Using the Steering Gear Arm Puller tool No. ST29020001, separate the pitman arm from the power steering pump.
7. To install, reverse the removal procedures. Torque the pitman arm-to-power steering pump to 101–130 ft. lbs. (137–177 Nm) and the ball joint-to-pitman arm nut to 40–72 ft. lbs. (54–98 Nm).

Idler Arm

1. Block the rear wheels.
2. Raise and support the front of the vehicle on jackstands.
3. Remove the cross link-to-idler arm cotter pin and the castle nut.
4. Using the Ball Joint Removal tool No.

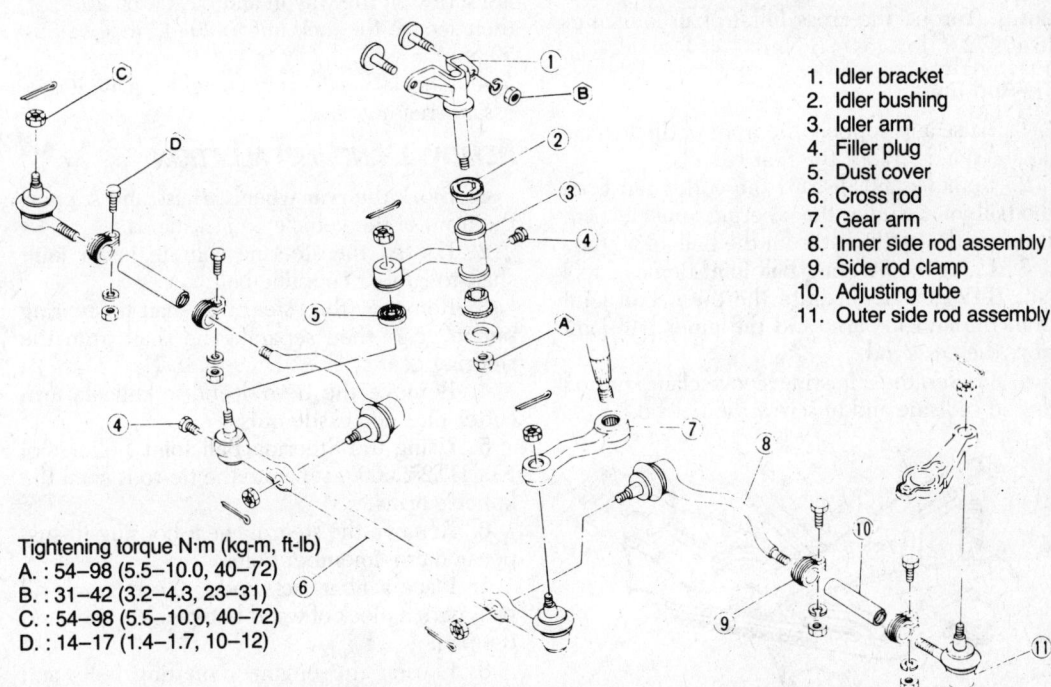

1. Idler bracket
2. Idler bushing
3. Idler arm
4. Filler plug
5. Dust cover
6. Cross rod
7. Gear arm
8. Inner side rod assembly
9. Side rod clamp
10. Adjusting tube
11. Outer side rod assembly

Tightening torque N·m (kg-m, ft-lb)
A.: 54–98 (5.5–10.0, 40–72)
B.: 31–42 (3.2–4.3, 23–31)
C.: 54–98 (5.5–10.0, 40–72)
D.: 14–17 (1.4–1.7, 10–12)

Exploded view of the power steering linkage, 1979–81

228 SUSPENSION AND STEERING

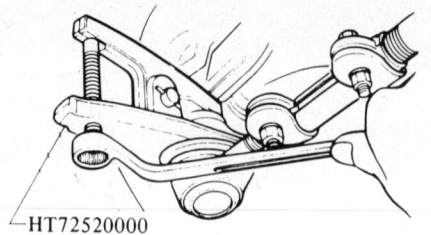

Removing the power steering ball joints, 1979–81

HT72520000, separate the cross link from the idler arm.

5. Remove the idler arm assembly-to-frame nuts, bolts and washer, then the assembly from the vehicle.

6. To install, reverse the removal procedures. Torque the idler arm assembly-to-frame nuts/bolts to 23–31 ft. lbs. (31–42 Nm) and the ball joint-to-idler arm nut to 40–72 ft. lbs. (54–98 Nm).

Center Link

1. Block the rear wheels.
2. Raise and support the front of the vehicle on jackstands.
3. Remove the cross link-to-pitman arm, the cross link-to-idler arm and the cross link-to-tie rods cotter pins and the castle nuts.
4. Using the Ball Joint Removal tool No. HT72520000, separate the cross link from the pitman arm, the idler arm and the tie-rod ends.
5. Remove the cross link from the vehicle.
6. To install, reverse the removal procedures. Torque the cross link-to-ball joint nuts to 40–72 ft. lbs. (54–98 Nm).

Tie-Rod Ends

1. Raise and support the front of the vehicle on jackstands. Block the rear wheels.
2. Remove and discard the cotter pin from the ball joint stud at the steering knuckle arm. Remove the castle nut from the ball joint stud.
3. Using the Steering Ball Joint Removal tool No. HT2520000, separate the outer ball joint from the knuckle arm and the inner ball joint from the cross rod.
4. Loosen the adjusting sleeve clamp nut on the tie-rod side and unscrew the tie-rod.

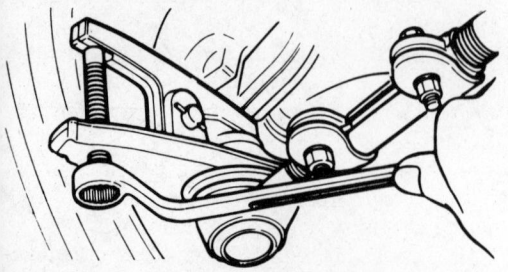

Separate the ball joint from the knuckle with a puller (power steering model shown)

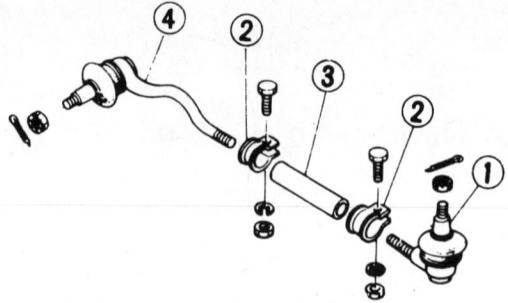

1. Tie-rod end
2. Clamp
3. Adjusting sleeve
4. Inner tie-rod

Exploded view of the power steering tie-rod

5. To install, reverse the removal procedures. Tighten the ball joint castle nut to 40 ft. lbs. (54 Nm), then continue to tighten until the cotter pin holes align. Torque limit is 72 ft. lbs. (100 Nm). Install a new cotter pin.
6. Check and/or adjust the toe-in as necessary.

Manual Steering Gear

ADJUSTMENTS

1970–83

1. Raise and support the front of the vehicle on jackstands.
2. Using a large wrench, loosen the large lock nut at the bottom of the steering gear.
3. Using a large screwdriver, while holding the lock nut with the wrench, turn the adjusting screw all the way in and back it off 20°–25°, then secure the lock nut to 29–43 ft. lbs. (39–59 Nm).
4. Check the steering wheel for play; if necessary, readjust it.

REMOVAL AND INSTALLATION

1. Block the rear wheels. Raise and support the front of the vehicle on jackstands.
2. Loosen the steering column lower joint shaft-to-rubber coupling bolt.
3. Remove the steering shaft-to-steering pinion gear, then separate the shaft from the steering gear.
4. Remove the tie-rod end-to-knuckle arm cotter pins and castle nuts.
5. Using the Steering Ball Joint Puller tool No. HT2520000, separate the tie-rods from the knuckle arms.
6. Remove the steering gear housing-to-suspension crossmember bolts.
7. Place a floor jack under the engine's oil pan, with a block of wood between the jack and the pan.
8. Loosen the engine mounting bolts and raise the engine approximately ½ in., then remove the steering gear and linkage from the vehicle.

SUSPENSION AND STEERING 229

9. To install, reverse the removal procedures. Torque the steering gear-to-suspension crossmember bolts to 33–44 ft. lbs. (45–60 Nm).

Power Steering Gear
ADJUSTMENTS
1982 and Later

1. Raise and support the front of the vehicle on jackstands.
2. Using a large wrench, loosen the large lock nut at the bottom of the steering gear.
3. Using a large screwdriver, while holding the lock nut with the wrench, turn the adjusting screw all the way in and back it off 20°–25°, then secure the lock nut to 29–43 ft. lbs. (39–59 Nm).
4. Check the steering wheel for play, (if necessary) readjust it.

REMOVAL AND INSTALLATION
1979–81

1. Block the rear wheels. Raise and support the front of the vehicle on jackstands.
2. Place an oil catch pan under the power steering gear, then remove the oil lines from the steering gear and drain the oil into the pan.
3. Loosen the steering column lower joint shaft bolt.
4. Remove the steering shaft-to-steering pinion gear, the separate the shaft from the steering gear.
5. Remove the pitman arm-to-steering gear nut and washer.
6. Using the Steering Gear Arm Puller tool No. ST29020001, separate the pitman arm from the steering gear.
7. Remove the steering gear-to-frame bolts and the steering gear from the vehicle.
8. To install, reverse the removal procedures. Torque the steering gear-to-frame bolts to 23–30 ft. lbs. (31–41 Nm) and the pitman arm-to-steering gear nut to 101–130 ft. lbs. (137–177).
9. Refill the power steering pump, start the engine and bleed the system.

1982 and Later

1. Block the rear wheels. Raise and support the front of the vehicle on jackstands.
2. Place an oil catch pan under the power steering gear, then remove the oil lines from the steering gear and drain the oil into the pan.
3. Loosen the steering column lower joint shaft bolt.
4. Remove the steering shaft-to-steering pinion gear, the separate the shaft from the steering gear.
5. Remove the tie-rod end-to-knuckle arm cotter pins and castle nuts.
6. Using the Steering Ball Joint Puller tool No. HT2520000, separate the tie-rods from the knuckle arms.
7. Remove the steering gear housing-to-suspension crossmember bolts.
8. Place a floor jack under the engine's oil pan, with a block of wood between the jack and the pan.
9. Loosen the engine mounting bolts and raise the engine approximately ½ in., then remove the steering gear and linkage from the vehicle.
10. To install, reverse the removal procedures. Torque the steering gear-to-suspension crossmember bolts to 22–29 ft. lbs. (29–39 Nm) and the ball joints to 40–72 ft. lbs. (54–98 Nm).
11. Refill the power steering pump, start the engine and bleed the power steering system.

Power Steering Pump
REMOVAL AND INSTALLATION

1. Loosen the power steering pump lock nut and turn the drive belt adjusting nut counterclockwise.
2. Remove the oil pump drive belt.
3. Loosen but do not remove the hoses at the pump.
4. Remove the pump bolts and the pump from the vehicle.
5. Disconnect the hoses from the pump and remove the pump from the vehicle.
6. To install, reverse the removal procedures. Torque the pump-to-bracket bolts to 14–19 ft. lbs. (19–25 Nm). Adjust the drive belt to 0.31–0.47 in. @ 22 lbs. Refill the reservoir and bleed the power steering system.

BLEEDING

1. Raise and support the front of the vehicle on jackstands.
2. Make sure that the oil reservoir is filled to the "MAX" level.
3. With the engine temperature at 140°–176°F (60°–80°C), quickly turn the wheels (all the way to the wheel stoppers) left and right, ten times.
4. Stop the engine and check the fluid level, (if necessary) add fluid.
5. Start the engine and repeat Step 3 until all of the air is bled from the pump.
CAUTION: *When performing the bleeding operation, DO NOT hold the steering wheel at the "LOCK" position for more than 15 seconds.*
6. With the steering wheel fully turned to the left, open the bleeder screw (on top of the power steering gear) to bleed off the air.
NOTE: *If the air cannot be expelled, repeat the bleeding operation while running the engine at 1,000–1,500 rpm.*

Brakes

BRAKES

The 240, 260 and 280-Z models are equipped with a vacuum-assisted proportioned braking system employing discs on the front and finned aluminum drums on the rear. The vacuum-assist cylinder is 6.0 in. in diameter on 1970–72 vehicles, and 7.5 in. in diameter on 1973 and later models (except 2 + 2 models which use a 9 in.). The S-16 Girling-Sumitomo disc brake calipers are the two-piston type and the rear brakes are self-adjusting, leading-trailing type. The hand-brake is mechanical, employing cables for actuation of the rear drum brakes.

The master cylinder is a dual cylinder design so that failure of either the front or rear brakes causes the brake system at the opposite end of the vehicle to be sealed off at the master cylinder and continue to operate normally.

The "Master-Vac" assist system employs manifold vacuum against a diaphragm to assist in application of the brakes. The vacuum is regulated to be proportional to the pressure placed on the pedal.

The system also incorporates a warning light which is operated by a hydraulic electric switch which connects the front and rear hydraulic systems. If pressure in one system is not counter-balanced by pressure in the other, as when a leak causes it to be sealed off at the master cylinder, the switch piston is forced to one side and closes the warning light switch.

Ordinarily in a hydraulic brake system, application of pressure at the master cylinder

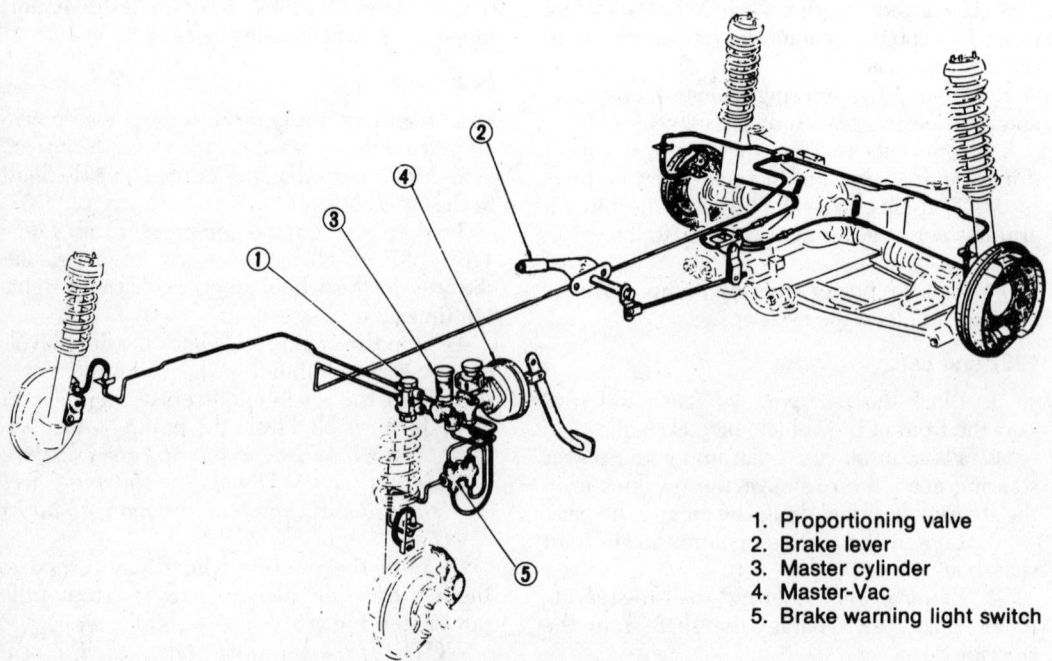

1. Proportioning valve
2. Brake lever
3. Master cylinder
4. Master-Vac
5. Brake warning light switch

The brake system, 1973–74; later models similar

BRAKES

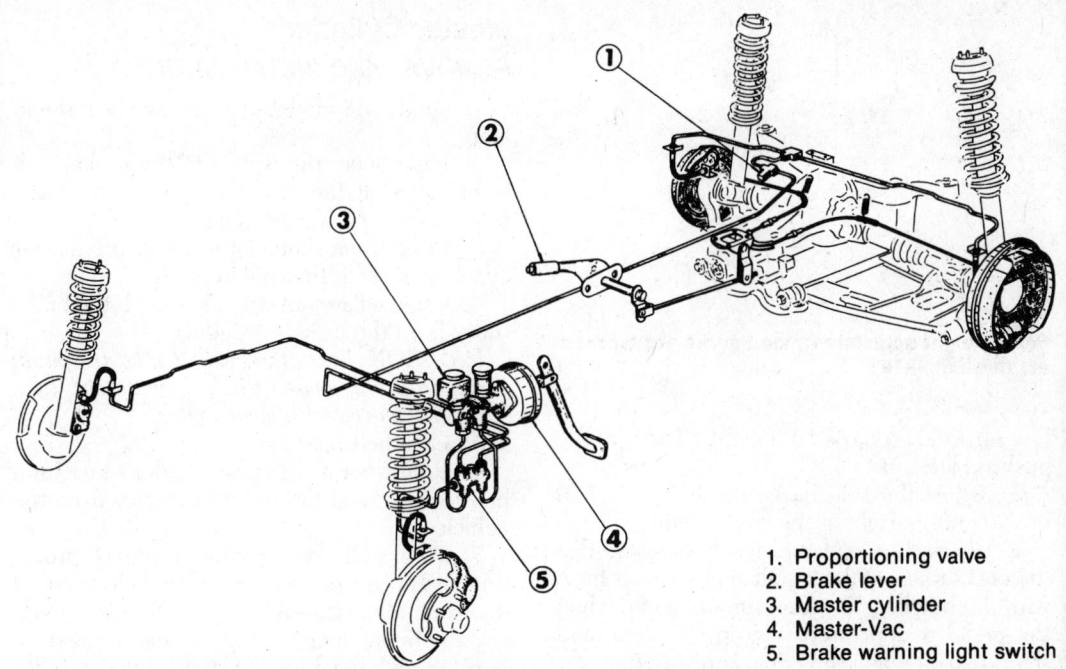

1. Proportioning valve
2. Brake lever
3. Master cylinder
4. Master-Vac
5. Brake warning light switch

The 1970-72 brake system

causes equal pressure to be built up at all wheel cylinders or caliper pistons at the wheels. While this is appropriate during normal braking, weight transfer from the back wheels to the front (under very hard braking) lessens the rear brake pressure requirements. Stable braking cannot be achieved if the rear wheels cease to turn as the tire will track only if it is rolling along the road. As a result, a proportioning valve is used. The valve permits equal pressure in all parts of the system until the system pressure reaches a certain point. Then, through the motion of spring pistons in the valve, the rear brake pressure is throttled and maintained at a reduced percentage of front brake pressure.

On the 1970-72 models, the proportioning valve is located in the rear of the main brake line (going to the back of the vehicle), while in later model vehicles, it is located in the engine compartment and links the front and rear systems.

The ZX models are equipped with vacuum-assisted disc brakes at all four wheels. The front discs are CL28V (1970-83), CL28VA or CL28VB (1984 and later) single piston sliding caliper models with ventilated rotors. The rear brakes are Annette AN14H (1979-81), CL14H or CL14HB single piston sliding caliper models. The inner piston is equipped with a toggle and strut actuated parking brake mechanism which locks the inner pad against the solid rotor. A 9 inch "Master-Vac" booster is used on all models and is similar to the one installed on the 1973-78 (2 + 2) Z but is not interchangeable. The warning light and proportioning valve systems are the same as those used on the Z series.

BRAKE SYSTEM

Adjustments

DRUM BRAKES

1970-78

The rear drum brakes are equipped with automatic adjusters actuated by the parking brake mechanism. No periodic adjustment of the drum brakes is necessary if this mechanism is working properly. If the brake shoe to drum clearance is incorrect, applying and releasing the parking brake a few times does not adjust it properly, the parts will have to be disassembled for repair.

DISC BRAKES

All disc brakes are inherently self-adjusting. No periodic adjustment is either necessary or possible.

PEDAL HEIGHT

1970-78

1. Loosen the locknut and turn the pushrod clevis to get a pedal height of 8.11 in. (206 mm). If necessary, loosen the locknut and adjust the pedal stop back and out of the way, so that it

BRAKES

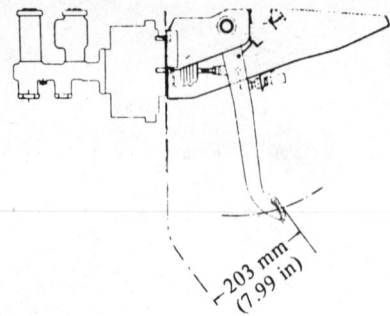

Pedal height adjustment; the figures are for models through 1978

has no effect on pedal height. Tighten the pushrod locknut.

2. Adjust the stop back until height is 7.99 in. (203 mm). Tighten the stop locknut.

3. Check the stop lamp switch to ensure that the end surface of the installation screw is flush with the bracket. The lamp should go on when the pedal is depressed 0.59 in. (15 mm) and should go off when the pedal is released.

1979 and Later

Pedal height is adjusted with the brake light switch and the pushrod.

1. Measure the pedal height from the floorboard (beneath the mat) to the front of the brake pedal. The distance should be 7.13–7.36 in. (1979–82), 6.97–7.36 in. (1983) or 7.17–7.56 in. (1984 and later) for manual transmission models; 7.48–7.72 in. (1979–82), 7.32–7.72 in. (1983) or 7.24–7.64 in. (1984 and later) for automatic transmission models.

2. If the pedal height is incorrect, loosen the brake light switch locknut and turn the body of the switch to screw it in or out. When the pedal height is correct, tighten the locknut.

3. In some cases, the switch adjustment will not have enough range. In this case, loosen the pushrod locknut and adjust the pedal height by turning the pushrod. Tighten the locknut after adjustment.

4. Check the operation of the brake lights after all adjustments are complete.

Brake Light Switch

REMOVAL AND INSTALLATION

1. Disconnect the negative battery cable.
2. Remove the lower instrument cover.
3. Disconnect the electrical connectors from the switch.
4. Loosen the lock nut, rotate the switch and remove it.
5. To install, reverse the removal procedures.

Master Cylinder

REMOVAL AND INSTALLATION

1. On the ZX models, remove the heat shield plate.

2. Disconnect the wiring to the brake fluid level gauge at the electrical connector. Early models do not have the gauge.

3. Place some shop cloths under the master cylinder to catch the spilled fluid.

4. Using a flare nut wrench, unbolt the brake tubes from the master cylinder.

CAUTION: *Brake fluid will damage the paint; wipe up any spilled fluid immediately, then flush the area with clear water.*

5. Cap the brake tubes.

6. Remove the master cylinder-to-vacuum booster nuts and the master cylinder from the vehicle.

7. To install, reverse the removal procedures. Torque the master cylinder-to-vacuum booster nuts to 5.0–8.0 ft. lbs. (6.8–10.8 Nm) and the brake lines to 11–13 ft. lbs. (14.9–17.6 Nm). Bleed the brake system and check for leaks. Adjust the brake pedal height, if necessary.

OVERHAUL

This is a tedious, time-consuming job. A lot of trouble can be saved by buying a rebuilt master cylinder from your dealer or a parts supply house. The small difference in cost between a rebuilding kit and a rebuilt part usually makes it more economical, in terms of time and work, to buy the rebuilt part.

NOTE: *Datsun has two suppliers of brake parts: Nabco and Tokico. These parts are not interchangeable. Be certain to get the correct rebuilding parts for the vehicle's master cylinder. The manufacturer's name is clearly stamped on the part.*

1. Remove the master cylinder from the vehicle.

2. Remove the reservoir caps and filters, then drain the brake fluid. Discard this fluid.

3. Using a small pry bar, pry the piston stopper snap-ring from the open end of the master cylinder.

4. Remove the stopper screw and the washer from the bottom of the master cylinder, then the primary and secondary piston assemblies from the master cylinder bore.

5. Remove the caps on the underside of the master cylinder to gain access to the check valves, for cleaning.

NOTE: *DO NOT disassemble the brake fluid level gauge, if equipped.*

6. Discard all the used rubber parts and gaskets. These parts should be replaced with

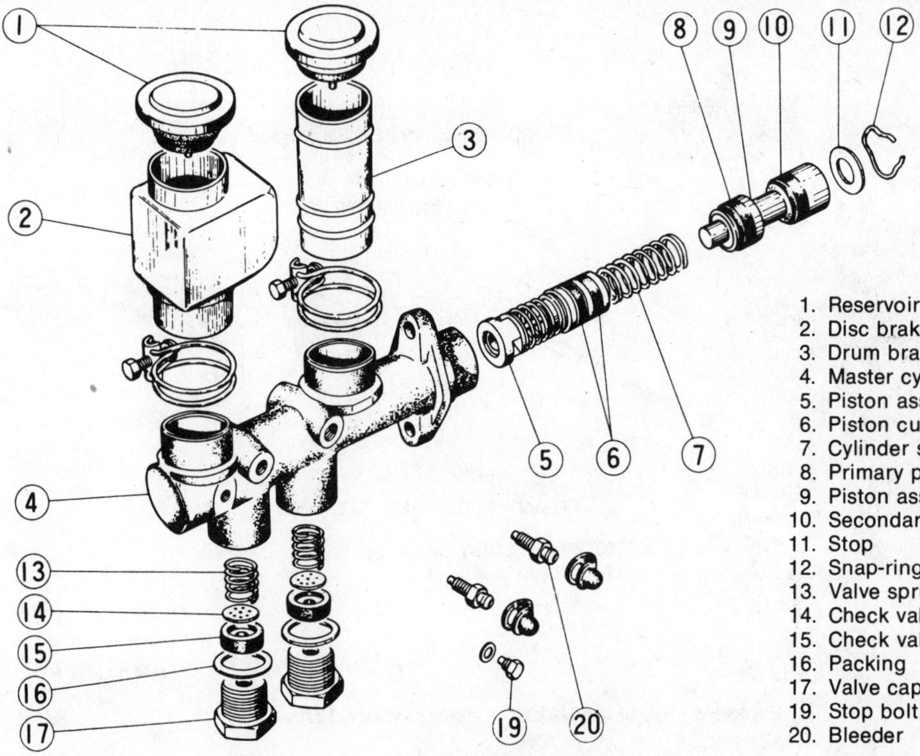

BRAKES 233

1. Reservoir cap
2. Disc brake reservoir
3. Drum brake reservoir
4. Master cylinder
5. Piston assembly (A)
6. Piston cup
7. Cylinder spring
8. Primary piston cup
9. Piston assembly (B)
10. Secondary piston cup
11. Stop
12. Snap-ring
13. Valve spring
14. Check valve assembly
15. Check valve assembly
16. Packing
17. Valve cap screw
19. Stop bolt
20. Bleeder

1970–72 master cylinder

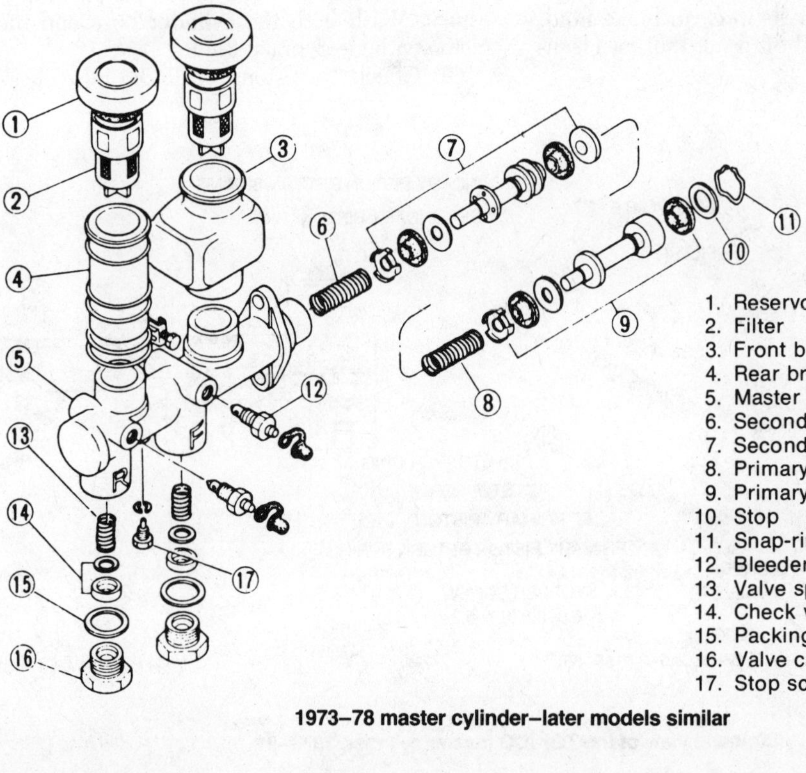

1. Reservoir cap
2. Filter
3. Front brake fluid reservoir
4. Rear brake fluid reservoir
5. Master cylinder body
6. Secondary piston return spring
7. Secondary piston assembly
8. Primary piston return spring
9. Primary piston assembly
10. Stop
11. Snap-ring
12. Bleeder
13. Valve spring
14. Check valve assembly
15. Packing
16. Valve cap
17. Stop screw

1973–78 master cylinder–later models similar

234 BRAKES

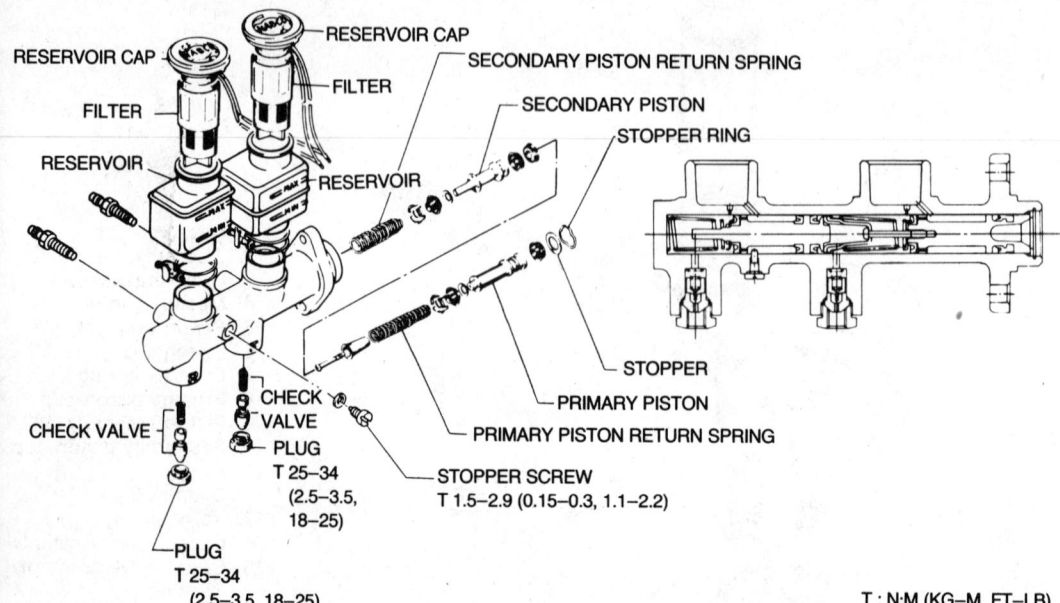

Exploded view of the NABCO master cylinder, 1979–81

the new components included in the rebuilding kit.

NOTE: *DO NOT remove the master cylinder reservoir tanks unless they are leaking. If they are removed for any reason, they must be replaced with new ones.*

7. Clean all the parts in clean brake fluid. DO NOT use mineral oil or alcohol for cleaning.

8. Check the cylinder bore and piston for wear, scoring, corrosion or any other damage. The piston and cylinder bore can be dressed with crocus cloth soaked in brake fluid. Move the crocus cloth around the cylinder bore, not in and out. Do the same to the piston, if necessary. Wash both the cylinder bore and the piston with clean brake fluid.

9. Check the piston-to-cylinder bore clear-

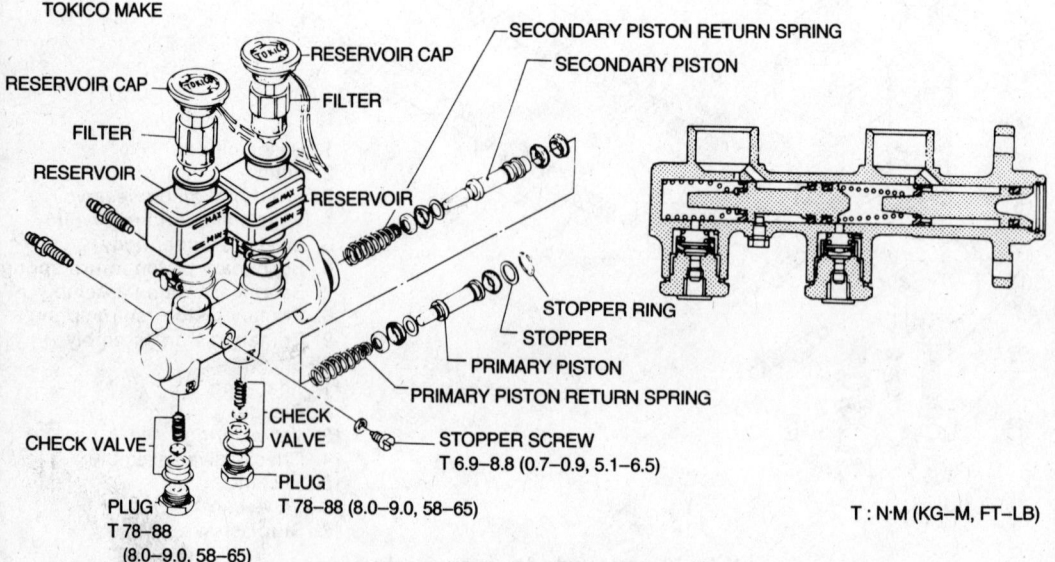

Exploded view of the TOKICO master cylinder, 1979–81

BRAKES 235

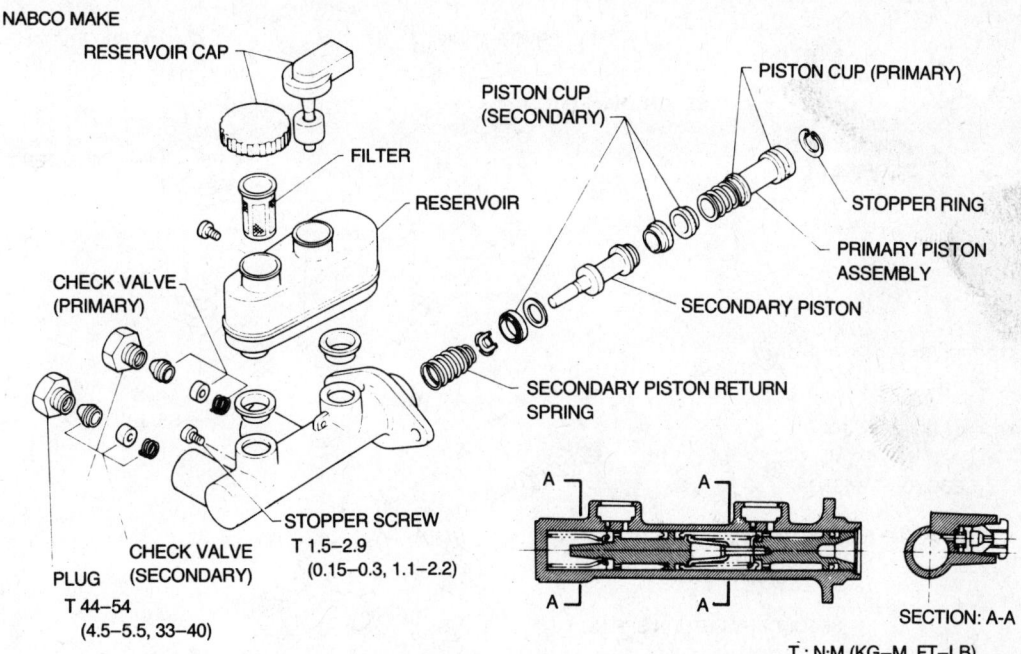

Exploded view of the NABCO master cylinder, 1982–83

ance; it should measure less than 0.0059 in. (0.15 mm) for all models. If a larger clearance exists, replace the piston, the cylinder or both. The cylinder bore diameter should be ⅞ in. (22.23 mm) for 1970–78 or 15/16 in. (23.81 mm) for 1979 and later.

10. Assemble the master cylinder in the reverse order of disassembly. Soak all of the components in clean brake fluid before assembling them.

11. Clamp the master cylinder in a vise by one of it's flanges. Fill the reservoirs with fresh

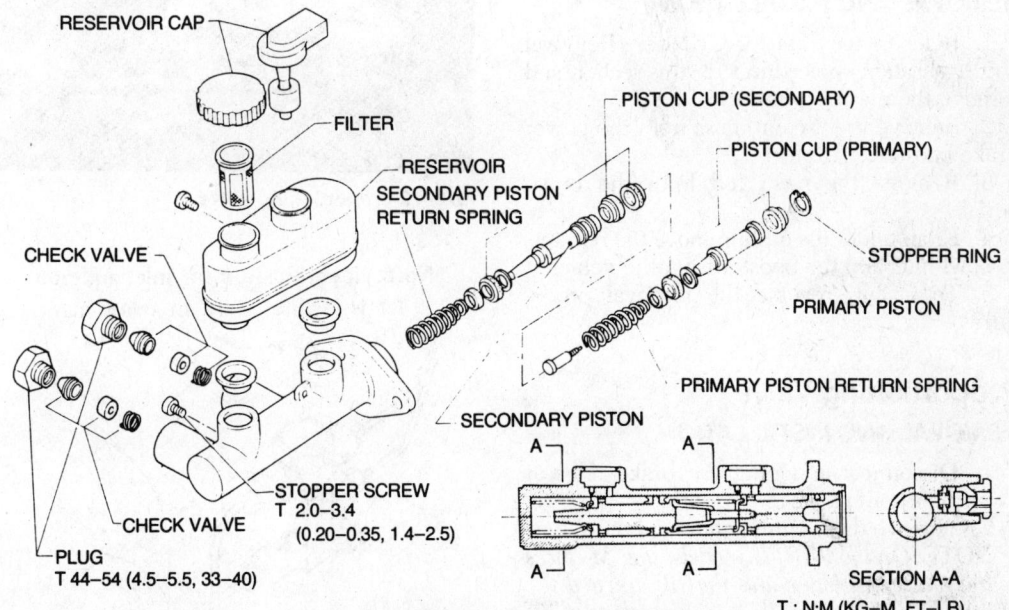

Exploded view of the TOKICO master cylinder, 1982–83

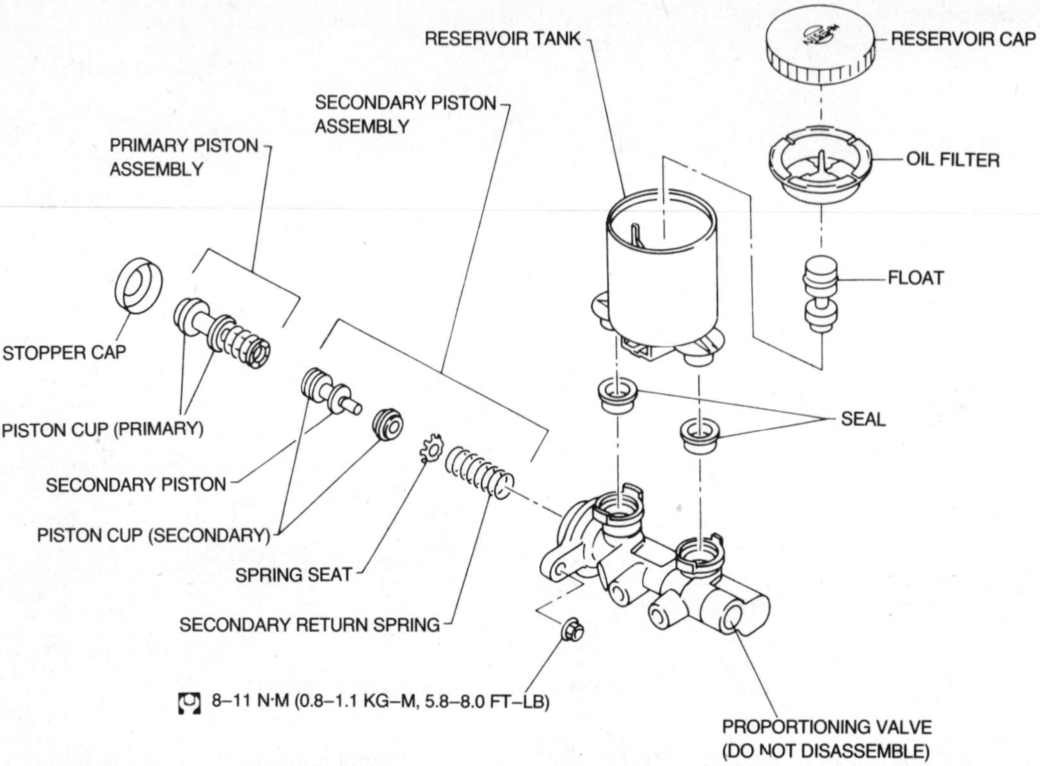

236 BRAKES

Exploded view of the master cylinder, 1984 and later

fluid and pump the piston with a screwdriver until fluid squirts from the outlet ports. Install the master cylinder and bleed the system.

Power Brake Booster
REMOVAL AND INSTALLATION

1. Refer to the "Master Cylinder, Removal and Installation" procedures, in this section and remove the master cylinder.
2. Remove the vacuum hose from the power brake booster.
3. Remove the push rod from the brake pedal.
4. From under the dash, remove the booster-to-cowl nuts and the booster from the vehicle.
5. To install, reverse the removal procedures.

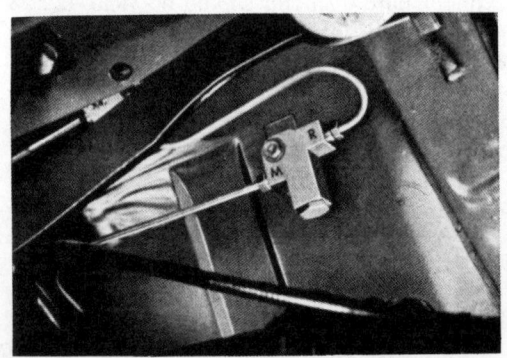

1970–72 proportioning valve

Proportioning Valve
REMOVAL AND INSTALLATION

1. Disconnect and plug the brake lines at the proportioning valve.
2. Remove the mounting bolt and the valve.
NOTE: *On the 1970–72 models, the "M" faces the master cylinder and the "R" toward the rear brakes. On the 1973–83 models, the "F" faces the front brakes and the arrow faces*

Note: Identification for inlet and outlet is facilitated by an arrow mark.

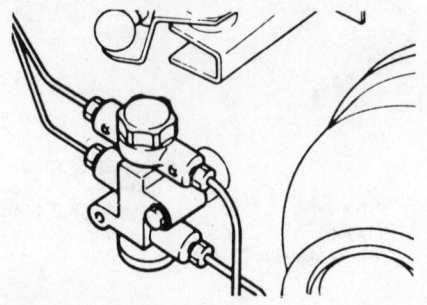

Typical proportioning valve

BRAKES

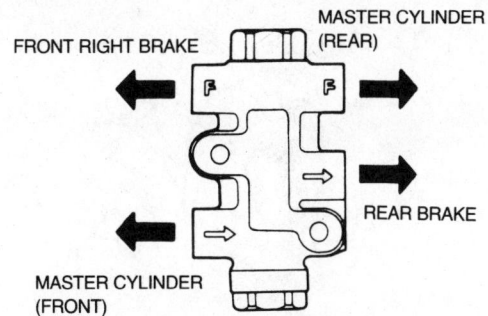

View of the proportioning valve, 1973–83

the rear brake side. On the 1984 and later models, the proportioning valve is part of the master cylinder. DO NOT disassemble the valve.

3. To install, reverse the removal procedures. Bleed the brake system.

Brake Warning Light System

1970–77

This assembly is unrepairable and must be replaced as a unit, if problems occur. Replacement is made by disconnecting the brake lines (use a flare nut wrench, to avoid damage to the lines) and removing the part. Install the lines onto the new switch and bleed the system.

1978–83

The warning light switch(s) are installed in the master cylinder reservoir cap(s) in these models. The switch(s) can be tested by removing the cap(s) in turn and holding it above the reservoir, allowing the switch float to drop to the bottom of it's travel. With the ignition switch ON and the parking brake released, the warning light should glow. If the switch(s) do not operate properly, they must be replaced. They are available only as complete units.

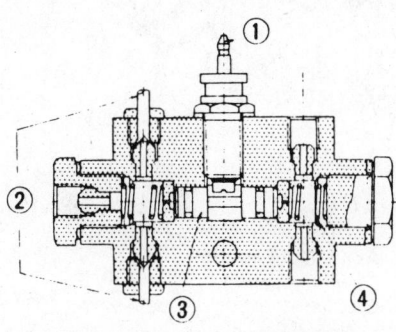

1. Wire terminal
2. Brake tubes
3. Valve assembly
4. Piston load spring

Cross-section of the brake warning light switch through 1977

1984 and Later

The warning switch is located at the bottom of the master cylinder reservoir. With the brake fluid removed from the reservoir, allow the float to settle to the bottom of the reservoir. With the ignition switch turned ON and the parking brake released, the warning light should glow. If the switch does not operate correctly, replace the reservoir tank.

Bleeding

The purpose of bleeding the brakes is to expel the air trapped in the hydraulic system. The system must be bled whenever the pedal feels spongy, indicating the that air has entered the system. It must also be bled whenever the system has been opened or repaired. An assistant will be needed for this job.

CAUTION: *Never reuse brake fluid which has been bled from the system.*

The sequence for bleeding is as follows:

a. 1970–78: Right rear, left rear, right front, then left front.

b. 1979–83: Master cylinder front, master cylinder rear, right rear, left rear, right front, then left front.

c. 1984 and later: Left rear, right rear, right front, then left front.

1. Clean the dirt from around the master cylinder reservoir cap(s). Remove the cap(s) and fill the master cylinder to the proper level with clean, fresh brake fluid meeting DOT 3 specifications.

NOTE: *Brake fluid picks up moisture from the air, which reduces it's effectiveness and causes brake line corrosion. Don't leave the master cylinder or the fluid container open any longer than necessary. Be careful not to spill brake fluid on painted surfaces; wipe up any spilled fluid immediately and rinse the area with clear water.*

2. Clean all the bleeder screws. Give each one a shot of penetrating solvent to loosen it; seizure is a common problem with bleeder screws, which often break off, sometimes requiring replacement of the part to which they are attached.

3. Attach a length of clear vinyl tubing to the bleeder screw on the wheel cylinder (or master cylinder). Insert the other end of the tube into a clear, clean jar, half filled with brake fluid.

4. Have the assistant slowly depress the brake pedal. As this is done, open the bleeder screw ⅓–½ of a turn and allow the fluid to run through the tube. Close the bleeder screw before the pedal reaches the end of it's travel. Have the assistant slowly release the pedal. Repeat this

238 BRAKES

process until no air bubbles appear in the expelled fluid.

5. Repeat the procedure on the other three brakes, checking the fluid level in the master cylinder reservoirs often. DO NOT allow the reservoirs to run dry, or the bleeding process will have to be repeated.

FRONT DISC BRAKES

CAUTION: *Brake discs contain asbestos, which has been determined to be a cancer causing agent. Never clean the brake surfaces with compressed air! Avoid inhaling any dust from any brake surface! When cleaning brake surfaces, use a commercially available brake cleaning fluid.*

Disc Brake Pads

INSPECTION
1970–78

The brake pads must be removed from the caliper for inspection. Refer to the removal procedures, in this section.

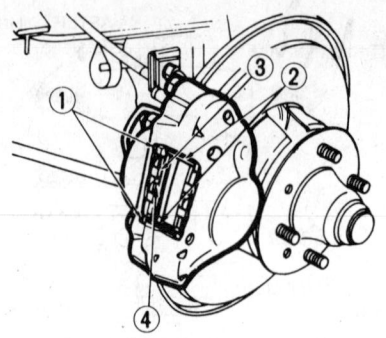

1. Clip
2. Retaining pin
3. Anti-squeal spring
4. Pad

Parts of the front disc brake through 1978

1. Clean the pad with a stiff brush.
2. Check the pad for:
   a. Heavy saturation with fluid or grease.
   b. Friction material thickness of less than 0.079 in. (2 mm) or overall thickness of less than 0.295 in. (7.5 mm).

NOTE: *If either "a" or "b" apply, replace both pads with a new set. This minimum thickness measurement may disagree with your state inspection laws.*

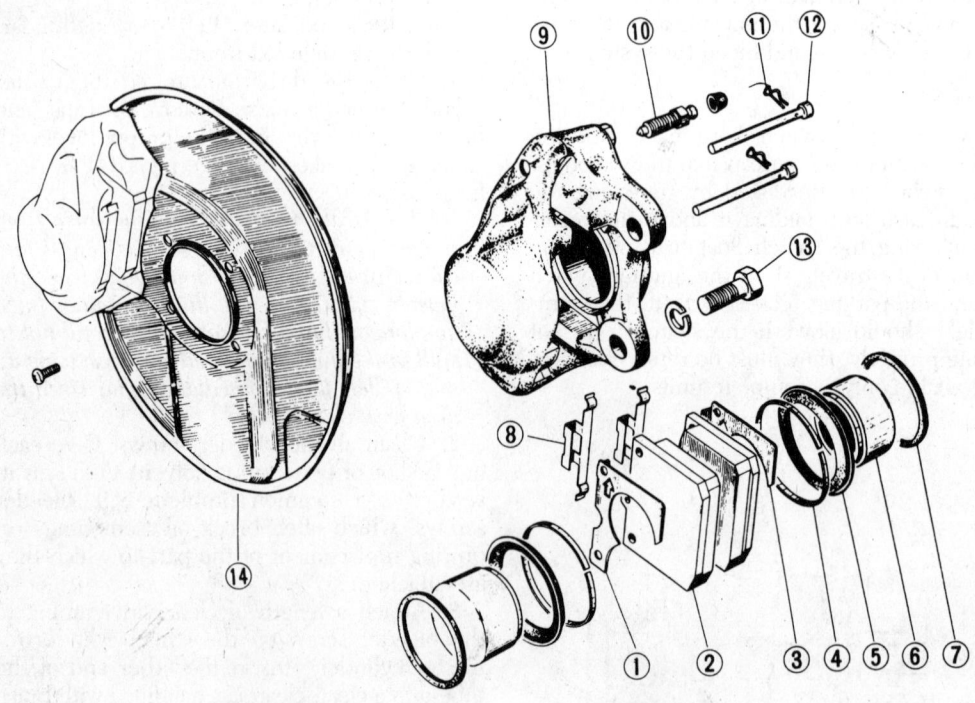

1. Anti-squeal shim (right-side)
2. Pad
3. Anti-squeal shim (left-side)
4. Retaining ring
5. Dust cover
6. Piston
7. Piston seal
8. Anti-squeal spring
9. Caliper assembly
10. Bleeder
11. Clip
12. Retaining pin
13. Caliper mounting bolt
14. Baffle plate

Exploded view of the S-16 Girling-Sumitomo front disc brake (1970–78)

1979 and Later

An inspection slot is provided in the top of the caliper for checking the pad thickness. However, if the thickness seems marginal, the pads should be removed from the caliper and checked. Minimum thickness for the pads is 0.08 in. (2 mm). This measurement may disagree with your state inspection laws.

NOTE: *Always replace all of the pads on both front wheels at the same time. When inspecting or replacing the pads, check the surface of the rotors for scoring or wear. The rotors should be removed for resurfacing if badly scored.*

REMOVAL AND INSTALLATION

1970–78

1. Raise and support the front of the vehicle on jackstands. Remove the wheel.
2. Remove the clips, the retaining pins and the anti-squeal spring.
3. Remove the pads and anti-squeal shim.
4. Clean all of the caliper and pad locating parts.
5. Loosen the master cylinder "F" reservoir cap. Using a C-clamp, force the piston back into the cylinder to accommodate the greater thickness of a new pad.
6. Apply a light coat of grease to the sliding surfaces of the caliper and both sides of the shim. The shim should only be greased along the round cut-out which fits around the piston.
7. Install the pad and anti-squeal shim. The shim arrow must point in the direction of forward rotation. Install the anti-squeal spring and retaining pin, then secure them with the clip.
8. Depress and release the brake pedal several times.

1979 and Later

1. Raise and support the front of the vehicle on jackstands. Remove the wheels.
2. Remove the lower pin bolt which retains the caliper to the torque member.
3. Rotate the caliper up and out of the way, exposing the pads. Do not try to move the caliper sideways.
4. Remove the pad retainers, the inner and outer shims, then the pads.
5. To install, clean the piston end and pin bolts.
6. Install a new inner pad. Rotate the caliper back down into place, slightly open the bleeder screw, then using a long bar, lever the caliper to the outside to press the piston into place. Rotate the caliper back up and out of the way.
7. Lightly coat the sliding surfaces of the torque member with grease. Install a new outer

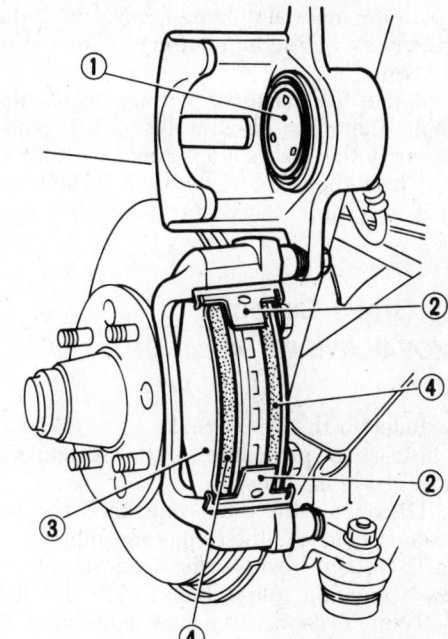

1. Inner shim   3. Outer shim
2. Pad retainer   4. Pads

Brake pad removal—typical 1979 and later

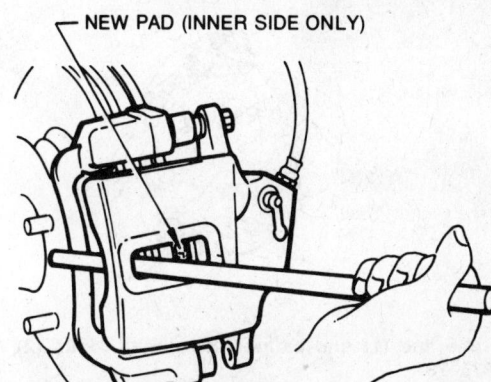

Lever the caliper to the outside to press the piston back—typical 1979 and later

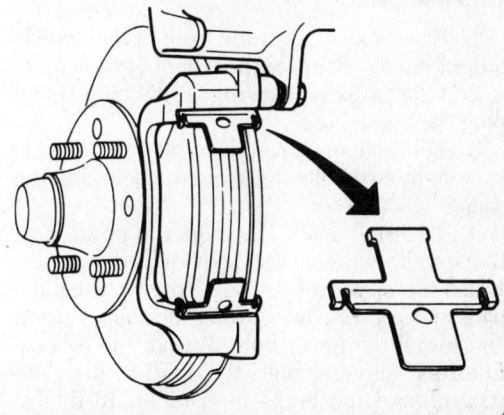

Pad retainer installation—typical 1979 and later

240 BRAKES

pad with the inner and outer shims. Install the pad retainers; be careful not to install them upside down.

8. Rotate the caliper down and install the pin bolt. Tighten to 16–23 ft. lbs. (22–31 Nm).

9. Apply the brakes a few times to seat the pads. Check the master cylinder level and add fluid if necessary. Bleed the brakes if necessary.

Disc Brake Calipers

REMOVAL AND INSTALLATION
1970–78

1. Refer to the "Disc Brake Pad, Removal and Installation" procedures, in this section and remove the brake pads.

2. Disconnect the brake line, then remove the caliper bolts and the caliper assembly.

3. To install, reverse the removal procedures. Torque the caliper bolts to 53–72 ft. lbs. (73–99 Nm). Reconnect the brake line and bleed the system.

NOTE: *When bleeding the brake system, it may be only necessary to bleed the line which was disconnected.*

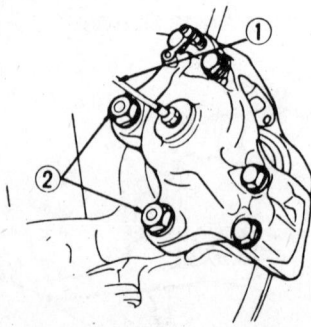

Brake line (1) and caliper installation bolts (2), 1970–78

1979 and Later

1. Raise and support the front of the vehicle on jackstands. Remove the wheel.

2. Using a flare nut wrench, disconnect and plug the brake hose.

3. The caliper is retained to the knuckle spindle by two bolts. Remove the bolts and the caliper assembly.

4. To install, place the caliper in position on the spindle without the pads or pad retainer. Install the upper caliper bolt loosely. Install the pads and pad retainer. Swing the caliper down and install the lower bolt. Torque the caliper-to-torque member bolts to 53–72 ft. lbs. (73–99 Nm) and the brake hose to 11–13 ft. lbs. (15–18 Nm). Bleed the brakes.

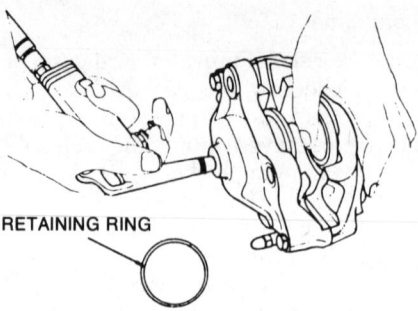

Removing the caliper piston, 1970–78

OVERHAUL
1970–78

The caliper halves must not be separated. If brake fluid leaks from the bridge seal, replace the caliper assembly.

1. Clean the caliper assembly of all accumulated mud and dust.

2. Remove the caliper from the steering knuckle.

3. Remove the retaining rings and the dust covers.

4. Hold one piston with a finger so that it will not come out and gradually apply air pressure to the brake line fitting. This should cause the other piston to come out but if the piston you are holding begins moving before the other, switch your finger over and remove the more movable one first.

5. Carefully push the other piston out.

6. With a finger, carefully remove both piston seals.

7. Thoroughly clean all parts in brake fluid.

8. Inspect, as follows:

 a. Check cylinder walls for damage or excessive wear. Light rust and etc., should be removed with fine emery paper. If the wall is heavily rusted, replace the caliper assembly.

 b. Inspect the pad, as previously described.

 c. Inspect the piston for uneven wear, damage or rust. Replace the piston if there is rust, as it is chrome plated and cannot be cleaned.

 d. Replace piston seals and dust covers.

9. Coat the piston seal with brake fluid and carefully install the piston seal.

10. Install the dust seal onto the piston. Coat the piston with brake fluid. Install the piston and seal assembly, then the retaining ring.

11. Repeat Steps 9 and 10 for the other piston.

1979 and Later

1. Raise and support the front of the vehicle on jackstands. Remove the wheels.

BRAKES 241

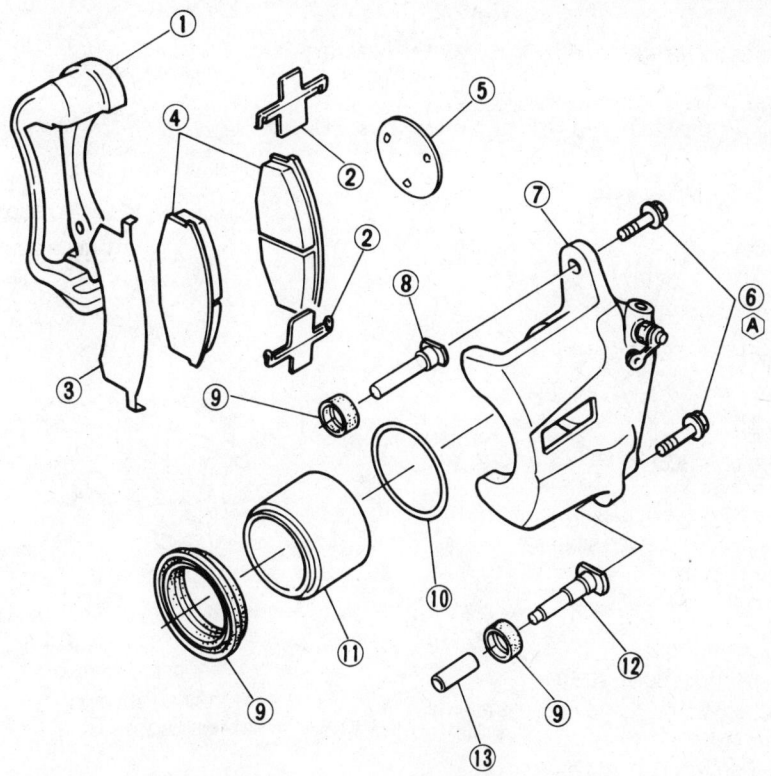

1. Torque member
2. Pad retainer
3. Outer shim
4. Pad
5. Inner shim
6. Pin bolt
7. Cylinder body
8. Main pin
9. Dust seal
10. Piston seal
11. Piston
12. Sub pin
13. Rubber seal

Tightening torque kg-m (ft-lb)
A : 2.2 to 3.2 (16 to 23)

Exploded view of the CL28V front disc brake—1979–83

2. Remove the brake hose, then plug the caliper and hose to prevent leakage.
3. Remove the two mounting bolts and the caliper from the spindle.
4. Remove the two pin bolts and separate the caliper from the torque member.
5. Remove the pad retainers and the pads.
6. Gradually apply compressed air to the fluid inlet, then remove the pistons and the dust seals. Remove the piston seals.
7. Check the caliper bore for scoring, wear, corrosion and/or etc. Minor damage can be cleaned up with crocus cloth but deep pits or wear warrant caliper replacement. The piston is plated and must not be polished.
8. Install the piston seals.
9. Lubricate the piston, dust seals and caliper bore with clean brake fluid. Install the dust seal to the piston, then install the other lip of the seal into the caliper bore groove. Install the piston.

10. Apply a thin coat of grease to the torque member (where it contacts the pads), the pin bushings and the pins.
11. Install the pin bolts, torquing them to 16–23 ft. lbs. (22–32 Nm).
12. Install the caliper.

Brake Disc (Rotor)

REMOVAL AND INSTALLATION

For further wheel bearing information, refer to "Wheel Bearing" in Chapter 6.

All Models

1. Refer to the "Caliper, Removal and Installation" procedures, in this section and remove the caliper.
2. Pry off the grease cap.
3. Remove the cotter pin, the adjusting cap, the wheel bearing locknut and the lock washer.

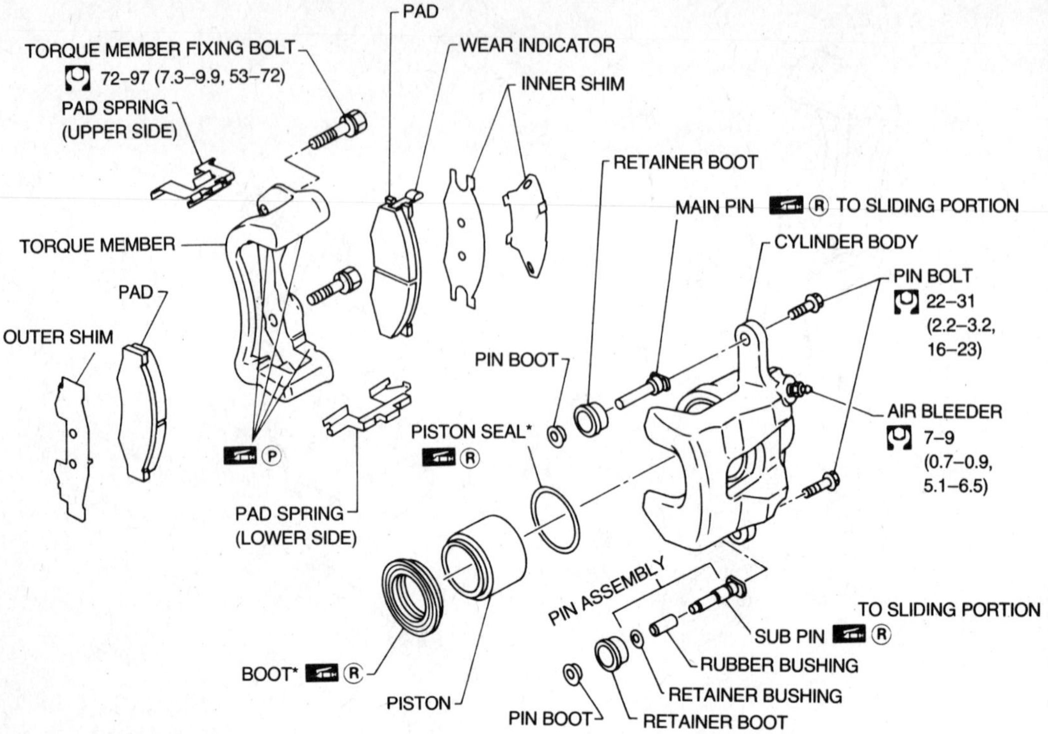

(P) : P.B.C. (POLY BUTYL CUPRYSIL) GREASE OR SILICONE-BASED GREASE POINT
(R) : RUBBER GREASE POINT
* : ALWAYS REPLACE WHEN DISASSEMBLED.

[torque] : N·M (KG-M, FT. LB.)

Exploded view of the CL28VA, CL28VB front disc brake—1984 and later

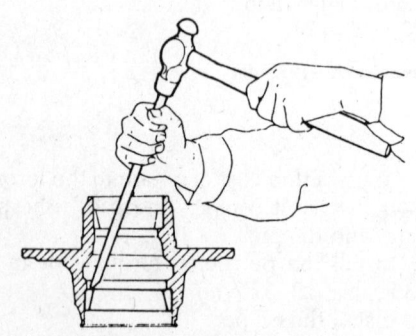

Removing the outer race

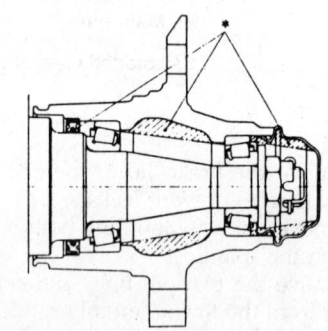

Greasing the points in the hub

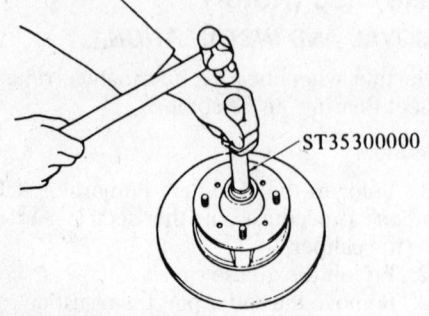

Installing the outer race

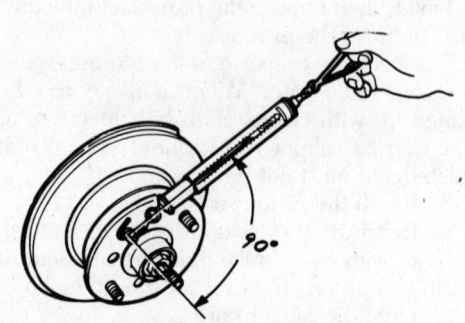

Checking wheel bearing rotation torque

BRAKES

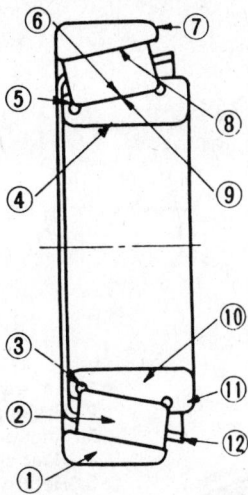

1. Outer race
2. Roller
3. Small collar
4. Collar surface
5. Inner race fitted surface
6. Inner race surface
7. Outer race fitted surface
8. Outer race surface
9. Roller rolling surface
10. Inner race
11. Large roller
12. Supporter

Wheel bearing

4. Remove the hub/rotor assembly from the spindle. Remove the seal and bearings from the hub.
5. Remove the rotor-to-hub bolts and the rotor.
6. To inspect the wheel bearings:
   a. Remove all of the old grease with solvent.
   b. Put the bearings back in position in the hub and slowly rotate to check for smooth rotation; check for roughness, burrs, discoloration or other defects. If any defects are noted, supply new parts.
7. Using a brass drift and a hammer, drive the outer bearing races from the hub.
8. Using the installation tool No. ST35300000, drive the new outer races into the wheel hub.
9. Install a new grease seal and grease in the wheel hub. Torque the rotor-to-hub bolts to 28–38 ft. lbs. (39–53 Nm) for 1970–79, 40–54 ft. lbs. (55–75 Nm) for 1980–83 or 36–51 ft. lbs. (49–69 Nm) for 1984 and later.

NOTE: *Fill the spaces between the rollers and the pocket in the seal lip with wheel bearing grease. Fill the hub and hub cap with grease as indicated in the illustration.*

10. To complete the installation, reverse the removal procedures. Torque the locknut to 18–22 ft. lbs. (25–30 Nm). Turn the hub back and forth several turns to seat the bearing and retorque the locknut to the same figure.
11. Turn the locknut back out at least 60° and up to 75° until the nut is aligned properly for the cotter pin.
12. Rotate the hub back and forth several times, then measure the starting torque at the wheel hub bolt with a spring scale. It should be 3.5–7.4 inch lbs. (0.40–0.83 Nm) with new parts or 0.9–3.9 in. lbs. (0.10–0.45 Nm) with used parts. Bleed the hydraulic system.

INSPECTION

1. Refer to the "Brake Caliper, Removal and Installation" procedures, in this section and remove the caliper.
2. Mount a dial indicator so that deflection at the center of pad contact surface can be measured. Maximum deflection is 0.0079 in. (0.2 mm) for 1970–78, 0.0039 in. (0.1 mm) for 1979–82 or 0.0028 in. (0.07 mm) for 1983 and later. If necessary, adjust the wheel bearing.
3. Measure the thickness of the rotor all the way around with a micrometer. Maximum variation should be 0.0012 in. (0.03 mm) or less with a used rotor and 0.0028 in. (0.07 mm) when new.
4. If the rotor is machined, the minimum thickness is 0.413 in. (10.5 mm) for 1970–78, 0.709 in. (18.0 mm) for 1979–83 or 0.787 (20.0 mm) for 1984 and later. Replace the disc if the minimum thickness will be less after machining.

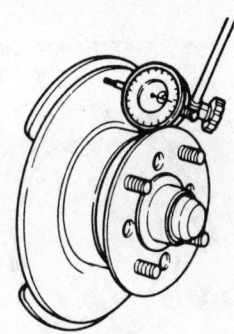

Measuring rotor deflection

REAR DRUM BRAKES

CAUTION: *Brake shoes contain asbestos, which has been determined to be a cancer causing agent. Never clean the brake surfaces with compressed air! Avoid inhaling any dust from any brake surface! When cleaning brake surfaces, use a commercially available brake cleaning fluid.*

244 BRAKES

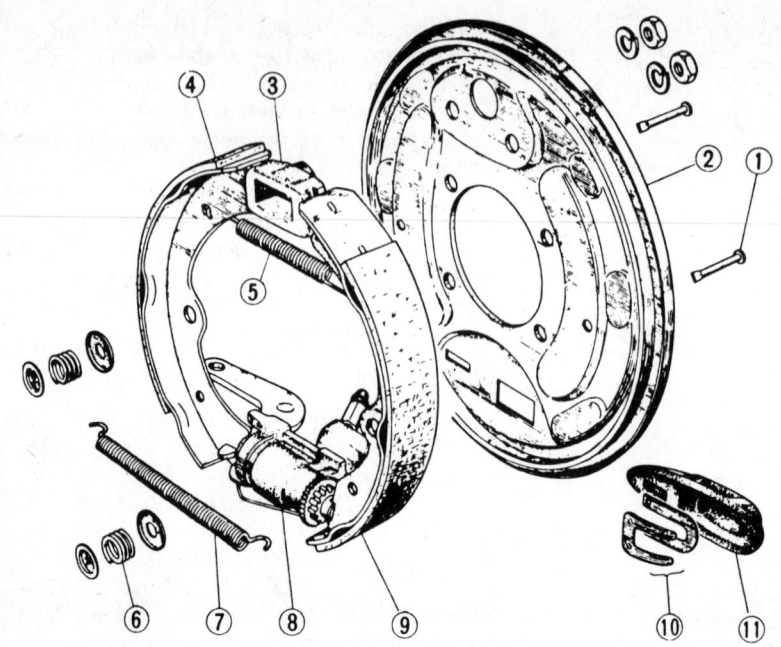

Disassembled view of the 1970–76 rear drum brake

1. Anti-rattle pin
2. Brake plate
3. Anchor block
4. Rear shoe assembly
5. Return spring
6. Anti-rattle spring
7. Return spring
8. Wheel cylinder
9. Front shoe
10. Retaining shim
11. Dust cover

Brake Drums

NOTE: *To remove the wheel bearings, refer to the "Wheel Bearing, Removal and Installation" procedures, in Chapter 6 and replace the wheel bearings.*

REMOVAL AND INSTALLATION

1. Raise and support the rear of the vehicle on jackstands.
2. Remove the wheel and the brake drum.
3. To remove a stubborn 1970–76 models drum, perform the following procedures:

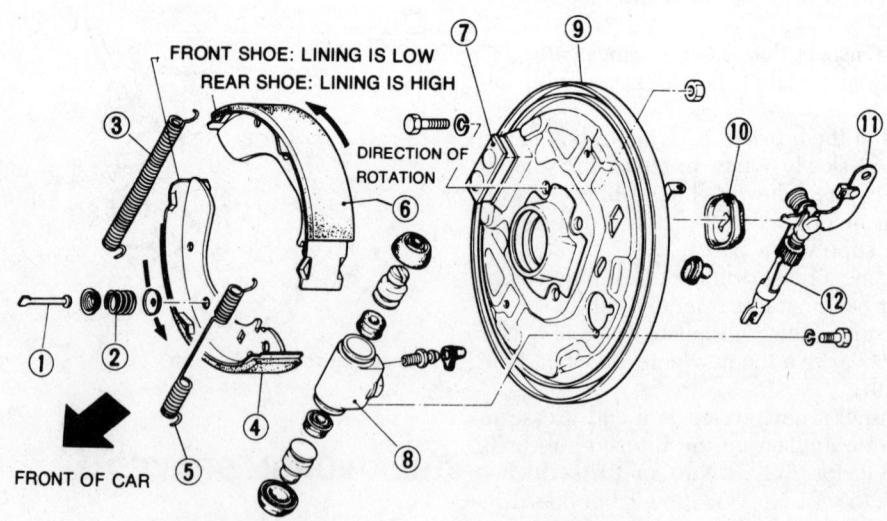

1. Anti-rattle pin
2. Anti-rattle spring
3. Return spring
4. Leading shoe assembly
5. Return spring
6. Trailing shoe assembly
7. Anchor block
8. Wheel cylinder
9. Backing plate
10. Dust cover
11. Parking brake toggle lever
12. Adjuster

Exploded view of the 1977–78 rear drum brake

BRAKES 245

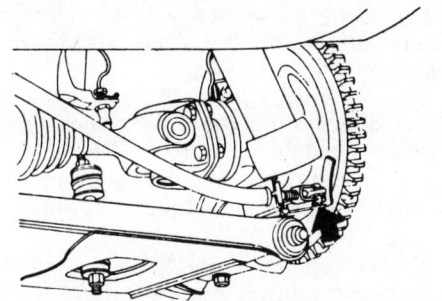

Disconnecting the handbrake cable (drum brakes)

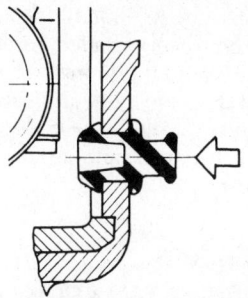

The adjusting hole plug (drum brakes)

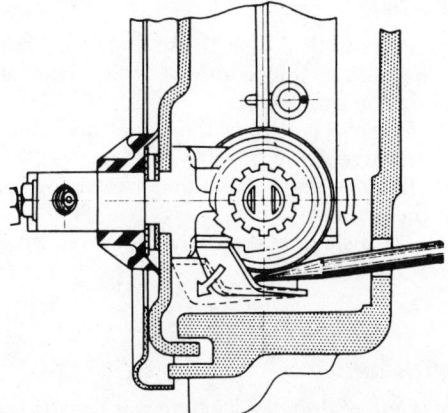

Turning the adjusting wheel (drum brakes)

a. Remove the handbrake clevis pin from the wheel cylinder lever and disconnect the handbrake cable.

b. Remove the plug from the adjusting hole in the drum, then using a screwdriver, remove the adjusting lever from the adjusting wheel.

c. Turn the adjusting wheel in a downward direction, using a screwdriver until the drum is movable. Remove the drum.

4. To remove a stubborn 1977–78 model drum, perform the following procedures:

a. Fully apply the handbrake.

b. Push or tap the cotter pin out and remove the stop from the parking brake lever on the rear of the drum.

c. Release the parking brake. Remove the drum.

5. To install the brake drum, perform the following procedures:

a. Install the drum onto the wheel studs.

b. Using a screwdriver and going in through the adjusting hole, turn the adjusting wheel in an upward direction until the brake shoes lightly touch the drum.

c. Reconnect the handbrake cable with the clevis pin. Operate the handbrake until the adjusting mechanism no longer clicks.

d. Install the adjusting hole plug making sure that it is installed so that the inner lip is on the inside of the drum all the way around.

e. Install the wheel and lower the vehicle.

INSPECTION

1. Remove the brake drum. Wipe out the accumulated dust with a damp cloth.

CAUTION: *DO NOT blow the brake dust out of the drums with compressed air or lungpower. Brake linings contain asbestos, a known cancer causing substance. Dispose of the cloth after use.*

2. Inspect the drum for uneven wear, wear in steps or scoring.

3. The drum may be machined until it reaches the wear limit shown in the "Brake Specifications" chart. The drum requires machining if the inner diameter is more than 0.0020 in. (0.05 mm) out-of-round.

Brake Shoes
INSPECTION

1. Clean the shoes with a stiff brush.
2. Check the shoes for:

a. Heavy saturation with fluid or grease.

b. Friction material thickness of less than 0.059 in. (1.5 mm).

NOTE: *If either "a" or "b" apply, replace both shoes with a new set. This minimum thickness measurement may disagree with your state inspection laws.*

REMOVAL AND INSTALLATION

1. Refer to the "Rear Brake Drum, Removal and Installation" procedures in this section and remove the brake drum.

2. Remove the anti-rattle springs.

3. Remove both brake shoes together.

4. To install, perform the following procedures:

a. Apply grease to the adjusting wheel, the threaded and the sliding portions of the adjust screw.

b. Apply multi-purpose grease to the

backing plate, the anchor block and sliding portions of the wheel cylinder, carefully avoid getting grease onto the lining surfaces.

c. Install the shoes, the anti-rattle springs and the return spring.

d. Install the drum and adjust the adjuster mechanism.

Wheel Cylinders

REMOVAL AND INSTALLATION

1970–76

1. Refer to the "Rear Brake Shoes, Removal and Installation" procedures, in this section and remove the brake shoes.

2. Disconnect the brake line (1) and remove the dust cover (2).

3. Drive out the locking shim (3) toward the front and remove the other shim by pulling it to the rear.

4. Remove the wheel cylinder.

5. To install the wheel cylinder, perform the following procedures:

a. Apply grease to the cylinder, the backing plate, the shims and the wheel cylinder lever fulcrum.

b. Place the cylinder into position and install shims in reverse of the removal procedure. Install the dust cover.

c. Measure the sliding resistance of the cylinder with a spring scale. It should be 4.41–15.43 lbs. (2–7 kg).

d. To complete the installation, reverse the removal procedures. Bleed the hydraulic system and adjust the adjuster.

1977–78

1. Refer to the "Rear Brake Shoes, Removal and Installation" procedures, in this section and remove the brake shoes.

2. Remove and plug the brake line. Use a flare nut wrench, if possible.

3. Remove the wheel cylinder retaining bolts and the wheel cylinder.

4. To install, reverse the removal procedures.

OVERHAUL

This is one of those jobs where it is usually easier to just replace the part rather than rebuild it. Rebuilding kits contain all the parts of a wheel cylinder except the body and piston.

NOTE: *Datsun has two suppliers of wheel cylinder parts: Nabco and Tokico. The parts are not interchangeable. Be sure to get the correct rebuilding kit for the parts on your vehicle. The name of the manufacturer is stamped on the wheel cylinder.*

1. Remove the wheel cylinder from the backing plate.

2. Remove the dust boots and the pistons. Discard the piston cup. The dust boots can be reused (if necessary) but it is better to replace them.

3. Wash all of the components in clean brake fluid.

4. Inspect the piston and piston bore. Replace them if corroded, scored or worn. The piston and bore can be polished lightly with crocus cloth. Move the crocus cloth around the piston bore, not in and out.

5. Wash the wheel cylinder and piston thoroughly in clean brake fluid, allowing them to remain wet for assembly. Lubricate the piston cups and dust seals with brake fluid.

6. Apply rubber grease sparingly to the inside of the dust boot lip.

7. Assemble the wheel cylinder and install it in the reverse order of removal. Assemble the remaining components and bleed the brakes.

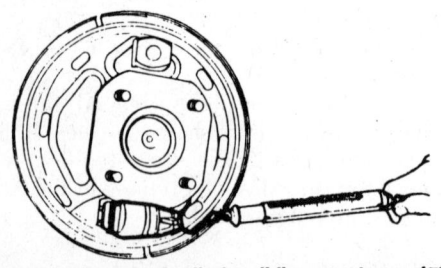

Measuring the wheel cylinder sliding resistance, 1970–76

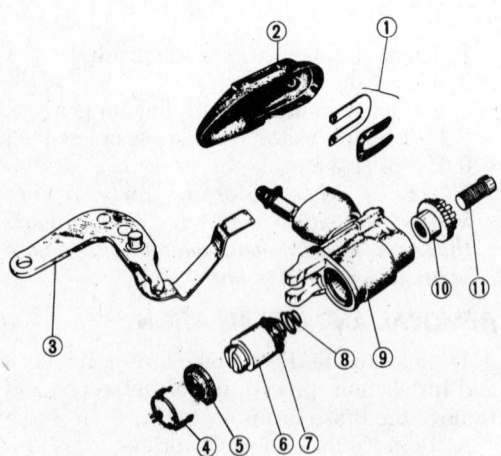

1. Retaining shim
2. Dust cover
3. Wheel cylinder lever
4. Retainer
5. Dust cover
6. Piston
7. Piston cup
8. Spring
9. Wheel cylinder
10. Adjust wheel
11. Adjust screw

Wheel cylinder components, 1970–76

REAR DISC BRAKES

CAUTION: *Brake discs contain asbestos, which has been determined to be a cancer causing agent. Never clean the brake surfaces with compressed air! Avoid inhaling any dust from any brake surface! When cleaning brake surfaces, use a commercially available brake cleaning fluid.*

Disc Pads

INSPECTION

1. Raise and support the rear of the vehicle on jackstands. Remove the wheel.
2. The pads can be inspected through the top of the yoke. However, it is better to remove the pads to measure their thickness.
3. Minimum pad thickness is 0.08 in. (2 mm). This minimum thickness may disagree with your state inspection laws.

NOTE: *If the pads are worn, always replace all of the pads on both wheels at the same time.*

4. Check the condition of the rotor while you are about the task of inspecting the pads. If it is scored, cracked or worn beyond the minimum thickness (0.339 in. (8.6 mm) replace it.

REMOVAL AND INSTALLATION

1. Raise and support the rear of the vehicle on jackstands. Remove the wheels.
2. Disconnect the parking brake cable.
3. Remove the clip at the outside of the pad pins.
4. Remove the pad pins. Hold the anti-squeal springs in place with your finger.
5. Remove the pads.
6. To install, perform the following procedures:

   a. Clean the end of the piston with clean brake fluid.

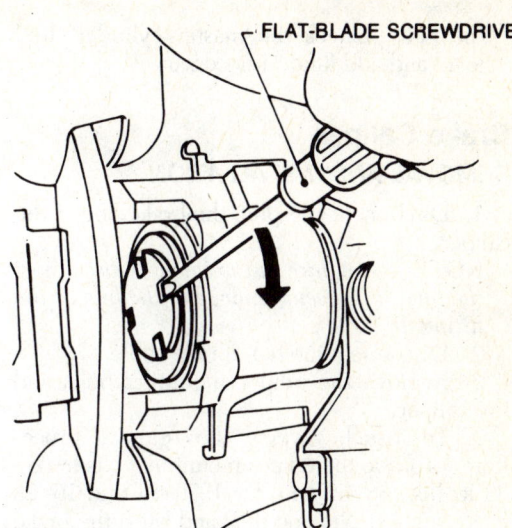

Push and turn the piston into the bore (rear disc brakes)

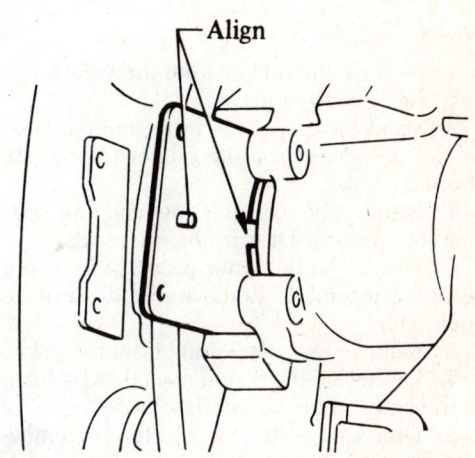

Align the tab with the piston notch (rear disc brakes)

   b. Lightly coat the caliper-to-pad, the yoke-to-pad, the retaining pin-to-pad and the retaining pin-to-bracket surfaces with grease. DO NOT allow grease to get on the rotor or pad surfaces.

   c. Push the piston into place with a screwdriver by pushing in on the piston while at the same time turning it clockwise into the bore. Then, with a lever between the rotor and yoke, push the yoke over until there is clearance to install the pads, equally.

   d. Install the shims, the pads, the anti-squeal springs and the pins. Install the clip. Note that the inner pad has a tab which must fit into the piston notch. Therefore, be sure that the piston notch is centered to allow proper pad installation.

   e. Apply the brakes a few times to center

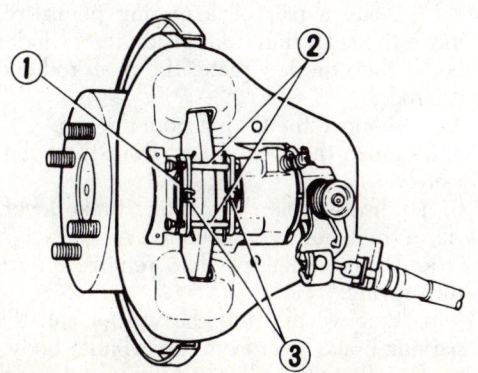

1. Clip   2. Pad pins   3. Anti-squeal springs

Rear disc brake pad removal, 1979 and later

the pads. Check the master cylinder fluid level and add fluid, if necessary.

Brake Caliper

REMOVAL AND INSTALLATION

1. Disconnect and plug the brake line at the caliper.
NOTE: *Use a flare nut wrench to disconnect the line, to prevent damage to the line or the fitting.*
2. Disconnect the handbrake cable.
3. Remove the caliper mounting bolts and the caliper.
4. To install, reverse the removal procedures. Torque the caliper mounting bolts to 28–38 ft. lbs. (38–52 Nm) for 1970–81 and 16–23 ft. lbs. (22–31 Nm) for 1982 and later; the brake line fitting to 11–13 ft. lbs. (15–18 Nm). Bleed the brake system.

OVERHAUL

1979–81

1. Remove the caliper from the vehicle.
2. Remove the pads.
3. Stand the caliper assembly on end, large end down and push on the caliper to separate it from the yoke.
4. Remove the retaining rings and dust seals from both pistons. Discard the dust seals.
5. Push in on the outer piston to force out the piston assembly. Remove and discard the piston seals.
6. Remove the yoke spring from the yoke.
7. Disengage the piston assembly by turning the outer piston counterclockwise.
8. Disassemble the outer piston by removing the snap ring.
9. Disassemble the inner piston by removing the snap ring. This will allow the spring cover, the spring and the spring seat to come out. Remove the inner snap ring, the key plate, the push rod and the strut.
10. To assemble the pistons, reverse the order of disassembly. Apply a thin coat of grease to the groove in the push rod, it's O-ring, the strut ends, the oil seal, the piston seal and the inside of the dust seal.
NOTE: *The piston seals, the dust seals, the oil seal and the push rod O-ring should be replaced with new ones whenever the caliper is disassembled. New parts are included in the rebuilding kit.*
11. Install the piston seals. Apply a thin coat of grease to the groove in the sliding surfaces of the piston and caliper bore. Install the pistons into the caliper. Install the retainers onto the dust seals.
12. Install the yoke springs on the yoke.
13. Lightly coat the yoke, the caliper body contact surfaces and the pad pin hole, with silicone grease. Assemble the yoke to the caliper.
14. Install the pads and the caliper.

1982 and Later

1. Remove the caliper from the vehicle.
2. Using a pair of needle-nose pliers, turn the caliper piston counterclockwise and remove it from the caliper.
3. To disassemble the piston, perform the following procedures:
   a. Using a small screwdriver, pry the snap ring from inside the piston.
   b. Remove the adjusting nut, the ball bearing, the wave washer and the spacers from the piston.
   c. Remove the cup from the adjusting nut.
4. To disassemble the cylinder body, perform the following procedures:
   a. Using a pair of snap ring pliers, remove the snap ring from inside the cylinder body, then the spring cover, the spring and the seat.
   b. Using a pair of snap ring pliers, remove the snap ring from inside the cylinder body, then the key plate, the push rod and the rod.
   c. Remove the O-ring from the rod.
5. Remove the O-ring seal from the cylinder body.
6. To disassemble the parking brake lever, perform the following procedures:
   a. Using a small pry bar, remove the return spring.
   b. Remove the nut, the washer and the parking brake lever from the cylinder body.
   c. Pull out the adjusting cam and the cam boot.
7. Before assembling the cylinder body, ap-

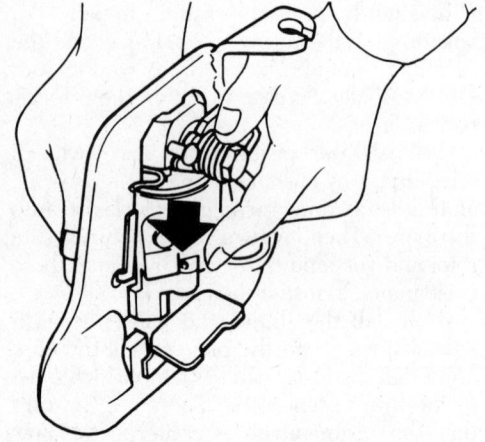

Push on the caliper to remove it from the yoke (rear disc brakes)

BRAKES 249

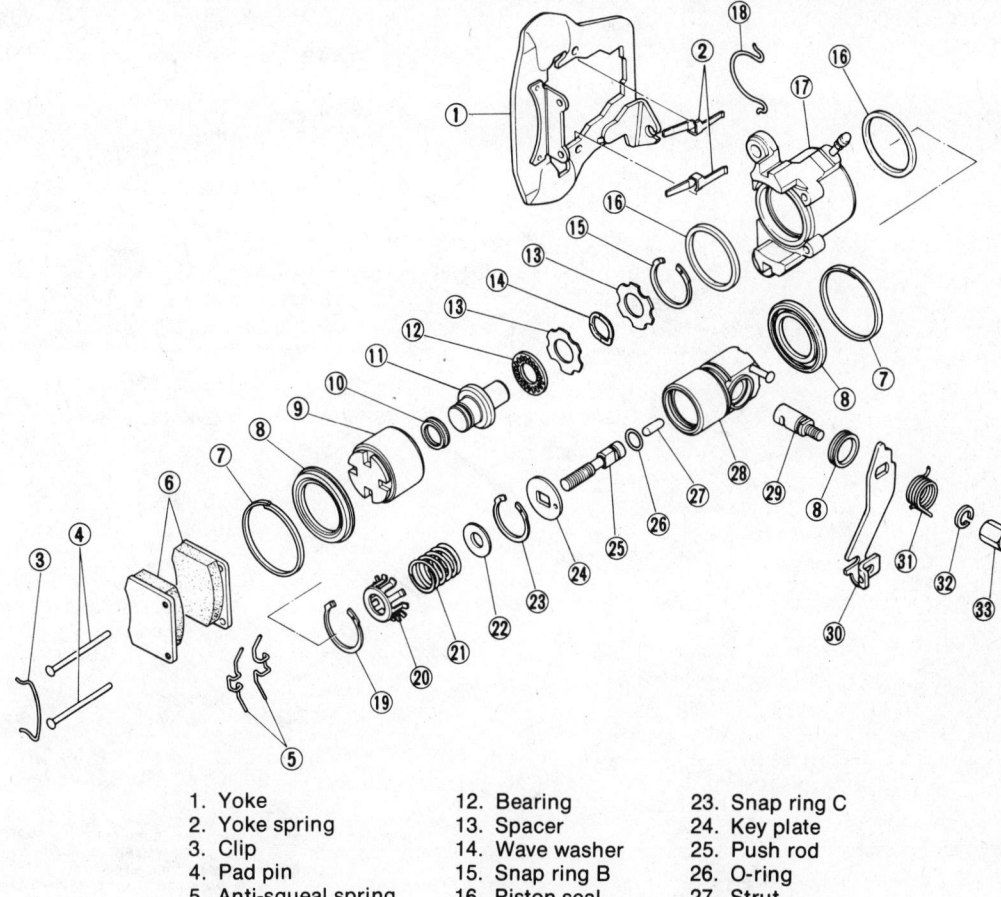

1. Yoke
2. Yoke spring
3. Clip
4. Pad pin
5. Anti-squeal spring
6. Pad
7. Retaining ring
8. Dust seal
9. Outer piston
10. Oil seal
11. Adjusting nut
12. Bearing
13. Spacer
14. Wave washer
15. Snap ring B
16. Piston seal
17. Cylinder body
18. Retainer
19. Snap ring A
20. Spring cover
21. Spring
22. Spring seat
23. Snap ring C
24. Key plate
25. Push rod
26. O-ring
27. Strut
28. Inner piston
29. Cam
30. Toggle lever
31. Spring
32. Washer
33. Nut

Annette AN14H rear disc brake assembly, 1979–81

ply a thin coat of rubber grease to the following items:

    a. The groove in the push rod and the new O-ring strut ends.

    b. The groove in the adjusting nut and the cup piston seal.

    c. Inside the boot.

    d. The sliding portions of the piston and the pins.

8. To assemble the cylinder body, use new seals and reverse the removal procedures. Use a hydraulic press to hold the spring in the compressed position, so that the snap ring may be installed.

Brake Disc (Rotor)

NOTE: *To remove the wheel bearings, refer to the "Wheel Bearing, Removal and Installation" procedures, in Chapter 6 and replace the wheel bearings.*

REMOVAL AND INSTALLATION

1. Refer to the "Rear Brake Caliper, Removal and Installation" procedures, in this section and remove the caliper.
2. Pull the rotor from the hub.
3. To install, reverse the removal procedures.

INSPECTION

1. Check the surface for wear or scoring. Deep scoring, grooves or rust pitting can be removed by refacing. Minimum thickness is 0.339 in. (8.6 mm) for 1970–83 and 0.354 in. (9.0 mm) for 1984 and later. If the rotor will be thinner than this after refinishing, it must be replaced.

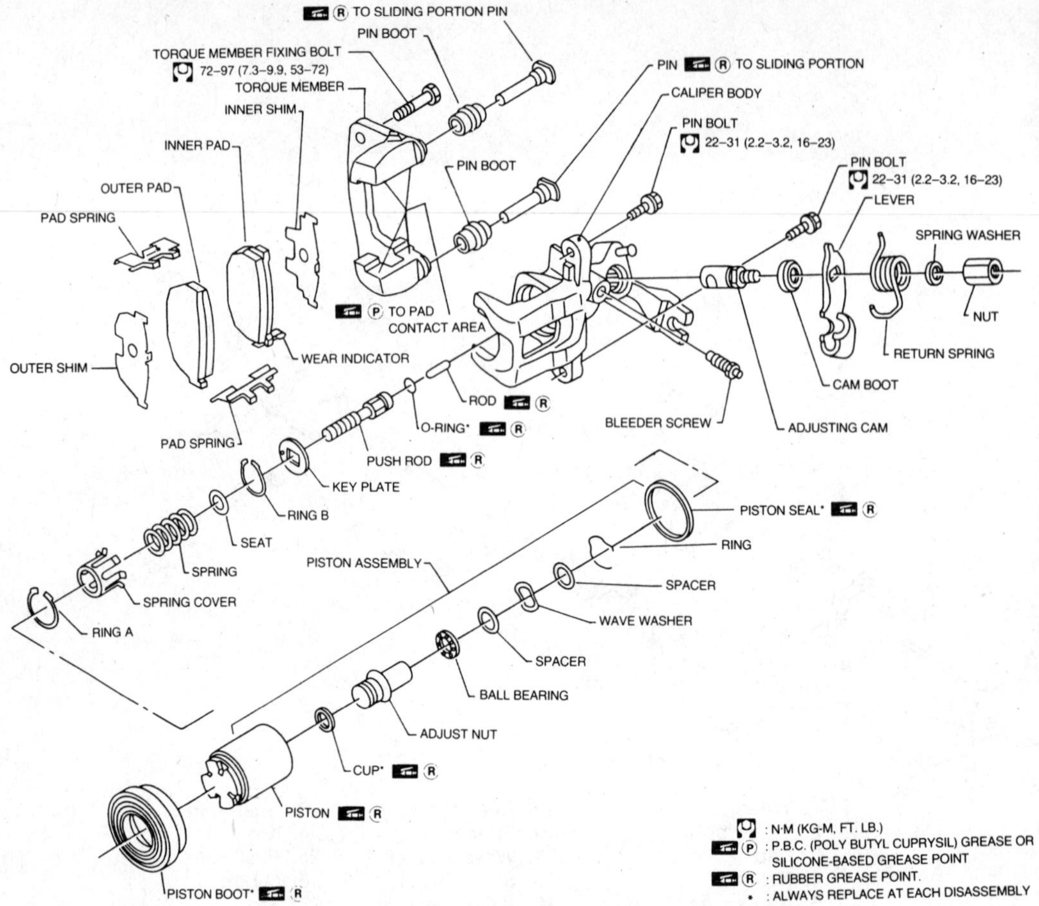

250 BRAKES

CL14H, CL14HB, rear disc brake assembly—1982 and later

2. Check the disc parallelism; it must be less than 0.0012 in. (0.03 mm). If over this specification, the disc must be replaced.
3. Install the disc and the wheel nuts. Check the runout with a dial indicator. If runout exceeds 0.0059 in. (0.15 mm) for 1970-81 and 0.0028 in. (0.07 mm) for 1982 and later, the disc needs to be refinished or replaced.

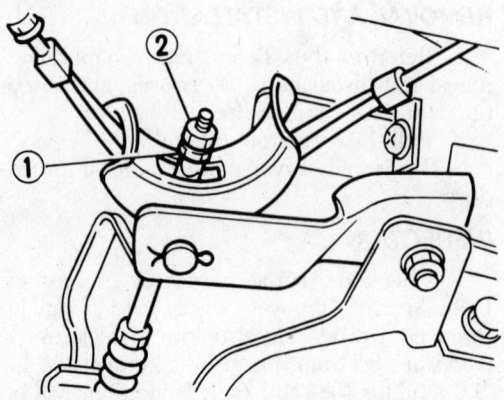

Parking brake equalizer; (1) is the adjusting nut and (2) is the locknut

PARKING BRAKE

Cable

NOTE: *The driveshaft must be removed, as described in Chapter 6, to adjust or replace the handbrake cable on the 1970-78 models.*

REMOVAL AND INSTALLATION

1970-78

1. Remove the hanger spring and clevis pin located at (3).

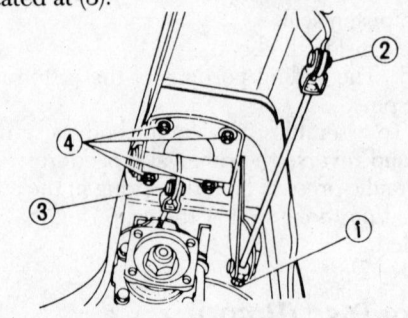

Handbrake locknut and adjusting nut (1), clevis pins (2 and 3), and brake handle mounting bracket bolts (4)—1970-78 models

BRAKES 251

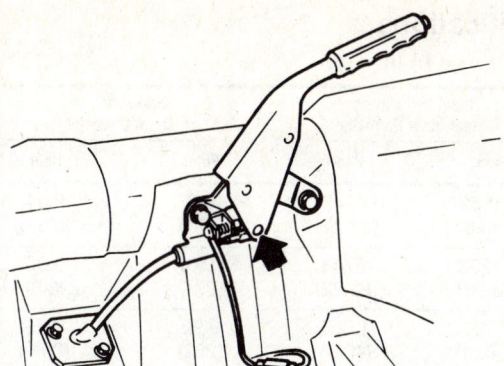

Front brake cable clevis pin—1984 and later

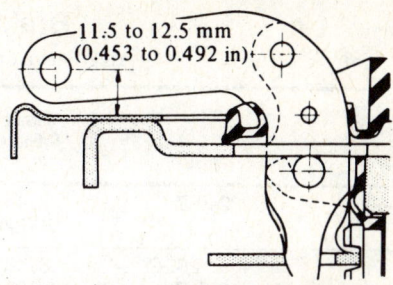

Handbrake adjustment dimensions, 1970–78

2. Remove the clevis pins at both wheel cylinder levers.
3. Remove the cable retainers at the wheels and disconnect the cable from both hanger springs.
4. Remove the retainers at the forward (equalizer end) and remove the cable.
5. To install, reverse the removal procedures. Adjust the cable.

1979 and Later

FRONT CABLE

1. Remove the passenger seat.
2. Disconnect the warning switch electrical connector.
3. Remove the two bolts securing the lever to the floor.
4. Working under the vehicle, remove the locknut, the adjusting nut and the equalizer.
5. Pull the cable out through the passenger compartment and remove it from the vehicle.
6. To install, reverse the removal procedures.

NOTE: *On the 1984 and later models, it may be necessary to separate the front cable from the lever by breaking the pin.*

REAR CABLE

1. Disconnect the cable at the equalizer.
2. Remove the cable lock plate from the rear suspension member and the rear discs.
3. Remove the clevis pin and clevis at the rear disc levers.
4. Disconnect the cable from the suspension arm. Remove the cable.
5. To install, reverse the removal procedures. Perform the adjustment procedures.

ADJUSTMENT

1970–78

1. Release the handbrake fully and block the wheels.
2. Loosen the locknut at the rear of the front rod.
3. Measure the dimension between the wheel cylinder lever pin hole centers and their respective buffer plates.
4. Rotate the front rod to bring the dimension to 0.453–0.492 in. (11.5–12.5 mm) on both sides.
5. Tighten the locknut at the rear of the front rod.

1979 and Later

1. Pull up the handbrake lever, counting the number of ratchet clicks for full engagement.

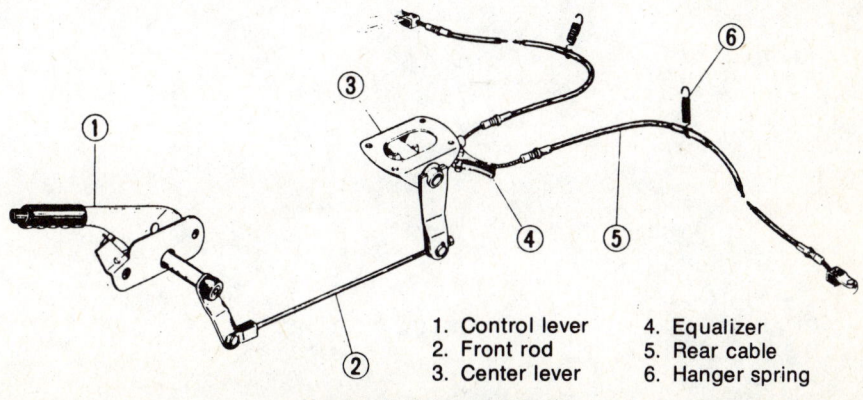

1. Control lever
2. Front rod
3. Center lever
4. Equalizer
5. Rear cable
6. Hanger spring

Handbrake linkage, 1970–78

Brake Specifications

All measurements are given in in. (mm)

Year	Model	Master Cylinder Bore	Wheel Cylinder or Caliper Inner Diameter		Brake Disc or Drum Diameter	
			Front	Rear	Front	Rear
1970–71	240-Z	.8748 (22.22)	2.1252 (53.98)	.8748 (22.22)	10.67 (271)	9.04 (229.6)
1972–78	240-Z, 260-Z, 280-Z	.8748 (22.22)	2.1252 (53.98)	.8748 (22.22)	10.67 (271)	9.00 (228.6) ①
1979–83	280-ZX	15/16 (23.81)	2.386 (60.6)	1.685 (42.8)	9.92 (252)	10.59 (2.69)
1984–86	300-ZX	15/16 (23.81)	2.386 (60.6)	1.685 (42.8)	9.84 (250) ②	10.16 (258) ③

① Wear limit: 9.055(230.0)
② GL, GL-L models—(274)10.79
③ GL, GL-L models—(290)11.42

Full engagement should be reached in 4–6 notches (79–83), 8–10 (1984 and later).

2. Release the parking brake.
3. Adjust the lever stroke at the cable equalizer under the vehicle: loosen the locknut and tighten the adjusting nut to reduce the number of ratchet clicks necessary for engagement. Tighten the locknut.
4. Check the adjustment and repeat as necessary.
5. After adjustment, check to see that the rear brake levers (at the calipers) return to their full off positions when the lever is released and that the rear cables are not slack when the lever is released.
6. To adjust the warning lamp, bend the warning lamp switch plate down so that the light comes on when the lever is engaged one notch.

Body and Trim

9

EXTERIOR

Doors

REMOVAL AND INSTALLATION

NOTE: *When removing the various components, be sure to place a cloth or padding onto the body to prevent scratching, soiling or damaging them.*

1. Refer to the "Door Panel, Removal and Installation" procedures in this section and remove the door panel.

NOTE: *If the doors are equipped with power components, it may be necessary to remove the lower trim panels (on each side of the vehicle) to disconnect the electrical connectors.*

2. Fully open the door and support it with a jack or jackstand.
3. Using the Door Hinge Wrench tool No. ST08720000, remove the door from the hinges.
4. To install, reverse the removal procedures. Adjust and torque the door hinges to 14–17 ft. lbs. (19–23 Nm) and the striker plate to 5.8–8.0 ft. lbs. (7.8–10.8 Nm).

ADJUSTMENT

NOTE: *On some models, it may be necessary to remove the front fender for adjustment purposes.*

1. Open the door fully.
2. Using the Door Hinge Wrench tool No. ST08720000, loosen the door hinges.
3. Loosen the striker plate.

NOTE: *With the hinges and the striker plate loosened, the adjustment can now be made by moving the hinges and striker plate up/down and in/out.*

4. Adjust so that the door can latch smoothly and aligns with the body.
5. Torque the hinges to 14-17 ft. lbs. (19–23

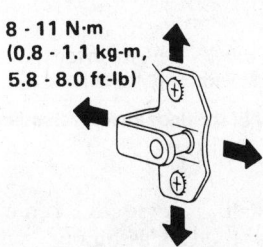

Adjusting the door striker on the 1984 and later models—other models are similar

Nm) and the striker plate to 5.8–8 ft. lbs. (7.8–10.8 Nm).

NOTE: *Be sure to grease the hinges.*

Door Locks

REMOVAL AND INSTALLATION

NOTE: *Some 1984 and later models are equipped with power door locks; removal and installation procedures are performed in the same manner as the manual systems. When removing the power lock, be sure to disconnect the electrical connector.*

1. Refer to the "Door Glass and Regulator, Removal and Installation" procedures, in this section and remove the door glass.
2. Remove the door inside handle retaining screws, disengage the control rods from the bell crank and door lock, then remove the inside handle assembly.

NOTE: *On the GS30 (2 + 2 seater), remove the rear remote control bracket retaining bolts and the rear inside handle.*

3. Loosen the bell crank assembly screws. Disconnect the key rod from the door lock and remove the door lock assembly with the bell crank.
4. Remove the door outside assembly.

NOTE: *Be sure to grease the sliding surfaces of the levers and the springs.*

254 BODY AND TRIM

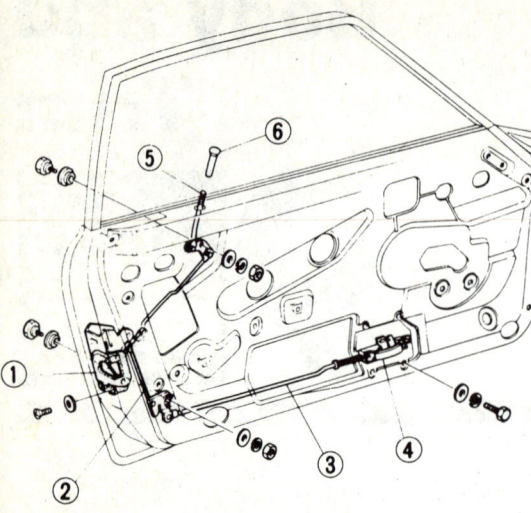

1. Door lock
2. Connecting rod
3. Remote control rod
4. Door remote control handle
5. Knob rod
6. Lock knob

Exploded view of the door lock mechanism, for 1970–78 S30

5. To install, reverse the removal procedures. Adjust the lock assembly.

ADJUSTMENT

NOTE: *On some models, it may be necessary to remove the door glass and regulator assembly to perform the adjustment procedure.*

1. Refer to the "Door Panel, Removal and Installation" procedures, in this section and remove the door panel.
2. Loosen the inside door handle assembly retaining screws and place it in the "Closed" position.
3. Adjust the inside door handle so that the lock inside lever can touch the lock base plate, then secure the inside handle.
4. Place the lock knob in the "Lock" position, then loosen and adjust the bell crank so that the lock knob play is minimal. Tighten the bell crank screws.
5. At the outside handle control rod, turn the nylon adjusting nut to obtain the clearance of 0.0–0.039 in. (0.0–0.53 Nm) for 1970–78, 0.0–0.020 in. (0.0–0.027 Nm) for 1979–83 or 0.020–0.059 in. (0.027–0.079 Nm) for 1984 and later, between the adjusting nut and the control lever.
6. With the adjustment complete, reverse the removal procedures.

Hood

REMOVAL AND INSTALLATION

CAUTION: *The removal and installation of the hood is awkward and cumbersome; two people are necessary to perform this operation.*

NOTE: *The hood of the 1970–83 models, open toward the front; it locks into place by a single stay. The hood of the 1984 and later models, open toward the rear; it is held open by two non-locking stays.*

1. Raise the hood. Place covers on the fenders to protect them from paint damage.
2. Using a scribing tool, mark the position of the hinges to the hood.

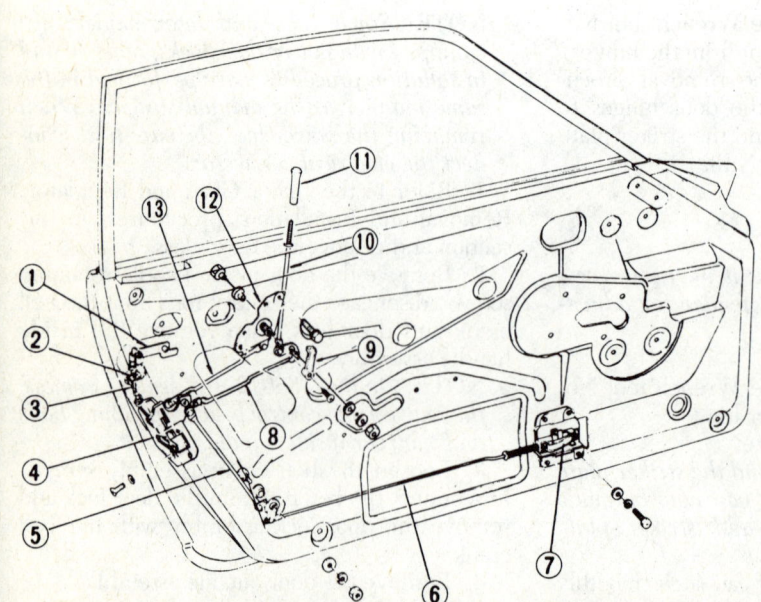

1. Outside door handle
2. Key cylinder
3. Outside door handle rod
4. Door lock
5. Connecting rod
6. Remote control rod
7. Door remote control handle
8. Rod
9. Rear inside handle
10. Knob rod
11. Lock knob
12. Rear inside handle bracket
13. Rod

Exploded view of the door lock mechanism, for 1970–78 GS30-2+2

BODY AND TRIM 255

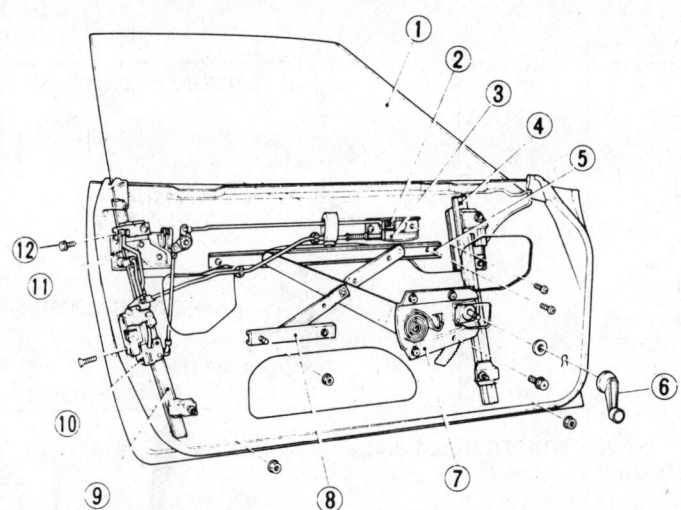

1. Door glass
2. Door lock knob
3. Door inside handle
4. Front guide rail assembly
5. Guide channel A
6. Regulator handle
7. Regulator assembly
8. Guide channel B
9. Rear guide rail assembly
10. Door lock assembly
11. Door outside handle
12. Rear guide rail upper securing bolt

View of the door lock and window regulator assemblies, for 1979–83 models—1984 and later models are similar

3. Holding both sides of the hood, remove the hinge-to-hood bolts, the stay(s) and the hood.
NOTE: *On the 1984 and later models, remove the stay-to-hood bolts.*
CAUTION: *The stays contents are under pressure. DO NOT take them apart, puncture or subject them to heat.*
4. To install, reverse the removal procedures. Align the hinge-to-hood scribe marks and torque the hinge-to-hood bolts to 5.8–8 ft. lbs. (7.8–10.8 Nm) for 1970–83 or 6.7–8.7 ft. lbs. (9.1–11.8 Nm) for 1984 and later, the stay-to-hood bolts to 12–15 ft. lbs. (16–21 Nm) for 1984 and later.

ALIGNMENT

1. For the fore and aft adjustment, perform the following procedures:
    a. Loosen the hinge-to-hood bolts and reposition the hood.
    b. Loosen the hood bumper lock nuts and lower the bumpers until they do not contact the hood when it is locked.
    c. Loosen the hood lock mounting bolts and set the striker at the center of the hood lock, then tighten the bolts temporarily.
    d. Torque the hinge-to-hood bolts to 5.8–8.0 ft. lbs. (8–11 Nm) for 1970–83 or 6.7–8.7 ft. lbs. (9.1–11.8 Nm) for 1984 and later.
2. To align the hood flush with the body, perform the following:
    a. Loosen the hinge-to-body bolts and the hood lock-to-body bolts.
    b. Move the hood and/or the hood lock up or down to obtain a flush fit.
    c. Torque the hinge-to-body bolts to 5.8–8.0 ft. lbs. (8–11 Nm) for 1970–83 or 6.7–8.7 ft. lbs. (9.1–11.8 Nm) for 1984 and later, the hood lock-to-body bolts to 5.8–8.0 ft. lbs.

(8–11 Nm) for 1970–83 or 12–15 ft. lbs. (16–21 Nm) for 1984 and later.
3. Raise the bumpers until they contact the hood in the locked position.

Hatch

REMOVAL AND INSTALLATION

CAUTION: *The removal and installation of the hood is awkward and cumbersome; two people are necessary to perform this operation.*
1. Open the hatch. Place covers on the body to protect them from paint damage.
2. Using a scribing tool, mark the position of the hinges to the hatch.
NOTE: *On the 1979 and later models, remove the rear roof rail trim, then disconnect the rear defogger and the rear window wiper electrical connectors and hose.*
3. Holding both sides of the hatch, remove the hatch-to-stay bolts, the hinge-to-hatch bolts and the hatch.
CAUTION: *The stays contents are under pressure. DO NOT take them apart, puncture or subject them to heat.*
4. To install, reverse the removal procedures. Align the hinge-to-hatch scribe marks, then torque the hinge-to-hatch bolts to 5.8–8.0 ft. lbs. (8–11 Nm) and the hatch-to-stay bolts to 2.7–3.7 ft. lbs. (3.7–5.0 Nm).

ALIGNMENT

NOTE: *The hatch adjustment is performed with the hatch hinges and the hatch door lock.*
1. To align the hatch to the body, perform the following procedures:
    a. Loosen the hatch-to-hinge bolts.
    b. Move the hatch left and right to obtain

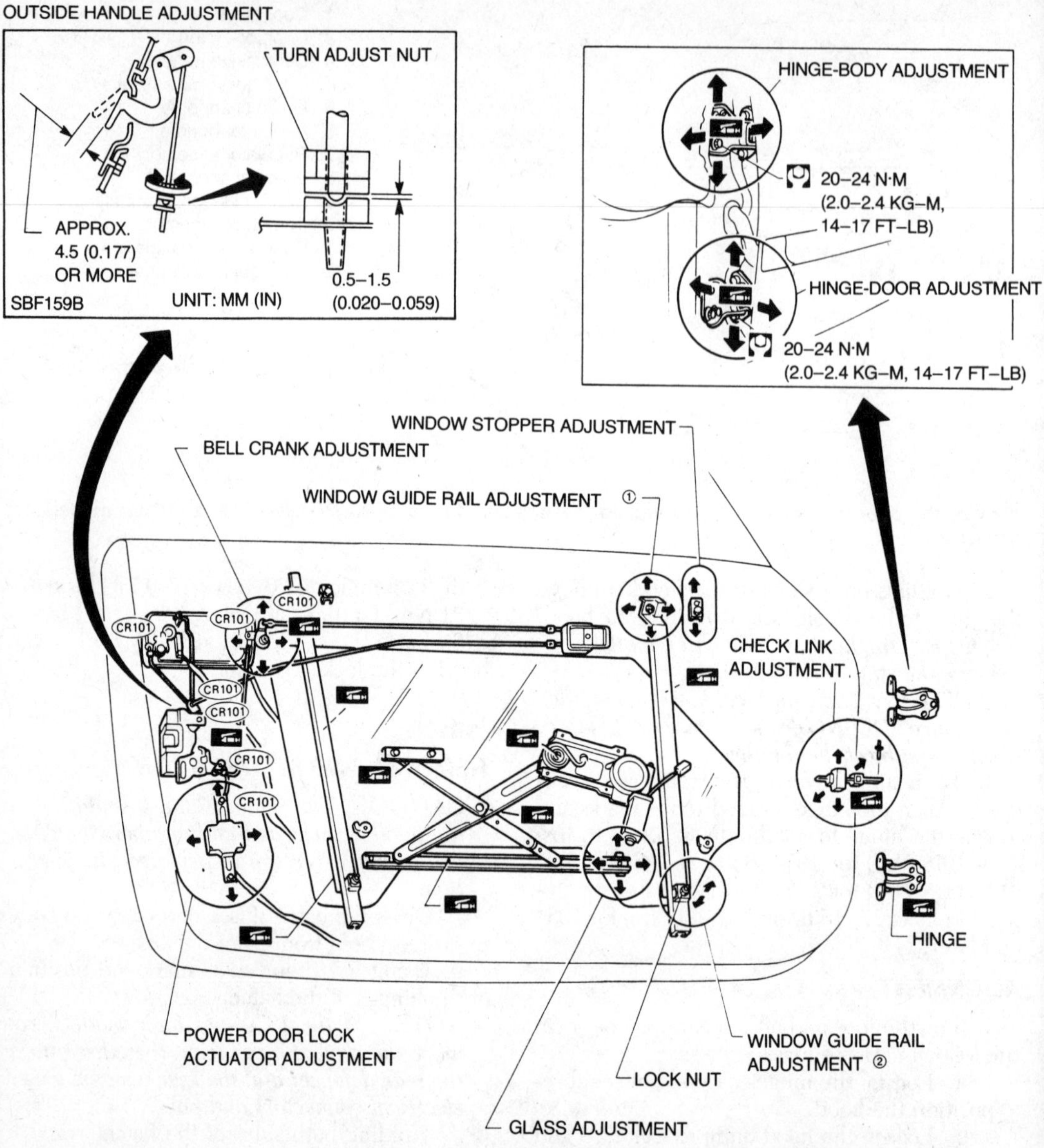

256 BODY AND TRIM

OUTSIDE HANDLE ADJUSTMENT

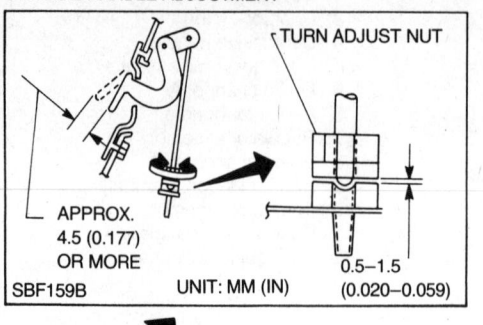

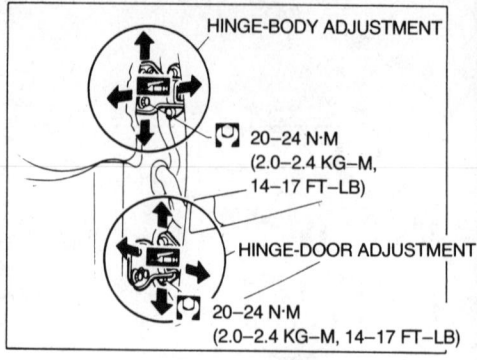

View of the 1984 and later door lock and window regulator adjustments—other models are similar

Centering the hood on the 1970–83 models

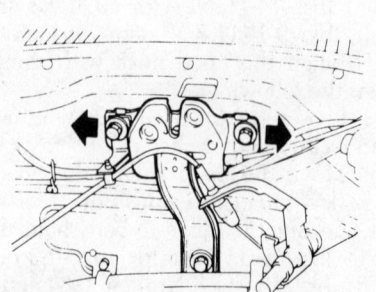

Centering the hood lock on the 1970–83 models

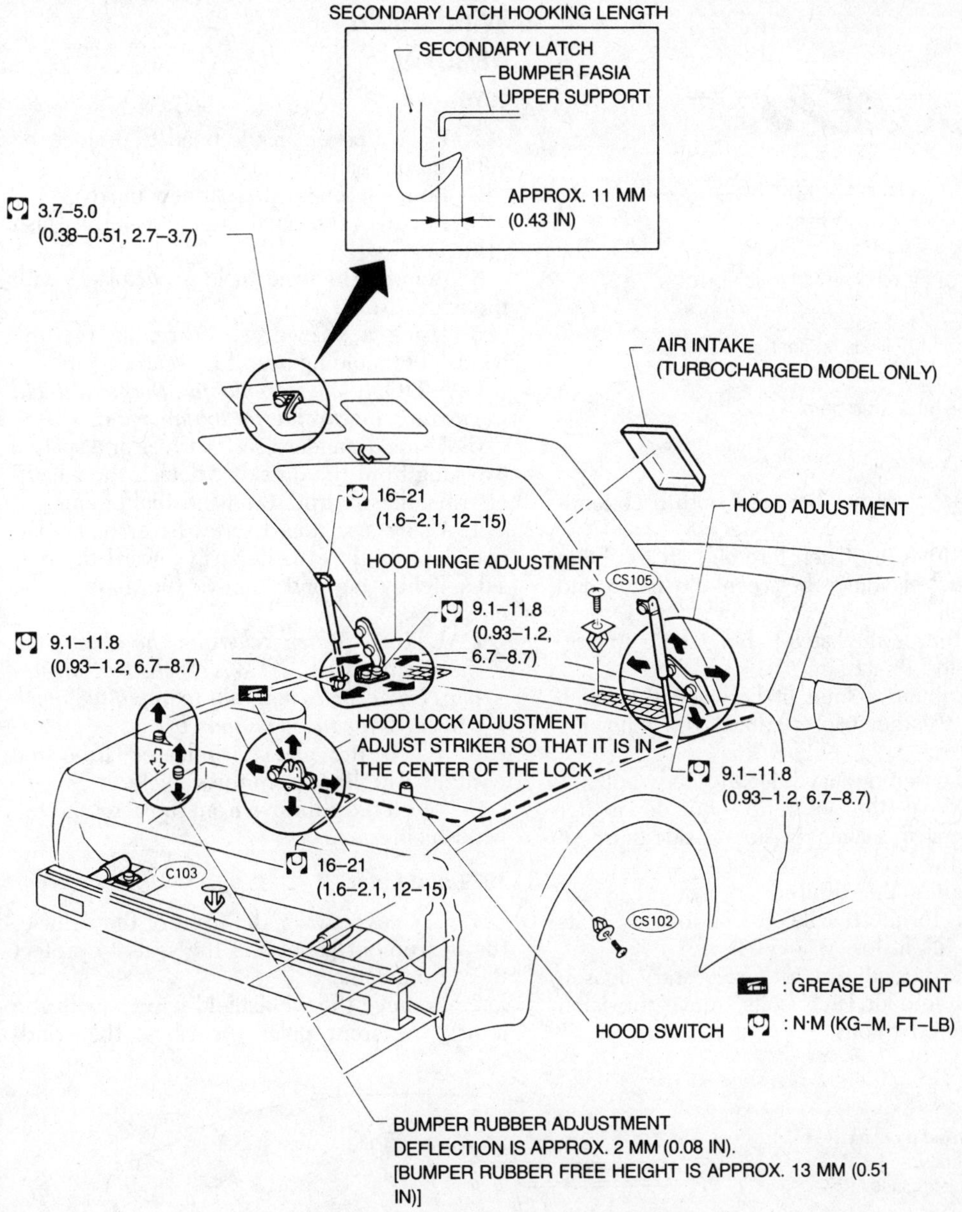

BODY AND TRIM 257

SECONDARY LATCH HOOKING LENGTH
- SECONDARY LATCH
- BUMPER FASIA
- UPPER SUPPORT

APPROX. 11 MM (0.43 IN)

3.7–5.0 (0.38–0.51, 2.7–3.7)

AIR INTAKE (TURBOCHARGED MODEL ONLY)

16–21 (1.6–2.1, 12–15)
HOOD HINGE ADJUSTMENT

HOOD ADJUSTMENT

9.1–11.8 (0.93–1.2, 6.7–8.7)

9.1–11.8 (0.93–1.2, 6.7–8.7)

HOOD LOCK ADJUSTMENT
ADJUST STRIKER SO THAT IT IS IN THE CENTER OF THE LOCK

9.1–11.8 (0.93–1.2, 6.7–8.7)

16–21 (1.6–2.1, 12–15)

CS102

: GREASE UP POINT
: N·M (KG–M, FT–LB)

HOOD SWITCH

BUMPER RUBBER ADJUSTMENT
DEFLECTION IS APPROX. 2 MM (0.08 IN).
[BUMPER RUBBER FREE HEIGHT IS APPROX. 13 MM (0.51 IN)]

View of the 1984 and later hood adjustments

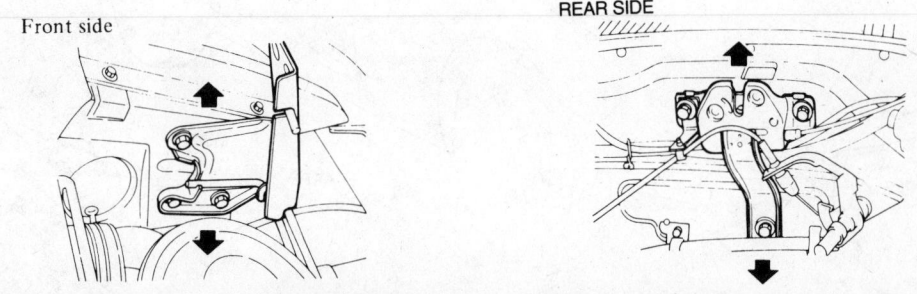

Front side | REAR SIDE

Adjusting the hood height on the 1970–83 models

258 BODY AND TRIM

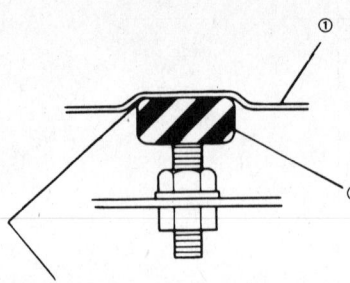

BE SURE TO CONTACT THIS PORTION.

1. Hood
2. Hood bumper rubber

View of the hood bumpers

an equal clearance between both back fenders.

   c. Move the hatch fore and aft to obtain an equal clearance between the hatch and the roof.

   d. Torque the hatch-to-hinge bolts to 5.8–8.0 ft. lbs. (8–11 Nm).

2. To obtain a snug fit between the hatch and the weatherstrip, perform the following procedures:

   a. Loosen the hatch lock-to-body bolts.

   b. Move the lock up and down (for weatherstrip sealing) or side-to-side (for centering the latch).

   c. After the desired adjustment is acquired, torque the hatch lock-to-body bolts to 2.7–3.7 ft. lbs. (3.7–5.0 Nm).

3. If further adjustment is necessary, loosen the hatch-to-door latch bolts, move the latch and tighten the bolts.

Windshield

REMOVAL

1970–78

1. Place a cover on the hood to protect the vehicle from paint damage.
2. Remove the inside rearview mirror.
3. Remove the instrument panel garnish plate.
4. Remove the windshield wiper blades with the wiper arms.
5. Using a screwdriver, carefully pry the windshield molding from the weatherstrip.

CAUTION: *When removing the windshield molding, be careful not to damage it.*

6. Using a standard screwdriver or a spatula (working from the outside), detach the weatherstrip adhesive from the windshield frame.
7. Using a standard screwdriver or a spatula, depress the weatherstrip toward the outside, lightly tap and remove the glass to the outside.

CAUTION: *When releasing the glass from the weatherstrip, ALWAYS start at an upper corner; be careful not to apply too much pressure, for the glass may break.*

8. When the glass is released from the weatherstrip, lift it from the vehicle.
9. Clean the adhesive from the glass and the windshield frame.

1979 and Later

1. Lay covers over the front of the vehicle, the instrument panel and the seats to protect them from damage.
2. Remove the windshield wipers (with the arms), the front pillar garnishes, the wind-

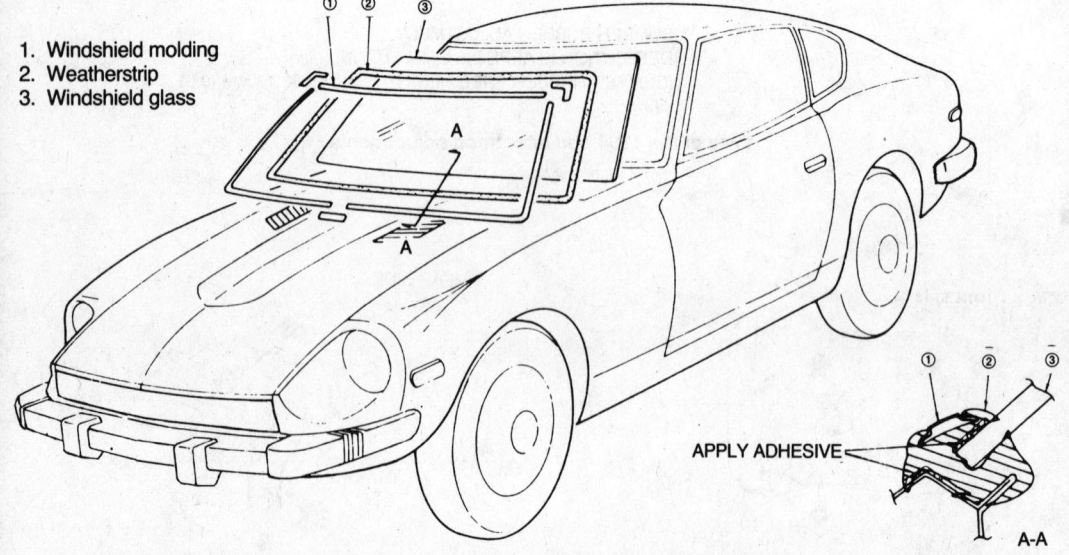

1. Windshield molding
2. Weatherstrip
3. Windshield glass

APPLY ADHESIVE

A-A

Exploded view of the 1970–78 windshield assembly and the cross-sectional view of the assembly

BODY AND TRIM 259

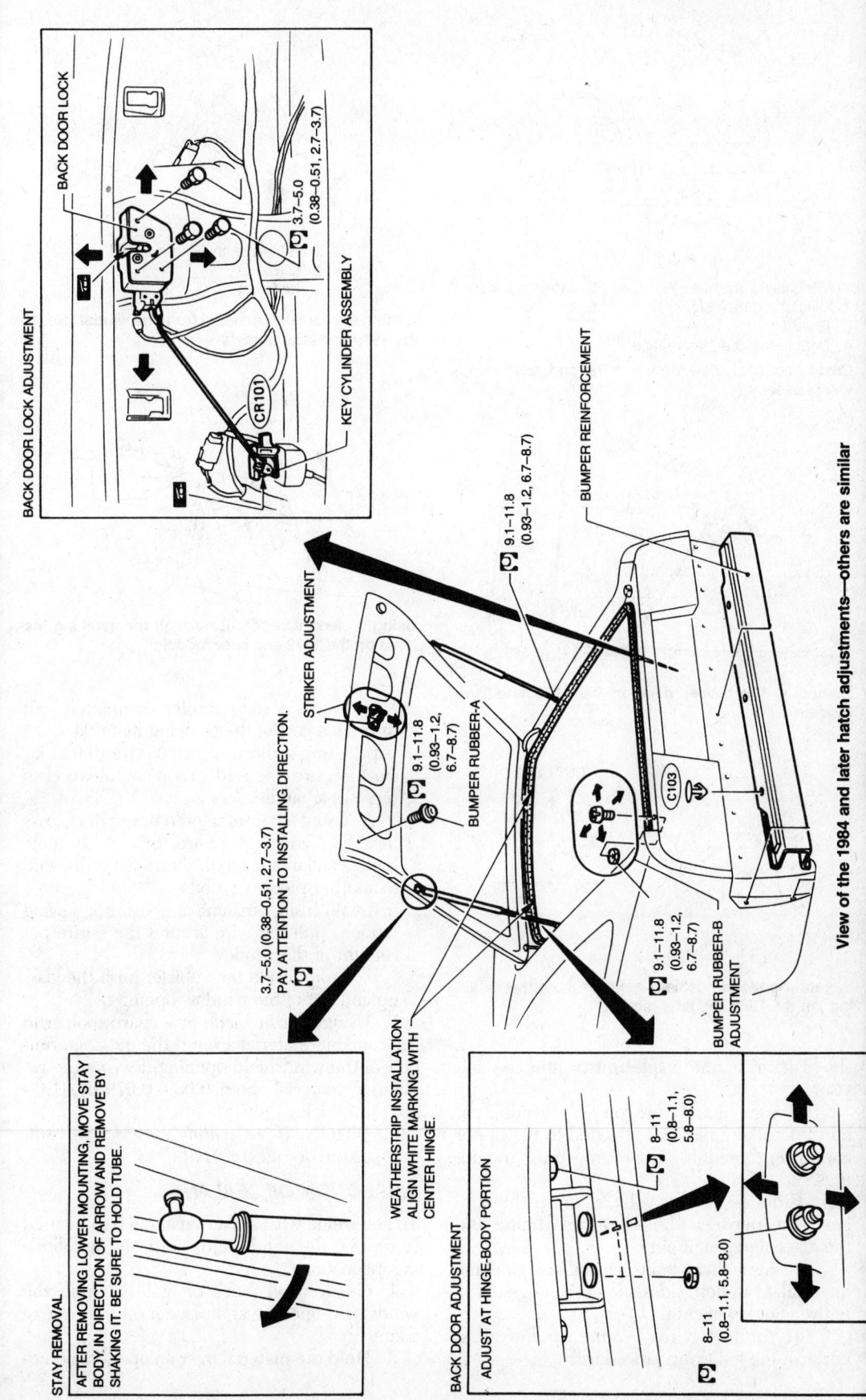

View of the 1984 and later hatch adjustments—others are similar

260 BODY AND TRIM

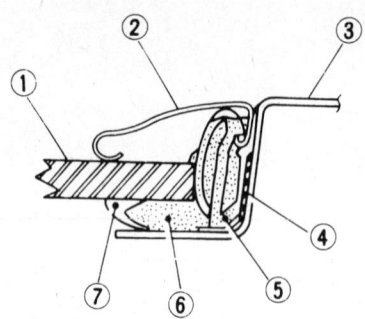

1. Windshield glass
2. Windshield molding
3. Body
4. Double-faced adhesive tape
5. Molding fastener
6. Sealant
7. Dam

Cross-sectional view of the 1979 and later windshield assembly

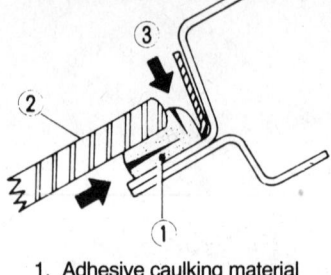

1. Adhesive caulking material
2. Glass
3. Knife cut

Cutting the caulking material from the windshield, on the 1979 and later models

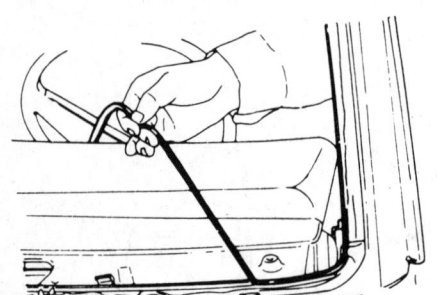

Removing the rubber dam on the 1979 and later models

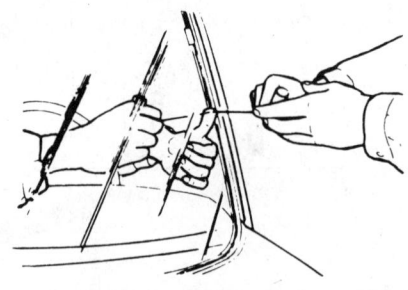

Using a piano wire to cut through the caulking material on the 1979 and later models

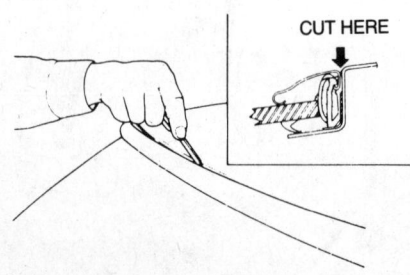

Separating the windshield molding from the caulking, on the 1979 and later models

shield garnish, the inside mirror and the sun visors.

3. Using a sharp knife (on the outside), cut off the caulking material attached to the upper and lower mouldings, then remove the mouldings.

4. From inside the vehicle, grasp the rubber dam (between the windshield frame and the glass) and pull it out.

5. Using a sharp knife, cut off the caulking material (from both sides) along the edge of the entire window opening.

6. To completely remove the window glass, perform the following procedure:

   a. Using a sharp knife, completely cut through a part of the caulking material.
   b. Using a piece of piano wire (0.020 in. dia.), secure one end to a piece of wood to serve as a handle.
   c. Using a pair of needle nose pliers, pass the other end of the wire through the hole in the caulking material, then secure that end to another piece of wood.
   d. With an assistant and using a sawing motion, pull the wire around the entire perimeter of the window.
   e. From inside the vehicle, push the glass up and out of the window opening.

7. Using a razor blade or a sharp tool, trim the caulking material around the entire perimeter of the windshield opening, leaving the remaining material about 0.039–0.079 in. (1.0–2.0 mm) thick.

CAUTION: *If the sealing material was silicone, remove all traces of it.*

INSPECTION OF SEALANT

To determine what sealant material is to be used to replace the windshield, perform the following inspection:

1. Cut a small piece of material from the windshield opening and place it on the edge of a knife.
2. Hold the material over an open flame un-

til it ignites, then determine the kind of material from the following descriptions:

  a. Polysulfide–Burns with a clear flame, a small amount of white smoke or no smoke and has heavy odor (sulfur dioxide).

  b. Polyurethane–Burns with a dirty flame, heavy black smoke and has very little odor.

  c. Silicone–Glows with little or no flame, white smoke, has very little odor and leaves white ash.

INSTALLATION

NOTE: *The installation of the window glass MUST be carried on by two people.*
CAUTION: *When installing the glass, make certain that no chipping occurs, for this can lead to future cracking.*

1970–78

1. Apply weatherstrip adhesive to the outer portion of the windshield frame.
2. Install the weatherstrip to the glass. Install a heavy string in the weatherstrip groove (side facing inside the vehicle).
3. Place the windshield onto the windshield frame with string inside the vehicle.

NOTE: *One person must work inside the vehicle and another person on the outside.*

4. The person on the inside will pull the string, in such a manner, so that the weatherstrip will correctly engage the windshield flange. The person on the outside will assist the operation by lightly tapping (by hand) on the glass.

NOTE: *If the weatherstrip does not seat correctly but is mounted on the windshield flange, use a spatula to work it into position.*

5. Lightly tap the overall glass area to settle the weatherstrip onto the windshield flange.
6. Raise the outer weatherstrip-to-glass seal and apply adhesive to the entire circumference.
7. To complete the installation, reverse the removal procedures.

1979 and Later

1. Clean the window glass, the sealing dam and the windshield frame contact surfaces with non-leaded gasoline.

CAUTION: *Make sure that oil, grease and/or water does not get on the cleaned surfaces from dirty hands or tools.*

2. Install the molding fasteners on the upper and the lower windshield opening by performing the following procedures:

  a. Using a heat gun, heat the molding fastener and the contacting face of the body to 104°F (40°C).

  b. Using a suitable roller, press the molding fastener into the body using more than 71 psi.

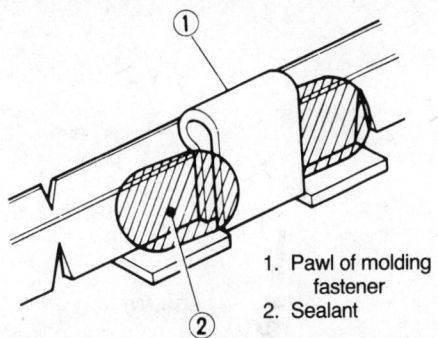

1. Pawl of molding fastener
2. Sealant

Installing the molding fasteners to the windshield frame, on the 1979 and later models

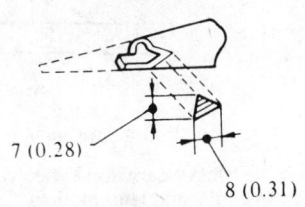

7 (0.28)
8 (0.31)
Unit: mm (in)

Preparing the adhesive nozzle

NOTE: *Make certain that the molding fastener stays in contact with the body and does not come off.*

  c. Apply sealant beside the molding fasteners.

3. Using new rubber dam material, install it (on the glass inboard edge) 0.35 in. (9 mm) from the edge of the glass and cut off the excess at its ends.
4. Using the sponge furnished with the Primer "A", apply a light coat of primer on the cleaned glass sealing surface.

CAUTION: *DO NOT apply primer to the glass opening flanges.*

5. With the sponge furnished with the Primer "E", apply a light coat of primer on the original caulking material left on the glass opening flange.

NOTE: *If the original sealant is silicone, remove all traces of it.*

CAUTION: *Allow all of the primers to dry for 10–15 minutes before proceeding to the next step.*

6. Obtain a cartridge of the correct window sealant, insert it into a dispensing gun, cut the nozzle to obtain an opening of 0.31 in. and pierce the sealing film with a needle.
7. Apply a continuous bead (0.43 in. high) of sealant on the glass contact surface (against the rubber dam) around the entire perimeter of the glass.

CAUTION: *Since the sealant starts to harden within 15 minutes after it is applied, the window glass MUST be installed within that time.*

8. Using the Glass Suction tools No.

262 BODY AND TRIM

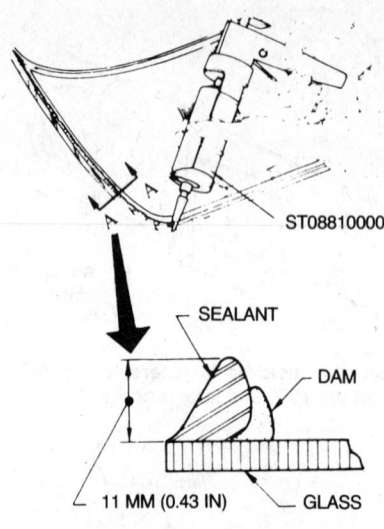

Installing the rubber dam and adhesive on the windshield on the 1979 and later models

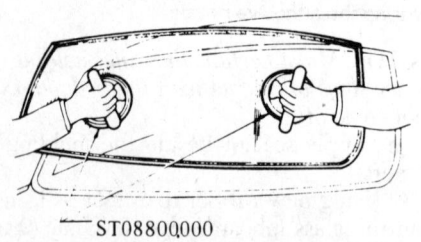

Installing the windshield on the 1979 and later models

ST08800000, attach them to the outer surface of the glass.

9. Using an assistant, install the glass into the window opening so that the clearances between the glass and the frame are about 0.28 in. (7 mm). Apply pressure on the glass to aid it's seating on the plate.

10. Wipe the excess caulking material from the molding fasteners, the edges of the glass and the body.

11. Remove the protective covers and water test immediately, using a cold water spray.

NOTE: *When using the cold water spray, allow the water to splash over the edges of the glass, not a direct stream on the fresh sealant. If a leak is detected, use the hand gun to force additional sealant into the leak area.*

CAUTION: *Allow the vehicle to set for 24 hrs. to give the sealant time to cure. DO NOT drive the vehicle on rough roads or surfaces and ALWAYS leave a window slightly open for at least 3 days, until the sealant has had time to vulcanize.*

12. To complete the installation, reverse the removal procedures.

Rear Window Glass

REMOVAL

1970–83

1. Place covers on the hatch and rear fenders to protect the vehicle from paint damage.
2. If equipped with a rear window wiper, remove the wiper blade with the wiper arm.

NOTE: *On the 1979–83 models, remove the rear roof rail trim, the rear finisher panel, the rear body side trim and the front body side trim. Disconnect the rear window defogger electrical harness.*

3. Using a screwdriver, carefully pry the window molding from the weatherstrip.

CAUTION: *When removing the window molding, be careful not to damage it.*

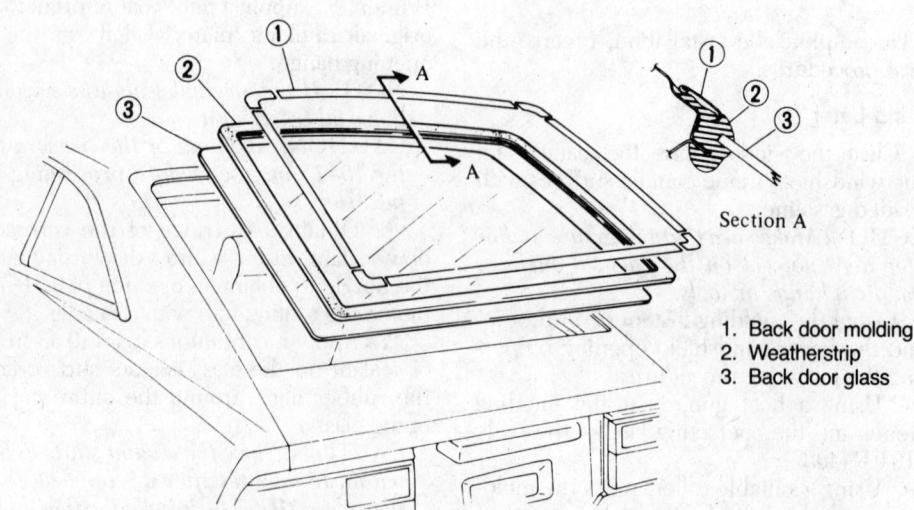

1. Back door molding
2. Weatherstrip
3. Back door glass

Exploded and cross-section views of the rear window assemblies for 1970–83 models

BODY AND TRIM

4. Using a standard screwdriver or a spatula (working from the outside), detach the weatherstrip sealing agent from the window frame.

5. Using a standard screwdriver or a spatula, depress the weatherstrip toward the outside, lightly tap and remove the glass to the outside.

CAUTION: *When releasing the glass from the weatherstrip, ALWAYS start at an upper corner; be careful not to apply too much pressure, for the glass may break.*

6. When the glass is released from the weatherstrip, lift it from the vehicle.

7. Clean the sealing agent from the glass and the window frame.

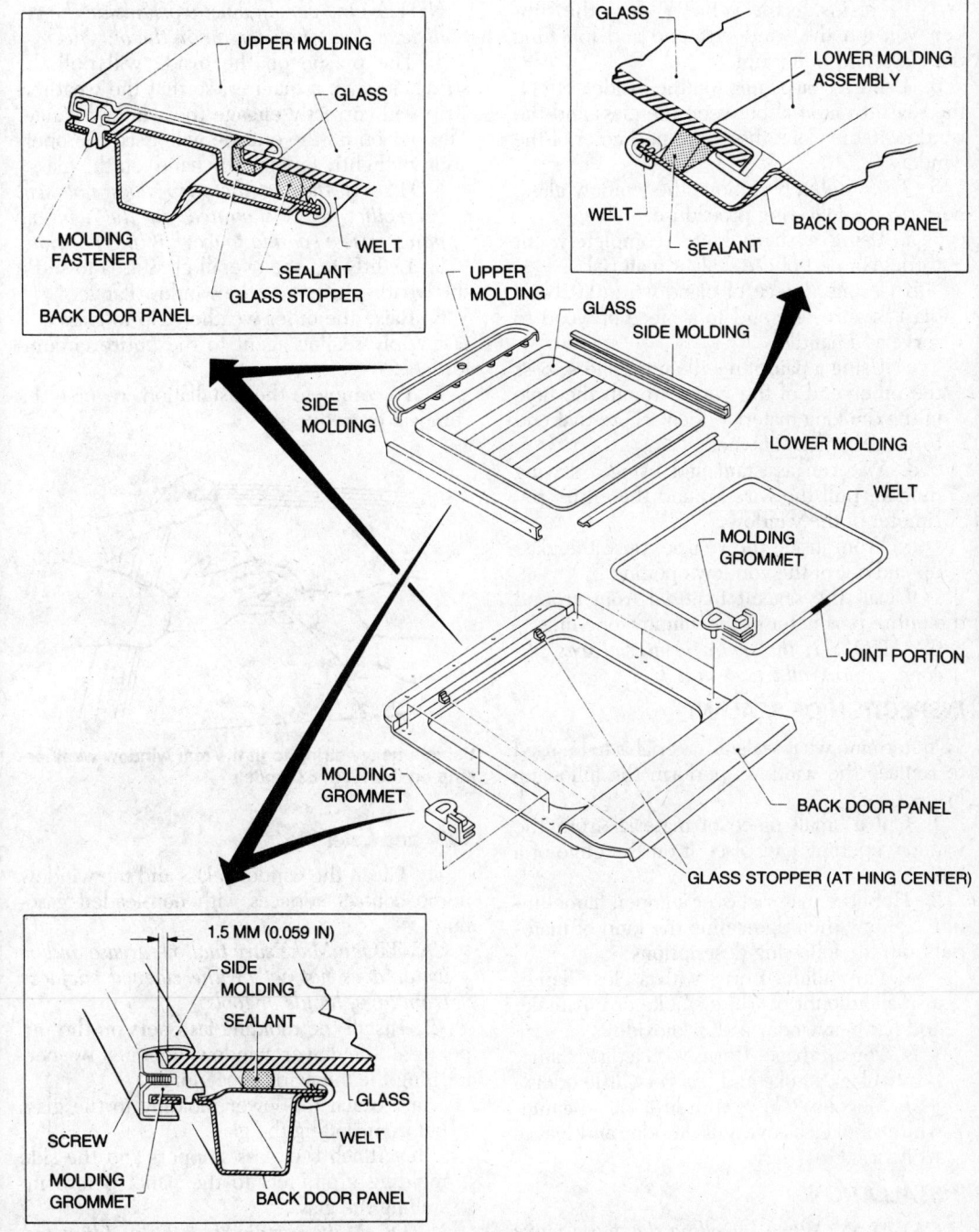

Exploded view of the 1984 and later, rear window assembly

1984 and Later

1. Lay covers over the hatch and the rear fenders of the vehicle to protect the paint from damage.
2. Remove the rear window wiper (with the arm), the upper molding, the side moldings and the lower molding.
3. Remove the rear roof rail trim and disconnect the rear window defogger electrical harness.
4. From inside the vehicle, grasp the rubber welt (on the window frame and touching the glass) and pull it out.
5. Using a sharp knife (on the inside), cut off the sealant material between the glass and the window frame along the entire perimeter of the window.
6. To completely remove the window glass, perform the following procedure:
   a. Using a sharp knife, completely cut through a part of the sealant material.
   b. Using a piece of piano wire (0.020 in. dia.), secure one end to a piece of wood to serve as a handle.
   c. Using a pair of needle nose pliers, pass the other end of the wire through the hole in the caulking material, then secure that end to another piece of wood.
   d. With an assistant and using a sawing motion, pull the wire around the entire perimeter of the window.
   e. From inside the vehicle, push the glass up and out of the window opening.
7. Clean the sealant material from around the entire perimeter of the window opening.

CAUTION: *If the sealing material was silicone, remove all traces of it.*

INSPECTION OF SEALANT

To determine what sealant material is to be used to replace the window, perform the following inspection:
1. Cut a small piece of material from the window opening and place it on the edge of a knife.
2. Hold the material over an open flame until it ignites, then determine the kind of material from the following descriptions:
   a. Polysulfide–Burns with a clear flame, a small amount of white smoke or no smoke and has heavy odor (sulfur dioxide).
   b. Polyurethane–Burns with a dirty flame, heavy black smoke and has very little odor.
   c. Silicone–Glows with little or no flame, white smoke, has very little odor and leaves white ash.

INSTALLATION

CAUTION: *When installing the glass, make certain that no chipping occurs, for this can lead to future cracking.*

1970–83

NOTE: *The installation of the window glass MUST be carried on by two people.*

1. Apply weatherstrip sealing agent to the outer portion of the window frame.
2. Install the weatherstrip to the glass. Install a heavy string in the weatherstrip groove (side facing inside the vehicle).
3. Place the window onto the window frame with string inside the vehicle.

NOTE: *One person must work inside the vehicle and another person on the outside.*

4. The person on the inside will pull the string, in such a manner, so that the weatherstrip will correctly engage the window flange. The person on the outside will assist the operation by lightly tapping (by hand) on the glass.

NOTE: *If the weatherstrip does not seat correctly but is mounted on the window flange, use a spatula to work it into position.*

5. Lightly tap the overall glass area to settle the weatherstrip onto the window flange.
6. Raise the outer weatherstrip-to-glass seal and apply sealing agent to the entire circumference.
7. To complete the installation, reverse the removal procedures.

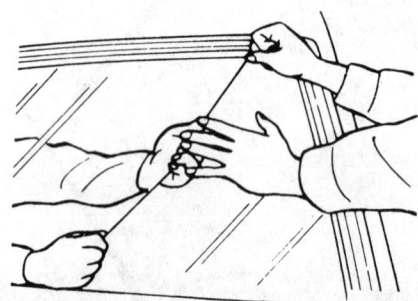

Using a heavy string to fit the rear window weatherstrip on the 1970–83 models

1984 and Later

1. Clean the window glass and the window frame contact surfaces with non-leaded gasoline.

CAUTION: *Make sure that oil, grease and/or water does not get on the cleaned surfaces from dirty hands or tools.*

2. Install the molding fasteners on the upper and the lower window opening by performing the following procedures:
   a. Attach the lower molding to the glass before installing the glass.
   b. Attach the glass stoppers and the side molding grommets to the panel before installing the glass.

NOTE: *Make certain that the molding fastener stays in contact with the window frame and does not come off.*

3. Using new rubber welt material, install it on the window frame edge and cut off the excess at its ends.

4. Using the sponge furnished with the Primer "A", apply a light coat of primer on the cleaned glass sealing surface.

CAUTION: *DO NOT apply primer to the glass opening flanges.*

5. With the sponge furnished with the Primer "E", apply a light coat of primer on the window frame flange.

NOTE: *If the original sealant is silicone, remove all traces of it.*

CAUTION: *Allow all of the primers to dry for 10–15 minutes before proceeding to the next step.*

6. Obtain a cartridge of the correct window sealant, insert it into a dispensing gun, cut the nozzle to obtain an opening of 0.31 in. and pierce the sealing film with a needle.

7. Apply a continuous bead (0.43 in. high) of sealant on the window frame contact surface, around the entire perimeter of the window frame.

CAUTION: *Since the sealant starts to harden within 15 minutes after it is applied, the window glass MUST be installed within that time.*

8. Using the Glass Suction tools No. ST08800000, attach them to the outer surface of the glass.

9. Install the glass into the window opening so that the clearances between the glass and the frame are equal distant. Apply pressure on the glass to aid it's seating on the plate.

10. Wipe the excess sealant material from the molding fasteners, the edges of the glass and the body.

11. Remove the protective covers and water test immediately, using a cold water spray.

NOTE: *When using the cold water spray, allow the water to splash over the edges of the glass, not a direct stream on the fresh sealant. If a leak is detected, use the hand gun to force additional sealant into the leak area.*

CAUTION: *Allow the vehicle to set for 24 hrs. to give the sealant time to cure. DO NOT drive the vehicle on rough roads and ALWAYS leave a window slightly open for at least 3 days, until the sealant has had time to vulcanize.*

12. To complete the installation, reverse the removal procedures.

INTERIOR

Door Panels

REMOVAL AND INSTALLATION

NOTE: *When removing the various components, be sure to place a cloth or padding onto the body to prevent scratching, soiling or damaging them.*

1. Remove the door release handle and the arm rest from the door.

2. If equipped with the manual window cranking handle, push in on the door panel and pry the spring clip from the back-side of the handle. If equipped with power windows and/or power door locks, remove the escutcheon plate(s) and disconnect the electrical connectors.

NOTE: *On the GS30 (2 + 2 seater), remove the rear inside handle escutcheon and the rear inside handle.*

3. If the door panel is retained by metallic fasteners, remove them. If the door panel is retained by plastic clips, place a flat blade of a screwdriver between the clip and the door, then lift the screwdriver handle to pry the clip from the door.

4. After removing the retaining fasteners or clips, remove the door panel.

5. To install, reverse the removal procedures. If equipped with plastic clips, push them back into the mounting holes.

Door Glass and Regulator

REMOVAL AND INSTALLATION

1970–78

1. Refer to the "Door Panel, Removal and Installation" procedures, in this section and remove the door panel.

2. Using the cranking handle, lower the window glass all the way.

3. Remove the outer door molding. Remove the door sash-to-door inner panel and draw the door sash UP.

4. Support the door glass (in the down position) and remove the glass back plate-to-guide channel "B."

5. Loosen the front and rear guide rail bolts, then raise the door glass and draw it upwards.

6. Remove the retaining bolts and the guide rails from the door.

7. Remove the retaining screws, then the guide channel "A", the regulator arm base and the regulator base; remove them through the large opening at the base of the door.

8. To install, reverse the removal procedures. Adjust the window glass.

1979 and Later

1. Refer to the "Door Panel, Removal and Installation" procedures, in this section and remove the door panel.

2. Using the cranking handle (manual) or switch (power), lower the window glass all the way.

3. Using a small screwdriver, turn the out-

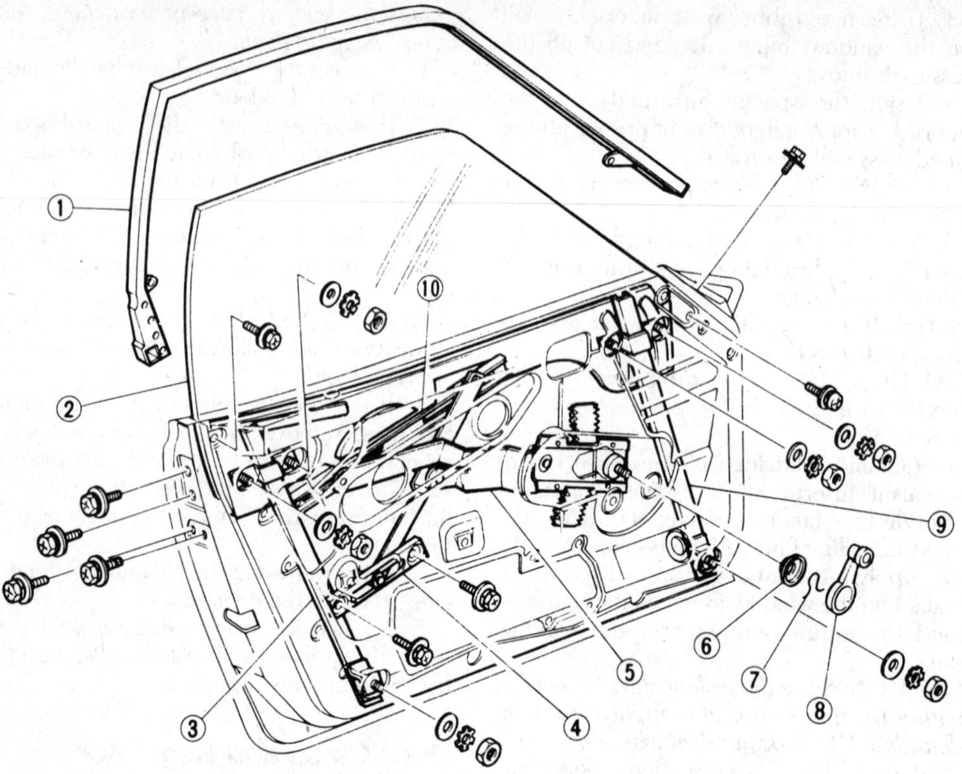

266 BODY AND TRIM

1. Door sash
2. Door glass
3. Rear guide rail
4. Guide channel A
5. Regulator assembly
6. Nylon washer
7. Retaining spring
8. Regulator handle
9. Front guide rail
10. Guide channel B

Exploded view of the 1970–78 door window glass, S30 model

side molding retaining clips 90° and remove the molding.

NOTE: *The retaining clips are made of plastic; DO NOT apply excessive force to them.*

4. Raise the window glass until the retaining screws appear at the access holes in the door inside panels. Remove the front and the rear stopper bolts.

5. Holding the glass in one hand, remove the regulator-to-glass retaining bolts, then raise the glass and draw it upwards.

NOTE: *When removing the window hardware from the door, use the large access hole.*

6. Remove the front guide rail assembly retaining screws and the assembly.

NOTE: *If equipped with power windows, disconnect the electrical harness connector.*

7. Remove the regulator assembly retaining screws and the assembly.

8. Remove the rear guide rail assembly retaining screws and the assembly.

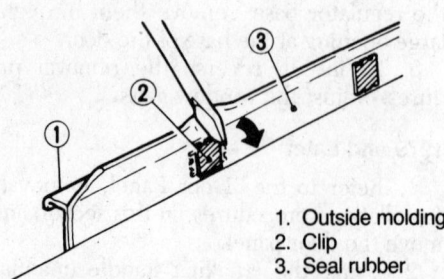

1. Outside molding
2. Clip
3. Seal rubber

Using a screwdriver to turn the outside door glass molding retaining clips on the 1979 and later models

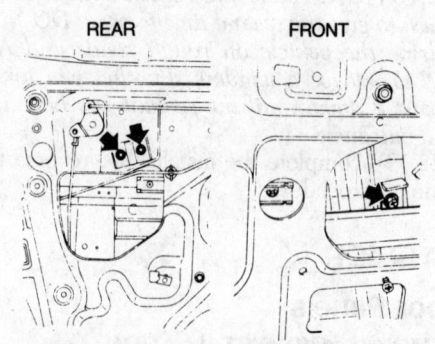

Removing the front and rear door glass regulator stopper bolts on the 1979 and later models

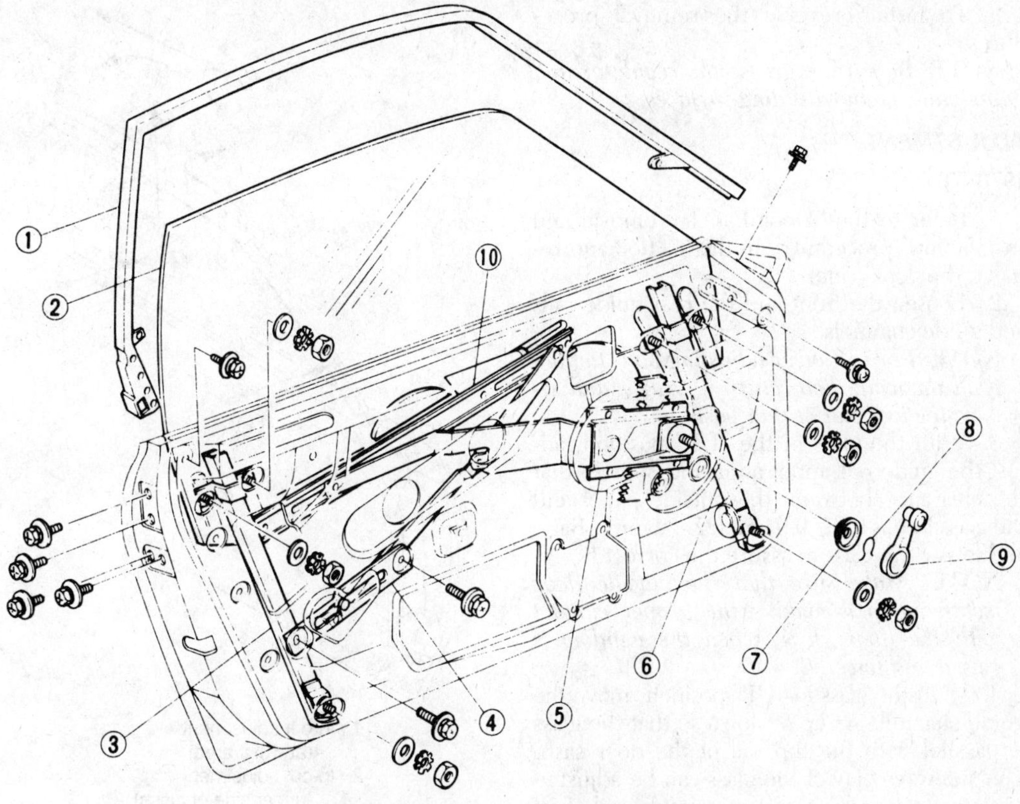

BODY AND TRIM 267

1. Door sash
2. Door glass
3. Rear guide rail
4. Guide channel A
5. Regulator assembly
6. Front guide rail
7. Nylon washer
8. Retaining spring
9. Regulator handle
10. Guide channel B

Exploded view of the 1970–78 door window glass, GS30–2+2 model

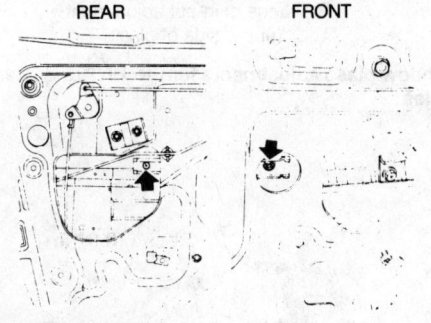

Removing the 1979 and later regulator-to-door glass retaining bolts

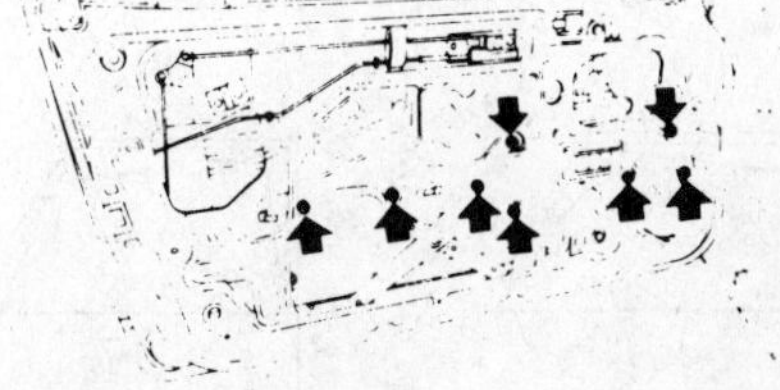

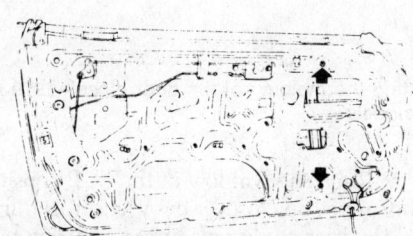

Removing the 1979 and later front guide rail

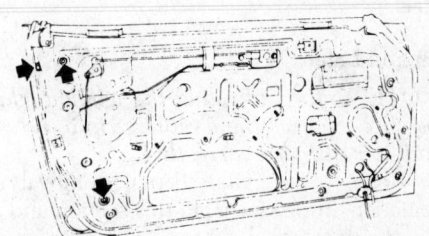

Removing the 1979 and later door glass regulator assembly

Removing the 1979 and later door glass rear regulator assembly

268 BODY AND TRIM

9. To install, reverse the removal procedures.

NOTE: *Be sure to grease the regulator and the guide channel sliding surfaces.*

ADJUSTMENT

1970–78

1. Refer to the "Door Panel, Removal and Installation" procedures, in this section and remove the door panel.
2. Loosen the front and the rear guide rails and guide channels.

NOTE: *For the lower adjusting bolt, tighten it all the way, then return it 4 turns and secure the lock nut at that position.*

3. With the glass in the "UP" position, adjust the guide rail upper adjusting bolts so that the clearance between the outside panel and the glass face is 0.87–0.94 in. (22–24 mm). Raise and lower the glass to assure the correct fit.

NOTE: *Make sure that the outside door weatherstrip is making the proper contact with the door glass, when the window is raised and lowered.*

4. With the glass in "UP" position, move the guide channel "A" up or down so that the glass is parallel with the top rail of the door sash. The sideways play of the glass can be adjusted by moving the front and rear guide rails fore and aft.
5. Tighten the adjusting bolts. The operating force of the control handle should be less than 7.7 lbs. (3.5 kg) at the knob.

NOTE: *Be sure to lubricate the guide rollers, the guide rails and the regulator linkage.*

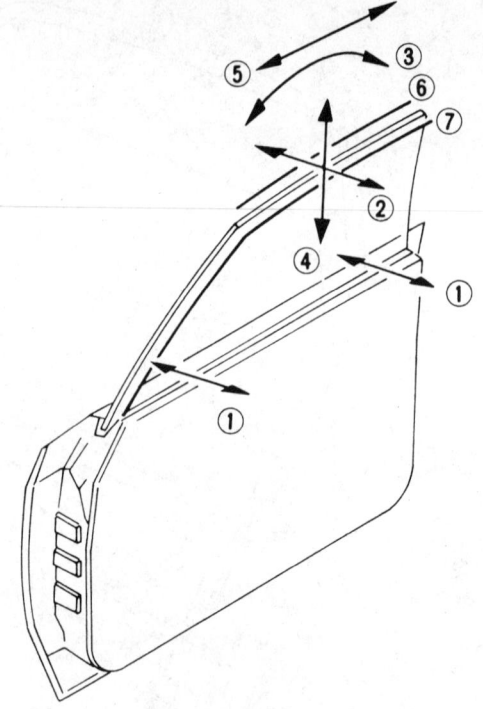

1. In-out adjustment (at waist area)
2. In-out adjustment (upper side of glass)
3. Tilt adjustment (upper side of glass)
4. Glass upper stop adjustment
5. Glass fore and aft adjustment
6. Range of glass upper stop adjustment
7. Range of in-out adjustment (upper side of glass)

Window glass adjustments for the 1979 and later vehicles

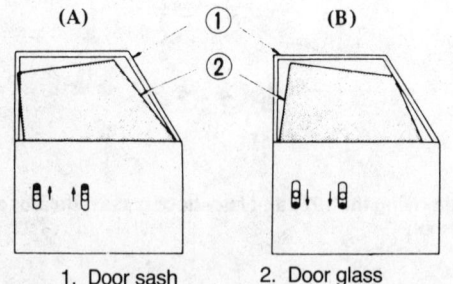

1. Door sash 2. Door glass

Adjusting the guide rail channel on the 1970–78 models

1979 and Later

NOTE: *Before adjusting the window glass, be sure to check the weatherstrip to be sure that it is installed correctly.*

1. Refer to the "Door Panel, Removal and Installation" procedures, in this section and remove the door panel.
2. For the In-Out Adjustment at the waist area, perform the following:

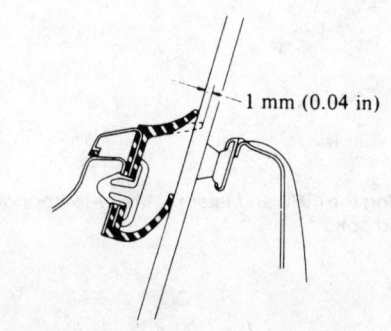

Adjusting the molding of the door glass—1979 and later models

a. Place the window in the "UP" position (door must be closed), then loosen the front and the rear guide rails upper securing bolt.
b. Adjust the upper adjusting bolts so that

BODY AND TRIM

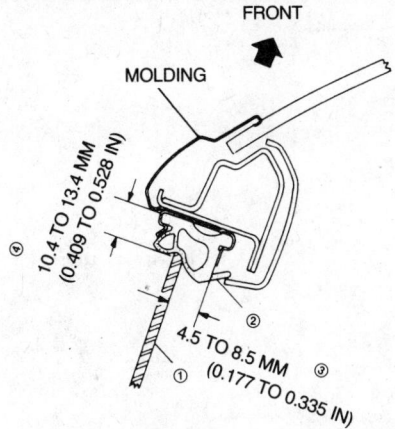

1. Door glass
2. Body side weatherstrip
3. In-out adjustment (Upper side of glass)
4. Fore and aft adjustment

Adjusting the window glass-to-roof molding—1979 and later

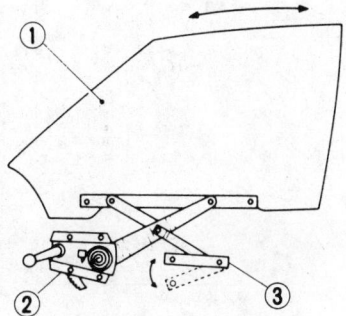

1. Door glass
2. Regulator
3. Guide channel

Adjusting the tilt of the upper glass—1979 and later

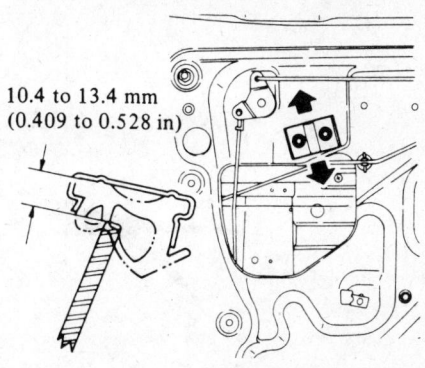

Adjusting the door glass upper rear stopper—1979 and later

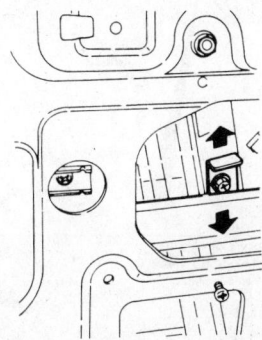

Adjusting the door glass upper front stopper—1979 and later

the window will push on the door's upper molding seal by 0.04 in. (1 mm), then tighten the upper adjusting bolts.

3. For the In-Out Adjustment at the roof molding, perform the following:

a. Place the window in the "UP" position (door must be closed).

b. Using the lower adjusting bolts, adjust the upper edge of the glass to obtain 0.177–0.335 in. (4.5–8.5 mm) between the inner surface of the glass and the weatherstrip inner edge.

4. For the Tilt Adjustment at the roof molding, perform the following:

a. Loosen the front/rear upper stopper securing bolts and the front/rear guide rail adjusting nuts.

b. Adjust the door regulator so that the upper side of the glass is parallel with the body side weatherstrip.

5. For the fore and aft adjustment, perform the following:

a. Loosen the front and rear guide rail adjusting bolts.

b. Adjust the door glass so that it is equally positioned on the weatherstrip.

6. For the Upper Stop Adjustment, perform the following:

a. Loosen the rear stopper bolt and position the rear of the window glass to 0.409–0.528 in. (10.4–13.4 mm) between the top of the glass and the base of the weatherstrip.

b. Loosen the front stopper bolt and position the front of the window glass to 0.409–0.528 in. (10.4–13.4 mm) between the top of the glass and the base of the weatherstrip.

7. After adjustment is complete, make sure that each alignment is within specifications.

Electric Window Motor—1979 and Later

REMOVAL AND INSTALLATION

NOTE: *It may be necessary to remove the lower trim panel to disconnect the electrical connector to the electric window motor.*

1. Refer to the "Door Glass and Regulator,

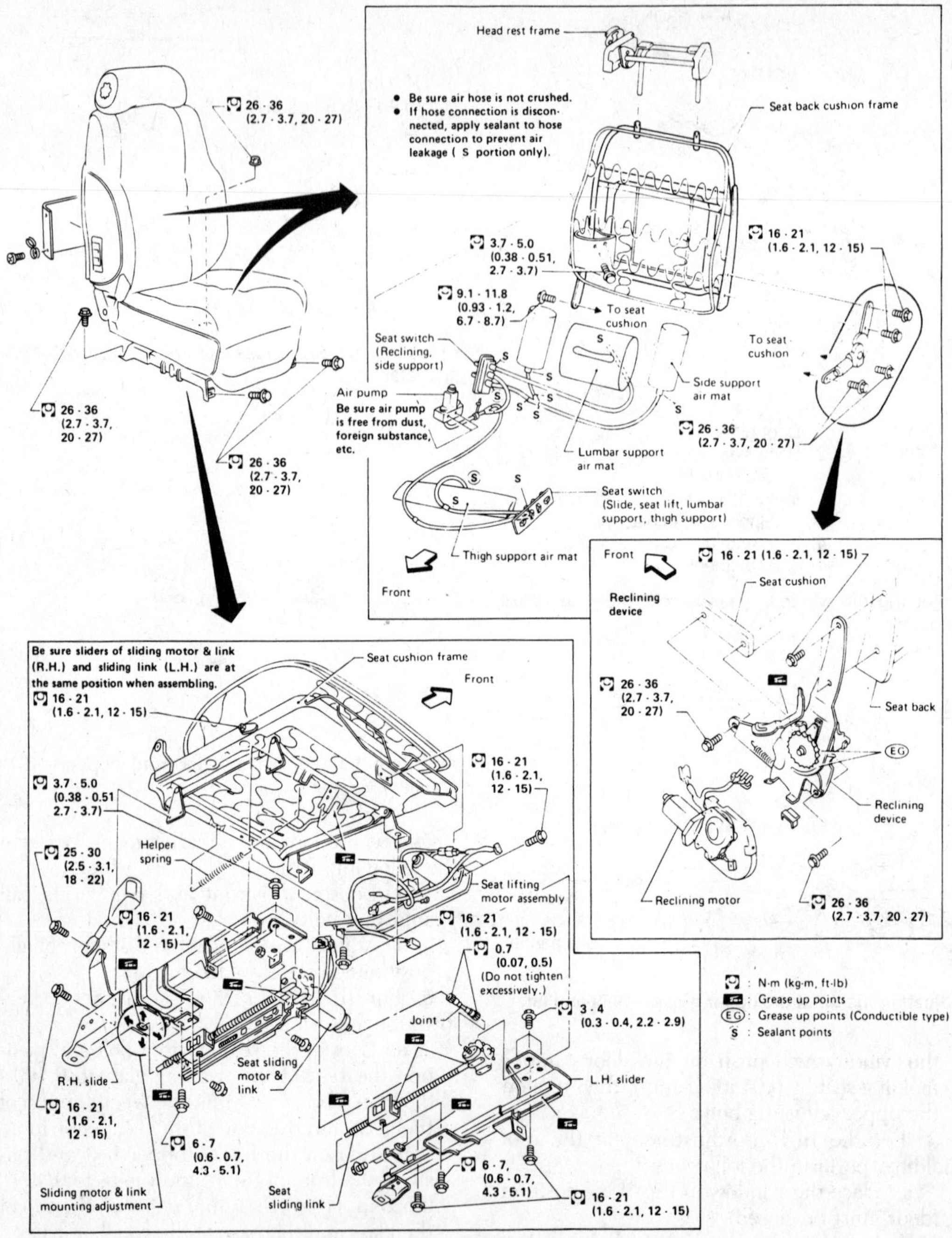

270 BODY AND TRIM

Exploded view of the power seat—1984 and later

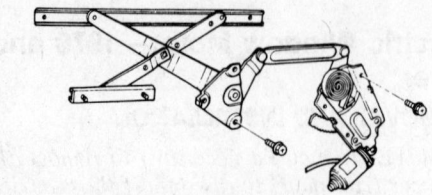

View of the power window regulator, for the 1979–83 models—others are similiar

Removal and Installation" procedures, in this section and remove the regulator.

2. To install, reverse the removal procedures. Adjust the window glass.

Power Seat Motor—1984 and Later
REMOVAL AND INSTALLATION

1. Remove the seat-to-floor mounting bolts (one at each corner).
2. Raise the seat, then disconnect the air hoses and the electrical connectors from the seat.
3. Remove the seat from the vehicle.
4. Remove the motor(s) from the drive mechanism(s).
5. To install, lubricate the drive mechanism(s) and reverse the removal procedures. Torque the seat mounting bolts to 20–27 ft. lbs. (26–36 Nm).

Headliner
REMOVAL AND INSTALLATION

1. Remove the interior roof and pillar trim strips.

NOTE: *The headliner is held in place by the weatherstrips.*

2. Pull back the weatherstrip lips to release the headliner.
3. To install, reverse the removal procedures.

Troubleshooting 10

This section is designed to aid in the quick, accurate diagnosis of automotive problems. While automotive repairs can be made by many people, accurate troubleshooting is a rare skill for the amateur and professional alike.

In its simplest state, troubleshooting is an exercise in logic. It is essential to realize that an automobile is really composed of a series of systems. Some of these systems are interrelated; others are not. Automobiles operate within a framework of logical rules and physical laws, and the key to troubleshooting is a good understanding of all the automotive systems.

This section breaks the car or truck down into its component systems, allowing the problem to be isolated. The charts and diagnostic road maps list the most common problems and the most probable causes of trouble. Obviously it would be impossible to list every possible problem that could happen along with every possible cause, but it will locate MOST problems and eliminate a lot of unnecessary guesswork. The systematic format will locate problems within a given system, but, because many automotive systems are interrelated, the solution to your particular problem may be found in a number of systems on the car or truck.

USING THE TROUBLESHOOTING CHARTS

This book contains all of the specific information that the average do-it-yourself mechanic needs to repair and maintain his or her car or truck. The troubleshooting charts are designed to be used in conjunction with the specific procedures and information in the text. For instance, troubleshooting a point-type ignition system is fairly standard for all models, but you may be directed to the text to find procedures for troubleshooting an individual type of electronic ignition. You will also have to refer to the specification charts throughout the book for specifications applicable to your car or truck.

TOOLS AND EQUIPMENT

The tools illustrated in Chapter 1 (plus two more diagnostic pieces) will be adequate to troubleshoot most problems. The two other tools needed are a voltmeter and an ohmmeter. These can be purchased separately or in combination, known as a VOM meter.

In the event that other tools are required, they will be noted in the procedures.

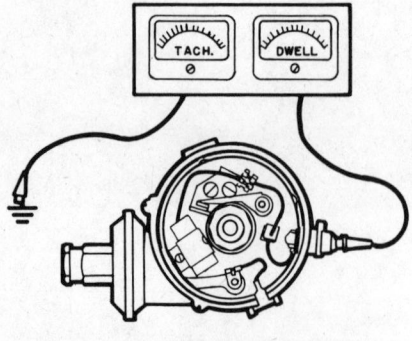

Tach-dwell hooked-up to distributor

TROUBLESHOOTING

Troubleshooting Engine Problems

See Chapters 2, 3, 4 for more information and service procedures.

Index to Systems

System	To Test	Group
Battery	Engine need not be running	1
Starting system	Engine need not be running	2
Primary electrical system	Engine need not be running	3
Secondary electrical system	Engine need not be running	4
Fuel system	Engine need not be running	5
Engine compression	Engine need not be running	6
Engine vacuum	Engine must be running	7
Secondary electrical system	Engine must be running	8
Valve train	Engine must be running	9
Exhaust system	Engine must be running	10
Cooling system	Engine must be running	11
Engine lubrication	Engine must be running	12

Index to Problems

Problem: Symptom	Begin at Specific Diagnosis, Number
Engine Won't Start:	
Starter doesn't turn	1.1, 2.1
Starter turns, engine doesn't	2.1
Starter turns engine very slowly	1.1, 2.4
Starter turns engine normally	3.1, 4.1
Starter turns engine very quickly	6.1
Engine fires intermittently	4.1
Engine fires consistently	5.1, 6.1
Engine Runs Poorly:	
Hard starting	3.1, 4.1, 5.1, 8.1
Rough idle	4.1, 5.1, 8.1
Stalling	3.1, 4.1, 5.1, 8.1
Engine dies at high speeds	4.1, 5.1
Hesitation (on acceleration from standing stop)	5.1, 8.1
Poor pickup	4.1, 5.1, 8.1
Lack of power	3.1, 4.1, 5.1, 8.1
Backfire through the carburetor	4.1, 8.1, 9.1
Backfire through the exhaust	4.1, 8.1, 9.1
Blue exhaust gases	6.1, 7.1
Black exhaust gases	5.1
Running on (after the ignition is shut off)	3.1, 8.1
Susceptible to moisture	4.1
Engine misfires under load	4.1, 7.1, 8.4, 9.1
Engine misfires at speed	4.1, 8.1
Engine misfires at idle	3.1, 4.1, 5.1, 7.1, 8.1

Sample Section

Test and Procedure	Results and Indications	Proceed to
4.1—Check for spark: Hold each spark plug wire approximately ¼" from ground with gloves or a heavy, dry rag. Crank the engine and observe the spark.	→ If no spark is evident:	→ 4.2
	→ If spark is good in some cases:	→ 4.3
	→ If spark is good in all cases:	→ 4.6

274 TROUBLESHOOTING

Specific Diagnosis

This section is arranged so that following each test, instructions are given to proceed to another, until a problem is diagnosed.

Section 1—Battery

Test and Procedure	Results and Indications	Proceed to
1.1—Inspect the battery visually for case condition (corrosion, cracks) and water level.	If case is cracked, replace battery:	1.4
	If the case is intact, remove corrosion with a solution of baking soda and water (**CAUTION**: *do not get the solution into the battery*), and fill with water:	1.2

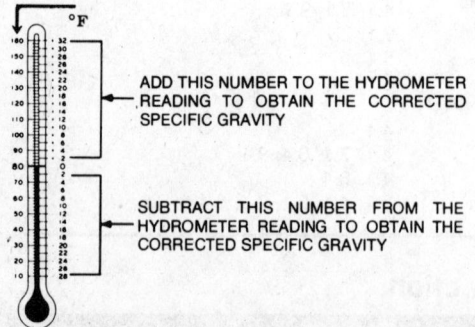

Inspect the battery case

1.2—Check the battery cable connections: Insert a screwdriver between the battery post and the cable clamp. Turn the headlights on high beam, and observe them as the screwdriver is gently twisted to ensure good metal to metal contact.	If the lights brighten, remove and clean the clamp and post; coat the post with petroleum jelly, install and tighten the clamp:	1.4
	If no improvement is noted:	1.3

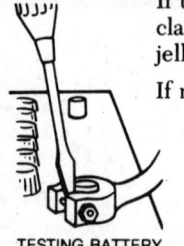

TESTING BATTERY CABLE CONNECTIONS USING A SCREWDRIVER

1.3—Test the state of charge of the battery using an individual cell tester or hydrometer.	If indicated, charge the battery. **NOTE**: *If no obvious reason exists for the low state of charge (i.e., battery age, prolonged storage), proceed to:*	1.4

Specific Gravity (@ 80° F.)

Minimum	Battery Charge
1.260	100% Charged
1.230	75% Charged
1.200	50% Charged
1.170	25% Charged
1.140	Very Little Power Left
1.110	Completely Discharged

ADD THIS NUMBER TO THE HYDROMETER READING TO OBTAIN THE CORRECTED SPECIFIC GRAVITY

SUBTRACT THIS NUMBER FROM THE HYDROMETER READING TO OBTAIN THE CORRECTED SPECIFIC GRAVITY

The effects of temperature on battery specific gravity (left) and amount of battery charge in relation to specific gravity (right)

1.4—Visually inspect battery cables for cracking, bad connection to ground, or bad connection to starter.	If necessary, tighten connections or replace the cables:	2.1

TROUBLESHOOTING 275

Section 2—Starting System
See Chapter 3 for service procedures

Test and Procedure	Results and Indications	Proceed to
Note: Tests in Group 2 are performed with coil high tension lead disconnected to prevent accidental starting.		
2.1—Test the starter motor and solenoid: Connect a jumper from the battery post of the solenoid (or relay) to the starter post of the solenoid (or relay).	If starter turns the engine normally:	2.2
	If the starter buzzes, or turns the engine very slowly:	2.4
	If no response, replace the solenoid (or relay).	3.1
	If the starter turns, but the engine doesn't, ensure that the flywheel ring gear is intact. If the gear is undamaged, replace the starter drive.	3.1
2.2—Determine whether ignition override switches are functioning properly (clutch start switch, neutral safety switch), by connecting a jumper across the switch(es), and turning the ignition switch to "start".	If starter operates, adjust or replace switch:	3.1
	If the starter doesn't operate:	2.3
2.3—Check the ignition switch "start" position: Connect a 12V test lamp or voltmeter between the starter post of the solenoid (or relay) and ground. Turn the ignition switch to the "start" position, and jiggle the key.	If the lamp doesn't light or the meter needle doesn't move when the switch is turned, check the ignition switch for loose connections, cracked insulation, or broken wires. Repair or replace as necessary:	3.1
	If the lamp flickers or needle moves when the key is jiggled, replace the ignition switch.	3.3

Checking the ignition switch "start" position

STARTER RELAY (IF EQUIPPED)

2.4—Remove and bench test the starter, according to specifications in the engine electrical section.	If the starter does not meet specifications, repair or replace as needed:	3.1
	If the starter is operating properly:	2.5
2.5—Determine whether the engine can turn freely: Remove the spark plugs, and check for water in the cylinders. Check for water on the dipstick, or oil in the radiator. Attempt to turn the engine using an 18" flex drive and socket on the crankshaft pulley nut or bolt.	If the engine will turn freely only with the spark plugs out, and hydrostatic lock (water in the cylinders) is ruled out, check valve timing:	9.2
	If engine will not turn freely, and it is known that the clutch and transmission are free, the engine must be disassembled for further evaluation:	Chapter 3

TROUBLESHOOTING

Section 3—Primary Electrical System

Test and Procedure	Results and Indications	Proceed to
3.1—Check the ignition switch "on" position: Connect a jumper wire between the distributor side of the coil and ground, and a 12V test lamp between the switch side of the coil and ground. Remove the high tension lead from the coil. Turn the ignition switch on and jiggle the key.	If the lamp lights:	3.2
	If the lamp flickers when the key is jiggled, replace the ignition switch:	3.3
	If the lamp doesn't light, check for loose or open connections. If none are found, remove the ignition switch and check for continuity. If the switch is faulty, replace it:	3.3

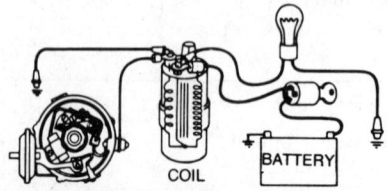

Checking the ignition switch "on" position

3.2—Check the ballast resistor or resistance wire for an open circuit, using an ohmmeter. See Chapter 3 for specific tests.	Replace the resistor or resistance wire if the resistance is zero. **NOTE:** *Some ignition systems have no ballast resistor.*	3.3

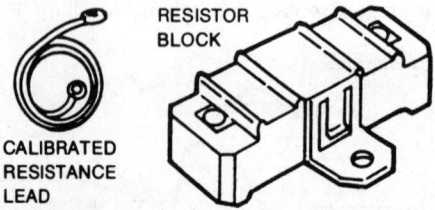

Two types of resistors

3.3—On point-type ignition systems, visually inspect the breaker points for burning, pitting or excessive wear. Gray coloring of the point contact surfaces is normal. Rotate the crankshaft until the contact heel rests on a high point of the distributor cam and adjust the point gap to specifications. On electronic ignition models, remove the distributor cap and visually inspect the armature. Ensure that the armature pin is in place, and that the armature is on tight and rotates when the engine is cranked. Make sure there are no cracks, chips or rounded edges on the armature.	If the breaker points are intact, clean the contact surfaces with fine emery cloth, and adjust the point gap to specifications. If the points are worn, replace them. On electronic systems, replace any parts which appear defective. If condition persists:	3.4

TROUBLESHOOTING 277

Test and Procedure	Results and Indications	Proceed to
3.4—On point-type ignition systems, connect a dwell-meter between the distributor primary lead and ground. Crank the engine and observe the point dwell angle. On electronic ignition systems, conduct a stator (magnetic pickup assembly) test. See Chapter 3.	On point-type systems, adjust the dwell angle if necessary. **NOTE:** *Increasing the point gap decreases the dwell angle and vice-versa.*	3.6
	If the dwell meter shows little or no reading;	3.5
	On electronic ignition systems, if the stator is bad, replace the stator. If the stator is good, proceed to the other tests in Chapter 3.	

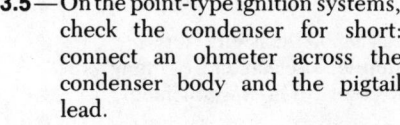

Dwell is a function of point gap

3.5—On the point-type ignition systems, check the condenser for short: connect an ohmeter across the condenser body and the pigtail lead.	If any reading other than infinite is noted, replace the condenser	3.6

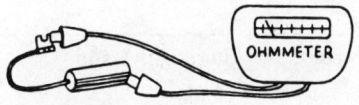

Checking the condenser for short

3.6—Test the coil primary resistance: On point-type ignition systems, connect an ohmmeter across the coil primary terminals, and read the resistance on the low scale. Note whether an external ballast resistor or resistance wire is used. On electronic ignition systems, test the coil primary resistance as in Chapter 3.	Point-type ignition coils utilizing ballast resistors or resistance wires should have approximately 1.0 ohms resistance. Coils with internal resistors should have approximately 4.0 ohms resistance. If values far from the above are noted, replace the coil.	4.1

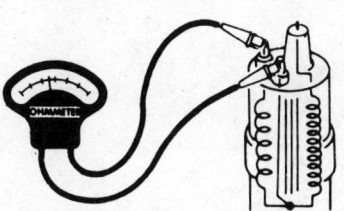

Check the coil primary resistance

278 TROUBLESHOOTING

Section 4—Secondary Electrical System
See Chapters 2–3 for service procedures

Test and Procedure	Results and Indications	Proceed to
4.1—Check for spark: Hold each spark plug wire approximately ¼″ from ground with gloves or a heavy, dry rag. Crank the engine, and observe the spark.	If no spark is evident:	4.2
	If spark is good in some cylinders:	4.3
	If spark is good in all cylinders:	4.6

Check for spark at the plugs

4.2—Check for spark at the coil high tension lead: Remove the coil high tension lead from the distributor and position it approximately ¼″ from ground. Crank the engine and observe spark. **CAUTION:** *This test should not be performed on engines equipped with electronic ignition.*	If the spark is good and consistent:	4.3
	If the spark is good but intermittent, test the primary electrical system starting at 3.3:	3.3
	If the spark is weak or non-existent, replace the coil high tension lead, clean and tighten all connections and retest. If no improvement is noted:	4.4
4.3—Visually inspect the distributor cap and rotor for burned or corroded contacts, cracks, carbon tracks, or moisture. Also check the fit of the rotor on the distributor shaft (where applicable).	If moisture is present, dry thoroughly, and retest per 4.1:	4.1
	If burned or excessively corroded contacts, cracks, or carbon tracks are noted, replace the defective part(s) and retest per 4.1:	4.1
	If the rotor and cap appear intact, or are only slightly corroded, clean the contacts thoroughly (including the cap towers and spark plug wire ends) and retest per 4.1: If the spark is good in all cases:	4.6
	If the spark is poor in all cases:	4.5

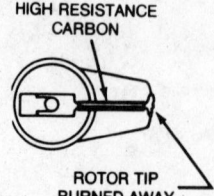

Inspect the distributor cap and rotor

TROUBLESHOOTING 279

Test and Procedure	Results and Indications	Proceed to
4.4—Check the coil secondary resistance: On point-type systems connect an ohmmeter across the distributor side of the coil and the coil tower. Read the resistance on the high scale of the ohmmeter. On electronic ignition systems, see Chapter 3 for specific tests.	The resistance of a satisfactory coil should be between 4,000 and 10,000 ohms. If resistance is considerably higher (i.e., 40,000 ohms) replace the coil and retest per 4.1. **NOTE:** *This does not apply to high performance coils.*	

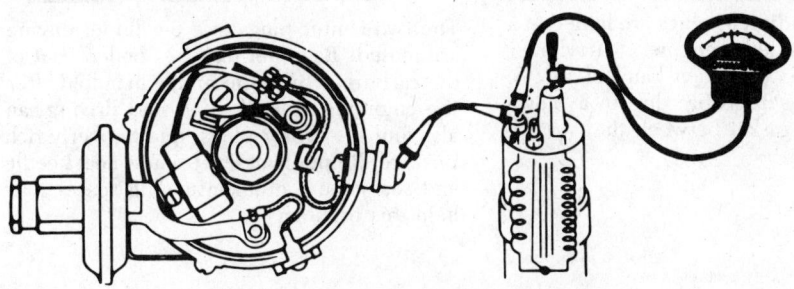

Testing the coil secondary resistance

4.5—Visually inspect the spark plug wires for cracking or brittleness. Ensure that no two wires are positioned so as to cause induction firing (adjacent and parallel). Remove each wire, one by one, and check resistance with an ohmmeter.	Replace any cracked or brittle wires. If any of the wires are defective, replace the entire set. Replace any wires with excessive resistance (over $8000\,\Omega$ per foot for suppression wire), and separate any wires that might cause induction firing.	4.6

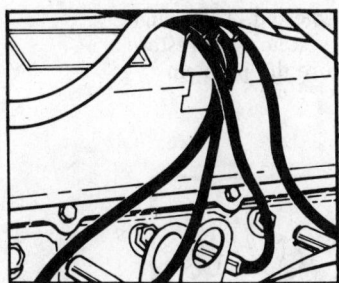 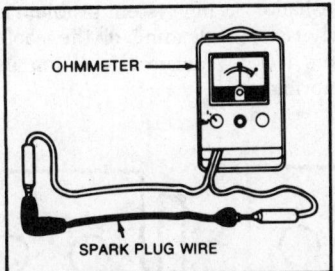 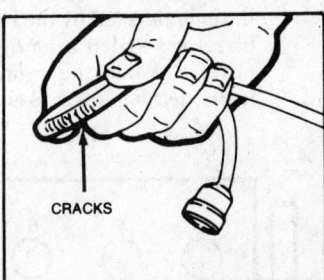

Misfiring can be the result of spark plug leads to adjacent, consecutively firing cylinders running parallel and too close together

On point-type ignition systems, check the spark plug wires as shown. On electronic ignitions, do not remove the wire from the distributor cap terminal; instead, test through the cap

Spark plug wires can be checked visually by bending them in a loop over your finger. This will reveal any cracks, burned or broken insulation. Any wire with cracked insulation should be replaced

4.6—Remove the spark plugs, noting the cylinders from which they were removed, and evaluate according to the color photos in the middle of this book.	See following.	See following.

280 TROUBLESHOOTING

Test and Procedure	Results and Indications	Proceed to
4.7—Examine the location of all the plugs.	The following diagrams illustrate some of the conditions that the location of plugs will reveal.	4.8

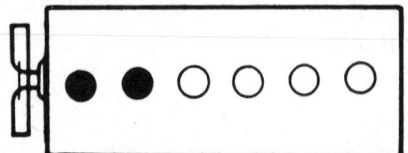

Two adjacent plugs are fouled in a 6-cylinder engine, 4-cylinder engine or either bank of a V-8. This is probably due to a blown head gasket between the two cylinders

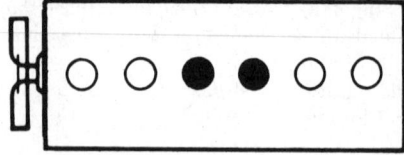

The two center plugs in a 6-cylinder engine are fouled. Raw fuel may be "boiled" out of the carburetor into the intake manifold after the engine is shut-off. Stop-start driving can also foul the center plugs, due to overly rich mixture. Proper float level, a new float needle and seat or use of an insulating spacer may help this problem

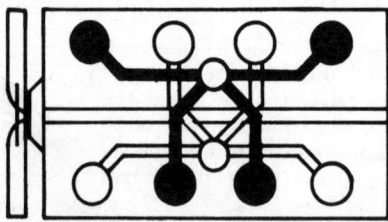

An unbalanced carburetor is indicated. Following the fuel flow on this particular design shows that the cylinders fed by the right-hand barrel are fouled from overly rich mixture, while the cylinders fed by the left-hand barrel are normal

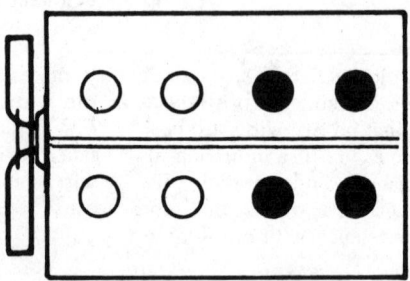

If the four rear plugs are overheated, a cooling system problem is suggested. A thorough cleaning of the cooling system may restore coolant circulation and cure the problem

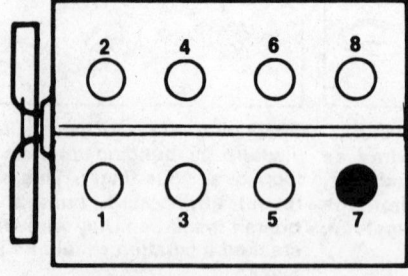

Finding one plug overheated may indicate an intake manifold leak near the affected cylinder. If the overheated plug is the second of two adjacent, consecutively firing plugs, it could be the result of ignition cross-firing. Separating the leads to these two plugs will eliminate cross-fire

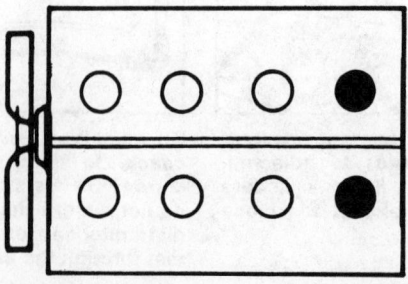

Occasionally, the two rear plugs in large, lightly used V-8's will become oil fouled. High oil consumption and smoky exhaust may also be noticed. It is probably due to plugged oil drain holes in the rear of the cylinder head, causing oil to be sucked in around the valve stems. This usually occurs in the rear cylinders first, because the engine slants that way

TROUBLESHOOTING 281

Test and Procedure	Results and Indications	Proceed to
4.8—Determine the static ignition timing. Using the crankshaft pulley timing marks as a guide, locate top dead center on the compression stroke of the number one cylinder.	The rotor should be pointing toward the No. 1 tower in the distributor cap, and, on electronic ignitions, the armature spoke for that cylinder should be lined up with the stator.	4.8
4.9—Check coil polarity: Connect a voltmeter negative lead to the coil high tension lead, and the positive lead to ground (**NOTE:** *Reverse the hook-up for positive ground systems*). Crank the engine momentarily. **Checking coil polarity**	If the voltmeter reads up-scale, the polarity is correct: If the voltmeter reads down-scale, reverse the coil polarity (switch the primary leads):	5.1 5.1

Section 5—Fuel System
See Chapter 4 for service procedures

Test and Procedure	Results and Indications	Proceed to
5.1—Determine that the air filter is functioning efficiently: Hold paper elements up to a strong light, and attempt to see light through the filter.	Clean permanent air filters in solvent (or manufacturer's recommendation), and allow to dry. Replace paper elements through which light cannot be seen:	5.2
5.2—Determine whether a flooding condition exists: Flooding is identified by a strong gasoline odor, and excessive gasoline present in the throttle bore(s) of the carburetor. 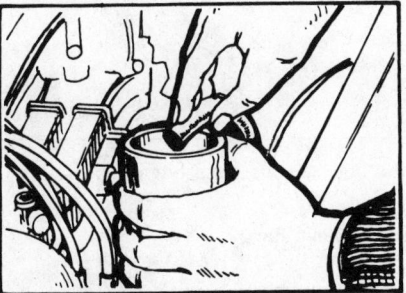 **If the engine floods repeatedly, check the choke butterfly flap**	If flooding is not evident: If flooding is evident, permit the gasoline to dry for a few moments and restart. If flooding doesn't recur: If flooding is persistent:	5.3 5.7 5.5
5.3—Check that fuel is reaching the carburetor: Detach the fuel line at the carburetor inlet. Hold the end of the line in a cup (not styrofoam), and crank the engine.	If fuel flows smoothly: If fuel doesn't flow (**NOTE:** *Make sure that there is fuel in the tank*), or flows erratically: **Check the fuel pump by disconnecting the output line (fuel pump-to-carburetor) at the carburetor and operating the starter briefly**	5.7 5.4

282 TROUBLESHOOTING

Test and Procedure	Results and Indications	Proceed to
5.4—Test the fuel pump: Disconnect all fuel lines from the fuel pump. Hold a finger over the input fitting, crank the engine (with electric pump, turn the ignition or pump on); and feel for suction.	If suction is evident, blow out the fuel line to the tank with low pressure compressed air until bubbling is heard from the fuel filler neck. Also blow out the carburetor fuel line (both ends disconnected):	5.7
	If no suction is evident, replace or repair the fuel pump: NOTE: *Repeated oil fouling of the spark plugs, or a no-start condition, could be the result of a ruptured vacuum booster pump diaphragm, through which oil or gasoline is being drawn into the intake manifold (where applicable).*	5.7
5.5—Occasionally, small specks of dirt will clog the small jets and orifices in the carburetor. With the engine cold, hold a flat piece of wood or similar material over the carburetor, where possible, and crank the engine.	If the engine starts, but runs roughly the engine is probably not run enough. If the engine won't start:	5.9
5.6—Check the needle and seat: Tap the carburetor in the area of the needle and seat.	If flooding stops, a gasoline additive (e.g., Gumout) will often cure the problem:	5.7
	If flooding continues, check the fuel pump for excessive pressure at the carburetor (according to specifications). If the pressure is normal, the needle and seat must be removed and checked, and/or the float level adjusted:	5.7
5.7—Test the accelerator pump by looking into the throttle bores while operating the throttle.	If the accelerator pump appears to be operating normally:	5.8
	If the accelerator pump is not operating, the pump must be reconditioned. Where possible, service the pump with the carburetor(s) installed on the engine. If necessary, remove the carburetor. Prior to removal:	5.8

Check for gas at the carburetor by looking down the carburetor throat while someone moves the accelerator

5.8—Determine whether the carburetor main fuel system is functioning: Spray a commercial starting fluid into the carburetor while attempting to start the engine.	If the engine starts, runs for a few seconds, and dies:	5.9
	If the engine doesn't start:	6.1

TROUBLESHOOTING

Test and Procedure	Results and Indications	Proceed to
5.9—Uncommon fuel system malfunctions: See below:	If the problem is solved: If the problem remains, remove and recondition the carburetor.	6.1

Condition	Indication	Test	Prevailing Weather Conditions	Remedy
Vapor lock	Engine will not restart shortly after running.	Cool the components of the fuel system until the engine starts. Vapor lock can be cured faster by draping a wet cloth over a mechanical fuel pump.	Hot to very hot	Ensure that the exhaust manifold heat control valve is operating. Check with the vehicle manufacturer for the recommended solution to vapor lock on the model in question.
Carburetor icing	Engine will not idle, stalls at low speeds.	Visually inspect the throttle plate area of the throttle bores for frost.	High humidity, 32–40° F.	Ensure that the exhaust manifold heat control valve is operating, and that the intake manifold heat riser is not blocked.
Water in the fuel	Engine sputters and stalls; may not start.	Pump a small amount of fuel into a glass jar. Allow to stand, and inspect for droplets or a layer of water.	High humidity, extreme temperature changes.	For droplets, use one or two cans of commercial gas line anti-freeze. For a layer of water, the tank must be drained, and the fuel lines blown out with compressed air.

Section 6—Engine Compression
See Chapter 3 for service procedures

6.1—Test engine compression: Remove all spark plugs. Block the throttle wide open. Insert a compression gauge into a spark plug port, crank the engine to obtain the maximum reading, and record.	If compression is within limits on all cylinders:	7.1
	If gauge reading is extremely low on all cylinders:	6.2
	If gauge reading is low on one or two cylinders: (If gauge readings are identical and low on two or more adjacent cylinders, the head gasket must be replaced.)	6.2
	Checking compression	
6.2—Test engine compression (wet): Squirt approximately 30 cc. of engine oil into each cylinder, and retest per 6.1.	If the readings improve, worn or cracked rings or broken pistons are indicated:	See Chapter 3
	If the readings do not improve, burned or excessively carboned valves or a jumped timing chain are indicated: NOTE: *A jumped timing chain is often indicated by difficult cranking.*	7.1

284 TROUBLESHOOTING

Section 7—Engine Vacuum
See Chapter 3 for service procedures

Test and Procedure	Results and Indications	Proceed to
7.1—Attach a vacuum gauge to the intake manifold beyond the throttle plate. Start the engine, and observe the action of the needle over the range of engine speeds.	See below.	See below

INDICATION: normal engine in good condition

Proceed to: 8.1

Normal engine
Gauge reading: steady, from 17–22 in./Hg.

INDICATION: sticking valves or ignition miss

Proceed to: 9.1, 8.3

Sticking valves
Gauge reading: intermittent fluctuation at idle

INDICATION: late ignition or valve timing, low compression, stuck throttle valve, leaking carburetor or manifold gasket

Proceed to: 6.1

Incorrect valve timing
Gauge reading: low (10–15 in./Hg) but steady

INDICATION: improper carburetor adjustment or minor intake leak.

Proceed to: 7.2

Carburetor requires adjustment
Gauge reading: drifting needle

INDICATION: ignition miss, blown cylinder head gasket, leaking valve or weak valve spring

Proceed to: 8.3, 6.1

Blown head gasket
Gauge reading: needle fluctuates as engine speed increases

INDICATION: burnt valve or faulty valve clearance. Needle will fall when defective valve operates

Proceed to: 9.1

Burnt or leaking valves
Gauge reading: steady needle, but drops regularly

INDICATION: choked muffler, excessive back pressure in system

Proceed to: 10.1

Clogged exhaust system
Gauge reading: gradual drop in reading at idle

INDICATION: worn valve guides

Proceed to: 9.1

Worn valve guides
Gauge reading: needle vibrates excessively at idle, but steadies as engine speed increases

White pointer = steady gauge hand   Black pointer = fluctuating gauge hand

CHILTON'S
AUTO BODY REPAIR TIPS

Tools and Materials • Step-by-Step Illustrated Procedures
How To Repair Dents, Scratches and Rust Holes
Spray Painting and Refinishing Tips

EASY STEP-BY-STEP TIPS FROM PROS

With a little practice, basic body repair procedures can be mastered by any do-it-yourself mechanic. The step-by-step repairs shown here can be applied to almost any type of auto body repair.

TOOLS & MATERIALS

You may already have basic tools, such as hammers and electric drills. Other tools unique to body repair — body hammers, grinding attachments, sanding blocks, dent puller, half-round plastic file and plastic spreaders — are relatively inexpensive and can be obtained wherever auto parts or auto body repair parts are sold. Portable air compressors and paint spray guns can be purchased or rented.

Auto Body Repair Kits

The best and most often used products are available to the do-it-yourselfer in kit form, from major manufacturers of auto body repair products. The same manufacturers also merchandise the individual products for use by pros.

Kits are available to make a wide variety of repairs, including holes, dents and scratches and fiberglass, and offer the advantage of buying the materials you'll need for the job. There is little waste or chance of materials going bad from not being used. Many kits may also contain basic body-working tools such as body files, sanding blocks and spreaders. Check the contents of the kit before buying your tools.

BODY REPAIR TIPS

Safety

Many of the products associated with auto body repair and refinishing contain toxic chemicals. Read all labels before opening containers and store them in a safe place and manner.
• Wear eye protection (safety goggles) when using power tools or when performing any operation that involves the removal of any type of material.
• Wear lung protection (disposabl[e] mask or respirator) when grinding, sand[-]ing or painting.

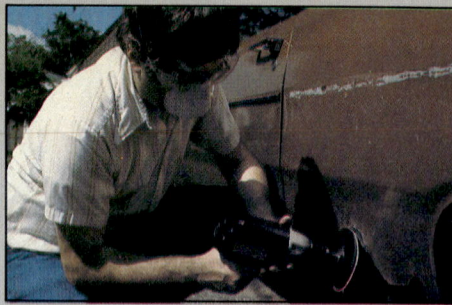

Sanding

1 Sand off paint before using a den[t] puller. When using a non-adhesiv[e] sanding disc, cover the back of the dis[c] with an overlapping layer or two o[f] masking tape and trim the edges. Th[e] disc will last considerably longer.

2 Use the circular motion of the sand[-]ing disc to grind *into* the edge of th[e] repair. Grinding or sanding away fro[m] the jagged edge will only tear the sand[-] paper.

3 Use the palm of your hand flat on the panel to detec[t] high and low spots. Do not use you[r] fingertips. Slide your hand slowly bac[k] and forth.

WORKING WITH BODY FILLER

Mixing The Filler

Cleanliness and proper mixing and application are extremely important. Use a clean piece of plastic or glass or a disposable artist's palette to mix body filler.

1 Allow plenty of time and follow directions. No useful purpose will be served by adding more hardener to make it cure (set-up) faster. Less hardener means more curing time, but the mixture dries harder; more hardener means less curing time but a softer mixture.

2 Both the hardener and the filler should be thoroughly kneaded or stirred before mixing. Hardener should be a solid paste and dispense like thin toothpaste. Body filler should be smooth, and free of lumps or thick spots.

Getting the proper amount of hardener in the filler is the trickiest part of preparing the filler. Use the same amount of hardener in cold or warm weather. For contour filler (thick coats), a bead of hardener twice the diameter of the filler is about right. There's about a 15% margin on either side, but, if in doubt use less hardener.

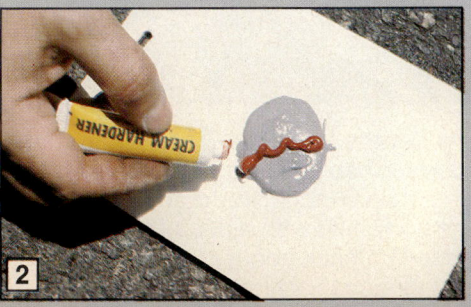

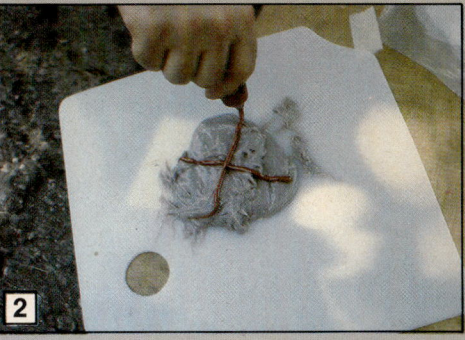

3 Mix the body filler and hardener by wiping across the mixing surface, picking the mixture up and wiping it again. Colder weather requires longer mixing times. Do not mix in a circular motion; this will trap air bubbles which will become holes in the cured filler.

Applying The Filler

1 For best results, filler should not be applied over 1/4" thick.

Apply the filler in several coats. Build it up to above the level of the repair surface so that it can be sanded or grated down.

The first coat of filler must be pressed on with a firm wiping motion.

Apply the filler in one direction only. Working the filler back and forth will either pull it off the metal or trap air bubbles.

REPAIRING DENTS

Before you start, take a few minutes to study the damaged area. Try to visualize the shape of the panel before it was damaged. If the damage is on the left fender, look at the right fender and use it as a guide. If there is access to the panel from behind, you can reshape it with a body hammer. If not, you'll have to use a dent puller. Go slowly and work the metal a little at a time. Get the panel as straight as possible before applying filler.

1 This dent is typical of one that can be pulled out or hammered out from behind. Remove the headlight cover, headlight assembly and turn signal housing.

2 Drill a series of holes ½ the size of the end of the dent puller along the stress line. Make some trial pulls and assess the results. If necessary, drill more holes and try again. Do not hurry.

3 If possible, use a body hammer and block to shape the metal back to its original contours. Get the metal back as close to its original shape as possible. Don't depend on body filler to fill dents.

4 Using an 80-grit grinding disc on an electric drill, grind the paint from the surrounding area down to bare metal. Use a new grinding pad to prevent heat buildup that will warp metal.

5 The area should look like this when you're finished grinding. Knock the drill holes in and tape over small openings to keep plastic filler out.

6 Mix the body filler (see Body Repair Tips). Spread the body filler evenly over the entire area (see Body Repair Tips). Be sure to cover the area completely.

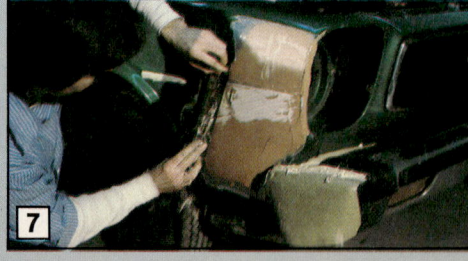

7 Let the body filler dry until the surface can just be scratched with your fingernail. Knock the high spots from the body filler with a body file ("Cheesegrater"). Check frequently with the palm of your hand for high and low spots.

8 Check to be sure that trim pieces that will be installed later will fit exactly. Sand the area with 40-grit paper.

9 If you wind up with low spots, you may have to apply another layer of filler.

10 Knock the high spots off with 40-grit paper. When you are satisfied with the contours of the repair, apply a thin coat of filler to cover pin holes and scratches.

11 Block sand the area with 40-grit paper to a smooth finish. Pay particular attention to body lines and ridges that must be well-defined.

12 Sand the area with 400 paper and then finish with a scuff pad. The finished repair is ready for priming and painting (see Painting Tips).

Materials and photos courtesy of Ritt Jones Auto Body, Prospect Park, PA.

REPAIRING RUST HOLES

There are many ways to repair rust holes. The fiberglass cloth kit shown here is one of the most cost efficient for the owner because it provides a strong repair that resists cracking and moisture and is relatively easy to use. It can be used on large and small holes (with or without backing) and can be applied over contoured areas. Remember, however, that short of replacing an entire panel, no repair is a guarantee that the rust will not return.

1 Remove any trim that will be in the way. Clean away all loose debris. Cut away all the rusted metal. But be sure to leave enough metal to retain the contour or body shape.

2 Grind away all traces of rust with a 24-grit grinding disc. Be sure to grind back 3-4 inches from the edge of the hole down to bare metal and be sure all traces of paint, primer and rust are removed.

3 Block sand the area with 80 or 100 grit sandpaper to get a clear, shiny surface and feathered paint edge. Tap the edges of the hole inward with a ball peen hammer.

4 If you are going to use release film, cut a piece about 2-3″ larger than the area you have sanded. Place the film over the repair and mark the sanded area on the film. Avoid any unnecessary wrinkling of the film.

5 Cut 2 pieces of fiberglass matte to match the shape of the repair. One piece should be about 1″ smaller than the sanded area and the second piece should be 1″ smaller than the first. Mix enough filler and hardener to saturate the fiberglass material (see Body Repair Tips).

6 Lay the release sheet on a flat surface and spread an even layer of filler, large enough to cover the repair. Lay the smaller piece of fiberglass cloth in the center of the sheet and spread another layer of filler over the fiberglass cloth. Repeat the operation for the larger piece of cloth.

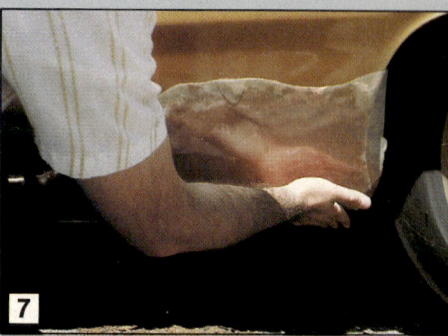

7 Place the repair material over the repair area, with the release film facing outward. Use a spreader and work from the center outward to smooth the material, following the body contours. Be sure to remove all air bubbles.

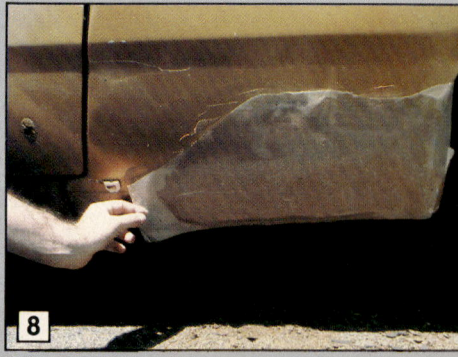

8 Wait until the repair has dried tack-free and peel off the release sheet. The ideal working temperature is 60°- 90° F. Cooler or warmer temperatures or high humidity may require additional curing time. Wait longer, if in doubt.

9 Sand and feather-edge the entire area. The initial sanding can be done with a sanding disc on an electric drill if care is used. Finish the sanding with a block sander. Low spots can be filled with body filler; this may require several applications.

10 When the filler can just be scratched with a fingernail, knock the high spots down with a body file and smooth the entire area with 80-grit. Feather the filled areas into the surrounding areas.

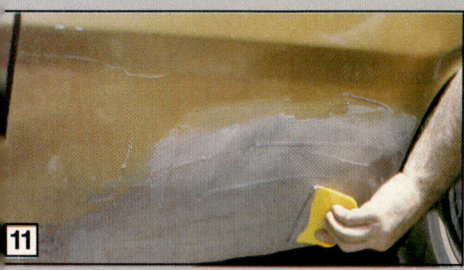

11 When the area is sanded smooth, mix some topcoat and hardener and apply it directly with a spreader. This will give a smooth finish and prevent the glass matte from showing through the paint.

12 Block sand the topcoat smooth with finishing sandpaper (200 grit), and 400 grit. The repair is ready for masking, priming and painting (see Painting Tips).

Materials and photos courtesy Marson Corporation, Chelsea, Massachusetts

PAINTING TIPS

Preparation

1 SANDING — Use a 400 or 600 grit wet or dry sandpaper. Wet-sand the area with a ¼ sheet of sandpaper soaked in clean water. Keep the paper wet while sanding. Sand the area until the repaired area tapers into the original finish.

2 CLEANING — Wash the area to be painted thoroughly with water and a clean rag. Rinse it thoroughly and wipe the surface dry until you're sure it's completely free of dirt, dust, fingerprints, wax, detergent or other foreign matter.

3 MASKING — Protect any areas you don't want to overspray by covering them with masking tape and newspaper. Be careful not get fingerprints on the area to be painted.

4 PRIMING — All exposed metal should be primed before painting. Primer protects the metal and provides an excellent surface for paint adhesion. When the primer is dry, wet-sand the area again with 600 grit wet-sandpaper. Clean the area again after sanding.

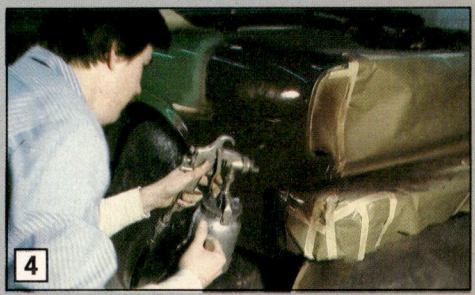

Painting Techniques

Paint applied from either a spray gun or a spray can (for small areas) will provide good results. Experiment on an old piece of metal to get the right combination before you begin painting.

SPRAYING VISCOSITY (SPRAY GUN ONLY) — Paint should be thinned to spraying viscosity according to the directions on the can. Use only the recommended thinner or reducer and the same amount of reduction regardless of temperature.

AIR PRESSURE (SPRAY GUN ONLY) — This is extremely important. Be sure you are using the proper recommended pressure.

TEMPERATURE — The surface to be painted should be approximately the same temperature as the surrounding air. Applying warm paint to a cold surface, or vice versa, will completely upset the paint characteristics.

THICKNESS — Spray with smooth strokes. In general, the thicker the coat of paint, the longer the drying time. Apply several thin coats about 30 seconds apart. The paint should remain wet long enough to flow out and no longer; heavier coats will only produce sags or wrinkles. Spray a light (fog) coat, followed by heavier color coats.

DISTANCE — The ideal spraying distance is 8"-12" from the gun or can to the surface. Shorter distances will produce ripples, while greater distances will result in orange peel, dry film and poor color match and loss of material due to overspray.

OVERLAPPING — The gun or can should be kept at right angles to the surface at all times. Work to a wet edge at an even speed, using a 50% overlap and direct the center of the spray at the lower or nearest edge of the previous stroke.

RUBBING OUT (BLENDING) FRESH PAINT — Let the paint dry thoroughly. Runs or imperfections can be sanded out, primed and repainted.

Don't be in too big a hurry to remove the masking. This only produces paint ridges. When the finish has dried for at least a week, apply a small amount of fine grade rubbing compound with a clean, wet cloth. Use lots of water and blend the new paint with the surrounding area.

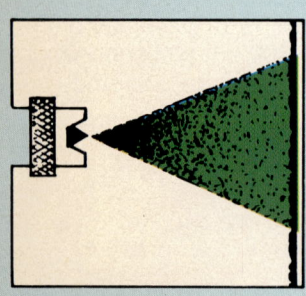

WRONG

Thin coat. Stroke too fast, not enough overlap, gun too far away.

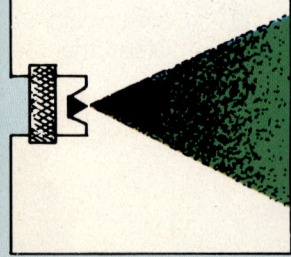

CORRECT

Medium coat. Proper distance, good stroke, proper overlap.

WRONG

Heavy coat. Stroke too slow, too much overlap, gun too close.

TROUBLESHOOTING 285

Test and Procedure	Results and Indications	Proceed to
7.2—Attach a vacuum gauge per 7.1, and test for an intake manifold leak. Squirt a small amount of oil around the intake manifold gaskets, carburetor gaskets, plugs and fittings. Observe the action of the vacuum gauge.	If the reading improves, replace the indicated gasket, or seal the indicated fitting or plug: If the reading remains low:	8.1 7.3
7.3—Test all vacuum hoses and accessories for leaks as described in 7.2. Also check the carburetor body (dashpots, automatic choke mechanism, throttle shafts) for leaks in the same manner.	If the reading improves, service or replace the offending part(s): If the reading remains low:	8.1 6.1

Section 8—Secondary Electrical System
See Chapter 2 for service procedures

Test and Procedure	Results and Indications	Proceed to
8.1—Remove the distributor cap and check to make sure that the rotor turns when the engine is cranked. Visually inspect the distributor components.	Clean, tighten or replace any components which appear defective.	8.2
8.2—Connect a timing light (per manufacturer's recommendation) and check the dynamic ignition timing. Disconnect and plug the vacuum hose(s) to the distributor if specified, start the engine, and observe the timing marks at the specified engine speed.	If the timing is not correct, adjust to specifications by rotating the distributor in the engine: (Advance timing by rotating distributor opposite normal direction of rotor rotation, retard timing by rotating distributor in same direction as rotor rotation.)	8.3
8.3—Check the operation of the distributor advance mechanism(s): To test the mechanical advance, disconnect the vacuum lines from the distributor advance unit and observe the timing marks with a timing light as the engine speed is increased from idle. If the mark moves smoothly, without hesitation, it may be assumed that the mechanical advance is functioning properly. To test vacuum advance and/or retard systems, alternately crimp and release the vacuum line, and observe the timing mark for movement. If movement is noted, the system is operating.	If the systems are functioning: If the systems are not functioning, remove the distributor, and test on a distributor tester:	8.4 8.4
8.4—Locate an ignition miss: With the engine running, remove each spark plug wire, one at a time, until one is found that doesn't cause the engine to roughen and slow down.	When the missing cylinder is identified:	4.1

Section 9—Valve Train
See Chapter 3 for service procedures

Test and Procedure	Results and Indications	Proceed to
9.1—Evaluate the valve train: Remove the valve cover, and ensure that the valves are adjusted to specifications. A mechanic's stethoscope may be used to aid in the diagnosis of the valve train. By pushing the probe on or near push rods or rockers, valve noise often can be isolated. A timing light also may be used to diagnose valve problems. Connect the light according to manufacturer's recommendations, and start the engine. Vary the firing moment of the light by increasing the engine speed (and therefore the ignition advance), and moving the trigger from cylinder to cylinder. Observe the movement of each valve.	Sticking valves or erratic valve train motion can be observed with the timing light. The cylinder head must be disassembled for repairs.	See Chapter 3
9.2—Check the valve timing: Locate top dead center of the No. 1 piston, and install a degree wheel or tape on the crankshaft pulley or damper with zero corresponding to an index mark on the engine. Rotate the crankshaft in its direction of rotation; and observe the opening of the No. 1 cylinder intake valve. The opening should correspond with the correct mark on the degree wheel according to specifications.	If the timing is not correct, the timing cover must be removed for further investigation.	See Chapter 3

Section 10—Exhaust System

Test and Procedure	Results and Indications	Proceed to
10.1—Determine whether the exhaust manifold heat control valve is operating: Operate the valve by hand to determine whether it is free to move. If the valve is free, run the engine to operating temperature and observe the action of the valve, to ensure that it is opening.	If the valve sticks, spray it with a suitable solvent, open and close the valve to free it, and retest.	
	If the valve functions properly:	10.2
	If the valve does not free, or does not operate, replace the valve:	10.2
10.2—Ensure that there are no exhaust restrictions: Visually inspect the exhaust system for kinks, dents, or crushing. Also note that gases are flowing freely from the tailpipe at all engine speeds, indicating no restriction in the muffler or resonator.	Replace any damaged portion of the system:	11.1

Section 11—Cooling System
See Chapter 3 for service procedures

Test and Procedure	Results and Indications	Proceed to
11.1—Visually inspect the fan belt for glazing, cracks, and fraying, and replace if necessary. Tighten the belt so that the longest span has approximately ½" play at its midpoint under thumb pressure (see Chapter 1).	Replace or tighten the fan belt as necessary: **Checking belt tension**	11.2
11.2—Check the fluid level of the cooling system.	If full or slightly low, fill as necessary: If extremely low:	11.5 11.3
11.3—Visually inspect the external portions of the cooling system (radiator, radiator hoses, thermostat elbow, water pump seals, heater hoses, etc.) for leaks. If none are found, pressurize the cooling system to 14–15 psi.	If cooling system holds the pressure: If cooling system loses pressure rapidly, reinspect external parts of the system for leaks under pressure. If none are found, check dipstick for coolant in crankcase. If no coolant is present, but pressure loss continues: If coolant is evident in crankcase, remove cylinder head(s), and check gasket(s). If gaskets are intact, block and cylinder head(s) should be checked for cracks or holes. If the gasket(s) is blown, replace, and purge the crankcase of coolant: **NOTE:** *Occasionally, due to atmospheric and driving conditions, condensation of water can occur in the crankcase. This causes the oil to appear milky white. To remedy, run the engine until hot, and change the oil and oil filter.*	11.5 11.4 12.6
11.4—Check for combustion leaks into the cooling system: Pressurize the cooling system as above. Start the engine, and observe the pressure gauge. If the needle fluctuates, remove each spark plug wire, one at a time, noting which cylinder(s) reduce or eliminate the fluctuation.	Cylinders which reduce or eliminate the fluctuation, when the spark plug wire is removed, are leaking into the cooling system. Replace the head gasket on the affected cylinder bank(s). 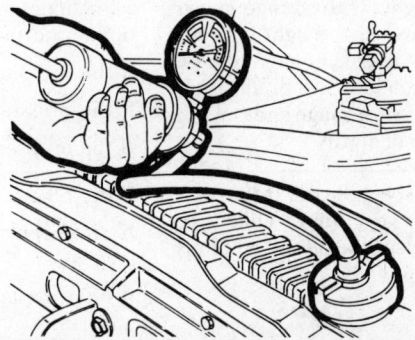 **Pressurizing the cooling system**	

288 TROUBLESHOOTING

Test and Procedure	Results and Indications	Proceed to
11.5—Check the radiator pressure cap: Attach a radiator pressure tester to the radiator cap (wet the seal prior to installation). Quickly pump up the pressure, noting the point at which the cap releases.	If the cap releases within ± 1 psi of the specified rating, it is operating properly:	11.6
	If the cap releases at more than ± 1 psi of the specified rating, it should be replaced:	11.6
11.6—Test the thermostat: Start the engine cold, remove the radiator cap, and insert a thermometer into the radiator. Allow the engine to idle. After a short while, there will be a sudden, rapid increase in coolant temperature. The temperature at which this sharp rise stops is the thermostat opening temperature.	If the thermostat opens at or about the specified temperature:	11.7
	If the temperature doesn't increase: (If the temperature increases slowly and gradually, replace the thermostat.)	11.7
11.7—Check the water pump: Remove the thermostat elbow and the thermostat, disconnect the coil high tension lead (to prevent starting), and crank the engine momentarily.	If coolant flows, replace the thermostat and retest per 11.6:	11.6
	If coolant doesn't flow, reverse flush the cooling system to alleviate any blockage that might exist. If system is not blocked, and coolant will not flow, replace the water pump.	

Checking radiator pressure cap

Section 12—Lubrication
See Chapter 3 for service procedures

Test and Procedure	Results and Indications	Proceed to
12.1—Check the oil pressure gauge or warning light: If the gauge shows low pressure, or the light is on for no obvious reason, remove the oil pressure sender. Install an accurate oil pressure gauge and run the engine momentarily.	If oil pressure builds normally, run engine for a few moments to determine that it is functioning normally, and replace the sender.	—
	If the pressure remains low:	12.2
	If the pressure surges:	12.3
	If the oil pressure is zero:	12.3
12.2—Visually inspect the oil: If the oil is watery or very thin, milky, or foamy, replace the oil and oil filter.	If the oil is normal:	12.3
	If after replacing oil the pressure remains low:	12.3
	If after replacing oil the pressure becomes normal:	—

TROUBLESHOOTING

Test and Procedure	Results and Indications	Proceed to
12.3—Inspect the oil pressure relief valve and spring, to ensure that it is not sticking or stuck. Remove and thoroughly clean the valve, spring, and the valve body.	If the oil pressure improves: If no improvement is noted:	— 12.4
12.4—Check to ensure that the oil pump is not cavitating (sucking air instead of oil): See that the crankcase is neither over nor underfull, and that the pickup in the sump is in the proper position and free from sludge.	Fill or drain the crankcase to the proper capacity, and clean the pickup screen in solvent if necessary. If no improvement is noted:	12.5
12.5—Inspect the oil pump drive and the oil pump:	If the pump drive or the oil pump appear to be defective, service as necessary and retest per 12.1:	12.1
	If the pump drive and pump appear to be operating normally, the engine should be disassembled to determine where blockage exists:	See Chapter 3
12.6—Purge the engine of ethylene glycol coolant: Completely drain the crankcase and the oil filter. Obtain a commercial butyl cellosolve base solvent, designated for this purpose, and follow the instructions precisely. Following this, install a new oil filter and refill the crankcase with the proper weight oil. The next oil and filter change should follow shortly thereafter (1000 miles).		

TROUBLESHOOTING EMISSION CONTROL SYSTEMS

See Chapter 4 for procedures applicable to individual emission control systems used on specific combinations of engine/transmission/model.

TROUBLESHOOTING THE CARBURETOR
See Chapter 4 for service procedures

Carburetor problems cannot be effectively isolated unless all other engine systems (particularly ignition and emission) are functioning properly and the engine is properly tuned.

TROUBLESHOOTING

Condition	Possible Cause
Engine cranks, but does not start	1. Improper starting procedure 2. No fuel in tank 3. Clogged fuel line or filter 4. Defective fuel pump 5. Choke valve not closing properly 6. Engine flooded 7. Choke valve not unloading 8. Throttle linkage not making full travel 9. Stuck needle or float 10. Leaking float needle or seat 11. Improper float adjustment
Engine stalls	1. Improperly adjusted idle speed or mixture **Engine hot** 2. Improperly adjusted dashpot 3. Defective or improperly adjusted solenoid 4. Incorrect fuel level in fuel bowl 5. Fuel pump pressure too high 6. Leaking float needle seat 7. Secondary throttle valve stuck open 8. Air or fuel leaks 9. Idle air bleeds plugged or missing 10. Idle passages plugged **Engine Cold** 11. Incorrectly adjusted choke 12. Improperly adjusted fast idle speed 13. Air leaks 14. Plugged idle or idle air passages 15. Stuck choke valve or binding linkage 16. Stuck secondary throttle valves 17. Engine flooding—high fuel level 18. Leaking or misaligned float
Engine hesitates on acceleration	1. Clogged fuel filter 2. Leaking fuel pump diaphragm 3. Low fuel pump pressure 4. Secondary throttle valves stuck, bent or misadjusted 5. Sticking or binding air valve 6. Defective accelerator pump 7. Vacuum leaks 8. Clogged air filter 9. Incorrect choke adjustment (engine cold)
Engine feels sluggish or flat on acceleration	1. Improperly adjusted idle speed or mixture 2. Clogged fuel filter 3. Defective accelerator pump 4. Dirty, plugged or incorrect main metering jets 5. Bent or sticking main metering rods 6. Sticking throttle valves 7. Stuck heat riser 8. Binding or stuck air valve 9. Dirty, plugged or incorrect secondary jets 10. Bent or sticking secondary metering rods. 11. Throttle body or manifold heat passages plugged 12. Improperly adjusted choke or choke vacuum break.
Carburetor floods	1. Defective fuel pump. Pressure too high. 2. Stuck choke valve 3. Dirty, worn or damaged float or needle valve/seat 4. Incorrect float/fuel level 5. Leaking float bowl

TROUBLESHOOTING

Condition	Possible Cause
Engine idles roughly and stalls	1. Incorrect idle speed 2. Clogged fuel filter 3. Dirt in fuel system or carburetor 4. Loose carburetor screws or attaching bolts 5. Broken carburetor gaskets 6. Air leaks 7. Dirty carburetor 8. Worn idle mixture needles 9. Throttle valves stuck open 10. Incorrectly adjusted float or fuel level 11. Clogged air filter
Engine runs unevenly or surges	1. Defective fuel pump 2. Dirty or clogged fuel filter 3. Plugged, loose or incorrect main metering jets or rods 4. Air leaks 5. Bent or sticking main metering rods 6. Stuck power piston 7. Incorrect float adjustment 8. Incorrect idle speed or mixture 9. Dirty or plugged idle system passages 10. Hard, brittle or broken gaskets 11. Loose attaching or mounting screws 12. Stuck or misaligned secondary throttle valves
Poor fuel economy	1. Poor driving habits 2. Stuck choke valve 3. Binding choke linkage 4. Stuck heat riser 5. Incorrect idle mixture 6. Defective accelerator pump 7. Air leaks 8. Plugged, loose or incorrect main metering jets 9. Improperly adjusted float or fuel level 10. Bent, misaligned or fuel-clogged float 11. Leaking float needle seat 12. Fuel leak 13. Accelerator pump discharge ball not seating properly 14. Incorrect main jets
Engine lacks high speed performance or power	1. Incorrect throttle linkage adjustment 2. Stuck or binding power piston 3. Defective accelerator pump 4. Air leaks 5. Incorrect float setting or fuel level 6. Dirty, plugged, worn or incorrect main metering jets or rods 7. Binding or sticking air valve 8. Brittle or cracked gaskets 9. Bent, incorrect or improperly adjusted secondary metering rods 10. Clogged fuel filter 11. Clogged air filter 12. Defective fuel pump

TROUBLESHOOTING FUEL INJECTION PROBLEMS

Each fuel injection system has its own unique components and test procedures, for which it is impossible to generalize. Refer to Chapter 4 of this Repair & Tune-Up Guide for specific test and repair procedures, if the vehicle is equipped with fuel injection.

TROUBLESHOOTING ELECTRICAL PROBLEMS

See Chapter 5 for service procedures

For any electrical system to operate, it must make a complete circuit. This simply means that the power flow from the battery must make a complete circle. When an electrical component is operating, power flows from the battery to the component, passes through the component causing it to perform its function (lighting a light bulb), and then returns to the battery through the ground of the circuit. This ground is usually (but not always) the metal part of the car or truck on which the electrical component is mounted.

Perhaps the easiest way to visualize this is to think of connecting a light bulb with two wires attached to it to the battery. If one of the two wires attached to the light bulb were attached to the negative post of the battery and the other were attached to the positive post of the battery, you would have a complete circuit. Current from the battery would flow to the light bulb, causing it to light, and return to the negative post of the battery.

The normal automotive circuit differs from this simple example in two ways. First, instead of having a return wire from the bulb to the battery, the light bulb returns the current to the battery through the chassis of the vehicle. Since the negative battery cable is attached to the chassis and the chassis is made of electrically conductive metal, the chassis of the vehicle can serve as a ground wire to complete the circuit. Secondly, most automotive circuits contain switches to turn components on and off as required.

Every complete circuit from a power source must include a component which is using the power from the power source. If you were to disconnect the light bulb from the wires and touch the two wires together (don't do this) the power supply wire to the component would be grounded before the normal ground connection for the circuit.

Because grounding a wire from a power source makes a complete circuit—less the required component to use the power—this phenomenon is called a short circuit. Common causes are: broken insulation (exposing the metal wire to a metal part of the car or truck), or a shorted switch.

Some electrical components which require a large amount of current to operate also have a relay in their circuit. Since these circuits carry a large amount of current, the thickness of the wire in the circuit (gauge size) is also greater. If this large wire were connected from the component to the control switch on the instrument panel, and then back to the component, a voltage drop would occur in the circuit. To prevent this potential drop in voltage, an electromagnetic switch (relay) is used. The large wires in the circuit are connected from the battery to one side of the relay, and from the opposite side of the relay to the component. The relay is normally open, preventing current from passing through the circuit. An additional, smaller, wire is connected from the relay to the control switch for the circuit. When the control switch is turned on, it grounds the smaller wire from the relay and completes the circuit. This closes the relay and allows current to flow from the battery to the component. The horn, headlight, and starter circuits are three which use relays.

It is possible for larger surges of current to pass through the electrical system of your car or truck. If this surge of current were to reach an electrical component, it could burn it out. To prevent this, fuses, circuit breakers or fusible links are connected into the current supply wires of most of the major electrical systems. When an electrical current of excessive power passes through the component's fuse, the fuse blows out and breaks the circuit, saving the component from destruction.

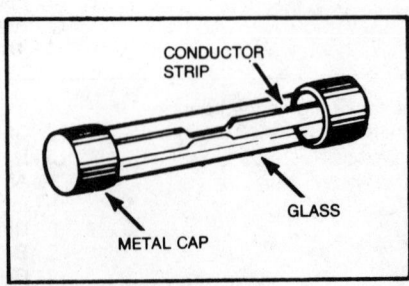

Typical automotive fuse

A circuit breaker is basically a self-repairing fuse. The circuit breaker opens the circuit the same way a fuse does. However, when either the short is removed from the circuit or the surge subsides, the circuit breaker resets itself and does not have to be replaced as a fuse does.

A fuse link is a wire that acts as a fuse. It is normally connected between the starter relay and the main wiring harness. This connection is usually under the hood. The fuse link (if installed) protects all the

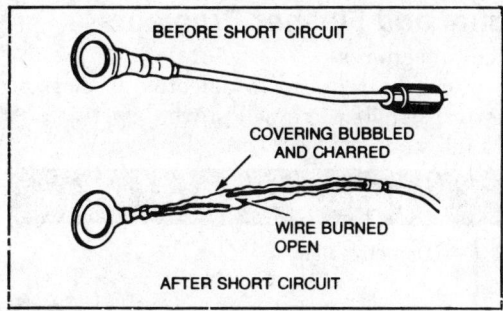

Most fusible links show a charred, melted insulation when they burn out

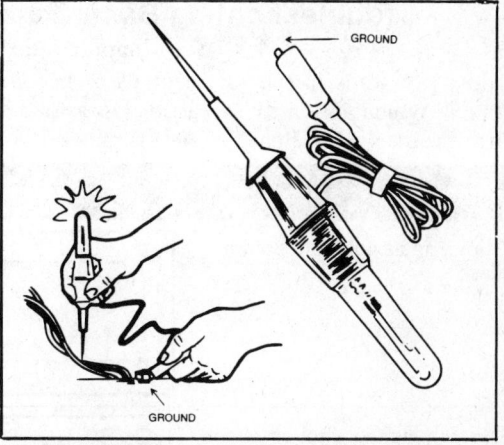

The test light will show the presence of current when touched to a hot wire and grounded at the other end

chassis electrical components, and is the probable cause of trouble when none of the electrical components function, unless the battery is disconnected or dead.

Electrical problems generally fall into one of three areas:

1. The component that is not functioning is not receiving current.
2. The component itself is not functioning.
3. The component is not properly grounded.

The electrical system can be checked with a test light and a jumper wire. A test light is a device that looks like a pointed screwdriver with a wire attached to it and has a light bulb in its handle. A jumper wire is a piece of insulated wire with an alligator clip attached to each end.

If a component is not working, you must follow a systematic plan to determine which of the three causes is the villain.

1. Turn on the switch that controls the inoperable component.
2. Disconnect the power supply wire from the component.
3. Attach the ground wire on the test light to a good metal ground.
4. Touch the probe end of the test light to the end of the power supply wire that was disconnected from the component. If the component is receiving current, the test light will go on.

NOTE: *Some components work only when the ignition switch is turned on.*

If the test light does not go on, then the problem is in the circuit between the battery and the component. This includes all the switches, fuses, and relays in the system. Follow the wire that runs back to the battery. The problem is an open circuit between the battery and the component. If the fuse is blown and, when replaced, immediately blows again, there is a short circuit in the system which must be located and repaired. If there is a switch in the system, bypass it with a jumper wire. This is done by connecting one end of the jumper wire to the power supply wire into the switch and the other end of the jumper wire to the wire coming out of the switch. If the test light lights with the jumper wire installed, the switch or whatever was bypassed is defective.

NOTE: *Never substitute the jumper wire for the component, since it is required to use the power from the power source.*

5. If the bulb in the test light goes on, then the current is getting to the component that is not working. This eliminates the first of the three possible causes. Connect the power supply wire and connect a jumper wire from the component to a good metal ground. Do this with the switch which controls the component turned on, and also the ignition switch turned on if it is required for the component to work. If the component works with the jumper wire installed, then it has a bad ground. This is usually caused by the metal area on which the component mounts to the chassis being coated with some type of foreign matter.

6. If neither test located the source of the trouble, then the component itself is defective. Remember that for any electrical system to work, all connections must be clean and tight.

294 TROUBLESHOOTING

Troubleshooting Basic Turn Signal and Flasher Problems
See Chapter 5 for service procedures

Most problems in the turn signals or flasher system can be reduced to defective flashers or bulbs, which are easily replaced. Occasionally, the turn signal switch will prove defective.

F = Front   R = Rear   ● = Lights off   ○ = Lights on

Condition		Possible Cause
Turn signals light, but do not flash	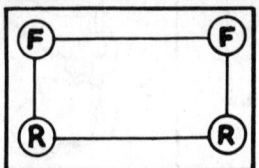	Defective flasher
No turn signals light on either side	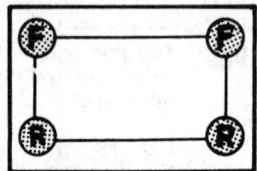	Blown fuse. Replace if defective. Defective flasher. Check by substitution. Open circuit, short circuit or poor ground.
Both turn signals on one side don't work	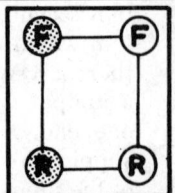	Bad bulbs. Bad ground in both (or either) housings.
One turn signal light on one side doesn't work	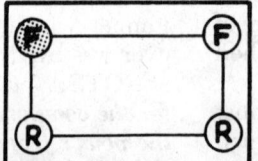	Defective bulb. Corrosion in socket. Clean contacts. Poor ground at socket.
Turn signal flashes too fast or too slowly	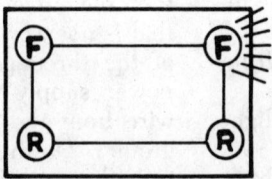	Check any bulb on the side flashing too fast. A heavy-duty bulb is probably installed in place of a regular bulb. Check the bulb flashing too slowly. A standard bulb was probably installed in place of a heavy-duty bulb. Loose connections or corrosion at the bulb socket.
Indicator lights don't work in either direction		Check if the turn signals are working. Check the dash indicator lights. Check the flasher by substitution.
One indicator light doesn't light		On systems with one dash indicator: See if the lights work on the same side. Often the filaments have been reversed in systems combining stoplights with taillights and turn signals. Check the flasher by substitution. On systems with two indicators: Check the bulbs on the same side. Check the indicator light bulb. Check the flasher by substitution.

TROUBLESHOOTING

Troubleshooting Lighting Problems
See Chapter 5 for service procedures

Condition	Possible Cause
One or more lights don't work, but others do	1. Defective bulb(s) 2. Blown fuse(s) 3. Dirty fuse clips or light sockets 4. Poor ground circuit
Lights burn out quickly	1. Incorrect voltage regulator setting or defective regulator 2. Poor battery/alternator connections
Lights go dim	1. Low/discharged battery 2. Alternator not charging 3. Corroded sockets or connections 4. Low voltage output
Lights flicker	1. Loose connection 2. Poor ground. (Run ground wire from light housing to frame) 3. Circuit breaker operating (short circuit)
Lights "flare"—Some flare is normal on acceleration—If excessive, see "Lights Burn Out Quickly"	High voltage setting
Lights glare—approaching drivers are blinded	1. Lights adjusted too high 2. Rear springs or shocks sagging 3. Rear tires soft

Troubleshooting Dash Gauge Problems

Most problems can be traced to a defective sending unit or faulty wiring. Occasionally, the gauge itself is at fault. See Chapter 5 for service procedures.

Condition	Possible Cause
COOLANT TEMPERATURE GAUGE	
Gauge reads erratically or not at all	1. Loose or dirty connections 2. Defective sending unit. 3. Defective gauge. To test a bi-metal gauge, remove the wire from the sending unit. Ground the wire for an instant. If the gauge registers, replace the sending unit. To test a magnetic gauge, disconnect the wire at the sending unit. With ignition ON gauge should register COLD. Ground the wire; gauge should register HOT.
AMMETER GAUGE—TURN HEADLIGHTS ON (DO NOT START ENGINE). NOTE REACTION	
Ammeter shows charge Ammeter shows discharge Ammeter does not move	1. Connections reversed on gauge 2. Ammeter is OK 3. Loose connections or faulty wiring 4. Defective gauge

TROUBLESHOOTING

Condition	Possible Cause
OIL PRESSURE GAUGE	
Gauge does not register or is inaccurate	1. On mechanical gauge, Bourdon tube may be bent or kinked. 2. Low oil pressure. Remove sending unit. Idle the engine briefly. If no oil flows from sending unit hole, problem is in engine. 3. Defective gauge. Remove the wire from the sending unit and ground it for an instant with the ignition ON. A good gauge will go to the top of the scale. 4. Defective wiring. Check the wiring to the gauge. If it's OK and the gauge doesn't register when grounded, replace the gauge. 5. Defective sending unit.
ALL GAUGES	
All gauges do not operate	1. Blown fuse 2. Defective instrument regulator
All gauges read low or erratically	3. Defective or dirty instrument voltage regulator
All gauges pegged	4. Loss of ground between instrument voltage regulator and frame 5. Defective instrument regulator
WARNING LIGHTS	
Light(s) do not come on when ignition is ON, but engine is not started	1. Defective bulb 2. Defective wire 3. Defective sending unit. Disconnect the wire from the sending unit and ground it. Replace the sending unit if the light comes on with the ignition ON.
Light comes on with engine running	4. Problem in individual system 5. Defective sending unit

Troubleshooting Clutch Problems

It is false economy to replace individual clutch components. The pressure plate, clutch plate and throwout bearing should be replaced as a set, and the flywheel face inspected, whenever the clutch is overhauled. See Chapter 6 for service procedures.

Condition	Possible Cause
Clutch chatter	1. Grease on driven plate (disc) facing 2. Binding clutch linkage or cable 3. Loose, damaged facings on driven plate (disc) 4. Engine mounts loose 5. Incorrect height adjustment of pressure plate release levers 6. Clutch housing or housing to transmission adapter misalignment 7. Loose driven plate hub
Clutch grabbing	1. Oil, grease on driven plate (disc) facing 2. Broken pressure plate 3. Warped or binding driven plate. Driven plate binding on clutch shaft
Clutch slips	1. Lack of lubrication in clutch linkage or cable (linkage or cable binds, causes incomplete engagement) 2. Incorrect pedal, or linkage adjustment 3. Broken pressure plate springs 4. Weak pressure plate springs 5. Grease on driven plate facings (disc)

TROUBLESHOOTING

Troubleshooting Clutch Problems (cont.)

Condition	Possible Cause
Incomplete clutch release	1. Incorrect pedal or linkage adjustment or linkage or cable binding 2. Incorrect height adjustment on pressure plate release levers 3. Loose, broken facings on driven plate (disc) 4. Bent, dished, warped driven plate caused by overheating
Grinding, whirring grating noise when pedal is depressed	1. Worn or defective throwout bearing 2. Starter drive teeth contacting flywheel ring gear teeth. Look for milled or polished teeth on ring gear.
Squeal, howl, trumpeting noise when pedal is being released (occurs during first inch to inch and one-half of pedal travel)	Pilot bushing worn or lack of lubricant. If bushing appears OK, polish bushing with emery cloth, soak lube wick in oil, lube bushing with oil, apply film of chassis grease to clutch shaft pilot hub, reassemble. NOTE: Bushing wear may be due to misalignment of clutch housing or housing to transmission adapter
Vibration or clutch pedal pulsation with clutch disengaged (pedal fully depressed)	1. Worn or defective engine transmission mounts 2. Flywheel run out. (Flywheel run out at face not to exceed 0.005") 3. Damaged or defective clutch components

Troubleshooting Manual Transmission Problems
See Chapter 6 for service procedures

Condition	Possible Cause
Transmission jumps out of gear	1. Misalignment of transmission case or clutch housing. 2. Worn pilot bearing in crankshaft. 3. Bent transmission shaft. 4. Worn high speed sliding gear. 5. Worn teeth or end-play in clutch shaft. 6. Insufficient spring tension on shifter rail plunger. 7. Bent or loose shifter fork. 8. Gears not engaging completely. 9. Loose or worn bearings on clutch shaft or mainshaft. 10. Worn gear teeth. 11. Worn or damaged detent balls.
Transmission sticks in gear	1. Clutch not releasing fully. 2. Burred or battered teeth on clutch shaft, or sliding sleeve. 3. Burred or battered transmission mainshaft. 4. Frozen synchronizing clutch. 5. Stuck shifter rail plunger. 6. Gearshift lever twisting and binding shifter rail. 7. Battered teeth on high speed sliding gear or on sleeve. 8. Improper lubrication, or lack of lubrication. 9. Corroded transmission parts. 10. Defective mainshaft pilot bearing. 11. Locked gear bearings will give same effect as stuck in gear.
Transmission gears will not synchronize	1. Binding pilot bearing on mainshaft, will synchronize in high gear only. 2. Clutch not releasing fully. 3. Detent spring weak or broken. 4. Weak or broken springs under balls in sliding gear sleeve. 5. Binding bearing on clutch shaft, or binding countershaft. 6. Binding pilot bearing in crankshaft. 7. Badly worn gear teeth. 8. Improper lubrication. 9. Constant mesh gear not turning freely on transmission mainshaft. Will synchronize in that gear only.

TROUBLESHOOTING

Condition	Possible Cause
Gears spinning when shifting into gear from neutral	1. Clutch not releasing fully. 2. In some cases an extremely light lubricant in transmission will cause gears to continue to spin for a short time after clutch is released. 3. Binding pilot bearing in crankshaft.
Transmission noisy in all gears	1. Insufficient lubricant, or improper lubricant. 2. Worn countergear bearings. 3. Worn or damaged main drive gear or countergear. 4. Damaged main drive gear or mainshaft bearings. 5. Worn or damaged countergear anti-lash plate.
Transmission noisy in neutral only	1. Damaged main drive gear bearing. 2. Damaged or loose mainshaft pilot bearing. 3. Worn or damaged countergear anti-lash plate. 4. Worn countergear bearings.
Transmission noisy in one gear only	1. Damaged or worn constant mesh gears. 2. Worn or damaged countergear bearings. 3. Damaged or worn synchronizer.
Transmission noisy in reverse only	1. Worn or damaged reverse idler gear or idler bushing. 2. Worn or damaged mainshaft reverse gear. 3. Worn or damaged reverse countergear. 4. Damaged shift mechanism.

TROUBLESHOOTING AUTOMATIC TRANSMISSION PROBLEMS

Keeping alert to changes in the operating characteristics of the transmission (changing shift points, noises, etc.) can prevent small problems from becoming large ones. If the problem cannot be traced to loose bolts, fluid level, misadjusted linkage, clogged filters or similar problems, you should probably seek professional service.

Transmission Fluid Indications

The appearance and odor of the transmission fluid can give valuable clues to the overall condition of the transmission. Always note the appearance of the fluid when you check the fluid level or change the fluid. Rub a small amount of fluid between your fingers to feel for grit and smell the fluid on the dipstick.

If the fluid appears:	It indicates:
Clear and red colored	Normal operation
Discolored (extremely dark red or brownish) or smells burned	Band or clutch pack failure, usually caused by an overheated transmission. Hauling very heavy loads with insufficient power or failure to change the fluid often result in overheating. Do not confuse this appearance with newer fluids that have a darker red color and a strong odor (though not a burned odor).
Foamy or aerated (light in color and full of bubbles)	1. The level is too high (gear train is churning oil) 2. An internal air leak (air is mixing with the fluid). Have the transmission checked professionally.
Solid residue in the fluid	Defective bands, clutch pack or bearings. Bits of band material or metal abrasives are clinging to the dipstick. Have the transmission checked professionally.
Varnish coating on the dipstick	The transmission fluid is overheating

TROUBLESHOOTING DRIVE AXLE PROBLEMS

First, determine when the noise is most noticeable.

Drive Noise: Produced under vehicle acceleration.

Coast Noise: Produced while coasting with a closed throttle.

Float Noise: Occurs while maintaining constant speed (just enough to keep speed constant) on a level road.

External Noise Elimination

It is advisable to make a thorough road test to determine whether the noise originates in the rear axle or whether it originates from the tires, engine, transmission, wheel bearings or road surface. Noise originating from other places cannot be corrected by servicing the rear axle.

ROAD NOISE

Brick or rough surfaced concrete roads produce noises that seem to come from the rear axle. Road noise is usually identical in Drive or Coast and driving on a different type of road will tell whether the road is the problem.

TIRE NOISE

Tire noise can be mistaken as rear axle noise, even though the tires on the front are at fault. Snow tread and mud tread tires or tires worn unevenly will frequently cause vibrations which seem to originate elsewhere; *temporarily, and for test purposes only,* inflate the tires to 40–50 lbs. This will significantly alter the noise produced by the tires, but will not alter noise from the rear axle. Noises from the rear axle will normally cease at speeds below 30 mph on coast, while tire noise will continue at lower tone as speed is decreased. The rear axle noise will usually change from drive conditions to coast conditions, while tire noise will not. Do not forget to lower the tire pressure to normal after the test is complete.

ENGINE/TRANSMISSION NOISE

Determine at what speed the noise is most pronounced, then stop in a quiet place. With the transmission in Neutral, run the engine through speeds corresponding to road speeds where the noise was noticed. Noises produced with the vehicle standing still are coming from the engine or transmission.

FRONT WHEEL BEARINGS

Front wheel bearing noises, sometimes confused with rear axle noises, will not change when comparing drive and coast conditions. While holding the speed steady, lightly apply the footbrake. This will often cause wheel bearing noise to lessen, as some of the weight is taken off the bearing. Front wheel bearings are easily checked by jacking up the wheels and spinning the wheels. Shaking the wheels will also determine if the wheel bearings are excessively loose.

REAR AXLE NOISES

Eliminating other possible sources can narrow the cause to the rear axle, which normally produces noise from worn gears or bearings. Gear noises tend to peak in a narrow speed range, while bearing noises will usually vary in pitch with engine speeds.

Noise Diagnosis

The Noise Is:	Most Probably Produced By:
1. Identical under Drive or Coast	Road surface, tires or front wheel bearings
2. Different depending on road surface	Road surface or tires
3. Lower as speed is lowered	Tires
4. Similar when standing or moving	Engine or transmission
5. A vibration	Unbalanced tires, rear wheel bearing, unbalanced driveshaft or worn U-joint
6. A knock or click about every two tire revolutions	Rear wheel bearing
7. Most pronounced on turns	Damaged differential gears
8. A steady low-pitched whirring or scraping, starting at low speeds	Damaged or worn pinion bearing
9. A chattering vibration on turns	Wrong differential lubricant or worn clutch plates (limited slip rear axle)
10. Noticed only in Drive, Coast or Float conditions	Worn ring gear and/or pinion gear

TROUBLESHOOTING

Troubleshooting Steering & Suspension Problems

Condition	Possible Cause
Hard steering (wheel is hard to turn)	1. Improper tire pressure 2. Loose or glazed pump drive belt 3. Low or incorrect fluid 4. Loose, bent or poorly lubricated front end parts 5. Improper front end alignment (excessive caster) 6. Bind in steering column or linkage 7. Kinked hydraulic hose 8. Air in hydraulic system 9. Low pump output or leaks in system 10. Obstruction in lines 11. Pump valves sticking or out of adjustment 12. Incorrect wheel alignment
Loose steering (too much play in steering wheel)	1. Loose wheel bearings 2. Faulty shocks 3. Worn linkage or suspension components 4. Loose steering gear mounting or linkage points 5. Steering mechanism worn or improperly adjusted 6. Valve spool improperly adjusted 7. Worn ball joints, tie-rod ends, etc.
Veers or wanders (pulls to one side with hands off steering wheel)	1. Improper tire pressure 2. Improper front end alignment 3. Dragging or improperly adjusted brakes 4. Bent frame 5. Improper rear end alignment 6. Faulty shocks or springs 7. Loose or bent front end components 8. Play in Pitman arm 9. Steering gear mountings loose 10. Loose wheel bearings 11. Binding Pitman arm 12. Spool valve sticking or improperly adjusted 13. Worn ball joints
Wheel oscillation or vibration transmitted through steering wheel	1. Low or uneven tire pressure 2. Loose wheel bearings 3. Improper front end alignment 4. Bent spindle 5. Worn, bent or broken front end components 6. Tires out of round or out of balance 7. Excessive lateral runout in disc brake rotor 8. Loose or bent shock absorber or strut
Noises (see also "Troubleshooting Drive Axle Problems")	1. Loose belts 2. Low fluid, air in system 3. Foreign matter in system 4. Improper lubrication 5. Interference or chafing in linkage 6. Steering gear mountings loose 7. Incorrect adjustment or wear in gear box 8. Faulty valves or wear in pump 9. Kinked hydraulic lines 10. Worn wheel bearings
Poor return of steering	1. Over-inflated tires 2. Improperly aligned front end (excessive caster) 3. Binding in steering column 4. No lubrication in front end 5. Steering gear adjusted too tight
Uneven tire wear (see "How To Read Tire Wear")	1. Incorrect tire pressure 2. Improperly aligned front end 3. Tires out-of-balance 4. Bent or worn suspension parts

TROUBLESHOOTING

HOW TO READ TIRE WEAR

The way your tires wear is a good indicator of other parts of the suspension. Abnormal wear patterns are often caused by the need for simple tire maintenance, or for front end alignment.

Excessive wear at the center of the tread indicates that the air pressure in the tire is consistently too high. The tire is riding on the center of the tread and wearing it prematurely. Occasionally, this wear pattern can result from outrageously wide tires on narrow rims. The cure for this is to replace either the tires or the wheels.

This type of wear usually results from consistent under-inflation. When a tire is under-inflated, there is too much contact with the road by the outer treads, which wear prematurely. When this type of wear occurs, and the tire pressure is known to be consistently correct, a bent or worn steering component or the need for wheel alignment could be indicated.

Feathering is a condition when the edge of each tread rib develops a slightly rounded edge on one side and a sharp edge on the other. By running your hand over the tire, you can usually feel the sharper edges before you'll be able to see them. The most common causes of feathering are incorrect toe-in setting or deteriorated bushings in the front suspension.

When an inner or outer rib wears faster than the rest of the tire, the need for wheel alignment is indicated. There is excessive camber in the front suspension, causing the wheel to lean too much putting excessive load on one side of the tire. Misalignment could also be due to sagging springs, worn ball joints, or worn control arm bushings. Be sure the vehicle is loaded the way it's normally driven when you have the wheels aligned.

Cups or scalloped dips appearing around the edge of the tread almost always indicate worn (sometimes bent) suspension parts. Adjustment of wheel alignment alone will seldom cure the problem. Any worn component that connects the wheel to the suspension can cause this type of wear. Occasionally, wheels that are out of balance will wear like this, but wheel imbalance usually shows up as bald spots between the outside edges and center of the tread.

Second-rib wear is usually found only in radial tires, and appears where the steel belts end in relation to the tread. It can be kept to a minimum by paying careful attention to tire pressure and frequently rotating the tires. This is often considered normal wear but excessive amounts indicate that the tires are too wide for the wheels.

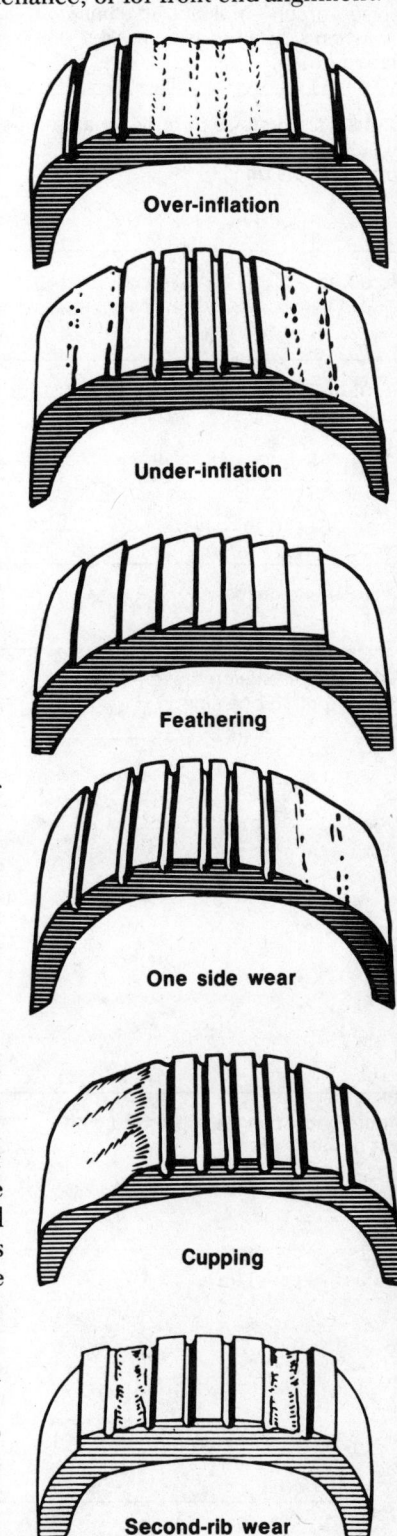

TROUBLESHOOTING

Troubleshooting Disc Brake Problems

Condition	Possible Cause
Noise—groan—brake noise emanating when slowly releasing brakes (creep-groan)	Not detrimental to function of disc brakes—no corrective action required. (This noise may be eliminated by slightly increasing or decreasing brake pedal efforts.)
Rattle—brake noise or rattle emanating at low speeds on rough roads, (front wheels only).	1. Shoe anti-rattle spring missing or not properly positioned. 2. Excessive clearance between shoe and caliper. 3. Soft or broken caliper seals. 4. Deformed or misaligned disc. 5. Loose caliper.
Scraping	1. Mounting bolts too long. 2. Loose wheel bearings. 3. Bent, loose, or misaligned splash shield.
Front brakes heat up during driving and fail to release	1. Operator riding brake pedal. 2. Stop light switch improperly adjusted. 3. Sticking pedal linkage. 4. Frozen or seized piston. 5. Residual pressure valve in master cylinder. 6. Power brake malfunction. 7. Proportioning valve malfunction.
Leaky brake caliper	1. Damaged or worn caliper piston seal. 2. Scores or corrosion on surface of cylinder bore.
Grabbing or uneven brake action—Brakes pull to one side	1. Causes listed under "Brakes Pull". 2. Power brake malfunction. 3. Low fluid level in master cylinder. 4. Air in hydraulic system. 5. Brake fluid, oil or grease on linings. 6. Unmatched linings. 7. Distorted brake pads. 8. Frozen or seized pistons. 9. Incorrect tire pressure. 10. Front end out of alignment. 11. Broken rear spring. 12. Brake caliper pistons sticking. 13. Restricted hose or line. 14. Caliper not in proper alignment to braking disc. 15. Stuck or malfunctioning metering valve. 16. Soft or broken caliper seals. 17. Loose caliper.
Brake pedal can be depressed without braking effect	1. Air in hydraulic system or improper bleeding procedure. 2. Leak past primary cup in master cylinder. 3. Leak in system. 4. Rear brakes out of adjustment. 5. Bleeder screw open.
Excessive pedal travel	1. Air, leak, or insufficient fluid in system or caliper. 2. Warped or excessively tapered shoe and lining assembly. 3. Excessive disc runout. 4. Rear brake adjustment required. 5. Loose wheel bearing adjustment. 6. Damaged caliper piston seal. 7. Improper brake fluid (boil). 8. Power brake malfunction. 9. Weak or soft hoses.

TROUBLESHOOTING

Troubleshooting Disc Brake Problems (cont.)

Condition	Possible Cause
Brake roughness or chatter (pedal pumping)	1. Excessive thickness variation of braking disc. 2. Excessive lateral runout of braking disc. 3. Rear brake drums out-of-round. 4. Excessive front bearing clearance.
Excessive pedal effort	1. Brake fluid, oil or grease on linings. 2. Incorrect lining. 3. Frozen or seized pistons. 4. Power brake malfunction. 5. Kinked or collapsed hose or line. 6. Stuck metering valve. 7. Scored caliper or master cylinder bore. 8. Seized caliper pistons.
Brake pedal fades (pedal travel increases with foot on brake)	1. Rough master cylinder or caliper bore. 2. Loose or broken hydraulic lines/connections. 3. Air in hydraulic system. 4. Fluid level low. 5. Weak or soft hoses. 6. Inferior quality brake shoes or fluid. 7. Worn master cylinder piston cups or seals.

Troubleshooting Drum Brakes

Condition	Possible Cause
Pedal goes to floor	1. Fluid low in reservoir. 2. Air in hydraulic system. 3. Improperly adjusted brake. 4. Leaking wheel cylinders. 5. Loose or broken brake lines. 6. Leaking or worn master cylinder. 7. Excessively worn brake lining.
Spongy brake pedal	1. Air in hydraulic system. 2. Improper brake fluid (low boiling point). 3. Excessively worn or cracked brake drums. 4. Broken pedal pivot bushing.
Brakes pulling	1. Contaminated lining. 2. Front end out of alignment. 3. Incorrect brake adjustment. 4. Unmatched brake lining. 5. Brake drums out of round. 6. Brake shoes distorted. 7. Restricted brake hose or line. 8. Broken rear spring. 9. Worn brake linings. 10. Uneven lining wear. 11. Glazed brake lining. 12. Excessive brake lining dust. 13. Heat spotted brake drums. 14. Weak brake return springs. 15. Faulty automatic adjusters. 16. Low or incorrect tire pressure.

TROUBLESHOOTING

Condition	Possible Cause
Squealing brakes	1. Glazed brake lining. 2. Saturated brake lining. 3. Weak or broken brake shoe retaining spring. 4. Broken or weak brake shoe return spring. 5. Incorrect brake lining. 6. Distorted brake shoes. 7. Bent support plate. 8. Dust in brakes or scored brake drums. 9. Linings worn below limit. 10. Uneven brake lining wear. 11. Heat spotted brake drums.
Chirping brakes	1. Out of round drum or eccentric axle flange pilot.
Dragging brakes	1. Incorrect wheel or parking brake adjustment. 2. Parking brakes engaged or improperly adjusted. 3. Weak or broken brake shoe return spring. 4. Brake pedal binding. 5. Master cylinder cup sticking. 6. Obstructed master cylinder relief port. 7. Saturated brake lining. 8. Bent or out of round brake drum. 9. Contaminated or improper brake fluid. 10. Sticking wheel cylinder pistons. 11. Driver riding brake pedal. 12. Defective proportioning valve. 13. Insufficient brake shoe lubricant.
Hard pedal	1. Brake booster inoperative. 2. Incorrect brake lining. 3. Restricted brake line or hose. 4. Frozen brake pedal linkage. 5. Stuck wheel cylinder. 6. Binding pedal linkage. 7. Faulty proportioning valve.
Wheel locks	1. Contaminated brake lining. 2. Loose or torn brake lining. 3. Wheel cylinder cups sticking. 4. Incorrect wheel bearing adjustment. 5. Faulty proportioning valve.
Brakes fade (high speed)	1. Incorrect lining. 2. Overheated brake drums. 3. Incorrect brake fluid (low boiling temperature). 4. Saturated brake lining. 5. Leak in hydraulic system. 6. Faulty automatic adjusters.
Pedal pulsates	1. Bent or out of round brake drum.
Brake chatter and shoe knock	1. Out of round brake drum. 2. Loose support plate. 3. Bent support plate. 4. Distorted brake shoes. 5. Machine grooves in contact face of brake drum (Shoe Knock). 6. Contaminated brake lining. 7. Missing or loose components. 8. Incorrect lining material. 9. Out-of-round brake drums. 10. Heat spotted or scored brake drums. 11. Out-of-balance wheels.

Troubleshooting Drum Brakes (cont.)

Condition	Possible Cause
Brakes do not self adjust	1. Adjuster screw frozen in thread. 2. Adjuster screw corroded at thrust washer. 3. Adjuster lever does not engage star wheel. 4. Adjuster installed on wrong wheel.
Brake light glows	1. Leak in the hydraulic system. 2. Air in the system. 3. Improperly adjusted master cylinder pushrod. 4. Uneven lining wear. 5. Failure to center combination valve or proportioning valve.

Mechanic's Data

General Conversion Table

Multiply By	To Convert	To	
LENGTH			
2.54	Inches	Centimeters	.3937
25.4	Inches	Millimeters	.03937
30.48	Feet	Centimeters	.0328
.304	Feet	Meters	3.28
.914	Yards	Meters	1.094
1.609	Miles	Kilometers	.621
VOLUME			
.473	Pints	Liters	2.11
.946	Quarts	Liters	1.06
3.785	Gallons	Liters	.264
.016	Cubic inches	Liters	61.02
16.39	Cubic inches	Cubic cms.	.061
28.3	Cubic feet	Liters	.0353
MASS (Weight)			
28.35	Ounces	Grams	.035
.4536	Pounds	Kilograms	2.20
—	To obtain	From	Multiply by

Multiply By	To Convert	To	
AREA			
.645	Square inches	Square cms.	.155
.836	Square yds.	Square meters	1.196
FORCE			
4.448	Pounds	Newtons	.225
.138	Ft./lbs.	Kilogram/meters	7.23
1.36	Ft./lbs.	Newton-meters	.737
.112	In./lbs.	Newton-meters	8.844
PRESSURE			
.068	Psi	Atmospheres	14.7
6.89	Psi	Kilopascals	.145
OTHER			
1.104	Horsepower (DIN)	Horsepower (SAE)	.9861
.746	Horsepower (SAE)	Kilowatts (KW)	1.34
1.60	Mph	Km/h	.625
.425	Mpg	Km/1	2.35
—	To obtain	From	Multiply by

Tap Drill Sizes

National Coarse or U.S.S.

Screw & Tap Size	Threads Per Inch	Use Drill Number
No. 5	40	39
No. 6	32	36
No. 8	32	29
No. 10	24	25
No. 12	24	17
1/4	20	8
5/16	18	F
3/8	16	5/16
7/16	14	U
1/2	13	27/64
9/16	12	31/64
5/8	11	17/32
3/4	10	21/32
7/8	9	49/64

National Coarse or U.S.S.

Screw & Tap Size	Threads Per Inch	Use Drill Number
1	8	7/8
1 1/8	7	63/64
1 1/4	7	1 7/64
1 1/2	6	1 11/32

National Fine or S.A.E.

Screw & Tap Size	Threads Per Inch	Use Drill Number
No. 5	44	37
No. 6	40	33
No. 8	36	29
No. 10	32	21

National Fine or S.A.E.

Screw & Tap Size	Threads Per Inch	Use Drill Number
No. 12	28	15
1/4	28	3
5/16	24	1
3/8	24	Q
7/16	20	W
1/2	20	29/64
9/16	18	33/64
5/8	18	37/64
3/4	16	11/16
7/8	14	13/16
1 1/8	12	1 3/64
1 1/4	12	1 11/64
1 1/2	12	1 27/64

MECHANIC'S DATA

Drill Sizes In Decimal Equivalents

Inch	Decimal	Wire	mm	Inch	Decimal	Wire	mm	Inch	Decimal	Wire & Letter	mm	Inch	Decimal	Letter	mm	Inch	Decimal	mm
1/64	.0156		.39		.0730	49			.1614		4.1		.2717		6.9		.4331	11.0
	.0157		.4		.0748		1.9		.1654		4.2		.2720	I		7/16	.4375	11.11
	.0160	78			.0760	48			.1660	19			.2756		7.0		.4528	11.5
	.0165		.42		.0768		1.95		.1673		4.25		.2770	J		29/64	.4531	11.51
	.0173		.44	5/64	.0781		1.98		.1693		4.3		.2795		7.1	15/32	.4688	11.90
	.0177		.45		.0785	47			.1695	18			.2810	K			.4724	12.0
	.0180	77			.0787		2.0	11/64	.1719		4.36	9/32	.2812		7.14	31/64	.4844	12.30
	.0181		.46		.0807		2.05		.1730	17			.2835		7.2		.4921	12.5
	.0189		.48		.0810	46			.1732		4.4		.2854		7.25	1/2	.5000	12.70
	.0197		.5		.0820	45			.1770	16			.2874		7.3		.5118	13.0
	.0200	76			.0827		2.1		.1772		4.5		.2900	L		33/64	.5156	13.09
	.0210	75			.0846		2.15		.1800	15			.2913		7.4	17/32	.5312	13.49
	.0217		.55		.0860	44			.1811		4.6		.2950	M			.5315	13.5
	.0225	74			.0866		2.2		.1820	14			.2953		7.5	35/64	.5469	13.89
	.0236		.6		.0886		2.25		.1850	13		19/64	.2969		7.54		.5512	14.0
	.0240	73			.0890	43			.1850		4.7		.2992		7.6	9/16	.5625	14.28
	.0250	72			.0906		2.3		.1870		4.75		.3020	N			.5709	14.5
	.0256		.65		.0925		2.35	3/16	.1875		4.76		.3031		7.7	37/64	.5781	14.68
	.0260	71			.0935	42			.1890		4.8		.3051		7.75		.5906	15.0
	.0276		.7	3/32	.0938		2.38		.1890	12			.3071		7.8	19/32	.5938	15.08
	.0280	70			.0945		2.4		.1910	11			.3110		7.9	39/64	.6094	15.47
	.0292	69			.0960	41			.1929		4.9		.3125		7.93		.6102	15.5
	.0295		.75		.0965		2.45		.1935	10		5/16	.3150		8.0	5/8	.6250	15.87
	.0310	68			.0980	40			.1960	9			.3160	O			.6299	16.0
1/32	.0312		.79		.0981		2.5		.1969		5.0		.3189		8.1	41/64	.6406	16.27
	.0315		.8		.0995	39			.1990	8			.3228		8.2		.6496	16.5
	.0320	67			.1015	38			.2008		5.1		.3230	P		21/32	.6562	16.66
	.0330	66			.1024		2.6		.2010	7			.3248		8.25		.6693	17.0
	.0335		.85		.1040	37		13/64	.2031		5.16		.3268		8.3	43/64	.6719	17.06
	.0350	65			.1063		2.7		.2040	6		21/64	.3281		8.33	11/16	.6875	17.46
	.0354		.9		.1065	36			.2047		5.2		.3307		8.4		.6890	17.5
	.0360	64			.1083		2.75		.2055	5			.3320	Q		45/64	.7031	17.85
	.0370	63		7/64	.1094		2.77		.2067		5.25		.3346		8.5		.7087	18.0
	.0374		.95		.1100	35			.2087		5.3		.3386		8.6	23/32	.7188	18.25
	.0380	62			.1102		2.8		.2090	4			.3390	R			.7283	18.5
	.0390	61			.1110	34			.2126		5.4		.3425		8.7	47/64	.7344	18.65
	.0394		1.0		.1130	33			.2130	3		11/32	.3438		8.73		.7480	19.0
	.0400	60			.1142		2.9		.2165		5.5		.3445		8.75	3/4	.7500	19.05
	.0410	59			.1160	32		7/32	.2188		5.55		.3465		8.8	49/64	.7656	19.44
	.0413		1.05		.1181		3.0		.2205		5.6		.3480	S			.7677	19.5
	.0420	58			.1200	31			.2210	2			.3504		8.9	25/32	.7812	19.84
	.0430	57			.1220		3.1		.2244		5.7		.3543		9.0		.7874	20.0
	.0433		1.1	1/8	.1250		3.17		.2264		5.75		.3580	T		51/64	.7969	20.24
	.0453		1.15		.1260		3.2		.2280	1			.3583		9.1		.8071	20.5
	.0465	56			.1280		3.25		.2283		5.8	23/64	.3594		9.12	13/16	.8125	20.63
3/64	.0469		1.19		.1285	30			.2323		5.9		.3622		9.2		.8268	21.0
	.0472		1.2		.1299		3.3		.2340	A			.3642		9.25	53/64	.8281	21.03
	.0492		1.25		.1339		3.4	15/64	.2344		5.95		.3661		9.3	27/32	.8438	21.43
	.0512		1.3		.1360	29			.2362		6.0		.3680	U			.8465	21.5
	.0520	55			.1378		3.5		.2380	B			.3701		9.4	55/64	.8594	21.82
	.0531		1.35		.1405	28			.2402		6.1		.3740		9.5		.8661	22.0
	.0550	54		9/64	.1406		3.57		.2420	C		3/8	.3750		9.52	7/8	.8750	22.22
	.0551		1.4		.1417		3.6		.2441		6.2		.3770	V			.8858	22.5
	.0571		1.45		.1440	27			.2460	D			.3780		9.6	57/64	.8906	22.62
	.0591		1.5		.1457		3.7		.2461		6.25		.3819		9.7		.9055	23.0
	.0595	53			.1470	26			.2480		6.3		.3839		9.75	29/32	.9062	23.01
	.0610		1.55		.1476		3.75	1/4	.2500	E	6.35		.3858		9.8	59/64	.9219	23.41
1/16	.0625		1.59		.1495	25			.2520		6.		.3860	W			.9252	23.5
	.0630		1.6		.1496		3.8		.2559		6.5		.3898		9.9	15/16	.9375	23.81
	.0635	52			.1520	24			.2570	F		25/64	.3906		9.92		.9449	24.0
	.0650		1.65		.1535		3.9		.2598		6.6		.3937		10.0	61/64	.9531	24.2
	.0669		1.7		.1540	23			.2610	G			.3970	X			.9646	24.5
	.0670	51		5/32	.1562		3.96		.2638		6.7		.4040	Y		31/64	.9688	24.6
	.0689		1.75		.1570	22		17/64	.2656		6.74	13/32	.4062		10.31		.9843	25.0
	.0700	50			.1575		4.0		.2657		6.75		.4130	Z		63/64	.9844	25.0
	.0709		1.8		.1590	21			.2660	H			.4134		10.5	1	1.0000	25.4
	.0728		1.85		.1610	20			.2677		6.8	27/64	.4219		10.71			

Index

A

Air cleaner, 8-9
Air conditioning inspection, 16-18
Air pump, 136-138
Alternator, 65-68
Antifreeze, 23-24, 29-30
Automatic transmission
   Adjustments, 195-198
   Filter change, 28-29
   Pan removal, 28-29, 194-195
   Removal and installation, 198
Axle
   Axle shaft bearings and seals
      Rear, 207-208
   CV joint, 199-26
   Fluid recommendations, 23
   Identification, 199
   Lubricant level, 29

B

Ball joints, 215, 226-227
Battery
   Fluid level, 11
   Jump starting, 34-35
   Maintenance, 11-13
   Removal and installation, 13, 72
Belts, 13-16
Brakes
   Adjustment, 231-232
   Bleeding, 237-238
   Brake light switch, 232, 237
   Disc brakes
      Caliper, 240-241, 248-249
      Pads, 231, 238-240, 247-248
      Rotor, 241-243, 249-250
   Drum brakes
      Drum, 243-245
      Shoes, 231, 245-246
      Wheel cylinder, 246-247
   Fluid level, 32
   Identification, 230-231, 243
   Master cylinder, 232-236
   Parking brake, 250-252
   Power booster, 236
   Proportioning valve, 236-237
   Specifications, 23, 252

C

Calipers, 240-241, 248-249
Camshaft and bearings, 81, 113-117
Capacities, 23
Carburetor
   Adjustments, 56-59, 152-156
   Overhaul, 153-156
   Replacement, 152
   Specifications, 33, 157
Catalytic converter, 10-11, 128-130, 145
Chassis electrical, 168-185
Chassis lubrication, 23, 33
Charging system, 65-72
Circuit breakers, 184-185
Clutch
   Adjustment, 187-190
   Description, 187
   Hydraulic system bleeding, 192-193
   Master cylinder, 32, 191
   Slave cylinder, 192
   Removal and Installation, 190-191
Coil (ignition), 62
Combination manifold, 91-92
Combination switch, 225
Compression testing, 77-79
Condenser, 42-44
Connecting rods and bearings, 82, 117-121
Constant velocity (CV) joints, 199-206
Control arm
   Lower, 216, 223-224
Cooling system, 24, 29-32, 94-97
Crankcase ventilation valve, 9-10, 132-133
Crankshaft, 82, 122-127
Cylinder head
   Inspection, 99
   Removal and installation, 97-101
Cylinders
   Inspection, 119
   Reboring & refinishing, 119-120

D

Differential
   Fluid level, 23, 29
   Rear, 199-207
Dimmer switch, 225
Disc brakes, 231, 240-243, 247-250
Distributor
   Breaker points, 42-45
   Condenser, 42-44
   Removal and installation, 62-65
Doors, 253
Door lock, 253-254
Door panels, 265
   Glass, 265-269
   Regulator, 265-269
Drive axle
   Identification, 199
   Rear, 199-207
Driveshaft
   Removal and Installation, 198-199
Drum brakes, 231, 243-247
Dwell angle, 38, 44-45

E

EGR valve, 139-143
Electrical
   Chassis, 168-185
   Engine, 41-42, 42-55, 72-75
Electronic Ignition, 52-55
Emission controls, 9-11, 132-150

Engine
    Camshaft, 113-117
    Combination manifold, 91-92
    Connecting rods, 117-121
    Crankshaft, 122-127
    Cylinder head, 97-101
    Cylinders, 119-120
    Design, 76
    Exhaust manifold, 91
    Fluids and lubricants, 22-27
    Flywheel, 127-128
    Front (timing) cover, 109-110
    Front seal, 109-110
    Identification, 7-8, 41-42
    Intake manifold, 90-91
    Main bearings, 122-127
    Oil pan, 107
    Oil pump, 107-108
    Oil seal, 121-122, 109-110
    Overhaul, 76
    Pistons, 117-121
    Rear main seal, 121-122
    Removal and installation, 79-88
    Rings, 117-121
    Rocker arms and/or shafts, 88-89
    Specifications, 23, 38-39, 78, 79-83
    Thermal reactor, 10-11, 128-130
    Timing belt, 110-113
    Timing chain, 110-113
    Turbocharger, 92-94
    Valve guides, 105-106
    Valves, 55-56, 101-102
    Valve seats, 103-105
    Valve springs, 103
    Valve timing, 55-56
    Water pump, 96-97
Evaporative canister, 10-11, 133-136
Exhaust Manifold, 91
Extension Tube, 130

F

Fan, 170-171
Firing orders, 41-42
Flashers, 185
Fluids and lubricants
    Automatic transmission, 23, 27-29
    Battery, 11-12
    Brake, 23, 32
    Chassis greasing, 23, 33
    Clutch, 23, 32
    Coolant, 23, 29-30
    Drive axle, 23, 29
    Engine oil, 23
    Manual transmission, 23, 27-28
    Master cylinder
        brake, 23, 32
        clutch, 23, 32
    Power steering, 23, 32-33
    Steering gear, 23, 32-33
    Steering knuckle, 23
Flywheel and ring gear, 127-128
Front brakes, 231, 238-243

Front suspension
    Ball joints, 215, 226-227
    Lower control arm, 216
    Radius arms, 217
    Shock absorbers, 210-213
    Springs, 210-213
    Struts, 213-214
    Sway bars, 216
    Torsion bars, 213
    Wheel alignment, 217-219
Fuel injection
    Injection pump, 158-162
    Injection timing
    Injectors, 163-165
    Testing, 161-162
    Throttle body, 162
Fuel filter, 21-22
Fuel pump, 150-151, 158-162
Fuel system
    Gasoline, 150
Fuel tank, 166-167
Fuses and circuit breakers, 185
Fusible links, 184-185

G

Gearshift linkage adjustment
    Automatic, 195-196
Generator, 65-68

H

Halfshafts, 199-208
Hatch, 255-258
Headlights, 182-184
Headlight switch, 181
Headliner, 271
Heater
    Blower, 170-171
    Core, 171-174
    Unit, 170-174
Hood, 254-255
Hoses, 16-17
How to buy a used car
Hubs, 207-208

I

Identification
    Axle, 29, 199
    Engine, 7-8
    Transmission, 8
    Vehicle, 6-7
Idle speed and mixture adjustment, 38-39, 57-61
Ignition switch, 226
Ignition timing, 38-39, 53-55
Injection pump, 158-162
Injectors, 163-165
Instrument cluster, 179-180
Instrument panel, 179-180
Intake manifold, 90-91

INDEX

J
Jacking points, 35-36
Jump starting, 35

K
Knuckles, 217

L
Lower control arm, 216
Lubrication
  Chassis, 23
  Differential, 23, 29
  Engine, 23, 107-108
  Transmission, 23, 27-29

M
MacPherson Struts
  Front, 213-214
  Rear, 223-224
Main bearings, 82, 122-127
Maintenance intervals, 24, 22-34
Manifolds
  Combination, 91-92
  Intake, 90-91
  Exhaust, 91
Manual transmission, 8, 27-28, 186-187
Master cylinder
  Brake, 32
  Clutch, 32, 191-192
Mechanic's data, 306-307
Model identification, 5-7
Muffler, 130

N
Neutral safety switch, 197-198

O
Oil and fuel recommendations, 22
Oil and filter change (engine), 23-27
Oil cooler
Oil level check, 24-25, 29
Oil pan, 28-29, 107
Oil pump, 107-108
Oxygen Sensor, 146-147

P
Pistons, 117-121
PCV valve, 9-10
Pivot pins, 120-121
Points, 42-45
Power brake booster, 250-252
Power steering pump, 229
Power window motor, 269-271
Power seat motor, 271

R
Radiator, 29-32, 94-96
Radio, 174-175
Rear axle, 29, 199-206
Rear brakes, 243-250
Rear main oil seal, 121-122
Rear suspension
  Alignment, 218, 224-225
  Control arms, 223-224
  Shock absorbers, 220
  Springs, 219-220
  Struts, 220-223
  Sway bars, 224
Rear wheel bearings, 207-208
Rear window, 262-265
Regulator, 68-72
Rings, 83, 117-121
Rocker arms' or shaft, 88-89
Routine maintenance, 24

S
Safety notice, ii, 4-5
Serial number location, 6-8
Shock absorbers
  Front, 210-213
  Rear, 220-223
Slave cylinder, 192
Solenoid, 75
Spark plugs, 37-41
Special tools, 2-4, 76
Specifications
  Alternator and regulator, 70-71
  Battery, 11-12
  Brakes, 252
  Camshaft, 81
  Capacities, 23
  Carburetor, 157
  Crankshaft and connecting rod, 82
  General engine, 79
  Generator, 70-71
  Piston and ring, 83
  Regulator, 70-71
  Starter, 75
  Torque, 78, 80
  Tune-up, 38-39
  Valves, 80
  Wheel alignment, 218
Speedometer cable, 181
Springs
  Front, 210-213
  Rear, 219-220
Starter, 72-75
Steering column, 226
Steering gear
  Manual, 32-33, 228-229
  Power, 32-33, 227-228
Steering knuckles, 217
Steering linkage, 227-229
Steering wheel, 225
Stripped threads, 76-77

INDEX

T

Thermal reactor, 128-130
Thermostat, 89-90
Throttle opener, 138-139
Tie rod ends, 226-227
Timing (ignition), 53-55
Timing belt, 110-113
Timing chain, 110-113
Tires, 18-21
Tools, 2-4, 76
Torsion bars, 213, 223-224
Towing, 35
Transmission
   Automatic, 8, 27-29, 193-194, 198
   Manual, 8, 27-28, 186-187
   Routine maintenance, 24, 27-29, 194-198
Troubleshooting, 272-305
Tune-up
   Procedures, 37, 42-55, 57-61
   Specifications, 38-39
Turbocharger, 92-94
Turn signal switch, 225-226

U

U-joints, 198-199

V

Valve guides, 105-106
Valves
   Adjustment, 55-56
   Service, 101-102
   Specifications, 80
Valve seats, 103-105
Valve springs, 103
Valve timing, 55-56
Vehicle identification, 6-7

W

Water pump, 96-97
Wheel alignment, 217-219, 224-225
Wheel bearings, 33
Wheel cylinders, 240-241, 248-249
Windshield, 258-262
Windshield wipers
   Arm, 175-177
   Blade, 18-19, 175-177
   Linkage, 177
   Motor, 177
   Rear window wiper, 177
   Switch, 180, 225-226
Wiring diagrams, 185

Chilton's Repair & Tune-Up Guides

The Complete line covers domestic cars, imports, trucks, vans, RV's and 4-wheel drive vehicles.

RTUG Title	Part No.
AMC 1975-82 Covers all U.S. and Canadian models	7199
Aspen/Volare 1976-80 Covers all U.S. and Canadian models	6637
Audi 1970-73 Covers all U.S. and Canadian models.	5902
Audi 4000/5000 1978-81 Covers all U.S. and Canadian models including turbocharged and diesel engines	7028
Barracuda/Challenger 1965-72 Covers all U.S. and Canadian models	5807
Blazer/Jimmy 1969-82 Covers all U.S. and Canadian 2- and 4-wheel drive models, including diesel engines	6931
BMW 1970-82 Covers U.S. and Canadian models	6844
Buick/Olds/Pontiac 1975-85 Covers U.S. and Canadian full size rear wheel drive models	7308
Cadillac 1967-84 Covers all U.S. and Canadian rear wheel drive models	7462
Camaro 1967-81 Covers all U.S. and Canadian models	6735
Camaro 1982-85 Covers all U.S. and Canadian models	7317
Capri 1970-77 Covers all U.S. and Canadian models	6695
Caravan/Voyager 1984-85 Covers all U.S. and Canadian models	7482
Century/Regal 1975-85 Covers all U.S. and Canadian rear wheel drive models, including turbocharged engines	7307
Champ/Arrow/Sapporo 1978-83 Covers all U.S. and Canadian models	7041
Chevette/1000 1976-86 Covers all U.S. and Canadian models	6836
Chevrolet 1968-85 Covers all U.S. and Canadian models	7135
Chevrolet 1968-79 Spanish	7082
Chevrolet/GMC Pick-Ups 1970-82 Spanish	7468
Chevrolet/GMC Pick-Ups and Suburban 1970-86 Covers all U.S. and Canadian $1/2$, $3/4$ and 1 ton models, including 4-wheel drive and diesel engines	6936
Chevrolet LUV 1972-81 Covers all U.S. and Canadian models	6815
Chevrolet Mid-Size 1964-86 Covers all U.S. and Canadian models of 1964-77 Chevelle, Malibu and Malibu SS; 1974-77 Laguna; 1978-85 Malibu; 1970-86 Monte Carlo; 1964-84 El Camino, including diesel engines	6840
Chevrolet Nova 1986 Covers all U.S. and Canadian models	7658
Chevy/GMC Vans 1967-84 Covers all U.S. and Canadian models of $1/2$, $3/4$, and 1 ton vans, cutaways, and motor home chassis, including diesel engines	6930
Chevy S-10 Blazer/GMC S-15 Jimmy 1982-85 Covers all U.S. and Canadian models	7383
Chevy S-10/GMC S-15 Pick-Ups 1982-85 Covers all U.S. and Canadian models	7310
Chevy II/Nova 1962-79 Covers all U.S. and Canadian models	6841
Chrysler K- and E-Car 1981-85 Covers all U.S. and Canadian front wheel drive models	7163
Colt/Challenger/Vista/Conquest 1971-85 Covers all U.S. and Canadian models	7037
Corolla/Carina/Tercel/Starlet 1970-85 Covers all U.S. and Canadian models	7036
Corona/Cressida/Crown/Mk.II/Camry/Van 1970-84 Covers all U.S. and Canadian models	7044

RTUG Title	Part No.
Corvair 1960-69 Covers all U.S. and Canadian models	6691
Corvette 1953-62 Covers all U.S. and Canadian models	6576
Corvette 1963-84 Covers all U.S. and Canadian models	6843
Cutlass 1970-85 Covers all U.S. and Canadian models	6933
Dart/Demon 1968-76 Covers all U.S. and Canadian models	6324
Datsun 1961-72 Covers all U.S. and Canadian models of Nissan Patrol; 1500, 1600 and 2000 sports cars; Pick-Ups; 410, 411, 510, 1200 and 240Z	5790
Datsun 1973-80 Spanish	7083
Datsun/Nissan F-10, 310, Stanza, Pulsar 1977-86 Covers all U.S. and Canadian models	7196
Datsun/Nissan Pick-Ups 1970-84 Covers all U.S. and Canadian models	6816
Datsun/Nissan Z & ZX 1970-86 Covers all U.S. and Canadian models	6932
Datsun/Nissan 1200, 210, Sentra 1973-86 Covers all U.S. and Canadian models	7197
Datsun/Nissan 200SX, 510, 610, 710, 810, Maxima 1973-84 Covers all U.S. and Canadian models	7170
Dodge 1968-77 Covers all U.S. and Canadian models	6554
Dodge Charger 1967-70 Covers all U.S. and Canadian models	6486
Dodge/Plymouth Trucks 1967-84 Covers all $1/2$, $3/4$, and 1 ton 2- and 4-wheel drive U.S. and Canadian models, including diesel engines	7459
Dodge/Plymouth Vans 1967-84 Covers all $1/2$, $3/4$, and 1 ton U.S. and Canadian models of vans, cutaways and motor home chassis	6934
D-50/Arrow Pick-Up 1979-81 Covers all U.S. and Canadian models	7032
Fairlane/Torino 1962-75 Covers all U.S. and Canadian models	6320
Fairmont/Zephyr 1978-83 Covers all U.S. and Canadian models	6965
Fiat 1969-81 Covers all U.S. and Canadian models	7042
Fiesta 1978-80 Covers all U.S. and Canadian models	6846
Firebird 1967-81 Covers all U.S. and Canadian models	5996
Firebird 1982-85 Covers all U.S. and Canadian models	7345
Ford 1968-79 Spanish	7084
Ford Bronco 1966-83 Covers all U.S. and Canadian models	7140
Ford Bronco II 1984 Covers all U.S. and Canadian models	7408
Ford Courier 1972-82 Covers all U.S. and Canadian models	6983
Ford/Mercury Front Wheel Drive 1981-85 Covers all U.S. and Canadian models Escort, EXP, Tempo, Lynx, LN-7 and Topaz	7055
Ford/Mercury/Lincoln 1968-85 Covers all U.S. and Canadian models of FORD Country Sedan, Country Squire, Crown Victoria, Custom, Custom 500, Galaxie 500, LTD through 1982, Ranch Wagon, and XL; MERCURY Colony Park, Commuter, Marquis through 1982, Gran Marquis, Monterey and Park Lane; LINCOLN Continental and Towne Car	6842
Ford/Mercury/Lincoln Mid-Size 1971-85 Covers all U.S. and Canadian models of FORD Elite, 1983-85 LTD, 1977-79 LTD II, Ranchero, Torino, Gran Torino, 1977-85 Thunderbird; MERCURY 1972-85 Cougar,	6696

continued on next page

RTUG Title	Part No.
1983-85 Marquis, Montego, 1980-85 XR-7; LINCOLN 1982-85 Continental, 1984-85 Mark VII, 1978-80 Versailles	
Ford Pick-Ups 1965-86	6913
Covers all $1/2$, $3/4$ and 1 ton, 2- and 4-wheel drive U.S. and Canadian pick-up, chassis cab and camper models, including diesel engines	
Ford Pick-Ups 1965-82 Spanish	7469
Ford Ranger 1983-84	7338
Covers all U.S. and Canadian models	
Ford Vans 1961-86	6849
Covers all U.S. and Canadian $1/2$, $3/4$ and 1 ton van and cutaway chassis models, including diesel engines	
GM A-Body 1982-85	7309
Covers all front wheel drive U.S. and Canadian models of BUICK Century, CHEVROLET Celebrity, OLDSMOBILE Cutlass Ciera and PONTIAC 6000	
GM C-Body 1985	7587
Covers all front wheel drive U.S. and Canadian models of BUICK Electra Park Avenue and Electra T-Type, CADILLAC Fleetwood and deVille, OLDSMOBILE 98 Regency and Regency Brougham	
GM J-Car 1982-85	7059
Covers all U.S. and Canadian models of BUICK Skyhawk, CHEVROLET Cavalier, CADILLAC Cimarron, OLDSMOBILE Firenza and PONTIAC 2000 and Sunbird	
GM N-Body 1985-86	7657
Covers all U.S. and Canadian models of front wheel drive BUICK Somerset and Skylark, OLDSMOBILE Calais, and PONTIAC Grand Am	
GM X-Body 1980-85	7049
Covers all U.S. and Canadian models of BUICK Skylark, CHEVROLET Citation, OLDSMOBILE Omega and PONTIAC Phoenix	
GM Subcompact 1971-80	6935
Covers all U.S. and Canadian models of BUICK Skyhawk (1975-80), CHEVROLET Vega and Monza, OLDSMOBILE Starfire, and PONTIAC Astre and 1975-80 Sunbird	
Granada/Monarch 1975-82	6937
Covers all U.S. and Canadian models	
Honda 1973-84	6980
Covers all U.S. and Canadian models	
International Scout 1967-73	5912
Covers all U.S. and Canadian models	
Jeep 1945-87	6817
Covers all U.S. and Canadian CJ-2A, CJ-3A, CJ-3B, CJ-5, CJ-6, CJ-7, Scrambler and Wrangler models	
Jeep Wagoneer, Commando, Cherokee, Truck 1957-86	6739
Covers all U.S. and Canadian models of Wagoneer, Cherokee, Grand Wagoneer, Jeepster, Jeepster Commando, J-100, J-200, J-300, J-10, J20, FC-150 and FC-170	
Laser/Daytona 1984-85	7563
Covers all U.S. and Canadian models	
Maverick/Comet 1970-77	6634
Covers all U.S. and Canadian models	
Mazda 1971-84	6981
Covers all U.S. and Canadian models of RX-2, RX-3, RX-4, 808, 1300, 1600, Cosmo, GLC and 626	
Mazda Pick-Ups 1972-86	7659
Covers all U.S. and Canadian models	
Mercedes-Benz 1959-70	6065
Covers all U.S. and Canadian models	
Mereceds-Benz 1968-73	5907
Covers all U.S. and Canadian models	

RTUG Title	Part No.
Mercedes-Benz 1974-84	6809
Covers all U.S. and Canadian models	
Mitsubishi, Cordia, Tredia, Starion, Galant 1983-85	7583
Covers all U.S. and Canadian models	
MG 1961-81	6780
Covers all U.S. and Canadian models	
Mustang/Capri/Merkur 1979-85	6963
Covers all U.S. and Canadian models	
Mustang/Cougar 1965-73	6542
Covers all U.S. and Canadian models	
Mustang II 1974-78	6812
Covers all U.S. and Canadian models	
Omni/Horizon/Rampage 1978-84	6845
Covers all U.S. and Canadian models of DODGE omni, Miser, 024, Charger 2.2; PLYMOUTH Horizon, Miser, TC3, TC3 Tourismo; Rampage	
Opel 1971-75	6575
Covers all U.S. and Canadian models	
Peugeot 1970-74	5982
Covers all U.S. and Canadian models	
Pinto/Bobcat 1971-80	7027
Covers all U.S. and Canadian models	
Plymouth 1968-76	6552
Covers all U.S. and Canadian models	
Pontiac Fiero 1984-85	7571
Covers all U.S. and Canadian models	
Pontiac Mid-Size 1974-83	7346
Covers all U.S. and Canadian models of Ventura, Grand Am, LeMans, Grand LeMans, GTO, Phoenix, and Grand Prix	
Porsche 924/928 1976-81	7048
Covers all U.S. and Canadian models	
Renault 1975-85	7165
Covers all U.S. and Canadian models	
Roadrunner/Satellite/Belvedere/GTX 1968-73	5821
Covers all U.S. and Canadian models	
RX-7 1979-81	7031
Covers all U.S. and Canadian models	
SAAB 99 1969-75	5988
Covers all U.S. and Canadian models	
SAAB 900 1979-85	7572
Covers all U.S. and Canadian models	
Snowmobiles 1976-80	6978
Covers Arctic Cat, John Deere, Kawasaki, Polaris, Ski-Doo and Yamaha	
Subaru 1970-84	6982
Covers all U.S. and Canadian models	
Tempest/GTO/LeMans 1968-73	5905
Covers all U.S. and Canadian models	
Toyota 1966-70	5795
Covers all U.S. and Canadian models of Corona, MkII, Corolla, Crown, Land Cruiser, Stout and Hi-Lux	
Toyota 1970-79 Spanish	7467
Toyota Celica/Supra 1971-85	7043
Covers all U.S. and Canadian models	
Toyota Trucks 1970-85	7035
Covers all U.S. and Canadian models of pick-ups, Land Cruiser and 4Runner	
Valiant/Duster 1968-76	6326
Covers all U.S. and Canadian models	
Volvo 1956-69	6529
Covers all U.S. and Canadian models	
Volvo 1970-83	7040
Covers all U.S. and Canadian models	
VW Front Wheel Drive 1974-85	6962
Covers all U.S. and Canadian models	
VW 1949-71	5796
Covers all U.S. and Canadian models	
VW 1970-79 Spanish	7081
VW 1970-81	6837
Covers all U.S. and Canadian Beetles, Karmann Ghia, Fastback, Squareback, Vans, 411 and 412	

Chilton's Repair & Tune-Up Guides are available at your local retailer or by mailing a check or money order for **$12.50** plus **$2.25** to cover postage and handling to:

**Chilton Book Company
Dept. DM
Radnor, PA 19089**

NOTE: When ordering be sure to include your name & address, book part No. & title.